CICERO

X

IN CATILINAM I–IV   PRO MURENA
PRO SULLA   PRO FLACCO

324

THE LOEB CLASSICAL LIBRARY

CICERO

IN TWENTY-EIGHT VOLUMES

X

IN CATILINAM I–IV · PRO MURENA
PRO SULLA · PRO FLACCO

WITH AN ENGLISH TRANSLATION BY
C. MACDONALD, M.A.
HEADMASTER OF UPPINGHAM SCHOOL

CAMBRIDGE, MASSACHUSETTS
HARVARD UNIVERSITY PRESS
LONDON
WILLIAM HEINEMANN LTD
MCMLXXVII

American
ISBN 0-674-99358-6

British
ISBN 0 434 99324 7

New edition by C. Macdonald 1976
(This replaces the edition by
Louis E. Lord, first published in 1937)

Printed in Great Britain

CONTENTS

	PAGE
LIST OF CICERO'S WORKS	vii
PREFACE	xi
INTRODUCTION	xv
The Political Background 70–59 . .	xvi
Table of Events 63	xxxvii

IN CATILINAM I–IV—

INTRODUCTION

Lucius Sergius Catilina. . . .	2
Policy and Supporters	10
The Course of the Conspiracy . .	13
The Manuscripts	31

IN CATILINAM I—
| Text and Translation . . . . | 32 |

IN CATILINAM II—
| Text and Translation . . . . | 68 |

IN CATILINAM III—
| Text and Translation . . . . | 100 |

IN CATILINAM IV—
| Text and Translation . . . . | 134 |

CONTENTS

PRO MURENA—

   Introduction 169

   The Manuscripts 185

   Text and Translation 186

PRO SULLA—

   Introduction 302

   The Manuscripts 313

   Text and Translation 314

PRO FLACCO—

   Introduction 413

   The Manuscripts 433

   Text and Translation 434

APPENDIX A : The *contio* and the *comitia* . 559

APPENDIX B : The *senatus consultum ultimum* . 567

BIBLIOGRAPHY 575

INDEX OF PROPER NAMES 585

LIST OF CICERO'S WORKS

SHOWING THEIR DIVISION INTO VOLUMES IN THIS EDITION

A. Rhetorical Treatises. 5 Volumes

volume

I. [Cicero], Rhetorica ad Herennium

II. De Inventione
De Optimo Genere Oratorum
Topica

III. De Oratore, Books I-II

IV. De Oratore, Book III
De Fato
Paradoxa Stoicorum
De Partitione Oratoria

V. Brutus
Orator

LIST OF CICERO'S WORKS

B. ORATIONS.   10 VOLUMES

VOLUME

VI. Pro Quinctio
Pro Roscio Amerino
Pro Roscio Comoedo
De Lege Agraria Contra Rullum I-III

VII. The Verrine Orations I :
In Q. Caecilium
In C. Verrem Actio I
In C. Verrem Actio II, Books I-II

VIII. The Verrine Orations II :
In C. Verrem Actio II, Books III-V

IX. De Imperio Cn. Pompei (Pro Lege Manilia)
Pro Caecina
Pro Cluentio
Pro Rabirio Perduellionis Reo

X. In Catilinam I-IV
Pro Murena
Pro Sulla
Pro Flacco

XI. Pro Archia
Post Reditum in Senatu
Post Reditum ad Quirites

LIST OF CICERO'S WORKS

VOLUME

      De Domo Sua
      De Haruspicum Responsis
      Pro Cn. Plancio

XII. Pro Sestio
      In Vatinium

XIII. Pro Caelio
      De Provinciis Consularibus
      Pro Balbo

XIV. Pro Milone
      In Pisonem
      Pro Scauro
      Pro Fonteio
      Pro Rabirio Postumo
      Pro Marcello
      Pro Ligario
      Pro Rege Deiotaro

XV. Philippics I-XIV

      C. PHILOSOPHICAL TREATISES. 6 VOLUMES

XVI. De Re Publica
      De Legibus

XVII. De Finibus Bonorum et Malorum

LIST OF CICERO'S WORKS

VOLUME

XVIII. Tusculan Disputations

XIX. De Natura Deorum
Academica I and II

XX. Cato Maior de Senectute
Laelius de Amicitia
De Divinatione

XXI. De Officiis

D. LETTERS. 7 VOLUMES

XXII. Letters to Atticus, Books I-VI

XXIII. Letters to Atticus, Books VII-XI

XXIV. Letters to Atticus, Books XII-XVI

XXV. Letters to His Friends, Books I-VI

XXVI. Letters to His Friends, Books VII-XII

XXVII. Letters to His Friends, Books XIII-XVI

XXVIII. Letters to His Brother Quintus
Letters to Brutus
Commentariolum Petitionis
Epistula ad Octavianum

PREFACE

THE seven speeches in this volume, five of them delivered in the year of Cicero's consulship, are not only sources of supreme interest for the history of their time, but also contain some of his finest oratory. In an age when rhetoric in the grand style is at a discount it is not easy to catch the spirit of the more vivid passages without making them sound unnatural to our ears. It must always be remembered that these speeches were delivered to a Mediterranean audience and often in the presence of large and noisy crowds. This translation seeks to combine an accurate rendering of the Latin with an appreciation of Cicero's qualities as orator, statesman and counsel for the defence ; not always an easy task when the tastes and assumptions of our two societies are so very different.

The importance of the subject-matter is no less striking than the quality of the oratory. Although Catiline's ill-fated outbreak was only one of a series of episodes in the death of the Roman republic, these speeches provide us with a mass of important material for our knowledge of the period and for our understanding of the framework of Roman politics and society. This fact is reflected in the output of modern scholarship, and an attempt to encompass even a fraction of what has been written about the

PREFACE

uneasy years that led up to the conspiracy of 63 and about that year itself is a daunting task. The Bibliography does not set out to be exhaustive, but it does point the way to works where fuller discussions and bibliographies may be found and where important problems arising out of these speeches are discussed in greater detail than the scale of this volume permits.

The text used is that of A. C. Clark in the *Oxford Classical Texts*, and there are few departures from it. Critical notes are confined to passages where variant readings or emendations should be known to the reader.

For all the speeches I have also consulted the Teubner text :

in Catilinam I-IV	P. Reis (1933)
pro Murena	H. Kasten (2nd ed. 1961)
pro Sulla	H. Kasten (3rd ed. 1966)
pro Flacco	L. Früchtel (1932)

and the Budé edition :

in Catilinam I-IV	Text : H. Bornecque ; translation : É. Bailly (1926)
pro Murena and *pro Sulla*	Text and translation : A. Boulanger (1943)
pro Flacco	Text and translation : A. Boulanger (1938)

Of the other editions that I have consulted, most helpful have been W. E. Heitland's *pro Murena* (2nd ed. 1876), J. S. Reid's *pro Sulla* (1882), and T. B. L. Webster's *pro Flacco* (1931).

This volume has been taking up much of my leisure for a number of years and its completion has

PREFACE

only been made possible by the very considerable help that I have received in a number of ways. In the first place, I must thank the generosity of my Governors at Portsmouth Grammar School, who gave me six months' leave of absence to take up a Fellowship at Harvard University from the Loeb Classical Library Foundation ; and of all those who helped to make my time at Harvard so enjoyable, my especial thanks are due to Professor Zeph Stewart, who went to great trouble on my behalf to smooth my path to Harvard and to enable me to reap the full benefit from my months here. My thanks are also due to Professor Herbert Bloch for his interest in my work and the encouragement and support that he has given to it.

For help with the work itself I am most grateful to friends on both sides of the Atlantic. In England to Professor R. G. M. Nisbet and in particular to Mr. M. W. Frederiksen, who devoted much time and effort to helping me fill the gaps in my knowledge of Roman history and the Latin language ; in America I have received much help from Professor E. Badian. To all three I express my deep gratitude for their efforts to overcome my ignorance. Where this has remained invincible, the responsibility is mine alone.

C. M.

INTRODUCTION

THE speeches in this volume cover the four years from 63 to 59,[a] but their subject-matter requires some knowledge of events at Rome from the beginning of the decade and a rather more detailed understanding of what happened between the consular elections of 66 and the defeat and death of Catiline early in 62. This introduction does not set out to give a detailed history of the 60s but attempts, in conjunction with the introductions to the individual speeches, to provide the background information that will enable the reader to understand the content of these speeches and to see them in their historical setting.

Our ancient sources for the crucial years from 66 to 63 are all too scanty and all too unreliable. We do well, therefore, to bear constantly in mind how fragile are the foundations upon which we seek to put together the story of these years and how perverted by subsequent expediency and political propaganda they became. In order to appreciate Cicero's calibre as statesman or counsel for the defence and to understand the line he took in his speeches, we must be aware of the shortcomings of our sources and of the limitations to what can be extracted from them.

It is with this warning in mind that we must seek to

---

[a] *in Catilinam* 1-4 and *pro Murena* in 63, *pro Sulla* in 62 and *pro Flacco* in 59.

disentangle the relationships between those on the
political stage at Rome : Cicero himself, Catiline,
Crassus, Caesar, the leading Optimates, consuls and
tribunes, as well as the absent Pompey.

THE POLITICAL BACKGROUND 70–59

In 70 the consuls were Gnaeus Pompeius Magnus
and Marcus Licinius Crassus. No detailed account of
their year of office is necessary, but one of Pompey's
actions was to have important repercussions during
the succeeding decades. It was in this year that he
restored their power to the tribunes of the plebs,[a] and
within three years the tribunate was once more a
force to be reckoned with in Rome. In 67 two

---

[a] This year also saw the establishment of juries drawn
from the Senate, *equites* and *tribuni aerarii* in equal numbers.
Thus, two of Sulla's policies—the elimination of the tribunate
as a force in politics and the removal of the juries from the
equestrian order—were finally reversed, but the idea that 70
saw the total overthrow of the Sullan constitution is a myth.
The system basically lasted until the end of the Republic.
Cf. pro Flacco 32, p.476; and see U. Laffi, " Il mito di Silla,"
Athenaeum 45 (1967), 177 f. and 255 f., especially 179 f. and
E. S. Gruen, *The Last Generation of the Roman Republic*
10 f.

It is no less mistaken to regard Pompey simply as a
popularis. His staff in the East was well stocked with
members of the *nobilitas* and four consulars spoke in support
of Manilius' bill (Cicero, *de imperio Gnaei Pompei* 68)
including those pillars of the Sullan establishment, Publius
Servilius Vatia Isauricus and Gaius Scribonius Curio. The
other two—Gaius Cassius Longinus and Gnaeus Cornelius
Lentulus Clodianus—were both *nobiles*. E. S. Gruen,
" Pompey, the Roman Aristocracy, and the Conference of
Luca," *Historia* 18 (1969), 71-108, especially 74-75 ; also
M. Griffin, " The Tribune C. Cornelius," *Journal of Roman
Studies* 63 (1973), 206-208.

tribunes became very active. Gaius Cornelius
carried measures that praetors should administer
justice in accordance with the edicts that they had
issued on entering office, that provincials in Rome
should not (in their own interests) be allowed to
borrow money, that foreign embassies should have
the right to meet the Senate, that dispensations to
individuals from a law (*privilegia*) should only be
granted when two hundred senators had voted ; he
also proposed a severe measure against electoral
corruption which was not carried but was passed in a
modified form by the consuls.[a] His subsequent
trial for *maiestas*—treason—was doubtless provoked
by optimate indignation at these attacks upon
senatorial interests.[b] A fellow tribune, Aulus Gabinius, proposed a measure which enabled Pompey
to advance his own career and obtain an extraordinary command against the pirates who infested
the Mediterranean. The senatorial opposition to this
proposal, led by the hard-core conservatives Quintus
Lutatius Catulus and Quintus Hortensius Hortalus,
did all it could to prevent the passage of this bill, but
its efforts were in vain. In the following year it was
no more successful in stopping the bill of Gaius
Manilius[c] which gave Pompey command of the provinces of Cilicia and of Bithynia and Pontus, and of
the war against Mithridates, king of Pontus. Cicero
supported the bill with all his eloquence,[d] and Pompey
was now launched upon his victorious progress in

---

[a] See p. 174.

[b] See M. Griffin, *op. cit.* 196-213.

[c] Another reforming tribune. *Cf. pro Murena* 47, p. 246,
n. *c.*

[d] In his speech *de imperio Gnaei Pompei.*

the East while Cicero looked after his interests at Rome.[a]

In the capital people viewed Pompey's enormous power and ever growing success with mounting alarm. Romans still had the return of Sulla from the East fresh in their minds, and years were to pass before the horrors of the *Sullanum regnum* were to be erased.[b]

The senatorial leadership saw Pompey as a general who held commands granted to him by the people in the teeth of their opposition and Crassus, one of the richest men in Rome, saw the rise of a military force that challenged his own financial resources as a means to political power. His aim, however, was to secure independence for himself from the Optimates as well as from Pompey ; his political stance was not openly anti-Pompeian and his activities in the mid-60s seem to have aimed at harassing the Optimates. Tales of anti-Pompeian collaboration between himself and Caesar in these years need to be treated with considerable reserve and Caesar, like other up-and-coming young politicians, certainly advertised his support for Pompey.[c]

[a] See *commentariolum petitionis* 51. Cicero remained on good terms with Pompey until December 63, when the activities of Metellus Nepos caused a breach which lasted until 60. See p. xxxii, n. *a* and p. 29, n. *a*. Cicero kept a watching brief on Pompey's interests in return for electoral support. The suppression of the Catilinarian Conspiracy changed their relationship and Cicero now addressed Pompey as an equal. See p. 130, n. *a*.

[b] On the face of it there was good cause for concern. Pompey had been Sulla's lieutenant in the late 80s, he had fought the oligarchy's battles against Lepidus and Sertorius in the 70s and he retained close links with the oligarchy (see p. xvi, n. *a* above). *Cf. in Catilinam* 2. 20, p. 88.

[c] G. V. Sumner, " Cicero, Pompeius, and Rullus,"

INTRODUCTION

In this year the consular elections resulted in the return of Publius Cornelius Sulla and Publius Autronius Paetus as consuls-elect for 65. They were promptly prosecuted for *ambitus* [a] by a fellow candidate, Lucius Aurelius Cotta, and by Lucius Manlius Torquatus.[b] In spite of an attempt to break up the proceedings [c] the prosecution was successful, and Sulla and Autronius were unseated. New elections were held in which Cotta and Torquatus were elected in their place.

At the time of the first election Catiline was nearing the end of his term of office as propraetor in Africa, but before he returned to Rome envoys had arrived to protest to the Senate about his conduct in the province.[d] Unconcerned at these protests and at the prospect of prosecution for extortion,[e] he declared his intention of standing as a candidate in the new elections, but the presiding consul, Lucius Volcacius Tullus, refused to accept him because he had not been one of the original candidates.[f]

Transactions of the American Philological Association 97 (1966), 573-575. See also pp. xxii-xxvii.

[a] See p. 171 for this offence. It is not unlikely that the cash had been provided by the wealthy Sulla. For his wealth *cf.* p. 302, n. *f.* [b] The other candidate's son. [c] *pro Sulla* 15, p. 328. [d] Asconius 85-87, 89 C. [e] See p. 415 for this offence.
[f] Volcacius ruled that no new candidates were to be accepted. Cotta and Torquatus had complained that they had been robbed of the consulship (*pro Sulla* 49, p. 362) and claimed that they should be elected automatically if Sulla and Autronius were disqualified. The second election was probably a mere formality with Cotta and Torquatus as the only candidates. E. G. Hardy, " The Catilinarian Conspiracy in its Context : A Re-Study of the Evidence," *Journal of Roman Studies* 7 (1917). 157 f., has shown that Catiline was not excluded because of any impending trial for extortion

INTRODUCTION

These events gave birth to a crop of rumours of intended violence which came to be known collectively as the First Catilinarian Conspiracy.[a] Our ancient sources [b] have some eight accounts of what is supposed to have taken place : Catiline and Gnaeus Calpurnius Piso planned to massacre the Optimates in 65 [c] ; Catiline was engaged in some murderous activity in the Forum on the 29th of December 66 [d] ; Sulla, Autronius and Catiline plotted in 66 to make Sulla and Autronius consuls on the 1st of January 65 [e] ; Sulla and Autronius plotted to make themselves consuls [f] ; Sulla and Autronius conspired with Caesar to restore themselves to office [g] ; Autronius, Catiline

---

although Volcacius and his advisers were doubtless subject to pressures that he should be prevented from standing. These pressures came both from those who wished to ensure that Catiline stood trial and from the powerful supporters backing Cotta and Torquatus.

[a] For the analysis of these events, see R. Seager, " The First Catilinarian Conspiracy," *Historia* 13 (1964), 338-347 ; also H. Frisch, " The First Catilinarian Conspiracy," *Classica et Mediaevalia* 9 (1947), 10-36 ; M. I. Henderson, " *De commentariolo petitionis,*" *Journal of Roman Studies* 40 (1950), 13-14 ; R. Syme, *Sallust* 86 f. ; E. S. Gruen, " Notes on the ' First Catilinarian Conspiracy,' " *Classical Philology* 64 (1969), 20-24. Much more has been written about this non-event ; some of it is highly ingenious, *e.g.* C. E. Stevens, " The ' Plotting ' of b.c. 66/65," *Latomus* 22 (1963), 397-435, but not necessarily very helpful to those who want to know what reliable evidence there is and what may be learnt from it.

[b] No source after 63 is to be trusted and earlier stories have to be carefully examined in the light of the circumstances of their origin.

[c] Cicero *apud* Asconius 92 C and *pro Murena* 81, p. 288.

[d] *in Catilinam* 1. 15, p. 46.

[e] *pro Sulla* 11 f., 67 f., 81, pp. 322 f., 378 f., 392 f.

[f] *Ib.* 67 f., p. 378 f.   [g] Suetonius, *Divus Iulius* 9.

and Piso plotted in 66 to make Autronius and Catiline consuls, and their plan was to be put into execution on the 1st of January 65 [a]; the same three men plotted to murder a number of the Senate on the 5th of February 65 [b]; Sulla, Autronius, Catiline and Piso plotted to make Autronius and Sulla consuls.[c]

We know that in fact nothing happened on the 1st of January 65, but this knowledge leaves two questions to be asked : did any plans for action exist ? If so, who was likely to have formed them ? Sulla and Autronius had a motive, but there is no reason why either Catiline or Piso should have wished to dispose of the consuls.[d] It is almost inconceivable that Sulla and Autronius, granted that they had a motive, intended to murder the consuls without apparently any thought for the inevitable counter-attack or plans to sustain their illegal power.

A further question must be asked : what was Catiline doing in the Forum on the 29th of December that could plausibly lead him to be associated with a plot to murder the consuls ? A possible answer is that the violence in which Catiline and Piso were involved at the turn of the year was part of the political upheaval surrounding the trials of Manilius [e]; and what —if anything—happened on the 5th of February 65, we do not know.

[a] Sallust, *Bellum Catilinae* 18. 5.
[b] *Ib.* 18. 6-7.   [c] Dio Cassius 36. 44. 3 f.
[d] For the introduction of Catiline into the affair, see p. 8.
[e] See Asconius 66 C ; but for the flimsiness of our information, see E. S. Gruen, *op. cit.* 23. For a highly speculative account of these trials and the parts played in them by Cicero, Catiline and Crassus, see A. M. Ward, " Politics in the Trials of Manilius and Cornelius," *Transactions of the American Philological Association* 101 (1970), 545-556.

INTRODUCTION

Two other names are linked by our sources with these alleged plots—Crassus and Caesar. In the resulting confusion Crassus was to have seized the dictatorship and Caesar was to have been his *magister equitum*. The charge against Caesar, however, first appeared in 59, and it is most unlikely that he would have joined a plot aiming to murder Cotta, who was his cousin.[a] His desire to be *magister equitum* and, along with it, Crassus' bid for the dictatorship are fictions prompted by political malice. The conduct of Crassus may have been such as to lead men to think that he was behind the prevailing unrest, but a bid to emulate Sulla did not form any part of his plans.

All that we can say is that after the *ambitus* trials and reversal of the electoral decision the frustrated rivals sought to retaliate or, at least, to make their annoyance known by some sort of demonstration. There is no evidence of big men manipulating small men, of deep laid plots, conspiracy, murder or revolution.

In 65 Crassus was censor and proposed to grant full citizenship to the Transpadanes,[b] but his Optimate colleague in the censorship fought the proposal so bitterly that it became impossible for them to perform the duties of their office and they resigned. Had his proposal become law Crassus would have obtained a large number of new clients [c] and increased his power in Rome. Even though he failed, he neverthe-

[a] M. Gelzer, *Caesar, Politician and Statesman* 39 ; P. A. Brunt, " Three Passages from Asconius," *Classical Review* 7 (1957), 193-195.
[b] Little time need be spent upon any scheme that Crassus may have had to extend his influence in Spain through Piso. Piso was speedily killed by local inhabitants or Pompeian agents.
[c] For the importance of clients in Roman politics, see p. 173.

less won the goodwill of the Transpadanes, a useful recruiting ground for the future. It was not long, indeed, since Caesar had interested himself in the Transpadanes on his return from his quaestorship in Spain, but there is no evidence of any form of collaboration between the two men in this matter. The whole affair may have been a political ploy that did him no harm and annoyed the Optimates, rather than a dedicated effort to extend the franchise.

In the same year a proposal was made to annex Egypt as a province. Our sources are divided on the identity of those responsible for the scheme,[a] and in the end it came to nothing. Catulus again rallied the Optimates against the proposal, and Cicero attacked it to good effect in his lost speech *de rege Alexandrino*.

The following year saw the atmosphere of suspicion and intrigue continue. Catiline had secured his

---

[a] According to Suetonius, *Divus Iulius* 11, the annexation was proposed by some tribunes who had been put up to it by Caesar in the hope that he would get the command for himself. Plutarch, *Crassus* 13. 1-2, says that Crassus was behind the scheme. The two versions are usually reconciled by saying that this is an example of Caesar and Crassus at work together, but of this there is in fact no evidence. (But see A. M. Ward in *Historia* vol. 21, see p. 582 below.) A possibility is that Suetonius' unknown tribunes, who tend to get overlooked, were working on behalf of Pompey. They would have been elected when Pompey was in high popular favour and may have been acting in the tradition of Gabinius and Manilius with the man on the spot in mind. The back of the Mithridatic War had been broken, and Pompey was well placed to handle the annexation of Egypt. This does not mean that Pompey was openly campaigning for the job. It would be characteristic of him to stay in the background, but it must not be assumed that because he was not in Rome he was not a powerful political force there. See G. V. Sumner, *op. cit.* 573-574. *Cf.* R. Syme, *Sallust* 102 with n. 88.

acquittal on the charge of extortion [a] and was now a candidate for the consulship of 63. The story of this year's elections and of Catiline's acquittal after another prosecution is told elsewhere.[b]

Later in the year, on a date before the 10th of December, Cicero learnt that some of the tribunes-elect were drafting an agrarian bill, and before the 1st of January the bill had been promulgated.[c] A commission of ten was to be elected by seventeen of the thirty-five tribes ; the commissioners were to have *praetoria potestas* for five years and they were to establish *coloniae* in Italy. The *ager Campanus* was to be distributed to five thousand colonists and, as more allotments were required, land was to be bought for the purpose. The commission was empowered to raise funds by selling certain land and domains outside Italy that had become the property of the Roman people in 88 or later. It was also authorized to impose taxes on public land outside Italy and to use the funds accruing from new *vectigalia* after the current year. War booty with certain exceptions—Pompey was specifically exempted—was to be handed over to it.

The tribune who proposed this bill, Publius Servilius Rullus, is a shadowy figure about whom we know very little and of whom no more is heard after this month. Three other members of this year's tribunician college are known to us : Lucius Caecilius Rufus, an opponent of the bill who undertook to veto it,[d] and two who supported it—Titus Ampius Balbus and Titus Labienus.

Cicero suggests that Rullus was a front-man and

[a] See p. 3.   [b] See pp. 4-5.
[c] *de lege agraria* 2. 11 f.   [d] *pro Sulla* 65, p. 378.

that the real sponsors of the bill were the powers behind the scene whom he never names. There has been general agreement that Cicero had Caesar and Crassus in mind, but other figures—there were ten seats on the commission—could well have been in men's minds: Catiline, Autronius, Cethegus, or even Cicero's colleague Antonius. Cicero's silence upon the identity of the sponsors left his audience free to make its own choice.

The political intentions of the bill have been variously interpreted. Rullus himself said in the Senate [a] that its purpose was to rid Rome of a dangerous proletariat and to improve the social, economic and political conditions of Rome and Italy.

This was undoubtedly true, but it was not the whole truth. Other theories are more dramatic: that it was a sort of coup d'état by Crassus and Caesar against Pompey or the Senate or both; that it was to give Crassus and Caesar control of Egypt and an army with which to combat Pompey; that it was an attempt by Crassus to corner allotment land and thus put himself in a strong bargaining position when Pompey returned seeking land for his veterans; that it was an attempt to provide something for everybody—land for the landless, profit for the landowners, business for the *negotiatores* and new taxes for the *publicani*; that it was never intended to become law at all but was meant to display Cicero in his true colours as a tool of the Optimates and to intensify the struggle between the people and the senatorial government.

Each of these theories has its own drawbacks and none carries total conviction. A case, however, can be made for the view that the law was at any rate in

[a] *de lege agraria* 2. 70.

INTRODUCTION

part designed to meet Pompey's need of land for his veterans.[a] The two tribunes who supported the measure had close links with Pompey. They are supposed to have proposed extravagant honours for him, Labienus was associated with Pompeian agents, and Balbus was a fanatical Pompeian, at least at a later date.[b] There were, of course, other benefits. The members of the commission stood to gain personally in their political careers, and the bill was genuinely conducive to social and economic advance. These may not have been the main purpose of the measure, but they are not to be ignored.

This theory inevitably raises the question: if the law was to further Pompey's interests, why did Cicero oppose it? The answer is to be found in a fundamental part of Cicero's political thinking, his attitude to agrarian reform.[c] In fact Cicero did little for Pompey during the year of his consulship, and Pompey's coolness towards him of which Cicero complained in the letter he wrote him the following year need not have surprised him.[d]

There is no convincing evidence that Crassus had any part in the affair, but Caesar may have backed the bill. He had done nothing overtly hostile to Pompey's interests, and various historical sources, even after allowance has been made for a certain amount of

[a] G. V. Sumner, *op. cit.* 579-582.

[b] R. Syme, "The Allegiance of Labienus," *Journal of Roman Studies* 28 (1938), 113-128.

[c] Compare his attitude to the bill proposed in Pompey's interest by the tribune, Lucius Flavius (*ad Atticum* 1. 19. 4) and the agrarian legislation of Caesar (*ad Atticum* 2. 16. 1-2).

[d] *ad familiares* 5. 7. 3. *Cf.* p. 131, n. *a.* The rebuff was a blow to his political status rather than to his personal pride.

exaggeration, record acts in Pompey's interests or in concert with Pompey's agents.[a] Any connection that he may have had would stand him in good stead for the future. He had kept well in the background and therefore suffered no loss of *dignitas* when the bill was thrown out. He would, however, have strengthened his ties of *amicitia* with Pompey, a valuable aid to his future career.[b]

Later in 63 there was a trial whose background is relevant to the relationship between Pompey and Caesar. One of the consuls of 67, Gaius Piso, was prosecuted by Caesar for, among other things, the illegal execution of a Transpadane,[c] but a stronger reason for the prosecution was the fact that Piso was an enemy of Pompey. In his consulship he had vehemently opposed the proposals of the Pompeian tribunes and had opposed Pompey in other ways[d]; Cicero defended him but his speech *pro Pisone* has not survived.

Another, more notorious and more important, trial was that of Gaius Rabirius Postumus in which Labienus played the active part while Caesar remained in the background. During these months there was a widespread fear of revolutionary violence at Rome, and Caesar realized the likelihood of serious disturbances which the Senate and Cicero would seek to hold in check, the one by passing the *senatus*

---

[a] See G. V. Sumner, *op. cit.* 579. It should also be noted that he was working with the Pompeian tribune, Nepos, at the beginning of 62.

[b] For the relationship between Pompey and Caesar in these years, see L. R. Taylor, " Caesar and the Roman Nobility," *Transactions of the American Philological Association* 73 (1942), 1-24.

[c] *Cf.* p. xxii.   [d] R. Syme, *op. cit.* 117-118.

consultum ultimum [a] and the other by acting upon it. For political reasons he was averse to its use because this would increase the influence and prestige of the Senate and because any success in the suppression of disturbances would be a set-back for the popular party.

Caesar, therefore, set about making his point by prosecuting Rabirius, now an elderly and respected senator, for *perduellio*—the old charge of treason—on the grounds that thirty-seven years previously he had killed a Roman citizen, Saturninus. The trial of Rabirius, initially in accordance with an obsolete and barbaric procedure, was not altogether in earnest, but the political points that Caesar was seeking to make were meant to be taken to heart by the senatorial government. One of his objects was to discredit a measure that was capable of condoning illegal acts. He wanted to make it clear that only armed and active enemies of the Republic could be killed by the magistrates and their forces. If legitimate action developed into a lynching, then the government was responsible for bringing to justice those who had committed illegal acts that sprang from its own decree. Cicero, on the other hand, saw the case as an attack upon the authority of the Senate and an attempt to deprive the State of the means of protecting itself in grave emergencies.

It is not necessary to recount here the details of the farce which ended in a fashion true to the spirit in which it had been conducted.[b] The proceedings

---

[a] See Appendix B, p. 567 f.

[b] On the whole question of the trial, see T. Rice Holmes, *The Roman Republic* 1. 452 f. and E. G. Hardy, *Some Problems in Roman History* 99 f.

were brought to an abrupt end after Cicero had delivered his speech *pro Rabirio perduellionis reo* by the lowering of the red flag on the Janiculum. This was the traditional signal that enemies were approaching and that any meeting of the *comitia centuriata* in the Campus Martius [a] below should break up immediately.

There was another occasion this year on which Labienus worked in concert with Caesar to assert the rights of the Roman people. By re-enacting the *lex Domitia* of 104 he abolished the oligarchic practice of filling vacancies in the priestly colleges by co-optation and returned to the previous system of election. When the vacant office of *pontifex maximus* came to be filled by the new method, the people chose Caesar, a mere aedilician, over the heads of two senior consulars, Quintus Lutatius Catulus and Publius Servilius Vatia Isauricus. Popular favour and bribery had combined to defeat the *principes*.[b]

The events of the remainder of the year are dealt with elsewhere,[c] but the Catilinarian Conspiracy was to have two important political consequences. Firstly, it provoked the hostility between Caesar and Marcus Porcius Cato ; and secondly, the alliance of all loyal citizens—senators, knights and commons—over which Cicero presided in 63 brought within the realm of practical politics his aim of a *concordia ordinum* or alliance between the senatorial and equestrian orders. This was to be his instrument for the preservation of

[a] See Appendix A, p. 562.
[b] The last three years had seen Caesar increase and Crassus maintain his influence. A number of demonstrations had been made and the Optimates harried and annoyed. For a concerted anti-Pompeian drive there is no evidence.
[c] See pp. 13-27.

the constitution of the Republic against the extreme oligarchs in the Senate and the would-be tyrants in the popular party.

Seeking to enlist Pompey's support for his objective, in mid-62 Cicero wrote to the general a letter that is important evidence for his own political thinking at the time. In it he sees Pompey as Scipio Aemilianus, casts himself in the rôle of Laelius, the counsellor of the great general of the day, and together the two men—military commander and civilian statesman— were to save the Republic.[a]

Within two years, however, the vision had faded— destroyed by political misfortunes and personal animosities.[b] Two events in 61 had re-opened the breach between Senate and knights, and Cicero was powerless to mend it. The consequences of this breach were to be grave and ultimately fatal to the Republic.

The first episode was the sacrilege committed in December 62 by a young patrician, Publius Clodius Pulcher, who violated the rites of the *Bona Dea* which were open only to women. Crassus and Caesar saw a man who might be useful to them and Crassus bribed the jury to acquit Clodius at his trial for impiety. This trial marked the beginning of a long and bitter feud between Clodius and Cicero because the latter gave evidence breaking Clodius' alibi and humiliated him with his sarcasm.[c] The Senate was incensed at the venality of the jury that had acquitted Clodius,

---

[a] *ad familiares* 5. 7. 3. For the importance of this rôle in Cicero's political thought, see C. Nicolet, " *Consul togatus*," *Revue des Études latines* 38 (1960), 248 and p. 130, n. *a*.

[b] *ad Atticum* 1. 18. 3.

[c] *Ib.* 1. 16. 9-10.

and Cato [a] led an attempt to deprive the non-senatorial jurors [b] of the anomalous immunity from prosecution for corruption that they had enjoyed for sixty years.[c] Bad blood between the orders was created by this move and the *concordia* was seriously compromised.

The second threat sprang from the wrangle that developed out of the refusal of the Senate to grant a rebate to a company of tax-gatherers. The company concerned had miscalculated in its bidding for the contract to collect the taxes of Asia and now found itself out of pocket.[d] The Senate was incited to opposition by Quintus Metellus Celer, consul-elect for 60, and by Cato who denounced the avarice of the *publicani* [e] ; Crassus, the protector of financial interests, was behind the application. In both conflicts Cicero, fearful for his *concordia*, urged concessions but without success. The long-standing prejudices of the two orders and the personal animosities of individuals proved too strong for him, and the *concordia* ceased to be a realistic aspiration.

It remained now to see whether the Senate would act in any more statesmanlike a fashion in their dealings with Pompey. Already the object of deep hostility among the die-hard conservatives before he

[a] Cato took over the leadership of the extreme conservatives in the Senate from Catulus and Hortensius.

[b] For the composition of the juries, see p. 172.

[c] *Ad Atticum* 1. 17. 8.

[d] *Ib.* 1. 17. 9 ; J. P. V. D. Balsdon, " Roman History 65–50 B.C. : Five Problems," *Journal of Roman Studies* 52 (1962), 135-137. For the system, see pp. 420-423.

[e] The word *publicani* describes those who enjoyed something obtained from the State (*publicum*), in this case the profit from the collection of taxes. *Cf. pro Murena* 62, p. 264.

left for the war against the pirates, Pompey by his behaviour towards other commanders in the East—Quintus Marcius Rex, Quintus Caecilius Metellus Creticus and Lucius Licinius Lucullus—only increased his unpopularity with the Senate. The efforts of Quintus Caecilius Metellus Nepos, his tribunician emissary of 63, to obtain for his master election to the consulship in his absence or recall to an extraordinary command against Catiline only culminated in the Senate passing the *senatus consultum ultimum.*[a] In the end Pompey and his army disembarked at Brundisium in December 62, and he quietly dismissed his soldiers to their homes. Rome breathed again. Now was the time for the Senate and Pompey to come to an agreement, but he was greeted with the envy and suspicion that seek to thwart a conquering hero on his return home. Once again prejudice was too deeply ingrained to permit the two parties to reach a *modus vivendi.* Too much had happened in the preceding years for the senatorial leaders to be able to treat him in an entirely rational fashion, and Pompey's unfortunate manner, suggesting a lack of sincerity and statesmanship, could only reinforce the senators' distaste for him.[b]

---

[a] See the Scholiast (p. 134 *ed.* Stangl). For a study of the events of the end of 63 and the beginning of 62 in the light of Pompey's original intentions when he despatched Metellus Nepos to Rome and of the changed circumstances created by the Catilinarian Conspiracy, see C. Meier, " Pompeius' Rückkehr aus dem Mithridatischen Kriege und die Catilinarische Verschwörung," *Athenaeum* 40 (1962), 103-125. He traces the moves of Pompey's supporters at the turn of the year. For the events of the 3rd of January 62, and the reasons for the turmoil of that day, see p. 29, n. *a.*

[b] *ad Atticum* 1. 13. 4.

In consequence, the Senate under the leadership of Lucullus alienated him by refusing to grant two requests: the ratification of his settlement in the East en bloc and the grant of land for allotments for his veterans. Not only should the Senate have dealt with both these requests as expeditiously as was reasonable, but any refusal to do so would be a personal affront to the general. The senators, because it was Pompey with whom they were dealing, deliberately procrastinated. The only result was that they antagonized him without securing any advantage to compensate them for the damage that they were doing to their own position.

Pompey attempted to circumvent their obstruction by securing the services of a tribune, Lucius Flavius, to propose an agrarian bill [a] under which all remaining public land in Italy was to be distributed to his veterans and to some of the poorer citizens. This land was to be supplemented by additional land purchased with the proceeds of the taxes from the new provinces in Asia. The Senate remained obdurate and, led once more by Quintus Metellus Celer, now consul, opposed the bill so vigorously that Pompey dropped it.[b]

Imagining that they had rendered Pompey impotent, the Senate now proceeded to humiliate Caesar in an equally foolish way. After his successful term of office in Further Spain, Caesar returned to Rome in the middle of the year 60. He was now seeking a triumph, election to the consulship and then a proconsular command in which to give further scope to the military talents for which Spain had proved a

[a] *Ad Atticum* 1. 18. 6.
[b] *Ib.* 1. 19. 4. *Cf.* p. xxvi, n. *c.*

useful proving ground. Constitutionally, a triumph and candidature for the consulship were incompatible. The former required the *triumphator* to remain outside the *pomerium* [a] until the day on which the triumph was to be celebrated ; the latter required the candidate to appear in the city in person. Caesar, therefore, sought the Senate's permission to sue for office *in absentia*. When Cato saw to it that the request, for which there were good precedents and which would have cost it nothing, was refused, Caesar chose the reality of power, forfeited his triumph and entered the city. The Senate had already ensured that he would not enjoy an attractive proconsular command. In anticipation of his election as consul, it had assigned to the consuls of 59 as their provinces in 58 the forests and cattle-paths of Italy.[b]

In December 60, Pompey and Caesar, thrown to-

[a] The augurally consecrated city boundary which the general could not cross without surrendering his *imperium* except on the occasion of his triumph.

[b] Suetonius, *Divus Iulius* 19. 2. The *lex Sempronia de provinciis consularibus* of Gaius Gracchus provided that the Senate should name the consular provinces before the consuls who would be going to them had been elected. The consuls then decided by lot or private agreement which province each should have.

An alternative explanation of the Senate's choice of provinces has been advanced by J. P. V. D. Balsdon, " Consular Provinces under the Late Republic," *Journal of Roman Studies* 29 (1939), 180-183. He takes it that their action was dictated by the unsettled state of Gaul at the time and the desire to leave their options open. The belief that it was a deliberate device of the Senate to deprive Caesar of an effective provincial command springs from Suetonius' misinterpretation of their motives.

Both views raise difficulties and doubtless the Senate's intentions were not as clear-cut as either would suggest.

gether by their treatment at the hands of the Senate, came to an agreement. An effort was made to obtain Cicero's support. Caesar had a high regard for his rhetorical skill and valued his influence in Italy ; but, although Cicero deplored the extremism of Cato and other optimate leaders, he remained loyal to the established constitution and refused to ally himself with Caesar against the Senate.[a] Not long afterwards an agreement was concluded with Crassus. Caesar was heavily indebted to him for financial assistance before taking up his Spanish command, and Crassus was seeking protection against Pompey and help for the tax-gatherers. The three men bound themselves by a solemn promise to take no political action of which one of the three disapproved,[b] and thus was born the *amicitia* [c] that has now come to be known as " The First Triumvirate."

Caesar was duly successful in the elections and as soon as he entered office started to discharge his obligations to the others. He brought an agrarian bill before the Senate in which he proposed that a commission should be established to acquire land and distribute it to Pompey's veterans and to some of the poorer citizens. Once more Cato was in the vanguard of the opposition, and the Senate rejected the measure. Caesar then submitted it to the Assembly and pushed it through with a ruthless disregard for the obstruction of his consular colleague, Marcus Calpurnius Bibulus. He also enlisted the aid of some of Pompey's veterans whom he brought into the

[a] *ad Atticum* 2. 3. 3-4 ; 4. 6. 2 ; *de provinciis consularibus* 41.

[b] Suetonius, *Divus Iulius* 19. 2.

[c] See p. 182, n. *a*.

Forum, and the bill became law. Soon afterwards he secured the passage of additional legislation, the *lex Iulia de agro Campano*, which settled veterans and civilians on public land around Capua.[a]

More laws were carried on Caesar's behalf by a tribune, Publius Vatinius. One measure discharged the second half of his obligation to Pompey and ratified Pompey's *acta* in the East en bloc; another repaid his debt to Crassus and relieved the Asiatic tax-gatherers of one third of their contract. For himself Caesar obtained the governorship of Cisalpine Gaul and Illyricum for five years from the 1st of March 59; subsequently the Senate added Narbonese Gaul where a vacancy had been created by the death of Quintus Metellus Celer.

At the beginning of the year Cicero had temporarily quitted politics and he took no part in the opposition to Caesar's activities during the latter's first weeks of office. In March, however, there occurred the trial of his consular colleague, Gaius Antonius Hybrida, who had not fulfilled the hopes set on him by Crassus and Caesar in 63.[b] They now dropped him and backed his prosecution. Cicero undertook his defence[c] and at the trial spoke critically of the current political situation. Within three hours Caesar had

[a] Suetonius, *Divus Iulius* 20. 3.

[b] Antonius had been strongly suspected of Catilinarian sympathies, but he was a trimmer (Cicero, *pro Sestio* 8), and Cicero had bought his support against Catiline with the lucrative province of Macedonia. See p. xxxvii, n. *f*.

[c] Cicero was never on particularly good terms with him, but probably felt it necessary to defend him as he had been in name at least commander of the army that had defeated the Catilinarians at Pistoria (see p. 29). An adverse verdict would reflect badly upon himself and weaken his own position.

INTRODUCTION

made Cicero's dangerous enemy, Publius Clodius, a
plebeian and so eligible for the tribunate from which
he could take his revenge upon Cicero. Antonius
was found guilty and his fall was celebrated on the
popular side as vengeance for the death of Catiline, a
banquet was held and wreaths were placed upon
Catiline's grave.[a]

Flaccus' trial later in the year has a similar background. The Triumvirs seem to have been behind
it,[b] and Flaccus' condemnation would have been
greeted in the same way by the popular party.
Cicero impresses upon the jury that the popular line
taken by the Triumvirs was endangering the good
order that he had established in 63 by the union of
Senate and Equites.[c] He could have gone further.
Asinius Pollio later dated the origins of the Civil War
to the consulship of Metellus,[d] the year that saw the
formation of the "Triumvirate," and he had good
cause to do so.

Table of Events 63

The praetor, Quintus Caecilius Metellus Celer, 1 Jan.
withdraws the bill of Lucius Caecilius.[e]

Cicero delivers his first speech *de lege agraria contra
Rullum.*

Rullus' bill is abandoned. Cicero exchanges provinces with Antonius and later in the year renounces his province.[f] Titus Labienus prosecutes

---

[a] *pro Flacco* 95, p. 544.   [b] See p. 430.
[c] *pro Flacco* 94-105, pp. 544-554.   [d] Horace, *Odes* 2. 1. 1-8.
[e] *pro Sulla* 62 f., p. 374 f.
[f] The Senate had assigned Cisalpine Gaul and Macedonia
to the consuls of 63. Cicero drew Macedonia, the more
lucrative province; Antonius received Cisalpine Gaul, the

Gaius Rabirius Postumus for *perduellio* ; the case is abandoned at the last minute. Caesar is elected *pontifex maximus.* Caesar prosecutes Gaius Calpurnius Piso ; Cicero defends him and he is acquitted. Cicero opposes the restoration of civil rights to the sons of the proscribed. Cicero carries a law limiting the tenure of a *libera legatio*[a] to one year. Cicero moves a proposal for a thanksgiving of ten days in honour of Pompey's victories. Cicero and Antonius carry a law against electoral corruption. Cicero moves a decree in the Senate defining the provisions of the *lex Calpurnia de ambitu.*[b]

July The consular elections are held after a delay to enable the Senate to debate Catiline's election address. Decimus Junius Silanus and Lucius Licinius Murena are elected.

Catiline starts to implement plans to seize power by force of arms.

18 Oct. Crassus brings anonymous letters to Cicero.

19 Oct. Cicero informs the Senate. The consuls are ordered to make a special investigation.

---

more important strategically. Early in 63 both parties gladly exchanged provinces (Sallust, *Bellum Catilinae* 26. 4) and then later in the year (? May or June) Cicero renounced his province and proceeded to take great credit for his unselfishness in surrendering something that he did not really want. See W. Allen, Jr., " Cicero's Governorship in 63 B.C.," *Transactions of the American Philological Association* 83 (1952), 233-241.

Cicero tells us in his speech *pro Plancio* 64-66 that when he returned from being quaestor at Lilybaeum he found that no one in Rome had heard of his good work in the province. He therefore decided to remain in Rome in the future and not take a province for fear of being forgotten in the capital.

[a] See p. 536, n. *a.*   [b] See p. 175.

INTRODUCTION

Cicero receives more detailed information. 19 or 20 Oct.

The *senatus consultum ultimum* is passed. 21 Oct.

Manlius in open insurrection. 27 Oct.

The Senate is informed about Manlius. 1 Nov. (approx.)

The conspirators meet at Laeca's house. 6 Nov.

Abortive attempt on Cicero's life. 7 Nov.

Cicero delivers *First Speech against Catiline* in the Senate. Catiline leaves Rome. 8 Nov.

Cicero delivers *Second Speech against Catiline* to the people. 9 Nov.

Catiline and Manlius outlawed. 17 Nov. (approx.)

Trial and acquittal of Murena on a charge of electoral corruption. Late Nov. or early Dec.

Arrest of the conspirators at the Mulvian Bridge. 2/3 Dec.

Examination of the arrested conspirators before the Senate. Cicero delivers *Third Speech against Catiline* to the people. 3 Dec.

Debate in the Senate to decide the fate of the arrested conspirators. Cicero delivers *Fourth Speech against Catiline* in the Senate. Execution of the conspirators. 5 Dec.

New tribunes enter office. Quintus Caecilius Metellus Nepos proceeds to attack Cicero. 10 Dec.

Nepos vetoes Cicero's delivery of the oration traditional to the last day of office. 31 Dec.

THE SPEECHES AGAINST
LUCIUS SERGIUS
CATILINA

INTRODUCTION

Lucius Sergius Catilina

Lucius Sergius Catilina [a] was a patrician member of a noble [b] family which had not provided Rome with a consul for more than three hundred years and whose decayed fortunes [c] he was determined to revive. Endowed with military talents of a high order,[d] he was a member of the staff of the consul Gnaeus Pompeius Strabo in 89 at the siege of the rebel town of Asculum.[e] We have no evidence that he played any very active rôle during the 80s but he certainly remained secure under the Cinnan government. Indeed, he may have had family ties with Marians because a fragment of Sallust's *Histories* [f] suggests that his first wife was Gratidia, a sister of Marcus Marius Gratidianus, and his Marian connexions were doubtless only severed when expediency dictated the

[a] M. Gelzer in Pauly-Wissowa, *Realencyclopädie* II A 2 (1923), L. Sergius Catilina (23), 1693-1711. For the modern literature, see N. Criniti, *Bibliografia Catilinaria*.

[b] His nobility is attested by *commentariolum petitionis* 9 and he must therefore be descended from the Sergii Fidenates who were consuls and consular tribunes in the fifth and fourth centuries. M. Gelzer, *The Nobility of the Roman Republic* 36.

[c] Politically, not financially; *cf.* Sallust, *Bellum Catilinae* 14. 2 ; likewise Sulla, p. 3, n. *a* below.

[d] Cicero, *pro Caelio* 12.

[e] Degrassi, *Inscriptiones Latinae Liberae Rei Publicae* 2 28-34, No. 515.　　　　　　[f] 1. 45.

transfer of his allegiance to Sulla. It was with the Dictator, himself born into a decayed patrician family,[a] and with the oligarchy established by him, that Catiline sought to restore his own family to fame.[b] Early in the 70s he saw service abroad, possibly in Cilicia with Publius Servilius Vatia, who was proconsul there from 78 until 74.[c]

In 73 he was accused of adultery with the Vestal Virgin, Fabia, who was a half-sister of Cicero's wife. Among those who testified in his favour was Quintus Lutatius Catulus, the consul of 78 and now the principal leader of the Optimates. Catiline was acquitted.[d]

Elected praetor in 68, he was propraetorian governor of Africa 67–66, but while he was still in the province a deputation appeared before the Senate with complaints about his misrule. On his return home he presented himself as a candidate in the consular elections for 65, but he was debarred from the elections by the consul Lucius Volcacius Tullus.[e] The complaints of the provincials led to his indictment for extortion, and the case finally came before the court in 65. After a hearing in which he received the support of many consulars, he was acquitted, but not

[a] But see E. Badian, *Sulla. The Deadly Reformer*, Todd Memorial Lecture, Sydney, 1970, p. 5 for Sulla's financial position and the peripeteia of the self-made man as the stock-in-trade of romantic biography.

[b] E. S. Gruen, " The Dolabellae and Sulla," *American Journal of Philology* 87 (1966), 393.

[c] C. Cichorius, *Römische Studien* 173. Some of his considerable military experience may conceivably have been with Pompey in Spain. E. Badian, " The Early Career of A. Gabinius (*cos.* 58 B.C.)," *Philologus* 103 (1959), 95.

[d] Asconius 91 C ; for the date, see *in Catilinam* 3. 9, p. 108.

[e] See p. xix.

CICERO

in time for him to stand in the consular elections
for 64.[a]

In the elections for 63 Catiline was accepted as a
candidate, and Cicero hoped that he would join him
in his election campaign.[b] There were five other
candidates, of whom Gaius Antonius Hybrida (the
uncle of Mark Antony) was reckoned to be the only
serious rival. Catiline and Antonius were said to have
been supported by Caesar and Crassus [c] and joined
forces in an effort to defeat Cicero, furthering their
campaign with extensive bribery. To curb their
lavish expenditure a measure was proposed which
would increase the penalties for this offence, but the
bill was vetoed by a tribune, Quintus Mucius
Orestinus.[d] Cicero thereupon took advantage of the
indignation this veto provoked in the Senate and

[a] Torquatus and other consulars turned up in force (pro
Sulla 81, p. 392), possibly in return for Catiline's acquiescence
in Volcacius' decision the previous year that he could not be
a consular candidate. Cicero (ad Atticum 1. 2. 1) has been
thought in the light of subsequent events to be alleging
collusion, but he is only saying that the prosecutor, Publius
Clodius, was agreeable in the reiectio of jurors and this may
mean no more than that the prosecution was supremely
confident of its case. Cicero (ad Atticum 1. 1. 1) thought that
Catiline had no chance of acquittal. He had good reason to
contemplate defending Catiline, even if he should fail,
because Catiline's support would be valuable in his forthcoming electoral plans (ad Atticum 1. 2. 1). Presumably
after Catiline's acquittal disgruntled men blamed Clodius, but
Catiline had an impressive array of supporters and they
carried the day for him. E. S. Gruen, " Some Criminal
Trials of the Late Republic: Political and Prosoprographical
Problems," Athenaeum 49 (1971), 60-61.

[b] See previous note.

[c] Asconius 83 C, but he got his information from the
notoriously unreliable de consiliis suis begun by Cicero in 59.

[d] See p. 304.

4

delivered a speech, *in toga candida*, attacking his two rivals.[a] The Optimates took fright and in default of a more suitable candidate helped Cicero in spite of his drawbacks—his *novitas*,[b] his support for Pompey and his equestrian connexions—to head the poll. Antonius came second with a narrow lead over Catiline.

Before the year was out Catiline survived another prosecution. At the instance of the quaestor, Marcus Porcius Cato, men who had profited by the Sullan proscriptions were charged with murder, and the flood of cases swamped the *quaestio de sicariis*—the murder court, one of the seven established or reconstituted by Sulla. As a result, aedilicians were co-opted to assist the praetor in charge and preside over trials for murder. Among these *iudices quaestionis* was Caesar, who accepted indictments against a number of Sullans, but when Lucius Lucceius, a praetorian who was closely linked with Pompey, prosecuted Catiline, the defendant was acquitted. As president of the court Caesar was, of course, not responsible for the verdict of the jury, but it does show that there existed influential men concerned to preserve Catiline from political extinction.

Free once more to stand as a consular candidate in 63, he again suffered defeat, this time at the hands of Decimus Junius Silanus and Lucius Licinius Murena. This defeat was conclusive.[c] The highest office in the State, the summit of his political ambitions, was not to be his by constitutional means, and it was the

[a] For the argument and fragments of this lost speech, see Asconius 82-94 C. The title derives from the whitened togas worn by the candidates.   [b] See p. 178, n. *e*.

[c] Catiline had hoped for the continued support of Antonius (*cf. pro Murena* 49, p. 250) but Cicero won over his colleague by exchanging provinces. See p. xxxvii, n. *f*.

realization of this fact that turned Catiline into an active revolutionary preparing a coup d'état in Rome and an insurrection in Italy. This was the only path now left open to him.

This account of Catiline's career hardly matches the version of his character that we find in our ancient sources. The man on whose behalf the leading optimate testified in 73, whom eminent consulars supported and Cicero thought of defending in 65, whom Cicero hoped to have as a political ally and who survived prosecution in 64, is not likely to have been the man depicted by Cicero in his speeches or by Sallust in his *Bellum Catilinae*. We must, therefore, examine what was alleged against Catiline and consider what credence can be attached to the allegations.[a]

In his speech *in toga candida*, delivered in the summer of 64, Cicero alleges a series of crimes committed over the past two decades. He says that at the time of the Sullan proscriptions Catiline had cut off the head of Marcus Marius Gratidianus and carried it through the streets of Rome,[b] and that he had murdered Quintus Caecilius, Marcus Volumnius and Lucius Tanusius[c]; that he had been discreditably involved with the Vestal Fabia (Cicero could not make much of this affair as Catiline had been acquitted and Fabia was his own sister-in-law)[d]; that he had entered into an incestuous marriage with his daughter, whose name, Aurelia Orestilla, is supplied for us by Sallust.[e] In the *First Speech Against*

---

[a] Anything written after 63 must be regarded with suspicion. *Cf.* p. 4, n. *c.* Nothing was now too bad for an active revolutionary.   [b] Asconius 84 C.   [c] *Ib.*
[d] *Ib.* 91 C.   [e] *Ib.* and Sallust, *Bellum Catilinae* 15. 2.

Catiline he adds the further allegation that after getting rid of his previous wife he committed another crime, the murder of his son.[a]

Two other writers add to his list. The author of the electioneering handbook, *commentariolum petitionis*, alleges that Catiline did away with his brother-in-law, a knight by the name of Quintus Caecilius, during the proscriptions.[b] Plutarch relates that he killed his own brother and committed incest with his daughter.[c]

In his monograph Sallust is seeking to characterize Catiline as symptomatic of all that was evil at Rome and a man foredoomed by the corruptness of society to a life of crime and violence.[d] We know that Sallust used speeches of Cicero for his own writing, and the crimes with which we are regaled in the speech *in toga candida* would be just what he wanted to make good his case. Yet there are surprisingly few of them in his work. No mention of the murders by Sulla's lieutenant, and of his moral depravity only a reference to Fabia and then the murder of his son introduced to provide the driving force of his revolutionary designs.[e]

In speeches delivered after the consular elections of 63 Cicero makes further allegations about Catiline's earlier plots : that he planned to murder Cicero in 64,[f] to murder Cicero and his rival candidates at the elections of 63,[g] to kill the consuls and the other

---

[a] *in Catilinam* 1. 14, p. 46 and Sallust, *Bellum Catilinae* 15. 2.   [b] 9.   [c] *Sulla* 32. 3 and *Cicero* 10. 3.
[d] *Bellum Catilinae* 14. 1-3. See R. Syme, *Sallust* 84 f.
[e] *Bellum Catilinae* 15. 2-5.
[f] *in Catilinam* 1. 11, p. 44. It must be remembered that our version of the speeches against Catiline did not appear until the summer of 60 (*ad Atticum* 2. 1. 3).
[g] *Ib.*

leading men on the 29th of December 66,[a] to massacre the Senate on the same occasion [b] and to take the place of one of the consuls for 65 who were to be murdered.[c]

These statements about Catiline's plans for violence at the end of 66 merit further study. In the speech *in toga candida* Cicero says that he will pass over the plot to massacre the Optimates,[d] but the speech *pro Sulla* can shed light on the origin of the myth. Cicero is engaged in the defence of Publius Cornelius Sulla and the prosecution has pointed out that in his letter to Pompey Cicero had linked the earlier affair with the conspiracy of 63.[e] Cicero therefore has to extricate Sulla from complicity in 66, and one of the devices he employs is the substitution of Catiline for Sulla as a principal in the affair and the implication that Catiline was to have taken the place of one of the murdered consuls.[f]

Sallust accepts Cicero's story and gives Catiline the leading rôle.[g] The story is highly appropriate for a man ever driven to violence and crime by the corruption of the times and by his bad conscience.

The evidence for Catiline's life of debauchery, murder and revolution derives from an electoral

[a] *in Catilinam* 1. 15, p. 46. See also pp. xx-xxi.
[b] *pro Murena* 81, p. 288.
[c] *pro Sulla* 67 f., p. 378 f. *Cf.* pp. xx and 311.
[d] Asconius 92 C.   [e] *pro Sulla* 67 f., p. 378 f.
[f] R. Syme, *Sallust* 90. See also R. Seager, *op. cit.* 34. The young Torquatus may have introduced Catiline's name in order to deepen Sulla's implication with Catiline. It is also possible that Cicero had, *e.g.* in lost portions of his speech *in toga candida*, linked Catiline with the alleged activities of Sulla and Autronius in order to discredit his opponent and later had to eat his words for the sake of his client.
[g] *Bellum Catilinae* 18.

8

address, an occasion upon which an almost total licence was allowed to Roman orators for heaping personal abuse upon their rivals; from a speech in a criminal case in which the truth may have been perverted in the interests of Cicero's client at Catiline's expense; from a monograph designed to show him to be the evil product of an evil system; and from speeches delivered after Catiline had revealed himself as an active revolutionary in the later months of 63. This is not to say that in the violent society in which he lived his hands were unstained by crime or that his behaviour was any better than that of many of his contemporaries with political ambitions. But it can be shown that some of the charges against him were in all probability false, that some were conventional slander and that some antedated his rôle as a revolutionary leader in 63. Men of standing and judgement were prepared to ignore his past and thought him worthy of their support until repeated electoral defeat drove him to take up arms against the system.

The portrait of Catiline in Cicero's speech *pro Caelio*, delivered in 56, is very different from that painted in the earlier denunciations. Cicero, admittedly, had an axe to grind but, in Syme's words, he found that " Catiline was not a monster after all : a blended and enigmatic individual, he possessed many virtues which for a time deceived excellent and unsuspecting persons including Cicero himself." [a] No worse morally than many others, Catiline was a man of ability and a leader; although he had his weaknesses, we must not allow the brilliance of Cicero's invective to hide his more desirable qualities from us.

[a] *The Roman Revolution* 150.

CICERO

Policy and Supporters [a]

The reasons for Catiline's emphasis upon his policy of *tabulae novae*, the cancellation of debts, are to be found in the economic conditions of the time. There had been previous occasions in Roman history when expenditure incurred in war had created widespread indebtedness and a serious shortage of currency, but the burden of debt had never been greater than in 63.[b] The fighting of the 80s and again in 78–77, followed by the slave revolt of 73–71 with all the attendant violence and devastation of the Italian countryside, led to a social and economic crisis which was exacerbated by the depredations of the pirates and the cost of the war against Mithridates.[c] The pirates had caused dear food and the expenditure incurred in defeating Mithridates had decreased the amount of money available for credit. The main grievances, however, were domestic in origin and concerned the plight of the urban poor [d] and the exactions of the rich. The consequent hatred of the

[a] Z. Yavetz, " The Failure of Catiline's Conspiracy," *Historia* 12 (1963), 485-499, is particularly illuminating. See also E. S. Gruen, *The Last Generation of the Roman Republic* 416-433.   [b] Cicero, *de officiis* 2. 84.

[c] P. A. Brunt, " The Army and the Land in the Roman Revolution," *Journal of Roman Studies* 52 (1962), 73 ; M. W. Frederiksen, " Caesar, Cicero and the Problem of Debt," *Journal of Roman Studies* 56 (1966), 132-133 ; and P. A. Brunt, *Italian Manpower 225 B.C.–A.D. 14* 108 f.

[d] Sallust, *Bellum Catilinae* 37. For the misery and squalor of the city population, see Z. Yavetz, " The Living Conditions of the Urban Plebs in Republican Rome," *Latomus* 17 (1958), 500-517 and P. A. Brunt, " The Roman Mob," *Past and Present* 35 (1966), 11-18. For agrarian discontent, see P. A. Brunt, *Social Conflicts in the Roman Republic* 131.

wealthy money-lenders [a] fostered popular propaganda against the payment of debts, and at the beginning of 63 a bill for the cancellation of debts had actually been promoted but it was never passed.[b] It was therefore sound politics for Catiline to make the cancellation of debts his prime concern. There were many in Italy, including the urban plebs, who were very ready to join a noble in refusing to pay their debts.[c]

In his *Second Speech against Catiline* [d] Cicero identifies six groups among Catiline's supporters :

(1) Wealthy men who are heavily in debt and who could repay their debts by selling land but are unwilling to do so.[e]

(2) Men who are in debt and see revolution as their road to power.

(3) Veterans of Sulla's army who had been settled in colonies, but have lived beyond their means and now want new proscriptions from which to recoup their fortunes.

(4) Men deep in financial difficulties who seek to evade their problems by joining Catiline.

(5) The criminal element in society.

(6) The dissolute youth of the capital.

Catiline's support was thus not confined to the lower classes, but there is a significant omission from this list—the urban plebs. There is no doubt that the

[a] Cicero was the champion of the money-lenders ; *ad Atticum* 2. 1. 11.

[b] Dio 37. 25 4.

[c] For Sallust's account of the background to the conspiracy, see *Bellum Catilinae* 33. 1 and 4-5, 37. 4-9.

[d] 17-23, pp. 84-92.

[e] For the explanation of their attitude, see M. W. Frederiksen, *op. cit.* 130 and 137-138.

Roman masses did at first support the conspiracy [a] and their omission is capable of explanation. The *Second Speech against Catiline* was delivered to a meeting open to the whole populace in which Cicero seeks to present Catiline's supporters in the worst possible light and to urge the lower classes not to join a conspiracy under the leadership of depraved aristocrats whose interests have nothing in common with theirs. He must therefore avoid identifying his audience with those whom he is attacking.

These efforts to split the urban plebs from the other conspirators were successful.[b] Cicero was able to convince his listeners that Catiline's aim was anarchy, but anarchy or the liberation of the slaves was not what they sought. No more was it the temporary alleviation of an economic crisis which would leave its root causes untouched. The prospect of radical social reform offering them a permanent improvement of their position in society might have led them to join Catiline, but this was not—according to Cicero— what they were being promised.

The leading individual supporters of the conspiracy were drawn from the misfits and failures of society. The most distinguished was Publius Cornelius Lentulus Sura, a consular who had been expelled from the Senate in 70. By 63 he had rehabilitated himself and become praetor, and was thus with Catiline able to bring some standing to the revolutionary leaders. A man, however, who was naïve enough to base his hopes of success upon oracles was in Cicero's view a man over whom no sleep need be

[a] *in Catilinam* 2. 8 and 4. 6, pp. 76 and 140; *pro Murena* 78-79, pp. 284-286; Sallust, *Bellum Catilinae* 37. 1.
[b] *Ib.* 48. 1.

lost. The most notable of the other senatorial adherents were Lucius Cassius Longinus, a corpulent rogue who had been one of the candidates at the consular elections in 64, and Gaius Cornelius Cethegus, a hot-head with no judgement.[a] There were also some knights involved, and men from the towns of Italy: Titus Volturcius from Croton, Marcus Ceparius from Terracina, and Publius Furius, a Sullan colonist from Faesulae. Freedmen, too, were among the members of the conspiracy, notably Publius Umbrenus who had been a businessman in Gaul; but Catiline in spite of the urging of his colleagues refused to the end to raise a slave revolt.[b]

Such men, although a potentially dangerous combination, were not the making of a successful revolution. Their conduct during the conspiracy only serves to confirm the view that their own shortcomings drove them to join Catiline as the sole means of achieving a better place in society. The main redeeming feature of Catiline's followers was their loyalty to their leader.

THE COURSE OF THE CONSPIRACY

Catiline's conduct during his election campaign in July 63 gave cause for alarm to all right-thinking citizens. Gaius Manlius, who had served as a centurion under Sulla, was enrolling men in Etruria, and Catiline himself was marching through the streets of Rome at the head of Sullan veterans and of men dispossessed by Sulla in his proscriptions.[c] It was also reported that in a private meeting Catiline had

---

[a] *in Catilinam* 3. 10, p. 108.　[b] See pp. 28 and 60, n. *a*.
[c] *pro Murena* 49, p. 248.

proclaimed himself the champion of the poor and oppressed and had stated his intention of assassinating Cicero at the forthcoming elections.[a] He continued to attend the meetings of the Senate and there was a note of ruthless menace in his reply to Cato's threat of prosecution.[b] As soon as Cicero heard of what had been said at the private meeting, he summoned the Senate, and his version of what transpired is recorded in the speech *pro Murena*.[c] After reporting what had taken place he moved that the elections which were due to be held the following day should be postponed so that the Senate might discuss his report. The Senate accepted his motion, but at the meeting on the next day took the view that there were no grounds for emergency measures, and Catiline stalked out of the House in triumph. Cicero, affirming that his life was threatened and seeing that he had failed to obtain official backing for his view that danger was imminent, formed a bodyguard of private citizens and entered the Campus Martius on the day of the poll surrounded by armed men and ostentatiously wearing a breastplate to overawe his enemies and to bring home to loyalists his own danger.[d] His plan succeeded. Catiline and his followers made no move—if they had ever intended one—and Decimus Junius Silanus and Lucius Licinius Murena were elected.[e]

When the result of the elections was known, Catiline sent Manlius back to Faesulae in northern Etruria, despatched two subordinates to Picenum and

[a] *Pro Murena* 50 and 52, pp. 250 and 252.
[b] *Ib.* 51, p. 252.   [c] *Ib.*   [d] *Ib.* 52, p. 252.
[e] *in Catilinam* 1. 11, p. 42 ; *pro Murena* 52, p. 252 ; *pro Sulla* 51, p. 364.

Apulia and others to other areas to raise new levies.[a] For the moment he remained himself in Rome to allay suspicion and to further his plans in the capital. We have no detailed knowledge of what was happening in Rome during August and September, but the existence of an active conspiracy should be dated from these months.

On the night of the 18th of October Cicero was roused from his bed by Crassus and two other nobles, Marcus Marcellus and Quintus Caecilius Metellus Pius Scipio, and was handed a bundle of letters which had been left at Crassus' house. Crassus had opened only that addressed to himself and had found that it warned him of impending massacre and urged him to flee Rome. Various theories about the origin of these letters are possible : that Cicero had forged them in order to check Crassus' reliability, that they were a device of Crassus himself to clear his name or that one of the conspirators was genuinely seeking to warn certain friends of their danger. No theory is susceptible of proof and none is entirely satisfactory, but the subsequent behaviour of the conspirators suggests that the third theory is the most likely. On the following morning Cicero convened the Senate and the letters were read out. Again the Senate refused to make any decisive move, but the consuls were instructed to make further inquiries. Later the same day or on the 20th of October Quintus Arrius, an expraetor, brought Cicero more explicit information of events in Etruria, and Cicero convened the Senate once more on the 21st of October and at this meeting the *senatus consultum ultimum* was passed.[b]

----

[a] Sallust, *Bellum Catilinae* 26. 5-27. 1.
[b] See Appendix B, pp. 567-574.

In his *First Speech against Catiline*, delivered on the 8th of November,[a] Cicero claimed that at this meeting he had forecast with complete accuracy that Manlius would take up arms on the 27th of October, that a massacre was planned for the 28th and that Praeneste, a stronghold of Latium, was to be seized on the 1st of November. We do not know how all this information came into Cicero's hands : whether from Arrius ; from Fulvia, the mistress of Quintus Curius, one of the conspirators, who kept Cicero posted on the conspirators' plans ; or from some other source. It is also possible that this claim in our version of the speech, published some three years later, may have replaced a less detailed version couched in more general terms.

Once the *senatus consultum ultimum* had been passed Cicero acted with all speed, arranged for forces to secure the capital, and despatched a specially raised levy to strengthen the defences of Praeneste. A few days later, at the very beginning of November, a senator named Lucius Saenius read to the Senate a letter that he had received from Faesulae telling him that Manlius had taken the field on the 27th as planned. It also contained the news that slaves were in revolt at Capua and in Apulia.[b] To deal with these emergencies two consulars who were awaiting triumphs outside the city, Quintus Marcius Rex, the ex-governor of Cilicia, and Quintus Metellus Creticus, the conqueror of Crete, were instructed to take control at Faesulae and in Apulia respectively. The

---

[a] *in Catilinam* 1. 7-8, p. 38-40. The date of this speech is still disputed. See T. Crane, " Times of the Night in Cicero's First Catilinarian," *Classical Journal* 61 (1965–66), 264-267 (with bibliography).   [b] Sallust, *Bellum Catilinae* 30. 1-2.

praetors, Quintus Pompeius Rufus and Quintus Metellus Celer, were given authority to raise troops and entrusted with Capua and Picenum.

Rewards were offered for information about the conspiracy : freedom and one hundred thousand sesterces for slaves and a pardon with two hundred thousand for citizens. This offer did not produce a single traitor to Catiline's cause. Arrangements were made to disperse the gladiators at Capua,[a] while at Rome itself Cicero's precautions created panic and caused the collapse of credit.[b]

Catiline still calmly remained in the city, and even when the young Lucius Aemilius Paulus gave notice of intent to prosecute him for violent crime (de vi) his nerve did not fail him. He offered to place himself in the custody of the consular Manius Lepidus, of Cicero, of Metellus Celer, and finally of a person whose identity is uncertain,[c] but none was willing to receive him and the threatened prosecution came to nothing.[d] Cicero was not yet in a position to prove Catiline's guilt. The Senate had shown itself reluctant to move unless totally convinced of imminent crisis, and the very success of Cicero's counter-measures had made him seem an alarmist. He wisely preferred to wait until he held incontrovertible evidence before he moved.

On the night of the 6th of November [e] the leading members of the conspiracy gathered at the house of Marcus Porcius Laeca in the street of the scythe-makers. Catiline announced that he had decided to leave Rome and take over the command of the rebels

---

[a] B.C. 30. 3-7.   [b] Ib. 31. 1-2 ; in Catilinam 1. 1, p. 32.
[c] For the possibility that it was Metellus Nepos, see p. 52, n. c.   [d] in Catilinam 1. 19, p. 52.   [e] pro Sulla 52, p. 364.

outside the city. He was going himself to join
Manlius, and those selected to take command of the
various areas were to proceed to Etruria, Picenum
and Cisalpine Gaul. Others were to remain behind
in Rome and arrange for the firing of certain regions
of the city and for Cicero's assassination. Gaius
Cornelius and Lucius Vargunteius volunteered to call
upon him the following morning on the pretext of
paying their respects and to kill him in his own home,
but Curius instructed Fulvia to warn Cicero, and
when the assassins arrived early on the morning of
the 7th they found the house strongly guarded
against them and abandoned their attempt.[a]

On the next day, the 8th of November, Cicero
convened the Senate in the temple of Jupiter Stator
at the foot of the Palatine Hill. The site was easier
to protect than the Senate-house itself, and Cicero
had surrounded the building with armed knights.[b]
To Cicero's astonishment Catiline took his place, but
as he sat down the other senators slipped away from
the seats around him and left him in isolation.[c]
Cicero then delivered his *First Speech against Catiline*,
a piece of invective that has remained unequalled.

When Cicero had finished, Catiline rose to reply.
Far from being cowed by the onslaught upon him he
rallied to the attack: his family had rendered great
service to Rome over the centuries and he, a patrician,
had followed their example and had nothing to win
from revolution; Cicero, the city's would-be saviour,

[a] *in Catilinam* 1. 1, p. 32; 8-10, pp. 40-42; 2. 6, p. 72;
pro Sulla 18 and 52, pp. 330 and 364; *Bellum Catilinae* 27. 3-
28. 3.
[b] *in Catilinam* 1. 21, p. 54.
[c] *Ib.* 1. 16 and 2. 12, pp. 48 and 78.

was a resident alien.[a] Shouted down by the Senate
he rushed from the House and went straight home.
There he urged Lentulus, Cethegus and the others to
carry out the instructions issued at Laeca's house on
the 6th, and then with a few followers he left Rome at
the dead of night to join Manlius.[b] Resourceful as
ever, he wrote to leading figures at Rome to say that
he was the victim of his enemies' malice and was
going into voluntary exile at Marseilles in order to
spare his country the horrors of civil war. His
accomplices who had been left behind at Rome spread
a similar report [c] with the object of discrediting Cicero
and casting doubt upon the necessity of his measures
against Catiline. He also sought to justify himself
in a letter to Quintus Catulus which Catulus read
out in the Senate and which Sallust claims to reproduce.[d]

On the following day, the 9th of November, Cicero
addressed a public meeting in the Forum and delivered his *Second Speech against Catiline* informing the
people of what had happened. A few days later (on
about the 17th of November) news reached Rome that
Catiline, accompanied like a consul by twelve lictors,
had arrived at Manlius' camp.[e] The two men were
immediately declared public enemies ; the consuls
instructed to enlist troops : Antonius was to pursue
Catiline without delay and Cicero was to remain in
Rome to defend the capital ; an amnesty was offered

---

[a] *Bellum Catilinae* 31. 7. Cicero came from Arpinum.
Cf. *pro Sulla* 22-23, p. 334 and n. *c*.
[b] *in Catilinam* 2. 1 and 6, pp. 68 and 72 ; *Bellum Catilinae* 32. 1-2.
[c] *in Catilinam* 2. 14 and 16, pp. 80 and 82.
[d] *Bellum Catilinae* 35.
[e] *in Catilinam* 2. 13, p. 80 ; *pro Sulla* 17, p. 328.

to those who laid down their arms by a certain day. Once again there was not a single defector from Catiline's ranks to take advantage of this offer.[a]

Of the conspirators left in Rome, Cethegus was all for instant action but was overruled by Lentulus. Plans were laid that on the 16th of December a tribune, Lucius Calpurnius Bestia, should attack Cicero and rouse the people against him for accusing innocent men and provoking a dangerous war. Then, on the night of the 17th, under cover of the uncontrolled revelry of the Saturnalia, Statilius and Gabinius were to start fires in twelve places, and in the resulting confusion Cethegus was to kill Cicero at his home and other leading men were to be assassinated. The conspirators were then to break out of the burning city and join Catiline who was to be at hand with his army to receive them.[b]

At this point a further call was made upon Cicero's time and energy. With a fine disregard for the perils of the hour Servius Sulpicius Rufus, one of the unsuccessful candidates for the consulship, combined with Marcus Porcius Cato to accuse Lucius Licinius Murena, consul-elect for 62, of electoral malpractice. Cicero interrupted his search for evidence against the conspirators and accepted the brief for the defence.[c] Scarcely was the trial over and the defendant safely acquitted than the evidence enabling him to arrest the conspirators came into his hands.

Envoys from the Allobroges, a tribe of Narbonese Gaul, had recently arrived in Rome to seek redress

[a] *Bellum Catilinae* 36. 5.
[b] *in Catilinam* 2. 1 and 6, pp. 68 and 72 ; 3. 10 and 17, pp. 108 and 118 ; *pro Sulla* 33 and 53, pp. 344 and 366.
[c] See p. 180.

against Roman misrule and the depredations of the
Italian financiers. At the request of Lentulus, a
certain Umbrenus who had been engaged on business
in Gaul approached the envoys with the proposal that
if they supported the conspiracy their grievances
would be remedied. After the initial approach
Publius Gabinius Capito, a leading conspirator of
equestrian rank, was introduced to them and details
of the conspiracy and the names of those involved
were given to them.[a] The envoys, however, had
more good sense than the conspirators and decided
that the dangers of the bargain outweighed its
benefits. They therefore made a clean breast of the
negotiations to Quintus Fabius Sanga, whose family
were the tribe's hereditary patrons. He promptly
informed Cicero of all that they had told him and,
acting on the consul's instructions, returned to the
envoys and told them to pretend to continue their
negotiations with the conspirators. They were to get
into touch with the other ringleaders, to promise the
help for which they had been asked and to exact
written promises from Lentulus, Cethegus, Statilius
and Cassius.[b] The first three complied, but Cassius,
more wary than his colleagues, replied that he was
going to Gaul in the near future and left Rome without delay. Late on the evening of the 2nd of December the Gauls, accompanied by Titus Volturcius,
left the city carrying with them the incriminating
documents. Volturcius' rôle was to lead them to Cati-

---

[a] *in Catilinam* 3. 4 and 9, pp. 102 and 108 ; *Bellum Catilinae*
40. For speculation upon the identity of this Gabinius, see
E. Badian, " The Early Career of A. Gabinius (*cos.* 58 B.C.),"
Philologus 103 (1959), 97-98.
[b] *Bellum Catilinae* 41.

line, for whom he carried a personal message from Lentulus.[a] As soon as he heard from the envoys the details of their plans, Cicero summoned Lucius Valerius Flaccus[b] and Gaius Pomptinus, two of the praetors and both men of wide military experience. He ordered them to take an armed force to the Mulvian bridge by which the *via Flaminia* crosses the Tiber two miles north of Rome. There they were to lie in wait for the party and arrest them as they passed. In the early hours of the 3rd of December the envoys' party reached the bridge and after a brief mêlée surrendered to the praetors.[c]

As dawn broke the envoys and Volturcius were brought before Cicero and the letters with their seals intact handed to him. Gabinius, Statilius, Cethegus and—after an interval—Lentulus were in turn interviewed and detained. Leading senators now began to join the group and urged Cicero to open the letters immediately to confirm that their contents were treasonable. Cicero, of course, knew what they were likely to contain and did not wish to be accused of tampering with them or to lessen their impact upon the Senate and so refused. Acting upon information received from the envoys he sent the praetor, Gaius Sulpicius, to search Cethegus' house and a large cache of arms was discovered there.[d]

Taking Lentulus by the hand out of consideration for his position as praetor, Cicero led the three other conspirators and Volturcius to the temple of Concord

---

[a] *in Catilinam* 3. 4 and 12, pp. 102 and 112; *Bellum Catilinae* 44.
[b] See p. 415.
[c] *in Catilinam* 3. 6, p. 104; *Bellum Catilinae* 45.
[d] *in Catil.* 3. 6-8, pp. 104-108; *B.C.* 46. 3-4.

where a meeting of the Senate had been convened. The temple was surrounded by armed guards and was closely packed inside.

Volturcius was questioned first and, prompted by the promise of immunity, revealed the conspirators' plans and related how he had been entrusted by Lentulus with the message for Catiline. The Gauls who had accompanied Cicero's party were then brought into the meeting and recounted all that had passed between them and the conspirators. The letters were now produced and their authors questioned—Cethegus first, then Statilius and Lentulus, and finally Gabinius. All four confessed and, even allowing for Cicero making the most of the material in his hands, the treasonable nature of the conspirators' activities could not remain in doubt.[a]

Cicero now invited the House to consider the situation revealed by these confessions. It was first resolved that Lentulus should resign his praetorship and be detained in custody. Cethegus, Statilius and Gabinius were also detained, and all four men were handed over to prominent senators for safe keeping. The Senate then went on to authorize the arrest of other conspirators, amongst them Cassius who had declined to provide a letter and the freedman, Umbrenus, who had made the first contact with the Gauls. Finally, a thanksgiving to the gods was decreed for Cicero, the first time that a magistrate had received this honour in recognition of the distinguished exercise of his civil, as opposed to his military, power.[b]

On Cicero's instructions copies of the evidence were

---

[a] *in Catil.* 3. 8-13, pp. 106-114; *B.C.* 46. 5-47. 2.
[b] *in Catil.* 3. 13-15, pp. 112-116; *B.C.* 47. 3-4.

posted throughout Italy [a] while Cicero himself went straight to the Forum where in his *Third Speech against Catiline* he informed the people of the events of the last few days and of the action taken by the Senate.

On the next day, the 4th of December, the Senate met again and an informer, Lucius Tarquinius, alleged that Crassus had ordered him to take a message to Catiline urging him not to lose heart. Some did not believe the story; others believed it, but felt it prudent to keep quiet. Some thought that Autronius was behind Tarquinius, others that he had been put up to his story by Cicero. This was Crassus' own version and the allegation provided him with a credible excuse for not attending the meeting of the Senate the following day and declaring his position publicly. The Senate decided that the evidence of Tarquinius was false and that he should be kept in custody until he revealed who was behind him.[b]

Enemies of Caesar also sought to exploit the crisis. Quintus Lutatius Catulus and Gaius Calpurnius Piso attempted to persuade Cicero to implicate Caesar by means of forged evidence, but he would have nothing to do with them.[c] The Gallic envoys and Volturcius

---

[a] *pro Sulla* 42, p. 354.

[b] *Bellum Catilinae* 48. 3-9.

[c] *Ib.* 49. During his election campaign Catiline was no doubt in touch with Crassus and Caesar, but when he became the leader of a revolutionary movement he ceased to represent their political aims.

The harsh reality of Caesar's consulship in 59 and the First Triumvirate provoked Cicero to write the pamphlet *de consiliis suis* in which he asserted that Crassus and Caesar had instigated the conspiracy, a belief to which he clung for the rest of his life. At the time he well knew that they only wanted to use Catiline for their own ends and that as soon as

were rewarded and the leading conspirators declared public enemies.[a] Meanwhile attempts were being made to gather parties to free the ringleaders. To counter these efforts Cicero posted guards and summoned the Senate for the following day to decide the fate of the conspirators.[b]

Early in the morning of the 5th of December the Senate met in the temple of Concord. All the approaches were guarded by armed men as were the Forum and the adjacent temples.[c] Cicero opened the debate upon the fate of the arrested men. It was his right as consul to take any action required, but he wanted the authority of the Senate behind him. The first speaker was the senior consul-designate, Junius Silanus.[d] He moved that the men already in custody together with Lucius Cassius Longinus, Publius Furius, Umbrenus and Quintus Annius, when they were caught, should be put to death. His fellow consul-designate, Lucius Licinius Murena, and fourteen consulars supported his motion. Caesar, as

---

his plans for revolution were put into practice, they ceased to support him.

[a] *in Catil.* 4. 5, p. 140 ; *B.C.* 50. 1. It is sad to record that the envoys' loyalty to Rome did not secure any redress for their people.

[b] *in Catil.* 4. 6, p. 140 ; *B.C.* 50. 1-3.

[c] *in Catil.* 4. 14-15, pp. 152-154 ; *B.C.* 50. 3.

[d] The earlier you spoke in a debate, the greater your *auctoritas*. Between election and taking office the consuls-elect spoke first, then the *consulares* followed in turn by the praetors-elect, the praetors and the *praetorii*. Junior senators were expected to be seen and not heard. The speech of the tribune-elect, Cato, who was a comparatively junior senator, far exceeded in its effect the *auctoritas* that he was expected to bring to the debate. J. P. V. D. Balsdon, " *Auctoritas, Dignitas, Otium*," *Classical Quarterly* 10 (1960), 44.

praetor-designate, was then asked to give his view. He acknowledged the guilt of the conspirators and maintained that no punishment could be too harsh for their crimes, but he opposed the death penalty. This opposition sprang from concern for the rule of law and out of fear that a dangerous precedent was being established. He proposed that the prisoners be detained in Italian towns which were to be held responsible for their safe custody. Even if it did not win wide support this suggestion raised doubts in men's minds, and in the succeeding speeches a variety of opinions was expressed until Cicero rose to intervene in the debate. In his *Fourth Speech against Catiline* he summed up the arguments advanced by the speakers and invited the Senate to come to its decision. He left little doubt where his own feelings lay, but other views were fairly represented. He was concerned that any decision to execute the conspirators should be seen to have the backing of the Senate. It needed little foresight on his part to visualize the capital that his enemies could make out of such a decision, and he did not wish to leave his political flank unnecessarily exposed.

Finally, Marcus Porcius Cato, tribune-designate for 62, rose and with his powerful oratory brought home to his audience the dangers of Caesar's suggestion. His personal authority and the force of his logic won the day, and he sat down to general applause. Cicero put Cato's motion proposing the punishment of death to the vote and it was carried by a large majority.[a]

There was no delay in putting the decision into effect. Fearful that attempts might be made to rescue the condemned men, Cicero personally con-

[a] *B.C.* 50. 3-53. 1.

ducted Lentulus to the Tullianum while the praetors escorted Gabinius. With them was Ceparius who had been caught shortly after the others. There they were all strangled and the waiting crowd heard the consul's announcement that the conspirators' lives were over.[a]

Praise and honours were now heaped upon Cicero. Catulus and Cato hailed him as " the father of his country," and the former censor Lucius Gellius moved that he be granted the " civic crown " for saving the lives of citizens.[b] On his journey home through the Forum after the executions the people hailed him as the saviour and second founder of the State, and that night lights shone at every door.[c]

This adulation was not to last long. On the 10th of December Quintus Caecilius Metellus Nepos entered the office of tribune and declared at a public meeting that a man who had executed citizens without trial should not be allowed to speak.[d] On the 31st of December when Cicero was about to make the customary speech to the people at the end of his consulship, he was compelled by Nepos to confine himself to the oath that he had faithfully performed the duties of his office. Cicero, however, was able on this occasion to turn the tables upon his opponent and swore that he alone had saved the State. His oath was greeted by the people with thunderous applause and he was again escorted home by the loyal citizens of Rome.[e] Three days later, on the 3rd of January, Nepos attacked him in the House, but the Senate

[a] B.C. 55.   [b] Cicero, in Pisonem 6.
        [c] Plutarch, Cicero 22. 3-4.
[d] ad familiares 5. 2. 7. On Nepos, see p. xxxii.
    [e] ad familiares ibid. ; pro Sulla 34, p. 346.

passed a resolution indemnifying all who had acted against the conspirators.[a]

Things had gone no better for Catiline outside the city after his departure for Rome. The risings in the Italian countryside had rapidly been rendered ineffectual. In the Apennines Metellus Celer and in Cisalpine Gaul Gaius Licinius Murena kept the situation under control. The conspirators at Capua were dealt with by the quaestor, Publius Sestius, and by December he was free to move north in support of Antonius who had been assigned to Etruria, the only area in which there was sustained opposition. Catiline succeeded in increasing his forces there from the two thousand men raised by Manlius to a total of ten thousand, but of these only a quarter was properly armed. He could easily have increased this total by enlisting the slaves who fled to his camp— Lentulus urged this course upon him—but he refused to do this for fear of the effect that it might have on citizens whom he hoped to attach to his cause. Any benefit, however, that he might have secured from this restraint was nullified by the lurid picture that Cicero was able to paint of Gallic hordes invited to join in the sack of Rome.[b]

When the news of the execution of the conspirators at Rome reached Catiline's camp, those who had joined his forces solely in the hope of booty deserted and left him even more heavily outnumbered. He therefore abandoned his designs upon Italy or Rome and set out across the Apennines en route for Transalpine Gaul. After an arduous march with the remains of his army, he reached the vicinity of

[a] *ad familiares* 5. 2. 8. For this day of frantic violence, see note below and p. xxxii, n. *a.* [b] *in Catilinam* 4. 12, p. 150.

Pistoria where he found the route blocked by Quintus Metellus Celer and three legions, and the forces of Antonius were by now not far away.

Faced by Metellus, Catiline turned back on his tracks towards Pistoria to face the reluctant Antonius in the hope that he might not fight too hard. Antonius, however, developed an opportune illness and handed over his command to an experienced subordinate, Marcus Petreius. Battle was joined and bitter fighting ensued. Only after the praetorian cohort had been flung against their centre did Catiline's forces break. Manlius was among the first to fall and when Catiline saw that all was lost he charged in the direction where the enemy were thickest and there fell fighting to the end. His troops had held their ground almost to a man ; even those who had been scattered were found with their wounds in front ; not a single freeborn citizen was taken alive and Catiline himself was found far in advance of his men, still breathing and with all his old spirit still showing upon his face.[a]

There remains one last question : do our sources give us an exaggerated idea of the conspiracy's importance ? The fate that has preserved both Ci-

---

[a] *Bellum Catilinae* 56-61. For the last days of Catiline, see G. V. Sumner, " The Last Journey of L. Sergius Catilina," *Classical Philology* 58 (1963), 215-219. He dates the final battle to the beginning of January and explains the hectic proceedings in Rome on the 3rd of January by assuming that the tribune, Nepos, knew that the decisive battle was about to take place and that he must get his bill for the recall of Pompey passed as soon as possible. The anti-Pompeian faction was equally determined that the bill should not be passed. News of the battle reached Rome on the night of the 3rd of January. There was nothing now that Nepos could do, and he left Rome without delay.

cero's speeches and Sallust's monograph may serve
to give Catiline a place in the history of the end of
the Republic that he does not deserve. The speeches
play up the danger to which Rome was exposed and,
when we have made allowance for Cicero's personal
pride in his achievement and for his self-justification
under political attack, Catiline falls into perspective.
He was no more dangerous or important than a
number of other men who attempted to rally bitter
discontent in city and countryside, but who mean less
to us because fate has not preserved the writings of a
Cicero or a Sallust to record their failure.[a]

[a] On the comparative unimportance of the Catilinarian
Conspiracy, see, for example, W. Hoffmann, " Catilina und
die römische Revolution," *Gymnasium* 66 (1959), 459-477 ;
Z. Yavetz, " The Failure of Catiline's Conspiracy," *Historia*
12 (1963), 498 ; and C. Meier, *Res Publica Amissa* 314.
But K. H. Waters, " Cicero, Sallust and Catiline," *Historia*
19 (1970), 195-215 goes too far.

IN CATILINAM I–IV

The Manuscripts

C = codex Cluniacensis 498, now Holkhamicus, 9th century (containing I. 1-5 Quo usque . . . iam pridem, 17-II. 11 viderem . . . quacumque, 15-III. 1 ne mihi sit . . . ac resti, 9-19 huius . . . urbis atque, 23-27 ac miserrimo . . . condicio, IV. 8-15 constituta . . . quo studio)

A = codex Ambrosianus, C. 29 inf., 10th century

V = codex Vossianus, Lat. O. 2, 11th century

a = codex Laurentianus XLV. 2, 13th century

h = codex Harleianus 2682, 11th century

b = codex Benedictoburanus, now Monacensis 4611, 12th century

l = codex Harleianus 2716, 10th/11th centuries (omitting II. 8-24 incredibile . . . cohortem)

s = codex Salisburgensis, now Monacensis 15964, 11th century

o = codex Oxoniensis, Coll. Corporis Christi 57, 12th century

t = codex Tegernseensis, now Monacensis 19472, 11th century

u = codex Egmontanus, now Bruxellensis 10060, 11th century

x = codex Laurentianus L. 45, 11th century

α = codices (C) AVa

β = codices $b(l)s$ in Speeches I-III
    = codices bs in Speech IV

γ = codices $otux$

---

i = codex Indersdorfensis now Monacensis 7809, 12th century

ORATIO
IN L. CATILINAM PRIMA

In Senatu Habita

1　Quo usque tandem abutere, Catilina, patientia nostra? quam diu etiam furor iste tuus nos eludet? quem ad finem sese effrenata iactabit audacia? Nihilne te nocturnum praesidium Palati, nihil urbis vigiliae, nihil timor populi, nihil concursus bonorum omnium, nihil hic munitissimus habendi senatus locus, nihil horum ora voltusque moverunt? Patere tua consilia non sentis, constrictam iam horum omnium scientia teneri coniurationem tuam non vides? Quid proxima, quid superiore nocte egeris, ubi fueris, quos convocaveris, quid consili ceperis quem nostrum ignorare arbitraris?
2　O tempora, o mores! Senatus haec intellegit, consul videt; hic tamen vivit. Vivit? immo vero etiam in senatum venit, fit publici consili particeps, notat et designat oculis ad caedem unum quemque nostrum. Nos autem fortes viri satis facere rei publicae videmur, si istius furorem ac tela vitamus.

ᵃ In the temple of Jupiter Stator on the Palatine, protected by a band of armed *equites*. It was vowed by Romulus during the fight against the Sabines, but was not built until 294. See E. Nash, *Pictorial Dictionary of Ancient Rome* 1. 534.

THE FIRST SPEECH
AGAINST LUCIUS SERGIUS CATILINA

DELIVERED IN THE SENATE

IN heaven's name, Catiline, how long will you take 1
advantage of our forebearance ? How much longer
yet will that madness of yours make playthings of
us ? When will your unbridled effrontery stop vaunt-
ing itself ? Are you impressed not at all that the
Palatine has a garrison at night, that the city is
patrolled, that the populace is panic-stricken, that all
loyal citizens have rallied to the standard, that the
Senate is meeting here behind stout defences,[a] and
that you can see the expression on the faces of the
senators ? Do you not appreciate that your plans are
laid bare ? Do you not see that your conspiracy is
held fast by the knowledge of all these men ? Do you
think that there is a man among us who does not
know what you did last night or the night before last,
where you were, whom you summoned to your meeting, what decision you reached ? What an age we 2
live in ! The Senate knows it all, the consul sees it,
and yet—this man is still alive. Alive did I say ?
Not only is he alive, but he attends the Senate, takes
part in our debates, picks us all out one by one and
with his gaze marks us down for death. We, however,
brave fellows that we are, think that we are doing our
duty to the Republic if only we avoid his frenzy and

Ad mortem te, Catilina, duci iussu consulis iam pridem oportebat, in te conferri pestem quam tu in 3 nos omnis iam diu machinaris. An vero vir amplissimus, P. Scipio, pontifex maximus, Ti. Gracchum mediocriter labefactantem statum rei publicae privatus interfecit : Catilinam orbem terrae caede atque incendiis vastare cupientem nos consules perferemus ? Nam illa nimis antiqua praetereo, quod C. Servilius Ahala Sp. Maelium novis rebus studentem manu sua occidit. Fuit, fuit ista quondam in hac re publica virtus ut viri fortes acrioribus suppliciis civem perniciosum quam acerbissimum hostem coercerent. Habemus senatus consultum in te, Catilina, vehemens et grave, non deest rei publicae consilium neque auctoritas huius ordinis : nos, nos, 4 dico aperte, consules desumus. Decrevit quondam senatus uti L. Opimius consul videret ne quid res publica detrimenti caperet : nox nulla intercessit : interfectus est propter quasdam seditionum suspiciones C. Gracchus, clarissimo patre, avo, maioribus, occisus est cum liberis M. Fulvius consularis. Simili

---

[a] Publius Cornelius Scipio Nasica Serapio, head of the college of pontiffs from 141 ? to 132, led the attack by senators and their clients in which Tiberius Gracchus, tribune in 133, was killed. He could legitimately be called a private citizen—in contrast with the consuls of the following sentence —because his religious office was not a magistracy.

[b] Ahala was Master of the Horse (*magister equitum*) to the dictator Cincinnatus and with his own hand killed Maelius, a wealthy plebeian, who had been accused of aiming at illegal power after selling corn to the populace at a low price during a famine in 440. This is one of the stories often introduced by Cicero to provide him with precedents for wishing to destroy political opponents.

[c] See p. xxxii and Appendix B, pp. 567-574.

his cold steel. You, Catiline, should have been led to your death long ago and on a consul's orders. It is upon yourself that the fate which you have long been planning for all of us ought to be visited. Publius 3 Scipio,[a] a man of distinction and the chief pontiff, was a private citizen when he killed Tiberius Gracchus even though he was not seriously undermining the constitution of the Republic. Shall we, the consuls, then tolerate Catiline whose aim it is to carry fire and the sword throughout the whole world? I pass over precedents that are too old, the fact that Gaius Servilius Ahala killed Spurius Maelius with his own hand when Maelius was planning revolution.[b] Gone, gone for ever is that valour that used to be found in this Republic and caused brave men to suppress a citizen traitor with keener punishment than the most bitter foe. We have a decree of the Senate against you, Catiline, a decree of power and authority.[c] It is not the deliberations and decisions of this body that the Republic lacks. It is we,—I say it openly—we consuls, who are lacking. Once the Senate passed a 4 decree [d] that the consul Lucius Opimius should see that the Republic came to no harm : not a single night intervened : Gaius Gracchus, for all the distinction of his father, grandfather and ancestors, was killed on vague suspicions of treason ; Marcus Fulvius, an ex-consul, was killed together with his children. A similar decree of the Senate entrusted

[d] Lucius Opimius, consul in 121, with the backing of the *senatus consultum ultimum* attacked the Aventine where Tiberius Gracchus' younger brother Gaius, tribune in 123 and 122, had assembled his supporters. Gaius and his supporter, Marcus Fulvius Flaccus, consul in 125, were killed in the attack. For the constitutional implications of this affair, see p. 571.

senatus consulto C. Mario et L. Valerio consulibus est permissa res publica : num unum diem postea L. Saturninum tribunum plebis et C. Servilium praetorem mors ac rei publicae poena remorata est ? At vero nos vicesimum iam diem patimur hebescere aciem horum auctoritatis. Habemus enim eius modi senatus consultum, verum inclusum in tabulis, tamquam in vagina reconditum, quo ex senatus consulto confestim te interfectum esse, Catilina, convenit. Vivis, et vivis non ad deponendam, sed ad confirmandam audaciam. Cupio, patres conscripti, me esse clementem, cupio in tantis rei publicae periculis non dissolutum videri, sed iam me ipse inertiae nequitiaeque condemno.

5   Castra sunt in Italia contra populum Romanum in Etruriae faucibus conlocata, crescit in dies singulos hostium numerus ; eorum autem castrorum imperatorem ducemque hostium intra moenia atque adeo in senatu videtis intestinam aliquam cotidie perniciem rei publicae molientem. Si te iam, Catilina, comprehendi, si interfici iussero, credo, erit verendum mihi ne non hoc potius omnes boni serius a me quam quisquam crudelius factum esse dicat. Verum ego hoc quod iam pridem factum esse oportuit certa de causa nondum adducor ut faciam. Tum denique inter-

---

a In 100.

b They had proposed revolutionary measures and the Senate, after passing the *senatus consultum ultimum*, called upon Marius for protection. In the subsequent disorders Saturninus and Servilius Glaucia were confined in the Senate-house and there stoned to death by their opponents. For the bizarre resurrection of this incident earlier this year, see p. xxviii.

c See E. G. Hardy, " A Catilinarian Date," *Journal of Roman Studies* 6 (1916), 56-58.

d *Cf. in Catilinam* 4. 10, p. 144.

e It must remain doubtful whether this emphasis upon his

the Republic to the consuls, Gaius Marius and Lucius Valerius [a]: did the tribune of the commons, Lucius Saturninus, and the praetor, Gaius Servilius, have to wait a single day for the death penalty imposed by the Senate?[b] For twenty days now [c] we have been allowing the edge of the Senate's authority to grow blunt. We have a decree of the Senate like theirs, but it is locked up with the records like a sword buried in its sheath; yet it is a decree under which you, Catiline, ought to have been executed immediately.[d] You still live and, as long as you live, you do not cease your acts of recklessness but add to their number. It is my wish, gentlemen, to be a man of compassion,[e] it is my wish not to seem easygoing at a time of serious danger for the Republic, but now I condemn myself for my inaction and my negligence.

There is in Italy a camp of enemies of the Roman 5 people situated in the passes of Etruria [f] and the number of those enemies is increasing daily. The commander of that camp and the leader of those enemies you see within the walls and even, indeed, in the Senate, plotting daily in our midst the destruction of the Republic. If I give orders, Catiline, for your instant arrest and execution, what I shall have to fear, I suppose, is not that all loyal citizens will say that I have acted too late but that some individual will say that I have acted too harshly. In fact there is one particular reason why I, for my part, cannot bring myself to do what I ought to have done long ago.

natural clemency in the speeches against Catiline and in others delivered this year or shortly afterwards appeared in the original versions. It would not be appropriate at the time and would be inserted in editing *post eventum* when Cicero was seeking to defend himself against political attack for his execution of the conspirators.   [f] At Faesulae.

ficiere, cum iam nemo tam improbus, tam perditus, tam tui similis inveniri poterit qui id non iure factum 6 esse fateatur. Quam diu quisquam erit qui te defendere audeat, vives, et vives ita ut nunc vivis, multis meis et firmis praesidiis obsessus ne commovere te contra rem publicam possis. Multorum te etiam oculi et aures non sentientem, sicut adhuc fecerunt, speculabuntur atque custodient.

Etenim quid est, Catilina, quod iam amplius exspectes, si neque nox tenebris obscurare coetus nefarios nec privata domus parietibus continere voces coniurationis tuae potest, si inlustrantur, si erumpunt omnia? Muta iam istam mentem, mihi crede, obliviscere caedis atque incendiorum. Teneris undique; luce sunt clariora nobis tua consilia omnia, quae 7 iam mecum licet recognoscas. Meministine me ante diem xii Kalendas Novembris dicere in senatu fore in armis certo die, qui dies futurus esset ante diem vi Kal. Novembris, C. Manlium, audaciae satellitem atque administrum tuae? Num me fefellit, Catilina, non modo res tanta tam atrox tamque incredibilis, verum, id quod multo magis est admirandum, dies? Dixi ego idem in senatu caedem te optimatium contulisse in ante diem v Kalendas Novembris, tum cum multi principes civitatis Roma non tam sui conservandi quam tuorum consiliorum reprimendorum causa profugerunt. Num infitiari potes te illo ipso die meis praesidiis, mea diligentia circumclusum commovere te contra rem publicam non potuisse, cum

You will only be executed when there can no longer be found a single individual so evil, so abandoned, so like yourself, as to say that it was an act of injustice. So long as there remains a single man bold enough to 6 defend you, you will live, and live as you live now, hemmed in by all my stout guards to prevent your making a move against the Republic. Furthermore, although you will not be aware of them, there will be, as there have been in the past, many eyes and ears observing you and keeping watch upon you.

What point is there, Catiline, in your waiting any longer, if night cannot conceal your criminal assemblies in its shadows nor a private house contain the voices of your conspirators within its walls, if they are all in a blaze of light and exposed to view ? Take my advice ; abandon your scheme and forget your murder and arson. You are trapped on every side ; all your plans are as clear as daylight to us. Let us go through them together. Do you remember that I 7 said in the Senate on the 21st of October that Gaius Manlius, your tool and lackey in your wild scheme, would take up arms on a certain day and that the day would be the 27th of October ? Was I not right, Catiline, both in the seriousness of the plot, beyond belief in its ferocity though it was, and—a much more remarkable feat—in the date ? I also said in the Senate that you had postponed the massacre of leading citizens until the 28th of October even though by that date many of the leading figures in the State had left Rome, not so much to save themselves as to thwart your plans. You cannot deny, can you, that, on that very day after the others had departed, my guards and my elaborate precautions had hemmed you in and you could not move against the

tu discessu ceterorum nostra tamen qui remansis-
8 semus caede contentum te esse dicebas ? Quid ? cum
te Praeneste Kalendis ipsis Novembribus occupatu-
rum nocturno impetu esse confideres, sensistin illam
coloniam meo iussu meis praesidiis, custodiis, vigiliis
esse munitam ? Nihil agis, nihil moliris, nihil cogitas
quod non ego non modo[1] audiam sed etiam videam
planeque sentiam.

Recognosce mecum tandem noctem illam superiorem ; iam intelleges multo me vigilare acrius ad
salutem quam te ad perniciem rei publicae. Dico te
priore nocte venisse inter falcarios—non agam obscure—in M. Laecae domum ; convenisse eodem compluris eiusdem amentiae scelerisque socios. Num
negare audes ? quid taces ? Convincam, si negas.
Video enim esse hic in senatu quosdam qui tecum
9 una fuerunt. O di immortales ! ubinam gentium
sumus ? quam rem publicam habemus ? in qua urbe
vivimus ? Hic, hic sunt in nostro numero, patres
conscripti, in hoc orbis terrae sanctissimo gravissimo-
que consilio, qui de nostro omnium interitu, qui de
huius urbis atque adeo de orbis terrarum exitio
cogitent. Hos ego video consul et de re publica
sententiam rogo, et quos ferro trucidari oportebat,
eos nondum voce volnero ! Fuisti igitur apud Laecam
illa nocte, Catilina, distribuisti partis Italiae, statuisti

---

[1] non ego non modo *Halm.* ego non modo non *V.* ego
non modo *the other* mss.

---

[a] A stronghold in the Hernican mountains, some twenty
miles S.E. of Rome.
[b] One of the colonies founded by Sulla. Its previous

Republic ? And that you said that you were quite content with the slaughter of those of us who had remained behind ? You confidently expected to take 8 Praeneste *a* in a night assault on the 1st of November, but were you aware that the defences of that colony *b* had been set on my orders with my garrison, my guard-posts, and my sentinels ? Nothing you do, no attempt you make, no plan you form, but I hear of it, see it, and know it all.

Go over with me, please, the events of the night before last. You will appreciate now that my concern for the safety of the Republic is much deeper than is yours for its destruction. I say that on the night before last you came to the street of the scythe-makers—I shall be precise—to the house of Marcus Laeca. There you were joined by many of your accomplices in your criminal folly. You do not have the effrontery to deny it, do you ? Why are you silent then ? If you deny it, I shall prove it. In fact, I see some of those who were with you here in the Senate. In heaven's name ! Where in the world 9 are we ? What State is ours ? What city are we living in ? Here, gentlemen, here in our very midst, in this, the most sacred and important council in the world, there are men whose plans extend beyond the death of us all and the destruction of this city to that of the whole world. As consul, I see these men and call for their views upon affairs of state, and as yet I am not even wounding with my tongue men who ought to be butchered with the sword. You were, then, at the house of Laeca on that night, Catiline ; you allocated the regions of Italy, you

inhabitants had been put to death for their support of the Marians.

quo quemque proficisci placeret, delegisti quos
Romae relinqueres, quos tecum educeres, discripsisti
urbis partis ad incendia, confirmasti te ipsum iam esse
exiturum, dixisti paulum tibi esse etiam nunc morae,
quod ego viverem. Reperti sunt duo equites Romani
qui te ista cura liberarent et se illa ipsa nocte paulo
ante lucem me in meo lecto interfecturos esse
10 pollicerentur. Haec ego omnia vixdum etiam coetu
vestro dimisso comperi; domum meam maioribus
praesidiis munivi atque firmavi, exclusi eos quos tu ad
me salutatum mane miseras, cum illi ipsi venissent
quos ego iam multis ac summis viris ad me id temporis
venturos esse praedixeram.

Quae cum ita sint, Catilina, perge quo coepisti:
egredere aliquando ex urbe; patent portae: proficiscere. Nimium diu te imperatorem tua illa
Manliana castra desiderant. Educ tecum etiam
omnis tuos, si minus, quam plurimos; purga urbem.
Magno me metu liberaveris, modo inter me atque te
murus intersit. Nobiscum versari iam diutius non
potes; non feram, non patiar, non sinam.

11 Magna dis immortalibus habenda est atque huic
ipsi Iovi Statori, antiquissimo custodi huius urbis,
gratia, quod hanc tam taetram, tam horribilem tamque infestam rei publicae pestem totiens iam effugi-

---

^a Gaius Cornelius and Lucius Vargunteius. Sallust, *Bel-
lum Catilinae* 28. 1, says that Vargunteius was a senator.
This conflict about his status, as was first suggested by Halm,
probably arises from the fact that Vargunteius, in all likelihood in 66, was indicted and eventually condemned on a
charge of electoral corruption under the *lex Calpurnia de
ambitu* (*cf. pro Sulla* 6, p. 318). One of the penalties under
this law was exclusion from the Senate for ever. This explanation has been rejected by, among others, R. F. Robin-
son, " *Duo Equites Romani*," *Classical Weekly* 40 (1947)

decided where you wanted each man to go, you chose those whom you were leaving at Rome and those whom you were taking with you, you assigned the parts of the city to be burnt, and you confirmed that you were on the point of departure yourself, but said that you still had to wait a little longer because I was alive. Two Roman knights [a] were found to free you from that particular anxiety and to promise that they would kill me in my bed that very night, shortly before dawn. Your meeting had scarcely broken up 10 when I learned all this. I strengthened the guards, made my house more secure, and barred the door against the men whom you had sent to call upon me early in the morning; and there duly arrived the very individuals whom, as I had already told many prominent citizens, I expected to come at that time.

In these circumstances, Catiline, finish the journey you have begun: at long last leave the city; the gates are open: be on your way. Manlius and that camp of yours have all too long been waiting for their general. Take all your men with you or, if you cannot take them all, take as many as you can. Cleanse the city. You will free me from my great fear, once there is a wall between us. You cannot remain among us any longer; I cannot, I will not, I must not permit it.

We owe a heavy debt of gratitude to the immortal 11 gods and not least to Jupiter Stator, the most venerable guardian of this city, in whose temple we are today, because so often in the past have we escaped this pestilence, so foul, so loathsome, so

138–143, who argues that the second knight was Marcus Ceparius. But Cicero is right to call Vargunteius a knight in 63 and he had been a senator. J. Linderski, " Cicero and Sallust on Vargunteius," *Historia* 12 (1963), 511–512.

mus. Non est saepius in uno homine summa salus periclitanda rei publicae. Quam diu mihi consuli designato, Catilina, insidiatus es, non publico me praesidio, sed privata diligentia defendi. Cum proximis comitiis consularibus me consulem in campo et competitores tuos interficere voluisti, compressi conatus tuos nefarios amicorum praesidio et copiis nullo tumultu publice concitato; denique, quotienscumque me petisti, per me tibi obstiti, quamquam videbam perniciem meam cum magna calamitate rei

12 publicae esse coniunctam. Nunc iam aperte rem publicam universam petis, templa deorum immortalium, tecta urbis, vitam omnium civium, Italiam totam ad exitium et vastitatem vocas. Qua re, quoniam id quod est primum, et quod huius imperi disciplinaeque maiorum proprium est, facere nondum audeo, faciam id quod est ad severitatem lenius, ad communem salutem utilius. Nam si te interfici iussero, residebit in re publica reliqua coniuratorum manus; sin tu, quod te iam dudum hortor, exieris, exhaurietur ex urbe tuorum comitum magna et perni-

13 ciosa sentina rei publicae. Quid est, Catilina? num dubitas id me imperante facere quod iam tua sponte faciebas? Exire ex urbe iubet consul hostem. Interrogas me, num in exsilium? Non iubeo, sed, si me consulis, suadeo.

ᵃ See Appendix A, p. 562.
ᵇ This word is a regular term for the urban proletariat and need not mean down-and-out unemployables. The epithet here, however, makes it opprobrious.
ᶜ Our oldest scrap of Cicero preserves part of this and the next two sections. It is a papyrus fragment from Upper Egypt (?) of the 3rd/4th centuries and contains parts or traces of nine lines of this section and nine of sections 14 and 15. W. H. Willis, " A Papyrus Fragment of Cicero,"
44

deadly to the Republic. Never again must one man have the power to imperil the very existence of the State. As long as you, Catiline, plotted against me when I was consul-designate, I protected myself not with a public guard but by my own alertness. At the last consular elections when I was consul you wanted to kill me and your fellow candidates in the Campus Martius [a]; I sounded no public call to arms but foiled your wicked efforts with a guard provided by a force of friends; whenever you went for me, I thwarted you in person, although I saw that my death would be a major disaster to the Republic. Now you are openly attacking the whole common-wealth; you are hailing to their destruction and devastation the temples of the immortal gods, the buildings of this city, the lives of all the citizens and the whole of Italy. I do not yet, however, presume to take the most obvious course, the course appropriate to the authority of my position and the stern tradition of our ancestors, and I shall therefore act in a way that is more lenient in degree of severity but more conducive to the common safety. If I give an order for you to be killed, there will remain in the State the rest of the conspirators; but if, as I have long been urging, you leave the city, there will then be drained from it that flood of the State's deadly sewage [b]—your accomplices. Well, Catiline? Surely you are not hesitating to do at my bidding what you were minded to do of your own free will? [c] The consul orders a public enemy to leave the city. You ask me, " You don't mean exile ? " I do not command that but, if you ask my opinion, that is my advice.

Transactions of the American Philological Association 94 (1963), 321–327.

Quid est enim, Catilina, quod te iam in hac urbe delectare possit ? in qua nemo est extra istam coniurationem perditorum hominum qui te non metuat, nemo qui non oderit. Quae nota domesticae turpitudinis non inusta vitae tuae est ? quod privatarum rerum dedecus non haeret in fama ?[1] quae libido ab oculis, quod facinus a manibus umquam tuis, quod flagitium a toto corpore afuit ? cui tu adulescentulo quem corruptelarum inlecebris inretisses non aut ad audaciam ferrum aut ad libidinem facem praetu-

14 listi? Quid vero ? nuper cum morte superioris uxoris novis nuptiis locum[2] vacuefecisses, nonne etiam alio incredibili scelere hoc scelus cumulavisti ? quod ego praetermitto et facile patior sileri, ne in hac civitate tanti facinoris immanitas aut exstitisse aut non vindicata esse videatur. Praetermitto ruinas fortunarum tuarum quas omnis proximis Idibus tibi impendere senties : ad illa venio quae non ad privatam ignominiam vitiorum tuorum, non ad domesticam tuam difficultatem ac turpitudinem, sed ad summam rem publicam atque ad omnium nostrum vitam

15 salutemque pertinent. Potestne tibi haec lux, Catilina, aut huius caeli spiritus esse iucundus, cum scias esse horum neminem qui nesciat te pridie Kalendas Ianuarias Lepido et Tullo consulibus stetisse in comitio cum telo, manum consulum et principum

---

[1] haeret in fama *Ant. Augustinus.* haeret (inhaeret *h*) infamiae (-ia *a*) *mss.* inhaeret in fama *Madvig.*
[2] locum *ah.* domum *βγ.*

---

[a] When interest upon loans fell due for payment.
[b] See pp. xx-xxii.
[c] The chief place of political assembly in Republican

What is there, Catiline, that can give you any pleasure in this city now ? There is not here outside that conspiracy of ruined men a single person who does not fear you, not one who does not hate you. What mark of family scandal is there not branded upon your life ? What deplorable episode in your personal affairs does not help form your reputation ? What lust has never shone in your eyes, what crime has never stained your hands, what shameful deed has never fouled your entire body ? What young man that you had ensnared with the allurements of your seduction have you not provided with a weapon for his crime or a torch for his passion ? Or again, 14 shortly after you had made room for a new bride by murdering your former wife, did you not compound this deed with yet another crime that defies belief ? I do not dwell on this and readily allow it to be glossed over in silence lest it be thought that this State has allowed so heinous a crime to have been committed or to have gone unpunished. I pass over the total ruin of your fortune which you will feel hanging over you on the coming Ides [a] ; I come to the events which are not concerned with the disgrace brought upon you by the scandals of your private life or with the poverty and shame of your family, but with the supreme interests of the State and the life and safety of us all. Can the light of this sun, Catiline, or can 15 the breath of this air give you any pleasure when you know that there is not one man present who does not know that on the last day of December, in the consulship of Lepidus and Tullus,[b] you were standing in the comitium [c] armed with a weapon, that you

Rome, it was situated to the north of the Forum. See E. Nash, *Pictorial Dictionary of Ancient Rome* 1. 287-289.

civitatis interficiendorum causa paravisse, sceleri ac furori tuo non mentem aliquam aut timorem tuum sed Fortunam populi Romani obstitisse? Ac iam illa omitto—neque enim sunt aut obscura aut non multa commissa postea—quotiens tu me designatum, quotiens vero consulem interficere conatus es! quot ego tuas petitiones ita coniectas ut vitari posse non viderentur parva quadam declinatione et, ut aiunt, corpore effugi! Nihil agis, nihil adsequeris, neque

16 tamen conari ac velle desistis. Quotiens iam tibi extorta est ista sica de manibus, quotiens excidit casu aliquo et elapsa est!¹ Quae quidem quibus abs te initiata sacris ac devota sit nescio, quod eam necesse putas esse in consulis corpore defigere.

Nunc vero quae tua est ista vita? Sic enim iam tecum loquar, non ut odio permotus esse videar, quo debeo, sed ut misericordia, quae tibi nulla debetur. Venisti paulo ante in senatum. Quis te ex hac tanta frequentia, tot ex tuis amicis ac necessariis salutavit? Si hoc post hominum memoriam contigit nemini, vocis exspectas contumeliam, cum sis gravissimo iudicio taciturnitatis oppressus? Quid, quod adventu tuo ista subsellia vacuefacta sunt, quod omnes consulares qui tibi persaepe ad caedem constituti fuerunt, simul atque adsedisti, partem istam subselliorum nudam atque inanem reliquerunt, quo tandem animo tibi

17 ferendum putas? Servi mehercule mei si me isto

¹ *The mss. have here* tamen ea carere diutius non potes, *which was deleted by Heumann on the grounds that it had been added from 24.*

ª If printed, as by Clark, with a capital letter, the goddess of good-fortune.

were organizing a band to kill the consuls and leading men in the State, and that it was not any reflection on your part or fear that foiled your mad crime but the Fortune *a* of the Roman people ? I omit these crimes too—they are no secret and you have committed many crimes since then; think of all the occasions on which you tried to kill me when I was consul-designate and even when I was consul ! Think of all your thrusts which seemed bound to find their mark but which I dodged with a slight swerve and, as they say, by a body-movement ! You achieve nothing, you accomplish nothing, but that does not stop you still trying and still hoping. Think of all the times when 16 your dagger has been wrenched from your grasp and when it has slipped out by some chance and fallen to the ground ! With what rites you have consecrated and dedicated it I do not know, that you must plunge it into the body of a consul.

At the end of it all what sort of a life are you living ? I shall speak to you now so as to show that I feel not the hatred that I ought to feel but the pity that you do not at all deserve. A short time ago you came into the Senate. Who out of all that crowd, out of all your many friends and intimates greeted you ? If no one else has received such treatment within the memory of man, are you waiting for condemnation to be voiced aloud, although you have been convicted by the hostile verdict of their silence ? What of the fact that at your arrival the seats near you emptied, that the moment you sat down all the ex-consuls whom you had repeatedly marked out for death left the seats around you bare and empty—how do you think you ought to feel about that ? Heavens 17 above ! If my slaves feared me as much as all your

49

pacto metuerent ut te metuunt omnes cives tui,
domum meam relinquendam putarem: tu tibi urbem non arbitraris ? et si me meis civibus iniuria sus-
pectum tam graviter atque offensum viderem, carere
me aspectu civium quam infestis omnium oculis con-
spici mallem: tu, cum conscientia scelerum tuorum agnoscas odium omnium iustum et iam diu tibi
debitum, dubitas quorum mentis sensusque volneras,
eorum aspectum praesentiamque vitare ? Si te
parentes timerent atque odissent tui neque eos
ratione ulla placare posses, ut opinor, ab eorum oculis
aliquo concederes. Nunc te patria, quae communis
est parens omnium nostrum, odit ac metuit et iam diu
nihil te iudicat nisi de parricidio suo cogitare: huius
tu neque auctoritatem verebere nec iudicium sequere
18 nec vim pertimesces ? Quae tecum, Catilina, sic agit
et quodam modo tacita loquitur: " Nullum iam aliquot annis facinus exstitit nisi per te, nullum flagitium sine te ; tibi uni multorum civium neces, tibi
vexatio direptioque sociorum impunita fuit ac libera ;
tu non solum ad neglegendas leges et quaestiones
verum etiam ad evertendas perfringendasque valuisti.
Superiora illa, quamquam ferenda non fuerunt, tamen
ut potui tuli ; nunc vero me totam esse in metu propter
unum te, quicquid increpuerit, Catilinam timeri,
nullum videri contra me consilium iniri posse quod
a tuo scelere abhorreat, non est ferendum. Quam ob
rem discede atque hunc mihi timorem eripe ; si est
verus, ne opprimar, sin falsus, ut tandem aliquando

[a] A reference to the part he was alleged to have played in
the Sullan proscriptions. See p. 6.
[b] Propraetor of Africa in 67, he was in 65 tried for extortion
and acquitted. See p. 3.

countrymen fear you, I would think that I should get out of my house. Do you not consider that *you* should leave the city ? And if I saw that—even undeservedly—I was so deeply suspected and loathed by my fellow-citizens, I should wish not to see a single one of them rather than meet the hostile gaze of them all. Yet you, recognizing as you do in your guilty knowledge of your crimes that the universal hatred you attract is justified and has long been your due, do you hesitate to avoid the sight and presence of those whose hearts and minds you are wounding ? If your own parents feared and hated you, and nohow could you be reconciled to them, you would, I imagine, retire somewhere out of their sight. As it is, your native land which is the mother of us all hates you and dreads you and has long since decided that you have been planning nothing but her destruction. Will you not respect her authority, bow to her judgement, or fear her power ? She addresses you, Catiline, 18 and though silent somehow makes this appeal to you : " For some years now you have been behind every crime, involved in every scandal. No one but you has killed a host of citizens[a] and oppressed and plundered the allies unpunished and scot-free. Not only have you been able to ignore the laws and law-courts but you have been able to overturn and shatter them.[b] I tolerated as well as I could those earlier crimes, insupportable as they were, but that I should now be in a state of total terror on your account, that Catiline should be feared at every sound, that no scheme can be hatched against me without assuming your criminal complicity, truly this is intolerable. Depart, then, and free me from this dread ; if it is well founded, that I may not be destroyed : if

51

19 timere desinam." Haec si tecum, ut dixi, patria loquatur, nonne impetrare debeat, etiam si vim adhibere non possit ?

Quid, quod tu te in custodiam dedisti, quod vitandae suspicionis causa ad M'. Lepidum te habitare velle dixisti ? A quo non receptus etiam ad me venire ausus es, atque ut domi meae te adservarem rogasti. Cum a me quoque id responsum tulisses, me nullo modo posse isdem parietibus tuto esse tecum, quia magno in periculo essem quod isdem moenibus contineremur, ad Q. Metellum praetorem venisti. A quo repudiatus ad sodalem tuum, virum optimum, M. Marcellum[1] demigrasti, quem tu videlicet et ad custodiendum te diligentissimum et ad suspicandum sagacissimum et ad vindicandum fortissimum fore putasti. Sed quam longe videtur a carcere atque a vinculis abesse debere qui se ipse iam dignum custodia iudicarit ?

20 Quae cum ita sint, Catilina, dubitas, si emori aequo animo non potes, abire in aliquas terras et vitam istam multis suppliciis iustis debitisque ereptam fugae solitudinique mandare ? " Refer " inquis " ad senatum "; id enim postulas et, si hic

---

[1] M. Marcellum *mss.* Metellum *a.* M. Metellum *Edd.*

---

[a] In answer to the charges of *vis* (see p. 17). A Roman citizen was not held in prison pending a criminal trial. He either gave surety or, as here, was placed in the charge of a fellow-citizen who became responsible for his appearance in court.

[b] Quintus Caecilius Metellus Celer, praetor this year and consul in 60.

[c] The identity of this man is uncertain. W. E. Gwatkin, Jr., " Cicero *in Catilinam* 1. 19," *Transactions of the American Philological Association* 65 (1934), 271-281, suggests that the correct reading is that of *a*, " Metellum "

groundless, that I may at long last cease to feel afraid." If our country were to appeal to you with 19 these words, should not her request be granted, even if she cannot force you?

What of the fact that you gave yourself into custody, that in order to avoid suspicion you said that you were willing to live at the house of Manius Lepidus? [a] And when he would not have you, you even had the effrontery to come to me and ask me to guard you at my home. I gave you the same answer and said that if I was in great danger because we lived together in the same city, I certainly would not be safe with you in the same house. You then came to the praetor, Quintus Metellus.[b] Rebuffed by him, you went off to your boon-companion, Marcus Marcellus,[c] clearly because you thought that he would be very careful guarding you, very astute at suspecting you and very active in punishing you. How far off do you think detention in prison ought to be for a man who already thinks that he should be kept in custody?

If in this situation, Catiline, you cannot face death 20 calmly, do you hesitate to leave for some other land and consign to exile and solitude a life that you have rescued from the numerous penalties that it so richly deserves? " Put the proposal," you say, " to the Senate." Yes, this is what you demand; and you say

without any initial, and that this refers to Quintus Caecilius Metellus Nepos. In pursuit of an opportunist policy he accepted Catiline and the heavy irony of the sentence is the result of Cicero's collision with Nepos at the turn of the year after which this passage was written. *Cf.* Quintilian 9. 2. 45. This identification is implausible. We know of two Marcelli, father and son, who were supporters of Catiline, and this passage may well refer to one of them.

ordo placere sibi decreverit te ire in exsilium, obtem-
peraturum te esse dicis. Non referam, id quod
abhorret a meis moribus, et tamen faciam ut intellegas quid hi de te sentiant. Egredere ex urbe,
Catilina, libera rem publicam metu, in exsilium, si
hanc vocem exspectas, proficiscere. Quid est ?
ecquid attendis, ecquid animadvertis horum silen-
tium ? Patiuntur, tacent. Quid exspectas auctoritatem loquentium, quorum voluntatem tacitorum
21 perspicis ? At si hoc idem huic adulescenti optimo P.
Sestio, si fortissimo viro M. Marcello dixissem, iam
mihi consuli hoc ipso in templo senatus iure optimo
vim et manus intulisset. De te autem, Catilina, cum
quiescunt, probant, cum patiuntur, decernunt, cum
tacent, clamant, neque hi solum quorum tibi
auctoritas est videlicet cara, vita vilissima, sed etiam
illi equites Romani, honestissimi atque optimi viri,
ceterique fortissimi cives qui circumstant senatum,
quorum tu et frequentiam videre et studia perspicere
et voces paulo ante exaudire potuisti. Quorum ego
vix abs te iam diu manus ac tela contineo, eosdem
facile adducam ut te haec quae vastare iam pridem
studes relinquentem usque ad portas prosequantur.
22   Quamquam quid loquor ? te ut ulla res frangat, tu
ut unquam te corrigas, tu ut ullam fugam meditere,

ᵃ His real reason was that the Senate was not a judicial
body and had no power to pass sentence upon an individual.
See Appendix B, p. 569 f.
ᵇ Publius Sestius was quaestor this year; Marcus Marcellus became consul in 51.

that, if they vote for you to go into exile, you will obey. I shall not put it to the Senate, for that is contrary to my practice,[a] but I shall see to it that you are left in no doubt about what the Senate feels about you. Leave the city, Catiline, free the commonwealth from fear and, if these are the words that you are waiting for, go into exile. Well, Catiline? What are you waiting for? Do you not notice the Senate's silence? They accept it, they are silent. Why are you waiting for them to voice their decision, when you see clearly their wish expressed by their silence? If I had spoken these same words to this 21 distinguished young man, Publius Sestius, or to the gallant Marcus Marcellus,[b] the Senate would have been fully justified in laying violent hands upon me this instant, consul though I am, and in the precincts of this temple. In your case, however, Catiline, their inaction signifies approval, their acquiescence a decision and their silence applause. And I am not only referring to these men whose decision presumably means a lot to you although you value their lives so lightly. I also mean those Roman knights, the most honourable and excellent of men, and the other citizens who are standing around the Senate, whose crowds you could see, whose support you could observe and whose voices you could hear just now. For a long time now only with difficulty have I kept their hands and weapons away from you, and I shall easily persuade them to accompany you as far as the city gates, when you leave all that you have for so long been longing to lay waste.

And yet, why do I bother to say this? Would any- 22 thing break your resolve? Would you ever take yourself in hand? Consider flight? Or ever think

tu ut ullum exsilium cogites ? Utinam tibi istam
mentem di immortales duint ! tametsi video, si mea
voce perterritus ire in exsilium animum induxeris,
quanta tempestas invidiae nobis, si minus in praesens
tempus recenti memoria scelerum tuorum, at in
posteritatem impendeat. Sed est tanti, dum modo
tua ista sit privata calamitas et a rei publicae periculis
seiungatur. Sed tu ut vitiis tuis commoveare, ut
legum poenas pertimescas, ut temporibus rei publicae
cedas non est postulandum. Neque enim is es,
Catilina, ut te aut pudor a turpitudine aut metus a
23 periculo aut ratio a furore revocarit. Quam ob rem,
ut saepe iam dixi, proficiscere ac, si mihi inimico, ut
praedicas, tuo conflare vis invidiam, recta perge in
exsilium ; vix feram sermones hominum, si id feceris,
vix molem istius invidiae, si in exsilium iussu consulis
iveris, sustinebo. Sin autem servire meae laudi et
gloriae mavis, egredere cum importuna sceleratorum
manu, confer te ad Manlium, concita perditos civis,
secerne te a bonis, infer patriae bellum, exsulta impio
latrocinio, ut a me non eiectus ad alienos, sed invi-
24 tatus ad tuos isse videaris. Quamquam quid ego te
invitem, a quo iam sciam esse praemissos qui tibi ad
Forum Aurelium praestolarentur armati, cui sciam
pactam et constitutam cum Manlio diem, a quo
etiam aquilam illam argenteam quam tibi ac tuis

---

^a A small town about fifty miles from Rome, situated on
the Aurelian Way en route to Faesulae.
^b This silver eagle, one of the legionary standards intro-
duced by Marius, had been carried in his army during the
war against the Cimbri.

of exile ? If only the immortal gods would put *that*
idea into your head ! Yet I see what a storm of
unpopularity would break over my head if you are
frightened by what I say and decide upon exile. It
may not come immediately, while the memory of
your crimes is still fresh, but in the future. But it is
worth it, provided that your ruin remains the ruin of
one man and is kept clear of peril to the Republic.
But that you should be shifted from your evil ways,
that you should fear the penalties of the law, that you
should yield to exigences of state, that is too much
to ask. No, Catiline, you are not the man to be
turned back from infamy by a sense of shame, from
danger by fear, or from an act of madness by rational
thought. Be on your way then !—I have said it often 23
enough—and, if you wish to fan men's hatred of me,
your enemy as you call me, go straight into exile. It
will be hard for me to bear men's criticism, if you do
that; hard to sustain the burden of that hostility,
if you go into exile at the consul's command. If,
however, you prefer to do my good name and my
reputation a service, depart with that reckless gang
of criminals and take yourself off to Manlius, gather to
your cause the citizens who have abandoned all hope,
separate yourself from loyal men, wage war upon
your native land, revel in the banditry of traitors ;
for then men will think not that I drove you into the
arms of men unlike yourself, but that I invited you to
join your own kind. And yet why should I be press- 24
ing you ? I know that you have already sent men
on ahead to await you under arms at Forum Aurelium [a] ; I know that you have agreed and fixed a day
with Manlius ; I know that you have also sent on
ahead that silver eagle [b] which will, I trust, bring

omnibus confido perniciosam ac funestam futuram,
cui domi tuae sacrarium sceleratum[1] constitutum fuit,
sciam esse praemissam ? Tu ut illa carere diutius
possis quam venerari ad caedem proficiscens solebas,
a cuius altaribus saepe istam impiam dexteram ad
necem civium transtulisti ?

25 Ibis tandem aliquando quo te iam pridem tua ista
cupiditas effrenata ac furiosa rapiebat; neque enim
tibi haec res adfert dolorem, sed quandam incredibilem voluptatem. Ad hanc te amentiam natura
peperit, voluntas exercuit, fortuna servavit. Numquam tu non modo otium sed ne bellum quidem nisi
nefarium concupisti. Nactus es ex perditis atque ab
omni non modo fortuna verum etiam spe derelictis
26 conflatam improborum manum. Hic tu qua laetitia
perfruere, quibus gaudiis exsultabis, quanta in
voluptate bacchabere, cum in tanto numero tuorum
neque audies virum bonum quemquam neque videbis!
Ad huius vitae studium meditati illi sunt qui feruntur
labores tui, iacere humi non solum ad obsidendum
stuprum verum etiam ad facinus obeundum, vigilare
non solum insidiantem somno maritorum verum etiam
bonis otiosorum. Habes ubi ostentes tuam illam
praeclaram patientiam famis, frigoris, inopiae rerum
omnium quibus te brevi tempore confectum esse
27 senties. Tantum profeci, cum te a consulatu reppuli,
ut exsul potius temptare quam consul vexare rem
publicam posses, atque ut id quod esset a te scelerate

[1] sceleratum *Clark.* scelerum *a.* scelerum tuorum *the other* MSS.

a See p. 19.

death and destruction to you and all your followers
and for which an evil shrine has been set up at your
house. Could you be parted any longer from that
eagle which you used to worship on your way to
commit murder and from whose altar your sacrilegious
hand often passed to the slaughter of citizens ?

You will, then, at last be going where your un- 25
governable and crazed greed was long taking you ;
and your path causes you no grief but a kind of pleasure that is incomprehensible to others. It was for
madness such as this that Nature bore you, that your
will has trained you, and that fortune has preserved
you. Never have you wanted—I will not mention
peace—even a war that was not a criminal enterprise.
You have got a band of evil men, swept together from
the refuse of society and from those who have been
abandoned by all fortune and all hope. What a 26
wonderful time you will have with them, what
pleasures will delight you and what evils will thrill
you in your debauchery, for among all those friends of
yours you will not see or hear a single decent man !
These exertions of yours that men are always talking
about have been good training for the pursuit of a
life such as this ; lying on the bare ground to attempt
an act of indecency—for committing a crime ; spending nights of wakefulness to trick husbands while
they sleep—for seizing the possessions of peaceful citizens. You have an opportunity to show your famous ability to endure hunger, cold and deprivation
of every necessity ; an ability which you will shortly
realize has destroyed you. I achieved this much when 27
I kept you from the consulship, that you would only
be able to attack the State as an exile and not harry
it as a consul,[a] and that this criminal attack upon

susceptum latrocinium potius quam bellum nomi-
naretur.

Nunc, ut a me, patres conscripti, quandam prope
iustam patriae querimoniam detester ac deprecer,
percipite, quaeso, diligenter quod dicam, et ea penitus animis vestris mentibusque mandate. Etenim si
mecum patria, quae mihi vita mea multo est carior,
si cuncta Italia, si omnis res publica loquatur : " M.
Tulli, quid agis ? Tune eum quem esse hostem com-
peristi, quem ducem belli futurum vides, quem ex-
spectari imperatorem in castris hostium sentis, auctorem sceleris, principem coniurationis, evocatorem
servorum et civium perditorum, exire patiere, ut abs
te non emissus ex urbe, sed immissus in urbem esse
videatur ? Nonne hunc in vincla duci, non ad mortem
rapi, non summo supplicio mactari imperabis ? Quid
28 tandem te impedit ? mosne maiorum ? At persaepe
etiam privati in hac re publica perniciosos civis morte
multarunt. An leges quae de civium Romanorum
supplicio rogatae sunt ? At numquam in hac urbe
qui a re publica defecerunt civium iura tenuerunt.
An invidiam posteritatis times ? Praeclaram vero
populo Romano refers gratiam qui te, hominem per
te cognitum, nulla commendatione maiorum tam

---

a This was not true of Catiline. Although urged by some
of his supporters to call upon the slaves to rise, he refused to
do this. A slave-revolt, particularly after the war against
Spartacus in 73–71, was a perpetual nightmare to Romans
and a useful bogey with which to frighten people away from
Catiline. See p. 13.

b See p. 34, n. *a*.   *c* See Appendix B, p. 571.

d Possibly not part of the speech as delivered. One of
Cicero's arguments justifying his execution of the conspirators was that by their behaviour they had forfeited their
rights as citizens and that his action was therefore no contra-

which you have embarked would go under the name of banditry not war.

At this point, gentlemen, in order most firmly to reject a complaint by our fatherland that might be thought justified, listen carefully, I beg of you, to what I say, and memorize it deep down in your hearts and minds. If my country, which means much more to me than my own life, if all Italy, if the whole commonwealth were to say this to me : " What are you doing, Marcus Tullius ? Are you going to let this man who is, as you have discovered, a public enemy ; who will, as you see, be the leader in war ; who, as you know, is awaited in the enemy's camp as their general, who is the instigator of crime, the leader of the conspiracy, the recruiter of slaves [a] and society's outcasts ; are you going to let him leave, not apparently despatched by you from the city but let into it ? Are you not going to order him to be put in chains, taken off to execution and suffer the supreme penalty ? What on earth is stopping you ? The practice of our ancestors ? In this Republic even private individuals have frequently punished dangerous citizens with death.[b] Is it the laws that have been passed concerning the punishment of Roman citizens ? [c] Never in this city have those who have rebelled against the State kept the rights of citizens.[d] Or do you fear the hatred of posterity ? Fine thanks indeed you are giving to the Roman people who have raised you so quickly through all the steps of office to the supreme power,[e] when you were a man known

28

vention of the laws protecting these rights. This argument is untenable because the crucial point of these laws was that only the people could make such a decision.

[e] Cicero held all his magistracies *suo anno*, *i.e.* in the first year in which he was eligible under the provisions of the

mature ad summum imperium per omnis honorum gradus extulit, si propter invidiam aut alicuius pe-
29 riculi metum salutem civium tuorum neglegis. Sed si quis est invidiae metus, non est vehementius severitatis ac fortitudinis invidia quam inertiae ac nequitiae pertimescenda. An, cum bello vastabitur Italia, vexabuntur urbes, tecta ardebunt, tum te non existimas invidiae incendio conflagraturum ? "

His ego sanctissimis rei publicae vocibus et eorum hominum qui hoc idem sentiunt mentibus pauca respondebo. Ego, si hoc optimum factu iudicarem, patres conscripti, Catilinam morte multari, unius usuram horae gladiatori isti ad vivendum non dedissem. Etenim si summi viri et clarissimi cives Saturnini et Gracchorum et Flacci et superiorum complurium sanguine non modo se non contaminarunt sed etiam honestarunt, certe verendum mihi non erat ne quid hoc parricida civium interfecto invidiae mihi in posteritatem redundaret. Quod si ea mihi maxime impenderet, tamen hoc animo fui semper ut invidiam virtute partam gloriam, non invidiam putarem.
30 Quamquam non nulli sunt in hoc ordine qui aut ea quae imminent non videant aut ea quae vident dissimulent ; qui spem Catilinae mollibus sententiis aluerunt coniurationemque nascentem non credendo conroboraverunt ; quorum auctoritate multi non solum improbi verum etiam imperiti, si in hunc animadvertissem, crudeliter et regie factum esse dicerent. Nunc intellego, si iste, quo intendit, in

---

various *leges annales* regulating the age at which a magistracy might be held. Before a man could become consul he had successively to be quaestor and praetor.

^a See p. 178, n. *e* and p. 204, n. *b*.
^b See p. 414, n. *a*.

only through your own efforts and without any backing from ancestors ! [a] Fine thanks if you neglect the safety of your fellow citizens because you are afraid of unpopularity or any danger to yourself ! If you are afraid of unpopularity, surely the unpopularity caused by severity and resoluteness is not to be feared any more than that caused by sloth and negligence. Or when Italy is laid waste by war, when her cities are destroyed, her dwellings in flames, do you not think that then you will be consumed by a blaze of unpopularity ? " 29

To these most solemn words of the Republic and of those who share her feelings I shall give a brief reply. If I judged it best, gentlemen, to punish Catiline with death, I would not have given that cutthroat another hour to live. If our leading men and most distinguished citizens have been honoured rather than besmirched by the blood of Saturninus, the Gracchi, Flaccus, [b] and of many before them, I certainly had no call to fear that any wave of unpopularity would flood over me because I had executed this murderer of citizens. If, however, it did seriously threaten me, I have always been of the opinion that unpopularity derived from doing what is right is not unpopularity but honour. Yet there are some in this body who either cannot see what threatens us or pretend that they cannot, who have fed Catiline's hopes by their feeble decisions [c] and put heart into the growing conspiracy by refusing to believe that it existed ; who would have influenced many, the merely naïve as well as those of ill will, into saying that my action was cruel and tyrannical, if I had punished Catiline. As it is, I am sure that, if he 30

[c] *Cf. pro Murena* 51, p. 252.

Manliana castra pervenerit, neminem tam stultum
fore qui non videat coniurationem esse factam, neminem tam improbum qui non fateatur. Hoc autem uno
interfecto intellego hanc rei publicae pestem paulisper reprimi, non in perpetuum comprimi posse.
Quod si sese eiecerit secumque suos eduxerit et
eodem ceteros undique conlectos naufragos adgre-
garit, exstinguetur atque delebitur non modo haec
tam adulta rei publicae pestis verum etiam stirps ac
semen malorum omnium.

31   Etenim iam diu, patres conscripti, in his periculis
coniurationis insidiisque versamur, sed nescio quo
pacto omnium scelerum ac veteris furoris et audaciae
maturitas in nostri consulatus tempus erupit. Nunc[1]
si ex tanto latrocinio iste unus tolletur, videbimur
fortasse ad breve quoddam tempus cura et metu esse
relevati, periculum autem residebit et erit inclusum
penitus in venis atque in visceribus rei publicae. Ut
saepe homines aegri morbo gravi, cum aestu febrique
iactantur, si aquam gelidam biberunt, primo relevari
videntur, deinde multo gravius vehementiusque
adflictantur, sic hic morbus qui est in re publica
relevatus istius poena vehementius reliquis vivis
32   ingravescet. Qua re secedant improbi, secernant se a
bonis, unum in locum congregentur, muro denique,
quod saepe iam dixi, secernantur a nobis ; desinant
insidiari domi suae consuli, circumstare tribunal
praetoris urbani, obsidere cum gladiis curiam, mal-

---

[1] nunc *Clark* ; *perhaps* hoc *should be read.* hic *CA V βtx.*
quod *ahou.*

---

[a] The senior of the eight praetors. Their business was
largely judicial and they tried their cases at a tribunal in the
Forum

arrives at Manlius' camp to which he is on his way, no one will be such a fool as not to see that a conspiracy has been formed and no one such a traitor as to deny it. Yet I believe that, if Catiline alone is killed, this cancer in the State can be held in check for a short time, but not eliminated for ever. If, however, he banishes himself and marches off his followers with him, and rounds up in one place the other castaways whom he has collected from every corner, then there will be wiped out and destroyed not only this cancer now grown so large in the State but with it the root and seed of all our ills.

We have lived among these dangers and plots of conspiracy for a long time, gentlemen, but it has turned out that all these crimes and the reckless frenzy of such long standing have come to a head in my consulship. If he alone is removed out of all this band of brigands, we shall appear perhaps to have gained a short respite from anxiety and fear, but the danger will remain and be set deep in the veins and vitals of the Republic. Men who are seriously ill often toss to and fro with the heat of their fever and, if they drink cold water, seem to get relief at first, but then are much more seriously and acutely distressed. In the same way this disease from which the Republic is suffering will be temporarily relieved by his punishment, but so long as the others remain alive will grow more serious. Let the traitors, then, depart; let them separate themselves from the loyal citizens, let them gather in one place and lastly, as I have now said so often, let them be separated from us by the city wall. Let them stop attacking the consul in his own home, surrounding the tribunal of the urban praetor,[a] besieging the Senate-house with swords,

leolos et faces ad inflammandam urbem comparare ; sit denique inscriptum in fronte unius cuiusque quid de re publica sentiat. Polliceor hoc vobis, patres conscripti, tantam in nobis consulibus fore diligentiam, tantam in vobis auctoritatem, tantam in equitibus Romanis virtutem, tantam in omnibus bonis consensionem ut Catilinae profectione omnia patefacta, inlustrata, oppressa, vindicata esse videatis.

33 Hisce ominibus, Catilina, cum summa rei publicae salute, cum tua peste ac pernicie cumque eorum exitio qui se tecum omni scelere parricidioque iunxerunt, proficiscere ad impium bellum ac nefarium. Tu, Iuppiter, qui isdem quibus haec urbs auspiciis a Romulo es constitutus, quem Statorem huius urbis atque imperi vere nominamus, hunc et huius socios a tuis ceterisque templis, a tectis urbis ac moenibus, a vita fortunisque civium omnium arcebis et homines bonorum inimicos, hostis patriae, latrones Italiae scelerum foedere inter se ac nefaria societate coniunctos aeternis suppliciis vivos mortuosque mactabis.

---

[a] See p. 32, n. *a*.

and preparing burning arrows and torches to set fire to the city ; finally, let there be written upon the brow of every man what he feels about the Republic. I make this promise to you, gentlemen, that we consuls will take such pains, that you senators will display such authority, the Roman knights such valour, all loyal citizens such close agreement that with Catiline's departure you will see everything not only revealed and illumined but crushed and punished.

With omens such as these, Catiline, go forth to 33 your impious and wicked war, and bring sure salvation to the Republic, disaster and ruin upon yourself, and destruction upon those who have joined you in every crime and act of treason. You, Jupiter,[a] whom Romulus established with the same auspices as this city, whom we justly call the Supporter of this city and empire, will keep him and his confederates from your temple and those of the other gods, from the houses and the walls of the city, from the lives and fortunes of all her citizens. And these men, the foes of loyal citizens, public enemies of their native land, plunderers of Italy, men who are joined together in an evil alliance and companionship of crime, these men alive or dead you will visit with eternal punishment.

ORATIO
IN L. CATILINAM SECUNDA

Habita ad Populum

1 Tandem aliquando, Quirites, L. Catilinam, furentem audacia, scelus anhelantem, pestem patriae nefarie molientem, vobis atque huic urbi ferro flammaque minitantem ex urbe vel eiecimus vel emisimus vel ipsum egredientem verbis prosecuti sumus. Abiit, excessit, evasit, erupit. Nulla iam pernicies a monstro illo atque prodigio moenibus ipsis intra moenia comparabitur. Atque hunc quidem unum huius belli domestici ducem sine controversia vicimus. Non enim iam inter latera nostra sica illa versabitur, non in campo, non in foro, non in curia, non denique intra domesticos parietes pertimescemus. Loco ille motus est, cum est ex urbe depulsus. Palam iam cum hoste nullo impediente bellum iustum geremus. Sine dubio perdidimus hominem magnificeque vicimus, cum illum ex occultis insidiis in apertum 2 latrocinium coniecimus. Quod vero non cruentum mucronem, ut voluit, extulit, quod vivis nobis egressus est, quod ei ferrum e manibus extorsimus, quod incolumis civis, quod stantem urbem reliquit, quanto tandem illum maerore esse adflictum et pro-

---

^a The Latin word is the regular term for the citizens meeting as civilians. For the nature of this meeting, see Appendix A, p. 559.

68

THE SECOND SPEECH
AGAINST LUCIUS SERGIUS CATILINA

At long last, citizens,[a] we have expelled Lucius 1
Catilina, or, if you prefer, sent him off, or followed him
on his way with our farewells as he left Rome of his
own accord, roused to a frenzy of audacity, breathing
crime, foully plotting the destruction of his country,
and ceaselessly threatening you and this city with
fire and the sword. He has gone, left us, got away,
broken out. No longer will that misbegotten monster
plan the destruction of our very walls within these
walls; no longer is our victory over the one true leader
of this civil war in doubt ; no longer will that dagger
be twisted in our sides ; no longer shall we tremble
in the Campus Martius, in the Forum, in the Senate-
house,—yes, even in our own homes. He was shifted
from his vantage-point when he was driven from the
city. We shall now wage open war without hindrance
upon a public enemy. There is no doubt that we
destroyed the man and won a glorious victory when
we drove him from secret plots to open banditry.
Because he did not bear off a dagger stained with 2
blood as he wished, because he left us still alive,
because we wrenched his weapon from his hands,
because he left the city still standing and its citizens
safe and sound—just think of the sense of desolation

fligatum putatis ? Iacet ille nunc prostratus, Quirites, et se perculsum atque abiectum esse sentit et
retorquet oculos profecto saepe ad hanc urbem quam
e suis faucibus ereptam esse luget : quae quidem
mihi laetari videtur, quod tantam pestem evomuerit
forasque proiecerit.

3   Ac si quis est talis qualis esse omnis oportebat, qui
in hoc ipso in quo exsultat et triumphat oratio mea
me vehementer accuset, quod tam capitalem hostem
non comprehenderim potius quam emiserim, non est
ista mea culpa, Quirites, sed temporum. Interfectum
esse L. Catilinam et gravissimo supplicio adfectum
iam pridem oportebat, idque a me et mos maiorum et
huius imperi severitas et res publica postulabat. Sed
quam multos fuisse putatis qui quae ego deferrem
non crederent, quam multos qui propter stultitiam
non putarent,[1] quam multos qui etiam defenderent,
quam multos qui propter improbitatem faverent ?
Ac si illo sublato depelli a vobis omne periculum
iudicarem, iam pridem ego L. Catilinam non modo
invidiae meae verum etiam vitae periculo sustulissem.

4 Sed cum viderem, ne vobis quidem omnibus etiam
tum re probata[2] si illum, ut erat meritus, morte
multassem, fore ut eius socios invidia oppressus persequi non possem, rem huc deduxi ut tum palam pugnare possetis cum hostem aperte videretis. Quem
quidem ego hostem, Quirites, quam vehementer
foris esse timendum putem, licet hinc intellegatis,
quod etiam illud moleste fero quod ex urbe parum

---

[1] quam ... putarent *comes after* defenderent *in* CA Vh ;
is omitted by a *and deleted by Halm.*

[2] re probata *Clark.* reprobatam *C.* rei p. probatam *V.*
A *has a gap of ten letters.* probata *the other* MSS.

that weighed him down! He lies helpless now, citizens, and realizes that he has been struck down and laid low. Again and again, I know, he gazes back at this city in his anguish that his prey has been snatched from his jaws. And the city? I think that it is thankful that it has vomited forth that deadly pestilence and rid itself of it.

One of you, however, may react with feelings that 3 all should share and make a violent attack upon me for the very decision that is the triumphant boast of my speech, that I did not arrest so fatal an enemy but let him go. That fault is not mine, citizens, but lies in the circumstances. Lucius Catilina ought to have suffered the supreme penalty and been put to death long ago, a course required of me by the practice of our ancestors, the stern tradition of my office, and by interests of state. But how many do you think there were who did not believe my charges, who were too stupid to have any views at all, who went so far as to defend him, or who were criminal enough to support him? If I thought that by removing him I could free you from all danger, I would long ago have risked not merely unpopularity but my very life and got rid of Lucius Catilina. At a time, however, when some 4 even of you still remained unconvinced of the facts, I saw that, if I had inflicted the death penalty that he deserved, the unpopularity of that action would have prevented me from tackling his confederates. I therefore created a situation in which you could see your enemy clearly and fight him in the open. You may judge too, citizens, how formidable an enemy I consider him to be, now that he has left the city, from my concern that he left Rome with so few companions.

comitatus exierit. Utinam ille omnis secum suas copias eduxisset! Tongilium mihi eduxit quem amare in praetexta[1] coeperat, Publicium et Minucium quorum aes alienum contractum in popina nullum rei publicae motum adferre poterat : reliquit quos viros, quanto aere alieno, quam valentis, quam nobilis !

5 Itaque ego illum exercitum prae Gallicanis legionibus et hoc dilectu quem in agro Piceno et Gallico Q. Metellus habuit, et his copiis quae a nobis cotidie comparantur, magno opere contemno, conlectum ex senibus desperatis, ex agresti luxuria, ex rusticis decoctoribus, ex eis qui vadimonia deserere quam illum exercitum maluerunt ; quibus ego non modo si aciem exercitus nostri, verum etiam si edictum praetoris ostendero, concident. Hos quos video volitare in foro, quos stare ad curiam, quos etiam in senatum venire, qui nitent unguentis, qui fulgent purpura, mallem secum suos milites eduxisset : qui si hic permanent, mementote non tam exercitum illum esse nobis quam hos qui exercitum deseruerunt pertimescendos. Atque hoc etiam sunt timendi magis quod quid cogitent me scire sentiunt neque tamen

6 permoventur. Video cui sit Apulia attributa, quis

---

[1] praetexta *i.* praetexta (-tata *A*) calumnia *the other* MSS. praetexta calumniatum *Reis.*

---

[a] The phrase means that he was still wearing the purple-edged *toga praetexta*, the dress for boys up to the age of sixteen (as well as for curule magistrates).

[b] Catiline took only the small fry with him. The debts of the men left behind were large enough to be politically and economically important. On *nobilis*, see p. 178, n. *e.*

[c] *i.e.* composed of the inhabitants of Cisalpine Gaul ; the regular forces there.

[d] Metellus Celer, see p. 17. As praetor he had been

If only he had left at the head of all his forces! I see
that he did take with him Tongilius with whom he had
started a liaison when he was still a lad.[a] He also
took Publicius and Minucius whose debts run up in
taverns could not cause the least disturbance in the
State, but the men he has left behind! What debts
they have![b] What power! What distinguished
birth!

If I compare that army of his with the Gallic 5
legions[c] and the levy which Quintus Metellus has
held in Picenum and Umbria[d] and with these forces
which we are building up every day, I treat it with
deep contempt—that collection of old men without
hope, of spendthrift peasants,[e] of bankrupts from the
country, of men who would rather jump their bail
than desert his ranks. They will collapse if I show
them the praetor's edict,[f] let alone our army's battle-
line. As for these men whom I see flitting about in the
Forum, standing in front of the Senate-house, even
coming into the Senate, who glisten with unguents,
who are resplendent in purple, these I would prefer
him to have taken with him as his soldiers. Remember that, if they remain here, it is not so much his
army that we ought to fear as those who have deserted it. They are all the more frightening because
they are unmoved in spite of their realization that I
know their plans. I see to whom Apulia has been 6

ordered by the Senate to levy troops in Picenum and the *ager
Gallicus*, the coastal district of Umbria between Ariminum
and Ancona, so called because it had been the land of the
Senones, the last Gauls to settle in Italy.

[e] Particularly Sulla's veterans who had been settled in his
colonies.

[f] Presumably the praetorian edict dealing with the seizure
of persons.

habeat Etruriam, quis agrum Picenum, quis Gallicum, quis sibi has urbanas insidias caedis atque incendiorum depoposcerit. Omnia superioris noctis consilia ad me perlata esse sentiunt ; patefeci in senatu hesterno die ; Catilina ipse pertimuit, profugit : hi quid exspectant ? Ne illi vehementer errant, si illam meam pristinam lenitatem perpetuam sperant futuram.

Quod exspectavi, iam sum adsecutus ut vos omnes factam esse aperte coniurationem contra rem publicam videretis ; nisi vero si quis est qui Catilinae similis cum Catilina sentire non putet. Non est iam lenitati locus ; severitatem res ipsa flagitat. Unum etiam nunc concedam : exeant, proficiscantur, ne patiantur desiderio sui Catilinam miserum tabescere. Demonstrabo iter : Aurelia via profectus est ; si accelerare 7 volent, ad vesperam consequentur. O fortunatam rem publicam, si quidem hanc sentinam urbis eiecerit ! Uno me hercule Catilina exhausto levata mihi et recreata res publica videtur. Quid enim mali aut sceleris fingi aut cogitari potest quod non ille conceperit ? quis tota Italia veneficus, quis gladiator, quis latro, quis sicarius, quis parricida, quis testamentorum subiector, quis circumscriptor, quis ganeo, quis nepos, quis adulter, quae mulier infamis, quis corruptor iuventutis, quis corruptus, quis perditus inveniri potest qui se cum Catilina non familiarissime vixisse fateatur ? quae caedes per hosce annos sine illo facta est, quod nefarium stuprum non per illum ?

---

[a] The road to Faesulae and to Marseilles where according to Cicero Catiline pretended that he was going.

assigned, who has Etruria, who Picenum, who Umbria, and who has demanded as his task the plans for murder and arson in Rome itself. They know that all their plans laid the other night have been reported to me. I revealed them in the Senate yesterday ; Catiline himself was terrified and fled. What are *these* men waiting for ? I can assure them that they are very much mistaken if they expect the clemency that I have shown in the past to last for ever.

I have now achieved what I have been waiting for —you all see that a conspiracy has been openly formed against the Republic ; unless, of course, anyone thinks that men like Catiline are not in agreement with him. There is no longer any place for clemency ; the situation demands severity but I shall even at this late hour make one concession ; let them leave, let them depart, so that they do not allow poor Catiline to pine away in longing for them. I will show them the road ; he left by the Aurelian Way,*a* and if they are prepared to hurry, they will catch him up by evening. What a relief for the Republic to have baled out of it 7 this bilge-water ! I feel that the disposal of Catiline alone has lightened the Republic and restored it. Can you rack your brain for a single misdeed or crime that has not already occurred to him ? What poisoner in the whole of Italy, what gladiator, what bandit, what assassin, what parricide, what forger of wills, what cheat, what glutton, what spendthrift, what adulterer, what whore, what corrupter of youth, what rogue, what scoundrel can be found who does not admit to having lived on the most intimate terms with Catiline ? What murder over all these years in which he has not had a hand ? What criminal debauchery for which he has not been responsible ?

8 Iam vero quae tanta umquam in ullo iuventutis inlecebra fuit quanta in illo ? qui alios ipse amabat turpissime, aliorum amori flagitiosissime serviebat, aliis fructum libidinum, aliis mortem parentum non modo impellendo verum etiam adiuvando pollicebatur. Nunc vero quam subito non solum ex urbe verum etiam ex agris ingentem numerum perditorum hominum conlegerat ! Nemo non modo Romae sed ne ullo quidem in angulo totius Italiae oppressus aere alieno fuit quem non ad hoc incredibile sceleris foedus asciverit.

9 Atque ut eius diversa studia in dissimili ratione perspicere possitis, nemo est in ludo gladiatorio paulo ad facinus audacior qui se non intimum Catilinae esse fateatur, nemo in scaena levior et nequior qui se non eiusdem prope sodalem fuisse commemoret. Atque idem tamen stuprorum et scelerum exercitatione adsuefactus frigore et fame et siti et vigiliis perferendis fortis ab istis praedicabatur, cum industriae subsidia atque instrumenta virtutis in libidine auda-

10 ciaque consumeret. Hunc vero si secuti erunt sui comites, si ex urbe exierint desperatorum hominum flagitiosi greges, o nos beatos, o rem publicam fortunatam, o praeclaram laudem consulatus mei ! Non enim iam sunt mediocres hominum libidines, non humanae et tolerandae audaciae; nihil cogitant nisi caedem, nisi incendia, nisi rapinas. Patrimonia sua profuderunt, fortunas suas obligaverunt; res eos iam pridem, fides nuper deficere coepit : eadem tamen illa

Who ever proved so active a seducer of the young as 8
he ? Upon some he satisfied his own foul passion, for
others he pandered to their filthy desires. To some
he offered the satisfaction of their lust and to others
the murder of their parents, offering encouragement
and even assistance. How quickly, too, he had collected a huge crowd of desperate men from the
countryside as well as from the city ! There was not
a single man overwhelmed by debt, whether in Rome
or in the furthest corner of Italy, whom he did not
enrol in this incredible alliance of crime.

Let me now help you to note his varied aptitudes 9
of a different sort. There is no one in a gladiatorial
school, rather more criminally inclined than the
others, who does not claim Catiline as a bosom friend ;
no actor, more frivolous and vicious than his fellows,
who does not claim to have been his almost constant
companion. Catiline, moreover, trained by his life of
debauchery and crime to endure cold, hunger, thirst
and lack of sleep, won in the eyes of these men a
reputation for endurance, although by his sexual
excesses and his violence he was exhausting those
faculties which foster long toil and provide the outlets
for a man's natural ability. If his companions follow 10
him, if the criminal bands of desperate men leave
Rome, how happy we shall be ! What good fortune
for the Republic ! What a glorious reward for my
consulship ! The depravity of these men is no longer
any ordinary depravity, their violence is no longer the
violence of men and we cannot endure it ; they think
of nothing but murder, arson and pillage. They have
squandered their inheritances ; they have mortgaged
their estates ; money began to fail them long ago and
their credit has now started to run out ; but the

77

CICERO

quae erat in abundantia libido permanet. Quod si in
vino et alea comissationes solum et scorta quaererent,
essent illi quidem desperandi, sed tamen essent
ferendi: hoc vero quis ferre possit, inertis homines
fortissimis viris insidiari, stultissimos prudentissimis,
ebrios sobriis, dormientis vigilantibus? qui mihi ac-
cubantes in conviviis, complexi mulieres impudicas,
vino languidi, conferti cibo, sertis redimiti, unguentis
obliti, debilitati stupris eructant sermonibus suis
11 caedem bonorum atque urbis incendia. Quibus ego
confido impendere fatum aliquod et poenam iam diu
improbitati, nequitiae, sceleri, libidini debitam aut
instare iam plane aut certe appropinquare. Quos si
meus consulatus, quoniam sanare non potest, sus-
tulerit, non breve nescio quod tempus sed multa
saecula propagarit rei publicae. Nulla enim est natio
quam pertimescamus, nullus rex qui bellum populo
Romano facere possit. Omnia sunt externa unius
virtute terra marique pacata: domesticum bellum
manet, intus insidiae sunt, intus inclusum periculum
est, intus est hostis. Cum luxuria nobis, cum amentia,
cum scelere certandum est. Huic ego me bello ducem profiteor, Quirites; suscipio inimicitias hominum perditorum; quae sanari poterunt quacumque
ratione sanabo, quae resecanda erunt non patiar ad
perniciem civitatis manere. Proinde aut exeant aut
quiescant aut, si et in urbe et in eadem mente
permanent, ea quae merentur exspectent.
12   At etiam sunt qui dicant, Quirites, a me eiectum

---

[a] Pompey had crushed the pirates in 67 and in the following years had defeated Mithridates, king of Pontus.

78

expensive tastes that they had in their days of plenty still remain. If in their drinking and gambling they only looked for wild revelry and whores, they would admittedly be beyond hope, but we could still tolerate them ; but who could stand by and watch wastrels hatch plots against men of action, fools against the wise, sots against the sober, sluggards against the wakeful ? Reclining at their banquets, embracing their whores, stupefied by wine, stuffed with food, crowned with garlands, reeking with scent, enfeebled by debauchery, they belch out in their conversation the murder of loyal citizens and the firing of Rome. I am confident that some doom 11 hangs over these men and that the punishment long due for their dishonesty, their wickedness, their crimes, and their depravity is—if not upon them this very instant—at least on its way. My consulship cannot cure these men but, if it removes them, then it will have prolonged the life of the Republic, not for a few fleeting seconds, but for many centuries. There is no foreign people left for us to fear, no king able to make war on the Roman people. Peace reigns abroad by land and sea thanks to the valour of one man.[a] The sole remaining war is on our own soil ; the plots, the danger, the enemy are in our own midst. The battles we have to fight are against luxury, folly, and crime. That is the war for which I offer myself as your leader, citizens. I accept the enmity of scoundrels. I shall find a way to cure what can be cured ; what needs excising, I shall not allow to remain to destroy the State. Let them either go, then, or keep the peace ; if they remain in Rome without a change of heart, they can expect their deserts.

There are others, however, who say that I have 12

esse Catilinam.[1] Quod ego si verbo adsequi possem,
istos ipsos eicerem qui haec loquuntur. Homo enim
videlicet timidus aut etiam permodestus vocem consulis ferre non potuit; simul atque ire in exsilium
iussus est, paruit. Quin[2] hesterno die, cum domi
meae paene interfectus essem, senatum in aedem
Iovis Statoris convocavi, rem omnem ad patres con-
scriptos detuli. Quo cum Catilina venisset, quis eum
senator appellavit, quis salutavit, quis denique ita
aspexit ut perditum civem ac non potius ut im-
portunissimum hostem? Quin etiam principes eius
ordinis partem illam subselliorum ad quam ille
13 accesserat nudam atque inanem reliquerunt. Hic ego
vehemens ille consul qui verbo civis in exsilium eicio
quaesivi a Catilina in nocturno conventu ad M.
Laecam fuisset necne. Cum ille homo audacissimus
conscientia convictus primo reticuisset, patefeci
cetera : quid ea nocte egisset, ubi fuisset, quid in
proximam constituisset, quem ad modum esset ei ratio
totius belli descripta edocui. Cum haesitaret, cum
teneretur, quaesivi quid dubitaret proficisci eo quo
iam pridem pararet, cum arma, cum securis, cum
fascis, cum tubas, cum signa militaria, cum aquilam
illam argenteam cui ille etiam sacrarium[3] domi suae
14 fecerat scirem esse praemissam. In exsilium eiciebam quem iam ingressum esse in bellum videram ?
Etenim, credo, Manlius iste centurio qui in agro
Faesulano castra posuit bellum populo Romano suo

---

[1] eiectum esse Catilinam *Clark*. *The* MSS. *contain the
words* in exilium *in various positions in the sentence.*
[2] quin *Clark*. qui *A Vo*[2]. quid ut *ah*. qui (quod *o*[1]) ut
the other MSS.
[3] sacrarium scelerum *ahot*. scelerum sacrarium *β*.

---

[a] See p. 65, n. *b*.

driven out Catiline. If I could achieve this merely by saying the word, I would drive out the men who are saying this. The fellow was so timid or even sensitive, of course, that he could not bear to hear what the consul said ; the minute he was ordered to go into exile, he obeyed. In fact, when I had come within an ace of death in my own home, I summoned the Senate yesterday to the temple of Jupiter Stator and brought the whole matter up before the House. When Catiline arrived, what senator spoke to him ? Who greeted him ? Who treated him as a citizen, though a scoundrel, and not as the most dangerous of outlaws ? They went further ; the most senior members of the House left empty and bare the benches around that upon which he had seated himself. Your stern consul who drives citizens into 13 exile with a mere word then asked Catiline whether or not he had been at the meeting the previous night at the house of Marcus Laeca. When the man for all his effrontery was overcome by the knowledge of his guilt and did not at first reply, I disclosed the rest of the story. I described what he had done that night, where he had been, what he had planned for the following night, and how he had mapped out the plan for the whole war. Since he was at a loss and was trapped, I asked him why he was hesitating to go where he had long been preparing to go, for I knew that the arms, the axes, the fasces, the trumpets, the military standards, that silver eagle *a* for which he had even built a shrine in his own home had been sent on ahead. Was I driving him into exile when I had 14 seen that he had already begun operations ? Manlius, that mere centurion, was acting on his own account, I suppose, when he set up camp in the territory of

nomine indixit, et illa castra nunc non Catilinam ducem exspectant, et ille eiectus in exsilium se Massiliam, ut aiunt, non in haec castra confert.

O condicionem miseram non modo administrandae verum etiam conservandae rei publicae! Nunc si L. Catilina consiliis, laboribus, periculis meis circumclusus ac debilitatus subito pertimuerit, sententiam mutaverit, deseruerit suos, consilium belli faciendi abiecerit, et ex hoc cursu sceleris ac belli iter ad fugam atque in exsilium converterit, non ille a me spoliatus armis audaciae, non obstupefactus ac perterritus mea diligentia, non de spe conatuque depulsus, sed indemnatus innocens in exsilium eiectus a consule vi et minis esse dicetur: et erunt qui illum, si hoc fecerit, non improbum sed miserum, me non diligentissimum consulem sed crudelissimum tyrannum existimari velint. Est mihi tanti, Quirites, huius invidiae falsae atque iniquae tempestatem subire, dum modo a vobis huius horribilis belli ac nefarii periculum depellatur. Dicatur sane eiectus esse a me, dum modo eat in exsilium. Sed mihi credite, non est iturus. Numquam ego ab dis immortalibus optabo, Quirites, invidiae meae relevandae causa ut L. Catilinam ducere exercitum hostium atque in armis volitare audiatis, sed triduo tamen audietis; multoque magis illud timeo ne mihi sit invidiosum aliquando

Faesulae and declared war upon the Roman people, and that camp is not at this moment waiting for its commander, Catiline; and Catiline himself, driven out into exile, is making for Marseilles—that's what they say—and not for this camp.

The preservation of the Republic no less than governing it—what a thankless task it is! If all the measures that I have taken and the efforts that I have made at such danger to myself have trapped Lucius Catilina and reduced him to impotence and if, as a result, he is now suddenly seized with panic, changes his mind, deserts his confederates, abandons his plan to make war, and turns from his path of war and crime to flight and exile, there are men who will claim, not that a violent criminal was stripped of his arms, baffled and terrified by my energy, frustrated of his hopes and thwarted in his enterprises, but that a man, untried and innocent, was driven into exile by the violent threats of the consul; and, if he does take this course, there will be others who will want to make him an object of pity rather than a criminal, and myself the cruellest of tyrants rather than the most vigilant of consuls. Citizens, it is worth my enduring 15 the storm of this ill-deserved and unfounded hatred, provided only that you are spared the horror and danger of civil war. By all means let men say that I drove him out, provided that he does go into exile. But he has no intention of going, take my word for it. I shall never pray to the immortal gods, citizens, to be cleared of this hatred at the cost of your hearing that Lucius Catilina is marching to and fro under arms at the head of an army of enemies; but that is what you will be hearing in three days' time. I am afraid of being attacked in the future much more for letting

quod illum emiserim potius quam quod eiecerim.
Sed cum sint homines qui illum, cum profectus sit,
eiectum esse dicant, idem, si interfectus esset, quid
16 dicerent? Quamquam isti qui Catilinam Massiliam
ire dictitant non tam hoc queruntur quam verentur.
Nemo est istorum tam misericors qui illum non ad
Manlium quam ad Massiliensis ire malit. Ille autem,
si me hercule hoc quod agit numquam antea cogitasset, tamen latrocinantem se interfici mallet quam
exsulem vivere. Nunc vero, cum ei nihil adhuc
praeter ipsius voluntatem cogitationemque acciderit,
nisi quod vivis nobis Roma profectus est, optemus
potius ut eat in exsilium quam queramur.

17 Sed cur tam diu de uno hoste loquimur et de eo
hoste qui iam fatetur se esse hostem, et quem, quia,
quod semper volui, murus interest, non timeo: de his
qui dissimulant, qui Romae remanent, qui nobiscum
sunt nihil dicimus? Quos quidem ego, si ullo modo
fieri possit, non tam ulcisci studeo quam sanare sibi
ipsos, placare rei publicae, neque id qua re fieri non
possit, si iam me[1] audire volent, intellego. Exponam
enim vobis, Quirites, ex quibus generibus hominum
istae copiae comparentur; deinde singulis medicinam
consili atque orationis meae, si quam potero, adferam.

18 Unum genus est eorum qui magno in aere alieno
maiores etiam possessiones habent quarum amore
adducti dissolvi nullo modo possunt. Horum hominum species est honestissima—sunt enim locupletes

---

[1] si iam me *Clark.* si a me *CAah.* si me *the other* MSS.

---

[a] Politics at Rome required large sums of ready cash but
the capital of most of those involved was tied up in land.
They therefore borrowed the money they required and ran up
huge debts. *Cf. pro Sulla* 56, p. 370.

him go than for driving him out. And if there are
men who say that he was driven into exile when in
fact he went voluntarily, what would they be saying,
if he had been killed ? Yet those who keep on saying 16
that Catiline is going to Marseilles are more afraid
than sorry. None of them is tender-hearted enough
to wish him to go there rather than join Manlius. If
he had never before even dreamt of doing what he is
doing now, he would still rather die a bandit than
live an exile. As it is, everything has so far gone for
him according to plan and just as he wished—except
that I was still alive when he left Rome—let us hope,
then, that he is going into exile, and not complain
about it.

Why, though, am I talking so long about one 17
enemy, an enemy at that who now admits that he is an
enemy and one of whom I am not afraid because—
and this is what I have always wanted—the city wall
lies between us, and yet do not mention those who
pretend that they are not enemies, who remain in
Rome, and are still among us ? I do not wish so
much to take revenge upon these men as to bring
them to their senses in any way that I can, and to
reconcile them to the Republic, a task that should not
prove impossible if only they are now willing to listen
to me. I shall list for you, citizens, the types of men
from which the revolutionary forces are recruited and
I shall then offer to each of them in my speech the
remedy of any advice that I can give.

One group consists of those who have heavy debts 18
and possess estates more than large enough to pay
them, but are so attached to their estates that they
cannot be parted from them.^a These men have the
most respectable outward appearance—for they are

—voluntas vero et causa impudentissima. Tu agris,
tu aedificiis, tu argento, tu familia, tu rebus omnibus
ornatus et copiosus sis, et dubites de possessione detrahere, adquirere ad fidem? Quid enim exspectas?
bellum? Quid ergo? in vastatione omnium tuas
possessiones sacrosanctas futuras putes? an tabulas
novas? Errant qui istas a Catilina exspectant: meo
beneficio tabulae novae proferuntur, verum auctio-
nariae; neque enim isti qui possessiones habent alia
ratione ulla salvi esse possunt. Quod si maturius
facere voluissent neque, id quod stultissimum est,
certare cum usuris fructibus praediorum, et locuple-
tioribus his et melioribus civibus uteremur. Sed
hosce homines minime puto pertimescendos, quod
aut deduci de sententia possunt aut, si permanebunt,
magis mihi videntur vota facturi contra rem publicam
quam arma laturi.

19 Alterum genus est eorum qui, quamquam premuntur aere alieno, dominationem tamen exspectant,
rerum potiri volunt, honores quos quieta re publica
desperant perturbata se consequi posse arbitrantur.
Quibus hoc praecipiendum videtur, unum scilicet et
idem quod reliquis omnibus, ut desperent id quod
conantur se consequi posse : primum omnium me
ipsum vigilare, adesse, providere rei publicae ; deinde
magnos animos esse in bonis viris, magnam concordiam,[1] maximam multitudinem, magnas praeterea
militum copias; deos denique immortalis huic invicto

[1] concordiam ordinum *Clark.*

---

[a] *i.e.* account books—the cancellation of their debts.
[b] At the auction sale of their estates to pay their debts.

wealthy—but their intentions and attitudes are quite unscrupulous. Could *you* be richly and abundantly supplied with lands, houses, silver plate, slaves and possessions of every sort and yet hesitate to give up part of your estate in order to improve your credit ? What are you waiting for ? War ? All right ; but would you think that your estates will be regarded as sacred in the general devastation ? Or are you waiting for new books ?[a] You need not expect them from Catiline ; but my good offices are indeed providing new books—auctioneers' catalogues.[b] This is the only way in which men who possess estates can be solvent. If they had been willing to do this earlier and had not been so stupid as to try to meet the interest on their debts from the income of their estates, we should find them both richer and better citizens. I think, however, that these men need cause us little concern because they can be induced to change their attitude or, if they persist, are in my view more likely to attack the Republic with vows than with arms.

The second group consists of those who are over- 19 whelmed by debt but still expect to enjoy absolute power. They want to gain control of the government and think that revolution can bring them the offices of which they have no hope in times of peace. This is my best advice to them—as it is, needless to say, to all the others—to give up all hope of attaining their goal. First of all, I personally am on the alert, I am right at hand, I am guarding the Republic ; in the second place, the body of loyal citizens has rare courage, complete harmony, and strength in their large numbers, and there is too a strong force of soldiers ; and finally, the immortal gods will bring

populo, clarissimo imperio, pulcherrimae urbi contra
tantam vim sceleris praesentis auxilium esse laturos.
Quod si iam sint id quod summo furore cupiunt
adepti, num illi in cinere urbis et in sanguine civium,
quae mente conscelerata ac nefaria concupiverunt,
consules se aut dictatores aut etiam reges sperant
futuros ? Non vident id se cupere quod, si adepti sint,
fugitivo alicui aut gladiatori concedi sit necesse ?

20   Tertium genus est aetate iam adfectum, sed tamen
exercitatione robustum; quo ex genere iste est Manlius cui nunc Catilina succedit. Hi sunt homines ex
eis coloniis quas Sulla constituit; quas ego universas
civium esse optimorum et fortissimorum virorum
sentio, sed tamen ei sunt coloni qui se in[1] insperatis ac
repentinis pecuniis sumptuosius insolentiusque iacta-
runt. Hi dum aedificant tamquam beati, dum praediis
lectis, familiis magnis, conviviis apparatis delectantur,
in tantum aes alienum inciderunt ut, si salvi esse
velint, Sulla sit eis ab inferis excitandus: qui etiam
non nullos agrestis homines tenuis atque egentis in
eandem illam spem rapinarum veterum impulerunt.
Quos ego utrosque in eodem genere praedatorum
direptorumque pono, sed eos hoc moneo, desinant fu-
rere ac proscriptiones et dictaturas cogitare. Tantus
enim illorum temporum dolor inustus est civitati ut
iam ista non modo homines sed ne pecudes quidem
mihi passurae esse videantur.

---

[1] in *added by Ernesti.*

---

[a] Cicero speaks so approvingly in deference to the Sullan
affiliations of some of those to whom he looked for support
against the conspirators.

help in person to this unconquered people, this most renowned of empires and fairest of cities. Let us suppose, however, that they were to attain the goal to which their utter madness directs them, do they then hope—for this is the heart's desire of these wicked criminals—to be consuls, dictators or even kings amid the ashes of their city and in the blood of their fellow-countrymen? Do they not see that, if they get what they want, they will be bound to lose it to some runaway slave or gladiator?

The third group comprises men who are now get- 20 ting on in years but whose active life has kept them physically fit. The Manlius from whom Catiline has taken over is in this class. They are men from those colonies which Sulla founded and which, I appreciate, are as a whole composed of men of complete loyalty and outstanding bravery.[a] Nevertheless there are some colonists who have used their sudden and un-expected wealth to give a display of luxury to which they were quite unaccustomed and which was beyond their means. Putting up buildings as men of wealth and enjoying their choice of farms, their large establishments, and their sumptuous banquets, they have run so deeply into debt that they would have to raise Sulla from the dead if they wanted to be in the clear. They have also induced some poor small-holders to share their hopes that earlier confiscations will be repeated. I include both these groups in the one class of thieves and robbers; but I give them this advice : let them give up their wild thoughts of proscriptions and dictatorships. The horror of that period is so deeply branded upon the State that not even the dumb animals, let alone men, will tolerate its return.

21 Quartum genus est sane varium et mixtum et
turbulentum; qui iam pridem premuntur, qui numquam emergunt, qui partim inertia, partim male
gerendo negotio, partim etiam sumptibus in vetere
aere alieno vacillant, qui vadimoniis, iudiciis, pro-
scriptione bonorum defetigati permulti et ex urbe et
ex agris se in illa castra conferre dicuntur. Hosce ego
non tam milites acris quam infitiatores lentos esse
arbitror. Qui homines quam[1] primum, si stare non
possunt, conruant, sed ita ut non modo civitas sed ne
vicini quidem proximi sentiant. Nam illud non intellego quam ob rem, si vivere honeste non possunt,
perire turpiter velint, aut cur minore dolore perituros
se cum multis quam si soli pereant arbitrentur.

22 Quintum genus est parricidarum, sicariorum, denique omnium facinerosorum. Quos ego a Catilina non
revoco; nam neque ab eo divelli possunt et pereant
sane in latrocinio, quoniam sunt ita multi ut eos carcer
capere non possit.

Postremum autem genus est non solum numero
verum etiam genere ipso atque vita quod proprium
Catilinae est, de eius dilectu, immo vero de complexu eius ac sinu; quos pexo capillo, nitidos, aut
imberbis aut bene barbatos videtis, manicatis et
talaribus tunicis, velis amictos, non togis; quorum
omnis industria vitae et vigilandi labor in antelucanis
23 cenis expromitur. In his gregibus omnes aleatores,

---

[1] quam *added by Halm.*

[a] *i.e.* are bankrupt.
[b] Imprisonment was not a punishment for which Roman
citizens were liable; the Tullianum under the Capitol, the
place of execution, was the sole prison in Rome. See E. Nash,
Pictorial Dictionary of Ancient Rome 1. 206-207.

The fourth group is a motley assortment of trouble- 21
makers; those who have been in financial straits for
years, who never get their heads above water, who are
staggering under age-old debts which result partly
from laziness, partly from failures in business, partly
too from extravagance. Many of them have been
worn down by summonses on bail, judgements given
against them and enforced sales of property, and are
said to be making off from town and country alike to
Catiline's camp. These men, I would say, are not so
much eager soldiers as reluctant defaulters. If these
men cannot stand on their own feet,[a] let them crash
as soon as possible, but don't let the State or even the
neighbours next door hear the thud. I do not understand why men who cannot live an honourable life
should want to die in disgrace or why they think that
it will be less painful to perish in a crowd than to die
alone.

The fifth group is composed of parricides, assassins 22
and every sort of criminal. These men I have no
wish to redeem from Catiline; indeed, they cannot
be torn from him. Let them perish in the course of
their crime, for there are too many of them for the
prison [b] to hold them all.

The last group is not only last in order but also in
character and way of life. It is Catiline's very own;
his special choice—let me say—or rather his most
intimate and bosom friends. These are the men you
see with their carefully combed hair, dripping with
oil, some smooth as girls, others with shaggy beards,
with tunics down to their ankles and wrists, and
wearing frocks not togas. All the activity of their
lives and all the efforts of their waking hours are
devoted to banquets that last till dawn. In this herd 23

omnes adulteri, omnes impuri impudicique versantur.
Hi pueri tam lepidi ac delicati non solum amare et
amari neque saltare et cantare sed etiam sicas vibrare
et spargere venena didicerunt. Qui nisi exeunt, nisi
pereunt, etiam si Catilina perierit, scitote hoc in re
publica seminarium Catilinarum futurum. Verum
tamen quid sibi isti miseri volunt ? num suas secum
mulierculas sunt in castra ducturi ? Quem ad modum
autem illis carere poterunt, his praesertim iam nocti-
bus ? Quo autem pacto illi Appenninum atque illas
pruinas ac nivis perferent ? nisi idcirco se facilius
hiemem toleraturos putant, quod nudi in conviviis
saltare didicerunt.

24   O bellum magno opere pertimescendum, cum hanc
sit habiturus Catilina scortorum cohortem praetoriam!
Instruite nunc, Quirites, contra has tam praeclaras
Catilinae copias vestra praesidia vestrosque exercitus. Et primum gladiatori illi confecto et saucio consules imperatoresque vestros opponite; deinde contra
illam naufragorum eiectam ac debilitatam manum florem totius Italiae ac robur educite. Iam vero arces[1]
coloniarum ac municipiorum respondebunt Catilinae
tumulis silvestribus. Neque ego ceteras copias, ornamenta, praesidia vestra cum illius latronis inopia
25 atque egestate conferre debeo. Sed si, omissis his
rebus quibus nos suppeditamur, eget ille, senatu,
equitibus Romanis, urbe, aerario, vectigalibus, cuncta
Italia, provinciis omnibus, exteris nationibus, si his

---

[1] arces *Garatoni.* urbes *MSS.* vires *Muretus.*

---

[a] Strictly speaking, a *municipium* was a self-governing
community that had become part of the Roman State, while
a *colonia* was in origin a settlement planted by Rome. The
phase *municipia et coloniae* means in effect " the towns of
Italy." A. N. Sherwin-White, *The Roman Citizenship* 143 f.

you find all the gamblers, all the adulterers, all the filthy minded lechers. These boys, so dainty and effeminate, have learnt not only to love and be loved, not only to dance and sing, but also to brandish daggers and sow poison. Unless they leave Rome, unless they perish, even if Catiline has perished, rest assured that there will remain in the Republic this spawning-ground of Catilines. Yet what do those wretches want for themselves? They are not going to take their mistresses to the camp with them, are they? How can they be parted from them, and on nights like these? How will they stand the frosts and snows of the Apennines? Perhaps they think that they will withstand the winter more easily because they have learned to dance naked at banquets.

What a truly terrifying war if Catiline is going to 24 have this élite force of ponces! Now, citizens, marshal your garrisons and your field forces against these brilliant troops of Catiline! First, pit your consuls and your generals against that part-worn gladiator; then lead out against that castaway band of shipwrecked men at their last gasp the flower and the pick of the whole of Italy. Why, the colonies and boroughs of Italy [a] will prove strongholds to match Catiline's wooded hills.[b] I do not need to compare all your other resources, your equipment, your garrisons, with that bandit's down-and-out and impoverished band. If, however, we were to ignore 25 all these resources with which we are supplied and which Catiline lacks, the Senate, the equestrian order, the capital itself, the treasury, the revenue, all Italy, all the provinces, the foreign nations; if, leaving all

[b] The haunt of bandits like Catiline and suitable for the guerrilla warfare of which alone he is capable.

rebus omissis causas ipsas quae inter se confligunt
contendere velimus, ex eo ipso quam valde illi ia-
ceant intellegere possumus. Ex hac enim parte pudor
pugnat, illinc petulantia ; hinc pudicitia, illinc stuprum ; hinc fides, illinc fraudatio ; hinc pietas, illinc
scelus ; hinc constantia, illinc furor ; hinc honestas,
illinc turpitudo ; hinc continentia, illinc libido ; hinc
denique aequitas, temperantia, fortitudo, prudentia,
virtutes omnes certant cum iniquitate, luxuria, igna-
via, temeritate, cum vitiis omnibus ; postremo copia
cum egestate, bona ratio cum perdita, mens sana cum
amentia, bona denique spes cum omnium rerum
desperatione confligit. In eius modi certamine ac
proelio nonne, si hominum studia deficiant, di ipsi
immortales cogant ab his praeclarissimis virtutibus
tot et tanta vitia superari ?

26   Quae cum ita sint, Quirites, vos, quem ad modum
iam antea dixi, vestra tecta vigiliis custodiisque defendite ; mihi ut urbi sine vestro metu[1] ac sine ullo
tumultu satis esset praesidi consultum atque provi-
sum est. Coloni omnes municipesque vestri certiores
a me facti de hac nocturna excursione Catilinae facile
urbis suas finisque defendent ; gladiatores, quam sibi
ille manum certissimam fore putavit, quamquam
animo meliore sunt quam pars patriciorum, potestate
tamen nostra continebuntur. Q. Metellus quem ego
hoc prospiciens in agrum Gallicum Picenumque
praemisi aut opprimet hominem aut eius omnis motus
conatusque prohibebit. Reliquis autem de rebus

---

[1] mutu *C, omitted by h.* motu βx.

[a] See p. 17.

these on one side, we were willing to make a comparison of the causes which are opposed to each other, we could tell from that alone how utterly abject is the position of our enemies. On our side fights decency, on theirs viciousness; on our side morality, on theirs debauchery; on ours good faith, on theirs deceit; on ours respect for right, on theirs crime; on ours firmness of purpose, on theirs wild irresponsibility; on ours honour, on theirs disgrace; on ours self-control, on theirs a surrender to passion; in short, justice, moderation, bravery, wisdom, all the virtues, contend with injustice, intemperateness, cowardice, folly, all the vices. In a word, plenty fights against poverty, incorrupt principles against corrupt, sanity against insanity, well-founded hope against general desperation. In a contest and battle of this sort, even if men's ardour fail them, would not the immortal gods by themselves force such a sink of iniquity to yield to these sterling virtues?

In such a situation as this, citizens, I urge you, as I 26 did before, to defend your homes with patrols and guards. For my part, I have made full provision for the protection of the city without alarming you or declaring a state of emergency. All your fellow-citizens in the colonies and boroughs of Italy have been informed by me of this night attack planned by Catiline and they will defend their cities and territories with ease. The gladiators who, he thought, would be his most valuable adherents, although they are better disposed towards us than some patricians, will be kept under control by our forces. I foresaw this and sent Quintus Metellus ahead to Umbria and Picenum.[a] He will either crush Catiline or prevent any movement or attempt on his part. I shall refer to

constituendis, maturandis, agendis iam ad senatum referemus, quem vocari videtis.

27 Nunc illos qui in urbe remanserunt atque adeo qui contra urbis salutem omniumque vestrum in urbe a Catilina relicti sunt, quamquam sunt hostes, tamen, quia nati sunt cives, monitos etiam atque etiam volo. Mea lenitas adhuc si cui solutior visa est, hoc exspectavit ut id quod latebat erumperet. Quod reliquum est, iam non possum oblivisci meam hanc esse patriam, me horum esse consulem, mihi aut cum his vivendum aut pro his esse moriendum. Nullus est portis custos, nullus insidiator viae : si qui exire volunt, conivere possum ; qui vero se in urbe commoverit cuius ego non modo factum sed vel[1] inceptum ullum conatumve contra patriam deprehendero, sentiet in hac urbe esse consules vigilantis, esse egregios magistratus, esse fortem senatum, esse arma, esse carcerem quem vindicem nefariorum ac manifestorum scelerum maiores nostri esse voluerunt.

28 Atque haec omnia sic agentur ut maximae res minimo motu, pericula summa nullo tumultu, bellum intestinum ac domesticum post hominum memoriam crudelissimum et maximum me uno togato duce et imperatore sedetur. Quod ego sic administrabo,

[1] sed vel *bs.* sed ne (ne quid *o*) *alo.* sed *hux.*

---

[a] The Tullianum.

[b] The word *togatus* makes its first appearance in these speeches in this passage. The toga is the dress of the civilian, of peace (*cf.* Cicero's famous line *Cedant arma togae, concedat laurea laudi* quoted in his speech *in Pisonem* 73-74) and Cicero develops his theme in his speeches *in Catilinam* 3. 15 and 23, pp. 116 and 126, and *pro Sulla* 85, p. 398, a speech in which he had to defend himself against charges of acting tyrannically. His civilian status and his suppression of the conspiracy in Rome without having resort to arms is

the Senate, whom, as you see, I am convening, the decision upon all other measures, their despatch and their execution.

To those who have remained in Rome, or rather to 27 those who have been left in Rome by Catiline to destroy both the city and all of you, I now wish to re-iterate my warning; for although they are enemies, still they were born citizens. My former clemency may have been thought too lax, but it was only waiting for what lay hidden to be revealed. For the future, no longer can I forget that this is my father-land, that I am consul of these men, and that I must either live with them or die for them. The city gates are not guarded, the road is not watched. If they want to leave, I can connive at it; but if anyone makes a move in the city, if I detect any plan or attempt upon our fatherland, let alone any act, he will find that there are vigilant consuls in this city, incomparable magistrates, a vigorous Senate, that there are arms and a place of execution *a* where following the ordinances of our ancestors we exact the penalty for heinous crimes when they have been ex-posed.

In all these measures I shall ensure that a major 28 crisis is resolved with the least disturbance, that acute dangers are averted without a state of emergency, and that the most bitter and widespread civil war within the memory of man is suppressed with a single civil magistrate as your general to lead you.*b* I shall

contrasted with the constant menace of intervention by the *imperatores*. They are men of war with violent solutions to Rome's political problems. C. Nicolet, " *Consul togatus*," *Revue des Études latines* 38 (1960), 240-245. Also, with particular reference to Pompey, p. 130, n. *a*.

Quirites, ut, si ullo modo fieri poterit, ne improbus quidem quisquam in hac urbe poenam sui sceleris sufferat. Sed si vis manifestae audaciae, si impendens patriae periculum me necessario de hac animi lenitate deduxerit, illud profecto perficiam quod in tanto et tam insidioso bello vix optandum videtur, ut neque bonus quisquam intereat paucorumque poena vos omnes salvi esse possitis.

29 Quae quidem ego neque mea prudentia neque humanis consiliis fretus polliceor vobis, Quirites, sed multis et non dubiis deorum immortalium significationibus, quibus ego ducibus in hanc spem sententiamque sum ingressus; qui iam non procul, ut quondam solebant, ab externo hoste atque longinquo, sed hic praesentes suo numine atque auxilio sua templa atque urbis tecta defendunt. Quos vos, Quirites, precari, venerari, implorare debetis ut, quam urbem pulcherrimam florentissimam potentissimamque esse voluerunt, hanc omnibus hostium copiis terra marique superatis a perditissimorum civium nefario scelere defendant.

ᵃ In a number of passages (*cf. in Catilinam* 3. 1 and 18-22, pp. 100 and 120-124 ; *pro Sulla* 40, p. 352) Cicero attributes the suppression of the conspiracy in part to the *virtus* of the Senate or the *providentia* of the gods. See Quintilian 11. 1. 23. Quintilian seems to think that Cicero only did this out of a sense of what was right and proper, but he surely had sound political reasons for making the Senate a partner in his actions, and *ad Atticum* 1. 16. 6 suggests that his belief in

handle the situation in such a way, citizens, that if it can possibly be avoided, not even a common criminal will suffer in this city the penalty for his crime. If, however, the extent of the conspiracy now revealed, if the danger that threatens our fatherland compels me to abandon my policy of clemency, then I shall certainly see to it—an aim that might be thought virtually hopeless in so extensive and treacherous a war—that no patriot perishes and that by the punishment of only a few you can all be saved.

When I make this promise, citizens, I do not rely 29 upon my own good sense or upon any human wisdom, but upon the many clear omens from the immortal gods under whose guidance I entertained these hopes and embarked upon this policy.[a] No longer, as was once their practice, do they guard us from afar against a foreign and distant enemy, but here at our side they defend their temples and the city's buildings with the protection of their divine power. These gods, citizens, have ordained that this city be the most beautiful, the most prosperous, the most powerful in the world, and now that all the forces of her foreign foes have been defeated on land and sea, you ought to pray to them, to worship them, to implore them to defend her from criminal attack by traitors among her own citizens.

divine assistance was to some extent genuine. See W. Allen, Jr., " Cicero's Conceit," *Transactions of the American Philological Association* 85 (1954), 142 f.

ORATIO
IN L. CATILINAM TERTIA

Habita ad Populum

1   Rem publicam, Quirites, vitamque omnium vestrum, bona, fortunas, coniuges liberosque vestros atque hoc domicilium clarissimi imperi, fortunatissimam
pulcherrimamque urbem, hodierno die deorum
immortalium summo erga vos amore, laboribus, consiliis, periculis meis e flamma atque ferro ac paene
ex faucibus fati ereptam et vobis conservatam ac
2 restitutam videtis.   Et si non minus nobis iucundi
atque inlustres sunt ei dies quibus conservamur quam
illi quibus nascimur, quod salutis certa laetitia est,
nascendi incerta condicio et quod sine sensu nascimur,
cum voluptate servamur, profecto, quoniam illum qui
hanc urbem condidit ad deos immortalis benivolen-
tia famaque sustulimus, esse apud vos posterosque
vestros in honore debebit is qui eandem hanc urbem
conditam amplificatamque servavit.   Nam toti urbi,
templis, delubris, tectis ac moenibus subiectos prope
iam ignis circumdatosque restinximus, idemque

---

   a Cf. *in Catilinam* 2. 29, p. 98 and n. *a.*
   b Cf. *pro Flacco* 102, p. 552.   In 63 Cicero's day of triumph
was the 3rd of December ; by 59 he regarded the 5th as the
summit of his achievement.
   c Romulus.

THE THIRD SPEECH
AGAINST LUCIUS SERGIUS CATILINA

Delivered before the People

The Republic, citizens, the lives of you all, your 1
property, your fortunes, your wives and your children,
together with this heart of our glorious empire, this
most blessed and beautiful of cities, have, as you see,
on this very day been snatched from fire and the
sword. The great love that the immortal gods hold
for you[a] has combined with the toil and the vigilance
that I have undertaken, and with the perils that I
have undergone, to bring them out of the very jaws
of destruction and restore them to you safe and
sound. The day on which we are saved is, I believe, 2
as bright and joyous as that on which we are born,
because delight at our salvation is assured while at
birth our future is uncertain, and because we are not
conscious of our birth but feel pleasure at our preservation.[b] If I am right, then surely when we have
out of gratitude and by our praises raised to the
immortal gods the man who founded this city,[c] you
and your descendants should hold in honour the man
who has saved this same city after its foundation and
growth to greatness. It is I who have quenched the
fires which were on the point of being set to the whole
city, to its temples, its shrines, its houses and its
walls and which were about to engulf them. It is I

101

gladios in rem publicam destrictos rettudimus mu-
3 cronesque eorum a iugulis vestris deiecimus. Quae
quoniam in senatu inlustrata, patefacta, comperta
sunt per me, vobis iam exponam breviter ut et
quanta et quam manifesta et qua ratione investigata
et comprehensa sint vos qui et ignoratis et exspectatis
scire possitis.

Principio, ut Catilina paucis ante diebus erupit ex
urbe, cum sceleris sui socios huiusce nefarii belli acer-
rimos duces Romae reliquisset, semper vigilavi et
providi, Quirites, quem ad modum in tantis et tam
absconditis insidiis salvi esse possemus. Nam tum cum
ex urbe Catilinam eiciebam—non enim iam vereor
huius verbi invidiam, cum illa magis sit timenda,
quod vivus exierit—sed tum cum illum exterminari
volebam, aut reliquam coniuratorum manum simul
exituram aut eos qui restitissent infirmos sine illo ac
4 debilis fore putabam. Atque ego, ut vidi, quos maximo furore et scelere esse inflammatos sciebam,
eos nobiscum esse et Romae remansisse, in eo omnis
dies noctesque consumpsi ut quid agerent, quid
molirentur sentirem ac viderem, ut, quoniam auribus
vestris propter incredibilem magnitudinem sceleris
minorem fidem faceret oratio mea, rem ita compre-
henderem ut tum demum animis saluti vestrae
provideretis cum oculis maleficium ipsum videretis.

---

a It is now the 3rd of December; Catiline had left Rome
on the night of the 8th of November.

who have thrust back the swords drawn against the Republic and have dashed away the daggers they held at your throats. It is through my efforts that 3 these plots have been detected, laid bare and displayed to the Senate and I shall therefore now give you a brief account of them so that you, who have not yet heard but wish to be told, can learn their extent, the nature of the evidence and my methods of investigation and detection.

In the first place, ever since Catiline dashed from the city a few days ago,[a] he has left in Rome accomplices in his crime, the most active leaders in this wicked war. I have, therefore, been constantly on the alert and seeking ways, citizens, of ensuring our safety in the midst of such wide-ranging and deep-laid plots. At the time when I drove Catiline from the city—and I no longer fear the hostility provoked by the word " drove " so much as that roused by his departure alive—at the time, I repeat, when I wanted him driven beyond our frontiers, I thought that either the remaining band of conspirators would leave with him or that those who remained would be impotent and ineffectual without him. When, however, it be- 4 came clear to me that the men whom I knew to be the most desperate criminals were still among us and had stayed back in Rome, all my time, night and day, was devoted to the task of finding out what they were doing and what they were working at. Since I realized that you would be the more reluctant to believe my story because the extent of their crime defies belief, this I did so that I might discover enough of the conspiracy to force you at long last to make plans for your own safety when you actually saw the crime with your own eyes. Discovering, then,

CICERO

Itaque ut comperi legatos Allobrogum belli Transalpini et tumultus Gallici excitandi causa a P. Lentulo esse sollicitatos, eosque in Galliam ad suos civis eodemque itinere cum litteris mandatisque[1] ad Catilinam esse missos, comitemque eis adiunctum esse T. Volturcium, atque huic esse ad Catilinam datas litteras, facultatem mihi oblatam putavi ut, quod erat difficillimum quodque ego semper optabam ab dis immortalibus, tota res non solum a me sed etiam a
5 senatu et a vobis manifesto deprenderetur. Itaque hesterno die L. Flaccum et C. Pomptinum praetores, fortissimos atque amantissimos rei publicae viros, ad me vocavi, rem exposui, quid fieri placeret ostendi. Illi autem, qui omnia de re publica praeclara atque egregia sentirent, sine recusatione ac sine ulla mora negotium susceperunt, et, cum advesperasceret, occulte ad pontem Mulvium pervenerunt atque ibi in proximis villis ita bipertito fuerunt ut Tiberis inter eos et pons interesset. Eodem autem et ipsi sine cuiusquam suspicione multos fortis viros eduxerant, et ego ex praefectura Reatina compluris delectos adulescentis quorum opera utor adsidue in rei
6 publicae praesidio cum gladiis miseram. Interim tertia fere vigilia exacta, cum iam pontem Mulvium

---

[1] cum litteris mandatisque *placed after* civis *by Nohl.*

---

[a] See p. 12.
[b] Lucius Valerius Flaccus, the defendant of p. 413 f.
[c] Where the road to Etruria crosses the Tiber, some two miles north of Rome. See E. Nash, *Pictorial Dictionary of Ancient Rome* 2. 191-192.
[d] A *municipium* in Umbria. It was the regular practice for Romans to use their clients or the clients of friends from the Italian countryside against their political enemies in the city. This meant that magistrates brought these men, often

104

that Publius Lentulus [a] had been tampering with the envoys of the Allobroges in an attempt to start a war on the other side of the Alps and a rebellion in Cisalpine Gaul, and that the envoys had been sent back to their fellow-citizens in Gaul, and on the way to Catiline himself with a letter and instructions by word of mouth, and that Titus Volturcius was accompanying them and was taking a letter for Catiline, I thought that there was within my grasp the chance to achieve something which was very difficult but which I was always hoping would be granted by the immortal gods—that the Senate and you citizens should share with me in the full disclosure of the whole affair. Accordingly, I yesterday sum- 5 moned the praetors, Lucius Flaccus [b] and Gaius Pomptinus, gallant soldiers and devoted supporters of the Republic ; I explained the situation to them and told them what I wanted done. Being men who were outstanding in their loyalty to the Republic, they undertook the mission without hesitation and without a moment's delay. As it was growing dark, they went secretly to the Mulvian Bridge [c] and there divided their party into two groups in the near-by houses, so that the Tiber and the bridge lay between them. They had taken with them without arousing any suspicion a good number of stout fellows and I had sent from the prefecture of Reate [d] a strong detachment of picked young men armed with swords whose services I have been constantly using in the protection of the Republic. At about three o'clock 6 in the morning when the envoys of the Allobroges

men with military experience, to pit against popular leaders and the urban proletariat who tended to come off second-best in the ensuing struggles.

magno comitatu legati Allobroges ingredi inciperent
unaque Volturcius, fit in eos impetus; ducuntur et
ab illis gladii et a nostris. Res praetoribus erat nota
solis, ignorabatur a ceteris. Tum interventu Pomp-
tini atque Flacci pugna quae erat commissa[1] sedatur.
Litterae quaecumque erant in eo comitatu integris
signis praetoribus traduntur; ipsi comprehensi ad me,
cum iam dilucesceret, deducuntur. Atque horum
omnium scelerum improbissimum machinatorem,
Cimbrum Gabinium, statim ad me nihil dum suspi-
cantem vocavi; deinde item arcessitus est L. Statilius
et post eum Cethegus; tardissime autem Lentulus
venit, credo quod in litteris dandis praeter con-
7 suetudinem proxima nocte vigilarat. Cum summis et
clarissimis huius civitatis viris qui audita re frequentes
ad me mane convenerant litteras a me prius aperiri
quam ad senatum deferri[2] placeret, ne, si nihil esset
inventum, temere a me tantus tumultus iniectus
civitati videretur, negavi me esse facturum ut de
periculo publico non ad consilium publicum rem inte-
gram deferrem. Etenim, Quirites, si ea quae erant
ad me delata reperta non essent, tamen ego non
arbitrabar in tantis rei publicae periculis esse mihi
nimiam diligentiam pertimescendam. Senatum fre-
8 quentem celeriter, ut vidistis, coegi. Atque interea
statim admonitu Allobrogum C. Sulpicium praetorem,

---

[1] quae erat commissa *omitted by two inferior* MSS. *and
deleted by Halm.*
[2] referrem *a.* deferrem *Halm.*

---

a Publius Gabinius Capito. Why Cicero calls him Cimber
Gabinius here is not clear. See F. Münzer in Pauly-Wissowa,
Realencyclopädie VII. 1 (1910), P. Gabinius Capito (15), 431.
b Ironical. Publius Cornelius Lentulus was notorious for

with a large retinue and accompanied by Volturcius were beginning to cross the Mulvian Bridge, these men fell upon them and both sides drew their swords. Only the praetors were apprised of the situation, the others knew nothing. Then Pomptinus and Flaccus intervened and stopped the fighting just as it had started. All the letters found in the possession of the party were handed over to the praetors with their seals intact; the men were arrested and brought before me as day was breaking. I promptly summoned the arch-villain behind all these crimes, Cimber Gabinius,[a] who as yet suspected nothing; I then summoned Lucius Statilius in the same way and after him Cethegus. Lentulus was the last to arrive, presumably because, contrary to his usual practice, he had stayed up late the previous night to write his letter.[b] When they had heard the news a 7 considerable number of Rome's most eminent and distinguished men had come to my house early in the morning. They wanted me to open the letters before referring them to the Senate so that, if they did not contain anything incriminating, I should not be thought to have raised a false alarm of insurrection.[c] I replied that in a matter of public safety I would bring the facts before the council of state without prejudice. Even, citizens, if the information that I had received had not been contained in the letters it still was not my view that when the Republic stood in such danger I needed to fear any charge of excessive zeal. As you saw, I quickly called a full meeting of the Senate. In the meantime, following the advice 8 of the Allobroges, I immediately sent that gallant man,

his idleness; for the length of the letter that kept him up so late, see 12, p. 122.   [c] For his real reason, see p. 22.

fortem virum, misi qui ex aedibus Cethegi si quid
telorum esset efferret ; ex quibus ille maximum si-
carum numerum et gladiorum extulit.

Introduxi Volturcium sine Gallis ; fidem publicam
iussu senatus dedi ; hortatus sum ut ea quae sciret
sine timore indicaret. Tum ille dixit, cum vix se ex
magno timore recreasset, a P. Lentulo se habere ad
Catilinam mandata et litteras ut servorum praesidio
uteretur, ut ad urbem quam primum cum exercitu
accederet ; id autem eo consilio ut, cum urbem ex
omnibus partibus quem ad modum descriptum dis-
tributumque erat incendissent caedemque infinitam
civium fecissent, praesto esset ille qui et fugientis ex-
ciperet et se cum his urbanis ducibus coniungeret.
9 Introducti autem Galli ius iurandum sibi et litteras a
P. Lentulo, Cethego, Statilio ad suam gentem datas
esse dixerunt, atque ita sibi ab his et a L. Cassio
esse praescriptum ut equitatum in Italiam quam
primum mitterent ; pedestris sibi copias non defutu-
ras. Lentulum autem sibi confirmasse ex fatis Sibyllinis haruspicumque responsis se esse tertium illum
Cornelium ad quem regnum huius urbis atque imperium pervenire esset necesse : Cinnam ante se et
Sullam fuisse. Eundemque dixisse fatalem hunc annum esse ad interitum huius urbis atque imperi qui
esset annus decimus post virginum absolutionem,
10 post Capitoli autem incensionem vicesimum. Hanc

---

[a] See p. 13.

[b] Lucius Cornelius Cinna, the Marian leader, consul in
87–85, and the Dictator.

[c] The original Sibylline books, containing prophecies in
Greek, were believed to have been brought to Tarquinius
Superbus by the Sibyl of Cumae. They were kept in the
Capitol and were consulted in times of national crisis. The
Capitol was burnt with its contents in 83 and a fresh collection

the praetor Gaius Sulpicius, to get from the house of Cethegus any weapons that were there, and he brought out a very large number of daggers and swords.

I had Volturcius led in without the Gauls; on the Senate's authority I gave him a guarantee of immunity; I urged him to reveal without fear what he knew. He then pulled himself together with difficulty in his abject terror and said that he had instructions from Lentulus and a letter to Catiline urging him to rally the slaves to his standard [a] and march on Rome with his army as soon as possible. The plan was to be that they should set fire to every part of the city according to the plan and dispositions already made, massacre the whole citizen body and that then he should be ready in person to intercept the fugitives and to join up with these leaders in the city. The 9 Gauls were then brought in and said that an oath had been administered, a letter addressed to their people given them by Publius Lentulus, Cethegus and Statilius, and that they had been requested by these men and by Lucius Cassius to send cavalry as soon as possible into Italy where there would be no lack of infantry. Lentulus had assured them that the Sibylline books and soothsayers had declared that he was that third Cornelius to whom the rule and dominion of Rome was fated to come: before him there had been Cinna and Sulla. [b] He also said that this was the year, the tenth after the acquittal of the Vestal Virgins and the twentieth after the burning of the Capitol, fated for the destruction of Rome and her empire. [c] They said too that Cethegus had had this 10

of Sibylline prophecies had to be made (cf. p. 414). For the trial of the Vestals, see p. 6. Any trial of a Vestal Virgin, even if she was acquitted, was a matter for grave concern.

autem Cethego cum ceteris controversiam fuisse
dixerunt quod Lentulo et aliis Saturnalibus caedem
fieri atque urbem incendi placeret, Cethego nimium
id longum videretur.

Ac ne longum sit, Quirites, tabellas proferri
iussimus quae a quoque dicebantur datae. Primo
ostendimus Cethego : signum cognovit. Nos linum
incidimus ; legimus. Erat scriptum ipsius manu Allobrogum senatui et populo sese quae eorum legatis
confirmasset facturum esse ; orare ut item illi facerent
quae sibi eorum legati recepissent. Tum Cethegus,
qui paulo ante aliquid tamen de gladiis ac sicis quae
apud ipsum erant deprehensa respondisset dixisset-
que se semper bonorum ferramentorum studiosum
fuisse, recitatis litteris debilitatus atque abiectus
conscientia repente conticuit. Introductus Statilius
cognovit et signum et manum suam. Recitatae sunt
tabellae in eandem fere sententiam ; confessus est.
Tum ostendi tabellas Lentulo et quaesivi cogno-
sceretne signum. Adnuit. " Est vero " inquam
" notum quidem signum, imago avi tui, clarissimi
viri, qui amavit unice patriam et civis suos ; quae
quidem te a tanto scelere etiam muta revocare
11 debuit." Leguntur eadem ratione ad senatum Allobrogum populumque litterae. Si quid de his rebus
dicere vellet, feci potestatem. Atque ille primo quidem negavit ; post autem aliquanto, toto iam indicio

---

[a] The festival of Saturn beginning on the 19th of December during which special licence was given to slaves.

[b] Publius Cornelius Lentulus, *consul suffectus* in 162 and
princeps senatus from 125 until after 120 ; he was wounded
in the fighting which resulted in the death of Gaius Gracchus
in 121.

argument with the other conspirators: Lentulus and the others proposed that the massacre and the burning of Rome should take place on the Saturnalia,[a] but Cethegus thought that this was too long to wait.

Not to make a long story of it, citizens, we ordered the letter to be produced which each man was alleged to have given them. We first showed Cethegus his letter and he identified his seal. We cut the string and read the letter. He had written in his own hand to the senate and people of the Allobroges that he would honour his undertakings to their envoys and asked them, on their side, to carry out the requests that their envoys had received from him. A little earlier Cethegus had managed a reply to questions about the swords and daggers which had been found at his house and had said that he had always been a keen collector of fine arms. Now, when his letter was read out, he stood paralysed and smitten by his guilty conscience and suddenly fell silent. Statilius was brought in and identified his seal and handwriting. His letter was read out and was in much the same vein. He admitted writing it. Then I showed Lentulus his letter and asked whether he recognized the seal. He nodded assent. " It is indeed," I said, " a well-known seal, a portrait of your illustrious grandfather [b] who loved his country and its citizens more than any other man. Surely this seal, even though it cannot speak, should have called you back from so heinous a crime." There was then read out 11 the letter that he had written along the same lines to the senate and people of the Allobroges. I offered him the chance to say anything he wanted about its contents. At first he refused, but shortly afterwards

exposito atque edito, surrexit, quaesivit a Gallis quid
sibi esset cum eis, quam ob rem domum suam venissent, itemque a Volturcio. Qui cum illi breviter
constanterque respondissent per quem ad eum quo-
tiensque venissent, quaesissentque ab eo nihilne
secum esset de fatis Sibyllinis locutus, tum ille subito scelere demens quanta conscientiae vis esset ostendit. Nam, cum id posset infitiari, repente praeter
opinionem omnium confessus est. Ita eum non modo
ingenium illud et dicendi exercitatio qua semper
valuit sed etiam propter vim sceleris manifesti atque
deprehensi impudentia qua superabat omnis impro-
12 bitasque defecit. Volturcius vero subito litteras proferri atque aperiri iubet quas sibi a Lentulo ad Catilinam datas esse dicebat. Atque ibi vehementissime
perturbatus Lentulus tamen et signum et manum
suam cognovit. Erant autem sine nomine, sed ita :
" Quis sim scies ex eo quem ad te misi. Cura ut vir
sis et cogita quem in locum sis progressus. Vide
ecquid[1] tibi iam sit necesse et cura ut omnium
tibi auxilia adiungas, etiam infimorum." Gabinius
deinde introductus, cum primo impudenter respondere coepisset, ad extremum nihil ex eis quae Galli
13 insimulabant negavit. Ac mihi quidem, Quirites, cum
illa certissima visa sunt argumenta atque indicia
sceleris, tabellae, signa, manus, denique unius cuiusque confessio, tum multo certiora illa, color, oculi, voltus, taciturnitas. Sic enim obstupuerant, sic terram
intuebantur, sic furtim non numquam inter sese aspi-

---

[1] vide ecquid *Halm*. vide et quid αβo. et vide quid *htwx*.

when all the evidence had been produced and read out, he rose to his feet and asked the Gauls and then Volturcius what he had to do with them that they had come to his house. They replied briefly and firmly, telling how often they had come, who was the agent, and asking him whether he had never mentioned the Sibylline books to them. Then, suddenly, his guilt made him lose his wits and he showed what a bad conscience can make a man do. Although he could have denied their statement, to everyone's surprise he suddenly confessed. Not only did the native wit and verbal facility in which he always excelled fail him, but his unequalled effrontery and depravity as well, so great was the effect of the revelation and detection of his crime. Volturcius, however, suddenly de- 12 manded that the letter which he said had been given him by Lentulus for Catiline should be produced and opened. Then, although he was badly shaken, Lentulus nevertheless identified his seal and hand-writing. The letter was unsigned but read as follows : " You will know who I am from the man whom I have sent to you. Be resolute and take stock of your position. See what you must now do and take care that you get the support of everyone, even the lowest." Gabinius was then brought in and, although he began to answer with assurance, in the end he admitted all the charges brought against him by the Gauls. In my view, citizens, completely convincing 13 as were the letter, seal, handwriting and confession of each man as arguments and proofs of their guilt, still more so were their pallor, eyes, expression and their silence. They were so dazed, kept their eyes so fixed upon the ground and from time to time cast such furtive glances at each other that their guilt

ciebant ut non iam ab aliis indicari sed indicare se
ipsi viderentur.

Indiciis expositis atque editis, Quirites, senatum
consului de summa re publica quid fieri placeret.
Dictae sunt a principibus acerrimae ac fortissimae
sententiae, quas senatus sine ulla varietate est secutus. Et quoniam nondum est perscriptum senatus
consultum, ex memoria vobis, Quirites, quid senatus
14 censuerit exponam. Primum mihi gratiae verbis amplissimis aguntur, quod virtute, consilio, providentia mea res publica maximis periculis sit liberata.
Deinde L. Flaccus et C. Pomptinus praetores, quod
eorum opera forti fidelique usus essem, merito ac iure
laudantur. Atque etiam viro forti, conlegae meo,
laus impertitur, quod eos qui huius coniurationis
participes fuissent a suis et a rei publicae consiliis removisset. Atque ita censuerunt ut P. Lentulus, cum
se praetura abdicasset, in custodiam traderetur; itemque uti C. Cethegus, L. Statilius, P. Gabinius qui
omnes praesentes erant in custodiam traderentur ;
atque idem hoc decretum est in L. Cassium qui sibi
procurationem incendendae urbis depoposcerat, in
M. Ceparium cui ad sollicitandos pastores Apuliam
attributam esse erat indicatum, in P. Furium qui est
ex eis colonis quos Faesulas L. Sulla deduxit, in
Q. Annium Chilonem qui una cum hoc Furio semper
erat in hac Allobrogum sollicitatione versatus, in

---

a Gaius Antonius Hybrida. See pp. xxxvi, n. *c* and
xxxvii, n. *f*.
b For Sulla's colonies, see references earlier in these

was proved more by their own behaviour than by others.

When the evidence had been produced and read out, citizens, I asked the Senate what action it proposed to take in the supreme interests of the Republic. The senior senators made vigorous and courageous proposals and the Senate adopted them without amendment. Since the resolution of the Senate has not yet been written out completely, I shall tell you from memory, citizens, what the Senate decided. Firstly, I am thanked in the most generous terms 14 because my courage, prudence and foresight freed the Republic from dire peril. Secondly, Lucius Flaccus and Gaius Pomptinus, the praetors, are justly and deservedly praised because they had given me their courageous and loyal assistance. Praise too is accorded to that gallant man, my colleague,[a] because he had excluded those who had been members of this conspiracy from his personal counsels and from those of the State. They voted, too, that Publius Lentulus should resign his praetorship and be given into custody, and that Gaius Cethegus, Lucius Statilius and Publius Gabinius who were all present should also be given into custody. The same decision was taken in the case of Lucius Cassius who had demanded for himself the supervision of the firing of Rome; and of Marcus Ceparius to whom, as had been shown, Apulia had been assigned for him to raise the shepherds there; and of Publius Furius, who is one of the colonists whom Lucius Sulla settled at Faesulae,[b] of Quintus Annius Chilo who had throughout been involved with this Furius in tampering with the

speeches on pp. 40 and 88; also *pro Murena* 49, p. 250 and *pro Sulla* 60 f., pp. 372–374.

P. Umbrenum, libertinum hominem, a quo primum
15 Gallos ad Gabinium perductos esse constabat. Atque
ea lenitate senatus est usus, Quirites, ut ex tanta
coniuratione tantaque hac multitudine domesticorum
hostium novem hominum perditissimorum poena re
publica conservata reliquorum mentis sanari posse
arbitraretur. Atque etiam supplicatio dis immortalibus pro singulari eorum merito meo nomine decreta
est, quod mihi primum post hanc urbem conditam
togato contigit, et his decreta verbis est : " quod
urbem incendiis, caede civis, Italiam bello liberas-
sem." Quae supplicatio si cum ceteris supplicationi-
bus conferatur, hoc interest, quod ceterae bene gesta,
haec una conservata re publica constituta est. Atque
illud quod faciendum primum fuit factum atque trans-
actum est. Nam P. Lentulus, quamquam patefactis
indiciis, confessionibus suis, iudicio senatus non modo
praetoris ius verum etiam civis amiserat, tamen magistratu se abdicavit, ut quae religio C. Mario, clarissimo viro, non fuerat quo minus C. Glauciam de quo
nihil nominatim erat decretum praetorem occideret,
ea nos religione in privato P. Lentulo puniendo li-
beraremur.
16   Nunc quoniam, Quirites, consceleratissimi peri-
culosissimique belli nefarios duces captos iam et
comprehensos tenetis, existimare debetis omnis Catilinae copias, omnis spes atque opes his depulsis urbis

---

[a] He had been a businessman in Gaul. Sallust, *Bellum Catilinae* 40. 2.   [b] *Cf. in Catilinam* 2. 28, p. 96 and n. *b*.
    [c] The Senate's authority to do this would not be accepted by champions of the people's rights. See Appendix B, p. 571.
    [d] Gaius Servilius Glaucia was a popular orator and tribune in 101 and praetor in 100. He co-operated with Saturninus and died with him in the riots of 100. They had worked with Marius, but when they went too far in their attempts to
116

Allobroges; and of Publius Umbrenus,[a] a freedman who, it was established, first introduced the Gauls to Gabinius. The Senate displayed such clemency, citizens, because, although the conspiracy was so widespread and the number of traitors so great, it thought that the punishment of nine desperate criminals would suffice to save the Republic and bring the others to their senses. Furthermore, a thanksgiving was decreed to the immortal gods in my honour for their exceptional favour, an honour that I was the first civilian to receive since the founding of Rome.[b] The terms of the resolution read as follows: " because I had saved Rome from burning, the citizens from massacre and Italy from war." A comparison of this thanksgiving with all others shows that it differs in this respect: the others were granted for the successful conduct of public business, this alone for saving the Republic. Yet what had to be done first was done and effected. Although the Senate judged, after the evidence had been given and his admissions heard, that Publius Lentulus had forfeited the rights of a citizen [c] as well as those of a praetor, he was nevertheless allowed to resign his office. This would enable us to punish him as a private individual without the restraint of any religious scruple, although such scruples did not prevent the illustrious Gaius Marius from killing the praetor Gaius Glaucia without his being named in any resolution.[d]

Now, citizens, that you have captured and hold under guard the arch-villains in this most criminal and dangerous of wars, you are bound to think that with Rome's escape from these dangers all Catiline's

acquire power independent of his own, he joined the Optimates and turned upon them.

periculis concidisse. Quem quidem ego cum ex urbe
pellebam, hoc providebam animo, Quirites, remoto
Catilina non mihi esse P. Lentuli somnum nec L. Cassi
adipes nec C. Cethegi furiosam temeritatem pertimescendam. Ille erat unus timendus ex istis omnibus,
sed tam diu dum urbis moenibus continebatur. Omnia norat, omnium aditus tenebat; appellare, temptare, sollicitare poterat, audebat. Erat ei consilium
ad facinus aptum, consilio autem neque lingua neque
manus deerat. Iam ad certas res conficiendas cer-
tos homines delectos ac descriptos habebat. Neque
vero, cum aliquid mandarat, confectum putabat:
nihil erat quod non ipse obiret, occurreret, vigila-
ret, laboraret; frigus, sitim, famem ferre poterat.

17 Hunc eo hominem tam acrem, tam audacem, tam
paratum, tam callidum, tam in scelere vigilantem,
tam in perditis rebus diligentem nisi ex domesticis
insidiis in castrense latrocinium compulissem—dicam
id quod sentio, Quirites—non facile hanc tantam
molem mali a cervicibus vestris depulissem. Non ille
nobis Saturnalia constituisset, neque tanto ante exiti
ac fati diem rei publicae denuntiavisset neque com-
misisset ut signum, ut litterae suae testes manifesti
sceleris deprehenderentur. Quae nunc illo absente
sic gesta sunt ut nullum in privata domo furtum umquam sit tam palam inventum quam haec in tota re
publica coniuratio manifesto comprehensa est. Quod

forces, all his hopes and all his resources have collapsed. At the time when I was driving him from the city, I foresaw, citizens, that with Catiline's removal I should have nothing to fear from the lethargy of Publius Lentulus, the corpulence of Lucius Cassius or the insensate impetuosity of Gaius Cethegus. Catiline was the only one out of all these men to be feared and he only so long as he was within the walls of Rome. He knew everything, he could go anywhere. He had the ability and nerve to approach men, sound them out and win them over. He had a genius for crime, a genius which his tongue and hand were always ready to serve. He now had certain individuals selected and assigned to perform allotted tasks, but he did not think that he only had to delegate some task for it to be completed. He toiled long hours in person to supervise and deal with every point that arose. He could endure cold, thirst, hunger. His energy, enterprise, preparedness, resourcefulness, the long hours spent in crime, the diligence in iniquity, were such that, if I had not driven him from his plots within the city to his bandits' camp—and I shall speak frankly, citizens—it would have been no easy matter for me to have lifted from your necks the burden of his evildoing. He would not have decided upon the Saturnalia for us and would not have proclaimed the day of ruin and destruction for the Republic so far ahead, nor would he have made the mistake of allowing seal and letter to be seized and provide clear evidence of his guilt. As it is, everything has been handled so incompetently in his absence that this conspiracy against the whole Republic has been detected more clearly than any theft from a private house. Had Catiline remained

si Catilina in urbe ad hanc diem remansisset, quamquam, quoad fuit, omnibus eius consiliis occurri atque
obstiti, tamen, ut levissime dicam, dimicandum nobis
cum illo fuisset, neque nos umquam, cum ille in urbe
hostis esset, tantis periculis rem publicam tanta pace,
tanto otio, tanto silentio liberassemus.

18 Quamquam haec omnia, Quirites, ita sunt a me
administrata ut deorum immortalium nutu atque
consilio et gesta et provisa esse videantur. Idque
cum coniectura consequi possumus, quod vix videtur
humani consili tantarum rerum gubernatio esse
potuisse, tum vero ita praesentes his temporibus opem
et auxilium nobis tulerunt ut eos paene oculis videre
possimus. Nam ut illa omittam, visas nocturno
tempore ab occidente faces ardoremque caeli, ut
fulminum iactus, ut terrae motus relinquam, ut omittam cetera quae tam multa nobis consulibus facta
sunt ut haec quae nunc fiunt canere di immortales
viderentur, hoc certe, Quirites, quod sum dicturus
neque praetermittendum neque relinquendum est.

19 Nam profecto memoria tenetis Cotta et Torquato
consulibus compluris in Capitolio res de caelo esse
percussas, cum et simulacra deorum depulsa sunt et
statuae veterum hominum deiectae et legum aera
liquefacta et tactus etiam ille qui hanc urbem condidit Romulus, quem inauratum in Capitolio, parvum
atque lactantem, uberibus lupinis inhiantem fuisse
meministis. Quo quidem tempore cum haruspices ex
tota Etruria convenissent, caedis atque incendia et

---

[a] *Cf. in Catilinam* 2. 29, p. 98 and n. *a.*
[b] In 65.
[c] The traditional home of augury.

in the city to this day, notwithstanding the way in which I countered and foiled all his plans while he was here, we should have had to fight him to the finish—I cannot put it less strongly—and, while that enemy was in the city, we should never have freed the Republic from its perils in such peace, tranquillity and quiet.

Even so, citizens, my conduct of this whole matter 18 may be thought to display both foresight and action that depended upon the wisdom and the will of the immortal gods.[a] We can make this assumption not only because it seems almost impossible that human reason can have directed matters of such importance, but also because so closely have the gods stood by us at this time to bring us their help and assistance that we can almost see them with our eyes. Even if I do not mention those portents, the meteors that were seen in the west at night and lit up the sky, even if I leave out the thunderbolts and the earthquakes, even if I omit the other portents which have occurred so frequently in my consulship that the immortal gods seemed to be foretelling these events which are now coming to pass, surely, citizens, I must not pass over or leave out what I am about to describe. You 19 remember, of course, that in the consulship of Cotta and Torquatus[b] a large number of objects on the Capitol was struck by lightning, images of the gods were overthrown and statues of men of old overturned and the bronze tablets of our laws melted; even the statue of Romulus, the founder of Rome, was struck—you remember that it was a gilt statue on the Capitol of a baby being given suck from the udders of a wolf. On that occasion the soothsayers assembled from the whole of Etruria[c] and said that

legum interitum et bellum civile ac domesticum et
totius urbis atque imperi occasum appropinquare
dixerunt, nisi di immortales omni ratione placati suo
20 numine prope fata ipsa flexissent. Itaque illorum
responsis tum et ludi per decem dies facti sunt neque
res ulla quae ad placandos deos pertineret praetermissa est. Idemque iusserunt simulacrum Iovis
facere maius et in excelso conlocare et contra atque
antea fuerat ad orientem convertere ; ac se sperare
dixerunt, si illud signum quod videtis solis ortum et
forum curiamque conspiceret, fore ut ea consilia quae
clam essent inita contra salutem urbis atque imperi
inlustrarentur ut a senatu populoque Romano perspici
possent. Atque illud signum conlocandum consules
illi locaverunt; sed tanta fuit operis tarditas ut neque
superioribus consulibus neque nobis ante hodiernum
21 diem conlocaretur. Hic quis potest esse tam aversus
a vero, tam praeceps, tam mente captus qui neget
haec omnia quae videmus praecipueque hanc urbem
deorum immortalium nutu ac potestate administrari?
Etenim cum esset ita responsum, caedis, incendia, interitum rei publicae comparari, et ea per civis, quae
tum propter magnitudinem scelerum non nullis in-
credibilia videbantur, ea non modo cogitata a nefariis civibus verum etiam suscepta esse sensistis.
Illud vero nonne ita praesens est ut nutu Iovis Optimi
Maximi factum esse videatur, ut, cum hodierno die
mane per forum meo iussu et coniurati et eorum

---

murder and arson, the end of the rule of law, rebellion and civil war, the destruction of the whole city and of our empire were upon us, unless the immortal gods were placated by every means and used their power virtually to alter the path of destiny. On the strength 20 of their replies games were then held for ten days and nothing with any bearing on placating the gods was left undone. They also ordered a larger statue of Jupiter to be made and placed in a prominent position facing east, in the opposite direction to that of its predecessor. They also said that they hoped that, if the statue which you now see faced the rising sun, the Forum and the Senate-house, the plots which had been hatched in secret against the safety of Rome and of her empire would be illuminated so brightly that they could be seen by the Senate and the people of Rome. The consuls gave a contract for its erection, but progress was so slow that it was not put in position during my predecessors' nor during my own consulship until this very day. Who here 21 can be so blind to the truth, so impetuous, so deranged in his mind as to deny that, more than any other city in the whole world that we see about us, Rome is governed by the will and the power of the immortal gods? When the answer was given that murder, arson and the destruction of the Republic were being planned, and by citizens at that, the enormity of the crimes made some people refuse to believe it, although you have seen that traitorous citizens have passed from plans to deeds. Surely the very fact that the statue was being erected early this morning at the time when the conspirators and witnesses against them were being taken on my orders through the Forum to the temple of Concord *a* is

indices in aedem Concordiae ducerentur, eo ipso tempore signum statueretur ? Quo conlocato atque ad vos senatumque converso omnia et senatus et vos quae erant contra salutem omnium cogitata inlustrata 22 et patefacta vidistis. Quo etiam maiore sunt isti odio supplicioque digni qui non solum vestris domiciliis atque tectis sed etiam deorum templis atque delubris sunt funestos ac nefarios ignis inferre conati. Quibus ego si me restitisse dicam, nimium mihi sumam et non ferendus : ille, ille Iuppiter restitit ; ille Capitolium, ille haec templa, ille cunctam urbem, ille vos omnis salvos esse voluit. Dis ego immortalibus ducibus hanc mentem voluntatemque suscepi atque ad haec tanta indicia perveni. Iam vero illa Allobrogum sollicitatio, iam ab Lentulo ceterisque domesticis hostibus tam dementer tantae res creditae et ignotis et barbaris commissaeque litterae numquam essent profecto, nisi ab dis immortalibus huic tantae audaciae consilium esset ereptum. Quid vero ? ut homines Galli ex civitate male pacata, quae gens una restat quae bellum populo Romano facere et posse et non nolle videatur, spem imperi ac rerum maximarum ultro sibi a patriciis hominibus oblatam neglegerent vestramque salutem suis opibus anteponerent, id non divinitus esse factum putatis, praesertim qui nos non pugnando sed tacendo superare potuerunt ?

---

a Cicero plays upon the credulity of the common people and must surely have contrived the timing of the statue's completion for its propaganda value with the superstitious. There is none of all this in his speech to the more sophisticated Senate.

clear proof of the intervention of Jupiter Optimus
Maximus ? [a] When the statue had been placed in
position and turned towards yourselves and the Senate, both Senate and people saw the plots against
the safety of you all brought into the light of day and
laid bare. Those men who have tried to fire with the 22
torches of death and crime not only your homes and
dwellings but the temples and shrines of the gods
deserve an even more bitter hatred and condign
punishment. If I were to say that I foiled them, I
should be taking too much credit for myself—an
intolerable presumption. It was Jupiter, the mighty
Jupiter, who foiled them ; it was Jupiter who secured
the salvation of the Capitol, of these temples, of the
whole city and of you all. The immortal gods have
been my guides in my purpose and determination and
have led me to this vital evidence. Again, surely
there would never have been the intrigue with the
Allobroges ; surely Lentulus and the other enemies
in our midst would never have so foolishly entrusted
matters of such importance to barbarians who were
not known to them and committed letters to their
care, if the immortal gods had not robbed their
boundless audacity of all discretion. What is more,
the fact that men from Gaul, from a state not completely pacified and the only remaining nation to
appear both able and not unwilling to make war upon
the Roman people, would disregard the hope of independence and great rewards, offered gratuitously to
them by patricians, and would set your safety before
their own again—do you think that the gods had no
hand in this ? Why, these Gauls did not need to
fight, only to keep silent, for them to be able to
overcome us.

CICERO

23 Quam ob rem, Quirites, quoniam ad omnia pulvinaria supplicatio decreta est, celebratote illos dies cum coniugibus ac liberis vestris. Nam multi saepe honores dis immortalibus iusti habiti sunt ac debiti, sed profecto iustiores numquam. Erepti enim estis e crudelissimo ac miserrimo interitu, erepti sine caede, sine sanguine, sine exercitu, sine dimicatione; togati me uno togato duce et imperatore vicistis.

24 Etenim recordamini, Quirites, omnis civilis dissensiones, non solum eas quas audistis sed eas quas vosmet ipsi meministis atque vidistis. L. Sulla P. Sulpicium oppressit[1]: C. Marium, custodem huius urbis, multosque fortis viros partim eiecit ex civitate, partim interemit. Cn. Octavius consul armis expulit ex urbe conlegam: omnis hic locus acervis corporum et civium sanguine redundavit. Superavit postea Cinna cum Mario: tum vero clarissimis viris interfectis lumina civitatis exstincta sunt. Ultus est huius victoriae crudelitatem postea Sulla: ne dici quidem opus est quanta deminutione civium et quanta calamitate rei publicae. Dissensit M. Lepidus a clarissimo

---

[1] eiecit ex urbe *added by ho and* ex urbe eiecit *by tux*; *deleted by Lambinus*.

---

[a] Cf. in Catilinam 2. 28, p. 96, n. b.

[b] Publius Sulpicius Rufus, tribune in 88, introduced a number of bills, among which was one to replace Sulla by Marius in the command against Mithridates. The consuls, Lucius Cornelius Sulla and Quintus Pompeius Rufus, opposed him and he had them expelled from the city and carried his bills. Sulla then appealed to the army and marched on Rome, annulled the laws of Sulpicius and decreed death and exile for the leaders of the opposition. Sulpicius was betrayed and put to death.

That is why, citizens, since a thanksgiving has been 23
decreed at all the shrines, you should celebrate the
days devoted to it with your wives and children.
Honours have on numerous occasions been decreed to
the immortal gods that were deserved and long due,
but none was ever more deserved than this. You
have been rescued from the cruellest and most piti-
able of deaths ; you have been rescued without
massacre, without bloodshed, without an army and
without fighting. As civilians, under the guidance
and command of one civilian—myself—you have won
your victory.[a] Think, citizens, of all the civil wars, 24
not only those of which you have been told, but those
too which you remember as eyewitnesses. Lucius
Sulla crushed Publius Sulpicius [b] : Gaius Marius, the
protector of this city,[c] and many gallant men he drove
into exile, many he massacred. The consul Gnaeus
Octavius expelled his colleague from Rome by force
of arms.[d] All this area was choked with piles of
corpses and awash with the blood of citizens. Later
Cinna and Marius won control [e] ; then the most distinguished men were killed and the shining lights of
the State snuffed out. Sulla subsequently avenged
the atrocities of this victory [f]; but there is no need
even to refer to the losses inflicted upon the citizen
body and the magnitude of the calamity for the
Republic. Marcus Lepidus was in conflict with the

[c] By his victories over the Teutones and Cimbri at Aquae
Sextiae in 102 and Vercellae in 101. He fled with Sulpicius
when Sulla captured Rome.
[d] Gnaeus Octavius, consul in 87, expelled Lucius Cornelius
Cinna, his colleague, who after swearing an oath not to interfere with Sulla's arrangements attempted to carry a bill
recalling Marius and other exiles.
[e] As consuls in 86.   [f] In 82.

et fortissimo viro Q. Catulo : attulit non tam ipsius
interitus rei publicae luctum quam ceterorum.

25   [Atque illae tamen omnes][1] dissensiones erant eius
modi quae non ad delendam sed ad commutandam
rem publicam pertinerent. Non illi nullam esse rem
publicam sed in ea quae esset se esse principes, neque
hanc urbem conflagrare sed se in hac urbe florere
voluerunt. Atque illae tamen omnes dissensiones,
quarum nulla exitium rei publicae quaesivit, eius
modi fuerunt ut non reconciliatione concordiae sed
internicione civium diiudicatae sint.[2] In hoc autem
uno post hominum memoriam maximo crudelissimo-
que bello, quale bellum nulla umquam barbaria cum
sua gente gessit, quo in bello lex haec fuit a Lentulo, Catilina, Cethego, Cassio constituta ut omnes
qui salva urbe salvi esse possent in hostium numero
ducerentur, ita me gessi, Quirites, ut salvi omnes
conservaremini, et, cum hostes vestri tantum civium
superfuturum putassent quantum infinitae caedi restitisset, tantum autem urbis quantum flamma obire
non potuisset, et urbem et civis integros incolumis-
que servavi.

26   Quibus pro tantis rebus, Quirites, nullum ego a
vobis praemium virtutis, nullum insigne honoris,
nullum monumentum laudis postulabo praeterquam
huius diei memoriam sempiternam. In animis ego
vestris omnis triumphos meos, omnia ornamenta
honoris, monumenta gloriae, laudis insignia condi
et conlocari volo. Nihil me mutum potest delectare,

---

[1] Atque . . . omnes *deleted by Clark* (tamen omnes
omitted by x).

[2] Atque . . . sint *deleted by Bloch*.

---

[a] Marcus Aemilius Lepidus, consul in 78, quarrelled with
his colleague Quintus Lutatius Catulus and began an in-

distinguished and gallant Quintus Catulus, but the Republic did not mourn his death as deeply as that of those who died with him.[a]

[Yet all those] conflicts were not concerned with 25 destroying the Republic but with changing it. Those men did not want there to be no Republic at all but they wanted there to be a Republic in which they were the leading men; they did not want to burn this city but wished to have power in it. Yet all those conflicts, not one of which sought the destruction of the Republic, were resolved not by a peaceful reconciliation but by the slaughter of citizens. In this war, however, the most important and the most savage within memory of man, a war such as no tribe of barbarians ever fought among its own people, a war in which Lentulus, Catiline, Cethegus and Cassius laid it down as a law that all who could be safe so long as Rome was safe should be counted among their enemies, in this war, citizens, my actions have secured the salvation of you all. Although your enemies thought that only those citizens would remain who had survived indiscriminate slaughter and only that area of Rome which the flames could not reach, I have preserved both city and citizens safe and sound.

In recognition of such great services, citizens, I shall 26 demand of you no reward for my valour, no signal mark of distinction, no monument in my honour except that this day be remembered for all time. It is in your hearts that I wish to have set all my triumphs, all the decorations of distinction, the monuments of fame, the tokens of praise. Nothing

surrection. Catulus led the forces of the Republic against him.

nihil tacitum, nihil denique eius modi quod etiam
minus digni adsequi possint. Memoria vestra,
Quirites, nostrae res alentur, sermonibus crescent,
litterarum monumentis inveterascent et conrobo-
rabuntur ; eandemque diem intellego, quam spero
aeternam fore, propagatam esse et ad salutem urbis
et ad memoriam consulatus mei, unoque tempore in
hac re publica duos civis exstitisse quorum alter finis
vestri imperi non terrae sed caeli regionibus termi-
naret, alter huius imperi domicilium sedisque servaret.
27 Sed quoniam earum rerum quas ego gessi non
eadem est fortuna atque condicio quae illorum qui
externa bella gesserunt, quod mihi cum eis vivendum
est quos vici ac subegi, illi hostis aut interfectos aut
oppressos reliquerunt, vestrum est, Quirites, si ceteris
facta sua recte prosunt, mihi mea ne quando obsint
providere. Mentes enim hominum audacissimorum
sceleratae ac nefariae ne vobis nocere possent ego
providi, ne mihi noceant vestrum est providere.
Quamquam, Quirites, mihi quidem ipsi nihil ab istis
iam noceri potest. Magnum enim est in bonis
praesidium quod mihi in perpetuum comparatum est,
magna in re publica dignitas quae me semper tacita
defendet, magna vis conscientiae quam qui neglegunt,
28 cum me violare volent, se indicabunt. Est enim nobis

ᵃ Cicero now addresses Pompey as an equal. Previously he
had been very much overshadowed by him. *Cf.* p. xxx, n. *a*
Contrasting the language of this passage with the letter to
Atticus (2. 1. 3) of June 60, C. Nicolet, " *Consul togatus*,"
Revue des Études latines 38 (1960), 247, notes that the rôles
of the civil and military powers are contrasted by Cicero
throughout the period between 63 and 60 (*cf. pro Murena*
19 f.). His new position *vis-à-vis* Pompey is developed by

mute can please me, nothing silent, nothing in short that can be shared with less deserving men. Your memories, citizens, will cherish my deeds, your conversation enhance them and the records of history will bring them age and strength. I know that the same length of days—and may it be unending—has been destined for the safety of Rome as for the memory of my consulship and that in this State there have arisen at one time two men, one of whom has carried the frontiers of your empire to the limits not of earth but of heaven [a] and one who has preserved the home and seat of this empire.

Yet the lot and circumstances of a man who has 27 done what I have done are different from the position of those who have fought wars abroad. I have to live with those whom I have overcome and conquered, while they have left their enemies either dead or subdued. It is, therefore, for you, citizens, since the others rightly profit from what they have done, to see that I do not ever suffer as a result of what I have done. My foresight has prevented the criminal plans of wicked desperados from injuring you ; it is for you to see that they do not injure me. Yet *I*, citizens, can no longer be harmed by these men. Stout is the protection from the body of loyal citizens that is always at my service ; strong is the authority of the Republic which, though silently, will ever be my defence ; powerful is the force of a guilty conscience and those who ignore it and want to do me violence will be their

Cicero into a political philosophy that finds the salvation of the Republic in the alliance of soldier and civilian. *Cf.* p. 96, n. *b* ; also *ad Atticum* 6. 1. 22.

For Pompey's cold reaction to Cicero's new-found rôle, see the scholiast's comment on *pro Plancio* 85 (p. 167 *ed.* Stangl).

is animus, Quirites, ut non modo nullius audaciae cedamus sed etiam omnis improbos ultro semper lacessamus. Quod si omnis impetus domesticorum hostium depulsus a vobis se in me unum converterit, vobis erit videndum, Quirites, qua condicione posthac eos esse velitis qui se pro salute vestra obtulerint invidiae periculisque omnibus : mihi quidem ipsi quid est quod iam ad vitae fructum possit adquiri, cum praesertim neque in honore vestro neque in gloria virtutis quicquam videam altius quo mihi libeat 29 ascendere ? Illud perficiam profecto, Quirites, ut ea quae gessi in consulatu privatus tuear atque ornem, ut, si qua est invidia in conservanda re publica suscepta, laedat invidos, mihi valeat ad gloriam. Denique ita me in re publica tractabo ut meminerim semper quae gesserim, curemque ut ea virtute non casu gesta esse videantur.

Vos, Quirites, quoniam iam est nox, venerati Iovem illum custodem huius urbis ac vestrum in vestra tecta discedite et ea, quamquam iam est periculum depulsum, tamen aeque ac priore nocte custodiis vigiliisque defendite. Id ne vobis diutius faciendum sit atque ut in perpetua pace esse possitis providebo, Quirites.

own downfall. I shall yield to the rash acts of no man, 28
citizens ; indeed, such is my spirit that I shall always
strike at the evildoer first. But if I become the sole
object of violence at the hands of those traitors from
whom you have been saved, you will have to consider,
citizens, what you want to see happen in the future to
those who expose themselves in preserving you to
unpopularity and every sort of danger. For myself,
what more can now be added to life's rewards ?
Neither in the honours that you can bestow nor in the
renown of my own achievement can I see any higher
peak that I would want to scale. Have no doubt, 29
citizens, that I shall ensure that upon my return to
private life I shall uphold and consolidate the work of
my consulship and see that any hatred incurred in
saving the Republic injures those who hate me and
redounds to my own glory. In short, my policy will
be to remain true to the memory of my achievements
and ensure that men realize that they were the work
of meritorious service and not of chance.

Do you, citizens, since it is now night, offer up your
prayers to Jupiter, the guardian of this city and of
yourselves, and then depart to your homes and
defend them, although the danger is now averted, as
you did last night with your pickets and sentries. I
shall see to it that you do not have to do this for too
long and that you can dwell, citizens, in peace for
evermore.

ORATIO
IN L. CATILINAM QUARTA

1 Video, patres conscripti, in me omnium vestrum ora
atque oculos esse conversos, video vos non solum de
vestro ac rei publicae verum etiam, si id depulsum sit,
de meo periculo esse sollicitos. Est mihi iucunda in
malis et grata in dolore vestra erga me voluntas, sed
eam per deos immortalis! deponite atque obliti salutis
meae de vobis ac de vestris liberis cogitate. Mihi si
haec condicio consulatus data est ut omnis acerbitates,
omnis dolores cruciatusque perferrem, feram non
solum fortiter verum etiam libenter, dum modo meis
laboribus vobis populoque Romano dignitas salusque
2 pariatur. Ego sum ille consul, patres conscripti, cui
non forum in quo omnis aequitas continetur, non
campus consularibus auspiciis consecratus, non curia,
summum auxilium omnium gentium, non domus,
commune perfugium, non lectus ad quietem datus,
non denique haec sedes honoris[1] umquam vacua
mortis periculo atque insidiis fuit. Ego multa tacui,

---

[1] sella (id est sella *t*) curulis *in the mss. and deleted by
Muretus as an obvious gloss.*

---

[a] See Appendix A, p. 561. *Cf. pro Murena* 1, p. 186.
[b] A reference to the abortive attempt upon his life; *in
Catilinam* 1. 9, p. 42.

THE FOURTH SPEECH
AGAINST LUCIUS SERGIUS CATILINA

Delivered in the Senate

I SEE, gentlemen, that the faces and eyes of you all
are turned upon me ; I see that you are concerned not
only at your own danger and that of the Republic but
also, if that is averted, at my own. Your goodwill
towards me comforts me in my troubles and gratifies
me in my anxiety, but in the name of the immortal
gods lay it aside, forget my safety, and think of yourselves and your children. For myself, if these were the
terms on which I was given the consulship, that I
should endure all the suffering, all the anguish and all
the afflictions, I shall bear them bravely and even
gladly, provided that my efforts secure for you and for
the Roman people your authority and your salvation.
I am that consul, gentlemen, for whom neither the
Forum, the home of all justice, nor the Campus
Martius, hallowed by the auspices of consuls,[a] nor
the Senate-house, the fount of security for the nations
of the world, nor home, every man's haven of refuge,
nor the bed, a place of repose,[b] nor, finally, this seat
of honour,[c] has ever been free from plots and the risk
of death. Yes, I have left many things unsaid, I have

---

[c] The *sella curulis* used by all magistrates with *imperium*
and by the curule aediles.

multa pertuli, multa concessi, multa meo quodam
dolore in vestro timore sanavi. Nunc si hunc exitum
consulatus mei di immortales esse voluerunt ut vos
populumque Romanum ex caede miserrima, coniuges
liberosque vestros virginesque Vestalis ex acerbissima
vexatione, templa atque delubra, hanc pulcherrimam
patriam omnium nostrum ex foedissima flamma, totam Italiam ex bello et vastitate eriperem, quaecumque mihi uni proponetur fortuna subeatur. Etenim
si P. Lentulus suum nomen inductus a vatibus
fatale ad perniciem rei publicae fore putavit, cur ego
non laeter meum consulatum ad salutem populi Romani prope fatalem exstitisse ?

3 Qua re, patres conscripti, consulite vobis, prospi-
cite patriae, conservate vos, coniuges, liberos for-
tunasque vestras, populi Romani nomen salutemque
defendite ; mihi parcere ac de me cogitare desinite.
Nam primum debeo sperare omnis deos qui huic urbi
praesident pro eo mihi ac mereor relaturos esse gratiam ; deinde, si quid obtigerit, aequo animo parato-
que moriar. Nam neque turpis mors forti viro potest
accidere neque immatura consulari nec misera sa-
pienti. Nec tamen ego sum ille ferreus qui fratris
carissimi atque amantissimi praesentis maerore non
movear horumque omnium lacrimis a quibus me cir-
cumsessum videtis. Neque meam mentem non domum saepe revocat exanimata uxor et abiecta metu

---

[a] To his colleague, Gaius Antonius Hybrida, for example.
See p. xxxvii, n. *f*.   [b] *in Catilinam* 3. 9, p. 108.
[c] A man who has reached the consulship can ask for
nothing more from life.   [d] Quintus, now praetor-designate.
[e] Terentia ; his daughter Tullia was now about thirteen
years old and his son Marcus two ; his son-in-law was Gaius
Calpurnius Piso Frugi, who was not yet a senator and would

endured much, I have made many concessions *a* and at some cost to myself I have put right much that frightened you. Now, if this is the end that the immortal gods have willed for my consulship, that I should rescue you and the Roman people from the horrors of massacre, your wives, children and the Vestal Virgins from vile outrage, the temples and shrines, this fairest fatherland of us all from the foulest of fires, and all Italy from war and devastation, then let me suffer alone whatever fortune has in store for me. If Publius Lentulus was persuaded by the soothsayers to think that his name was destined by fate for the destruction of the Republic,*b* why should not I rejoice that my consulship has been destined by fate, as I might put it, for the salvation of the Roman people ?

Take thought for yourselves, therefore, gentlemen ; 3 look to the preservation of your fatherland, save yourselves, your wives, your children and your fortunes, defend the name of the Roman people and their very existence ; stop protecting me and cease your concern for me. Firstly, I am bound to hope that all the gods who watch over this city will recompense me as I deserve ; and secondly, if anything happens to me, I shall die calm and resigned. A brave man's death cannot bring dishonour, a consul's cannot be before its time,*c* a philosopher's cannot bring sorrow. But I do not have such a heart of steel that I am unmoved by the anguish of the most dear and most loving of brothers *d* and by the tears of all these gentlemen whom you see around me. My thoughts often go back to my home and to my terror-stricken wife,*e*

therefore have to stand with the crowd in the doorway of the temple and not among the body of the Senate.

filia et parvolus filius, quem mihi videtur amplecti res
publica tamquam obsidem consulatus mei, neque ille
qui exspectans huius exitum diei stat in conspectu
meo gener. Moveor his rebus omnibus, sed in eam
partem uti salvi sint vobiscum omnes, etiam si me vis
aliqua oppresserit, potius quam et illi et nos una rei
publicae peste pereamus.

4 Qua re, patres conscripti, incumbite ad salutem rei
publicae, circumspicite omnis procellas quae im-
pendent nisi providetis. Non Ti. Gracchus[a] quod
iterum tribunus plebis fieri voluit, non C. Gracchus
quod agrarios concitare conatus est, non L. Saturninus quod C. Memmium occidit, in discrimen aliquod
atque in vestrae severitatis iudicium adducitur : tenentur ei qui ad urbis incendium, ad vestram omnium
caedem, ad Catilinam accipiendum Romae restiterunt,
tenentur litterae, signa, manus, denique unius
cuiusque confessio : sollicitantur Allobroges, servitia
excitantur, Catilina arcessitur, id est initum consilium ut interfectis omnibus nemo ne ad deplorandum
quidem populi Romani nomen atque ad lamentandam
tanti imperi calamitatem relinquatur.

5 Haec omnia indices detulerunt, rei confessi sunt,
vos multis iam iudiciis iudicavistis, primum quod mihi
gratias egistis singularibus verbis et mea virtute
atque diligentia perditorum hominum coniurationem
patefactam esse decrevistis, deinde quod P. Lentulum
se abdicare praetura coegistis ; tum quod eum et

---

[a] Tiberius Gracchus, tribune in 133, unconstitutionally
sought re-election for the following year and was killed in the
course of his election campaign.   [b] See p. 35, n. *d*.
  [c] See p. 36, n. *b.*   [d] See p. 13, n. *b.*

to my daughter prostrated by fear and my little boy whom the Republic seems to be clasping as a hostage for my consulship, and to my son-in-law whom I see there awaiting the outcome of this day. I am moved by all these thoughts, but only to wish that, if some blow fells me, my family may all be safe with you, and that we do not all perish together in a single disaster to the State.

Devote your energies, therefore, gentlemen, to the 4 salvation of the State, guard well against all the storms that threaten you unless you take precautions against them. It is no Tiberius Gracchus that is brought to trial before the bar of your severity for wishing to become a tribune a second time,[a] no Gaius Gracchus for attempting to incite to violence those who sought agrarian reform,[b] no Lucius Saturninus for the murder of Gaius Memmius.[c] There are in custody men who stayed back here in Rome to burn the city, to massacre you all, to welcome Catiline ; their letters, their seals, their handwriting and finally the confession of each one of them, are in our possession. The Allobroges are being tampered with, the slaves are being called out,[d] the summons to Catiline is on its way. Their plan is that in the universal slaughter there should not survive a single individual even to mourn the name of the Roman people or to lament the destruction of so mighty an empire.

The informants have disclosed all these facts, the 5 accused men have confessed and you have already given your verdict in numerous decisions ; firstly, you thanked me in unprecedented terms and proclaimed that by my courage and exertions a conspiracy of criminals had been revealed ; secondly, you forced Publius Lentulus to resign his praetorship ; next, you

139

ceteros de quibus iudicastis in custodiam dandos
censuistis, maximeque quod meo nomine supplicationem decrevistis, qui honos togato habitus ante
me est nemini; postremo hesterno die praemia legatis
Allobrogum Titoque Volturcio dedistis amplissima.
Quae sunt omnia eius modi ut ei qui in custodiam
nominatim dati sunt sine ulla dubitatione a vobis
damnati esse videantur.

6 Sed ego institui referre ad vos, patres conscripti,
tamquam integrum, et de facto quid iudicetis et de
poena quid censeatis. Illa praedicam quae sunt
consulis. Ego magnum in re publica versari furorem et nova quaedam misceri et concitari mala iam
pridem videbam, sed hanc tantam, tam exitiosam haberi coniurationem a civibus numquam putavi. Nunc
quicquid est, quocumque vestrae mentes inclinant
atque sententiae, statuendum vobis ante noctem est.
Quantum facinus ad vos delatum sit videtis. Huic si
paucos putatis adfinis esse, vehementer erratis. Latius opinione disseminatum est hoc malum; mana-
vit non solum per Italiam verum etiam transcendit
Alpis et obscure serpens multas iam provincias
occupavit. Id opprimi sustentando et prolatando
nullo pacto potest; quacumque ratione placet celeriter vobis vindicandum est.

7 Video duas adhuc esse sententias, unam D. Silani
qui censet eos qui haec delere conati sunt morte esse
multandos, alteram C. Caesaris qui mortis poenam

---

[a] See p. 96, n. *b*.
[b] Sallust, *Bellum Catilinae* 47. 4, supplies the names:
Lentulus, Cethegus, Statilius, Gabinius and Ceparius.
[c] Silanus spoke first as senior consul designate. See p. 25,
n. *d*.
140

voted that he and the others on whom you passed judgement should be given into custody ; and most important of all, you decreed a thanksgiving in my name, an honour which I was the first civilian ever to receive [a] ; finally, yesterday you gave extremely generous rewards to the envoys of the Allobroges and to Titus Volturcius. All these acts go to show that the men who have been given into custody by name [b] have incurred your unhesitating condemnation.

I have decided, however, to refer the matter to you, 6 gentlemen, as if it were still an open question and you were giving both your verdict about the deed and your decision about the punishment. I shall, however, first say what as consul I must say. It had long been observed by me that a dangerous madness was abroad and that evils as yet unknown were seething and welling up in the Republic, but I never thought that so widespread and deadly a conspiracy was the work of citizens. Now, whatever your decision is, wherever your intentions and your feelings take you, you must decide today, before nightfall. You see the extent of the crime reported to you. If you think that there are only a few men involved in it, you are very much mistaken. This evil has been sown more widely than you think ; it has spread throughout Italy, it has even crossed the Alps, and it has now crept in unnoticed and taken hold of many provinces. Holding back and delay are quite useless in crushing it ; your punishment, whatever form it takes, must be a swift one.

I see that so far there are two proposals : one of 7 Decimus Silanus [c] who proposes that those who have attempted to destroy Rome should be punished by death ; the other of Gaius Caesar who opposes the

141

removet, ceterorum suppliciorum omnis acerbitates
amplecititur. Uterque et pro sua dignitate et pro
rerum magnitudine in summa severitate versatur.
Alter eos qui nos omnis, qui populum Romanum[1] vita
privare conati sunt, qui delere imperium, qui populi
Romani nomen exstinguere, punctum temporis frui
vita et hoc communi spiritu non putat oportere atque
hoc genus poenae saepe in improbos civis in hac re
publica esse usurpatum recordatur. Alter intellegit
mortem a dis immortalibus non esse supplici causa
constitutam, sed aut necessitatem naturae aut labo-
rum ac miseriarum quietem. Itaque eam sapientes
numquam inviti, fortes saepe etiam libenter oppeti-
verunt. Vincula vero et ea sempiterna certe ad singularem poenam nefarii sceleris inventa sunt. Municipiis
dispertiri iubet. Habere videtur ista res iniquitatem,
si imperare velis, difficultatem, si rogare. Decernatur
8 tamen, si placet. Ego enim suscipiam et, ut spero,
reperiam qui id quod salutis omnium causa statueritis
non putent esse suae dignitatis recusare. Adiungit
gravem poenam municipiis, si quis eorum vincula
ruperit; horribilis custodias circumdat et dignas
scelere hominum perditorum; sancit ne quis eorum
poenam quos condemnat aut per senatum aut per
populum levare possit; eripit etiam spem quae sola
hominem in miseriis consolari solet. Bona praeterea

---

[1] qui populum Romanum *deleted by Bloch.*

[a] It is not clear whether this sentence continues Cicero's
account of Caesar's argument or, as I take it, is a sly counter-
thrust of his own.

[b] At Rome imprisonment was only a temporary measure
and imprisonment for life could plausibly be represented as
worse than death.

death penalty but advocates the full rigour of the law with other punishments. Each, as befits the responsibility of his position and the gravity of the offences, envisages the utmost severity. Silanus urges the view that men who have tried to deprive of life the whole Senate and people of Rome, who have tried to destroy the empire and erase the name of the Roman people, ought not to enjoy life and this air that we all breathe for a single minute, remembering as he does that this kind of punishment has often been invoked in our country against traitorous citizens. Caesar, however, feels that death has been ordained by the immortal gods not as a means of punishment but as a necessity of nature or a relief from all our toil and woe. That is why philosophers have never been reluctant to face it and brave men have often faced it even gladly.[a] Confinement, however, and for life at that, is an exemplary punishment indeed for a heinous crime.[b] He proposes that the prisoners be dispersed among the towns of Italy. This is a course that appears to involve injustice, if you intend to command them to do it, and difficulty, if you only ask them. Still, let this be your decree, if it is your will. I shall 8 undertake to put it into effect and shall—I hope— find men who think that their position cannot allow them to refuse to do what you have decided for the security of the whole nation. He also proposes a heavy penalty for a town which allows a prisoner to escape ; he surrounds the criminals with a grim guard that matches their crime ; he makes it illegal for anyone to mitigate the penalty of the men whom he is condemning whether by decree of the Senate or vote of the people ; he removes even hope, the sole consolation of men in their misfortune. He further

publicari iubet; vitam solam relinquit nefariis
hominibus : quam si eripuisset, multas uno dolore
animi atque corporis[1] et omnis scelerum poenas
ademisset. Itaque ut aliqua in vita formido improbis
esset proposita, apud inferos eius modi quaedam illi
antiqui supplicia impiis constituta esse voluerunt,
quod videlicet intellegebant his remotis non esse
mortem ipsam pertimescendam.

9   Nunc, patres conscripti, ego mea video quid intersit.
Si eritis secuti sententiam C. Caesaris, quoniam hanc
is in re publica viam quae popularis habetur secutus
est, fortasse minus erunt hoc auctore et cognitore
huiusce sententiae mihi populares impetus perti-
mescendi; sin illam alteram, nescio an amplius mihi
negoti contrahatur. Sed tamen meorum periculorum
rationes utilitas rei publicae vincat. Habemus enim a
Caesare, sicut ipsius dignitas et maiorum eius amplitudo postulabat, sententiam tamquam obsidem perpetuae in rem publicam voluntatis. Intellectum est
quid interesset inter levitatem contionatorum et
animum vere popularem saluti populi consulentem.[a]

10 Video de istis qui se popularis haberi volunt abesse
non neminem, ne de capite videlicet civium Romanorum sententiam ferat. Is et nudius tertius in custodiam civis Romanos dedit et supplicationem mihi
decrevit et indices hesterno die maximis praemiis[b]

---

[1] miserias *added after* corporis *by Clark*; aerumnas *Halm*.
Many other suggestions have been made.

---

[a] This rationalization of ancient beliefs for the Senate is in
sharp contrast to the list of portents retailed to the people.
Cf. in Catilinam 3. 18-22, pp. 120-124.

[b] In particular Quintus Caecilius Metellus Nepos and
Lucius Calpurnius Bestia. For Cicero's earlier suspicions of
such men, *cf. pro Murena* 83, p. 290.

orders their property to be confiscated; the only thing that he leaves these wicked men is their life; and if he had taken that from them, he would in one painful act have relieved them of much mental and bodily suffering and of all the penalties for their crimes. In the same way, to confront evil-doers with some fear in this life, those men of old would have had us believe that punishments of this kind were ordained for malefactors in the next world because, obviously, they realized that without this prospect, death by itself was nothing very frightening.[a]

Now, gentlemen, it is clear to me where my own 9 interest lies. If you adopt the motion of Gaius Caesar, since he has taken what we call the democratic side in politics, it may be that I shall have less need to fear the attacks of the people because it is he who is proposing and advocating this motion; but if you adopt the alternative, I fear that more trouble may be brought down upon my head. But let the interests of the Republic count for more than considerations of danger to myself. Now we have from Caesar, as his standing and the distinction of his ancestors required, a proposal—a pledge almost—of his lasting attachment to the Republic. We well know how deep lies the gulf between the fickleness of demagogues [b] and the true democratic spirit which has the interests of the people at heart. I see that a 10 certain person,[c] one of those who claim to be democrats, is absent; I presume because he wants to avoid voting on the life or death of Roman citizens. Yet this is the man who the day before yesterday gave Roman citizens into custody and voted me a thanksgiving, and yesterday gave the informants lavish

[c] Crassus.

adfecit. Iam hoc nemini dubium est qui reo custodiam, quaesitori gratulationem, indici praemium decrerit, quid de tota re et causa iudicarit. At vero C. Caesar intellegit legem Semproniam esse de civibus Romanis constitutam; qui autem rei publicae sit hostis eum civem esse nullo modo posse : denique ipsum latorem Semproniae legis iussu[1] populi poenas rei publicae dependisse. Idem ipsum Lentulum, largitorem et prodigum, non putat, cum de pernicie populi Romani, exitio huius urbis tam acerbe, tam crudeliter cogitarit, etiam appellari posse popularem. Itaque homo mitissimus atque lenissimus non dubitat P. Lentulum aeternis tenebris vinculisque mandare et sancit in posterum ne quis huius supplicio levando se iactare et in pernicie populi Romani posthac popularis esse possit. Adiungit etiam publicationem bonorum, ut omnis animi cruciatus et corporis etiam egestas ac mendicitas consequatur.

11 Quam ob rem, sive hoc statueritis, dederitis mihi comitem ad contionem populo carum atque iucundum, sive Silani sententiam sequi malueritis, facile me atque vos crudelitatis vituperatione populus Romanus

---

[1] iniussu *Bucherius.*

---

a The law of Gaius Gracchus, passed in 123, which reaffirmed the citizen's right of appeal to the people in capital cases and rendered magistrates who transgressed it liable to prosecution.

b Cicero is making the very assumption that Gracchus' law forbade—that a citizen could be treated as other than a citizen without being free to exercise the right of appeal to the people. Ch. Wirszubski, *Libertas as a Political Idea at Rome during the Late Republic and Early Principate* 60, n. 1, quotes Thomas Paine " He that would make his own liberty secure, must guard even his enemy from oppression ;

146

rewards. A man who has voted custody for the defendant, public thanks for the investigator and a reward for the informant, leaves no doubt about his judgement upon the whole case and its merits. But Gaius Caesar recognizes by his presence that the Sempronian law *a* was passed in the interests of Roman citizens; that an enemy of the Republic cannot in any respect be regarded as a citizen *b*; and he knows, too, that the author of the Sempronian law himself paid the supreme penalty to the Republic with the authority of the people. At the same time he thinks that Lentulus, prodigal and spendthrift though he is, does not deserve even the title " friend of the people " because he planned the massacre of the Roman people and the destruction of Rome with such vicious cruelty. In this way the kindest and gentlest of men does not hesitate to consign Publius Lentulus to darkness and chains for the rest of his life and makes it illegal for anyone to be able to advance his own cause in the future by lightening his punishment or subsequently to win popularity at the expense of the Roman people. And he then adds the confiscation of their property so that every mental and physical torment, even poverty and beggary, may be heaped upon them.

If, then, you vote for Caesar's proposal, you will 11 give me a companion at the public meeting *c* who is popular with the people and welcome to them; but if you prefer to adopt the motion of Silanus the Roman people will readily release both you and myself from

for if he violates this duty, he establishes a precedent that will each to himself."

c At which Cicero will inform the people of the Senate's decision. See Appendix A, p. 560.

liberabit,[1] atque obtinebo eam multo leniorem fuisse. Quamquam, patres conscripti, quae potest esse in tanti sceleris immanitate punienda crudelitas ? Ego enim de meo sensu iudico. Nam ita mihi salva re publica vobiscum perfrui liceat ut ego, quod in hac causa vehementior sum, non atrocitate animi moveor —quis enim est me mitior ?—sed singulari quadam humanitate et misericordia. Videor enim mihi videre hanc urbem, lucem orbis terrarum atque arcem omnium gentium, subito uno incendio concidentem. Cerno animo sepulta in patria miseros atque insepultos acervos civium, versatur mihi ante oculos aspectus Cethegi et furor in vestra caede bacchantis.

12 Cum vero mihi proposui regnantem Lentulum, sicut ipse se ex fatis sperasse confessus est, purpuratum esse huic Gabinium, cum exercitu venisse Catilinam, tum lamentationem matrum familias, tum fugam virginum atque puerorum ac vexationem virginum Vestalium perhorresco, et, quia mihi vehementer haec videntur misera atque miseranda, idcirco in eos qui ea perficere voluerunt me severum vehementemque praebebo. Etenim quaero, si quis pater familias, liberis suis a servo interfectis, uxore occisa, incensa domo, supplicium de servis non[2] quam acerbissimum sumpserit, utrum is clemens ac misericors an inhumanissimus et crudelissimus esse videatur ? Mihi vero importunus ac ferreus qui non dolore et cruciatu nocentis suum dolorem cruciatumque lenierit. Sic

---

[1] liberabit *Clark* ; *omitted by a.* exsolvitis *βh.* defendetis *lγ.* eripiam *i.* purgabo *Müller.*
[2] non *added by Lambinus.*

---

[a] The extent of the assonance in the Latin of this passage can scarcely be matched in English.

the accusation of cruelty and it will be easy for me to maintain that this motion was much more merciful. What cruelty, gentlemen, can there be in the punishment of a crime of such enormity ? My view springs from what I feel. My wish to enjoy with you the Republic that I have saved is as genuine as the truth that I am moved not by cruelty, although in this case with a greater severity than is natural for me—for who is gentler than I ?—but by an exceptional humanity and compassion. A vision comes to me of this city, the light of the whole world and the citadel of all nations, suddenly collapsing in a single sheet of flame. In my mind's eye I see the pitiful heaps of citizens lying unburied upon the grave of our fatherland ; there passes before my eyes the sight of Cethegus as he prances upon your corpses in his frenzied revels. Whenever I have pictured Lentulus 12 as potentate, as he admitted was his hope of what fate held for him, with Gabinius as his grand vizier, and Catiline there with his army, I shudder when I think of the mothers weeping, the boys and girls fleeing, the violation of Vestal Virgins [a] ; and it is because this vision arouses in me such strong feelings of pity and anguish that I am acting with severity and vigour against those who have wanted to perpetrate such horrors. Answer me this : if the head of a household were to find his children killed by a slave, his wife murdered and his house burned, and not to inflict the extreme penalty upon his slaves, would he be thought kindly and compassionate or the most inhuman and cruel of men ? To my mind a man who does not soften his own grief and suffering by inflicting similar distress upon the man responsible is unfeeling and has a heart of stone. So in the case of

nos in his hominibus qui nos, qui coniuges, qui liberos
nostros trucidare voluerunt, qui singulas unius
cuiusque nostrum domos et hoc universum rei publicae domicilium delere conati sunt, qui id egerunt ut
gentem Allobrogum in vestigiis huius urbis atque in
cinere deflagrati imperi conlocarent, si vehementis-
simi fuerimus, misericordes habebimur ; sin remis-
siores esse voluerimus, summae nobis crudelitatis in
13 patriae civiumque pernicie fama subeunda est. Nisi
vero cuipiam L. Caesar, vir fortissimus et amantissimus rei publicae, crudelior nudius tertius visus est,
cum sororis suae, feminae lectissimae, virum prae-
sentem et audientem vita privandum esse dixit, cum
avum suum iussu consulis interfectum filiumque eius
impuberem legatum a patre missum in carcere
necatum esse dixit. Quorum quod simile factum,
quod initum delendae rei publicae consilium ?
Largitionis voluntas tum in re publica versata est et

---

^a Lentulus was married to Julia, the sister of Lucius
Caesar, consul in 64. His grandfather was Marcus Fulvius
Flaccus, an adherent of Gaius Gracchus who was killed with
him. He had sent his young son to treat with Opimius but
the consul had him arrested and executed. The family tree is :

those men who planned to slaughter us, our wives and our children, who have attempted to destroy the homes of each one of us and this centre of the whole Republic, who have done this in order to establish the tribe of the Allobroges upon the ruins of Rome and the ashes of the Empire that they have burnt to the ground, the harshest punishment will be judged compassion ; but when our fatherland and our fellow-citizens have been destroyed, a desire to be more lenient will win us a reputation for extreme cruelty. At least, this is the case unless it be thought that the 13 courageous patriot, Lucius Caesar, was too cruel the day before yesterday when he said in the presence and hearing of the husband of that estimable lady, his sister,[a] that he deserved to be put to death, and recalled that his own grandfather had been killed at a consul's command and that his son, although he was only a youth and had been sent by his father to act as an intermediary, had been executed in prison. What deed had those men done, what plan to destroy the Republic had they made as terrible as the plots of these conspirators ? At that time plans to distribute

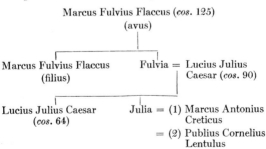

Marcus Fulvius Flaccus (*cos.* 125)
(avus)

Marcus Fulvius Flaccus (filius)

Fulvia = Lucius Julius Caesar (*cos.* 90)

Lucius Julius Caesar (*cos.* 64)

Julia = (1) Marcus Antonius Creticus
= (2) Publius Cornelius Lentulus

partium quaedam contentio. Atque illo tempore
huius avus Lentuli, vir clarissimus, armatus Gracchum
est persecutus. Ille etiam grave tum volnus accepit,
ne quid de summa rei publicae minueretur; hic ad
evertenda fundamenta rei publicae Gallos arces-
sit, servitia concitat, Catilinam vocat, attribuit nos
trucidandos Cethego et ceteros civis interficiendos
Gabinio, urbem inflammandam Cassio, totam Italiam
vastandam diripiendamque Catilinae. Vereamini minus[1] censeo ne in hoc scelere tam immani ac nefando
aliquid severius statuisse videamini: multo magis
est verendum ne remissione poenae crudeles in patriam quam ne severitate animadversionis nimis vehementes in acerbissimos hostis fuisse videamur.

14   Sed ea quae exaudio, patres conscripti, dissimulare
non possum. Iaciuntur enim voces quae perveniunt ad
auris meas eorum qui vereri videntur ut habeam satis
praesidi ad ea quae vos statueritis hodierno die trans-
igenda. Omnia et provisa et parata et constituta
sunt, patres conscripti, cum mea summa cura atque
diligentia tum multo etiam maiore populi Romani ad
summum imperium retinendum et ad communis
fortunas conservandas voluntate. Omnes adsunt
omnium ordinum homines, omnium generum,[2] omnium denique aetatum; plenum est forum, plena
templa circum forum, pleni omnes aditus huius templi
ac loci. Causa est enim post urbem conditam haec
inventa sola in qua omnes sentirent unum atque

---

[1] minus *added by Clark. The* mss. *have* nimis *before*
aliquid.
[2] omnium generum *added by Putsche.*

---

[a] Cicero plays down Gracchus' measures in order to
strengthen his argument.

largesse were being canvassed in the State and there was a certain amount of party strife.[a] On that occasion the distinguished grandfather of this Lentulus took vengeance on Gracchus with armed force. He even received a severe wound in his efforts to ensure that the majesty of the Republic should be in no way impaired. His grandson, however, summons Gauls to overthrow the foundations of the Republic, urges the slaves to rise, sends for Catiline, assigns us to Cethegus to be slaughtered, the other citizens to Gabinius to be killed, the city to Cassius to be burnt, the whole of Italy to Catiline to be sacked and laid waste. You are less apprehensive, I suppose, that your measures against a crime as monstrous and unspeakable as this may show an excessive severity. Much more should we fear that by reducing our punishment we may appear cruel towards our fatherland than that by the severity of our retribution we may seem too harsh towards her most bitter enemies.

But, gentlemen, I cannot pretend to be deaf to 14 what comes to my ears. Comments are being made, which I can plainly hear, by those who apparently fear that my forces are inadequate to carry out the decisions that you have taken today. Everything has been provided for, gentlemen, everything prepared and arranged by me with all my care and pains reinforced by the even stronger desire of the Roman people to defend the sovereignty of their power and preserve their common possessions. Everyone is here —men of every order, every class and every age ; the Forum is crowded, the temples around the Forum are crowded, all the approaches and grounds of this temple are crowded. This is the only known case since the foundation of Rome on which there has been

idem praeter eos qui, cum sibi viderent esse pereun-
dum, cum omnibus potius quam soli perire voluerunt.
15 Hosce ego homines excipio et secerno libenter, neque
in improborum civium sed in acerbissimorum hostium
numero habendos puto. Ceteri vero, di immortales !
qua frequentia, quo studio, qua virtute ad communem salutem dignitatemque consentiunt ! Quid
ego hic equites Romanos commemorem ? qui vobis
ita summam ordinis consilique concedunt ut vobiscum
de amore rei publicae certent ; quos ex multorum
annorum dissensione huius ordinis ad societatem
concordiamque revocatos hodiernus dies vobiscum
atque haec causa coniungit. Quam si coniunctionem
in consulatu confirmatam meo perpetuam in re publica
tenuerimus, confirmo vobis nullum posthac malum
civile ac domesticum ad ullam rei publicae partem
esse venturum. Pari studio defendendae rei publicae
convenisse video tribunos aerarios, fortissimos viros ;
scribas item universos, quos cum casu hic dies ad
aerarium frequentasset, video ab exspectatione sortis
16 ad salutem communem esse conversos. Omnis in-
genuorum adest multitudo, etiam tenuissimorum.
Quis est enim cui non haec templa, aspectus urbis,
possessio libertatis, lux denique haec ipsa et com-

---

a *e.g.* the struggle for control of the juries of the criminal
courts. See pp. 417-419.

b Formerly officers of the tribes, they now formed a new
class in the State with a property rating slightly below that
of the knights.

c The *scribae*, the clerical grade of the Civil Service, were
professional clerks who made the service their life's career.
They were usually free-born, but if freedmen, were often
men of a certain standing either through the eminence of
their patron or on their own merits. They formed an *ordo*

agreement that is unanimous apart from those who, seeing that perish they must, would rather die in a general massacre than alone. These men I am only 15 too glad to except and set apart, for in my view they are to be classed as mortal public enemies, not just wicked citizens. But the rest—heavens above !— look at the crowds, the enthusiasm, the valour with which they unite for the salvation and honour of us all ! Why should I mention the Roman knights at this point ? They may yield to you the first place in rank and councils of state but they rival you in patriotism. After many years' strife *a* this day and this cause renews their harmonious alliance with your order and reunites them with you. If we maintain for ever in the Republic this union that we have cemented in my consulship, I assure you that hereafter no civil and domestic strife will touch any part of the State. I see that the same zeal to defend the Republic has gathered here the gallant tribunes of the treasury.*b* I see too that the entire body of clerks,*c* which happens to be here at the treasury today, has been diverted from waiting for the drawing of their lots to concern for our common safety. The whole mass of 16 freeborn citizens is here, even the poorest. There is not a single one of us for whom these temples, the sight of the city, the possession of liberty, the very

in their own right and claimed to be of equestrian standing. They were a body to be reckoned with ; *cf. pro Murena* 42, p. 240. See A. H. M. Jones, *Studies in Roman Government and Law* 154 and Th. Mommsen, *Römisches Staatsrecht* 1. 346 f.

They were present because on the 5th of December the quaestors for the following year entered office and the *scribae* met at the treasury in view of the Temple of Concord to draw lots for their posts for the following year.

mune patriae solum cum sit carum tum vero dulce
atque iucundum ? Operae pretium est, patres conscripti, libertinorum hominum studia cognoscere qui,
sua virtute fortunam huius civitatis consecuti, vere
hanc suam patriam esse iudicant quam quidam hic
nati, et summo nati loco, non patriam suam sed
urbem hostium esse iudicaverunt. Sed quid ego
hosce ordines atque homines commemoro quos
privatae fortunae, quos communis res publica, quos
denique libertas ea quae dulcissima est ad salutem
patriae defendendam excitavit ? Servus est nemo,
qui modo tolerabili condicione sit servitutis, qui non
audaciam civium perhorrescat, qui non haec stare
cupiat, qui non quantum audet et quantum potest
17 conferat ad salutem voluntatis. Qua re si quem
vestrum forte commovet hoc quod auditum est,
lenonem quendam Lentuli concursare circum tabernas, pretio sperare sollicitari posse animos egentium
atque imperitorum, est id quidem coeptum atque
temptatum, sed nulli sunt inventi tam aut fortuna
miseri aut voluntate perditi qui non illum ipsum sellae
atque operis et quaestus cotidiani locum, qui non
cubile ac lectulum suum, qui denique non cursum
hunc otiosum vitae suae salvum esse velint. Multo
vero maxima pars eorum qui in tabernis sunt, immo
vero—id enim potius est dicendum—genus hoc universum amantissimum est oti. Etenim omne instru-
mentum, omnis opera atque quaestus frequentia

---

[a] In the last century of the Republic the *libertini* became a
distinguishable force in politics, an *ordo* in its own right
alongside the other orders. Their order's new prominence in
political life and the rise of individual freedmen indicates
that there were in their number men of considerable political
awareness, competence and drive.

[b] The treatment of slaves ranged from the kindness shown

light of day and the soil of the fatherland we all share are not only precious but a joy and a delight. It is worth our while, gentlemen, to recognize the enthusiasm of the freedmen,[a] men who have won the advantages of our citizenship on their own merit and genuinely feel that this is their own land, while others born here, members of the aristocracy at that, have judged it to be not their homeland but a city of the enemy. Why do I mention these classes and individuals who have been roused to defend the safety of their fatherland by their private fortunes, their community of political interest and by that sweetest of all possessions—liberty? There is no slave—none at least whose condition of slavery is tolerable [b]—who does not shudder at the rash folly of such citizens, who does not wish Rome to remain standing, who does not work with all his heart for our salvation so far as he dares or is able. Some of you, 17 then, may perhaps be alarmed by the rumour that an agent of Lentulus is making the rounds of the shops hoping to buy the support of the poor and the naïve. It is true, certainly, that he began an attempt to do this, but no one has been found so poverty-stricken or disaffected as not to wish to preserve intact his workshop where he daily pursues his trade and wins his livelihood, his couch and his bed, in short, the peaceful tenour of his life.[c] By far the greater part, indeed the whole class—for surely that is the truth—of those who work in shops are the strongest supporters of peace. Their whole means of trade, their labour and their livelihood are supported by the number of their

to educated friends of the family to appalling cruelty in the countryside and mines.

[c] See p. 12.

civium sustentatur, alitur otio ; quorum si quaestus occlusis tabernis minui solet, quid tandem incensis futurum fuit ?

18 Quae cum ita sint, patres conscripti, vobis populi Romani praesidia non desunt : vos ne populo Romano desse videamini providete. Habetis consulem ex plurimis periculis et insidiis atque ex media morte non ad vitam suam sed ad salutem vestram reservatum. Omnes ordines ad conservandam rem publicam mente, voluntate, voce consentiunt. Obsessa facibus et telis impiae coniurationis vobis supplex manus tendit patria communis, vobis se, vobis vitam omnium civium, vobis arcem et Capitolium, vobis aras Penatium, vobis illum ignem Vestae sempiternum, vobis omnium deorum templa atque delubra, vobis muros atque urbis tecta commendat. Praeterea de vestra vita, de coniugum vestrarum atque liberorum anima, de fortunis omnium, de sedibus, de focis 19 vestris hodierno die vobis iudicandum est. Habetis ducem memorem vestri, oblitum sui, quae non semper facultas datur ; habetis omnis ordines, omnis homines, universum populum Romanum, id quod in civili causa hodierno die primum videmus, unum atque idem sentientem. Cogitate quantis laboribus fundatum imperium, quanta virtute stabilitam libertatem, quanta deorum benignitate auctas exaggeratasque fortunas una nox paene delerit. Id ne umquam posthac non modo non confici sed ne cogitari quidem possit a civibus hodierno die providendum est.

ᵃ For the view that this section is an earlier version of sections 9-14 which are an elaborated account written subsequently for publication in 60, see H. Fuchs, " Eine Doppel-

customers and promoted by peace. If their profits
decline when their shops are closed, what on earth
would have happened if they had been burnt ?

Such being the case, gentlemen, the protection of 18
the Roman people does not fail you ; see to it then
that you do not fail the Roman people.[a] You have a
consul kept from a multitude of dangers and plots,
from the very jaws of death, not just to cling to life
but to save you. All classes are united in purpose,
will and voice to preserve the Republic. Beset by
the brands and weapons of this vile conspiracy, the
fatherland we all share extends to you the hands of
a suppliant. To you she commends herself, the lives
of all her citizens, the citadel and the Capitol, the
altars of her household gods, the never dying fire of
Vesta over there, the temples and shrines of all her
gods, the walls and buildings of the city. Your lives,
too, and the lives of your wives and children, the
fortunes of you all, your houses and your hearths,
depend upon the decision you have to make this day.
You have as your leader a man who is heedless of 19
himself and thinks only of you, an advantage that
you do not always enjoy ; you have the support of all
classes, of all men, of the whole Roman people—something that we have never seen before today in a domestic issue—in complete agreement. Think how
one night [b] nearly destroyed all the toil that founded
our empire, all the valour that established our freedom, all the bounty of the gods that has built up our
fortunes to their present size. You must see to it
this day that never again are citizens able even to
think of this, much less to achieve it. I have spoken

fassung in Ciceros Catilinarischen Reden," *Hermes* 87 (1959),
463-469.   [b] The night of 2nd/3rd of December.

Atque haec, non ut vos qui mihi studio paene prae-
curritis excitarem, locutus sum, sed ut mea vox quae
debet esse in re publica princeps officio functa consulari videretur.

20 Nunc ante quam ad sententiam redeo, de me
pauca dicam. Ego, quanta manus est coniuratorum,
quam videtis esse permagnam, tantam me inimicorum
multitudinem suscepisse video ; sed eam turpem
iudico et infirmam et abiectam. Quod si aliquando
alicuius furore et scelere concitata manus ista plus
valuerit quam vestra ac rei publicae dignitas, me
tamen meorum factorum atque consiliorum numquam, patres conscripti, paenitebit. Etenim mors,
quam illi fortasse minitantur, omnibus est parata :
vitae tantam laudem quanta vos me vestris decretis
honestastis nemo est adsecutus ; ceteris enim semper
bene gesta, mihi uni conservata re publica gratulatio-
21 nem decrevistis. Sit Scipio clarus ille cuius consilio
atque virtute Hannibal in Africam redire atque Italia decedere coactus est, ornetur alter eximia laude
Africanus qui duas urbis huic imperio infestissimas
Karthaginem Numantiamque delevit, habeatur vir
egregius Paulus ille cuius currum rex potentissi-
mus quondam et nobilissimus Perses honestavit, sit
aeterna gloria Marius qui bis Italiam obsidione et
metu servitutis liberavit, anteponatur omnibus Pompeius cuius res gestae atque virtutes isdem quibus solis cursus regionibus ac terminis continentur :

---

a Publius Cornelius Scipio Africanus, who invaded Africa
while Hannibal was in Italy and forced him to return to
Africa to protect Carthage. He defeated him at the Battle of
Zama in 202.

b Publius Cornelius Scipio Aemilianus Africanus Numantinus destroyed Carthage in 146 and Numantia in 133.

in this way, not to stir you to action—for your energy usually surpasses mine—but because it is my responsibility to speak first upon affairs of state and I therefore want you to hear me fulfil my obligations as a consul.

At this point, before I start again to ask you for 20 your views, I shall say a few words about myself. I recognize that I have made every member of the conspiracy my enemy and you see how numerous they are ; but I regard them as vile, feeble and craven. But if that band is ever again roused by some leader's criminal frenzy and vanquishes your authority and the authority of the Republic, I shall even so, gentlemen, never regret what I have said and done. They may threaten me with death, but that is in store for us all, and no man has ever been accorded such praise as you have bestowed upon me in your decrees. Others have received public thanksgivings from you for serving the Republic well, none but I for preserving it. I acknowledge the renown of that Scipio whose 21 skill and valour compelled Hannibal to quit Italy and return to Africa *a* ; the signal fame of that other Africanus who destroyed the cities of Carthage and Numantia, those twin foes of our empire *b* ; the distinction of that Paulus whose triumph was adorned by Perses, once the most powerful and noble of kings *c* ; the undying glory of Marius who twice freed Italy from occupation and the fear of enslavement *d* ; and greater than all these, Pompeius whose exploits and deeds of valour span the world from the rising to the

---

c Lucius Aemilius Paulus defeated and captured Perses, king of Macedonia, at the Battle of Pydna in 168.
d By defeating the Teutones at Aquae Sextiae in 102 and the Cimbri near Vercellae in 101.

erit profecto inter horum laudes aliquid loci nostrae
gloriae, nisi forte maius est patefacere nobis provincias quo exire possimus quam curare ut etiam illi
22 qui absunt habeant quo victores revertantur. Quamquam est uno loco condicio melior externae victoriae
quam domesticae, quod hostes alienigenae aut
oppressi serviunt aut recepti beneficio se obligatos
putant, qui autem ex numero civium dementia aliqua
depravati hostes patriae semel esse coeperunt, eos,
cum a pernicie rei publicae reppuleris, nec vi coercere
nec beneficio placare possis. Qua re mihi cum perditis
civibus aeternum bellum susceptum esse video. Id
ego vestro bonorumque omnium auxilio memoriaque
tantorum periculorum, quae non modo in hoc populo
qui servatus est sed in omnium gentium sermonibus
ac mentibus semper haerebit, a me atque a meis facile
propulsari posse confido. Neque ulla profecto tanta
vis reperietur quae coniunctionem vestram equi-
tumque Romanorum et tantam conspirationem bonorum omnium confringere et labefactare possit.
23 Quae cum ita sint, pro imperio, pro exercitu, pro
provincia quam neglexi, pro triumpho ceterisque
laudis insignibus quae sunt a me propter urbis ves-
traeque salutis custodiam repudiata, pro clientelis
hospitiisque provincialibus quae tamen urbanis opibus

---

a See p. 130, n. *a.*   *b* See p. xxix.
c See p. xxxvii, n. *f.*

setting sun.[a] There will certainly be some place for my fame amid the praise of these men, unless of course it is a greater achievement to open up provinces to which we may go as governors than to ensure that those who have gone out to them have a homeland to which they may return from their victories. Yet in one respect a victory won abroad is **22** preferable to a victory gained in a civil war because foreign enemies are either conquered and become subjects or are accepted as allies and feel themselves bound by ties of gratitude; but when some of your own citizens have been unhinged by an attack of madness and have once become traitors to their own country, and you have repulsed their attempt to destroy the State, you can never coerce them by force or win them over by kindness. I realize, therefore, that there lies before me an unending war against evil citizens. It is my confident belief that your support and the support of all loyal citizens, the recollection of the seriousness of these dangers, a recollection that will always remain fixed not only among our own people because of its salvation, but upon the lips and in the minds of every nation, can easily repel these perils from me and my supporters. Nor, surely, will any force be found strong enough to break or dissolve the bond between yourselves and the Roman knights [b] and the complete harmony among all loyal citizens.

Accordingly, in place of the supreme command, of **23** the army, of the province to which I have shown myself indifferent,[c] in place of the triumph and the other marks of honour which I have rejected in order to have the safety of Rome and of yourselves in my care, in place of the ties formed with clients and hosts

non minore labore tueor quam comparo, pro his igitur omnibus rebus, pro meis in vos singularibus studiis
proque hac quam perspicitis ad conservandam rem
publicam diligentia nihil a vobis nisi huius temporis
totiusque mei consulatus memoriam postulo : quae
dum erit in vestris fixa mentibus, tutissimo me muro
saeptum esse arbitrabor. Quod si meam spem vis
improborum fefellerit atque superaverit, commendo
vobis parvum meum filium, cui profecto satis erit
praesidi non solum ad salutem verum etiam ad dignitatem, si eius qui haec omnia suo solius periculo
24 conservarit illum filium esse memineritis. Quapropter
de summa salute vestra populique Romani, de vestris
coniugibus ac liberis, de aris ac focis, de fanis atque
templis, de totius urbis tectis ac sedibus, de imperio
ac libertate, de salute Italiae, de universa re publica
decernite diligenter, ut instituistis, ac fortiter. Habetis eum consulem qui et parere vestris decretis non
dubitet et ea quae statueritis, quoad vivet, defendere
et per se ipsum praestare possit.

in a province—although I still strive by means of my influence in Rome to acquire them as energetically as I maintain them—in place of all these lost opportunities, then, and in return for my exceptional devotion to your cause and for the painstaking efforts with which, as you see, I have preserved the Republic, I ask nothing of you except that you remember this occasion and the whole of my consulship. So long as they remain fixed in your minds, I shall feel that I am protected by an impregnable wall. But if the power of these traitors dashes my hopes and wins the day, I entrust to you my little son and he will surely receive protection enough to ensure not only his safety but also the career that is his due, if only you remember that he is the son of the man who imperilled no life but his own to save the entire country. With the care, 24 therefore, and the courage that you have displayed from the beginning, take your decision upon the salvation of yourselves and of the Roman people, upon your wives and children, your altars and hearths, your shrines and temples, the buildings and homes of the entire city, your dominion and your freedom, the safety of Italy and upon the whole Republic. You have a consul who will not shrink from obeying your decrees and, while he lives, from defending your decisions and answering for them in person.

THE SPEECH IN DEFENCE OF
LUCIUS LICINIUS MURENA

INTRODUCTION

Lucius Licinius Murena was a member of a plebeian family of the *gens Licinia* which came originally from Lanuvium, a *municipium* situated about sixteen miles from Rome.[a] Most of our knowledge about him is gained from this speech. He was the first member of his family or of his town to attain the consulship, although both his grandfather and his great-grandfather had risen to the praetorship.[b] The most famous member of the family was his father who, after his praetorship,[c] was left by Sulla in command in Asia, probably as propraetor. In the two following years he invaded Pontic territory in violation of Sulla's agreement with Mithridates, was repulsed in 82 with serious losses and was subsequently ordered by Sulla to cease hostilities. These events are grossly misrepresented by Cicero in this speech.[d]

In this campaign his son served under him and took part in the ill-deserved triumph that he eventually celebrated.[e] At some uncertain date before 74

---

[a] 15 and 90, pp. 202 and 298. For Murena, see F. Münzer in Pauly-Wissowa, *Realencyclopädie* XIII. 1 (1926), L. Licinius Murena (123) 446-449.

[b] 15, p. 202. Many families, old and new, at all periods of the Republic settled in praetorian status.

[c] In 84.

[d] 15 and 32, pp. 202 and 226.

[e] 15, p. 202.

Cicero's client may have been a personal adjutant [a] and was in that year elected quaestor together with Servius Sulpicius Rufus,[b] who was later to be his fellow-candidate for the consulship of 62 and one of the prosecutors in this trial.

In 73 he served as a subordinate commander under Lucius Licinius Lucullus in Asia, Bithynia and Pontus, and in the following year was placed in charge of the siege of Amisus.[c] Some time before 66, possibly in 70, ten commissioners were appointed and sent to advise Lucullus on the organization of the territory taken from Mithridates. A Lucius Licinius Murena is one of the two members of the commission named by our sources, but it is not clear whether this man is to be identified with the defendant or with his father. No reference to this special position is made in this speech when describing the son's service in Pontus and Armenia [d] and, although the father had died before 63, the exact date is not known.[e] It is therefore possible that either father or son could have been this commissioner.

He never held the aedileship,[f] but in 65 was elected praetor [g] and in the following two years was proconsul in command of Transalpine Gaul.[h] In 63

[a] On the assumption that his name is to be supplied in the *lacuna* at the beginning of 73, p. 276.

[b] 18, p. 206. For the date, see T. R. S. Broughton, *The Magistrates of the Roman Republic* 2. 109, n. 5.

[c] 20 and 89, pp. 208 and 296.

[d] 20, p. 208. See also T. R. S. Broughton, *op. cit.* 2. 131, n. 6.   [e] 88 and 90, pp. 296 and 298.

[f] 37, p. 234.   [g] 35-41 and 53, pp. 232-238 and 254.

[h] 42, 68 and 89, pp. 240, 272 and 296. For the province, see E. Badian, " Notes on *Provincia Gallia* in the Late Republic," *Mélanges Piganiol*, Paris, 1966, 913-916. W. Allen, Jr., " The Acting Governor of Cisalpine Gaul in 63 B.C.,"

he left his brother Gaius as temporary governor of his province and returned home for the election campaign.[a]

There were three other candidates for the consulship : Servius Sulpicius Rufus, Decimus Iunius Silanus and Lucius Sergius Catilina. The consular elections, due to be held in July, were postponed on Cicero's initiative to enable an emergency debate to be held in the Senate to discuss Catiline's menacing pre-election speech. The Senate decided to take no action and the elections were held later the same month.[b] Having failed in his attempt to get Catiline's candidacy disallowed, Cicero assisted Murena to defeat Catiline by granting Lucullus his triumph. Cicero's action secured the presence of Lucullus' army at the elections, where it duly voted for its general's man.[c] Murena and Silanus were elected. This blow to Catiline's ambitions set in motion his plans for an insurrection which, it now seemed to him, was the only way to power left open.

The offence with which Murena was charged— *ambitus* or electoral malpractice [d]—had been the subject of intervention by the State for three centuries, and by 181 it required the enactment of still

---

Classical Philology 48 (1953), 176, had argued that he was governor of both Cisalpine and Transalpine Gaul.

[a] 89, p. 296.

[b] 51, p. 252. For the date of the elections, see T. Rice Holmes, *The Roman Republic* 1. 458-461 and D. Stockton, *Cicero* 336-337.

[c] 37-38 and 69, pp. 234-236 and 272. For the close ties between Murena and Lucullus, see *ad Atticum* 13. 6. 4.

[d] For *ambitus* see Th. Mommsen, *Römisches Strafrecht* 865 f. and L. R. Taylor, *Party Politics in the Age of Caesar* 67 f.

more legislation to deal with it. In that year the consuls carried a law providing disqualification from office for ten years for any person found guilty of influencing an election through bribery or other illegal means.[a] This measure proved inadequate and in 159 another consular law increased the penalty to death but with no greater success than its predecessor.[b] A *quaestio de ambitu* or standing court to deal with cases of bribery appears to have been set up shortly before 116, when three *ambitus* trials took place, and in all likelihood the juries who served in this court were drawn from the ranks of the knights.[c] Sulla appears to have sponsored a law on the subject as part of his judicial reforms but nothing is known about it except that it prescribed a penalty of ten years' prohibition from candidature for magistracies.[d]

Another of Sulla's reforms had been to place the juries of the *ambitus* court together with those of the other permanent courts in the hands of the Senate. But the *lex Aurelia iudiciaria*, a measure of Lucius Aurelius Cotta, praetor in 70, reconstituted the juries, and they were now drawn in equal numbers from senators, knights and *tribuni aerarii*.[e] The last named were previously officers of the tribes and now formed a new class in the State with a property rating slightly below that of the knights. The panel was nine hundred strong and composed of equal numbers of each class. Under the terms of the *lex Cassia tabellaria* of Lucius Cassius Longinus Ravilla, a tribune of 137, they gave their verdict by ballot.

[a] Livy 40. 19. 11.　　　　[b] Livy, *Periocha* 47.
[c] E. S. Gruen, *Roman Politics and the Criminal Courts 149–78 B.C.* 124–125.
[d] The scholiast on *pro Sulla* 17 (p. 78, *ed.* Stangl).
[e] Asconius 67 C.

PRO MURENA

The final decades of the Roman Republic from 70 onwards saw an intensification of electoral malpractices accompanying the bitter rivalry for office. A succession of laws increasing the penalties for this crime was passed during this period but all efforts to eradicate the blight proved ineffectual. By 61 even Cato, it was said, had succumbed.

The laws of the second century had succeeded in eliminating the more direct forms of bribery but more devious ways of distributing largesse had been devised. Electoral malpractice at Rome was facilitated by a traditional code of behaviour which lent itself to abuse, and the difficulty of distinguishing between behaviour condoned by custom and criminal practice rendered virtually ineffective all legislation attempting to draw such a distinction.

Much ingenuity was employed in the search for legal bases for the distribution of benefits to citizens in such a way as to influence their votes. Such bases were found within the framework of the client system. The essence of this system was that the patron was expected to undertake certain responsibilities for his clients, and they to provide him with support in his career in public life. A passage in this speech [a] describes the relationship in some detail and enables us to appreciate how easily a situation in which political support was given in return for services rendered could degenerate into an indiscriminate purchase of votes. A benefit conferred in the context of a personal relationship is quite different from an indiscriminate distribution, and the laws of this period attempt to define this distinction. Cicero is concerned here both to defend the traditional

[a] 70-73, pp. 274-278.

practice and to prove that Murena has not gone beyond it.[a]

In 67 the lex (Acilia) Calpurnia of the consul Gaius Calpurnius Piso, warmly supported by his colleague Manius Acilius Glabrio, imposed a heavy fine, permanent disqualification from holding office or sitting in the Senate and loss of the ius imaginum, the right to display the busts of one's distinguished ancestors.[b] This law attempted to make the agents who distributed the bribes share the guilt of the candidates for whom they were acting.[c] It was subsequently supplemented by a measure carried by an otherwise unknown Fabius to limit the number of those who attended upon the candidates.[d] In 63 Cicero and his colleague, Antonius, carried a law against bribery which replaced Sulpicius' more comprehensive demands.[e] In it the penalty on the agents was increased, the penalty on the convicted

[a] E. S. Staveley, Greek and Roman Voting and Elections 202 f. For clients, see L. R. Taylor, Party Politics in the Age of Caesar 41 f.

[b] 46, p. 244; pro Sulla 88, p. 402. Contemporary opinion thought this law an extremely harsh measure.

[c] Asconius 74-76 C.

[d] This law may have been de vi rather than de ambitu since it was concerned not with the hiring of sectatores but with their number. Its object was to prevent the gathering of large crowds of sectatores and its penalty must have been imposed upon the sectatores, not the candidates. The fact that Murena had a large number could not form the basis of a crimen against him (see pro Murena 73, p. 276). T. R. S. Broughton, op. cit. 2. 164, n. 4, dates it to 64, following D. Niccolini, I fasti dei tribuni della plebe 266, but it is not possible with any degree of safety to go further than " the recent past." Cf. T. E. Kinsey, " Cicero, pro Murena 71," Revue belge de Philologie et d'Histoire 43 (1965), 57-59.

[e] 47, p. 246.

candidate was ten years' exile, and there was provision that candidates should not give gladiatorial shows during the two years preceding their candidacy except in the execution of the provisions of a will and that defendants who absented themselves from a trial, even on grounds of illness, should be fined.[a] At some time during the same year, after the campaigns of the consular candidates had got under way, Cicero passed through the Senate a decree enacting that the law of 67 should be interpreted as applying to the hiring of the candidate's retinue, the granting of free seats at gladiatorial shows to tribes other than the candidate's own and the entertainment of those with whom he had no personal connexion.[b] The provisions of this decree were presumably included in the *lex Tullia*. The problem was not abated, however, and further legislation had to be passed throughout the remainder of the republican period.

Before the elections had taken place Marcus Porcius Cato Uticensis (95–46), shocked by the extent of the bribery employed in the campaign, had announced in the Senate that he would prosecute any

---

[a] A. H. J. Greenidge, *The Legal Procedure of Cicero's Time* 474, n. 3, doubts whether this last provision did in fact find its way into the *lex Tullia*.

[b] 67, p. 270. This decree was demanded by one or more of the honest candidates in their indignation at the way in which a dishonest rival or rivals were violating the provisions of the *lex Calpurnia*. Such a demand would clearly not be made by a guilty candidate, but Murena joined in the demand to avoid admitting guilt by implication and because the practical effects of the decree were nil—hence *pro Murena* 68 : " omnibus postulantibus candidatis." The Senate was merely humouring some of the candidates. *Cf.* T. E. Kinsey, "A *senatus consultum* in the *pro Murena*," *Mnemosyne* 19 (1966), 272-273.

candidate guilty of corruption.[a] The great-grandson of the famous Cato Censorius, he appears to have been unpleasant in character, but his adherence to a mixture of Stoic and traditional Roman principles was genuine. As a Stoic he was more concerned with wrong-doing itself than with the political consequences that would flow from his efforts to remove or punish it. Cicero, while freely acknowledging his high ideals and good intentions, held little brief for him as a politician, but expresses himself less forcefully in this speech [b] than he did three years later in a letter to his friend Atticus.[c]

Cato acted in his prosecution of Murena without regard either for personalities or for the welfare of the State. His principles allowed him to exclude his brother-in-law, the other successful candidate, from his promise to prosecute offending candidates but in his speech against Murena he belittled the Mithridatic War [d] for which Lucullus, another brother-in-law, had just celebrated his belated triumph. This disparagement of the achievements of Roman arms under his leadership was a gratuitous insult to a powerful optimate who was personally present in court to support his former subordinate.[e] Furthermore, Cato could be pilloried for showing a reckless indifference to the safety of the State when, after Catiline had joined his forces under arms in Etruria and a state of emergency had been declared, he was ready to launch a prosecution upon a consul-designate. An instant politician, Cato lacked the foresight—Cicero does not impugn his motives—to appreciate

[a] 62, p. 264.   [b] 78, p. 284.
[c] ad Atticum 2. 1. 8.
[d] 31, p. 224.   [e] 20, p. 210.

176

the perilous situation into which he could thrust the
State if his prosecution was successful.[a]

Cato was joined in his prosecution by Servius
Sulpicius Rufus, who had also decided to prosecute his
successful rival, before the elections had taken
place.[b] That he was concerned about electoral corruption is clear from this speech,[c] and this concern
forms a bond between him and Cato. There were
other motives, however, which led him to join the
attack upon Murena. In him he saw an energetic
consul who would continue Cicero's own line of
action, and the popular legislation that he had proposed earlier in the year [d] reveals him as a man out
of sympathy with Cicero's political objectives. Indeed, Catiline had looked in his direction.[e] Of
paramount importance, however, was his failure in
the polls, a disaster that could only be remedied by
the prosecution and unseating of a successful candidate. One of the perils in public life was the endless
succession of prosecutions brought by unsuccessful
candidates and their friends in the course of the
struggle for office. The elimination of rivals by
means of lawsuits was constantly being attempted.
Before the elections were held extortion in a province
was a common charge, and between election and

[a] 78, p. 284.   [b] 46, p. 244.
[c] 46-47, pp. 244-248.   [d] 47, p. 246.
[e] 49, p. 250. For Sulpicius' position, see C. Nicolet,
" Confusio suffragiorum," Mélanges d'Archéologie et
d'Histoire 71 (1959), 160, n. 1 and " Le Sénat et les amendements aux lois à la fin de la République," Revue historique
de Droit français et étranger 36 (1958), 267-269. Nicolet sees
(267, n. 42) Sulpicius' proposals as a popular attempt to
counteract the alliance between the novus homo and the
moderate Optimates.

177

entry into office a man was still liable to prosecution, usually for *ambitus*.[a]

Sulpicius led for the prosecution. He was the son of a knight and an almost exact contemporary of Cicero, with whom he had studied rhetoric at Rhodes before turning to the study of the law in which he won a justly high reputation. He was known and well respected for his upright character and his ability both as an orator and as a jurisconsult. He was elected quaestor in 74 and was allotted Ostia as his province.[b] He then became *praetor de peculatu*—in charge of the embezzlement court—in 65[c] and lived an active political life until his death in 43 on the embassy to Antony. He eventually became consul in 51 and remained throughout his life a close friend of Cicero, who attributed his success as an orator to his extreme clarity of thought and exposition.[d]

Sulpicius' case appears to have been that the electoral victory of a " new man " like Murena over a noble of ancient lineage provided *prima facie* evidence of corrupt practices.[e] Cicero devotes a large part of his speech[f] to a detailed refutation of

[a] L. R. Taylor, *Party Politics in the Age of Caesar* 7 and 31 f. [b] 18, p. 206.

[c] 35 and 42, pp. 232 and 240.

[d] Cicero's *Ninth Philippic* is a eulogy of him.

[e] The term *novus homo*—" the new man "—was ambiguous in the usage of the late Republic. It could be applied to the first member of a family to enter the Senate, but in particular it could refer to a consul or consular candidate whose ancestors had been senators of praetorian rank but had not attained the consulship. From the time of the Gracchi onwards the word *nobilis* is used of a man whose family has already supplied the State with a consul. M. Gelzer, *The Roman Nobility* 27 f. [f] 15-53, pp. 202-254.

this presumption which he takes in deadly earnest. He goes to great pains to show that Murena is even better endowed than Sulpicius with all the personal qualifications required for success in the consular elections and therefore, it could be argued, had no need of recourse to bribery.[a]

Of the other two members of the prosecution nothing is known except the little that can be gleaned from this speech. The other Servius Sulpicius Rufus was *adulescens* [b] and his father a friend of Murena [c]; about Gaius Postumus there is virtually nothing.[d] If Cicero's statement about them, that they prosecuted Murena not out of personal enmity but because they were eager for a prosecution, is true, they either took a sterner view of bribery than did Cicero or were young men hoping to make a name for themselves by taking part in a successful prosecution.[e]

Appearing with Cicero for the defence were Quintus Hortensius Hortalus (114–50) and Marcus Licinius Crassus (*c.* 112–53). For many years Cicero's great rival in the courts, Hortensius had until the trial of Verres in 70 been the leader of the Roman Bar.[f]

---

[a] T. P. Wiseman, *New Men in the Roman Senate 139 b.c.– 14 a.d.* 1, n. 2, calls this " a mere lawyer's ploy." Cicero in fact took this justification of a *novus homo* seriously and expected his audience to do so. E. Badian, *Roman Imperialism in the Late Republic* 61.

[b] 57, p. 258.   [c] 56, p. 256.

[d] 54, 56, 57 and 69, pp. 254, 256, 258 and 272. All attempts at identification have failed through lack of evidence.

[e] In Cicero's day it was normally young men in search of an oratorical reputation who prosecuted a man on charges involving his *caput*. P. A. Brunt, " ' Amicitia ' in the late Roman Republic," *Proceedings of the Cambridge Philological Society* 11 (1965), 13; reprinted in *The Crisis of the Roman Republic*.   [f] Cicero, *Brutus* 308.

Cicero's success at this trial enabled him to eclipse Hortensius and when in 61 the consul, Marcus Pupius Piso, called upon the senators to speak, he named Cicero second and Hortensius fourth. An exponent of the Asiatic school of oratory, Hortensius had an exceptionally accurate memory, a brilliant mastery of language, and he enhanced his natural talents by assiduous practice. He was meticulous in the preparation of his case, presented it with great clarity, never omitted anything that was relevant and had the advantage of an attractive voice. Only in his delivery and gestures did Cicero feel that he tended to exaggeration,[a] although his speeches were more effective when delivered than their written form suggested.[b]

Crassus is better known to us for his political activities but he was in fact one of the leading speakers at the Roman Bar. This position he reached, in spite of limited rhetorical training and little natural ability, by his industry and personal influence. He spoke good Latin and arranged his material carefully but without elaboration. He had a lively intellect but his voice and delivery were dull to the point of monotony. In short, he was a painstaking and more than competent speaker rather than an inspired orator.[c]

Cicero's motives for joining these two distinguished members of the Bar are not as simple as he would have us believe. He may have seen the acceptance of this brief as part of a consul's duty to protect Rome from Catiline's threat to law and order, and he may have genuinely believed that Murena's acquittal was

---

[a] *Brutus* 301-303. In 317-330 Cicero contrasts his own career with that of Hortensius.
[b] Cicero, *Orator* 132.   [c] *Brutus* 233.

essential to the national security.[a] Yet there were
other considerations that will have played their part
in his decision. Murena was like himself a " new
man " and likely to prove sympathetic to his own
policies and prepared to continue them in the following year.[b] More important than this was Cicero's
obligation to put himself at the service of the Optimates, men like Hortensius and Lucullus, without
whose support he could never, as a " new man," have
become consul. These men may well have thought
Murena's acquittal essential to their interests, not for
the defeat of Catiline's spent force, but for their
protection against the impending return of Pompey
from the East. Murena was well suited in his military
experience and by his personal ties to organize and
lead the forces of senatorial government in any clash
that might occur.[c] Another consideration was that
the strong line that Cicero had taken against the
Catilinarians might not go unchallenged, and a consul
in his debt for a successful defence might prove a
welcome ally in the following year should there be
any attack upon his actions during his consulship.[d]
Again, a thwarted consul-designate of Murena's
wealth and power would be an additional hazard in a
political situation that was already dangerous enough.

Had Cicero refused to take up Murena's case, he
would not have been without justification. There is
little reason to doubt Murena's guilt, even allowing
for the fact that Hortensius and Crassus may have
produced more telling answers to the charges than
appear in Cicero's speech. The recent introduction of

[a] 4, p. 190. *Cf.* p. 176 above.   [b] *Cf.* p. 178 above.
[c] See pp. 170-171 above.
[d] *Cf.* the introduction to the speech *pro Sulla*, p. 308.

CICERO

his law against *ambitus*, even if he was as reluctant to promote it as he would have us believe, and his friendship with Sulpicius, whom he had recently supported against Murena in the consular elections, could have given him further grounds for hesitation.

One of the problems confronting Roman politicians was how to act in the face of conflicting claims of friendship. Cicero looked upon both Murena and Sulpicius as friends, but his links were closer with the latter. Sulpicius felt aggrieved by Cicero's defence of Murena which he thought was a breach of their friendship, and Cicero has to defend himself against this resentment. He argues that Sulpicius has no cause to feel resentful, but considerations of *amicitia* had to be carefully weighed.[a]

Murena with his powerful support might still have been acquitted if Cicero had refused the brief. It was almost unprecedented for a consul-designate to be prevented from taking up office by being convicted in the courts. This had, indeed, happened to Sulla and Autronius only three years previously, but Murena had the backing of powerful forces which could prevent him from sharing their fate.

In the event, Cicero joined the defence and his speech clinched the matter. Its rebuttal of charges is very slender, but it is a brilliant piece of oratory.[b] It has a deep feeling for how the minds of a Roman

[a] For *amicitia* see R. Syme, *The Roman Revolution* 12 f., L. R. Taylor, *Party Politics in the Age of Caesar* 7 f. and P. A. Brunt, *op. cit.* 14 f. In at least eleven speeches Cicero was a friend of his client's prosecutors. In this volume *cf. pro Murena* 7 and 10, pp. 192 and 196; *pro Sulla* 2 and 47, pp. 314 and 360; *pro Flacco* 2, p. 436.

[b] E. G. Hardy, *The Catilinarian Conspiracy* 73, strangely thought it " the dullest of dull speeches."

jury worked, for their instinctive admiration for the practical man of action and for their prejudice against the academic lawyer and idealistic philosopher. Its appeal for a man of action to suppress the Catilinarian conspiracy struck a responsive chord in Roman breasts, while the wit and the spirit of ridicule that he heaped upon the pettifogging jurisconsult and unworldly Stoic found their mark. Cato may have been provoked to his sourly double-edged comment " What a comic consul we have ! " [a] and irrelevant this may all have been by our standards, but the counter-attack had the desired effect. The prosecution was revealed as not capable of appreciating the seriousness of the crisis that faced Rome, much less of dealing with it.

From internal evidence [b] it is clear that the speech was delivered after Catiline and Manlius had openly taken the field, but before the conspirators had been apprehended at Rome and the debate on their punishment been held. The arrest of the conspirators took place on the night of the 2nd-3rd of December, and Catiline had left Rome on the evening of the 8th of November. He must have reached Manlius' camp about the middle of the month, and Murena's trial will therefore have taken place between then and early December. Cicero spoke last for the defence.[c]

[a] Plutarch, *Cato Minor* 21. 5 and *Demosthenes and Cicero* 1. 5. *Cf.* Cicero, *de finibus* 4. 74. This speech was a famous example of how to win your case by means of jokes. *Cf.* Macrobius, *Saturnalia* 2. 1. 13, p. 427, n. *e*, on the speech *pro Flacco*, for Cicero's technique of helping the cases of guilty clients by means of his jokes. See also R. Syme, *The Roman Revolution* 151 f.

[b] 79 and 84, pp. 286 and 292. See p. 20.

[c] 48, p. 248. For Quintilian's rules for delivery, see 11. 3.

He was accorded this place in view of his unrivalled capacity for playing upon the sympathies of a jury.[a] Murena was unanimously [b] acquitted and entered upon his stormy consulship.

On the 10th of December, Quintus Caecilius Metellus Nepos became tribune, and Cicero did not have long to wait for the attack upon his execution of the conspirators. On the last day of the month Cicero was about to follow precedent and address the people at the end of his term of office, but Metellus prevented him from doing more than taking the oath that he had done his duty. January, 62, saw violence in Rome as well as the defeat of Catiline in the field.[c] Cato had been elected tribune with the express purpose of opposing Metellus [d] and was subjected to such violence that Murena had to come to the rescue of his prosecutor.

After his consulship Murena passes into oblivion. He does not appear to have held any further command or office and the date of his death is not known.

---

70. Cicero must have been a good actor to get his material across effectively.

[a] Cicero, *Orator* 130 and *Brutus* 190. See also L. Laurand, *Le Style des discours de Cicéron* 327-331 ; *pro Murena* 86-90, pp. 292-298, especially 88-89, pp. 296-298, *pro Sulla* 86-93, pp. 400-408, especially 91, p. 404, and *pro Flacco* 100-106, pp. 548-556, especially 102-103, pp. 550-552. Much of these passages is irrelevant but it was the function of oratory to persuade jurors as well as to prove facts ; see *Orator* 69.

[b] If *pro Flacco* 98, p. 548 is to be taken literally.

[c] For their connexion, see p. 29, n. *a*.   [d] 81, p. 288.

PRO MURENA

THE MANUSCRIPTS

Σ   =codex Parisiensis 14749, formerly codex S.
     Victoris 91, 15th century

B   =The excerpts of Bartolommeo of Monte-
     pulciano from the codex Cluniacensis which
     are found in the codex Laurentianus LIV. 5

A   =codex Laurentianus XLVIII. 10, written in
     A.D. 1416 by Ioannes Arretinus (Lagomar-
     sinianus 10)

π   =codex Perusinus E 71, written in A.D. 1416

φ   =codex Laurentianus LII. 1 (Lagomarsinianus
     65)

χ   =codex Laurentianus XLVIII. 25 (Lagomar-
     sinianus 25)

ψ   =codex Laurentianus (Gadd.) XC sup. 69

ω   =codex Laurentianus XLVIII. 26 (Lagomar-
     sinianus 26)

s   =codex Monacensis 15734

w   =codex Guelferbytanus 205

Schol. =Scholiasta Gronovianus

PRO L. MURENA ORATIO

1   Quod precatus a dis immortalibus sum, iudices,
more institutoque maiorum illo die quo auspicato
comitiis centuriatis L. Murenam consulem re-
nuntiavi, ut ea res mihi fidei magistratuique meo,
populo plebique Romanae bene atque feliciter
eveniret, idem precor ab isdem dis immortalibus ob
eiusdem hominis consulatum una cum salute obtinen-
dum, et ut vestrae mentes atque sententiae cum
populi Romani voluntatibus suffragiisque consentiant,
eaque res vobis populoque Romano pacem, tranquil-
litatem, otium concordiamque adferat. Quod si illa
sollemnis comitiorum precatio consularibus auspiciis
consecrata tantam habet in se vim et religionem
quantam rei publicae dignitas postulat, idem ego sum
precatus ut eis quoque hominibus quibus hic consulatus me rogante datus esset ea res fauste feliciter
2 prospereque eveniret. Quae cum ita sint, iudices, et
cum omnis deorum immortalium potestas aut translata sit ad vos aut certe communicata vobiscum, idem
consulem vestrae fidei commendat qui antea dis

---

^a See Appendix A, p. 561.

^b For Th. Mommsen's reconstruction of the *rogationis
carmen* : " velitis iubeatis, si consules duos rogaro, uti hi in
annum proximum sint, vos Quirites rogo," see *Römisches
Staatsrecht* 3. 391, n. 1.

SPEECH IN DEFENCE OF
LUCIUS LICINIUS MURENA

On that day, gentlemen of the jury, on which after I 1
had taken the auspices I announced Lucius Murena's
election as consul to the assembly of the centuries,[a]
I prayed to the immortal gods according to the traditional usage of our ancestors[b] that his election
should bring all good fortune to myself, my trust,[c]
my office and to the people and commons of Rome.
Today I pray again to those same immortal gods
that Murena's acquittal may preserve him for his
consulship, that your opinion given in your verdict
may tally with the wishes of the Roman people expressed in their votes, and that this agreement may
bring peace, calm, tranquillity and harmony to yourselves and to the people of Rome. Believing that that
customary election prayer, hallowed by the auspices
taken by a consul, has the force and religious weight
that the majesty of the Republic demands, I prayed
too that the election over which I presided should
bring to the successful candidates all good fortune and
prosperity. Accordingly, gentlemen, since the im- 2
mortal gods have either transferred to you their
whole power or at least have allowed you to share it,
I now commend to your protection the consul whom I

[c] In which as their *patronus* he has promised his protection
to the citizens.

immortalibus commendavit, ut eiusdem hominis voce
et declaratus consul et defensus beneficium populi
Romani cum vestra atque omnium civium salute tuea-
tur.

Et quoniam in hoc officio studium meae defensionis
ab accusatoribus atque etiam ipsa susceptio causae
reprensa est, ante quam pro L. Murena dicere in-
stituo, pro me ipso pauca dicam, non quo mihi potior
hoc quidem tempore sit offici mei quam huiusce
salutis defensio, sed ut meo facto vobis probato maiore
auctoritate ab huius honore fama fortunisque omnibus
inimicorum impetus propulsare possim.

3 Et primum M. Catoni vitam ad certam rationis
normam derigenti et diligentissime perpendenti
momenta officiorum omnium de officio meo respondebo. Negat fuisse rectum Cato me et consulem et
legis ambitus latorem et tam severe gesto consulatu
causam L. Murenae attingere. Cuius reprehensio
me vehementer movet, non solum ut vobis, iudices, quibus maxime debeo, verum etiam ut ipsi
Catoni, gravissimo atque integerrimo viro, rationem
facti mei probem. A quo tandem, M. Cato, est
aequius consulem defendi quam a consule ? Quis
mihi in re publica potest aut debet esse coniunctior
quam is cui res publica a me nunc[1] traditur sustinenda
magnis meis laboribus et periculis sustentata ?
Quod si in eis rebus repetendis quae mancipi sunt is

---

[1] nunc *Nisbet, Classical Review 12 (1962), 311.* una mss.
iam *Klotz. Many other suggestions have been made.*

---

[a] *Cf. pro Sulla 2, p. 316.*
[b] A technical term from Stoic ethical teaching. See 61
and n. *a* on p. 264. [c] See p. 174.

previously entrusted to the immortal gods. He will thus be defended by the voice of the man who declared him consul and preserve along with the office conferred upon him by the Roman people the safety of yourselves and of the whole citizen body.

Because in this fulfilment of my obligation I have been attacked by the prosecution for the vigour of my defence and even for the fact that I have taken on Murena's case at all, before I begin to speak in his defence, I shall say a few words on my own behalf. I do so, not because I feel at this moment that self-justification is more important than the acquittal of my client, but so that by winning your approval for my conduct I may be able to repel with greater authority the attacks of his enemies upon his public honour, his good name and his whole position.[a]

I shall deal with the fulfilment of my obligation first 3 and reply to Marcus Cato who organizes life according to the fixed pattern of a system and weighs with scrupulous care the importance of all obligations. Cato says that it was not a " right act " [b] for me to accept Murena's case because I am a consul, have carried a law against electoral corruption [c] and have displayed such severity during my consulship. His criticism impels me to justify my motives not only to you, gentlemen, with whom my first duty lies, but to Cato himself as well, for he is a man of the highest authority and integrity. I ask you, Marcus Cato : who more appropriate to defend a consul than another consul ? Who in the Republic can or should be more closely tied to me than the man to whom, after defending it with such efforts and at such peril to myself, I am now handing it over for him to preserve ? If, in a case for the recovery of goods which have been

periculum iudici praestare debet qui se nexu obligavit,
profecto etiam rectius in iudicio consulis designati is
potissimum consul qui consulem declaravit auctor
benefici populi Romani defensorque periculi esse
4 debebit. Ac si, ut non nullis in civitatibus fieri solet,
patronus huic causae publice constitueretur, is potissimum summo[1] honore adfecto defensor daretur qui
eodem honore praeditus non minus adferret ad
dicendum auctoritatis quam facultatis. Quod si e
portu solventibus ei qui iam in portum ex alto inve-
huntur praecipere summo studio solent et tempestatum rationem et praedonum et locorum, quod natura
adfert ut eis faveamus qui eadem pericula quibus nos
perfuncti sumus ingrediantur, quo tandem me esse
animo oportet prope iam ex magna iactatione terram
videntem in hunc cui video maximas rei publicae
tempestates esse subeundas ? Qua re si est boni
consulis non solum videre quid agatur verum etiam
providere quid futurum sit, ostendam alio loco quantum salutis communis intersit duos consules in re
5 publica Kalendis Ianuariis esse. Quod si ita est, non
tam me officium debuit ad hominis amici fortunas
quam res publica consulem ad communem salutem
defendendam vocare. Nam quod legem de ambitu
tuli, certe ita tuli ut eam quam mihimet ipsi iam

---

[1] potissimum summo *Madvig.* potissimo MSS.

---

a Murena's consulship is a *res mancipi* of which Cicero is
the seller and Murena the purchaser. A *res mancipi* changes
hands by the formal process of *mancipatio* = a taking in the
hand. In this process the purchaser took hold of what was
to become his property and received a guarantee from the
seller that, if challenged on his right to the property, he
would either prove it or reimburse the purchaser. The risk
of the court decision is that the property may be assigned to
the third party who has laid claim to it.

sold under contract, a man who has assumed the contractual obligation should incur the risk of a court decision,[a] then it is surely even more appropriate in the trial of a consul-designate that the consul above all who has declared his election should be the guarantor of the office conferred by the Roman people and defend it from all danger. If, as is the practice in 4 some states, an advocate were officially appointed for this case, it would be most appropriate that a man elected to the highest office should be granted counsel who by virtue of holding that same office would plead with as much authority as eloquence. Sailors who are just putting into harbour from the high seas are usually eager to give those weighing anchor an account of storms, pirates and places of danger, because nature inclines us to help those who are entering the dangers through which we have ourselves passed. Such, I can tell you, are the feelings that I, who am now in sight of land after a severe buffeting, have for this man who has to face the most violent political storms. If, then, it is the mark of a good consul to foresee the future as well as to see the present, I shall show elsewhere [b] how vital it is for the preservation of us all that there are two consuls in the Republic on the 1st of January.[c] If this is indeed the case, it was 5 not so much a personal obligation that should have called me to defend the position of a friend as the Republic that should have summoned a consul to defend the safety of all her citizens. I admittedly carried a law against electoral corruption but I did

[b] 79, p. 286.
[c] If convicted, Murena would be debarred from office; consuls end their term of office on the last day of December, whether there are validly elected successors or not.

pridem tulerim de civium periculis defendendis non
abrogarem. Etenim si largitionem factam esse con-
fiterer idque recte factum esse defenderem, facerem
improbe, etiam si alius legem tulisset; cum vero nihil
commissum contra legem esse defendam, quid est
quod meam defensionem latio legis impediat?

6   Negat esse eiusdem severitatis Catilinam exitium
rei publicae intra moenia molientem verbis et paene
imperio ex urbe expulisse et nunc pro L. Murena
dicere. Ego autem has partis lenitatis et misericordiae quas me natura ipsa docuit semper egi libenter, illam vero gravitatis severitatisque personam
non appetivi, sed ab re publica mihi impositam
sustinui, sicut huius imperi dignitas in summo periculo civium postulabat. Quod si tum, cum res publica
vim et severitatem desiderabat, vici naturam et tam
vehemens fui quam cogebar, non quam volebam, nunc
cum omnes me causae ad misericordiam atque ad
humanitatem vocent, quanto tandem studio debeo
naturae meae consuetudinique servire? Ac de officio
defensionis meae ac de ratione accusationis tuae
fortasse etiam alia in parte orationis dicendum nobis
erit.

7   Sed me, iudices, non minus hominis sapientissimi
atque ornatissimi, Ser. Sulpici, conquestio quam
Catonis accusatio commovebat qui gravissime et
acerbissime se ferre[1] dixit me familiaritatis necessi-
tudinisque oblitum causam L. Murenae contra se

[1] se ferre *Lambinus.* ferme MSS.

---

[a] See pp. 18-19.   [b] For this theme *cf. pro Sulla* 8, p. 320.
[c] 67 f., p. 270 f.   [d] See p. 180 f.

not repeal that long standing private rule of mine, to protect my fellow-citizens in their hour of danger. If, however, I admitted that bribery had taken place and argued that nothing wrong had been done, then I should be acting improperly, even if another had carried the law ; but since my case is that there has been no breach of the law, I fail to see how my responsibility for the law can interfere with my appearance for the defence.

Cato says that my present defence of Murena is **6** inconsistent with the severity which I employed in expelling Catiline from Rome by my speeches and virtually by my consular edict when he was contriving the destruction of the State within the city's walls.[a] I have always been happy to play this rôle of leniency and mercy which I learned from Mother Nature [b] ; I have not sought the part of sternness and severity, but when I had it thrust upon me by the State I have sustained it as the majesty of this realm demanded in her citizens' supreme peril. If I did overcome my natural inclination and, loth though I was, display the necessary vigour at a time when the State required the use of force and severity, should I not be eager to indulge my temperament and usual practice now that every consideration invites mercy and human feeling ? Perhaps I shall have to deal further with my obligation to act for the defence and with the grounds for your accusation in another part of my speech.[c]

The complaint, gentlemen, of my learned and eminent friend Servius Sulpicius affected me as deeply **7** as Cato's accusation. He said that he was pained and bitterly hurt that I had forgotten the ties of friendship and was defending Murena against him.[d]

defendere. Huic ego, iudices, satis facere cupio
vosque adhibere arbitros. Nam cum grave est vere
accusari in amicitia, tum, etiam si falso accuseris, non
est neglegendum. Ego, Ser. Sulpici, me in petitione
tua tibi omnia studia atque officia pro nostra necessitudine et debuisse confiteor et praestitisse arbitror.
Nihil tibi consulatum petenti a me defuit quod esset
aut ab amico aut a gratioso aut a consule postulandum.
Abiit illud tempus ; mutata ratio est. Sic existimo,
sic mihi persuadeo, me tibi contra honorem Murenae
quantum tu a me postulare ausus sis, tantum debuisse,
8 contra salutem nihil debere. Neque enim, si tibi tum
cum peteres consulatum studui nunc[1] cum Murenam
ipsum petas, adiutor eodem pacto esse debeo. Atque
hoc non modo non laudari sed ne concedi quidem
potest ut amicis nostris accusantibus non etiam
alienissimos defendamus. Mihi autem cum Murena,
iudices, et magna et vetus amicitia est, quae in capitis
dimicatione a Ser. Sulpicio non idcirco obruetur quod
ab eodem in honoris contentione superata est. Quae
si causa non esset, tamen vel dignitas hominis vel
honoris eius quem adeptus est amplitudo summam
mihi superbiae crudelitatisque infamiam[2] inussisset,
si hominis et suis et populi Romani ornamentis
amplissimi causam tanti periculi repudiassem. Neque
enim iam mihi licet neque est integrum ut meum
laborem hominum periculis sublevandis non imper-
tiam. Nam cum praemia mihi tanta pro hac industria

---

[1] consulatum studui, nunc *Clark, from Quintilian 9. 1. 68.*
consulatum adfui, nunc ψ^2 ; *omitted by the other MSS.*
[2] infamiam *Gulielmius.* famam *MSS.*

I wish, gentlemen, to justify myself to him and to have you decide between us. An accusation of neglecting the ties of friendship is a serious matter if it is true, and must not be ignored even if it is false. I agree, Sulpicius, that in the election the claims of friendship demanded all the support that I could give you and I think that I discharged my obligations. When you were a consular candidate, I failed you in nothing that could have been asked of a friend, or a man of influence, or of a consul. That time has passed; other considerations prevail. It is my conviction and firm belief that I was bound to give you as much as you dared ask of me in opposing Murena's political advancement, but I am under no obligation to you not to defend him. Even though I supported you when you were going for the consulship, I am not obliged to support you in the same way now that you are going for Murena himself. I cannot even concede, let alone applaud, the principle that when our friends appear for the prosecution we may not defend even complete strangers. I have for a long time, gentlemen, had close ties of friendship with Murena, but they will not be overridden by Servius Sulpicius in a case involving his civil rights because they took second place in an electoral campaign. Even were this not so, the standing of the accused or the regard for the high office which he has attained would have branded me with the stigma of arrogance and a hard heart, had I refused to defend in his hour of peril a man distinguished both for his own achievement and for the honours conferred upon him by the Roman people. I do not have the right nor am I at liberty to withhold my efforts to relieve the dangers of my fellow-men. Seeing that I have received

sint data quanta antea nemini, sic existimo laborem,
quem honores adepturus exceperis,[1] eos, cum adeptus
sis, deponere, esse hominis et astuti et ingrati.
9 Quod si licet desinere, si te auctore possum, si nulla
inertiae infamia,[2] nulla superbiae turpitudo, nulla
inhumanitatis culpa suscipitur, ego vero libenter
desino. Sin autem fuga laboris desidiam, repudiatio
supplicum superbiam, amicorum neglectio improbitatem coarguit, nimirum haec causa est eius modi
quam nec industrius quisquam[3] nec misericors nec
officiosus deserere possit. Atque huiusce rei coniecturam de tuo ipsius studio, Servi, facillime ceperis.
Nam si tibi necesse putas etiam adversariis amicorum tuorum de iure consulentibus respondere, et si
turpe existimas te advocato illum ipsum quem contra
veneris causa cadere, noli tam esse iniustus ut, cum
tui fontes vel inimicis tuis pateant, nostros etiam
10 amicis putes clausos esse oportere. Etenim si me tua
familiaritas ab hac causa removisset, et si hoc idem
Q. Hortensio, M. Crasso, clarissimis viris, si item
ceteris a quibus intellego tuam gratiam magni
aestimari accidisset, in ea civitate consul designatus
defensorem non haberet in qua nemini umquam
infimo maiores nostri patronum desse voluerunt.
Ego vero, iudices, ipse me existimarem nefarium si
amico, crudelem si misero, superbum si consuli de-
fuissem. Qua re quod dandum est amicitiae, large
dabitur a me, ut tecum agam, Servi, non secus ac si

---

[1] *Suggested by M. Brożek, " Emendationes Murenianae,"
Eos 55 (1965), 117 : it gives the sense required. The mss. are
unintelligible and many suggestions have been made.*

[2] infamia *added by Wesenberg.*

[3] quisquam *Gulielmius.* quam *mss.*

greater rewards than any of my predecessors for my hard work at the Bar, I think that it is the sign of calculation and ingratitude to abandon the effort that you made to obtain office as soon as you have secured it. If, however, I am allowed to abandon it, if you take the responsibility for my action, if I incur no bad name for idleness, no disgrace for high-handedness, no blame for insensitivity, I for my part am glad to give up. But if the avoidance of hard work indicates idleness, the rejection of petitioners high-handedness, the neglect of friends lack of principle, then this case is undoubtedly one such as no active, compassionate or loyal friend can abandon. You will very easily divine my position, Servius, from your own profession. If you think that you are obliged to give opinions even to your friends' opponents when they consult you upon a point of law, and if you think it a slur upon you that your former opponent should lose his case after taking your opinion, then do not be so unreasonable as to think that my fount of wisdom should be closed even to my friends when yours is open even to your enemies. If our friendship had kept me out of this case and if my distinguished friends Quintus Hortensius and Marcus Crassus, with all the others who, I know, set great store by your good-will, had acted in the same way, then in a city in which our ancestors did not wish even the humblest man ever to be without an advocate, a consul-designate would not have counsel to defend him. For my part, gentlemen, I would think myself beyond the pale had I failed a friend, hard hearted had I failed a man in trouble, arrogant had I failed a consul. I shall, therefore, make full concession to friendship and treat you, Servius, as if my brother, who is very dear

meus esset frater, qui mihi est carissimus, isto in loco ;
quod tribuendum est officio, fidei, religioni, id ita
moderabor ut meminerim me contra amici studium
pro amici periculo dicere.

11   Intellego, iudices, tris totius accusationis partis
fuisse, et earum unam in reprehensione vitae, alteram
in contentione dignitatis, tertiam in criminibus
ambitus esse versatam. Atque harum trium partium
prima illa quae gravissima debebat esse ita fuit in-
firma et levis ut illos lex magis quaedam accusatoria
quam vera male dicendi facultas de vita L. Murenae
dicere aliquid coegerit. Obiecta est enim Asia ; quae
ab hoc non ad voluptatem et luxuriam expetita est
sed in militari labore peragrata. Qui si adulescens
patre suo imperatore non meruisset, aut hostem aut
patris imperium timuisse aut a parente repudiatus
videretur. An cum sedere in equis triumphantium
praetextati potissimum filii soleant, huic donis mili-
taribus patris triumphum decorare fugiendum fuit, ut
rebus communiter gestis paene simul cum patre
12 triumpharet ? Hic vero, iudices, et fuit in Asia et viro
fortissimo, parenti suo, magno adiumento in periculis,
solacio in laboribus, gratulationi in victoria fuit. Et si
habet Asia suspicionem luxuriae quandam, non
Asiam numquam vidisse sed in Asia continenter
vixisse laudandum est. Quam ob rem non Asiae
nomen obiciendum Murenae fuit ex qua laus familiae,
memoria generi, honos et gloria nomini constituta est,

ᵃ For the temptations of this province, see p. 421.

to me, were standing in your place. I shall temper
the regard that I must have for my obligations, my
duty and my conscience, and remember that it is
against the case made by one friend that I speak
for another in his hour of peril.

I see, gentlemen, that the prosecution as a whole 11
was divided into three parts. One contained an
attack upon Murena's private life, the second a comparison of the merits of the candidates, and the third
the charges of corruption. Of these three, the first,
which should have been the most telling, was so
feeble and trivial that a sort of convention rather than
any true ground for abuse compelled the prosecution
to say something about Murena's private life. Asia
was cast in his teeth.[a] This province, however, he did
not seek deliberately for self-indulgence and high
living but traversed in the course of hard service in
the field. If in his youth he had not served under the
command of his father, it would be said that he had
been afraid of the enemy or of his father's command
or had been disowned by him. The young sons of a
general celebrating a triumph enjoy the privilege of
riding upon their father's horses ; should he then
have refused to adorn his father's triumph with the
trophies of his service or virtually to ride in triumph
with his father after sharing his campaigns ? He was 12
indeed in Asia and a great help to his gallant father in
danger, a comfort to him in hardship, a joy to him in
victory. If Asia arouses a suspicion of soft living, it is
more praiseworthy to have lived modestly in Asia than
never to have seen it. Murena, therefore, should not
have been reproached with the mere word " Asia "
from which his family has won praise, his house
immortality, his name honour and glory, but rather

sed aliquod aut in Asia susceptum aut ex Asia deportatum flagitium ac dedecus. Meruisse vero stipendia in eo bello quod tum populus Romanus non modo maximum sed etiam solum gerebat virtutis, patre imperatore libentissime meruisse pietatis, finem stipendiorum patris victoriam ac triumphum fuisse felicitatis fuit. Maledicto quidem idcirco nihil in hisce rebus loci est quod omnia laus occupavit.

13 Saltatorem appellat L. Murenam Cato. Maledictum est, si vere obicitur, vehementis accusatoris, sin falso, maledici conviciatoris. Qua re cum ista sis auctoritate, non debes, M. Cato, adripere maledictum ex trivio aut ex scurrarum aliquo convicio neque temere consulem populi Romani saltatorem vocare, sed circumspicere quibus praeterea vitiis adfectum esse necesse sit eum cui vere istud obici possit. Nemo enim fere saltat sobrius, nisi forte insanit, neque in solitudine neque in convivio moderato atque honesto. Tempestivi convivi, amoeni loci, multarum deliciarum comes est extrema saltatio. Tu mihi adripis hoc quod necesse est omnium vitiorum esse postremum, relinquis illa quibus remotis hoc vitium omnino esse non potest ? Nullum turpe convivium, non amor, non comissatio, non libido, non sumptus ostenditur, et, cum ea non reperiantur quae voluptatis nomen habent quamquam vitiosa sunt, in quo ipsam luxuriam reperire non potes, in eo te 14 umbram luxuriae reperturum putas ? Nihil igitur in vitam L. Murenae dici potest, nihil, inquam, omnino, iudices. Sic a me consul designatus defenditur ut

---

a i.e. a solo performer at riotous parties. Such accusations are conventional and, although Cicero is indignant when his own client is accused, he does not hesitate to make similar charges when acting as a prosecutor himself.

with scandalous behaviour in Asia or disgrace brought
back from it. However, by serving in the war which
was the most important—in fact the only—war then
being fought by the Roman people he gave proof of
his bravery, by serving of his own free will under his
father he gave proof of his filial obedience, by ending
his service with his father's victory and triumph he
gave proof of his good fortune. Slander has indeed
no place in this story because there is only room for
praise.

Cato calls Murena a dancer.[a] Strong language 13
from a forceful prosecution, if there is any truth in it ;
slanderous abuse, if it is false. A man of your stature,
then, Marcus Cato, should not pick a piece of dirt
from the street corner or from parasites' invective or
lightly abuse a consul of the Roman people in this
way. You should look around for the other vices with
which a man must be tainted before you can sustain
this charge. Hardly anyone dances except in his
cups, either by himself or at any respectable party,
unless of course he is out of his mind. Dancing comes
at the end of a seasonable meal, in attractive surround-
ings and after a wealth of sensuous enjoyment. You
are seizing upon this climax of debauchery but leave
out those attendant vices without which it cannot
exist. You do not produce any disgraceful party, any
love-making, riotous behaviour, loose and extravagant
living, and since there is no sign of behaviour that
goes by the name of pleasure but is really vice, do you
think that you can find the shadow of debauchery
where you cannot find the substance ? Nothing, 14
then, can be said against Murena's private life ; not
one single word, gentlemen. My defence of the
consul-designate is that his whole life is free from

eius nulla fraus, nulla avaritia, nulla perfidia, nulla
crudelitas, nullum petulans dictum in vita proferatur.
Bene habet; iacta sunt fundamenta defensionis.
Nondum enim nostris laudibus, quibus utar postea,
sed prope inimicorum confessione virum bonum atque
integrum hominem defendimus. Quo constituto
facilior est mihi aditus ad contentionem dignitatis,
quae pars altera fuit accusationis.

15　　Summam video esse in te, Ser. Sulpici, dignitatem
generis, integritatis, industriae ceterorumque orna-
mentorum omnium quibus fretum ad consulatus
petitionem adgredi par est. Paria cognosco esse ista
in L. Murena, atque ita paria ut neque ipse dignitate
vinci a te[1] potuerit neque te dignitate superarit.
Contempsisti L. Murenae genus, extulisti tuum.
Quo loco si tibi hoc sumis, nisi qui patricius sit,
neminem bono esse genere natum, facis ut rursus
plebes in Aventinum sevocanda esse videatur. Sin
autem sunt amplae et honestae familiae plebeiae, et
proavus L. Murenae et avus praetor fuit, et pater,
cum amplissime atque honestissime ex praetura
triumphasset, hoc faciliorem huic gradum consulatus
adipiscendi reliquit quod is iam patri debitus a filio
16　petebatur. Tua vero nobilitas, Ser. Sulpici, tametsi
summa est, tamen hominibus litteratis et historicis
est notior, populo vero et suffragatoribus obscurior.

---

[1] a te *added in this position by Clark*; a te vinci *Campe.*

---

[a] *Plebs,* the commons, is the general body of Roman
citizens, to be distinguished from the privileged patricians.
Tradition relates that on five occasions the plebeians with-
drew completely from the life of the city, usually to the
Aventine, one of the seven hills which lay outside the
pomerium—the city boundary—in the hope of redress for
their grievances.

deceit, greed, treachery, cruelty or intemperate
language. Excellent! The foundations of his
defence have been laid. My defence of this good and
upright man does not at this stage depend upon praise
from me—this will come later—but in the tacit
admission of his enemies. It is now easier for me,
having established this fact, to tackle the comparison
of the candidates' suitability for office which formed
the second part of the prosecution's case.

I see, Servius Sulpicius, that you are outstanding 15
in your lineage, character, application and in all the
other marks of distinction upon which it is right for a
consular candidate to rely. I know that Murena's
equality with you in these respects means that
neither of you is inferior in standing to the other.
You poured scorn on Murena's birth and exalted
your own. If for this line of argument you presume
that only a patrician is well born, you are making
another secession of the plebs to the Aventine
inevitable.[a] But if there do exist plebeian families of
honour and distinction, both the grandfather and
great-grandfather of Murena were praetors, and his
father, after celebrating a magnificent and thoroughly
deserved triumph at the end of his praetorship,[b] left
my client an easier path to the consulship because
the son was only claiming an office that had already
been his father's due. Although, Servius Sulpicius, 16
your nobility [c] is second to none, it is better known
to men of letters and antiquarians and less familiar
to the people and the voters. Your father was only

A gross misrepresentation of the facts ; see p. 169.
[c] For the meaning of this word, see p. 178, n. *e*. There
had been consular tribunes, treated as the equivalent of
consuls, in the family in 388, 384 and 383.

Pater enim fuit equestri loco, avus nulla inlustri laude celebratus. Itaque non ex sermone hominum recenti sed ex annalium vetustate eruenda memoria est nobilitatis tuae. Qua re ego te semper in nostrum numerum adgregare soleo, quod virtute industriaque perfecisti ut, cum equitis Romani esses filius, summa tamen amplitudine dignus putarere. Nec mihi umquam minus in Q. Pompeio, novo homine et fortissimo viro, virtutis esse visum est quam in homine nobilissimo, M. Aemilio. Etenim eiusdem animi atque ingeni est posteris suis, quod Pompeius fecit, amplitudinem nominis quam non acceperit tradere et, ut Scaurus, memoriam prope intermortuam generis sua

17 virtute renovare. Quamquam ego iam putabam, iudices, multis viris fortibus ne ignobilitas generis obiceretur meo labore esse perfectum, qui non modo Curiis, Catonibus, Pompeiis, antiquis illis fortissimis viris,[1] sed his recentibus, Mariis et Didiis et Caeliis, commemorandis id agebam.[2] Cum vero ego tanto

---

[1] novis hominibus *follows in the MSS. ; deleted by Boot.*
[2] id agebam *Badham.* iacebant *V.* iacebam *ψ².* iacebant *the other MSS.* studebam *Kasten.*

---

[a] Cicero was himself a " new man." See p. 5.
[b] The Latin word *virtus* is almost untranslatable, but fundamentally means the quality of the man—*vir.* In Cicero it is explicitly the quality peculiar to the *novus homo,* as *nobilitas*—something derived from his ancestors—was that peculiar to the noble. It " consisted in the winning of personal pre-eminence and glory by the commission of great deeds in the service of the Roman state." *Cf.* D. C. Earl, *The Moral and Political Tradition of Rome* 21. This, not ancestry, was the proper criterion of a man's fitness for the consulship.
[c] Consul in 141, the first member of the *gens Pompeia* to become consul, and in 131 the first plebeian censor.
[d] Marcus Aemilius Scaurus was consul in 115, censor in

of equestrian rank and your grandfather was not particularly distinguished. The evidence for your nobility, then, has to be unearthed not from current talk but from ancient documents. I have for this reason always included you in my own company [a] because, although you were only the son of a Roman knight, by your ability [b] and energy you made good your claim to the highest distinction. I have never thought that Quintus Pompeius, [c] a gallant soldier but a new man, displayed less ability than Marcus Aemilius, [d] a true member of the aristocracy. It requires the same qualities of character and intellect to pass on to his descendants, as did Pompeius, a distinction which he did not inherit, as to revive by his own ability, as did Scaurus, the almost extinct memory of his family. Yet I used to think, gentlemen, that many gallant men had by my efforts escaped the taunt of their family's lack of nobility; efforts that were rewarded not only in the case of those valiant men of old—men like Curius, Cato, and Pompeius [e]—but also of more recent figures like Marius, Didius, and Caelius. [f] After breaking down

109, *consul suffectus* in 108 and for a number of years *princeps senatus*.

[e] Manius Curius Dentatus, who defeated the Samnites in 290, and in 275 Pyrrhus, king of Epirus, at the Battle of Beneventum. He was consul in 290, 275 and 274, and censor in 272. Marcus Porcius Cato Censorius was consul in 195. For Pompeius see note above.

[f] Gaius Marius, consul 107, 104, 103, 102, 101, 100 and 86; reorganizer of the Roman army and conqueror of Jugurtha and the Germanic invaders of Italy. Titus Didius was consul in 98 and fought in Macedonia and Spain. Gaius Caelius Caldus was consul in 94 and a partisan of Marius. These lists of heroes become a cliché in Cicero. *Cf. pro Sulla* 23, p. 336.

intervallo claustra ista nobilitatis refregissem, ut
aditus ad consulatum posthac, sicut apud maiores
nostros fuit, non magis nobilitati quam virtuti pateret,
non arbitrabar, cum ex familia vetere et inlustri
consul designatus ab equitis Romani filio consule
defenderetur, de generis novitate accusatores esse
dicturos. Etenim mihi ipsi accidit ut cum duobus
patriciis, altero improbissimo atque audacissimo,
altero modestissimo atque optimo viro, peterem ;
superavi tamen dignitate Catilinam, gratia Galbam.
Quod si id crimen homini novo esse deberet, profecto
18 mihi neque inimici neque invidi defuissent. Omittamus igitur de genere dicere cuius est magna in
utroque dignitas ; videamus cetera.

" Quaesturam una petiit et sum ego factus prior."
Non est respondendum ad omnia. Neque enim
vestrum quemquam fugit, cum multi pares dignitate
fiant, unus autem primum solus possit obtinere, non
eundem esse ordinem dignitatis et renuntiationis,
propterea quod renuntiatio gradus habeat, dignitas
autem sit persaepe eadem omnium. Sed quaestura
utriusque prope modum pari momento sortis fuit.
Habuit hic lege Titia provinciam tacitam et quie-
tam, tu illam cui, cum quaestores sortiuntur, etiam
adclamari solet, Ostiensem, non tam gratiosam et

---

[a] Only a tiny proportion of men from non-consular families moved from the praetorship into the consulship.

[b] Publius Sulpicius Galba.

[c] Distinction attached not merely to election, but to
priority of election. See Appendix A, p. 563. Cicero pre-
tends here that the order of *renuntiatio* does not matter, but
this passage reveals what most Romans felt about it. The
general Roman view emerges from the passages listed by
Th. Mommsen, *Römisches Staatsrecht* 3. 414, n. 3.

[d] Perhaps a law of Sextus Titius, a tribune in 99.

the barriers which had protected nobility for so many years [a] and making the way to the consulship open, as it was in the time of our ancestors, to talent as much as to birth, I did not think that when a consul-designate, the member of an old and illustrious family, was being defended by a consul, the son of a Roman knight, the prosecution would attack his family's lack of nobility. It was my own experience to have two patricians as fellow candidates for the consulship, one an utterly reckless desperado, the other a law-abiding citizen of complete loyalty. Yet I defeated Catiline in merit and Galba [b] in popularity. If my success were a valid ground for accusing a new man, then I would certainly have had no shortage of enemies or rivals. Let us, then, stop talking about 18 their birth, for in this respect they are equally distinguished. Let us consider the other points of comparison.

" He was a fellow-candidate for the quaestorship and I was elected first." [c] I need not reply to every point. You all appreciate that, when there are many candidates of equal merit but only one can come first in the election, their order of merit does not correspond with the order in which their election is announced. This is because the announcement of election creates degrees of precedence whereas very often all the candidates are of equal merit. But the lot gave to each a quaestorship of much the same importance. In accordance with Titius' law [d] Murena was allotted a quiet and peaceful province, while you had Ostia which is always greeted by an uproar when the praetors draw the lots.[e] It is a province that

[e] Apart from the quaestors attached to provincial governors and commanders in the field, there were two

inlustrem quam negotiosam et molestam. Consedit
utriusque nomen in quaestura. Nullum enim vobis
sors campum dedit in quo excurrere virtus cognoscique
posset.

19 Reliqui temporis spatium in contentionem vocatur.
Ab utroque dissimillima ratione tractatum est.
Servius hic nobiscum hanc urbanam militiam respon-
dendi, scribendi, cavendi plenam sollicitudinis ac
stomachi secutus est ; ius civile didicit, multum
vigilavit, laboravit, praesto multis fuit, multorum
stultitiam perpessus est, adrogantiam pertulit, difficultatem exsorbuit ; vixit ad aliorum arbitrium, non
ad suum. Magna laus et grata hominibus unum
hominem elaborare in ea scientia quae sit multis
20 profutura. Quid Murena interea ? Fortissimo et
sapientissimo viro, summo imperatori legatus, L. Lucullo, fuit ; qua in legatione duxit exercitum, signa
contulit, manum conseruit, magnas copias hostium
fudit, urbis partim vi, partim obsidione cepit, Asiam
istam refertam et eandem delicatam sic obiit ut in ea
neque avaritiae neque luxuriae vestigium reliquerit,
maximo in bello sic est versatus ut hic multas res et
magnas sine imperatore gesserit, nullam sine hoc

quaestores urbani, who remained in Rome and were chiefly
concerned with criminal prosecutions and control of the
treasury, and four quaestores classici established after the
subjugation of Italy and dealing primarily with naval
matters. One of these was assigned to Ostia, a busy port
with the problem of handling Rome's supply of imported
corn, which could be a headache for the magistrate in charge.
Yet, Cicero may perhaps be trying deliberately to mislead his
audience. The opportunity of providing plentiful grain, if it
was there to provide, could have been politically advantageous.

⁶ For this comparison between the civil and military

brings more trouble and anxiety than fame and popularity. The reputation of each of you declined in his quaestorship, because the lot gave neither a field in which his ability could spread itself and win recognition.

The period that follows provides a comparison 19 between them.[a] It was employed by each in an entirely different way. Servius soldiered with me here at Rome, giving opinions, engrossing documents and drawing up formulas of security ; a life full of worry and vexation. He became an expert in civil law, worked long hours, spared no efforts, readily helped his many clients, put up with their stupidity, endured their arrogance and stomached those who were hard to please. He lived for others, not for himself. When a single individual takes great pains in a profession that will benefit so many, he wins great credit with men and widespread gratitude. What of 20 Murena at this time ? He was a subordinate commander under Lucius Lucullus,[b] an able and gallant soldier and a distinguished commander-in-chief. In this command he led an army, fought pitched battles, engaged in hand to hand fighting, routed strong forces of the enemy, took cities, some by storm, some after a siege, crossed the face of that Asia of yours, so crammed with wealth and luxury, and yet left behind in it not a trace of acquisitiveness or of extravagant living. In his conduct of a major war he performed many feats of arms without his commander, but his

powers as a reflection of Cicero's current political philosophy, see C. Nicolet, " Consul togatus," *Revue des Études latines* 38 (1960), 248-251.

[b] Lucius Licinius Lucullus (c. 117-56) had been appointed to an extraordinary proconsular command in 74 to fight Mithridates.

imperator. Atque haec quamquam praesente L.
Lucullo loquor, tamen ne ab ipso propter periculum
nostrum concessam videamur habere licentiam
fingendi, publicis litteris testata sunt omnia, quibus
L. Lucullus tantum laudis impertiit quantum neque
ambitiosus imperator neque invidus tribuere alteri in
21 communicanda gloria debuit. Summa in utroque est
honestas, summa dignitas ; quam ego, si mihi per
Servium liceat, pari atque eadem in laude ponam.
Sed non licet : agitat rem militarem, insectatur totam
hanc legationem, adsiduitatis et operarum harum
cotidianarum putat esse consulatum. " Apud exercitum mihi fueris " inquit " tot annos ; forum non
attigeris ; afueris tam diu et, cum longo intervallo
veneris, cum his qui in foro habitarint de dignitate
contendas ? " Primum ista nostra adsiduitas, Servi,
nescis quantum interdum adferat hominibus fastidi,
quantum satietatis. Mihi quidem vehementer ex-
pediit positam in oculis esse gratiam ; sed tamen
ego mei satietatem magno meo labore superavi et tu
item fortasse ; verum tamen utrique nostrum deside-
22 rium nihil obfuisset. Sed ut hoc omisso ad studiorum
atque artium contentionem revertamur, qui potest
dubitari quin ad consulatum adipiscendum multo plus
adferat dignitatis rei militaris quam iuris civilis
gloria ? Vigilas tu de nocte ut tuis consultoribus
respondeas, ille ut eo quo intendit mature cum
exercitu perveniat ; te gallorum, illum bucinarum
cantus exsuscitat ; tu actionem instituis, ille aciem

commander performed none without him. Although
I say this in Lucullus' presence, yet to avoid the
appearance of having his permission to exaggerate
because of my client's danger, I add that the official
despatches confirm everything. In allocating praise
in them Lucius Lucullus commends Murena more
highly than would any commander who sought glory
for himself or grudged it to others. The high distinc- 21
tion and prestige enjoyed by them both are equal in
my judgement, if Servius allows me to say so, and
deserve equal credit. He does not allow me. He
ridicules the profession of arms, he attacks the whole
of this command and thinks that the consulship is a
matter of persistent attention to the familiar daily
round. " You've been away with the army for
years," he says, " and you've been nowhere near the
Forum. You've been away all that time and now that
at last you're back, are you going to compete for
office with these men who have made their homes in
the Forum ? " Firstly, Servius, you do not realize
how tired and bored men get at seeing us always on
the job. Admittedly, it worked very much to my
advantage that my popularity was won in front of
men's very eyes but I worked hard—as no doubt did
you—to prevent them from becoming bored with me.
Yet neither of us would have suffered had we been
missed. Let me leave this topic, however, and return 22
to the comparison of their professions and careers.
Can there be any doubt that a distinguished war
record confers a much stronger claim to the consulship than eminence in civil law ? You are up before
dawn to give opinions to your clients, he to bring his
army betimes to its objective ; you are woken by the
call of cocks, he by the call of trumpets ; you draw up

instruit ; tu caves ne tui consultores, ille ne urbes aut
castra capiantur ; ille tenet et scit ut hostium copiae,
tu ut aquae pluviae arceantur ; ille exercitatus est in
propagandis finibus, tuque in regendis. Ac nimirum
—dicendum est enim quod sentio—rei militaris virtus
praestat ceteris omnibus. Haec nomen populo
Romano, haec huic urbi aeternam gloriam peperit,
haec orbem terrarum parere huic imperio coegit ;
omnes urbanae res, omnia haec nostra praeclara studia
et haec forensis laus et industria latet[1] in tutela ac
praesidio bellicae virtutis. Simul atque increpuit
suspicio tumultus, artes ilico nostrae conticiscunt.

23   Et quoniam mihi videris istam scientiam iuris tamquam filiolam osculari tuam, non patiar te in tanto
errore versari ut istud nescio quid quod tanto opere
didicisti praeclarum aliquid esse arbitrere. Aliis ego
te virtutibus, continentiae, gravitatis, iustitiae, fidei,
ceteris omnibus, consulatu et omni honore semper
dignissimum iudicavi ; quod quidem ius civile didicisti,
non dicam operam perdidisti, sed illud dicam, nullam
esse in ista disciplina munitam ad consulatum viam.
Omnes enim artes, quae nobis populi Romani studia
concilient,[2] et admirabilem dignitatem et pergratam
24 utilitatem debent habere. Summa dignitas est in eis
qui militari laude antecellunt ; omnia enim quae sunt
in imperio et in statu civitatis ab his defendi et firmari

---

[1] latet *Clark*. latent *mss*.
[2] concilient *Ernesti*. conciliant *mss*.

---

[a] The Italian weather and terrain, without any extensive
system of drainage, were responsible for many lawsuits
involving the disposal of surface water.

[b] This theme is developed for the purposes of his case and
does not represent what Cicero and his contemporaries really

a form of proceedings, he a line of battle ; you protect your clients against surprise, he his cities or camps ; he understands how to keep off the enemy's forces, you rain water [a] ; he has been engaged in extending boundaries, you in defining them. In truth there is no doubt—for I must speak my mind—that success in a military career counts for more than any other. It is this which has won renown for the people of Rome and eternal glory for their city, which has compelled the world to obey our rule. All the activities of this city, all this noble profession of ours, our hard work and recognition here at the Bar lurk in obscurity under the care and protection of prowess in war. The moment that there is a distant rumble of warfare, our arts immediately fall silent.

Since you seem to me to be hugging your knowledge of jurisprudence as if it were a darling daughter, 23 I shall not allow you to be so mistaken as to think that this whatever-it-is that you have taken such pains to learn is in any way remarkable.[b] I have always felt that other qualities—self-control, dignity, uprightness, sense of duty and all the others— have made you thoroughly deserving of the consulship and every other office. I shall not say that you have wasted your time in learning the civil law, but I shall say that there is no royal road to the consulship in your profession. Any career which is to win us the support of the Roman people must have a splendour to impress and a utility to please them. The most 24 distinguished military commanders have the greatest splendour because they are thought to give protection and backing to anything concerned with the

thought of jurisconsults. For a more favourable view, see Cicero, *Orator* 142.

putantur; summa etiam utilitas, si quidem eorum
consilio et periculo cum re publica tum etiam nostris
rebus perfrui possumus. Gravis etiam illa est et plena
dignitatis dicendi[1] facultas quae saepe valuit in
consule deligendo, posse consilio atque oratione et
senatus et populi et eorum qui res iudicant mentis
permovere. Quaeritur consul qui dicendo non numquam comprimat tribunicios furores, qui concitatum
populum flectat, qui largitioni resistat. Non mirum,
si ob hanc facultatem homines saepe etiam non
nobiles consulatum consecuti sunt, praesertim cum
haec eadem res plurimas gratias, firmissimas amicitias,
maxima studia pariat. Quorum in isto vestro artificio,
25 Sulpici, nihil est. Primum dignitas in tam tenui scientia non potest esse; res enim sunt parvae, prope
in singulis litteris atque interpunctionibus verborum
occupatae. Deinde, etiam si quid apud maiores
nostros fuit in isto studio admirationis, id enuntiatis
vestris mysteriis totum est contemptum et abiectum.
Posset agi lege necne pauci quondam sciebant; fastos
enim volgo non habebant. Erant in **magna** potentia
qui consulebantur; a quibus etiam dies tamquam a
Chaldaeis petebatur. Inventus est scriba quidam,
Cn. Flavius, qui cornicum oculos confixerit et singulis
diebus ediscendis fastos populo proposuerit et **ab**

---

[1] dicendi *deleted by Boot.*

---

[a] One of the most important ways of securing *gratia* was
by success as counsel for the defence. The acquitted
defendant was then under an obligation—*officium*—to his
counsel, and this obligation was not infrequently met in the
shape of electoral support. For this emphasis upon the

dominion of Rome and the condition of the State; they have the greatest utility because our enjoyment of the common weal and of our private possessions depends upon their decisions and their danger. The ability in speaking, which has often carried weight in the choice of a consul, by argument and eloquence to sway the opinions of the Senate, the people and the jury-class is also important and highly regarded. A consul must when required have the ability as a speaker to check the follies of tribunes, to calm the passions of the people and to stand up against bribery. It is not surprising that even men who are not nobles have often reached the consulship because they were good orators, particularly since the self-same ability wins the most widespread influence,[a] the closest political ties and the greatest popular support. There is none of these, Sulpicius, in that craft of you and your colleagues. Firstly, no prestige 25 can be gained from a knowledge of such trivialities. The subject matter is insignificant, almost entirely composed of questions of a single letter or a division between words. Secondly, even if our ancestors did once have some respect for your profession, it was brought into complete contempt and disregard after the publication of your secrets. At one time few knew whether legal business could be transacted, for the court-days were not public knowledge. Those who were consulted exercised tyrannical power; they were even asked about the day as if they were Chaldaean astrologers. A certain clerk, Gnaeus Flavius, materialized to peck out the crows' eyes and by learning off the days one by one published a

defensive rôle in oratory, see Cicero, *de oratore* 1. 32 and *de officiis* 2. 49-50.

ipsis his cautis iuris consultis eorum[1] sapientiam compilarit. Itaque irati illi, quod sunt veriti ne dierum ratione pervolgata et cognita sine sua opera lege agi[2] posset, verba quaedam composuerunt ut omnibus in
26 rebus ipsi interessent. Cum hoc fieri bellissime posset : " Fundus Sabinus meus est." " Immo meus," deinde iudicium, noluerunt. " Fundus " inquit " qui est in agro qui Sabinus vocatur." Satis verbose ; cedo quid postea ? " Eum ego ex iure Quiritium meum esse aio." Quid tum ? " Inde ibi ego te ex iure manum consertum voco." Quid huic tam loquaciter litigioso responderet ille unde petebatur non habebat. Transit idem iuris consultus tibicinis Latini modo. " Unde tu me " inquit " ex iure manum consertum vocasti, inde ibi ego te revoco." Praetor interea ne pulchrum se ac beatum putaret atque aliquid ipse sua sponte loqueretur, ei quoque carmen compositum est

[1] his *added by Clark* ; cautis *Beroaldus* ; causis iuris consultis eorum *mss.* ; consultorum *Madvig.*
[2] agi *added by editio Guariniana.*

---

[a] Gnaeus Flavius was the son of a freedman and a *scriba* of Appius Claudius Caecus. He became curule aedile in 304 and either while he was still a *scriba* or when in office he published the *Ius Flavianum*, an account of the legal procedures—*legis actiones*—and a calendar. What Flavius did and why he did it are not wholly clear and the part that he played in the development of the Roman calendar is controversial. *Cf.* A. K. Michels, *The Calendar of the Roman Republic* 108-118. For his career, see T. R. S. Broughton, *The Magistrates of the Roman Republic* 1. 168.
For the proverb, *cf. pro Flacco* 46, p. 494. See Macrobius, *Saturnalia* 7. 5. 11.
[b] The process by which a Roman sought to recover a violated right was known as *legis actio*. Such an action directed at a thing was known as *in rem actio* and originally the only means open to a plaintiff to assert his right to the object—*vindicatio rei*—was the *legis actio sacramento* in

calendar for the people and out of their own mouths robbed these canny lawyers of their wisdom.[a] Angry and afraid that since the list of days was now public knowledge legal processes could be set in motion without them, these lawyers devised certain formulas to ensure that they still took part in every case. When a case [b] could perfectly well go like this : 26 " The Sabine estate is mine," " No, mine," then a decision, they wouldn't have it. " An estate," he says, " which is in the territory which is called Sabine." That's long-winded enough, but listen to what follows : " I maintain that it is mine according to my legal rights as a Roman citizen." Where does that take us ? " I therefore summon you from the court to contest ownership at the property." The defendant did not know how to reply to so long-winded a litigant. The same lawyer crosses to the other side like a Latin pipe-player.[c] " Because," he says, " you have summoned me from the court to contest ownership, I therefore in my turn summon you there." Meanwhile to keep the praetor from getting too good an opinion of himself and saying something on his own, a jingle was composed for him

which the *sacramentum* was a wager recovered by the winner and forfeited by the loser. The stages in the legal drama of the action can be partially reconstructed from passages such as this which show that it survived in all its old vigour in the Ciceronian period. Cicero's account of the form of the *legis actio* is confirmed by Gaius, *Institutions* 4. 16. See A. H. J. Greenidge, *The Legal Procedure of Cicero's Time* 49 f. and 164 f. and A. Watson, *The Law of Property in the Later Roman Republic* 96.

[c] These musicians were traditionally Latins, not Romans. The lawyers are represented as crossing from one side to the other like the musicians accompanying first one singer and then another.

cum ceteris rebus absurdum tum vero in illo : " Suis utrisque superstitibus praesentibus istam viam dico ; ite viam." Praesto aderat sapiens ille qui inire viam doceret. " Redite viam." Eodem duce redibant. Haec iam tum apud illos barbatos ridicula, credo, videbantur, homines, cum recte atque in loco constitissent, iuberi abire ut, unde abissent, eodem statim redirent. Isdem ineptiis fucata sunt illa omnia : " Quando te in iure conspicio " et haec : " Anne tu dicas qua ex causa vindicaveris ? " Quae dum erant occulta, necessario ab eis qui ea tenebant petebantur ; postea vero pervolgata atque in manibus iactata et excussa, inanissima prudentiae reperta sunt, fraudis autem et stultitiae plenissima. Nam, cum permulta praeclare legibus essent constituta, ea iure consultorum ingeniis pleraque corrupta ac depravata sunt. Mulieres omnis propter infirmitatem consili maiores in tutorum potestate esse voluerunt ; hi invenerunt genera tutorum quae potestate mulierum continerentur. Sacra interire illi noluerunt ; horum ingenio senes ad coemptiones faciendas interimendorum sacrorum causa reperti sunt. In omni denique iure civili aequitatem reliquerunt, verba ipsa tenuerunt, ut, quia in alicuius libris exempli causa id nomen invenerant, putarent[1] omnis mulieres quae coemp-

27

---

[1] putarent *mss.* putarunt *editio Romana.*

---

[a] The practice of shaving came into Italy at about the end of the fourth century.

[b] *Coemptio* was a symbolic sale by which a woman passed into the power of a man ; if *matrimonii causa*, it was in effect a secular form of marriage. In the cases described here the woman found an old man who had neither children nor money and when he had become her husband and thus the owner of her property, including the obligation to perform *sacra familiaria*, he returned her tangible possessions as

too, and this is a particularly absurd example : " In the presence of the witnesses of both parties I indicate your route. Proceed by that route." Our learned friend was on hand to show them the road. " Return by that route." The same guide led them back. It already seemed absurd, I am sure, when our ancestors were still wearing beards,[a] for men to report as instructed to the right place only to be told to go somewhere else and then straight away to return to the original place. The same absurdity infects all that business about : " Whereas I see you before the court " and " Would you state the grounds on which you base your claim ? " While these formulas were secret, you had to beg for them from those who knew them. Later, however, when they had been published, bandied about, and thoroughly sifted, they were seen to be not only devoid of all sense but positively brimming with stupidity and trickery as well. After many forms of procedure 27 had been admirably established by law, most of them were ruined and spoiled by the subtleties of lawyers. Our ancestors required all women owing to the instability of their judgement to be under the control of guardians ; but these lawyers thought up kinds of guardian to be under the control of the women. Our ancestors wished religious rites to exist in perpetuity ; but these lawyers' ingenuity produced old men to go through a civil form of marriage [b] in order to end the rites. In short, throughout the whole of the civil law they abandoned its spirit but stuck to the letter, so as actually to think that all women who went through this form of

dona. The obligation to perform the *sacra* remained with him, but when he died leaving no heirs, it became extinct.

tionem facerent " Gaias " vocari. Iam illud mihi
quidem mirum videri solet, tot homines, tam in-
geniosos, post tot annos etiam nunc statuere non
potuisse utrum " diem tertium " an " perendinum,"
" iudicem " an " arbitrum," " rem " an " litem " dici
oporteret.

28   Itaque, ut dixi, dignitas in ista scientia consularis
numquam fuit, quae tota ex rebus fictis commenti-
ciisque constaret, gratiae vero multo etiam minus.
Quod enim omnibus patet et aeque promptum est
mihi et adversario meo, id esse gratum nullo pacto
potest. Itaque non modo benefici conlocandi spem
sed etiam illud quod aliquamdiu fuit " Licet consulere ? " iam perdidistis. Sapiens existimari nemo
potest in ea prudentia quae neque extra Romam
usquam neque Romae rebus prolatis quicquam valet.
Peritus ideo haberi nemo potest quod in eo quod
sciunt omnes nullo modo possunt inter se discrepare.
Difficilis autem res ideo non putatur quod et per-
paucis et minime obscuris litteris continetur. Itaque
si mihi, homini vehementer occupato, stomachum
moveritis, triduo me iuris consultum esse profitebor.
Etenim quae de scripto aguntur, scripta sunt omnia,
neque tamen quicquam tam anguste scriptum est quo
ego non possim " Qua de re agitur " addere ; quae
consuluntur autem, minimo periculo respondentur.
Si id quod oportet responderis, idem videare respon-

---

a Before crossing the threshold the bridegroom asked the
bride " Quaenam vocaris ? " to which she replied " Ubi tu
Gaius, ego Gaia." Cf. Quintilian 1. 7. 28 " Quia tam Gaias
esse vocitatas quam Gaios etiam ex nuptialibus sacris apparet." The bride's reply was the traditional, but not wholly
essential, formula which was used to show the marriage
consent. Cf. P. E. Corbett, The Roman Law of Marriage 74

marriage were called " Gaia," because in someone's works they had met that name used in a formula.[a] For my part, I never cease to wonder that so many intelligent men are still after all these years unable to decide whether they should say " two days later " or " the day after tomorrow," " judge " or " arbitrator," " case " or " suit."

Your profession, then, as I have already said, has 28 never conferred the prestige, much less the public support, required for the consulship, for it consists of nothing but fabrication and deceit. Since, moreover, its services are open to everyone and available to me and my opponent alike, you are quite unable to confer a favour. You have, therefore, now lost not only the hope of investing in a good turn but also your position in which would-be clients long had to ask " Is consultation permitted ? " You cannot have a reputation for wisdom if it is based on knowledge which has no value anywhere outside Rome and not even at Rome during the vacation. You cannot be an expert on a subject which everyone knows and about which, therefore, there can be no disagreement. You cannot say that the subject is difficult because it is contained in a very few extremely simple documents. If you provoke me, desperately busy as I am, I shall set myself up as a qualified lawyer within three days. In actions that depend upon a written formula everything is already in writing but nothing is written with such precision that I could not add " which is the matter at issue." Answers to requests for verbal advice can be given without risk. If you gave the right answer, you would get credit for agreeing with Servius ; if

and A. Watson, *The Law of Persons in the Later Roman Republic* 25.

disse quod Servius ; sin aliter, etiam controversum ius
29 nosse et tractare videare. Quapropter non solum illa
gloria militaris vestris formulis atque actionibus ante-
ponenda est verum etiam dicendi consuetudo longe et
multum isti vestrae exercitationi ad honorem ante-
cellit. Itaque mihi videntur plerique initio multo hoc
maluisse, post, cum id adsequi non potuissent, istuc
potissimum sunt delapsi. Ut aiunt in Graecis artifici-
bus eos auloedos esse qui citharoedi fieri non potuerint,
sic nos videmus, qui oratores evadere non potuerint,
eos ad iuris studium devenire. Magnus dicendi labor,
magna res, magna dignitas, summa autem gratia.
Etenim a vobis salubritas quaedam, ab eis qui dicunt
salus ipsa petitur. Deinde vestra responsa atque
decreta et evertuntur saepe dicendo et sine de-
fensione orationis[1] firma esse non possunt. In qua si
satis profecissem, parcius de eius laude dicerem ;
nunc nihil de me dico, sed de eis qui in dicendo magni
sunt aut fuerunt.

30   Duae sint artes igitur[2] quae possint locare homines
in amplissimo gradu dignitatis, una imperatoris, altera
oratoris boni. Ab hoc enim pacis ornamenta reti-
nentur, ab illo belli pericula repelluntur. Ceterae
tamen virtutes ipsae per se multum valent, iustitia,
fides, pudor, temperantia ; quibus te, Servi, excellere
omnes intellegunt. Sed nunc de studiis ad honorem
appositis, non de insita cuiusque virtute disputo.

---

[1] orationis *Clark.* oratoris *mss.*
[2] igitur *added by Clark* ; sint Σ*A* sunt *the other mss.* ;
possint Σ*A*π possunt *the other mss.*

---

[a] See p. 274, n. *a.*

not, you would be thought to have recognized a difficult point of law and to be arguing it. Not only, 29 then, must the renown of a military career be preferred to your formulas and processes, but even experience in speaking far and away surpasses your profession for political advancement. In my opinion most people at first strongly preferred my profession but when they could not achieve it slid down to yours for preference. They say of Greek musicians that those sing to the pipe who could not learn to sing to the lyre, and in just the same way we see that those who have not made orators find their way to the study of the law. Speaking means arduous toil, work of importance, capacity for the task, but powerful influence.[a] Clients come to you for a kind of well-being, but to orators for life itself. Furthermore, your legal opinions and pronouncements are often overturned by a speech and cannot be upheld without oratory to defend them. Had I achieved anything worthwhile in oratory, I should be speaking in its praise rather more hesitantly, but, as it is, I am not speaking of myself but of the great orators both past and present.

Let us agree, therefore, that there are two profes- 30 sions which can raise men to the highest level of distinction : that of a successful general and that of a good orator. The latter maintains the trappings of peace while the former averts the perils of war. Yet virtues of a different sort are valuable in their own right : justice, good faith, a sense of honour, moderation, and everyone recognizes, Servius, that you possess them in the fullest measure. I am now talking, however, about careers that lead to office, not about individuals' personal qualities. All those acti-

CICERO

Omnia ista nobis studia de manibus excutiuntur,
simul atque aliqui motus novus bellicum canere
coepit. Etenim, ut ait ingeniosus poeta et auctor
valde bonus, proeliis promulgatis " pellitur e medio "
non solum ista vestra verbosa simulatio prudentiae
sed etiam ipsa illa domina rerum, " sapientia ; vi
geritur res, spernitur orator " non solum odiosus in
dicendo ac loquax verum etiam " bonus ; horridus
miles amatur," vestrum vero studium totum iacet.
" Non ex iure manum consertum, sed mage ferro "
inquit " rem repetunt." Quod si ita est, cedat,
opinor, Sulpici, forum castris, otium militiae, stilus
gladio, umbra soli ; sit denique in civitate ea prima
res propter quam ipsa est civitas omnium princeps.

31 Verum haec Cato nimium nos nostris verbis magna
facere demonstrat et oblitos esse bellum illud omne
Mithridaticum cum mulierculis esse gestum. Quod
ego longe secus existimo, iudices ; deque eo pauca
disseram ; neque enim causa in hoc continetur. Nam
si omnia bella quae cum Graecis gessimus con-
temnenda sunt, derideatur de rege Pyrrho triumphus
M'. Curi, de Philippo T. Flaminini, de Aetolis M.
Fulvi, de rege Perse L. Pauli, de Pseudophilippo
Q. Metelli, de Corinthiis L. Mummi. Sin haec bella
gravissima victoriaeque eorum bellorum gratissimae

---

^a Quintus Ennius (239–169), the author of the *Annales*, an
epic recounting Roman history down to 171. These quota-
tions come from Book 8 of which the relevant portion is
preserved in Aulus Gellius, *Noctes Atticae* 20. 10. 4.

    pellitur e medio sapientia, vi geritur res ;
    spernitur orator bonus, horridus miles amatur.
    haut doctis dictis certantes nec maledictis
    miscent inter sese inimicitiam agitantes ;
    non ex iure manum consertum, sed magis ferro
    rem repetunt regnumque petunt, vadunt solida vi.

vities of yours are dashed from our hands the moment any fresh disturbance sounds the call to arms. In the words of a poet of genius [a] and a very reliable authority, at the declaration of war " there is banished " not only your wordy pretence of wisdom but also that mistress of the world " good sense ; force is in control, the orator is rejected " whether he is tiresome and long-winded or whether he is " a good speaker ; the rough soldier is courted," but your profession lies abandoned. " They do not go from court to join issue,[b] but rather," he says, " they seek redress with the sword." If this is so, Sulpicius, in my view, let the Forum give way to the camp, peace to war, the pen to the sword, shade to the heat of the sun ; in short, concede first place in the State to that profession which has given the State dominion over the world.

Cato, however, asserts that I am making too much 31 of this in my speech and have forgotten that the whole of that war against Mithridates [c] was only fought against a lot of women. I disagree entirely, gentlemen, but I shall speak only briefly on the matter since it is not relevant to my case. If we are to despise all the wars that we have ever fought against the Greeks, we must ridicule the triumphs of Manius Curius over King Pyrrhus, of Titus Flamininus over Philip, of Marcus Fulvius over the Aetolians, of Lucius Paulus over King Perses, of Quintus Metellus over the false Philip, of Lucius Mummius over Corinth.[d] But if these wars were major struggles

[b] See pp. 216-218.

[c] Mithridates VI Eupator, king of Pontus, against whom Rome fought three wars.

[d] Manius Curius Dentatus, consul in 290, 275 and 274, celebrated a triumph over the Samnites in 290 and over

fuerunt, cur Asiaticae nationes atque ille a te hostis
contemnitur ? Atqui ex veterum rerum monumentis
vel maximum bellum populum Romanum cum Anti-
ocho gessisse video ; cuius belli victor L. Scipio aequa
parta cum P. fratre gloria, quam laudem ille Africa
oppressa cognomine ipso prae se ferebat, eandem hic
32 sibi ex Asiae nomine adsumpsit. Quo quidem in bello
virtus enituit egregia M. Catonis, proavi tui ; quo ille,
cum esset, ut ego mihi statuo, talis qualem te esse
video, numquam cum Scipione[1] esset profectus, si
cum mulierculis bellandum arbitraretur. Neque vero
cum P. Africano senatus egisset ut legatus fratri
proficisceretur, cum ipse paulo ante Hannibale ex
Italia expulso, ex Africa eiecto, Carthagine oppressa
maximis periculis rem publicam liberasset, nisi illud
grave bellum et vehemens putaretur. Atqui si
diligenter quid Mithridates potuerit et quid effecerit
et qui vir fuerit consideraris, omnibus quibuscum[2]
populus Romanus bellum gessit hunc regem nimi-

[1] cum Glabrione *Klotz* (*cf. Livy* 37. 57) *; deleted by Ernesti.*
[2] omnibus quibuscum *Clark.* omnibus quibus regibus
cum Σ. omnibus quibuscum regibus *Aχψ.* omnibus
regibus quibuscum πφω.

Pyrrhus in 275. Titus Quinctius Flamininus, consul in 198,
won the Battle of Cynoscephalae in 197 and returned to Rome
in 194 to celebrate a triumph over Macedonia and Philip.
Marcus Fulvius Nobilior, consul in 189, returned from his
campaigns in 187 to celebrate a triumph over the Aetolians
and Cephallenians. Lucius Aemilius Paulus, consul in 168,
celebrated a triumph over King Perses and the Macedonians
whom he had defeated at the Battle of Pydna. Quintus
Caecilius Metellus Macedonicus recaptured Macedonia from
the pretender Andriscus and celebrated a triumph in 146.
Lucius Mummius, consul in 146, sacked Corinth and reduced
the other Achaean cities and in the following year celebrated
his triumph over them.
[a] Antiochus III, the Great, king of Syria. Born in 241,

and their victories hailed with great rejoicing, why do you despise the peoples of Asia and an enemy like Mithridates ? Yet I read in accounts of past history that perhaps the most serious war ever fought by the Roman people was that against Antiochus.[a] Lucius Scipio was the victor in that war in Asia and won from it as much glory as his brother Publius won from his victory in Africa ; for each took an additional name to honour his success [b] from the scene of his victory. In that war too your great-grandfather, Marcus Cato,[c] displayed exceptional bravery ; and since, as I conclude, he possessed the qualities that I now see in you, he would never have gone out with Scipio if he had thought that he would only have to fight against a lot of women. No more would the Senate ever have asked Publius Africanus to join his brother's staff shortly after he had expelled Hannibal from Italy, driven him from Africa, defeated Carthage and freed the Republic from desperate peril, if they had not considered it an important war involving hard fighting. Yet, if you consider carefully what Mithridates was capable of doing, what he actually achieved and the sort of man he was, you will surely rate this king more highly than any against whom

he succeeded to his kingdom in 223. In 196 he invaded Europe and was defeated by the Romans at Thermopylae in 191 and at Magnesia in 189. The Peace of Apamea in 188 brought the effective power of his kingdom to an end.

[b] Lucius Cornelius Scipio Asiaticus celebrated a triumph over Antiochus in 188 but was a lesser man than his brother Publius Cornelius Scipio Africanus Maior, the conqueror of Hannibal, who was his brother's *legatus* because, having been consul in 184, he could not constitutionally hold a magistracy again at this date.

[c] Marcus Porcius Cato Censorius (234–149) served with distinction at Thermopylae in 191.

rum antepones. Quem L. Sulla maximo et fortissimo exercitu, pugnax et acer et non rudis imperator, ut aliud nihil dicam, cum bello invectum totam in Asiam cum pace dimisit ; quem L. Murena, pater huiusce, vehementissime vigilantissimeque vexatum repressum magna ex parte, non oppressum reliquit ; qui rex sibi aliquot annis sumptis ad confirmandas rationes et copias belli tantum spe conatuque valuit ut se Oceanum cum Ponto, Sertori copias cum suis

33 coniuncturum putaret. Ad quod bellum duobus consulibus ita missis ut alter Mithridatem persequeretur, alter Bithyniam tueretur, alterius res et terra et mari calamitosae vehementer et opes regis et nomen auxerunt ; L. Luculli vero res tantae exstiterunt ut neque maius bellum commemorari possit neque maiore consilio et virtute gestum. Nam cum totius impetus belli ad Cyzicenorum moenia constitisset eamque urbem sibi Mithridates Asiae ianuam fore putasset qua effracta et revolsa tota pateret provincia, perfecta a Lucullo haec sunt omnia ut urbs fidelissimorum sociorum defenderetur et omnes copiae regis diuturnitate obsessionis consumerentur. Quid ? illam pugnam navalem ad Tenedum, cum contento cursu acerrimis ducibus hostium classis Italiam spe atque animis inflata peteret, mediocri certamine et parva dimicatione commissam arbitraris ? Mitto proelia, praetereo oppugnationes oppidorum ; expul-

---

[a] Under the terms of the Peace of Dardanus in 85.

[b] Cf. p. 169.

[c] Negotiations took place in the winter of 76/75 with Sertorius who was at this time holding Spain against the government at Rome.

[d] The consuls of 74, Lucius Licinius Lucullus and Marcus Aurelius Cotta.

the Roman people has ever fought. Lucius Sulla, the aggressive, spirited and, to put it no higher, not inexperienced commander of a large and valiant army, allowed him to depart in peace although he had carried war through the length and breadth of Asia.[a] Lucius Murena, my client's father, harried him with the utmost energy and persistence and left him largely contained but not crushed.[b] After spending a number of years building up his position and his forces, the king entertained such high hopes for the war he was undertaking that he expected to link the Atlantic with the Black Sea and the forces of Sertorius with his own.[c] Two consuls [d] were despatched to this war : one with orders to pursue Mithridates, the other to protect Bithynia. The latter's operations were disastrous on both land and sea and greatly enhanced the king's resources and prestige. Lucius Lucullus, however, conducted such extensive operations that I cannot think of a more important campaign or one conducted with greater skill and valour. Mithridates thought that Cyzicus would prove to be the gateway to Asia for him and therefore directed the whole force of his campaign against its walls in the belief that he had only to breach and raze them for the entire province to be at his mercy, but Lucullus' conduct of the operation ensured that the city of our loyalest allies was saved and all the king's forces frittered away on the protracted siege. Do you think that the naval battle off Tenedus, when a fleet of the enemy under spirited leadership was making for Italy under full sail with high hopes and confidence, was some half-hearted encounter or trivial clash ? I omit the battles, I pass over the storming of towns. Even after Mithridates

sus regno tandem aliquando tantum tamen consilio
atque auctoritate valuit ut se rege Armeniorum
adiuncto novis opibus copiisque renovarit. Ac si mihi
nunc de rebus gestis esset nostri exercitus impera-
torisque dicendum, plurima et maxima proelia com-
34 memorare possem; sed non id agimus. Hoc dico: Si
bellum hoc, si hic hostis, si ille rex contemnendus
fuisset, neque tanta cura senatus et populus Romanus
suscipiendum putasset neque tot annos gessisset
neque tanta gloria L. Lucullus,[1] neque vero eius belli
conficiendum exitum tanto studio populus Romanus
ad Cn. Pompeium detulisset. Cuius ex omnibus
pugnis, quae sunt innumerabiles, vel acerrima mihi
videtur illa quae cum rege commissa est et summa
contentione pugnata. Qua ex pugna cum se ille
eripuisset et Bosphorum confugisset quo exercitus
adire non posset, etiam in extrema fortuna et fuga
nomen tamen retinuit regium. Itaque ipso[2] Pompeius regno possesso ex omnibus oris ac notis sedibus
hoste pulso tamen tantum in unius anima posuit ut,
cum ipse[3] omnia quae tenuerat, adierat, speraverat,
victoria possideret, tamen non ante quam illum vita
expulit bellum confectum iudicarit. Hunc tu hostem,
Cato, contemnis quocum per tot annos tot proeliis tot
imperatores bella gesserunt, cuius expulsi et eiecti
vita tanti aestimata est ut morte eius nuntiata

---

[1] L. Lucullus *Angelius.* Luculli ψ^2. L. (*before a gap in*
χ) *the other* MSS.
[2] ipso MSS. ipse *w, Angelius, followed by Clark.*
[3] ipse *Clark.* ille MSS. omnia quae ille *Manutius.* illa
Zumpt.

---

[a] Tigranes.   [b] At Nicopolis in Pontus in 66.

was finally driven from his kingdom, he still had the resolution and the authority to enter into an alliance with the king of Armenia [a] and thus restore his position with fresh troops and resources. If I had now to recount the exploits of our army and its commander, I could mention many important battles ; but this is not my concern. I say only this : if this war, if this 34 enemy, if that king had really been contemptible, then the Senate and the Roman people would not have felt the need to plan their enterprise with such care, Lucius Lucullus would not have conducted it with such distinction for so many years, and the Roman people would not have been so eager to give Gnaeus Pompeius the task of bringing that war to an end. I think, too, that perhaps the fiercest of all his many battles is that bitter contest with the king.[b] Although Mithridates was in dire distress and a fugitive after he had escaped from this battle and taken refuge in the Bosporus [c] where our army could not reach him, even so he still kept the title of king. This is why Pompeius, although he had taken possession of his kingdom proper and had driven his foe from all his borders and all his known bases, attached such importance to the life of one man. Although he had himself won possession of all that the king had ever held, attacked or hoped to hold, Pompeius did not consider the war over until he had driven him from life itself. Is this, Cato, the enemy you despise ? An enemy with whom numerous generals have for years now fought many battles and wars ? An enemy whose very survival even as a fugitive and exile was so mportant that they did not think that the war was finally over until news of his

[c] The Cimmerian Bosporus, now the Straits of Kerch.

denique bellum confectum arbitrarentur ?[1] Hoc igitur in bello L. Murenam legatum fortissimi animi, summi consili, maximi laboris cognitum esse defendimus, et hanc eius operam non minus ad consulatum adipiscendum quam hanc nostram forensem industriam dignitatis habuisse.

35 At enim in praeturae petitione prior renuntiatus est Servius. Pergitisne vos tamquam ex syngrapha agere cum populo ut, quem locum semel honoris cuipiam dederit, eundem in[2] reliquis honoribus debeat ? Quod enim fretum, quem Euripum tot motus, tantas, tam varias habere putatis agitationes commutationesque fluctuum,[3] quantas perturbationes et quantos aestus habet ratio comitiorum ? Dies intermissus aut nox interposita saepe perturbat omnia, et totam opinionem parva non numquam commutat aura rumoris. Saepe etiam sine ulla aperta causa fit aliud atque existimaris, ut non numquam ita factum esse etiam populus admiretur, quasi vero non 36 ipse fecerit. Nihil est incertius volgo, nihil obscurius voluntate hominum, nihil fallacius ratione tota comitiorum. Quis L. Philippum summo ingenio, opera, gratia, nobilitate a M. Herennio superari posse arbitratus est ? quis Q. Catulum humanitate, sapientia, integritate antecellentem a Cn. Mallio ? quis M. Scaurum, hominem gravissimum, civem egregium, fortissimum senatorem, a Q. Maximo ? Non modo

---

[1] arbitrarentur *Zumpt.* arbitraretur ᴍss.

[2] in *added by Ernesti.*

[3] agitationes commutationesque fluctuum *Kayser.* agitationes quos fluctus ψ^2. agitationesque (que *omitted by* $\pi\phi\omega$) fluctuum *the other* ᴍss.

---

[a] The Euripus was the strait between the coast of Attica and the island of Euboea, notorious for its tricky currents.

[b] Lucius Philippus was unexpectedly defeated in the

death had been received ? Such, then, is the war in which, I maintain, Lucius Murena was recognized to be an officer of outstanding courage, high ability and tireless industry. Such, too, is the service which carried at least as much weight in winning the consulship as my labours here at the Bar.

" But in the election for the praetorship Servius 35 was declared elected first." Are you going to suggest to the people that it is obliged, as if under contract, to give a man in all subsequent magistracies the precedence that it has accorded him in one ? Can you think of any strait, any Channel,[a] that has the currents and variety of rough patches and changes of tide strong enough to match the upsets and the ebb and flow that accompany the working of elections ? The whole situation is often changed by having to break off for a day or by night intervening and the merest breath of a rumour sometimes changes everyone's views. Often, too, for no apparent reason the turn of events takes you by surprise and at times even the people is amazed at a result as if it were not itself responsible. Nothing is more fickle than 36 people in a crowd, nothing harder to discover than how men intend to vote, nothing trickier than the whole way in which elections work. Who thought that a man of Lucius Philippus' exceptional talents, public service, high esteem and nobility could be defeated by Marcus Herennius ? That a man of Quintus Catulus' culture, intelligence and integrity could be defeated by Gnaeus Mallius ? That a man of Marcus Scaurus' influence, outstanding qualities as a citizen and distinction as a senator could be defeated by Quintus Maximus ?[b] All these defeats

consular elections for 93 by Marcus Herennius, a *novus*

horum nihil ita fore putatum est sed, ne cum esset
factum quidem, qua re ita factum esset intellegi
potuit. Nam, ut tempestates saepe certo aliquo caeli
signo commoventur, saepe improviso nulla ex certa
ratione obscura aliqua ex causa concitantur, sic in
hac comitiorum tempestate populari saepe intellegas quo signo commota sit, saepe ita obscura causa[1]
37 est ut casu excitata esse videatur. Sed tamen si est
reddenda ratio, duae res vehementer in praetura
desideratae sunt quae ambae in consulatu multum
Murenae profuerunt, una exspectatio muneris quae
et rumore non nullo et studiis sermonibusque com-
petitorum creverat, altera quod ei quos in provincia
ac legatione omni[2] et liberalitatis et virtutis suae
testis habuerat nondum decesserant.[3] Horum utrumque ei fortuna ad consulatus petitionem reservavit.
Nam et L. Luculli exercitus qui ad triumphum con-
venerat idem comitiis L. Murenae praesto fuit, et
munus amplissimum quod petitio praeturae desidera-
38 rat praetura restituit. Num tibi haec parva videntur
adiumenta et subsidia consulatus, voluntas militum,
quaeque[4] cum per se valet multitudine, cum apud suos
gratia, tum vero in consule declarando multum etiam
apud universum populum Romanum auctoritatis habet, suffragatio militaris ? Imperatores enim comitiis
consularibus, non verborum interpretes deliguntur.
Qua re gravis est illa oratio : " Me saucium recrea-

---

[1] causa *added by Clark.*
[2] omni Σ. omnis *the other* mss.
[3] exercitum Luculli significat *follows in the* mss. ; *deleted
by* ψ².   [4] quaeque *Clark.* quae mss.

---

homo ; Catulus was defeated three times ; by Gaius Atilius
Serranus for 106, by Gnaeus Mallius, another *novus homo*,
for 105, and by Gaius Flavius Fimbria for 104 ; Marcus

were unexpected and could not even be explained when they had occurred. Storms are frequently raised by a particular constellation, but often break unexpectedly for some obscure reason that defies explanation. In the same way you may often recognize in elections the sign responsible for the storm brought on by the voters, but the cause is often so obscure that it appears to have blown up quite by chance. But if I have got to provide an explanation, 37 Murena badly missed two advantages in his campaign for the praetorship which helped him greatly for the consulship. One was the expectation of games which had been fanned by gossip and the ridicule of his fellow candidates' campaign; the other was the fact that those who had witnessed his generosity and ability in the province and throughout his military command had not yet returned to Rome. Both these advantages were kept by fortune for his campaign for the consulship. The army of Lucius Lucullus which had assembled for his triumph was at hand to help Lucius Murena in the election, and his praetorship supplied the magnificent games whose absence handicapped his campaign for that praetorship. Do 38 you really think that this help and assistance for the consulship is unimportant? I mean the goodwill of the soldiers and their voting power which derives its strength from their very number, from their influence with their friends and, most important of all, from the great weight that they carry with the whole people of Rome in electing a consul. Generals, not interpreters of words, are chosen at consular elections. Hence, talk like this is important: " He saved my

Aemilius Scaurus was defeated by Quintus Fabius Maximus Eburnus for 116.

vit, me praeda donavit; hoc duce castra cepimus,
signa contulimus; numquam iste plus militi laboris
imposuit quam sibi sumpsit ipse, cum fortis tum
etiam felix." Hoc quanti putas esse ad famam hominum ac voluntatem ? Etenim, si tanta illis comitiis
religio est ut adhuc semper omen valuerit praeroga-
tivum, quid mirum est in hoc felicitatis famam ser-
monemque valuisse ?

Sed si haec leviora ducis quae sunt gravissima et
hanc urbanam suffragationem militari anteponis, noli
ludorum huius elegantiam et scaenae magnificentiam
tam valde contemnere ; quae huic admodum profuerunt. Nam quid ego dicam populum ac volgus
imperitorum ludis magno opere delectari ? Minus
est mirandum. Quamquam huic causae id satis est ;
sunt enim populi ac multitudinis comitia. Qua re, si
populo ludorum magnificentia voluptati est, non est
mirandum eam L. Murenae apud populum profuisse.
39 Sed si nosmet ipsi qui et ab delectatione communi
negotiis impedimur et in ipsa occupatione delecta-
tiones alias multas habere possumus, ludis tamen
oblectamur et ducimur, quid tu admirere de multi-
40 tudine indocta ? L. Otho, vir fortis, meus necessarius,
equestri ordini restituit non solum dignitatem sed

***

ᵃ See Appendix A, p. 563. Cicero describes the *praerogativa* as the *omen comitiorum* in *de divinatione* 1. 103 and
2. 83. See L. R. Taylor, *Roman Voting Assemblies* 143, n.
30.

ᵇ Lucius Roscius Otho, one of the tribunes of 67, had
carried a law to reserve for the knights the front fourteen
rows in the theatre. T. P. Wiseman, " The Definition of
Eques Romanus," *Historia* 19 (1970), 80 explains this
passage as referring to a restoration of their dignity to the
real equestrian order. E. Badian, *Publicans and Sinners* 144,
n. 10 makes the valid objection that if the law conferred

life when I was wounded ; he gave me a share of the booty ; he was our leader when we took the camp and engaged the enemy ; he never asked a soldier to endure more hardship than himself ; he was lucky as well as brave." How important do you think this is for winning a reputation with men and their support ? If, moreover, the religious feeling of elections has always been so strong that the votes of the first century have been regarded as an omen,[a] there is no cause for surprise that Murena's reputation for luck and talk about it had a powerful effect.

But if you think that these extremely important considerations are quite trivial and attach more weight to the votes of civilians than to soldiers', do not treat with such complete contempt the fine arrangements for his games and the splendour of his show which helped him so much. Need I mention that games have a great attraction for the people and the ignorant herd ? There is nothing less surprising. Yet that is enough for my case ; elections are decided by the people and the masses. If, then, the splendour of games has such an attraction for the people, it is not surprising that it won their support for Lucius Murena. If we, who are able to derive many 39 pleasures of a different kind from our work which keeps us from the entertainments enjoyed by the people, are delighted and attracted by games, why be surprised at the attraction they hold for the ignorant masses ? My close friend, the gallant 40 Lucius Otho,[b] restored to the equestrian order both

dignity on the *equites* in the strict sense and left out the *tribuni aerarii* who were calling themselves *equites*, then Cicero should have had more sense than to try to please one third of his jury at the cost of offending another third. Otho

etiam voluptatem. Itaque lex haec quae ad ludos
pertinet est omnium gratissima, quod honestissimo
ordini cum splendore fructus quoque iucunditatis est
restitutus. Qua re delectant homines, mihi crede,
ludi etiam illos qui dissimulant, non solum eos qui
fatentur ; quod ego in mea petitione sensi. Nam nos
quoque habuimus scaenam competitricem. Quod si
ego qui trinos ludos aedilis feceram tamen Antoni
ludis commovebar, tibi qui casu nullos feceras nihil
huius istam ipsam quam inrides argenteam scaenam
adversatam putas ?

41 Sed haec sane sint paria omnia, sit par forensis
opera militari,[1] militaris suffragatio urbanae, sit idem
magnificentissimos et nullos umquam fecisse ludos ;
quid ? in ipsa praetura nihilne existimas inter tuam
et huius sortem interfuisse ? Huius sors ea fuit quam
omnes tui necessarii tibi optabamus, iuris dicundi ;
in qua gloriam conciliat magnitudo negoti, gratiam
aequitatis largitio ; qua in sorte sapiens praetor qualis
hic fuit offensionem vitat aequabilitate decernendi,
benivolentiam adiungit lenitate audiendi. Egregia
et ad consulatum apta provincia in qua laus aequitatis, integritatis, facilitatis ad extremum ludorum
42 voluptate concluditur. Quid tua sors ? Tristis, atrox,

---

[1] militari *added by Halm.*

---

was restoring a privilege to the *ordo* that had in all likelihood,
since at Rome privileges indicated power, been removed by
Sulla as part of his policy of stripping the *equites* of political
power.

[a] In 69 ; dedicated to Ceres, to Liber and Libera and to
Flora. Gaius Antonius Hybrida, Cicero's colleague in the
consulship, had given magnificent games when *praetor
urbanus* in 66.

[b] Murena drew the lot for the *praetura urbana* ; Sulpicius
that for the *quaestio de peculatu.*

their position and their pleasure. This law dealing with the games is the most popular of all because it has restored to that illustrious order both its distinction and the enjoyment of pleasure. Games, then, do give men pleasure, believe me, and not only those who admit it, but those too who pretend that they do not ; a fact that I observed in my own election campaign. I too had a stage-show in competition with mine ; and if I was dismayed at Antonius' games even after I had given three sets of games as aedile,[a] do you think that you were not put at a disadvantage by that silvered show of Murena which you ridicule when, as it happened, you had never given any games yourself ?

Let us agree, however, that all these factors are of 41 equal weight, that a lawyer's services are as important as a soldier's, civilians' votes as important as soldiers', that it is the same thing to have given the most splendid games as never to have given any at all. Then do you think that in the praetorship itself there was nothing between the provinces assigned by the lot to each of you ?[b] Murena was allotted what all your friends wanted for you, civil jurisdiction, a field in which the importance of the business confers distinction and the administration of justice in the spirit of the law wins gratitude. In this office a wise praetor, such as he, avoids unpopularity by the fairness of his decisions and creates goodwill by the courtesy with which he hears cases. It is a distinguished rôle and one suited to a candidate for the consulship because the reputation won by his impartiality, incorruptibility and affability is, to crown all, rounded off with delight at his games. What was your lot ? Dismal and depressing, the 42

quaestio peculatus ex altera parte lacrimarum et squaloris, ex altera plena accusatorum[1] atque indicum ; cogendi iudices inviti, retinendi contra voluntatem ; scriba damnatus, ordo totus alienus ; Sullana gratificatio reprehensa, multi viri fortes et prope pars civitatis offensa est ; lites severe aestimatae ; cui placet obliviscitur, cui dolet meminit. Postremo tu in provinciam ire noluisti. Non possum id in te reprehendere quod in me ipso et praetore et consule probavi. Sed tamen L. Murenae provincia multas bonas gratias cum optima existimatione attulit. Habuit proficiscens dilectum in Umbria ; dedit ei facultatem res publica liberalitatis, qua usus multas sibi tribus quae municipiis Umbriae conficiuntur adiunxit. Ipse autem in Gallia ut nostri homines desperatas iam pecunias exigerent aequitate diligentiaque perfecit. Tu interea Romae scilicet amicis praesto fuisti ; fateor ; sed tamen illud cogita non nullorum amicorum studia minui solere in eos a quibus provincias contemni intellegunt.

---

[1] accusatorum *Novák.* catenarum *mss.* calumniarum *Richter.*

---

[a] For the importance of the order, see p. 154, n. *c.*

[b] The property allotted by Sulla to his veterans who might now be attacked in the courts by dispossessed owners or political enemies.

[c] *Cf.* Cicero, *pro Plancio* 64–66 and p. xxxvii, n. *f.*

[d] The governor of a province was authorized by the Senate to hold a levy on his way to his province to provide *supplementa* to bring the standing army in the province up to strength and to replace losses by death, sickness or retirement. The recruitment of troops had provided other generous commanders besides Murena with grateful clients. Umbria, however, brought him particularly valuable support owing to the multiplicity of the tribes in the area. He no

embezzlement court; on one side nothing but tears and rags, on the other nothing but prosecutors and informers; a reluctant panel of jurors who have to be summoned to attend and kept against their will; a decision against a clerk and the whole order is up in arms against you *a*; a criticism of Sulla's grants *b* and many stout veterans, almost a class in the State, are your enemies; heavy damages awarded and the plaintiff forgets but the defendant remembers. Finally, you refused to go out to a province. I cannot criticize you for a course I took in my own praetorship and consulship.*c* His province nevertheless won many tokens of favour and a distinguished reputation for Lucius Murena. On his way to it he held a levy in Umbria.*d* The political situation enabled him to display a generosity which won him the support of the many tribes which are composed of the towns of Umbria. In Gaul by his justice and untiring efforts he personally enabled our men to recover sums already written off.*e* You in the meantime were at Rome and of course, I agree, were helping your friends; but just reflect that the enthusiasm of some friends tends to grow weaker for those whom they see spurning provinces.

doubt showed favouritism of some sort in the levy, perhaps to the richer inhabitants whose votes would count for more in elections. *Cf.* R. E. Smith, *Service in the Post-Marian Roman Army* 47; L. R. Taylor, *The Voting Districts of the Roman Republic* 114-115; T. P. Wiseman, *New Men in the Roman Senate 139 B.C.–A.D. 14* 44 and 139.

e Moneylending was the main activity of the Roman businessmen in provinces. Others were in business in law and banking. Murena appears to have looked after equestrian interests in his province, a concern that would have drawn him to Cicero and his equestrian protégés. See p. 181.

For identification of the province, see p. 170, n. *h*.

43 Et quoniam ostendi, iudices, parem dignitatem ad consulatus petitionem, disparem fortunam provincialium negotiorum in Murena atque in Sulpicio fuisse, dicam iam apertius in quo meus necessarius fuerit inferior, Servius, et ea dicam vobis audientibus amisso iam tempore quae ipsi soli re integra saepe dixi. Petere consulatum nescire te, Servi, persaepe tibi dixi; et in eis rebus ipsis quas te magno et forti animo et agere et dicere videbam tibi solitus sum dicere magis te fortem accusatorem mihi videri quam sapientem candidatum. Primum accusandi terrores et minae quibus tu cotidie uti solebas sunt fortis viri, sed et populi opinionem a spe[1] adipiscendi avertunt et amicorum studia debilitant. Nescio quo pacto semper hoc fit—neque in uno aut altero animadversum est sed iam in pluribus—simul atque candidatus accusationem meditari visus est, ut honorem desperasse vi-

44 deatur. Quid ergo? acceptam iniuriam persequi non placet? Immo vehementer placet; sed aliud tempus est petendi, aliud persequendi. Petitorem ego, praesertim consulatus, magna spe, magno animo, magnis copiis et in forum et in campum deduci volo. Non placet mihi inquisitio candidati, praenuntia repulsae, non testium potius quam suffragatorum comparatio, non minae magis quam blanditiae, non denuntiatio[2] potius quam persalutatio, praesertim cum iam hoc novo more omnes fere domos omnium concursent et ex voltu candidatorum coniecturam

---

[1] aspem . . . Σ; *Clark suggests* a spe mag[istratum].
[2] denuntiatio *Bake.* declamatio *mss.*

Now that I have shown, gentlemen, that **Murena** **43**
and Sulpicius had an equal claim to the consulship,
but had not been equally fortunate in their spheres
of office, I shall say more explicitly why my friend
Servius was the weaker candidate and I shall tell him
in your hearing, now that it is too late, what I often
told him in private before the election was decided.
I repeatedly told you, Servius, that you did not know
how to conduct a campaign for the consulship, and I
was always telling you that the spirit and energy that
you brought to all you said and did made you look to
me more like a vigorous prosecutor than an astute
candidate. Firstly, the warnings of prosecution and
the threats that you were uttering daily may prove
your energy but they stop people thinking that you
expect to win office and they weaken your friends'
support. Somehow or other it always happens—not
just once or twice but on most occasions—that as
soon as a candidate seems to be contemplating a
prosecution men think that he has given up all hope
of office. All right; but do I not approve of a man **44**
seeking satisfaction for an injury he has received?
Of course I do, but do not start proceedings when
you are a candidate for the consulship. I like a
candidate, particularly one for the consulship, to be
escorted to the Forum and to the Campus Martius
with high hopes, great enthusiasm and huge crowds.
I do not like a candidate to be gathering evidence—a
harbinger of defeat—, to be collecting witnesses
rather than voters, uttering threats rather than
compliments, giving notices rather than greetings to
all comers, particularly in view of this new practice of
running in a crowd from house to house and inferring
from the expression of the candidates how confident

faciant quantum quisque animi et facultatis habere
45 videatur. " Videsne tu illum tristem, demissum ?
iacet, diffidit, abiecit hastas." Serpit hic rumor.
" Scis tu illum accusationem cogitare, inquirere in
competitores, testis quaerere ? Alium fac iam,[1]
quoniam sibi hic ipse desperat." Eius modi rumoribus[2] candidatorum amici intimi debilitantur, studia
deponunt ; aut certam[3] rem abiciunt aut suam operam
et gratiam iudicio et accusationi reservant.

  Accedit eodem ut etiam ipse candidatus totum
animum atque omnem curam operam diligentiamque
suam in petitione non possit ponere. Adiungitur
enim accusationis cogitatio, non parva res sed nimirum omnium maxima. Magnum est enim te comparare ea quibus possis hominem e civitate, praesertim
non inopem neque infirmum, exturbare, qui et per se
et per suos et vero etiam per alienos defendatur.
Omnes enim ad pericula propulsanda concurrimus et
qui non aperte inimici sumus etiam alienissimis in
capitis periculis amicissimorum officia et studia
46 praestamus. Qua re ego expertus et petendi et
defendendi et accusandi molestiam sic intellexi in
petendo studium esse acerrimum, in defendendo
officium, in accusando laborem. Itaque sic statuo
fieri nullo modo posse ut idem accusationem et
petitionem consulatus diligenter adornet atque in-
struat. Unum sustinere pauci possunt, utrumque
nemo. Tu cum te de curriculo petitionis deflexisses

[1] fac iam ω. faci iam *the other* MSS. faciam *editiones Veneta et Romana.* [2] rumoribus *added by Clark.*
[3] certam ψ², *editio Romana.* testam *the other* MSS. *Numerous other suggestions have been made.*

[a] Roman elections had a strong " bandwagon " element
in them and it worked both ways.

each is and what appear to be his chances of success.
" Do you see him sad and dejected ? He's down, he 45
has given up, he has thrown away his weapons." The
rumour spreads. " Do you know ? He's thinking
of prosecuting, he's investigating his fellow candidates, he's looking for witnesses. Vote for another
candidate ; he has given up hope." Close friends of
candidates are unnerved by this sort of rumour and
their enthusiasm cools. They either abandon the
campaign as already decided or keep their services
and support for the prosecution and trial.[a]

A further result is that even the candidate himself
cannot devote all his attention, all his care and all his
unremitting effort to the campaign. He is also working on the plans for his prosecution, and this is of
course his main concern and no mere side line. It is a
big undertaking for you to collect the evidence with
which to drive a man into exile, especially a man who
is not friendless and without support and one who is
defended by his own efforts, by his friends and even
by strangers. We all rush to repel danger and those
of us who are not open enemies fulfil the obligations
and good offices of the closest friendship even in the
case of total strangers when their civil rights are in
danger. Knowing from experience how much work 46
is involved in fighting an election or conducting a
defence or a prosecution, I have observed that in an
election the driving force is the spirit of partisanship,
in a defence the sense of obligation and in a prosecution sheer hard work. It is, therefore, my view that it
is quite impossible for a man simultaneously to prepare and organize with due care both a prosecution
and a campaign for the consulship. Few can tackle
one, no man both. You thought that, when you had

animumque ad accusandum transtulisses, existimasti
te utrique negotio satis facere posse. Vehementer
errasti. Quis enim dies fuit, postea quam in istam
accusandi denuntiationem ingressus es, quem tu non
totum in ista ratione consumpseris ? Legem ambitus
flagitasti, quae tibi non deerat ; erat enim severissime
scripta Calpurnia. Gestus est mos et voluntati et
dignitati tuae. Sed tota illa lex accusationem tuam,
si haberes nocentem reum, fortasse armasset ; peti-
47 tioni vero refragata est. Poena gravior in plebem
tua voce efflagitata est ; commoti animi tenuiorum.
Exsilium in nostrum ordinem ; concessit senatus pos-
tulationi tuae, sed non libenter duriorem fortuna[1]
communi condicionem te auctore constituit. Morbi
excusationi poena addita est ; voluntas offensa multorum quibus aut contra valetudinis commodum labo-
randum est aut incommodo morbi etiam ceteri vitae
fructus relinquendi. Quid ergo ? haec quis tulit ?
Is qui auctoritati senatus, voluntati tuae paruit,
denique is tulit cui minime proderant. Illa quidem[2]
quae mea summa voluntate senatus frequens re-
pudiavit mediocriter adversata tibi esse existimas ?
Confusionem suffragiorum flagitasti, †praerogatio-

---

[1] fortuna *Nisbet, Classical Review 12 (1962), 312.* fortunae
MSS.   [2] quidem *added by Clark.*

---

[a] See p. 174.   [b] See p. 175, n. *a.*
[c] The text is printed as a *locus desperatus* because no
acceptable restoration has yet been made. Sulpicius'
proposal was that the voting groups should vote in an order
determined by lot. This would diminish the advantage of the
higher census classes and the privileged position of the
praerogativa which made it such a target for bribery. There
appears to be a reference to the *praerogativa* in the corrupt
praerogationum, but the only *lex Manilia* of which we have
any knowledge is that *de libertinorum suffragiis* which was

turned aside from the race for office and had transferred your attention to a prosecution, you could pay proper attention to both. How very wrong you were! Was there a single day after you had set in motion the process of your prosecution that was not entirely taken up with putting your plan into effect? You demanded a law against bribery; but you did not need it, for you already had the stringent provisions of Calpurnius' law available.[a] Your wishes and your standing were deferred to. That law as a whole would perhaps have put teeth into your prosecution, if you had a guilty defendant; but in fact it wrecked your campaign. Your voice demanded a heavier 47 penalty for the commons; the anger of the poorer people was aroused. There was to be exile for our order; the Senate yielded to your demand although reluctant to impose at your request a harsher fate than the common lot. A penalty was attached to the plea of ill-health[b]; this lost the good-will of many who either have to exert themselves to the detriment of their health or in addition to suffering ill-health have to forgo their remaining rewards in life. Who was it, then, that secured the passage of these provisions? A man who obeyed the authority of the Senate and your wishes, the man, in short, who stood to get least from them. Do you think that the other provisions which a crowded Senate rejected at my express request were not particularly damaging to your interests? You demanded a random order of voting for the centuries[c] ... of Manilius' law, the

passed at the end of 67 and was promptly annulled. It could be said, in a rhetorical passage such as this, to seek to achieve " the equal distribution of influence, prestige and voting-power "—it proposed that freedmen should be dis-

num legis Maniliae†,[1] aequationem gratiae, dignitatis, suffragiorum. Graviter homines honesti atque in suis vicinitatibus[2] et municipiis gratiosi tulerunt a tali viro esse pugnatum ut omnes et dignitatis et gratiae gradus tollerentur. Idem editicios iudices esse voluisti, ut odia occulta civium quae tacitis nunc discordiis continentur in fortunas optimi cuiusque erumperent.

48 Haec omnia tibi accusandi viam muniebant, adipiscendi obsaepiebant.

Atque ex omnibus illa plaga est iniecta petitioni tuae non tacente me maxima, de qua ab homine ingeniosissimo et copiosissimo, Q. Hortensio, multa gravissime dicta sunt. Quo etiam mihi durior locus est dicendi datus ut, cum ante me et ille dixisset et vir summa dignitate et diligentia et facultate dicendi, M. Crassus, ego in extremo non partem aliquam agerem causae sed de tota re dicerem quod mihi videretur. Itaque in isdem rebus fere versor et quoad possum, iudices, occurro vestrae satietati.

Sed tamen, Servi, quam te securim putas iniecisse petitioni tuae, cum populum Romanum in eum metum adduxisti ut pertimesceret ne consul Catilina fieret, dum tu accusationem comparares deposita

49 atque abiecta petitione? Etenim te inquirere vide-

---

1 praerogationum MSS. (ψ¹). prorogationem ψ², *editiones Veneta et Romana.* perrogationem *Mommsen.*
2 vicinitatibus Σ; *cf. commentariolum petitionis 24.* civitatibus *the other* MSS.

---

tributed throughout all the tribes. Alternatively, there may have been a proposal by Manilius to abolish the *praerogativa* that never reached the statute book and for which we have no evidence. See Appendix A, p. 564.

ᵃ The system proposed by Sulpicius had the prosecution select one hundred and twenty-five *equites* and *tribuni aerarii* from the register of jurors. The defence then re-

equal distribution of influence, prestige, and voting-power. Men of standing, influential in their neigh-bourhoods and towns, objected to a man such as you fighting to remove all distinctions of prestige and influence. You also wanted the jury to be your own choice, so that the secret enmities of citizens which are now confined to silent disagreements might be let loose upon the fortunes of all our finest men.[a] All this paved your way to a prosecution but blocked 48 your path to office.

I said at the time that this was the greatest blow of all struck at your campaign, and my talented and eloquent friend, Quintus Hortensius, has spoken about it at length and with authority. The position of my speech makes my task even harder than his, for both he and Marcus Crassus, a man of immense prestige, conscientiousness and eloquence,[b] have spoken before me. I am speaking last and am not dealing with any one part of the case but am saying what I feel is required by it as a whole. I am there-fore concerned for the most part with the same topics as they but I am doing my best, gentlemen, not to bore you.

But what sort of a hatchet-blow, Servius, do you think that you struck at your campaign when you frightened the Roman people so badly that they were afraid that Catiline would be elected consul while you were jettisoning and abandoning your campaign and making preparations for your prosecution? They saw you making inquiries, despondent your- 49

jected seventy-five. See *pro Plancio* 41 and *cf.* p. 406, n. *a.* The personal antagonisms would emerge out of the public rejection of seventy-five individuals by the defence.

[b] *Cf.* p. 180.

bant, tristem ipsum, maestos amicos; observationes, testificationes, seductiones testium, secessiones subscriptorum animadvertebant, quibus rebus certe ipsi candidatorum voltus[1] obscuriores videri solent; Catilinam interea alacrem atque laetum, stipatum choro iuventutis, vallatum indicibus atque sicariis, inflatum cum spe militum tum[2] conlegae mei, quem ad modum dicebat ipse, promissis, circumfluentem colonorum Arretinorum et Faesulanorum exercitu; quam turbam dissimillimo ex genere distinguebant homines perculsi Sullani temporis calamitate. Voltus erat ipsius plenus furoris, oculi sceleris, sermo adrogantiae, sic ut ei iam exploratus et domi conditus consulatus videretur. Murenam contemnebat, Sulpicium accusatorem suum numerabat non competitorem; ei vim 50 denuntiabat, rei publicae minabatur. Quibus rebus qui timor bonis omnibus iniectus sit quantaque desperatio rei publicae, si ille factus esset, nolite a me commoneri velle; vosmet ipsi vobiscum recordamini. Meministis enim, cum illius nefarii gladiatoris voces percrebruissent quas habuisse in contione domestica dicebatur, cum miserorum fidelem defensorem negasset inveniri posse nisi eum qui ipse miser esset; integrorum et fortunatorum promissis saucios et miseros credere non oportere; qua re qui consumpta replere, erepta reciperare vellent, spectarent quid ipse deberet, quid possideret, quid auderet; minime timidum et valde calamitosum esse oportere eum qui

---

[1] voltus *added by editio Veneta.*
[2] militum tum ψ^2. militum *the other MSS.*

---

[a] See p. xxxvi, n. *b.*
[b] See *in Catilinam* 2. 20, p. 88 and *pro Sulla* 60 f., p. 372. For the Sullan allotments, see P. A. Brunt, *Italian Manpower 225 B.C.–A.D. 14* 300-312.

self and your friends deep in gloom, they noted the investigations, the depositions, the confidential chats with witnesses, the conferences with juniors, and of course these all tend to make the very features of candidates less familiar. At the same time they watched Catiline, brisk and cheerful, accompanied by his troop of youths, entrenched behind informers and assassins, buoyant with the hopes of his soldiers and the promises which he said my colleague had made to him,[a] surrounded by an army of colonists from Arretium and Faesulae,[b] a throng with here and there men of a very different type, victims of disaster at the time of Sulla. The frenzy of his expression, the crime in his eyes, the insolence of his talk were such that the consulship seemed to have been already confirmed as his and stored ready for him at his home. He despised Murena and regarded Sulpicius more as a prosecutor on his behalf than as a rival. He threatened him with violence, he menaced the State. Do not ask me to remind you of the fear that was 50 inspired in all loyal citizens by these events or the despair that overtook the Republic at the prospect of his election. Recall it for yourselves. You remember how the report of a speech which that evil cut-throat was said to have made in a meeting at his home spread throughout the city: that the only trust-worthy protector of the poor able to be found was poor himself; that broken men and those down on their luck should not trust the promises of the prosperous and successful; that those who wished to replace what they had spent and to recover what had been taken from them had only to consider the debts, the scanty possessions, the audacity that were his ; that the man who was to be the standard-bearer and

51 esset futurus dux et signifer calamitosorum. Tum
igitur, his rebus auditis, meministis fieri senatus consultum referente me ne postero die comitia habe-
rentur, ut de his rebus in senatu agere possemus.
Itaque postridie frequenti senatu Catilinam excitavi
atque eum de his rebus iussi, si quid vellet, quae ad
me adlatae essent dicere. Atque ille, ut semper fuit
apertissimus, non se purgavit sed indicavit atque
induit. Tum enim dixit duo corpora esse rei publicae,
unum debile infirmo capite, alterum firmum sine
capite; huic, si ita de se meritum esset, caput se vivo
non defuturum. Congemuit senatus frequens neque
tamen satis severe pro rei indignitate decrevit; nam
partim ideo fortes in decernendo non erant, quia
nihil timebant, partim, quia omnia.[1] Erupit[2] e senatu
triumphans gaudio quem omnino vivum illinc exire
non oportuerat, praesertim cum idem ille in eodem
ordine paucis diebus ante Catoni, fortissimo viro,
iudicium minitanti ac denuntianti respondisset, si
quod esset in suas fortunas incendium excitatum, id
52 se non aqua sed ruina restincturum. His tum rebus
commotus et quod homines iam tum coniuratos cum
gladiis in campum deduci a Catilina sciebam, descendi
in campum cum firmissimo praesidio fortissimorum
virorum et cum illa lata insignique lorica, non quae
me tegeret—etenim sciebam Catilinam non latus aut

[1] omnia *Clark.* timebant *mss.* timebant nimium *Müller.*
[2] *There appears to be a word or words missing before*
Erupit *Clark.* Atque erupit *Mommsen.*

---

[a] There is no evidence that it was unconstitutional for the
comitia to meet when the Senate was sitting, but simultaneous
meetings would be inconvenient if not impossible since both
required the presence of magistrates. A. K. Michels, *The
Calendar of the Roman Republic* 44.
[b] *Cf. in Catilinam* 1. 30, p. 62.

leader of ruined men should himself be the least timid and the most completely ruined. You recall, 51 too, that on receipt of this news I then proposed and carried a decree of the Senate to stop the election on the following day so that we could debate these events in the Senate.[a] On the next day, then, in a crowded Senate I called upon Catiline to rise and invited him to give any explanation he wished about the matters which had been reported to me. He, frank as ever, instead of justifying himself, incriminated and entangled himself. For he then said that the State had two bodies, one frail with a weak head, the other strong but with no head at all; and provided that it showed itself worthy of his leadership this body would never go short of a head so long as he was alive. There was a groan from the crowded Senate but it still did not pass a decree of the severity merited by his outrageous speech. Some senators were disinclined to take firm measures because they saw nothing to fear, others because they were afraid of everything.[b] Catiline dashed from the Senate in triumphant delight although he should never have left alive, not least because a few days previously he had in this same Senate told the gallant Cato who was threatening to bring him to court that he would put out any fire set to his property not with water but by destroying everything. Stirred then by these 52 events and by the knowledge that men who had at that time already formed a conspiracy were being led by Catiline to the Campus Martius with swords in their hands, I too went to the Campus Martius with a strong bodyguard of valiant men and displayed that broad cuirass, not to protect myself—for I knew that it was Catiline's practice to thrust at the head or

ventrem sed caput et collum solere petere—verum ut
omnes boni animadverterent et, cum in metu et
periculo consulem viderent, id quod est factum, ad
opem praesidiumque concurrerent. Itaque cum te,
Servi, remissiorem in petendo putarent, Catilinam et
spe et cupiditate inflammatum viderent, omnes qui
illam ab re publica pestem depellere cupiebant ad
53 Murenam se statim contulerunt. Magna est autem
comitiis consularibus repentina voluntatum inclinatio,
praesertim cum incubuit ad virum bonum et multis
aliis adiumentis petitionis ornatum. Qui cum
honestissimo patre atque maioribus, modestissima
adulescentia, clarissima legatione, praetura probata
in iure, grata in munere, ornata in provincia petisset
diligenter, et ita petisset ut neque minanti cederet
neque cuiquam minaretur, huic mirandum est magno
adiumento Catilinae subitam spem consulatus adipiscendi fuisse ?

54   Nunc mihi tertius ille locus est relictus orationis, de
ambitus criminibus, perpurgatus ab eis qui ante me
dixerunt, a me, quoniam ita Murena voluit, retrac-
tandus ; quo in loco C.[1] Postumo, familiari meo,
ornatissimo viro, de divisorum indiciis et de deprehen-
sis pecuniis, adulescenti ingenioso et bono, Ser.
Sulpicio, de equitum centuriis, M. Catoni, homini in
omni virtute excellenti, de ipsius accusatione, de
55 senatus consulto, de re publica respondebo. Sed

---

[1] C. *added by Zumpt.* P. *added by Halm.*

---

[a] For the order in which the centuries of the knights
voted, see Appendix A, p. 563.

neck and not at the flank or stomach—but for all loyal citizens to observe and, seeing the fear and danger in which their consul was placed, to rush to his help and defence ; and this is what they did. Thinking, Servius, that you were not active enough in your campaign and seeing Catiline ablaze with hope and lust for power, all who wished to drive that plague from the Republic immediately turned to Murena. In a consular election a sudden movement 53 of opinion is important, particularly when it has swung to a good man whose candidature has many other sources of support. Is it surprising that a candidate who had fought a vigorous campaign backed by a distinguished father and forebears, by a blameless youth, by illustrious service as a lieutenant-general, by a praetorship in which his administration of justice won him acclaim, his games popularity and his conduct in his province distinction, a candidate who had fought it without either threatening anyone or himself yielding to threats, is it surprising that he received great assistance from Catiline's sudden hope of winning the consulship ?

It now remains for me to deal with the third topic 54 of my speech—the charges of bribery. It has been fully dealt with by those who have spoken before me but I must accede to Murena's wish and examine it again. In what follows I shall reply to my distinguished friend, Gaius Postumus, on the disclosures of the financial agents and the sums of money seized. I shall also reply to the talented young Servius Sulpicius on the centuries of the knights,[a] and to Marcus Cato, that paragon of all the virtues, on the charge he made, on the decree of the Senate and on the state of the Republic. But first let me briefly 55

pauca quae meum animum repente moverunt prius de
L. Murenae fortuna conquerar. Nam cum saepe
antea, iudices, et ex aliorum miseriis et ex meis curis
laboribusque cotidianis fortunatos eos homines iudicarem qui remoti a studiis ambitionis otium ac tran-
quillitatem vitae secuti sunt, tum vero in his L.
Murenae tantis tamque improvisis periculis ita sum
animo adfectus ut non queam satis neque communem
omnium nostrum condicionem neque huius eventum
fortunamque miserari. Qui primum, dum ex honoribus continuis familiae maiorumque suorum unum
ascendere gradum dignitatis conatus est, venit in
periculum ne et ea quae ei[1] relicta, et haec quae ab
ipso parta sunt amittat, deinde propter studium
novae laudis etiam in veteris fortunae discrimen
56 adducitur. Quae cum sunt gravia, iudices, tum illud
acerbissimum est quod habet eos accusatores, non qui
odio inimicitiarum ad accusandum, sed qui studio
accusandi ad inimicitias descenderint. Nam ut omittam Servium Sulpicium quem intellego non iniuria
L. Murenae sed honoris contentione permotum, accusat paternus amicus, C.[2] Postumus, vetus, ut ait
ipse, vicinus ac necessarius, qui necessitudinis causas
compluris protulit, simultatis nullam commemorare
potuit. Accusat Ser. Sulpicius, sodalis filius, cuius ingenio paterni omnes necessarii munitiores esse debe-
bant. Accusat M. Cato qui cum[3] a Murena nulla re
umquam alienus fuit, tum[3] ea condicione nobis[4] erat
in hac civitate natus ut eius opes, ut ingenium

---

[1] ei *added by Halm.*
[2] C. *Zumpt.* tum *mss.*
[3] cum . . . tum *Kayser.* quamquam . . . tamen *mss.*
[4] nobis *editio Veneta.* nobilis *mss ; deleted by Mommsen.*

---

[a] But see p. 177.

voice the distress that has suddenly welled up within me at Lucius Murena's misfortune. The distress of others, gentlemen, no less than my own daily anxieties and labours has often in the past made me envy the peace and tranquillity of those free from the pressures of ambition. Today, however, I have been so deeply moved by the extent and suddenness of Lucius Murena's peril that I cannot deplore strongly enough either the situation in which we all find ourselves or the unhappy course that his life has taken. Firstly, in trying to rise a single step in office beyond the rank attained repeatedly by his family and his ancestors he is risking both what he has inherited and what he has won himself. Secondly, in his eagerness for new distinction he is endangering even his previous good fortune. Painful as this may be, 56 gentlemen, the most bitter blow of all is to have as his accusers not men who have sunk to prosecuting him from political enmity but men who have become enemies out of their eagerness to launch a prosecution. I do not include Servius Sulpicius, for I realize that his motive lies not in any wrong done him by Lucius Murena but in their election rivalry.[a] But Murena is accused by Gaius Postumus, his father's friend and on his own admission an old friend and neighbour; he produced a number of reasons why he should be a friend but could recall none for enmity. He is accused by Servius Sulpicius whose father was a boon companion and whose talents should rather have been devoted to protecting all his father's friends. He is accused by Marcus Cato who has never had cause to be an enemy of Murena and whose birth had given him a position with us in Rome from which he should direct his resources and native talent

praesidio multis etiam alienis, exitio vix cuiquam
57 inimico esse deberet. Respondebo igitur Postumo
primum qui nescio quo pacto mihi videtur praetorius
candidatus in consularem quasi desultorius in quadri-
garum curriculum incurrere. Cuius competitores si
nihil deliquerunt, dignitati eorum concessit, cum
petere destitit ; sin autem eorum aliquis largitus est,
expetendus amicus est qui alienam potius iniuriam
quam suam persequatur.

De Postumi criminibus, de Servi adulescentis

58 Venio nunc ad M. Catonem, quod est fundamen-
tum ac robur totius accusationis ; qui tamen ita gravis est accusator et vehemens ut multo magis eius
auctoritatem quam criminationem pertimescam. In
quo ego accusatore, iudices, primum illud deprecabor
ne quid L. Murenae dignitas illius, ne quid exspectatio
tribunatus, ne quid totius vitae splendor et gravitas
noceat, denique ne ea soli huic obsint bona M. Catonis
quae ille adeptus est ut multis prodesse possit. Bis
consul fuerat P. Africanus et duos terrores huius
imperi, Carthaginem Numantiamque, deleverat cum
accusavit L. Cottam. Erat in eo[1] summa eloquentia,

---

[1] in eo χψ. in *the other mss.*

---

[a] Cicero plays upon the meaning of the words "Postumus"
—"last"—and "primus"—"first."

[b] Postumus would have done better to worry about
bribery among his fellow-candidates for the praetorship and
not concern himself with the election of superior magistrates.

[c] This *titulus* marks an abridgement made by Cicero
himself. *Cf.* Pliny, *Epistulae* 1. 20. 7. For discussion of the
desirability of editing a speech, and of the difference between
the spoken and the written versions, see Quintilian 12. 10.
49 f. *Cf.* L. Laurand, *Le Style des discours de Cicéron* 5 f.

[d] He was tribune-elect for 62.

to the constant protection even of strangers and only
rarely to the destruction even of an enemy. I shall 57
reply therefore to Postumus posthaste.[a] In some
way or other I feel that this candidate for the praetorship is interfering with a candidate for the consulship
like a trick rider running into the chariot of a four-
horse team. If his fellow candidates observed the law,
he conceded their superior claims when he ceased to
run, but if one of them was guilty of bribery, then he
really is a friend to be cultivated since he is prosecuting an injury done to someone else and not that done
to himself.[b]

Reply to the Charges of Postumus and of the Young Servius [c]

I come now to Marcus Cato who is the root and 58
core of the whole prosecution. He is, indeed, so
important and forceful a prosecutor that I fear his
prestige more than his charges. In the case of this
prosecutor, gentlemen, I shall first offer this prayer :
that his authority, his expectation of the tribunate,[d]
the lustre and dignity of his whole life may not do
Lucius Murena any harm ; and secondly, that
Murena may not be the only man ever to be harmed
by the resources which have enabled Marcus Cato
to help so many. Publius Africanus had been consul
twice and had destroyed Carthage and Numantia,[e]
those twin threats to our empire, when he accused
Lucius Cotta.[f] He was a man of outstanding elo-

---

[e] He had been consul in 147 and 134, and had destroyed
Carthage in 146 and Numantia in 133.

[f] Lucius Aurelius Cotta, a consul in 144, was in 138
accused of extortion and, after several adjournments of the
case, acquitted by a bribed jury.

summa fides, summa integritas, auctoritas tanta
quanta in imperio populi Romani quod illius opera
tenebatur. Saepe hoc maiores natu dicere audivi,
hanc accusatoris eximiam vim et[1] dignitatem plurimum L. Cottae profuisse. Noluerunt sapientissimi
homines qui tum rem illam iudicabant ita quemquam
cadere in iudicio ut nimiis adversarii viribus abiec-
59 tus videretur. Quid ? Ser. Galbam—nam traditum
memoriae est—nonne proavo tuo, fortissimo atque
florentissimo viro, M. Catoni, incumbenti ad eius
perniciem populus Romanus eripuit ? Semper in hac
civitate nimis magnis accusatorum opibus et populus
universus et sapientes ac multum in posterum prospi-
cientes iudices restiterunt. Nolo accusator in iudicium potentiam adferat, non vim maiorem aliquam,
non auctoritatem excellentem, non nimiam gratiam.
Valeant haec omnia ad salutem innocentium, ad opem
impotentium, ad auxilium calamitosorum, in periculo
60 vero et in pernicie civium repudientur. Nam si quis
hoc forte dicet, Catonem descensurum ad accusandum
non fuisse, nisi prius de causa iudicasset, iniquam
legem, iudices, et miseram condicionem instituet
periculis hominum, si existimabit iudicium accusatoris
in reum pro aliquo praeiudicio valere oportere.

Ego tuum consilium, Cato, propter singulare enim,

---

[1] vim et *a few inferior* mss. vim mss.; *omitted by editio*
Veneta.

---

[a] Servius Sulpicius Galba was praetor in Further Spain in
151 and propraetor in the following year. Lucius Scribonius
Curio, a tribune of 149, proposed that Galba should be condemned for his massacre of the Lusitanians. Cato supported

quence, sense of duty and integrity, and his prestige was as great as that of the dominion of the Roman people which his service preserved. I have often heard older men say that the exceptional power and prestige of his accuser helped Lucius Cotta immensely. The wise men who at that time were the jury in the case did not want any man to be condemned, to all appearances crushed by the excessive resources of his adversary. Again, did not the Roman 59 people, according to the story, snatch Servius Galba from your gallant great-grandfather, Marcus Cato, when at the height of his power and doing his utmost to destroy him? [a] In Rome the whole people and its wise and far-sighted jurors [b] have always resisted prosecutors with too much power. I do not like a prosecutor to come into court with overweening power, an excessive force, overwhelming influence or too much popularity. Let all these assets be used to deliver the innocent, protect the weak and help those in trouble; for the trial and destruction of fellow-citizens, let them be rejected. Yet it will 60 perhaps be said that Cato would not have agreed to prosecute had he not first reached his decision upon the case. It will be creating an unjust precedent, gentlemen, and a wretched state of affairs for men on trial if the prosecutor's judgement is to count against the defendant as presumption of guilt.

The high opinion, Cato, that I have formed of your

him but Galba pleaded for mercy and was acquitted. This case and that of Cotta became bywords for the miscarriage of justice. See Cicero, *Brutus* 89 f.; also p. 416.

[b] The techniques for winning the goodwill of the jury were taught in the rhetorical schools as were the ways of discrediting your opponent by allusions to his power, clique, nobility or *clientela*.

mei de tua virtute iudicium vituperare non possum[1];
non nulla forsitan conformare et leviter emendare
possim. " Non multa peccas," inquit ille fortissimo
viro senior magister," sed peccas; te regere possum."
At ego non te; verissime dixerim peccare te nihil
neque ulla in re te esse huius modi ut corrigendus
potius quam leviter inflectendus esse videare. Finxit
enim te ipsa natura ad honestatem, gravitatem,
temperantiam, magnitudinem animi, iustitiam, ad
omnis denique virtutes magnum hominem et excel-
sum. Accessit istuc doctrina non moderata nec mitis
sed, ut mihi videtur, paulo asperior et durior quam
61 aut veritas aut natura patitur. Et quoniam non est
nobis haec oratio habenda aut in imperita multitudine
aut in aliquo conventu agrestium, audacius paulo de
studiis humanitatis quae et mihi et vobis nota et
iucunda sunt disputabo. In M. Catone, iudices, haec
bona quae videmus divina et egregia ipsius scitote
esse propria; quae non numquam requirimus, ea sunt
omnia non a natura verum a magistro. Fuit enim
quidam summo ingenio vir, Zeno, cuius inventorum
aemuli Stoici nominantur. Huius sententiae sunt et
praecepta eius modi. Sapientem gratia numquam
moveri, numquam cuiusquam delicto ignoscere;
neminem misericordem esse nisi stultum et levem;
viri non esse neque exorari neque placari; solos sa-

---

[1] non possum ψ^2. non audeo *Lag. 24; omitted by the
other* MSS. nolo *Boot.*

---

^a Phoenix to Achilles. A quotation from an unknown
play.
^b A wholly insincere compliment. *Cf.* Cicero, *de finibus* 4.
74 (referring to this speech) " apud imperitos tum illa dicta
sunt."

moral standards stops me from censuring your conduct, but I may, perhaps, reshape parts of it and improve them slightly. " You do not make many mistakes," said the old tutor to the brave warrior, " but you do make some. I can correct you." [a] I do not say the same of you; I might perhaps put it best by saying that you do not make mistakes and that you seem to be the sort of man who needs not so much straightening out as a little guidance. Nature has framed you for integrity, serious-mindedness, self-control, strength of character and justice; in short, a paragon of every virtue. To these virtues there has been added a stern and uncompromising set of beliefs and one in my view that is a little too harsh and hard for reality or human nature to endure. Seeing, too, that I do not have to address an ignorant 61 crowd or some gathering of rustics,[b] I shall be a little more venturesome in discussing the liberal studies which are so familiar and agreeable to us both. Rest assured, gentlemen, that the exceptional and almost superhuman qualities that we see in Marcus Cato are innate; the absence of the qualities that we sometimes miss in him is entirely due not to Nature but to his master. For there was a man of genius, Zeno, and the disciples of his teaching are called Stoics.[c] Here are examples of his maxims and precepts : the wise man is never moved by favour, never forgives anyone's misdeed ; only the fool or the trifler feels pity ; a real man does not yield to entreaty or appeasement ; only the wise man is handsome how-

---

[c] Zeno of Citium in Cyprus (335–263) was the founder of the Stoic school of philosophy, so called from the Stoa Poikile or Painted Colonnade in which his followers met at Athens.

pientes esse, si distortissimi sint, formosos, si mendi-
cissimi, divites, si servitutem serviant, reges; nos
autem qui sapientes non sumus fugitivos, exsules,
hostis, insanos denique esse dicunt; omnia peccata
esse paria; omne delictum scelus esse nefarium, nec
minus delinquere eum qui gallum gallinaceum, cum
opus non fuerit, quam eum qui patrem suffocaverit;
sapientem nihil opinari, nullius rei paenitere, nulla in
62 re falli, sententiam mutare numquam. Hoc homo
ingeniosissimus, M. Cato, auctoribus eruditissimis
inductus adripuit, neque disputandi causa, ut magna
pars, sed ita vivendi. Petunt aliquid publicani; cave
ne[1] quicquam habeat momenti gratia. Supplices
aliqui veniunt miseri et calamitosi; sceleratus et
nefarius fueris, si quicquam misericordia adductus
feceris. Fatetur aliquis se peccasse et sui delicti
veniam petit; "nefarium est facinus ignoscere." At
leve delictum est. "Omnia peccata sunt paria."
Dixisti quippiam: "fixum et statutum est." Non re
ductus es sed opinione; "sapiens nihil opinatur."
Errasti aliqua in re; male dici putat. Hac ex disciplina nobis illa sunt: "Dixi in senatu me nomen
consularis candidati delaturum." Iratus dixisti.
"Numquam" inquit "sapiens irascitur." At temporis causa. "Improbi" inquit "hominis est mendacio
fallere; mutare sententiam turpe est, exorari scelus,
63 misereri flagitium." Nostri autem illi—fatebor enim,
Cato, me quoque in adulescentia diffisum ingenio meo

---

[1] cave ne *Clark.* cave . . . Σ. cave *the other* mss.

---

[a] A technical term from their philosophy. L. Laurand,
Le Style des discours de Cicéron 97-98.
[b] In all likelihood a later addition to the speech and containing a reference to the tax-collectors' request for a remis-

ever misshapen, rich however needy, a king however much a slave. We who are not wise are by their account runaways, exiles, enemies or even madmen. All misdeeds are equal; every misdemeanour is a heinous crime. The casual killing of a cock is no less a crime than strangling one's father. The wise man never " supposes " [a] anything, never regrets anything, is never wrong, never changes his mind. Marcus Cato with his outstanding intellectual gifts 62 was induced by the teaching of these savants to seize upon this doctrine not just as a topic for discussion, as do most people, but as a way of life. The tax-collectors make a request; take care that you are not swayed by favour.[b] Some wretched down-and-outs appear as suppliants; you will be a wicked criminal if pity leads you to do anything for them. A man admits that he has done wrong and asks pardon for his misdeed. " It is a crime to forgive." But it is only a trivial wrong. " All wrongs are equal." You passed a casual remark: " It is fixed and settled," making a supposition, not stating a fact. " The wise man never ' supposes ' anything." You made a slip; he thinks that you spoke with malice. It is from teaching like this that we get : " I said in the Senate that I would prosecute a consular candidate." You spoke in anger. " The wise man," he says, " is never angry." Well, you said it as a matter of expediency. " To deceive by lying is dishonest, to change one's mind shameful, to allow oneself to be prevailed upon a crime, to feel pity a disgrace." My 63 masters—for I shall admit, Cato, that I too in my youth distrusted my natural ability and sought the

sion of part of the price of the Asiatic tax-contract. The opposition to this request was led by Cato. See p. xxxi.

quaesisse adiumenta doctrinae—nostri, inquam, illi a
Platone et Aristotele, moderati homines et temperati,
aiunt apud sapientem valere aliquando gratiam ; viri
boni esse misereri ; distincta genera esse delictorum
et disparis poenas ; esse apud hominem constantem
ignoscendi locum ; ipsum sapientem saepe aliquid
opinari quod nesciat, irasci non numquam, exorari
eundem et placari, quod dixerit interdum, si ita
rectius sit, mutare, de sententia decedere aliquando ;
omnis virtutes mediocritate quadam esse moderatas.

64 Hos ad magistros si qua te fortuna, Cato, cum ista
natura detulisset, non tu quidem vir melior esses nec
fortior nec temperantior nec iustior—neque enim esse
potes—sed paulo ad lenitatem propensior.   Non
accusares nullis adductus inimicitiis, nulla lacessitus
iniuria, pudentissimum hominem summa dignitate
atque honestate praeditum ; putares, cum in eiusdem
anni custodia te atque L. Murenam fortuna posuisset,
aliquo te cum hoc rei publicae vinculo esse coniunctum ; quod atrociter in senatu dixisti, aut non dixisses
aut, si potuisses,[1] mitiorem in partem interpretarere.

65 Ac te ipsum, quantum ego opinione auguror, nunc et
animi quodam impetu concitatum et vi naturae atque
ingeni elatum et recentibus praeceptorum studiis

---

[1] aut si potuisses *Hotoman.* aut si posuisses *Halm (2).*
aut si dixisses *Campe.* aut seposuisses aut *mss.*

---

[a] Plato, the Athenian philosopher, lived *c.* 429–347 and *c.*
385 founded the Academy. His pupil, Aristotle of Stagira
(384–322), in 335 founded the Peripatetic School, named
after the covered court (peripatos) at Athens in which he
worked.

Cicero affects diffidence in revealing his philosophical
interests because a Roman statesman was liable to be mistaken for a dilettante if he knew too much about Greek art or
philosophy.

support of philosophy—my masters, the schools of
Plato and Aristotle,[a] men who do not hold violent or
extreme views, say that favour can on occasions
influence the wise man ; that a good man can feel
pity ; that there are different degrees of wrongdoing
and different punishments ; that there is a place for
forgiveness in a man of principle. The wise man
himself often " supposes " something that he does
not know for certain, is angry at times, yields to
entreaty and appeasement, sometimes alters what he
has said if it is better so and sometimes changes his
mind ; all virtues are saved from excess by a so-called
mean.[b] If some happy chance, Cato, had carried a 64
man of your character off to these masters, you would
not indeed be a better man or a braver or a more
temperate or more just—for that is impossible—but
you would be a little more disposed to kindness.
You would not, unprompted by any personal hostility
and unprovoked by any private injury, be prosecuting
a man with a deep sense of honour and one who
enjoys so high a position and reputation. You would
think that the chance which has placed you and
Lucius Murena as guards of the same year would
have united you in some political bond,[c] and that
you would either not have spoken with such violence
in the Senate or, if you had been able, would now be
expressing your views more mildly. You have at the 65
present time, so far as I can surmise, been excited
by some impulse, carried away by the force of your
character and intellect, and fired by your recent

---

[b] Another technical philosophical term. Virtues are half
way between two opposed excesses ; e.g. the virtue " courage "
is half way between the two excesses " rashness " and
" cowardice."   [c] Murena as consul and Cato as tribune.

flagrantem iam usus flectet, dies leniet, aetas miti-
gabit. Etenim isti ipsi mihi videntur vestri praecep-
tores et virtutis magistri finis officiorum paulo
longius quam natura vellet protulisse ut, cum ad
ultimum animo contendissemus, ibi tamen ubi
oporteret consisteremus. " Nihil ignoveris." Immo
aliquid, non omnia. " Nihil gratiae causa feceris."[1]
Immo resistito gratiae, cum officium et fides postu-
labit. " Misericordia commotus ne sis." Etiam, in
dissolvenda severitate ; sed tamen est laus aliqua
humanitatis. " In sententia permaneto." Vero, nisi
66 sententiam sententia alia vicerit melior. Huiusce
modi Scipio ille fuit quem non paenitebat facere idem
quod tu, habere eruditissimum hominem Panaetium
domi ; cuius oratione et praeceptis, quamquam erant
eadem ista quae te delectant, tamen asperior non est
factus sed, ut accepi a senibus, lenissimus. Quis vero
C. Laelio comior fuit,[2] quis iucundior eodem ex studio
isto, quis illo gravior, sapientior ? Possum de L.
Philo, de C. Gallo[3] dicere haec eadem, sed te domum
iam deducam tuam. Quemquamne existimas Catone,
proavo tuo, commodiorem, communiorem, moderatio-
rem fuisse ad omnem rationem humanitatis ? De
cuius praestanti virtute cum vere graviterque diceres,

---

[1] causa feceris *Naugerius.*   confeceris *Clark's MSS.* con-
cesseris *Lag. 9.*   [2] fuit *added by Clark.*
[3] Gallo *MSS.* Galo *Müller from the Fasti Capitolini for*
243 and 166 B.C.

---

[a] Africanus Minor (185–129).
[b] The Stoic philosopher of Rhodes (*c.* 185–109) who was
entertained by Scipio just as a Stoic contemporary, Athenodorus, was entertained by Cato.
[c] Gaius Laelius Minor, consul in 140 and named *Sapiens*
for his Stoic learning.

philosophical studies; but experience will soon soften you, time calm you and age mellow you. Indeed, those tutors of yours and your teachers of ethics have, I think, extended the bounds of moral duty a little further than nature intended in order that our efforts of will to achieve perfection should bring us at least to the standards that we should attain. " Never forgive ! " No: not on every occasion, but do forgive sometimes. " Never show favour ! " No: stand out against it when obligation and good faith require. " Do not be moved by pity ! " Certainly not, if you are going to relax discipline; but there is some merit in sympathy. " Stand by your opinion ! " Yes, of course, so long as a better opinion does not replace it. The famous Scipio [a] was a man like that. He was 66 not ashamed to do what you are doing and entertain the philosopher Panaetius [b] in his own home. His guest's conversation and teaching, although it was the same as that which gives you such pleasure, did not make Scipio more harsh but, as I have heard from old men, extremely gentle. What member of that school was more kindly and agreeable than Gaius Laelius [c]; who more dignified or wise ? I can say the same of Lucius Philus and Gaius Gallus,[d] but I shall bring you now to your own house. Can you think of anyone, Cato, more affable, more sociable, more inclined in every way to accommodate his fellow-men than your great-grandfather ? [e] When you spoke with truth and conviction of his exceptional

[d] Lucius Furius Philus, a friend of Scipio and consul in 136; Gaius Sulpicius Gallus, consul in 166.

[e] Marcus Porcius Cato Censorius (234–149). A surprising description of a man notorious for his rustic bluntness and boorish manners, but one dictated by the requirements of the argument and produced to help laugh Cato out of court.

domesticum te habere dixisti exemplum ad imitandum. Est illud quidem exemplum tibi propositum domi, sed tamen naturae similitudo illius ad te magis qui ab illo ortus es quam ad unum quemque nostrum pervenire potuit, ad imitandum vero tam mihi propositum exemplar illud est quam tibi. Sed si illius comitatem et facilitatem tuae gravitati severitatique asperseris, non ista quidem erunt meliora, quae nunc sunt optima, sed certe condita iucundius.

67 Qua re, ut ad id quod institui revertar, tolle mihi e causa nomen Catonis, remove vim,[1] praetermitte auctoritatem quae in iudiciis aut nihil valere aut ad salutem debet valere, congredere mecum criminibus ipsis. Quid accusas, Cato, quid adfers ad iudicium, quid arguis ? Ambitum accusas ; non defendo. Me reprehendis, quod idem defendam quod lege punierim. Punivi ambitum, non innocentiam ; ambitum vero ipsum vel tecum accusabo, si voles. Dixisti senatus consultum me referente esse factum, si mercede[2] obviam candidatis issent, si conducti sectarentur, si gladiatoribus volgo locus tributim et item prandia si volgo essent data, contra legem Calpurniam factum videri. Ergo ita senatus iudicat, contra legem facta haec videri, si facta sint ; decernit quod nihil opus est, dum candidatis morem gerit. Nam factum sit necne vehementer quaeritur ; sin factum sit, quin contra legem sit dubitare nemo potest.

68 Est igitur ridiculum, quod est dubium, id relinquere incertum, quod nemini dubium potest esse, id iudi-

---

[1] vim *Clark.* in Σ, ac *s.* *Omitted by the other* MSS.
[2] mercede conducti Σχψ. corrupti *the other* MSS. *Deleted by Garatoni.*

---

[a] See p. 276, n. *c.*

virtue, you said that you had an example to imitate in your own family. You certainly do have an example in front of you at home, but it has been easier for his character to be passed on to you who are a descendant than to each one of us, and yet his example is there for me to copy as much as for you. If you sprinkle your sternness and severity with his courtesy and affability, your qualities will not become better—that is impossible—but they will at least be more agreeably seasoned.

To return, then, to my first point, please take the 67 name of Cato out of the case, remove his power, ignore his influence which in the criminal courts should either be powerless or a power for acquittal. Let us look at the charges together. What accusation do you make, Cato, what allegation are you bringing into court, what is your charge ? Bribery ? I do not defend it. You censure me for defending the very offence for which I have fixed penalties in my law. I fixed penalties for bribery, not for innocence. I shall certainly join you in prosecuting a real case of bribery, if you wish it. You said that on my proposal the Senate passed a decree that it be deemed a contravention of Calpurnius' law if men were paid to meet the candidates, if their companions were hired, if places were given to the tribes indiscriminately at the gladiatorial games and if dinners were given indiscriminately.[a] If the Senate resolves that these practices when employed be deemed illegal, its resolution may humour the candidates but is pointless. The crucial question is whether such practices took place. If they did, they were obviously illegal. It is ridiculous to leave uncertain what is in doubt and 68 seek a decision upon what is agreed by everybody.

care. Atque id decernitur omnibus postulantibus candidatis, ut ex senatus consulto neque cuius intersit, neque contra quem sit intellegi possit. Qua re doce ab L. Murena illa esse commissa ; tum egomet tibi contra legem commissa esse concedam.

" Multi obviam prodierunt de provincia decedenti." Consulatum petenti solet fieri ; eccui autem non proditur revertenti ? " Quae fuit ista multitudo ? " Primum, si tibi istam rationem non possim reddere, quid habet admirationis tali viro advenienti, candidato consulari, obviam prodisse multos ? quod nisi esset

69 factum, magis mirandum videretur. Quid ? si etiam illud addam quod a consuetudine non abhorret, rogatos esse multos, num aut criminosum sit aut mirandum, qua in civitate rogati infimorum hominum filios prope de nocte ex ultima saepe urbe deductum venire soleamus, in ea non esse gravatos homines prodire hora tertia in campum Martium, praesertim talis viri nomine rogatos ? Quid ? si omnes societates venerunt quarum ex numero multi sedent iudices ;[a] quid ? si multi homines nostri ordinis honestissimi ; quid ? si illa officiosissima quae neminem patitur non honeste in urbem introire tota natio candidatorum, si denique ipse accusator noster Postumus[b] obviam cum bene magna caterva sua venit, quid habet ista multitudo admirationis ? Omitto clientis, vicinos, tribulis, exercitum totum Luculli qui ad triumphum per eos dies venerat ; hoc dico, frequentiam in isto officio

---

[a] Two-thirds of the jury were equestrian (see p. 172) as were the members of these *societates*.
[b] See p. 171.
272

This decree was passed at the request of all the candidates so that you cannot tell whom it helps or whom it harms. Prove, therefore, that Murena employed these practices and then I shall concede to you that they were illegal.

"Crowds went out to meet him on his return from his province." That is the normal practice in the case of a consular candidate. Do not people go out to meet anyone on his return home? "Who formed that large crowd?" Firstly, even if I could not render you an account of it, does it surprise you that crowds went out to greet the arrival of a man like Murena when he was a candidate for the consulship? It would be more surprising if they had not done so. Moreover, 69 I might add that, following the usual practice, many had been asked to go. In Rome it is quite usual for us to be asked to escort to the Forum at first light the sons of the humblest citizens—and often from the remotest parts of the city. It is surely not illegal, then, or surprising, particularly in view of the individual concerned, that men were prepared to come to the Campus Martius at the third hour. Again, if all the companies to which many of the jurors belong,[a] if a host of our own distinguished order, if the whole of that tribe of candidates, always so ready to please and allowing nobody to enter the city without due honour, if even our own prosecutor Postumus came in person to meet him with a good large crowd of his own, what is surprising in the size of the throng? I leave out the clients, neighbours, fellow-tribesmen, the whole army of Lucullus [b] which was present at the time for his triumph; and I say this: a crowd ready to provide this courteous attention without payment has never failed any man,

273

gratuitam non modo dignitati nullius umquam sed ne
70 voluntati quidem defuisse. " At sectabantur multi."
Doce mercede ; concedam esse crimen. Hoc quidem
remoto quid reprendis ? " Quid opus est " inquit
" sectatoribus ? " A me tu id quaeris, quid opus sit
eo quo semper usi sumus ? Homines tenues unum
habent in nostrum ordinem aut promerendi aut
referendi benefici locum, hanc in nostris petitionibus
operam atque adsectationem. Neque enim fieri
potest neque postulandum est a nobis aut ab equitibus Romanis ut suos necessarios candidatos[1] adsec-
tentur totos dies ; a quibus si domus nostra celebratur,
si interdum ad forum deducimur, si uno basilicae
spatio honestamur, diligenter observari videmur et
coli ; tenuiorum amicorum et non occupatorum est ista
adsiduitas, quorum copia bonis viris et beneficis
71 deesse non solet. Noli igitur eripere hunc inferiori
generi hominum fructum offici, Cato ; sine eos qui
omnia a nobis sperant habere ipsos quoque aliquid
quod nobis tribuere possint. Si nihil erit praeter
ipsorum suffragium, tenues, etsi[2] suffragantur, nil
valent gratia. Ipsi denique, ut solent loqui, non
dicere pro nobis non spondere, non vocare domum
suam possunt. Atque haec a nobis petunt omnia
neque ulla re alia quae a nobis consequuntur nisi opera
sua compensari putant posse. Itaque et legi Fabiae

[1] candidatos *deleted by Kayser.*
[2] tenues, etsi *Clark.* tenue est si ut Σ. tenue est si (sed ω)
ut *the other* mss. *Many other suggestions have been made.*

---

[a] These sections contain invaluable information about the
working of the client system. See p. 173 and L. R. Taylor,
Party Politics in the Age of Caesar 42.
[b] Owing to the system of group voting the individual
votes of citizens in the lower census classes who were in
larger groups had less effect upon the outcome of elections

whether his position deserved it or whether it was only something that he wanted. " But he was fol- 70 lowed by a large crowd." Show that they were paid, and then I shall admit that a crime was committed. What accusation do you make, if that charge is dismissed ? " What need is there," he says, " of this retine ? " Am I the man to ask what is the need of something that we have always had ? Men of small means are only able to earn favours from our order or pay us back in one way and that is by helping us and following us about when we are candidates for office.[a] It is not possible and it cannot be asked of us senators or of the Roman knights that they should attend for whole days their friends who are candidates. If they come in large numbers to our houses and on occasion accompany us down to the Forum, if they condescend to walk with us the length of a public hall, we think that we are receiving great attention and respect. It is the poorer men with the time available who provide the constant attention that is habitually given to men of standing and to those who confer benefits. Do not, then, Cato, take from the lower 71 class this fruit of their attention. Allow the men who hope for everything from us to have something to give us in return. If poor men have nothing but their vote, then, even if they vote, their support is valueless.[b] Finally, as they are always saying, they cannot plead for us, stand surety for us, or invite us to their homes. They ask us for all these favours but think that they can only repay us for what they receive from us by personal service. For this reason they

than the votes of the well-to-do. Furthermore, the election was often decided before the lower classes were called upon to vote. See Appendix A, pp. 562-564.

quae est de numero sectatorum, et senatus consulto
quod est L. Caesare consule[1] factum restiterunt.
Nulla est enim poena quae possit observantiam tenuiorum ab hoc vetere instituto officiorum excludere.
72 " At spectacula sunt tributim data et ad prandium
volgo vocati." Etsi hoc factum a Murena omnino,
iudices, non est, ab eius amicis autem more et modo
factum est, tamen admonitus re ipsa recordor quantum hae conquestiones in senatu habitae punctorum
nobis, Servi, detraxerint. Quod enim tempus fuit aut
nostra aut patrum nostrorum memoria quo haec sive
ambitio est sive liberalitas non fuerit ut locus et in
circo et in foro daretur amicis et tribulibus ? Haec
homines tenuiores praemia commodaque a suis tribulibus vetere instituto adsequebantur * * *

[*Deest non nihil.*]

73 . . . praefectum fabrum semel locum tribulibus suis
dedisse, quid statuent in viros primarios qui in circo
totas tabernas tribulium causa compararunt ? Haec
omnia sectatorum, spectaculorum, prandiorum item
crimina a multitudine in tuam nimiam diligentiam,

---

[1] consule ⟨referente⟩ *Kinsey.*

---

[a] See p. 174.
[b] In 64 the *collegia* concerned with the *Compitalia*, celebrated on the 1st of January, were together with many others
outlawed by a decree of the Senate. At this festival of the
Lares their cult was performed by *collegia* which contained many members of the poorer section of the community.
In 67 the tribune Gaius Manilius appears to have exploited
them in his attempt to pass his law distributing the freedmen's votes among the tribes (*cf.* p. 246, n. *c*) and the Senate
was reacting against this and subsequent violence. A. W.
Lintott, *Violence in Republican Rome* 80-81.
[c] The tribal headquarters (the sites of which are not

opposed the law of Fabius limiting the number of those following a candidate[a] and the decree of the Senate passed in the consulship of Lucius Caesar.[b] There is no penalty that can prevent men of the lower class from showing their gratitude in this old-established way of fulfilling their obligations. " But shows were given to the tribes and invitations to dinner were given indiscriminately." Even though Murena took no part in this, gentlemen, and his friends followed traditional practices with moderation, the occasion prompts me to recall, Servius, the number of votes that these complaints in the Senate lost us.[c] Can we or our fathers ever remember a time when there has not been this wish—whether self-interested or out of a disinterested generosity— to provide a seat in the circus and the Forum for our friends and fellow-tribesmen ? Those are the rewards and bounties that poorer men receive from their fellow-tribesmen by ancient custom.

[Part of the speech is lost here]

⟨If they attack Murena⟩ for providing seats for his fellow-tribesmen on a single occasion when he was only a personal adjutant,[d] what will they do to our leading citizens who have provided whole blocks of seats in the circus for theirs ? These charges relating to retinues, shows, public banquets, have all alike been put down by the people to your officious-

known) apparently had enough space for shows and dinners. It was illegal to provide shows for tribes other than your own, but there was nothing to stop your friends entertaining their fellow-tribesmen on your behalf so long as the cost came out of their own pocket.

[d] For this post, see J. Suolahti, *The Junior Officers of the Roman Army in the Republican Period* 205 f.

Servi, coniecta sunt, in quibus tamen Murena ab
senatus auctoritate defenditur. Quid enim ? senatus
num obviam prodire crimen putat ? "Non, sed
mercede." Convince. Num sectari multos ? "Non,
sed conductos." Doce. Num locum ad spectandum
dare aut ad[1] prandium invitare ? "Minime, sed
volgo, passim."[2] Quid est volgo ? Universos. Non
igitur, si L. Natta, summo loco adulescens, qui et quo
animo iam sit et qualis vir futurus sit videmus, in
equitum centuriis voluit esse et ad hoc officium necessitudinis et ad reliquum tempus gratiosus, id erit
eius vitrico fraudi aut crimini, nec, si virgo Vestalis,
huius propinqua et necessaria, locum suum gladia-
torium concessit huic, non et illa pie fecit et hic a
culpa est remotus. Omnia haec sunt officia necessa-
riorum, commoda tenuiorum, munia candidatorum.

74 At enim agit mecum austere et Stoice Cato, negat
verum esse adlici benivolentiam cibo, negat iudicium
hominum in magistratibus mandandis corrumpi volup-
tatibus oportere. Ergo, ad cenam petitionis causa si
quis vocat, condemnetur ? "Quippe" inquit "tu
mihi summum imperium, tu summam auctoritatem,
tu gubernacula rei publicae petas fovendis hominum
sensibus et deleniendis animis et adhibendis voluptati-

---

[1] aut ad χψ. aut *the other* mss.
[2] passim *omitted by Lag. 9 and deleted by Beck, but cf.*
commentariolum petitionis 44.

---

[a] *i.e.* to every tribal headquarters.
[b] Lucius Pinarius Natta, of whom Cicero speaks elsewhere
with considerably less enthusiasm ; see *ad Atticum* 4. 8a. 3,
written in 56—" oderam hominem." The phrase *summo loco
adulescens* shows that he was a senatorial *eques.* The votes
of these centuries were important (see Appendix A, p. 563)
and Natta made a special effort on his step-father's behalf.

ness, Servius; but Murena has the authority of the
Senate to back him against them. How so? The
Senate does not think that it is illegal to go out to
meet a candidate, does it? "No; only if payment
was made." Prove that it was. To be escorted by a
large crowd? "No; only if they were hired."
Show that they were. To provide a seat at a show or
give an invitation to dinner? "Not at all; unless it
was given indiscriminately throughout the city." [a]
What does "indiscriminately" mean? "Given to
everybody." If, then, Lucius Natta,[b] a young man
of good birth,—and we see his present character and
the sort of man that he is going to become—wanted
to win favour with the centuries of knights in order
to fulfil the obligation of his close relationship with
Murena and with an eye to the future, no injury or
charge will be suffered by his stepfather as a result.
If a Vestal Virgin, a relative and friend, has given
Murena her seat at the gladiatorial games, her gift
is a mark of affection and his acceptance of it above
reproach. All these acts are the obligation of friends
and relatives, the services of poorer men and the
duties of candidates.

Cato, however, deals sternly with me like a true 74
Stoic. He says that it is wrong to promote good-will
with food and warp men's judgement by means of
pleasure in an election of magistrates. Are we then
to condemn everyone who gives an invitation to
dinner for this purpose? "Am I," he says, "going
to have you seek supreme power, supreme authority,
the very government of the State by pandering to
men's senses, bewitching their minds and plying

By 63 attendance at the ballot by members of these centuries
was casual; group voting encouraged non-attendance.

bus ? Utrum lenocinium " inquit " a grege delicatae
iuventutis, an orbis terrarum imperium a populo Romano petebas ? " Horribilis oratio ; sed eam usus,
vita, mores, civitas ipsa respuit. Neque tamen Lacedaemonii, auctores istius vitae atque orationis,
qui cotidianis epulis in robore accumbunt, neque vero
Cretes quorum nemo gustavit umquam cubans, melius
quam Romani homines qui tempora voluptatis la-
borisque dispertiunt res publicas suas retinuerunt ;
quorum alteri uno adventu nostri exercitus deleti
sunt, alteri nostri imperi praesidio disciplinam suam
75 legesque conservant. Qua re noli, Cato, maiorum instituta quae res ipsa, quae diuturnitas imperi com-
probat nimium severa oratione reprehendere. Fuit
eodem ex studio vir eruditus apud patres nostros et
honestus homo et nobilis, Q. Tubero. Is, cum epulum
Q. Maximus P. Africani, patrui sui, nomine populo
Romano daret, rogatus est a Maximo ut triclinium
sterneret, cum esset Tubero eiusdem Africani sororis
filius. Atque ille, homo eruditissimus ac Stoicus,
stravit pelliculis haedinis lectulos Punicanos et ex-
posuit vasa Samia, quasi vero esset Diogenes Cy-
nicus mortuus et non divini hominis Africani mors

---

^a *i.e.* brief ; " laconic " from Laconia.
^b Both Spartans and Cretans ate in common messes and
the latter sat to eat rather than reclining like the Romans.
^c By Quintus Caecilius Metellus Creticus in 68/67 with
three legions.
^d Sparta was a *civitas foederata*, *i.e.* had her own *foedus*
or treaty with Rome, and retained her own laws and institutions.
^e Quintus Fabius Maximus Allobrogicus gave the banquet
in honour of Publius Cornelius Scipio Aemilianus Africanus
Numantinus (185–129), the destroyer of Carthage and
Numantia, and asked Quintus Tubero to assist. The latter,
however, was a pupil of the Stoic Panaetius and displayed a

them with pleasures ? Were you asking," he says,
" a gang of spoilt youths for a job as a pimp or the
Roman people for world dominion ? " What monstrous talk ! It is repugnant to our practice, our
lives, our customs, the very spirit of Rome herself.
The Spartans, who invented your way of life and
speech *a* and who recline on hard wood at their daily
meals, have not succeeded any more than the
Cretans, none of whom ate a mouthful lying down,*b*
in preserving their countries better than the Romans
who divide their time between work and pleasure.
The Cretans were destroyed at a single appearance
of our army *c* and the Spartans only preserve their
laws and way of life under the protection of our rule.*d*
Do not then, Cato, condemn in too harsh terms the 75
customs of our ancestors which are vindicated by
experience and by the longevity of our government.
There was in our fathers' day a scholar and a Stoic
like yourself, a fine man and an aristocrat, Quintus
Tubero. When Quintus Maximus was giving a
funeral banquet to the Roman people in honour of
his uncle Publius Africanus, Tubero who was the
son of the sister of this same Africanus was asked
by Maximus to provide coverings for the couches.*e*
Whereupon, being deeply versed in Stoicism, he
covered the Punic couches with shabby goat skins and
set out Samian crockery more appropriate for the
death of Diogenes the Cynic *f* than a banquet to

Stoic indifference—hence the ironical " philosophy " below
—to the trappings of civilized life. Instead of elaborate and
expensive coverings he provided goat skins, and earthenware
crocks instead of silver cups.

f Diogenes of Sinope, a Cynic philosopher. The Cynics
were the moral predecessors of the Stoics and displayed an
even greater contempt for the refinements of civilization.

honestaretur ; quem cum supremo eius die Maximus laudaret, gratias egit dis immortalibus quod ille vir in hac re publica potissimum natus esset ; necesse enim fuisse ibi esse terrarum imperium ubi ille esset. Huius in morte celebranda graviter tulit populus Romanus hanc perversam sapientiam Tuberonis, 76 itaque homo integerrimus, civis optimus, cum esset L. Pauli nepos, P. Africani, ut dixi, sororis filius, his haedinis pelliculis praetura deiectus est. Odit populus Romanus privatam luxuriam, publicam magnificentiam diligit ; non amat profusas epulas, sordis et inhumanitatem multo minus ; distinguit rationem[1] officiorum ac temporum, vicissitudinem laboris ac voluptatis. Nam quod ais nulla re adlici hominum mentis oportere ad magistratum mandandum nisi dignitate, hoc tu ipse in quo summa est dignitas non servas. Cur enim quemquam ut studeat tibi, ut te adiuvet rogas ? Rogas tu me ut mihi praesis, ut committam ego me tibi. Quid tandem ? istuc me rogari oportet abs te, an te potius a me ut pro mea 77 salute laborem periculumque suscipias ? Quid quod habes nomenclatorem ? in eo quidem fallis et decipis. Nam, si nomine appellari abs te civis tuos honestum est, turpe est eos notiores esse servo tuo quam tibi. Sin iam[2] noris, tamenne[3] per monitorem

---

[1] rationem *mss.* ratione *Klotz.*
[2] iam *Clark.* etiam *mss.* etiam si *Lambinus.*
[3] tamenne *Clark.* tamen *mss.*

---

[a] *Cf. pro Flacco* 28, p. 470.

honour the death of the mighty Africanus. On the day of Africanus' funeral Maximus pronounced the funeral eulogy and gave thanks to the immortal gods that Africanus had been born in Rome and not elsewhere; for the seat of the world's government had of necessity been where he was. The Roman people took hard Tubero's ill-timed philosophy in the ceremony commemorating Africanus' death. These goat skins 76 cost this most upright of men and best of citizens the praetorship although he was the grandson of Lucius Paulus and, as I have said, the son of Publius Africanus' sister. The Roman people loathe private luxury, but they love public splendour.[a] They do not like extravagant banquets but much less do they like shabbiness and meanness; they take into account the variety of obligations and circumstances and recognize the alternation of work and pleasure. You, for all your own merit, do not adhere to your principle that the candidate's merit should be the only consideration to influence men in their choice of a magistrate. Why otherwise do you ask anyone to support you or assist you? You ask me to help you win office over myself, to entrust myself to you. Is it really for you to be asking me? Should it not be I asking you to take on toil and danger to preserve me? Do you not 77 have a slave to tell you the names of men and enable you to cheat and deceive people?[b] If it is creditable to greet your fellow-citizens by name, it is discreditable for your slave to know them better than yourself. But if you know them already, do you still have to greet them through your prompter when you

[b] Candidates were accompanied by a slave whose duty it was to whisper in his master's ear the names of citizens whom he met while out canvassing.

appellandi sunt cum[1] petis, quasi[2] incertus sis ?[3]
Quid quod,[4] cum admoneris, tamen, quasi tute noris, ita salutas ?   Quid, postea quam es designatus,
multo salutas neglegentius ?   Haec omnia ad rationem civitatis si derigas, recta sunt; sin perpendere
ad disciplinae praecepta velis, reperiantur pravissima.
Qua re nec plebi Romanae eripiendi fructus isti sunt
ludorum, gladiatorum, conviviorum, quae omnia
maiores nostri comparaverunt, nec candidatis ista
benignitas adimenda est quae liberalitatem magis
significat quam largitionem.

78   At enim te ad accusandum res publica adduxit.
Credo, Cato, te isto animo atque ea opinione venisse ;
sed tu imprudentia laberis.   Ego quod facio, iudices,
cum amicitiae dignitatisque L. Murenae gratia facio,
tum me pacis, oti, concordiae, libertatis, salutis,
vitae denique omnium nostrum causa facere clamo
atque testor.   Audite, audite consulem, iudices, nihil
dicam adrogantius, tantum dicam totos dies atque
noctes de re publica cogitantem !   Non usque eo
L. Catilina rem publicam despexit atque contempsit
ut ea copia quam secum eduxit se hanc civitatem
oppressurum arbitraretur.   Latius patet illius sceleris
contagio quam quisquam putat, ad pluris pertinet.
Intus, intus, inquam, est equus Troianus ; a quo num-

---

[1] cum *Clark.* curam *mss.* (cur ante ψ[2], *Naugerius*).
[2] quasi *Zumpt.* quam *mss.*
[3] incertus sis *Clark.* incertum sit *Lag. 9.* insusurravit
Naugerius.   [4] quidem (quid enim ψ[2]) χ ψ.   quod *Lag. 9.*
284

are a candidate as if you did not know them ? What of your greeting them as if you knew them personally when you are being prompted ? And what of your greeting them much less attentively when you have been elected ? If you judged all this behaviour by political considerations, they are right acts; but if you chose to weigh them scrupulously against philosophical dogmas, they would be found utterly wrong. The Roman commons, therefore, should not be robbed of the enjoyment it gets from games, gladiatorial shows and banquets, which were all established by our ancestors, nor should candidates be prevented from displaying an open-handedness which is the token of liberality rather than of bribery.

You say that the public interest led you to start **78** proceedings. I readily accept, Cato, that you have been brought here by your well-known patriotism and by the belief that it was in the national interest, but you slip up because you did not stop to think. What I am doing, gentlemen, I am doing not only out of friendship with Lucius Murena and for his good name but also for the sake of peace, quiet, unity, liberty, our preservation, in short the very lives of us all. This I publicly declare and I call upon you to bear witness to it. Listen, gentlemen, listen to a consul—I shall not claim too much but this much I shall say—a consul who spends all his days and nights thinking of the Republic! Lucius Catilina did not so despise and disregard the Republic as to think that he would overthrow our institutions with the force that marched out with him. The infection of his crime is more widely spread and affects more people than anyone imagines. The Trojan horse is within our walls, yes, within our very walls ; but never while I

79 quam me consule dormientes opprimemini. Quaeris
a me ecquid ego Catilinam metuam. Nihil, et curavi
ne quis metueret, sed copias illius quas hic video dico
esse metuendas; nec tam timendus est nunc exercitus
L. Catilinae quam isti qui illum exercitum deseruisse
dicuntur. Non enim deseruerunt sed ab illo in specu-
lis atque insidiis relicti in capite atque in cervicibus
nostris restiterunt. Hi et integrum consulem et bonum imperatorem et natura et fortuna cum rei publicae salute coniunctum deici de urbis praesidio et de
custodia civitatis vestris sententiis deturbari volunt.
Quorum ego ferrum et audaciam reieci in campo,
debilitavi in foro, compressi etiam domi meae saepe,
iudices, his vos si alterum consulem tradideritis, plus
multo erunt vestris sententiis quam suis gladiis consecuti. Magni interest, iudices, id quod ego multis
repugnantibus egi atque perfeci, esse Kalendis Ia-
80 nuariis in re publica duo consules. Nolite arbitrari,
mediocribus consiliis aut usitatis viis eos uti.[1] Non
lex improba, non perniciosa largitio, non auditum
aliquando aliquod malum rei publicae quaeritur.
Inita sunt in hac civitate consilia, iudices, urbis
delendae, civium trucidandorum, nominis Romani
exstinguendi. Atque haec cives, cives, inquam, si eos
hoc nomine appellari fas est, de patria sua et cogitant
et cogitaverunt. Horum ego cotidie consiliis occurro,
audaciam debilito, sceleri resisto. Sed moneo,

[1] eos uti *Clark*. aut ᴍss. aut ... eos uti *Kasten*.

---

[a] See pp. 7-8.

am consul will you be surprised in your sleep. You 79
ask me what I fear in Catiline. Nothing, and I have
seen to it that nobody need fear him, but I do say
that there is good reason to fear his forces which I see
here ; and it is not now so much the army of Lucius
Catilina that we have to fear as those who by their
story have deserted it. They have not deserted but
have been posted by him on the look-out and in
ambush, and have been left hanging over our heads.
These men want your verdict to dislodge from his
defence of the city and his protection of the citizen
body, an uncorrupt consul, a skilful general and a
man bound up by his character and circumstances
with the safety of the Republic. If you hand over
one of the two consuls to these men whose armed
aggression, gentlemen, I have repelled in the
Campus Martius, crippled in the Forum, crushed
time and again in my own home,^a they will have
achieved much more by your verdict than by their
own daggers. It is vital, gentlemen, that there are
two consuls in the State on the 1st of January and
that is what in the face of strong opposition I have
worked so hard to achieve. Do not imagine that 80
those men are employing any ordinary plans or
commonplace methods. It is not a question of an
unjust law, or ruinous bribery, or the sort of plot
against the Republic with which we are familiar.
Plans have been laid in this State, gentlemen, to
destroy the city, slaughter the citizens and obliterate
the name of Rome. And citizens, citizens, I say, if
it is right to call them by that name, are continuing
to plan these crimes against their fatherland. Every
day I counter their plans, I undermine their aggression, I resist their crime. I give you warning,

iudices. In exitu iam est meus consulatus; nolite mihi subtrahere vicarium meae diligentiae, nolite adimere eum cui rem publicam cupio tradere incolumem ab his tantis periculis defendendam.

81 Atque ad haec mala, iudices, quid accedat aliud non videtis? Te, te appello, Cato; nonne prospicis tempestatem anni tui? Iam enim in[1] hesterna contione intonuit vox perniciosa designati tribuni, conlegae tui; contra quem multum tua mens, multum omnes boni providerunt qui te ad tribunatus petitionem vocaverunt. Omnia quae per hoc triennium agitata sunt, iam ab eo tempore quo a L. Catilina et Cn. Pisone initum consilium senatus interficiendi scitis esse, in hos dies, in hos mensis, in hoc tempus

82 erumpunt. Qui locus est, iudices, quod tempus, qui dies, quae nox cum ego non ex istorum insidiis ac mucronibus non solum meo sed multo etiam magis divino consilio eripiar atque evolem? Neque isti me meo nomine interfici sed vigilantem consulem de rei publicae praesidio demoveri volunt. Nec minus vellent, Cato, te quoque aliqua ratione, si possent, tollere; id quod, mihi crede, et agunt et moliuntur. Vident quantum in te sit animi, quantum ingeni, quantum auctoritatis, quantum rei publicae praesidi; sed, cum consulari auctoritate et auxilio spoliatam vim tribuniciam viderint, tum se facilius inermem et debilitatum te oppressuros arbitrantur. Nam ne

---

[1] in *added by Halm.*

---

[a] Quintus Caecilius Metellus Nepos. See p. 184.
[b] See pp. xx f.

gentlemen. My consulate is now reaching its dying days; do not take from me the man whose vigilance should succeed mine, do not remove the man to whom I desire to hand over the Republic still intact for him to defend against these deadly perils.

Do you not see, gentlemen, what further disaster 81 is being added to this list ? It is you, Cato, you to whom I am speaking. Do you not look out to a storm in your year of office ? In yesterday's public meeting there was already thundering the sinister voice of one, a tribune-designate like yourself, against whom your own decision and all the loyal citizens who urged you to stand for the tribunate have taken elaborate precautions.[a] All the plots hatched over the past three years, ever since the time when, as you know, Lucius Catilina and Gnaeus Piso formed a plan to massacre the Senate, are coming to the boil during these days, these months, this very moment.[b] What place is there, gentlemen, what time, what 82 day, what night, on which divine providence fails to outdo my own precautions in snatching me off and carrying me clear of the plots and daggers of those assassins ? Those men do not want me to be killed on my own account but they want a vigilant consul to be removed from the defence of the Republic. They would be just as eager to find a way of removing you, Cato, if they could, and all their efforts, believe me, have this end in view. They see the extent of your courage, of your ability, your authority, and the protection you offer the Republic; but when they see the tribune's power deprived of a consul's lead and assistance, then they think that weakened and unarmed he will be crushed more easily. They are not afraid that another consul will be

sufficiatur consul non timent. Vident in tuorum
potestate conlegarum fore; sperant sibi D.[1] Sila-
num, clarum virum, sine conlega, te sine consule, rem
83 publicam sine praesidio obici posse. His tantis in
rebus tantisque in periculis est tuum, M. Cato, qui
mihi non tibi, sed patriae natus esse videris,[2] videre
quid agatur, retinere adiutorem, defensorem, socium
in re publica, consulem non cupidum, consulem, quod
maxime tempus hoc postulat, fortuna constitutum
ad amplexandum otium, scientia ad bellum gerendum, animo et usu ad quod velis negotium sustinendum.[3]

Quamquam huiusce rei potestas omnis in vobis sita
est, iudices; totam rem publicam vos in hac causa
tenetis, vos gubernatis. Si L. Catilina cum suo
consilio nefariorum hominum quos secum eduxit hac
de re posset iudicare, condemnaret L. Murenam, si
interficere posset, occideret. Petunt enim rationes
illius ut orbetur auxilio res publica, ut minuatur contra suum furorem imperatorum copia, ut maior
facultas tribunis plebis detur depulso adversario
seditionis ac discordiae concitandae. Idemne igitur
delecti ex amplissimis ordinibus honestissimi atque
sapientissimi viri iudicabunt quod ille importunissimus
84 gladiator, hostis rei publicae iudicaret? Mihi credite,
iudices, in hac causa non solum de L. Murenae verum
etiam de vestra salute sententiam feretis. In discrimen extremum venimus; nihil est iam unde nos

---

[1] D. *added by Hirschfelder.*
[2] videris *added by Klotz.* videare *added by Halm.*
[3] sustinendum *added by Völkel.*

---

[a] Tribunes could obstruct the election of a second consul
to replace Murena.   [b] *Cf. in Catilinam* 4. 9, p. 144.
[c] See p. 172 for its composition and *cf.* p. 248, n. *a* and
p. 406, n. *a.*

elected in Murena's place.[a] They see that your colleagues will be able to prevent this, and so they hope that the illustrious Decimus Silanus can be thrown to them without a colleague, yourself without a consul and the Republic without a defender. In 83 such important and dangerous times as these it is the duty of a man like you, Marcus Cato, born in my view to serve your fatherland more than yourself, to see what is to be done and to preserve as your helper, defender and ally in the Republic not a self-seeking consul, but—and this is the present situation's crying need—one fitted by his station to embrace peace, by his professional skill to wage war, by his spirit and experience to perform any task you like.

Yet the control of this situation lies completely in your hands, gentlemen. In this case you have complete control and mastery over the Republic. If Lucius Catilina and his council of criminals whom he marched out with him could decide this case, he would condemn Lucius Murena; if he could cut him short, he would kill him. His plans require the Republic to be bereft of succour, the number of commanders against his maniac attacks to be reduced, greater power to arouse sedition and dissension to be given to the tribunes of the people by toppling their opponent.[b] Shall, then, a jury of such distinction and intelligence, selected from the most distinguished orders,[c] give the same verdict as that ruthless cutthroat and enemy of the Republic ? Believe me, 84 gentlemen, you are going to give your verdict in this case not only on Lucius Murena's life but upon your own as well. We have come to the end of the road. There is no longer any reserve from which to make

reficiamus aut ubi lapsi resistamus. Non solum
minuenda non sunt auxilia quae habemus sed etiam
nova, si fieri possit, comparanda. Hostis est enim non
apud Anienem, quod bello Punico gravissimum visum
est, sed in urbe, in foro—di immortales ! sine gemitu
hoc dici non potest—non nemo etiam in illo sacrario
rei publicae, in ipsa, inquam, curia non nemo hostis
est. Di faxint ut meus conlega, vir fortissimus, hoc
Catilinae nefarium latrocinium armatus opprimat !
ego togatus vobis bonisque omnibus adiutoribus hoc
quod conceptum res publica periculum parturit con-
85 silio discutiam et comprimam. Sed quid tandem fiet,
si haec elapsa de manibus nostris in eum annum qui
consequitur redundarint ? Unus erit consul, et is non
in administrando bello sed in sufficiendo conlega
occupatus. Hunc iam qui impedituri sint * * *[1] illa
pestis immanis importuna Catilinae prorumpet, qua
po * * *[1] minatur; in agros suburbanos repente advolabit[2] ; versabitur in urbe[3] furor, in curia timor, in
foro coniuratio, in campo exercitus, in agris vastitas ;
omni autem in sede ac loco ferrum flammamque me-
tuemus. Quae iam diu comparantur, eadem ista omnia, si ornata suis praesidiis erit res publica, facile
et magistratuum consiliis et privatorum diligentia
comprimentur.
86 Quae cum ita sint, iudices, primum rei publicae
causa, qua nulla res cuiquam potior debet esse, vos
pro mea summa et vobis cognita in re publica dili-

[1] *The* mss. *are defective at these points.*

[2] advolabit *editiones Veneta et Romana.* advolavit mss.

[3] in urbe *Halm.* in castris πφψω. in rostris *Lag. 24.*
There is a gap in Σχ.

---

[a] A river some three miles from Rome to which Hannibal
advanced in 211 during the Second Punic War—the nearest
he ever came to the city.

good our losses or place in which to rise again when
we have fallen. Not only must we not weaken the
forces we have but, if we can, we must strengthen
them with new. The enemy is not on the Anio,[a] which
in the Punic War seemed desperate enough, but in
the city, in the Forum, and—immortal gods! I cannot
say it without a groan—there are even some in our
national holy of holies, yes, in the very Senate-house.
May the gods grant that my gallant colleague smash
Catiline's evil force of bandits in the field ![b] I, a
civilian,[c] with your help and with that of all loyal
citizens shall lay plans to break up and crush the
danger which the nation has engendered and to
which it is now giving birth. What will happen, 85
though, if these dangers slip from our fingers and
spill over into next year ? There will be only one
consul and he occupied in seeing to the election of a
new colleague instead of conducting the war. Already men to hinder him . . . that monstrous plague
that is Catiline will break out in all its violence where
it threatens . . . it will suddenly swoop on the areas
near the city ; frenzy will be rampant in the city,
terror in the Senate-house, conspiracy in the Forum,
an army in the Campus Martius and desolation in the
country-side. In every dwelling and every neighbour-
hood we shall fear fire and the sword. Yet, if only
the Republic is furnished with its proper means of
defence, all these plans, so long contrived, will easily
be crushed by the measures taken by the magistrates
and the watchful care of private citizens.

In this state of affairs, gentlemen, firstly, for the 86
sake of the Republic—which should come first for all
of us—as a notable and ardent patriot I warn you,

[b] See p. 28. [c] Cf. p. 96, n. b.

gentia moneo, pro auctoritate consulari hortor, pro
magnitudine periculi obtestor, ut otio, ut paci, ut
saluti, ut vitae vestrae et ceterorum civium consula-
tis; deinde ego idem et[1] defensoris et amici officio
adductus oro atque obsecro, iudices, ut ne hominis
miseri et cum corporis morbo tum animi dolore
confecti, L. Murenae, recentem gratulationem nova
lamentatione obruatis.   Modo maximo beneficio
populi Romani ornatus fortunatus videbatur, quod
primus in familiam veterem, primus in municipium
antiquissimum consulatum attulisset; nunc idem in[2]
squalore et sordibus, confectus morbo, lacrimis ac
maerore perditus vester est supplex, iudices, vestram
fidem obtestatur, vestram[3] misericordiam implorat,
87 vestram potestatem ac vestras opes intuetur.   Nolite,
per deos immortalis! iudices, hac eum cum[4] re qua
se honestiorem fore putavit etiam ceteris ante partis
honestatibus atque omni dignitate fortunaque privare.
Atque ita vos L. Murena, iudices, orat atque obsecrat,
si iniuste neminem laesit, si nullius auris volun-
tatemve violavit, si nemini, ut levissime dicam, odio
nec domi nec militiae fuit, sit apud vos modestiae
locus, sit demissis hominibus perfugium, sit auxilium
pudori. Misericordiam spoliatio consulatus magnam
habere debet, iudices; una enim eripiuntur cum consulatu omnia; invidiam vero his temporibus habere
consulatus ipse nullam potest; obicitur enim contionibus seditiosorum, insidiis coniuratorum, telis
Catilinae, ad omne denique periculum atque ad

[1] idem et *Clark.* fidem vel Σχ. fide in vos *the other MSS.*
idem vos *Madvig.*
[2] in *added by Clark.*
[3] vestram *added by Halm.*
[4] eum cum *Garatoni.* cum *B.* eum *the other MSS.*

294

with my authority as consul I exhort you, alert to the extent of the danger I implore you, to assure tranquillity, peace, security, your own lives and those of the other citizens. Secondly, true to my duty as both counsel and friend, I plead with you, gentlemen, not to drown with grief this day the words of congratulation still ringing in the ears of the unfortunate Lucius Murena, shattered as he is by bodily disease and mental anguish. Only the other day, honoured with the highest office in the gift of the Roman people, he seemed blessed by fortune because he had been the first man to bring the consulship into an old family and to an ancient town. Today, gentlemen, clad in sack-cloth and ashes, consumed by disease, worn out by his tears and his distress, he is your suppliant, gentlemen, he calls upon your protection, implores your pity, and looks to your power and resources. Do not, gentlemen, in the name of the 87 immortal gods, deprive him of this office which he thought would win him greater distinction, or of all the other distinctions that he has already won, or of all his rank and fortune. Lucius Murena begs and implores you, gentlemen, that if, as is the case, he has injured nobody unjustly, if he has offended nobody's sensibilities, if he has made no enemies—the least that I can say—either at Rome or in the field, there may be with you a place for the unassertive, a refuge for the down-cast and succour for the humiliated. We should feel deep compassion, gentlemen, for loss of the consulship, for with the consulship all else is lost. At a time like this, however, you cannot envy the office itself, for it is exposed to the demagoguery of traitors, the plots of conspirators, the weapons of Catiline ; in short, it alone bears the brunt of every

88 omnem iniuriam solus opponitur. Qua re quid
invidendum Murenae aut cuiquam nostrum sit in hoc
praeclaro consulatu non video, iudices; quae vero
miseranda sunt, ea et mihi ante oculos versantur et
vos videre et perspicere potestis. Si, quod Iuppiter
omen avertat! hunc vestris sententiis adflixeritis,
quo se miser vertet? domumne? ut eam imaginem
clarissimi viri, parentis sui, quam paucis ante diebus
laureatam in sua gratulatione conspexit, eandem
deformatam ignominia lugentemque videat? An
ad matrem quae misera modo consulem osculata
filium suum nunc cruciatur et sollicita est ne eundem
paulo post spoliatum omni dignitate conspiciat?
89 Sed quid eius matrem[1] aut domum appello quem nova
poena legis et domo et parente et omnium suorum
consuetudine conspectuque privat? Ibit igitur in
exsilium miser? Quo? ad Orientisne partis in quibus
annos multos legatus fuit, exercitus duxit, res maximas gessit? At habet magnum dolorem, unde cum
honore decesseris, eodem cum ignominia reverti. An
se in contrariam partem terrarum abdet, ut Gallia
Transalpina, quem nuper summo cum imperio
libentissime viderit, eundem lugentem, maerentem,
exsulem videat? In ea porro provincia quo animo C.
Murenam fratrem suum aspiciet? Qui huius dolor,
qui illius maeror erit, quae utriusque lamentatio,
quanta autem perturbatio fortunae atque sermonis,
cum, quibus in locis paucis ante diebus factum esse
consulem Murenam nuntii litteraeque celebrassent et

[1] eius matrem *Zumpt.* ego matrem *mss.* ego matrem eius
Halm.

---

[a] The Roman noble kept the busts of those of his ancestors
who had held curule office in the *atrium* of his house. They

danger and every outrage. I see, therefore, gentle- 88
men, no cause to envy Murena or any of us our
glorious consulships ; but pathetic indeed are the
events being enacted before my eyes which you too
can see and watch. If you crush him with your
verdict—may Jupiter avert the omen !—where will
the poor man turn ? To his home ? To see that bust
of his distinguished father,[a] which a few days ago he
saw wreathed in laurel in his own honour, now disfigured and saddened by his disgrace ? Or to his
mother who, unhappy woman, yesterday kissed a
consul when she kissed her son and today is tortured
by the anxiety that she may see this same son robbed
a little later of all his honours ? Yet why do I suggest 89
his mother or his home when the penalty of the new
law [b] deprives him of both home and parent and of all
sight of his people and intercourse with them ? Will
the poor man, then, go into exile ? Where ? To the
East where for many years he was a lieutenant-
general, commanded armies, performed mighty
exploits ? But it is deeply humiliating to return in
disgrace to a place from which you departed with
honour. Or will he hide himself at the other end of
the world to let Transalpine Gaul see the man whom
she lately welcomed as her governor return a sad
and sorrowing exile ? What, too, will be his feelings
when he sees his brother, Gaius Murena, in that
province ? Picture Gaius' grief, Lucius' despair, the
distress of both, the reversal of their fortunes and
change in their conversation when there suddenly
appears in person the courier of his own calamity
where a few days before messengers and letters had

were paraded on family occasions and garlanded at times of
family rejoicing.   [b] See p. 174.

unde hospites atque amici gratulatum Romam concurrerent, repente exstiterit[1] ipse nuntius suae cala-
90 mitatis ! Quae si acerba, si misera, si luctuosa sunt, si alienissima a mansuetudine et misericordia vestra, iudices, conservate populi Romani beneficium, reddite rei publicae consulem, date hoc ipsius pudori, date patri mortuo, date generi et familiae, date etiam Lanuvio, municipio honestissimo, quod in hac tota causa frequens maestumque vidistis. Nolite a sacris patriis Iunonis Sospitae, cui omnis consules facere necesse est, domesticum et suum consulem potissimum avellere. Quem ego vobis, si quid habet aut momenti commendatio aut auctoritatis confirmatio mea, consul consulem, iudices, ita commendo ut cupidissimum oti, studiosissimum bonorum, acerrimum contra seditionem, fortissimum in bello, inimicissimum huic coniurationi quae nunc rem publicam labefactat futurum esse promittam et spondeam.

[1] exstiterit *Clark.* exciderit ψ^2. excidet *the other MSS.* existet *Gulielmius.*

---

[a] An ancient Italian goddess, originally closely connected with the life of women, who developed other functions and became a great goddess of the State. This was notably so at Lanuvium where she was capable of leading the State into

spread the news of Murena's election as consul, and his hosts and friends rushed off to Rome to congratulate him ! If these are cruel, wretched or lamentable 90 fates, if they are repellent to your mercy and compassion, gentlemen, then preserve a distinction conferred by the Roman people, restore a consul to the Republic, grant this for the sake of his honour, for his dead father, for his home and family, grant it too for the distinguished town of Lanuvium which you have seen represented throughout this case by its sorrowing crowds. Do not tear from the hereditary worship of Juno Sospita, to whom all consuls must sacrifice, the consul who is her fellow-townsman and her own above all others ! [a] Myself a consul, gentlemen, I commend this consul to you. If my commendation carries any weight or my support any authority, I commend him with the promise and guarantee that he will be devoted to the cause of peace, zealous in the support of all loyal citizens, active in the suppression of rebellion, intrepid in war and a bitter enemy of this conspiracy which is now rocking the foundations of the Republic.

battle and defending it by force of arms. Her title, Sospita or Sispita, means " Preserver."

THE SPEECH IN DEFENCE OF
PUBLIUS CORNELIUS SULLA

INTRODUCTION

Publius Cornelius Sulla *ᵃ* was a member of the
Roman nobility *ᵇ* and a nephew of the Dictator.*ᶜ*
Cicero in his speech in his defence puts his client's
past in the best light that he can and records *ᵈ* that
in the proscriptions Sulla saved the lives of many
knights and senators by personal intervention with
the Dictator. Elsewhere Cicero's account of his
client's activities makes less pleasant reading. He
describes him as brandishing his kinsman's bloody
spear *ᵉ* and amassing a huge fortune from the sale of
confiscated property *ᶠ* ; and thirty-six years later in
the still more extensive sales of the Caesarian proscriptions Sulla was an eager participant.*ᵍ*

The only other information about his activities at
this time is that he had been one of the founders of
the Sullan colony settled at Pompeii.*ʰ* Thereafter
there is silence until 66 when he was a consular
candidate. The two successful candidates in these
elections were Sulla, who was elected by all the

ᵃ See F. Münzer in Pauly-Wissowa, *Realencyclopädie* IV.
1 (1900), P. Cornelius Sulla (386), 1518-1521.

ᵇ 37, p. 350. For the meaning of the term, see M. Gelzer,
The Roman Nobility 27 f. *Cf.* p. 178, n. *e.*

ᶜ A son of his brother. Dio 36. 44. 3 calls him ἀδελφιδοῦς ;
Cicero only *propinquus.*

ᵈ 72, p. 384.   *ᵉ* The sign of the auctioneer.
ᶠ *de officiis* 2. 29.   *ᵍ* *Ib.*   *ʰ* 60-62, pp. 372-376.

centuries,[a] and Publius Autronius Paetus, a man who is represented by Cicero as having a deplorable record that compromised his fellow consul-designate.[b]

Immediately after election both Sulla and Autronius were prosecuted for *ambitus*, electoral malpractice, under the provisions of the *lex Calpurnia*. The bribery in which they had indulged during their electoral campaign left them vulnerable to the hostility of their political rivals and two of the unsuccessful candidates launched the prosecutions.[c] Sulla was accused by Lucius Manlius Torquatus, who again prosecuted him in this case.[d] Autronius was accused by Lucius Aurelius Cotta and appears to have made an attempt to halt his trial by violence.[e] Sulla is said to have held aloof and Autronius' attempt came to nothing. In the end both defendants were convicted, and the vacant consulships went to Cotta and to Lucius Manlius Torquatus, the father of Sulla's accuser in this trial.[f]

After his conviction Sulla is represented as feeling his disgrace keenly [g] and keeping clear of the murky politics of the succeeding months.[h] Much of his time was spent at Naples although he appears to have been back in Rome on a number of occasions. On the 10th of December 64 one of the newly elected tribunes, a half-brother of Sulla named Lucius Caecilius Rufus, proposed a bill to provide that Sulla and Autronius

---

[a] 91, p. 404. It was considered a mark of distinction to have all the centuries vote for you. See Appendix A, p. 563.

[b] 1 and 66, pp. 314 and 378.

[c] On *ambitus*, see pp. 171-175 and on the political purposes of these trials, see p. 177.

[d] Cicero, *de finibus* 2. 62, establishes that this Torquatus was not the consul of 65, but his son.   [e] 15, p. 328.

[f] See p. xix.   [g] 15, p. 328.   [h] 1, p. 314.

should only undergo the penalties fixed by legislation prior to the *lex Calpurnia*. This would have enabled them to stand for office after an interval of ten years and to rehabilitate themselves by prosecuting others whose positions they would secure if they won their case, but the measure failed to win the support necessary to make it law. The Senate was unwilling to assist its passage because in 64 bribery had been more flagrant than ever and their efforts to secure the passage of a law providing for penalties even harsher than those of the *lex Calpurnia* had proved ineffectual. Cicero too was unable to help because he had been bitterly attacked by Quintus Mucius Orestinus, the tribune who had vetoed this bill.[a] Sulla accepted the situation and asked the praetor, Quintus Caecilius Metellus Celer, to say in the Senate on the 1st of January 63 that he did not wish the matter to be taken any further.[b]

While the Catilinarian conspiracy was running its course in Rome, Sulla continued at Naples [c] apart, possibly, from the occasion of the consular elections for 62 over which Cicero presided.[d] After the defeat of Catiline in the field, the regular processes of the law were set in motion against a number of the surviving conspirators.[e]

Legislation aimed at curbing political violence is not found at Rome until late in the Republic. The first accusation *de vi* belongs to 63, when Catiline

[a] Asconius 83, 85-86, and 88 C. *Cf.* C. Nicolet, "Le Sénat et les amendements aux lois à la fin de la République," *Revue historique de Droit français et étranger* 36 (1958), 266-267.

[b] 62-65, pp. 374-378.   [c] 53, p. 366.

[d] 51-52, pp. 364-366. The form of the argument suggests that Sulla was known to have been in the city or within easy reach of it.   [e] See p. 305 below.

PRO SULLA

himself was charged *lege Plautia* by Lucius Aemilius
Paulus, but left Rome before he could be brought to
trial. Gaius Cethegus too was charged with the same
offence, but his case was not heard either. In the
following year the same law was the basis of the
accusations against Publius Autronius Paetus, against
Servius and another Publius Sulla, both sons of a
brother of the Dictator, and against Lucius Vargunteius, Marcus Porcius Laeca and Gaius Cornelius.[a]
In this mopping-up operation against surviving
Catilinarians Cicero himself gave evidence against
Autronius and probably against the others.[b] All
were condemned.[c]

Sulla too was prosecuted under the provisions of
the *lex Plautia de vi*.[d] The date of his trial can be

---

[a] 6, 7 and 18, pp. 318-320 and 330.

[b] 10, 21, 48 and 83, pp. 322, 332, 360 and 396.

[c] 71, p. 382.

[d] See A. W. Lintott, *Violence in Republican Rome*
Chapter V and Appendix B. The *lex Plautia de vi* is
attested in our sources for a number of the cases occurring in
the 60s and 50s as the law under which these prosecutions
were brought, but in 56 Marcus Caelius Rufus was accused
de vi, according to Cicero (*pro Caelio* 1 and 70) " under the
law proposed and carried by Quintus Catulus." This law
was identified by Th. Mommsen, *Römisches Strafrecht* 654,
with the *lex Plautia* in the belief that Catulus got a tribune to
pass the bill for him. H. Last, *Cambridge Ancient History*,
ix. 896, rejects this view, as do J. N. Hough, " The *lex
Lutatia* and the *lex Plautia de vi*," *American Journal of
Philology* 51 (1930), 135-147 ; J. Cousin, " *lex Lutatia de
vi*," *Revue historique de Droit français et étranger* 22 (1943),
88-94 ; and R. G. Austin, Commentary on Cicero *pro Caelio*,
notes on 1 and 70. The *lex Lutatia* is a consular law of 78
and the *lex Plautia* either a tribunician or a praetorian
measure (A. W. Lintott, *op. cit.* 110-111). Why were there
two laws ? Various theories have been put forward. J. N.
Hough (*op. cit.* 142 and 146) suggests that the *lex Lutatia* was

fixed quite accurately from both internal and external evidence. It cannot have taken place much before the turn of the year, since the trials of Vargunteius and the others had been in progress for some months [a] and are not likely to have been started before Catiline's defeat in the field.[b] In two passages [c] Marcus Valerius Messalla Niger is mentioned in such a way as to indicate that the consular elections of 62 had not yet been held. We know that they were somewhat later than usual this year and may not have taken place until August. For a *terminus ante quem* we have the letter to Sestius [d] written between the 10th of December 62 and the 1st of January 61 showing that Sulla had been a *reus* some time before. The most likely time is therefore the month of July.

The jury would have been composed of equal numbers of senators, knights and *tribuni aerarii*,[e] as were all the juries of this period, under the provisions of the *lex Aurelia iudiciaria* of a praetor of 70, Lucius Aurelius Cotta.[f] The verdict would be given by

a law passed to deal specifically with the insurrection of Marcus Aemilius Lepidus in 78 and that the *lex Plautia* was a purely preventive measure of late 65 or 64. Cousin's view (*op. cit.*) is that the *lex Plautia* only dealt with violence against private citizens, but the *lex Lutatia* probably covered cases of violence directed against the State. A. W. Lintott's solution (*op. cit.* 115 f.) is that the *lex Lutatia* was passed to deal with Lepidus' rebellion by setting up a permanent *quaestio* to replace the earlier special tribunals and was aimed at *seditio*. The *lex Plautia* extended the competence of the court so that it also dealt with cases of violence against private citizens that were held to be against the interests of the State. It cannot be dated accurately but must have been passed between 78 and 63.

[a] 82, p. 394.
[b] In January 62.
[c] 20 and 42, pp. 332 and 354.
[d] *ad familiares* 5. 6. 2.
[e] See p. 419.
[f] The consul of 65.

ballot as provided by the *lex Cassia tabellaria* of a tribune of 137, Lucius Cassius Longinus Ravilla.

Cicero's colleague for the defence was Quintus Hortensius Hortalus,[a] while Lucius Manlius Torquatus was assisted in his prosecution by Gaius Cornelius, the son of the conspirator of that name.[b] Nothing is known about him other than what we can learn from this speech. Torquatus had been a close friend of Cicero for many years and shared his literary tastes and political views. He appears later in Cicero's dialogue *de finibus*, in which he defends Epicureanism.[c]

Cicero found himself in some personal difficulty in this trial and his situation goes some way to accounting for the tactics he employs. It is surprising at first sight that he was ready to take the part of a man whom he clearly did not like against so close a friend as Torquatus, but we have to realize what deep personal differences could be over-ridden in the interests of *amicitia*.[d] Nonetheless Torquatus was deeply offended by Cicero's unexpected defence of Sulla—after all the story was that his father was to have been murdered by Sulla. He attacked Cicero violently in his prosecution, accusing him of tyrannical behaviour, of setting himself up as judge and jury

[a] See p. 179.   [b] 51, p. 364.
[c] 2 and 34, pp. 314 and 346. *de finibus* 1. 28 f. For the family, see J. F. Mitchell, " The Torquati," *Historia* 15 (1966), 23-31.
[d] See P. A. Brunt, " ' Amicitia ' in the Late Roman Republic," *Proceedings of the Cambridge Philological Society* 11 (1965), 1-20, especially 15, n. 2. Torquatus never threatened to renounce his friendship: *pro Sulla* 21 f. and 47, pp. 332 f. and 360 ; this attitude had good precedent, *ib.* 49, p. 362. *Cf.* p. 182, n. *a*.

and of being the third foreign king of Rome after Tarquin and Numa.[a] So strong was the attack and so dangerous its allegations that Cicero felt that he had to devote more than a third of his speech to defending not his client but himself.[b] This defence he conducts with considerable adroitness. He carefully dissociates Sulla and Autronius and, with an eye on the fact that the court must have known how close a friend of Torquatus he was, adopts towards the younger man a patronizing tone with just a hint of menace in the background. He plays the rôle of the acknowledged master addressing an over-excited youngster, calming him with a condescension that must have been infuriating.[c]

To the question " Why did Cicero accept this brief ? " there is again [d] no simple answer. The reasons that Cicero himself advances are certainly not the whole story nor even the most important part of it. He maintains that he is the man in the best position to establish Sulla's innocence and therefore wishes to help him ; that he wishes to prove that he is capable of showing mercy when that is the right course and to clear himself of the charge of vindictiveness ; and that it was natural for him to wish to join the other distinguished figures who were supporting Sulla.[e] In fact Cicero was also seeking support against attacks upon his firm handling of the Catilinarian conspiracy and saw a powerful ally in a noble of Sulla's immense wealth and influence. If he had Sulla tied to him by the debt of a successful defence, his own situation would be greatly strengthened.

[a] 21 f., p. 332 f. [b] 1-35, pp. 314-348. [c] 47, p. 360.
[d] Cf. pp. 180-182 on Cicero's motives for defending Murena.
[e] 20, p. 332 ; 8-9, pp. 320-322 ; 5, p. 318.

PRO SULLA

Another source of concern to him was the coolness of Pompey, disappointed by his failure to obtain a command against Catiline, and Sulla was Pompey's brother-in-law.[a] He may also have hoped to conciliate the more moderate members of the popular party by easing his pressure upon the remaining Catilinarians. Cicero was in no position to let slip an opportunity of winning support in any quarter and could not afford to incur the hostility of men like Sulla by refusing to assist them. It may not be irrelevant, either, that Sulla's half-brother, Caecilius Rufus, the tribune of 63 mentioned above, had assisted those who opposed Rullus' land bill and thus placed them under an obligation to him.[b] We know too that Cicero had borrowed a very large sum of money from Sulla in order to buy from Crassus a house on the Palatine. The news of this loan got out and Cicero had some difficulty in living it down.[c]

The prosecution had charged Sulla with complicity both in the earlier affair and in the conspiracy of 63.[d] Hortensius opened for the defence and it was arranged that he should deal with the first charge while Cicero should concentrate on the events of 63[e] and deliver the final emotional appeal to the jury, a task at which he was unrivalled.[f] Since neither Torquatus' nor Hortensius' speech is extant we have

[a] This may be inferred from Cicero, ad Quintum fratrem 3. 3. 2. See R. Syme, Sallust 102, n. 88. For Pompey's maintenance of his connexions with the house of the Dictator, see E. S. Gruen, " Pompey, the Roman Aristocracy, and the Conference of Luca," Historia 18 (1969), 75 f.

[b] 65, p. 378. See also p. xxiv. [c] Aulus Gellius, 12. 12. 2-4.
[d] 11, p. 322. [e] 13, p. 326.
[f] 86 f., p. 400 f. See Cicero, Orator 130 and Brutus 190. Cf. p. 183.

virtually no knowledge of the details of the charges relating to the earlier affair or of the defence's reply.

Cicero's speech, even if not always wholly convincing, was an extremely able piece of pleading. Throughout his defence of Sulla against the second charge he makes much of his own central position in Rome in 63 and of his own version of the events of that year.[a] He relies first and foremost upon his own *auctoritas* and argues that the man who discovered the conspiracy, saved the State and dealt with the conspirators would never defend Sulla if he were guilty. But much of the speech is devoted to rebutting charges which were probably flimsy or not likely to have been an important part of Torquatus' case. The charge that Cicero had falsified official documents,[b] that Sulla had hired gladiators, had connexions with Publius Sittius, the troubles between the original inhabitants and new colonists at Pompeii, the attack upon Lucius Caecilius' bill, may all come in this category.[c] Elsewhere it is clear that Cicero is on more difficult ground. His justification for the division of duties between himself and Hortensius cannot be accepted. The excuse that he was ignorant of the events leading to the first charge because he had not yet reached the consulship is

[a] 14, p. 326.
[b] 40 f., p. 352 f. E. Gabba, " Cicerone e la falsificazione dei senatoconsulti," *Studi Classice e Orientali* 10 (1961), 92, concludes that the minutes of the evidence given by the Allobroges need not be free from manipulation, and that Torquatus, who was close to Cicero at the time, would be in a position to know certain things that Cicero would have preferred to be kept quiet.
[c] 54-55, pp. 366-368 ; 56-59, pp. 368-372 ; 60-62, pp. 372-374 ; 62-66, pp. 374-378.

310

clearly untenable.[a] In 66 he was a senior magistrate, a praetor, and in the following year seriously considered defending Catiline and running with him for the consulship.[b] He must have had sufficient knowledge to deal with the events of those years. If he did not, the lack of it did not inhibit him from making explicit and sweeping statements in other speeches.[c] It is much more likely that he had taken up a position elsewhere which made it prudent for him to leave this part of the charge to Hortensius.

His letter to Pompey was another source of trouble. In this letter, as the prosecution pointed out, he had linked the earlier allegations and the conspiracy of 63. In order to free Sulla from involvement in what was going on in 66, he, firstly, lays all the blame for the riots when Autronius and Sulla were on trial that year upon the violent Autronius and, secondly, he manages to substitute Catiline for Sulla among the names of those behind the plots that were allegedly being hatched, implying that Catiline and Autronius were to have become consuls in place of the murdered men. This solution, however, created a further problem because the alleged victim, Manlius Torquatus, had spoken up for Catiline at his trial for extortion in 65, but Cicero managed to play that awkward fact down.[d]

The facts behind the case are not easy to determine. The prosecution does not appear to have had any solid evidence with which to press home their

[a] 11-13, pp. 322-326. [b] ad Atticum 1. 2. 1.
[c] in toga candida ap. Asconius 92 C ; pro Murena 81, p. 288 ; in Catilinam 1. 15, p. 46.
[d] 67-68, pp. 378-380. See also p. 4, n. a. Cf. R. Syme, Sallust 89-90.

charges. It may well have been that the wily Sulla had supported Catiline and Autronius, but without doing anything to incriminate himself. He would then stand to share in the benefits flowing from their success without incurring any of the risks. At all events Cicero's skill was rewarded and Sulla acquitted.

Of his later life we know little. His house was used by Clodius as a base for his violence—in all probability with its owner's connivance [a]—and in 54, after a contest with Torquatus, Sulla secured the right to prosecute Gabinius on a charge of bribery. He fought with Caesar in the Civil War and was one of his senior commanders in 48 and 47. He saw service at Dyrrachium and commanded the right wing of Caesar's army at Pharsalus.[b] In the following year he nearly lost his life in a mutiny and he died in 45.

Cicero's reaction to his death recorded in letters to two friends, Dolabella and Cassius,[c] is a far cry from his attitude towards his client in this speech. There can be little doubt that the version of Cicero's feelings for the man contained in his letters is closer to the truth than the lawyer's account of his client.

[a] ad Atticum 4. 3. 3.
[b] Caesar, de bello civili 3. 51. 1 and 89. 3.
[c] ad familiares 9. 10. 3 and 15. 17. 2.

PRO SULLA

The Manuscripts

T	=codex Tegernseensis, now Monacensis 18787, 11th century
E	=codex Erfurtensis, now Berolinus 252, 12th-13th centuries (containing 81-93. Gulielmius and Zinzerlingus preserve a number of readings from an earlier part of the codex that was subsequently lost)
e	=codex Palatinus 1525, written in A.D. 1467 (43 is missing)
a	=codex Laurentianus (S. Crucis) xxiii. Sin. 3 (Lagomarsinianus 43), 14th century
p	=codex Palatinus 1820, written in A.D. 1394
Σ	=codex Parisiensis 14749, formerly codex S. Victoris 91, 15th century
g	=codex Parisiensis 16228
b	=codex S. Marci 255, Flor. Bibl. Nat. I. iv. 4 (Lagomarsinianus 6), 15th century
π	=codex Parcensis, now Bruxellensis 14492, 14th century
χ	=codex S. Marci 254, Flor. Bibl. Nat. I. iv. 5 (Lagomarsinianus 3)
ψ	=codex Laurentianus (Gadd.) xc. sup. 69
c	=codex Oxoniensis Canonici 226, 15th century
k	=codex Parisiensis 7779, written in A.D. 1459
ς	= codices *ck*
Schol.	=Scholiasta Bobiensis

PRO P. SULLA ORATIO

1 Maxime vellem, iudices, ut P. Sulla et antea dignitatis suae splendorem obtinere et post calamitatem acceptam modestiae fructum aliquem percipere potuisset. Sed quoniam ita tulit casus infestus ut in amplissimo honore cum communi ambitionis invidia tum singulari Autroni odio everteretur, et in his pristinae fortunae reliquiis miseris et adflictis tamen haberet quosdam quorum animos ne supplicio quidem suo satiare posset, quamquam ex huius incommodis magnam animo molestiam capio, tamen in ceteris malis facile patior oblatum mihi tempus esse in quo boni viri lenitatem meam misericordiamque, notam quondam omnibus, nunc quasi intermissam agnoscerent, improbi ac perditi cives domiti[1] atque victi praecipitante re publica vehementem me fuisse atque fortem, conservata mitem ac misericordem faterentur.

2 Et quoniam L. Torquatus, meus familiaris ac necessarius, iudices, existimavit, si nostram in accusatione sua necessitudinem familiaritatemque violasset, ali-

---

[1] domiti *Clark.* re domiti *T.* redomiti *the other MSS.*

---

[a] The consulship; see p. 303. [b] See p. 311.
[c] See p. 308. [d] See p. 307.

SPEECH IN DEFENCE OF
PUBLIUS CORNELIUS SULLA

It would be my dearest wish, gentlemen of the jury, 1
that Publius Sulla could on the previous occasion have
preserved the lustre of his office [a] and after his
conviction could have reaped some reward for his
obedience to the law. An unkind fate, however,
ensured that the jealousy which invariably accom-
panies a political career and the unique hatred felt for
Autronius [b] combined to deprive him of the highest office. It also ensured that in that pitiful and battered debris of his former good fortune there were
found men whose spite was not to be satisfied even
by his punishment. Deeply grieved though I am by
his misfortunes, yet in the midst of my other problems
I am well pleased that an occasion has been offered
me of enabling loyal citizens to recognize my leniency and mercy that used to be known universally
but are today virtually suspended. [c] I am pleased too
that I can force unprincipled and abandoned citizens,
now that they have been subdued and defeated, to
admit that, unrelenting and firm as I was when the
State was collapsing about us, I became mild and
compassionate once it had been saved. My close and 2
intimate friend, Lucius Torquatus,[d] has thought,
gentlemen, that a violation of our friendship and
intimacy in his speech for the prosecution can in some

quid se de auctoritate meae defensionis posse detrahere, cum huius periculi propulsatione coniungam defensionem offici mei. Quo quidem genere non uterer orationis, iudices, hoc tempore, si mea solum interesset; multis enim locis mihi et data facultas est et saepe dabitur de mea laude dicendi ; sed, ut ille vidit, quantum de mea auctoritate deripuisset, tantum se de huius praesidiis deminuturum, sic hoc ego sentio, si mei facti rationem vobis constantiamque huius offici ac defensionis probaro, causam quoque me P. Sullae probaturum.

3   Ac primum abs te illud, L. Torquate, quaero, cur me a ceteris clarissimis viris ac principibus civitatis in hoc officio atque in defensionis iure secernas. Quid enim est quam ob rem abs te Q. Hortensi factum, clarissimi viri atque ornatissimi, non reprehendatur, reprehendatur meum ? Nam, si est initum a P. Sulla consilium inflammandae huius urbis, exstinguendi imperi, delendae civitatis, mihi[1] maiorem hae res dolorem quam Q. Hortensio, mihi maius odium adferre debent, meum denique gravius esse iudicium, qui adiuvandus in his causis, qui oppugnandus, qui defendendus, qui deserendus esse videatur ? "Ita," inquit ; "tu enim investigasti, tu patefecisti coniura-

4 tionem." Quod cum dicit, non attendit eum qui patefecerit hoc curasse, ut id omnes viderent quod antea fuisset occultum. Qua re ista coniuratio, si patefacta per me est, tam patet Hortensio quam mihi. Quem cum videas hoc honore, auctoritate, virtute,

---

[1] mihi me *e.* mihine *Halm.* mihi nonne *Kasten.*

---

[a] Cf. *pro Murena 2*, p. 188.   [b] See p. 307 ; also p. 179.
[c] Because Cicero, not Hortensius, had exposed the conspiracy.

way diminish the authority of my speech for the defence. I shall therefore justify the fulfilment of my obligation to Sulla at the same time as I rebut the charge against him. I should not, of course, be taking this line in my speech now, if only my own interests were involved,[a] for I have already had many opportunities and I shall have many more in the future of singing my own praises ; but he realized that any damage that he inflicted upon my prestige would to that extent weaken the defence of my client, and I therefore now feel that, if I convince you that I have acted reasonably and consistently in undertaking this obligation to defend him, I shall also convince you of the case for Publius Sulla.

Now, my first question, Lucius Torquatus, is this: 3 why do you make a distinction between me and the other distinguished figures and leading men in the State over this fulfilment of an obligation and the right to appear for the defence ? Why is it that you attack my action but not that of the distinguished and illustrious Hortensius ? [b] If Sulla planned to burn this city, to annihilate our empire, to destroy the State, ought these acts to inspire greater anguish, greater hatred in me than in Hortensius ? [c] Ought I to be the more severe judge in deciding who should be supported in these cases, who attacked, who defended and who abandoned ? " Yes," he says, " for you investigated, you exposed the conspiracy." When 4 he says this, he fails to note that the man who exposed it took good care that what had been secret previously should become public knowledge. As a result, although that conspiracy was exposed by my efforts, it is now as familiar to Hortensius as it was to me. Hortensius, distinguished as he is by high office,

317

consilio praeditum non dubitasse quin innocentiam P.
Sullae defenderet, quaero cur qui aditus ad causam
Hortensio patuerit mihi interclusus esse debuerit;
quaero illud etiam, si me, qui defendo, reprehendendum putas esse, quid tandem de his existimes
summis viris et clarissimis civibus, quorum studio
et dignitate celebrari hoc iudicium, ornari causam,
defendi huius innocentiam vides. Non enim una
ratio est defensionis ea quae posita est in oratione;
omnes qui adsunt, qui laborant, qui salvum volunt,
5 pro sua parte atque auctoritate defendunt. An vero,
in quibus subselliis haec ornamenta ac lumina rei
publicae viderem, in his me apparere nollem, cum
ego illum in locum atque in hanc excelsissimam sedem dignitatis atque honoris multis meis ac magnis
laboribus et periculis ascendissem? Atque ut intellegas, Torquate, quem accuses, si te forte id offendit
quod ego, qui in hoc genere quaestionis defenderim
neminem, non desim P. Sullae, recordare de ceteris
ris quos adesse huic vides; intelleges et de hoc et
de aliis iudicium meum et horum par atque unum
6 fuisse. Quis nostrum adfuit Vargunteio? Nemo, ne
hic quidem Q. Hortensius, praesertim qui illum solus
antea de ambitu defendisset. Non enim iam se ullo
officio cum illo coniunctum arbitrabatur, cum ille
tanto scelere commisso omnium officiorum societatem
diremisset. Quis nostrum Serv. Sullam, quis Publium,

---

^a The *consulares viri* who were in court to lend Sulla their
support. ^b *i.e.* of Catilinarians.
^c See *in Catilinam* 1. 9, p. 42 and note.

prestige, ability and intelligence, had no doubt, as you see, that in Publius Sulla he was defending an innocent man, and so I ask why access to this case was open to Hortensius but should be closed to me. If you think, moreover, that I deserve censure as counsel for the defence, I ask: what do you think of these leading figures and distinguished citizens, men of drive and distinction, whom you can see thronging this court, making this case famous and proclaiming my client's innocence? There are other ways of conducting a defence than by a speech. Everybody who supports a defendant by his presence, by his exertions, by his desire to see him acquitted is defending him so far as his part and his influence go. Or was I really likely to refuse to appear on those 5 benches on which I saw these ornaments and luminaries of the Republic *a* when I had by my own exertions fraught with peril to myself risen to that exalted position, to that eminent throne of high rank and office? To enable you to understand, Torquatus, who it is that you are accusing,—in case you are annoyed that I am not failing Publius Sulla seeing that I have not defended anyone else in a trial of this nature *b*—bear in mind the others whom you see supporting him. You will then understand that I summed up the defendant and the others in exactly the same way as did those here in court. Who of us 6 supported Vargunteius? Not one, not even my learned friend Quintus Hortensius, and that although he had defended him previously on a charge of bribery whereas we had not.*c* He did not think that he remained bound by any obligation to a man who by committing so heinous a crime had broken the bond of all obligations. Who of us thought that Servius

319

quis M. Laecam, quis C. Cornelium defendendum
putavit, quis eis horum adfuit ? Nemo. Quid ita ?
Quia ceteris in causis etiam nocentis viri boni, si
necessarii sunt, deserendos esse non putant; in hoc
crimine non solum levitatis est culpa verum etiam
quaedam contagio sceleris, si defendas eum quem
7 obstrictum esse patriae parricidio suspicere. Quid ?
Autronio nonne sodales, non conlegae sui, non veteres
amici, quorum ille copia quondam abundarat, non hi
omnes qui sunt in re publica principes defuerunt ?
Immo etiam testimonio plerique laeserunt. Statu-
erant tantum illud esse maleficium quod non modo
non occultari per se sed etiam aperiri inlustrarique
deberet. Quam ob rem quid est quod mirere, si cum
isdem me in hac causa vides adesse cum quibus in
ceteris intellegis afuisse ? Nisi vero me unum vis
ferum praeter ceteros, me asperum, me inhumanum
existimari, me singulari immanitate et crudelitate
8 praeditum. Hanc mihi tu si propter meas res gestas
imponis in omni vita mea, Torquate, personam,
vehementer erras. Me natura misericordem, patria
severum, crudelem nec patria nec natura esse voluit ;
denique istam ipsam personam vehementem et acrem
quam mihi tum tempus et res publica imposuit iam
voluntas et natura ipsa detraxit. Illa enim ad breve
tempus severitatem postulavit, haec in omni vita

---

a For Servius and the others, see p. 305. Publius Sulla is
not to be confused with the defendant in this trial.
320

Sulla, Publius Sulla, Marcus Laeca or Gaius Cornelius
deserved to be defended ? [a] Who of those here in
court came to their aid ? Not one. Why was this ?
Because men loyal to their friends think that in other
types of case they should not desert them even if they
are guilty, but in a case such as this you would not
only be guilty of irresponsibility but also in danger
of infection, as it were, from the crime if you were to
defend a man whom you suspect of being implicated
in high treason. Look at Autronius ! Did not his 7
boon companions, his colleagues and his old friends,
of whom he had formerly enjoyed a wide circle, did
not all of them who are leading men in the State fail
him ? The majority, indeed, went further and gave
evidence against him. They had decided that his
crime was so heinous that it was their duty not only
not to conceal it but in addition to lay it bare and
bring it to the light of day. What cause, then, for
you to be surprised that in this case you see me giving
my support in the company of men with whom, as
you know, I withheld it in the other cases ? It may,
of course, be that you want me to be singled out for a
reputation of being fiercer, more hard-hearted and
less compassionate than the others, possessed of an
unparalleled savagery and cruelty. If you char- 8
acterize the whole of my life, Torquatus, on the basis
of my consulship, you are very much mistaken.
Nature meant to me be merciful, my country meant
me to be firm, neither country nor Nature meant
me to be cruel. Furthermore, my disposition and
Nature have now caused me to shed that harsh and
stern rôle which the State's circumstances forced
upon me at the time. My country demanded
severity for a short time ; Nature has sought com-

9 misericordiam lenitatemque desiderat. Qua re nihil
est quod ex tanto comitatu virorum amplissimorum
me unum abstrahas ; simplex officium atque una
bonorum est omnium causa. Nihil erit quod admirere
posthac, si in ea parte in qua hos animum adverteris
me videbis. Nulla est enim in re publica mea causa
propria ; tempus agendi fuit magis proprium quam
ceteris, doloris vero et timoris et periculi fuit illa
causa communis ; neque enim ego tunc princeps ad
salutem esse potuissem, si esse alii comites noluissent.
Qua re necesse est, quod mihi consuli praecipuum
fuit praeter alios, id iam privato cum ceteris esse
commune. Neque ego hoc partiendae invidiae, sed
communicandae laudis causa loquor ; oneris mei par-
10 tem nemini impertio, gloriae bonis omnibus. "In
Autronium testimonium dixisti," inquit ; " Sullam
defendis." Hoc totum eius modi est, iudices, ut, si
ego sum inconstans ac levis, nec testimonio fidem
tribui convenerit nec defensioni auctoritatem ; sin est
in me ratio rei publicae, religio privati offici, studium
retinendae voluntatis bonorum, nihil minus accusator
debet dicere quam a me defendi Sullam, testimonio
laesum esse Autronium. Videor enim iam non solum
studium ad defendendas causas verum etiam opinionis
aliquid et auctoritatis adferre ; qua ego et moderate
utar, iudices, et omnino non uterer, si ille me non
coegisset.
11 Duae coniurationes abs te, Torquate, constituun-

---

^a Cf. pro Murena 6, p. 192. This theme is prominent in
Cicero's speeches after 63 in self-justification of his execution
of the Catilinarians.

^b i.e. the Optimates. For the political considerations be-
hind Cicero's defence of Sulla, see p. 308.

^c i.e. that the two actions are inconsistent.

passion and mildness throughout my whole life.[a]
There is, then, no reason why you should pick upon 9
me to omit from this great company of distinguished
men. Duty is indivisible and the cause of loyal men
is common to all. You will have no ground for
surprise after this, if you see me in the party in which
you observe these men.[b] There is no political interest
that is mine exclusively. The occasion for action fell
to me and not to them but we all shared the distress,
the terror and the danger. Indeed, I could not at
the time have been the guide to safety, had not others
been willing to accompany me. For this reason, as a
private citizen, I must now share with everybody else
that responsibility which during my consulship was
peculiarly mine and shared with only a few others.
I say this, not to divide out the odium, but to share
the praise ; part of my burden I share with no man,
a share in the renown I give to all loyal citizens.
" You gave evidence against Autronius," he says, 10
" and yet you are defending Sulla." The long and
the short of it, gentlemen, is that if I am inconsistent
and unstable, no credence should have been given to
my evidence then nor weight to my defence now.
But if I do show regard for the public interest, respect
for personal obligation and a desire to retain the
good-will of loyal men, the last thing that the prosecutor should say is that I gave damaging evidence
against Autronius but am defending Sulla.[c] I think
that I now bring to my briefs for the defence not only
enthusiasm but some reputation and prestige as well.
This, gentlemen, I shall use in moderation, and I
would not be using it at all, had not Torquatus forced
me to do so.

You assume two conspiracies, Torquatus : one is 11

tur, una quae Lepido et Volcacio consulibus patre tuo
consule designato facta esse dicitur, altera quae me
consule; harum in utraque Sullam dicis fuisse. Patris tui, fortissimi viri atque optimi consulis, scis me
consiliis non interfuisse; scis me, cum mihi summus
tecum usus esset, tamen illorum expertem temporum et sermonum fuisse, credo quod nondum penitus
in re publica versabar, quod nondum ad propositum
mihi finem honoris perveneram, quod me ambitio
et forensis labor ab omni illa cogitatione abstrahebat.
12 Quis ergo intererat vestris consiliis? Omnes hi quos
vides huic adesse et in primis Q. Hortensius; qui cum
propter honorem ac dignitatem atque animum exi-
mium in rem publicam, tum propter summam familia-
ritatem summumque amorem in patrem tuum cum
communibus tum praecipuis patris tui periculis com-
movebatur. Ergo istius coniurationis crimen defen-
sum ab eo est qui interfuit, qui cognovit, qui particeps
et consili vestri fuit et timoris; cuius in hoc crimine
propulsando cum esset copiosissima atque ornatissima
oratio, tamen non minus inerat auctoritatis in ea
quam facultatis. Illius igitur coniurationis quae facta
contra vos, delata ad vos, a vobis prolata esse dicitur,
ego testis esse non potui; non modo animo nihil
comperi, sed vix ad auris meas istius suspicionis fama
13 pervenit. Qui vobis in consilio fuerunt, qui vobiscum
illa cognorunt, quibus ipsis periculum tum conflari

---

[a] In 66. [b] For this statement, see p. 310.

said to have been formed when Lepidus and Volcacius were consuls and your father consul-designate,[a] the other during my consulship. You say that Sulla took part in both. You know that I was not present at the deliberations of that gallant man and excellent consul, your father. You know that, in spite of the very close relationship between the two of us, I played no part in that crisis and those discussions; I believe because I was not yet at the heart of political life and had not yet attained that goal of office which I had set myself, and because my desire for advancement and my work at the Bar continued to divert me from all thought about the matter.[b] Who, then, did share your 12 deliberations? All these men whom you see here in support of my client and foremost was Quintus Hortensius. His high office, his prestige, his deep devotion to the Republic, his close friendship and affection for your father caused him to be upset by the dangers that beset us all but most deeply by those confronting your father. The accusation of complicity in the first conspiracy has been rebutted by a man who was involved with it, who investigated it and who shared your deliberations and your fears. Although his speech in rebuttal of this charge was delivered with a wealth of detail and a wide command of language, yet its authoritativeness did not fall short of its technical skill. I was not able, then, to give evidence about the first conspiracy of which, according to the prosecution, you were to be the victims, which was denounced to you and exposed by you. Not only did I know nothing of it, but scarcely a hint of a suspicion of its existence reached my ears. Those who were your advisers, who were investigat- 13 ing the affair with you, the very men believed to be

putabatur, qui Autronio non adfuerunt, qui in illum testimonia gravia dixerunt, hunc defendunt, huic adsunt, in huius periculo declarant se non crimine coniurationis, ne adessent ceteris, sed hominum maleficio deterritos esse. Mei consulatus autem tempus et crimen maximae coniurationis a me defendetur. Atque haec inter nos partitio defensionis non est fortuito, iudices, nec temere facta ; sed cum videremus eorum criminum nos patronos adhiberi quorum testes esse possemus, uterque nostrum id sibi suscipiendum putavit de quo aliquid scire ipse atque

14 existimare potuisset. Et quoniam de criminibus superioris coniurationis Hortensium diligenter audistis, de hac coniuratione quae me consule facta est hoc primum attendite.

Multa, cum essem consul, de summis rei publicae periculis audivi, multa quaesivi, multa cognovi ; nullus umquam de Sulla nuntius ad me, nullum indicium, nullae litterae pervenerunt, nulla suspicio. Multum haec vox fortasse valere deberet eius hominis qui consul insidias rei publicae consilio investigasset, veritate aperuisset, magnitudine animi vindicasset, cum is se nihil audisse de P. Sulla, nihil suspicatum esse diceret. Sed ego nondum utor hac voce ad hunc defendendum ; ad purgandum me potius utar, ut mi-

the intended victims of the attempt being organized at the time, men who did not support Autronius, who gave damaging evidence against him, these men are defending Sulla, are supporting him and in his trial are revealing that they were deterred from supporting the others not by the charge of conspiracy but by the criminality of the accused. Concerning the events of my consulship and on the charge relating to the more important of the conspiracies Sulla will be defended by me. Moreover, gentlemen, this division of the defence between us has not been made at random or recklessly; but when we saw that we were being retained as advocates to rebut charges upon which we could give evidence, each of us thought that he should deal with the events about which he had been able to acquire some personal knowledge and form a personal opinion. You heard Hortensius 14 with attention on the charges relating to the first conspiracy, so now listen first to what I have to say about the second conspiracy which was formed during my consulship.

When I was consul, I heard many reports about the desperate perils threatening the State. I made many inquiries, I learnt many facts. No message about Sulla ever reached me, no information, no letter, not a breath of suspicion. When a man who as consul had by his measures for the State's well-being unearthed a conspiracy, by his frankness disclosed it and by his resoluteness punished it, said that he had received no information about Publius Sulla and entertained no suspicion about him, this assertion of his ought perhaps to carry considerable weight. I am not yet, however, using this assertion to defend Sulla; I shall use it rather to clear myself and enable

rari Torquatus desinat me qui Autronio non ad-
15 fuerim Sullam defendere. Quae enim Autroni fuit
causa, quae Sullae est ? Ille ambitus iudicium tollere
ac disturbare primum conflato voluit gladiatorum
ac fugitivorum tumultu, deinde, id quod vidimus
omnes, lapidatione atque concursu; Sulla, si sibi
suus pudor ac dignitas non prodesset, nullum auxilium requisivit. Ille damnatus ita se gerebat non
solum consiliis et sermonibus verum etiam aspectu
atque voltu ut inimicus esse amplissimis ordinibus,
infestus bonis omnibus, hostis patriae videretur; hic
se ita fractum illa calamitate atque adflictum putavit
ut nihil sibi ex pristina dignitate superesse arbitrare-
16 tur, nisi quod modestia retinuisset. Hac vero in
coniuratione quid tam coniunctum quam ille cum
Catilina, cum Lentulo ? quae tanta societas ullis inter
se rerum optimarum quanta ei cum illis sceleris,
libidinis, audaciae ? quod flagitium Lentulus non
cum Autronio concepit ? quod sine eodem illo Catilina facinus admisit ? cum interim Sulla cum isdem
illis non modo noctem solitudinemque non quaereret
sed ne mediocri quidem sermone et congressu
17 coniungeretur. Illum Allobroges, maximarum rerum
verissimi indices, illum multorum litterae ac nuntii
coarguerunt ; Sullam interea nemo insimulavit, nemo
nominavit. Postremo eiecto sive emisso iam ex urbe

---

[a] For the prevalence of violence in Rome at this time, see
P. A. Brunt, " The Roman Mob," *Past and Present* 35 (1966),
3-27.   [b] The Senate and knights.
[c] 36 f., p. 348 f.

Torquatus to stop expressing his surprise that I am defending Sulla when I have not supported Autronius. What was Autronius' case and what was Sulla's? 15 Autronius wanted to break up the court that was trying him for bribery and stop the case, first by organizing a riot of gladiators and runaway slaves and then, as we all saw, by stone-throwing and an attack on the court.[a] Sulla sought no aid if the propriety of his behaviour and his personal standing were not going to help him. After Autronius' conviction, his proposals and conversation, even his appearance and expression, declared him to be an opponent of the most distinguished orders in the State,[b] a foe to all loyal citizens and the open enemy of his country. Sulla thought himself so broken and shattered by the disaster of that conviction that he felt that there was nothing left him of his former position except what he would retain by his obedience to the law. Who was more closely linked in this con- 16 spiracy with Catiline and Lentulus than Autronius? What association for noble deeds have men ever had so close as that which he had with them for crime, lawlessness, and wild recklessness? What scandalous conduct did Lentulus conceive without Autronius? What crime did Catiline commit without him? At this time Sulla, far from seeking a secret meeting with them by night, did not even talk to them or meet them in normal intercourse. It was 17 Autronius whom the Allobroges, the most reliable informants upon the crucial points, whom letters and messages proved guilty.[c] In this period no one accused Sulla, no one mentioned him by name. Finally, when Catiline had already left the city, whether expelled or allowed to go, it was Autronius

329

Catilina ille arma misit, cornua, tubas,[1] fascis, signa legionis,[2] ille relictus intus, exspectatus foris, Lentuli poena compressus convertit se aliquando ad timorem, numquam ad sanitatem; hic contra ita quievit ut eo tempore omni Neapoli[a] fuerit, ubi neque homines fuisse putantur huius adfines suspicionis et locus est ipse non tam ad inflammandos calamitosorum animos quam ad consolandos accommodatus.

Propter hanc igitur tantam dissimilitudinem hominum atque causarum dissimilem me in utroque 18 praebui. Veniebat enim ad me et saepe veniebat Autronius multis cum lacrimis supplex ut se defenderem, et se meum condiscipulum in pueritia, familiarem in adulescentia, conlegam in quaestura[b] commemorabat fuisse; multa mea in se, non nulla etiam sua in me proferebat officia. Quibus ego rebus, iudices, ita flectebar animo atque frangebar ut iam ex memoria quas mihi ipsi fecerat insidias deponerem, ut iam immissum esse ab eo C. Cornelium qui me in meis sedibus, in conspectu uxoris ac liberorum meorum trucidaret obliviscerer. Quae si de uno me cogitasset, qua mollitia sum animi ac lenitate, numquam me hercule illius lacrimis ac precibus restitissem; 19 sed cum mihi patriae, cum vestrorum periculorum, cum huius urbis, cum illorum delubrorum atque templorum, cum puerorum infantium, cum matronarum ac virginum veniebat in mentem, et cum illae infestae ac funestae faces universumque totius urbis incendium, cum tela, cum caedes, cum civium cruor, cum cinis patriae versari ante oculos atque animum

[1] tubas, secures *Kasten*; *cf. in Catilinam 2. 13.*
[2] legionis *A. Augustinus.* legiones *mss.* legionum *suggested by Clark.*

---

[a] In Etruria. [b] In 75.

who sent arms, bugles, trumpets, rods and legionary standards. He was the one left within the city and awaited by Catiline in the country,[a] whose mind, brought up short by the punishment of Lentulus, was at last struck by fear if not by reason. Sulla on the other hand remained inactive, so much so that throughout this period he was at Naples where men are not thought to have been touched by suspicion of this conspiracy and the very locality is more suited to consoling the spirits of men struck by disaster than to firing them.

It was, therefore, because the two men and their cases were so very dissimilar that I treated them differently. Autronius came to me and came re- 18 peatedly in tears imploring me to defend him and recounting how we had been school-fellows in boy-hood, friends in our youth and colleagues in the quaestorship[b]; he cited the many services that I had done him and some too that he had done me. These pleas, gentlemen, so weakened and shook my resolve that I was ready to shut out from my memory the plot which he had recently formed against my person and to forget that Gaius Cornelius had recently been sent by him to assassinate me in my own home before the eyes of my wife and children. If I had been the sole target of these plans, I would never—heaven knows—have resisted his tears and prayers; I am too kind and tender-hearted. But when I thought of our 19 country, of your perils, of this city, of those sanctu-aries and temples, of the little children, of our wives and daughters, and when those fatal fire-brands of our foes, the whole city in flames, the fighting, the slaughter, the blood of citizens, the ashes of our country, began to play before my eyes and their

331

memoria refricare coeperat, tum denique ei resiste-
bam, neque solum illi hosti ac parricidae sed his etiam
propinquis illius, Marcellis, patri et filio, quorum alter
apud me parentis gravitatem, alter fili suavitatem
obtinebat; neque me arbitrabar sine summo scelere
posse, quod maleficium in aliis vindicassem, idem in
20 illorum socio, cum scirem, defendere. Atque idem
ego neque P. Sullam supplicem ferre, neque eosdem
Marcellos pro huius periculis lacrimantis aspicere,
neque huius M. Messalae, hominis necessarii, preces
sustinere potui; neque enim est causa adversata naturae, nec homo nec res misericordiae meae repug-
navit. Nusquam nomen, nusquam vestigium fuerat,
nullum crimen, nullum indicium, nulla suspicio. Suscepi causam, Torquate, suscepi, et feci libenter ut me,
quem boni constantem, ut spero, semper existi-
massent, eundem ne improbi quidem crudelem dicerent.

21   Hic ait se ille, iudices, regnum meum ferre non
posse. Quod tandem, Torquate, regnum? Consulatus, credo, mei; in quo ego imperavi nihil et contra patribus conscriptis et bonis omnibus parui; quo
in magistratu non institutum est videlicet a me
regnum, sed repressum. An tum in tanto imperio,
tanta potestate non dicis me fuisse regem, nunc
privatum regnare dicis? quo tandem nomine?
" Quod, in quos testimonia dixisti," inquit, " damnati

---

^a Both were named Gaius Claudius Marcellus. The
father was praetor in 80, proconsular governor of Sicily in 79,
and one of the jury assembled to try Verres; the son was
consul in 50.

^b Consul in 61.

^c The word *regnum* was part of the stock-in-trade of
popular political invective.

recollection to gall my heart, only then did I bring myself to resist his pleas; and that particular enemy and traitor to his country was not alone; there were, too, his relatives here now in court, the Marcelli, father and son, of whom I revered the one as a father and cherished the other as a son.[a] I did not, however, think that I could defend their accomplice, who was charged with the very crime that I had punished in others and who was known by me to be guilty, without committing a serious crime myself. Yet I could not 20 bear to have Publius Sulla a suppliant, nor to see these same Marcelli in tears for his danger, nor could I withstand the prayers of my friend here, Marcus Messala,[b] for the case was not uncongenial to my nature, and the man and his circumstances were a fit subject for my compassion. Nowhere had his name been mentioned, nowhere had there been any trace of him; there was no charge, no information, no hint of suspicion. I have undertaken the case, Torquatus, I have undertaken the case and done so gladly. I flatter myself that I have always had a reputation with loyal citizens for firmness and hope that by this decision I shall avoid a name for cruelty even among traitors.

At this point, gentlemen, Torquatus says that he 21 cannot bear my tyranny.[c] What tyranny are you talking about, Torquatus? My consulship, I suppose. I gave no orders; on the contrary I obeyed the Senate and all loyal citizens. During this magistracy, far from establishing a tyranny, I suppressed one. Or do you mean not that I was a tyrant when I wielded an all-embracing power but that I am a tyrant now as a private citizen? On what account? " Because," he says, " those against whom you gave

sunt ; quem defendis, sperat se absolutum iri." Hic
tibi ego de testimoniis meis hoc respondeo, si falsum
dixerim, te in eosdem dixisse ; sin verum, non esse
hoc regnare, cum verum iuratus dicas, probare. De
huius spe tantum dico, nullas a me opes P. Sullam,
nullam potentiam, nihil denique praeter fidem
22 defensionis exspectare. " Nisi tu," inquit, " causam
recepisses, numquam mihi restitisset, sed indicta
causa profugisset." Si iam hoc tibi concedam, Q.
Hortensium, tanta gravitate hominem, si hos talis viros
non suo stare iudicio, sed meo ; si hoc tibi dem quod
credi non potest, nisi ego huic adessem, hos adfuturos
non fuisse, uter tandem rex est, isne cui innocentes
homines non resistunt, an is qui calamitosos non
deserit ? At hic etiam, id quod tibi necesse minime
fuit, facetus esse voluisti, cum Tarquinium et Numam
et me tertium peregrinum regem esse dixisti. Mitto
iam de rege quaerere ; illud quaero peregrinum cur
me esse dixeris. Nam si ita sum, non tam est
admirandum regem esse me, quoniam, ut tu ais, duo
iam[1] peregrini reges Romae fuerunt, quam consulem
Romae fuisse peregrinum. " Hoc dico," inquit, " te
23 esse ex municipio." Fateor et addo etiam : ex eo
municipio unde iterum iam salus huic urbi imperioque

---

[1] duo iam *Clark.* etiam MSS. iam *Müller.*

---

[a] *i.e.* Sulla, although innocent, would go into exile rather
than face Torquatus' charges.

[b] Two of the early kings of Rome, members of an
Etruscan dynasty.

[c] Arpinum. The Latin word *municipium* means an
Italian town which has full citizen rights. These were
acquired by Arpinum in 188.

evidence were condemned and the man whom you defend hopes to be acquitted." My reply to you regarding the evidence I gave is this : if I lied, you too gave evidence against those defendants ; but if I spoke the truth, it is not tyranny, when one tells the truth on oath, to make good one's case. Of Sulla's hopes I have only this to say : Publius Sulla expects from me no limitless resources, no misuse of my power, nothing but the conscientious discharge of the duties of a counsel for the defence. "If you had not 22 accepted the case," he says, "he would never have opposed me but would have gone into exile without standing trial." Suppose for the moment that Quintus Hortensius with all his authority, that the men like him whom you see here in court take their stand, not on their own judgement, but on mine ; suppose, incredible though it is, that if I were not supporting Sulla they would not have done so, tell me : which is the tyrant ? The man whom the in- nocent dare not face *a* or the man who does not aban- don those afflicted by disaster ? At this point too you were pleased, quite unnecessarily, to be funny when you said that there were three foreign tyrants, Tarquin, Numa,*b* and myself. I am not going to ask now about this word "tyrant," but I do ask why you said that I was a foreigner. If I am, it is less sur- prising that I am a tyrant, since you say that Rome has already had two foreign tyrants, than that Rome has had a foreign consul. "I mean," he says, "that you came from an Italian borough." *c* I admit it and 23 I also add that I am from a town which has twice now brought salvation to this city and her empire.*d* I

---

a By Marius who defeated the Germanic invaders and by Cicero himself.

missa est. Sed scire ex te pervelim quam ob rem qui
ex municipiis veniant peregrini tibi esse videantur.
Nemo istuc M. illi Catoni seni, cum plurimos haberet
inimicos, nemo Ti. Coruncanio, nemo M'. Curio, nemo
huic ipsi nostro C. Mario, cum ei multi inviderent,
obiecit umquam. Equidem vehementer laetor eum
esse me in quem tu, cum cuperes, nullam contumeliam
iacere potueris quae non ad maximam partem civium
conveniret. Sed tamen te a me pro magnis causis
nostrae necessitudinis monendum esse etiam atque
etiam puto. Non possunt omnes esse patricii; si
verum quaeris, ne curant quidem; nec se aequales tui
24 propter istam causam abs te anteiri putant. Ac si
tibi nos peregrini videmur, quorum iam et nomen et
honos inveteravit et urbi huic et hominum famae ac
sermonibus, quam tibi illos competitores tuos peregrinos videri necesse erit qui iam ex tota Italia delecti
tecum de honore ac de omni dignitate contendent!
Quorum cave tu quemquam peregrinum appelles, ne
peregrinorum suffragiis obruare. Qui si attulerint
nervos et industriam, mihi crede, excutient tibi istam
verborum iactationem et te ex somno saepe excita-
bunt nec patientur se abs te, nisi virtute vincentur,
25 honore superari. Ac si, iudices, ceteris patriciis me et
vos peregrinos videri oporteret, a Torquato tamen
hoc vitium sileretur; est enim ipse a materno genere
municipalis, honestissimi ac nobilissimi generis, sed

---

[a] Marcus Porcius Cato Censorius (234–149), Tiberius
Coruncanius (consul in 280) and Manius Curius Dentatus
(a plebeian hero of the first half of the third century). All
came from Tusculum and are frequently mentioned together
by Cicero as types portraying the virtues of Romans in early
times. *Cf. pro Murena* 17, p. 205 and note.
[b] See p. 204, n. *b*.

should, however, very much like you to tell me why
you count those who come from Italian boroughs as
foreigners. No one ever reproached with his place of
birth that fine old man Marcus Cato, although he had
a host of enemies, no one ever reproached Tiberius
Coruncanius, no one ever reproached Manius Curius,
nor my fellow-townsman Gaius Marius, although he
too had numerous political enemies.[a] Indeed I am
highly delighted that I am a man against whom you
have been able to fling no insult, however much you
wanted, that did not apply to the majority of citizens.
I still repeatedly feel, though, that I ought to warn
you as the closeness of our friendship dictates. Not
all men are able to be patricians and, to tell the truth,
they do not even care about it ; nor do men of your
own age think that they are your inferiors because
they are not patricians. If in your eyes we whose 24
name and position have become familiar to this city
and a common topic of men's talk and conversation
are foreigners, how much more will be those fellow-
candidates of yours who are the élite of the whole of
Italy and are now going to contend with you for office and every position of importance ! Take care that
you do not call any of them a foreigner or you will
be swamped by your foreigners' votes ! If they bring
to the election vigour and drive, believe me, they
will knock your boastful talk out of you and make
you wake up ; the only way in which they will let you
defeat them for office is by merit.[b] Even, gentlemen, 25
if it had been right for the other patricians to think
the two of us foreigners, Torquatus at any rate should
have kept quiet about this defect ; for he is himself
the citizen of an Italian borough on his mother's side,
a very honourable and distinguished family, but still

tamen Asculani. Aut igitur doceat Picentis solos non
esse peregrinos aut gaudeat suo generi me meum non
anteponere. Qua re neque tu me peregrinum posthac dixeris, ne gravius refutere, neque regem, ne deri-
deare. Nisi forte regium tibi videtur ita vivere ut non
modo homini nemini sed ne cupiditati quidem ulli
servias, contemnere omnis libidines, non auri, non
argenti, non ceterarum rerum indigere, in senatu
sentire libere, populi utilitati magis consulere quam
voluntati, nemini cedere, multis obsistere. Si hoc
putas esse regium, regem me esse confiteor ; sin te
potentia mea, si dominatio, si denique aliquod dictum
adrogans aut superbum movet, quin tu id potius
profers quam verbi invidiam contumeliamque male-
dicti ?

26   Ego, tantis a me beneficiis in re publica positis, si
nullum aliud mihi praemium ab senatu populoque
Romano nisi honestum otium postularem, quis non
concederet ? Ceteri[1] sibi haberent honores, sibi im-
peria, sibi provincias, sibi triumphos, sibi alia prae-
clarae laudis insignia ; mihi liceret eius urbis quam
conservassem conspectu tranquillo animo et quieto
frui. Quid si hoc non postulo ? si ille labor meus
pristinus, si sollicitudo, si officia, si operae, si vigiliae deserviunt amicis, praesto sunt omnibus ; si

---

[1] Ceteri *added by Clark.*

---

[a] A town in Picenum with the same status as Arpinum.
[b] This sentence is strongly reminiscent of Stoic philosophy.
[c] A life of retirement, voluntary or enforced, from the
conduct of affairs of state and from public office ; not the
same as *cum dignitate otium* which is leisure enjoyed in the
midst of an active and successful political career. Ch.

one from Asculum.[a] Let him then either show that only the people of Picenum are not foreigners or be glad that I do not rate my family more highly than his. Do not, then, repeat the reproach that I am a foreigner, if you do not want to be refuted more conclusively; nor that I am a tyrant, if you do not want to make yourself more ridiculous. You may of course think it tyrannical to live in such a way that you are in bondage to no man nor even to any passion; to make light of all excesses; to need neither gold, nor silver, nor any other possession; to give your opinion freely in the Senate; to consult the people's interests more than their wishes; to yield to no man; to resist many.[b] If you think that this is tyrannical, then I admit that I am a tyrant; but if my despotic power, my tyranny, if some overbearing or arrogant utterance angers you, why do you not produce this rather than a prejudicial phrase and abusive slander?

If I were asking the Senate and the Roman people 26 for no reward for myself other than an honourable retirement [c] in return for the great benefits that I have conferred upon the State, who would not grant it? The others would then keep for themselves their offices, commands, provinces, triumphs and other marks of exceptional distinction; but I would be allowed to enjoy with a calm and tranquil mind the sight of the city that I had preserved. What if I do not ask for this? If my drudgery over long years, if my anxious care, my sense of obligation, the help I have given, the vigilance I have shown, are active in the service of friends and readily available to anyone;

Wirszubski, " Cicero's *cum dignitate otium* : a Reconsideration," *Journal of Roman Studies* 44 (1954), 12.

neque amici in foro requirunt studium meum neque
res publica in curia ; si me non modo non rerum
gestarum vacatio sed neque honoris neque aetatis
excusatio vindicat a labore ; si voluntas mea, si in
dustria, si domus, si animus, si aures patent omnibus
si mihi ne ad ea quidem quae pro salute omnium
gessi recordanda et cogitanda quicquam relinquitu
temporis : tamen hoc regnum appellabitur, cuius
27 vicarius qui velit esse inveniri nemo potest ? Longe
abest a me regni suspicio ; si quaeris qui sint Romae
regnum occupare conati, ut ne replices annalium
memoriam, ex domesticis imaginibus invenies. Res
enim gestae, credo, meae me nimis extulerunt ac
mihi nescio quos spiritus attulerunt. Quibus de
rebus tam claris, tam immortalibus, iudices, hoc
possum dicere, me qui ex summis periculis eripuerim
urbem hanc et vitam omnium civium satis adeptum
fore, si ex hoc tanto in omnis mortalis beneficio nullum
28 in me periculum redundarit. Etenim in qua civitate
res tantas gesserim memini, in qua urbe verser
intellego. Plenum forum est eorum hominum quos
ego a vestris cervicibus depuli, iudices, a meis non
removi. Nisi vero paucos fuisse arbitramini qui
conari aut sperare possent se tantum imperium posse
delere. Horum ego faces eripere de manibus et
gladios extorquere potui, sicuti feci, voluntates vero
consceleratas ac nefarias nec sanare potui nec tollere.
Qua re non sum nescius quanto periculo vivam in

ª Marcus Manlius Vulso Capitolinus, an ancestor of
Torquatus, was consul in 392 and saved the Capitol from the

if my loyal support never fails friends at the Bar or
the Republic in the House; if no respite after my
exertions nor plea on the grounds either of office or of
age frees me from toil; if my goodwill, my unremitting efforts, my house, my brain and my ears are at
the service of all comers; if time is not left me to
record and recollect even those measures which I
took for the general safety; will this still be called
tyranny when no one can be found willing to succeed
to it? The suspicion of being a tyrant is quite 27
foreign to my character; but if you ask who have
tried to establish tyrannies at Rome, do not search
through historical records, you will find them in your
own family-tree.[a] Yes, I suppose my achievements
have made me too proud and bred in me a sort of
arrogance; but of these glorious and deathless
achievements, gentlemen, I can say this: I shall be
amply rewarded for saving this city and the lives of
all its citizens from direst peril if no danger falls upon
my person from this great service to all mankind.
I remember the situation in the State in which I 28
wrought these great deeds and I understand the
situation in the city in which I live. The Forum is
full of those men whom I have driven from your
throats, gentlemen, but have not removed from
mine. You may, of course, think that those who
could attempt or expect to be able to destroy so
powerful an Empire were few in number. I could—
and did—snatch their torches and twist their swords
from their grasp, but their criminal and evil intent I
could not heal or remove. I am not ignorant, then, of
the danger involved in my living among such a crowd

Gauls. He was accused of attempting to set up a tyranny
(Livy 6. 20. 4), condemned to death and executed.

tanta multitudine improborum, cum mihi uni cu▯
omnibus improbis aeternum videam bellum esse su▯
29 ceptum. Quod si illis meis praesidiis forte invide▯
et si ea tibi regia videntur quod omnes boni omniu▯
generum atque ordinum suam salutem cum me
coniungunt, consolare te quod omnium mentes impr▯
borum mihi uni maxime sunt infensae et adversae
qui me non modo[1] idcirco oderunt quod eorum con▯
tus impios et furorem conscceleratum repressi, sed e
etiam magis quod nihil iam se simile me vivo cona▯
30 posse arbitrantur. At vero quid ego mirer, si qu▯
ab improbis de me improbe dicitur, cum L. Torqu▯
tus primum ipse his fundamentis adulescentiae iacti▯
ea spe proposita amplissimae dignitatis, deinde I
Torquati, fortissimi consulis, constantissimi senatori▯
semper optimi civis filius, interdum efferatur im▯
moderatione verborum ? Qui cum suppressa voce d
scelere P. Lentuli, de audacia coniuratorum omniu▯
dixisset, tantum modo ut vos qui ea probatis exaudir▯
possetis, de supplicio,[2] de carcere magna et quer▯
31 bunda voce dicebat. In quo primum illud era▯
absurdum quod, cum ea quae leviter dixerat vobi▯
probare volebat, eos autem qui circum iudiciu▯
stabant audire nolebat, non intellegebat ea quae clar▯
diceret ita illos audituros quibus se venditabat ut vo▯
quoque audiretis, qui id non probabatis. Deind▯
alterum iam oratoris est vitium non videre quid quae▯

[1] non modo ψ^2. non solum $\pi\chi\psi^1\varsigma$. non modo solum *th*
other MSS.
[2] supplicio de Lentulo *Tea*. supplicio P. Lentuli *the othe*▯
MSS. P. Lentuli *deleted by Halm*. de laqueo *Reid*. d▯
supplicio sumpto de Lentulo *Kasten*.

[a] Because Lentulus had been executed by Cicero withou▯

of traitors, for I see that I alone have on my hands an
unending war against all traitors. If, however, by 29
any chance you look with disfavour upon the protection I afford and if you think it an act of tyranny that
all loyal men of every class and rank link their
security with mine, console yourself with the thought
that I alone am the chief target for the traitors'
hostility and fury. Not only am I the sole object of
their hate because I suppressed their wicked designs
and criminal lunacy, but all the more because they
think that they cannot repeat their attempt so long
as I am alive. Yet why should I be surprised if evil 30
men speak evil of me ? Even Lucius Torquatus who
laid the foundations of his young life so well and had
such hope before him of winning the highest office,
the son, moreover, of Lucius Torquatus, most valiant
of consuls, most resolute of senators and always the
loyalest of citizens, is sometimes carried away by
exaggerated language. When he had spoken in a
low voice of the crime of Publius Lentulus, of the
recklessness of all the conspirators—just loud enough
to be heard by you who approve what he was saying
—he then began to speak of punishment and of the
condemned cell in a loud and indignant voice.[a] In 31
the first place, a ridiculous side to the proceedings
was that, after he had said in a whisper what he
wanted you to approve and did not want those who
were standing round the court-room to hear, he did
not appreciate that those whose support he was seeking would not hear what he spoke out loud without
you who did not approve hearing it also. Secondly,
it is a further fault in an orator that he did not

being allowed to exercise his right of appeal to the people.
See Appendix B, p. 571.

que causa postulet. Nihil est enim tam alienum ab eo qui alterum coniurationis accuset quam videri coniuratorum poenam mortemque lugere. Quod cum is tribunus pl. facit qui unus videtur ex illis ad lugendos coniuratos relictus, nemini mirum est; difficile est enim tacere, cum doleas; te, si quid eius modi facis, non modo talem adulescentem sed in ea causa in qua te vindicem coniurationis velis esse vehementer 32 admiror. Sed reprehendo tamen illud maxime quod isto ingenio et prudentia praeditus causam rei publicae non tenes, qui arbitrere plebi Romanae eas non probari quas me consule omnes boni pro communi salute gesserunt.

Ecquem tu horum qui adsunt, quibus te contra ipsorum voluntatem venditabas, aut tam sceleratum statuis fuisse ut haec omnia perire voluerit, aut tam miserum ut et se perire cuperet et nihil haberet quod salvum esse vellet? An vero clarissimum virum generis vestri ac nominis nemo reprehendit, qui filium suum vita privavit ut in ceteros firmaret imperium; tu rem publicam reprehendis, quae domesticos hos-33 tis, ne ab eis ipsa necaretur, necavit? Itaque attende, Torquate, quam ego defugiam auctoritatem consulatus mei! Maxima voce ut omnes exaudire possint dico semperque dicam. Adeste omnes animis, Quirites,[1] quorum ego frequentia magno opere laetor; erigite mentis aurisque vestras et me de invidiosis

---

[1] Quirites *Clark.* qui adestis *mss., with* corpore *or* corporibus *in the margin.* qui adstatis *Reid.*

---

[a] According to the scholiast (p. 82 *ed.* Stangl), either Lucius Calpurnius Bestia or Quintus Metellus Nepos. The former is the more likely; for his implication in the conspiracy, see Sallust, *Bellum Catilinae* 17. 3 and 43. 1.

[b] Titus Manlius Torquatus, consul in 340, who sentenced

see what each case requires. There is nothing so damaging to a man who is accusing another of conspiracy as the appearance of regret at the punishment and death of conspirators. When the tribune of the commons [a] who seems to be the only one of them left to mourn the conspirators does just this, no one is surprised; for it is hard to remain silent, when your grief is genuine. I am greatly surprised, however, at any behaviour like that on the part of a young man such as yourself and particularly in a case in which you are setting out to punish conspirators. Your **32** greatest fault, though, is that for all your ability and good sense you do not grasp the State's case when you believe that the Roman commons do not approve those measures which all patriots took for the common safety when I was consul.

Do you believe that any of these men here whose reluctant support you were courting has been so criminal as to have planned the destruction of Rome, or is so wretched as to desire death and to have nothing that he wanted to keep safe? No one blames that famous member of your family and name who put his own son to death in order to strengthen his authority over the rest [b]; do you, then, blame the State which has destroyed the enemies in its midst to avoid being itself destroyed by them? Observe, **33** then, Torquatus, how much I repudiate my responsibility for my acts as consul! At the top of my voice, so that all can hear, I say it now and I shall never stop saying it. All you citizens—and I am delighted that there are so many of you here—give me your attention; alert your minds and ears, and listen to what I

his son to death for engaging the enemy against his father's orders.

rebus, ut ille putat, dicentem attendite ! Ego consul,
cum exercitus perditorum civium clandestino scelere
conflatus crudelissimum et luctuosissimum exitium
patriae comparasset, cum ad occasum interitumque
rei publicae Catilina in castris, in his autem templis
atque tectis dux Lentulus esset constitutus, meis
consiliis, meis laboribus, mei capitis periculis, sine
tumultu, sine dilectu, sine armis, sine exercitu, quinque hominibus comprehensis atque confessis incen-
sione urbem, internicione civis, vastitate Italiam,
interitu rem publicam liberavi ; ego vitam omnium
civium, statum orbis terrae, urbem hanc denique,
sedem omnium nostrum, arcem regum ac nationum
exterarum, lumen gentium, domicilium imperi,
quinque hominum amentium ac perditorum poena
34 redemi.   An me existimasti haec iniuratum in iudicio
non esse dicturum quae iuratus in maxima contione
dixissem ?   Atque etiam illud addam, ne qui forte
incipiat improbus subito te amare, Torquate, et aliquid sperare de te, atque ut idem omnes exaudiant
clarissima voce dicam.   Harum omnium rerum quas
ego in consulatu pro salute rei publicae suscepi atque
gessi L. ille Torquatus, cum esset meus contubernalis
in consulatu atque etiam in praetura fuisset, cum
princeps, cum auctor, cum signifer esset iuventutis,[1]
actor,[2] adiutor, particeps exstitit ; parens eius, homo
amantissimus patriae, maximi animi, summi consili,

---

[1] cum princeps . . . iuventutis *placed here by Clark*. exstitit cum princeps . . . iuventutis ᴍss.

[2] actor *Orelli*. auctor ᴍss.

---

[a] The execution of Lentulus, Cethegus, Statilius, Gabinius
and Ceparius.

[b] His oath on the last day of his consulship ; see p. 184.

am saying about the actions which he finds so odious. An army of abandoned citizens had been scraped together in a secret plot and had prepared for their country the most cruel and grievous destruction, Catiline had been placed in command of the camp to destroy and annihilate the Republic and Lentulus in command among our temples and homes ; but I, as consul, by my decisions, by my efforts and at the risk of my life, but without any state of emergency, without a levy, without use of arms, without an army, by the arrest and confession of five men, I rescued the city from burning, the citizens from slaughter, Italy from devastation and the Republic from destruction. By the punishment of five demented desperados [a] I saved the lives of all the citizens, the peace of the world, this city, the home of each one of us, the defence of foreign kings and peoples, the glory of all nations and the heart of empire. Did you think that I would not repeat in a 34 court of law when I was not on oath, what I had said on oath at a packed meeting of the people ? [b] Furthermore, to avoid the possibility of some scoundrel suddenly taking a liking to you, Torquatus, and building up his hopes of something from you, I shall add this too ; and to enable everyone to hear it, I shall say it loudly and clearly. In all the decisions and measures which I took during my consulship for the safety of the State, Lucius Torquatus who had been my comrade in the praetorship as well as in the consulship came forward in his capacity as the leader, the organizer and the standard-bearer of the youth to be my agent, my lieutenant and my associate. Indeed his father, a devoted patriot and a man of very great courage, excellent judgement and exceptional

singularis constantiae, cum esset aeger, tamen omnibus rebus illis interfuit, nusquam est a me digressus, studio, consilio, auctoritate unus adiuvit plurimum, cum infirmitatem corporis animi virtute superaret.
35 Videsne ut eripiam te ex improborum subita gratia et reconciliem bonis omnibus ? qui te et diligunt et retinent retinebuntque semper nec, si a me forte desciveris, idcirco te a se et a re publica et a tua dignitate deficere patientur. Sed iam redeo ad causam atque hoc vos, iudices, testor : mihi de memet ipso tam multa dicendi necessitas quaedam imposita est ab illo. Nam si Torquatus Sullam solum accusasset, ego quoque hoc tempore nihil aliud agerem nisi eum qui accusatus esset defenderem ; sed cum ille tota illa oratione in me esset invectus et cum, ut initio dixi, defensionem meam spoliare auctoritate voluisset, etiam si dolor me meus respondere non cogeret, tamen ipsa causa hanc a me orationem flagitavisset.
36 Ab Allobrogibus nominatum Sullam esse dicis. Quis negat ? Sed lege indicium et vide quem ad modum nominatus sit. L. Cassium dixerunt commemorasse cum ceteris Autronium secum facere. Quaero num Sullam dixerit Cassius. Nusquam. Sese aiunt quaesisse de Cassio quid Sulla sentiret. Videte diligentiam Gallorum ; qui vitam hominum naturamque non nossent ac tantum audissent eos pari calamitate esse, quaesiverunt essentne eadem voluntate. Quid tum Cassius ? Si respondisset idem sentire et secum fa-

---

[a] See pp. 20-23. [b] Their conviction for *ambitus* in 66.

resolution, was present in person at all these events
even though he was ill. He never left my side and,
his strength of will triumphing over the frailty of his
body, more than anyone else he helped me so far as a
man could with his support, advice and personal
influence. Do you see how I cut you off from any 35
sudden popularity with scoundrels and reconcile you
with all patriots ? They hold you in high esteem and
will not now or ever let you go. If you ever abandon
me, they will not allow you on that account to fail
them, the State or your own good name. Now, however, I return to the case and I call you, gentlemen, to
witness this fact : it was he who imposed upon me a
compulsion of a sort to say so much about myself. If
Torquatus had only accused Sulla, I too would now be
confining myself to the defence of the accused ; but
throughout his speech he attacked me and, as I said
at the beginning, he tried to rob my defence of its
authority. Even if my indignation did not compel
me to answer him, the case alone would still have
demanded of me the reply that I have just made.

You say that Sulla was named by the Allobroges.[a] 36
Who denies it ? But read their information and see
how Sulla's name came into it. They said that Lucius
Cassius had mentioned that Autronius and the others
were acting with him. My question is : did Cassius
say that Sulla was ? Nowhere. They say that they
asked Cassius what Sulla's attitude was. Observe
what pains the Gauls took. Not knowing the man's
way of life or character and only hearing that they
had both been convicted on the same charge,[b] they
inquired whether both were of the same way of
thinking. What did Cassius say then ? If he had
replied that their views were identical and that Sulla

349

cere Sullam, tamen mihi non videretur in hunc id
criminosum esse debere. Quid ita ? Quia, qui bar-
baros homines ad bellum impelleret, non debebat mi-
nuere illorum suspicionem et purgare eos de quibus
37 illi aliquid suspicari viderentur. Non respondit tamen
una facere Sullam. Etenim esset absurdum, cum ceteros sua sponte nominasset, mentionem facere Sullae
nullam nisi admonitum et interrogatum ; nisi forte
veri simile est P. Sullae nomen in memoria Cassio non
fuisse. Si nobilitas hominis, si adflicta fortuna, si re-
liquiae pristinae dignitatis non tam inlustres fuissent,
tamen Autroni commemoratio memoriam Sullae rettulisset ; etiam, ut arbitror, cum auctoritates principum coniurationis ad incitandos animos Allobrogum
conligeret Cassius, et cum sciret exteras nationes maxime nobilitate moveri, non prius Autronium quam
38 Sullam nominavisset. Iam vero illud minime probari
potest, Gallos Autronio nominato putasse propter calamitatis similitudinem sibi aliquid de Sulla esse
quaerendum, Cassio, si hic esset in eodem scelere, ne
cum appellasset quidem Autronium, huius in mentem
venire potuisse. Sed tamen quid respondit de Sulla
Cassius ? Se nescire certum. " Non purgat," inquit.
Dixi antea : ne si argueret quidem tum denique,
cum esset interrogatus, id mihi criminosum videretur.
39 Sed ego in iudiciis et in quaestionibus non hoc
quaerendum arbitror, num purgetur aliquis, sed num
arguatur. Etenim cum se negat scire Cassius, utrum

---

^a *i.e.* he wanted the Allobroges to think that the conspiracy
was widely supported by leading men and might therefore
have said that Sulla was involved even when he was not.

^b The onus of proof should be on the prosecution, not on
the defence.

was working with him, I still should not think that it ought to incriminate my client. I say this because Cassius, trying to involve foreigners in the war, did not want to lessen their suspicion or to clear those of whom they seemed to suspect something.[a] He did 37 not in fact reply that Sulla was working with him. Indeed it would be ridiculous for him, when he had named the others without prompting, only to mention Sulla after being reminded or specifically asked about him. Perhaps you think it likely that the name of Publius Sulla had slipped Cassius' mind. Even if the man's aristocratic birth, if his ill-fortune, if the remains of his former position had not been so conspicuous, still the mention of Autronius would have reminded him of Sulla. Moreover, as I see it, Cassius was using the prestige of the leading figures in the conspiracy to spur on the Allobroges and, knowing that foreign peoples are very impressed by aristocratic birth, he would not have named Autronius before Sulla. The view cannot possibly be accepted 38 that, when Autronius' name had been given, the Gauls thought that they ought to make some inquiry about Sulla because the two men had been convicted of the same offence while Cassius, even when he had given Autronius' name, could not remember Sulla, if he were indeed a fellow-conspirator. Apart from that ; what did Cassius reply about Sulla ? That he did not know for certain. "He does not clear him," says Torquatus. I have already said that not even if he had in the end accused Sulla in reply to a direct question, would I think it proof of his guilt. I 39 think that in the criminal courts the question at issue should not be whether a man is innocent but whether he is guilty.[b] When Cassius says that he does not

sublevat Sullam an satis probat se nescire ? " Sublevat apud Gallos." Quid ita ? " Ne indicent." Quid ?
si periculum esse putasset ne illi umquam indicarent,
de se ipse confessus esset ? " Nesciit videlicet."
Credo celatum esse Cassium de Sulla uno ; nam de
ceteris certe sciebat ; etenim domi eius pleraque con-
flata esse constabat. Qui negare noluit esse in eo
numero Sullam quo plus spei Gallis daret, dicere
autem falsum non ausus est, se nescire dixit. Atque[1]
hoc perspicuum est, cum is qui de omnibus scierit de
Sulla se scire negarit, eandem vim esse negationis
huius quam si extra coniurationem hunc esse se scire
dixisset. Nam cuius scientiam de omnibus constat
fuisse, eius ignoratio de aliquo purgatio debet videri.
Sed iam non quaero purgetne Cassius Sullam ; illud
mihi tantum satis est contra Sullam nihil esse in
indicio.

40   Exclusus hac criminatione Torquatus rursus in me
inruit, me accusat ; ait me aliter ac dictum sit in
tabulas publicas rettulisse. O di immortales !—vobis
enim tribuo quae vestra sunt, nec vero possum meo
tantum ingenio dare ut tot res tantas, tam varias, tam
repentinas in illa turbulentissima tempestate rei
publicae mea sponte dispexerim—vos profecto animum meum tum conservandae patriae cupiditate
incendistis, vos me ab omnibus ceteris cogitationibus

---

[1] Atque *Teaπb[1]*. Atqui *the other mss.*

---

[a] Cicero here assumes what he has to prove.
[b] See p. 310, n. *b*.

know, is he trying to clear Sulla or does he convince
us that he really does not know ? "He is trying to
clear him with the Gauls." Why ? "To stop them
including him in their information." If he had
thought that there was a danger that they might ever
lay an information, would he have confessed about
his own part ? "He evidently did not know." I
suppose that it was only Sulla of whom Cassius was
kept in ignorance; for he certainly knew about the
others and it was established that most of the plot
was hatched at his house. In order to give the Gauls
more confidence he did not want to say that Sulla
was not of their number, but he did not dare to say
what was untrue,[a] so he said that he did not know.
It is abundantly clear that, if a man who has known
about all those involved has denied that he knew
about Sulla, his denial is the equivalent of saying that
he knew that Sulla was not involved in the conspiracy. For, when it is accepted that somebody has
known about all those involved, his ignorance about
an individual ought to be taken as clearing him. But
I am not inquiring now whether Cassius clears
Sulla ; it is quite sufficient for me that there is nothing against Sulla in the information.

Thwarted on this charge, Torquatus returns to 40
the attack and makes another accusation against me.
He says that I falsified the entry in the public records
of what was said.[b] Immortal gods !—for I grant you
your due and cannot with honesty claim for myself
the sole credit for distinguishing unaided the number,
variety and speed of the dangers in that storm which
burst so furiously upon the State—it was surely you
who then kindled in my mind the desire to preserve
my country, you who turned me from all other con-

ad unam salutem rei publicae convertistis, vos denique in tantis tenebris erroris et inscientiae clarissi-
41 mum lumen menti meae praetulistis. Vidi ego hoc,
iudices, nisi recenti memoria senatus auctoritatem
huius indici monumentis publicis testatus essem, fore
ut aliquando non Torquatus neque Torquati quispiam
similis—nam id me multum fefellit—sed ut aliquis
patrimoni naufragus, inimicus oti, bonorum hostis,
aliter indicata haec esse diceret, quo facilius vento
aliquo in optimum quemque excitato posset in malis
rei publicae portum aliquem suorum malorum in-
venire. Itaque introductis in senatum indicibus con-
stitui senatores qui omnia indicum dicta, interrogata,
42 responsa perscriberent. At quos viros ! non solum
summa virtute et fide, cuius generis erat in senatu
facultas maxima, sed etiam quos sciebam memoria,
scientia,[1] celeritate scribendi facillime quae dicerentur
persequi posse, C. Cosconium, qui tum erat praetor,
M. Messalam, qui tum praeturam petebat, P. Nigi-
dium, App. Claudium. Credo esse neminem qui his
hominibus ad vere referendum aut fidem putet aut
ingenium defuisse.

Quid ? deinde quid feci ? Cum scirem ita esse indicium relatum in tabulas publicas ut illae tabulae

---

[1] scientia e, Scholiast. scientia, consuetudine et the other
MSS.

---

[a] Cf. in Catilinam 2. 29, p. 98 and note.
[b] Shorthand was introduced at Rome by Cicero according
to Plutarch, Cato Minor 23. 3. His system was probably
derived from Greece (ad Atticum 13. 32. 3) and is closely
linked with the name of his freedman, Tiro. See Oxford
Classical Dictionary 2nd Ed., s.v. tachygraphy, 1033-1034.
[c] Gaius Cosconius, praetor in 63, proconsul in Further
Spain in 62 and one of the commissioners appointed to as-

siderations to the single thought of delivering the Republic, you in short who amid the deep shadow of uncertainty and ignorance illumined my thoughts with the brightness of your light.[a] I realized, gentle- 41 men, that unless I had attested in official records the authenticity of this information while memory of it was still fresh in the Senate, one day, not Torquatus or anyone like Torquatus—a possibility far from my thoughts—but someone who had wrecked his inherit- ance, a foe of peace, an enemy of loyal citizens, might say that the record of this information was inaccurate in order that he might the more easily raise a storm against all the best men and find in the troubles of the State some harbour for his own. When, therefore, the informants had been brought into the Senate I appointed senators to take down all they said, the questions put to them and their replies. What men 42 they were ! Not only were they men of complete integrity and honour, a class that was very well re- presented in the Senate, but men, I knew, whose memory, skill, and speed in writing [b] enabled them to follow what was said with complete ease : Gaius Cosconius who was praetor at the time, Marcus Messala who was then a candidate for the praetor- ship, Publius Nigidius, and Appius Claudius.[c] I do not believe that there is anyone who thinks that these men had not the honesty and competence to make a true record.

Well, what did I do next ? Since I knew that the information had been entered in the public records,

sign land under Caesar's agrarian legislation of 59 ; Marcus Valerius Messala Rufus, consul in 53 ; Publius Nigidius Figulus, praetor in 56 ; and Appius Claudius Pulcher, con- sul in 54.

privata tamen custodia more maiorum continerentur, non occultavi, non continui domi, sed statim describi ab omnibus librariis, dividi passim et pervolgari atque edi populo Romano imperavi. Divisi tota Italia,[1] emisi in omnis provincias; eius indici ex quo oblata salus esset omnibus expertem esse neminem volui.

43 Itaque dico locum in orbe terrarum esse nullum, quo in loco populi Romani nomen sit, quin eodem perscriptum hoc indicium pervenerit. In quo ego tam subito et exiguo et turbido tempore multa divinitus, ita ut dixi, non mea sponte providi, primum ne quis posset tantum aut de rei publicae aut de alicuius periculo meminisse quantum vellet; deinde ne cui liceret umquam reprehendere illud indicium aut temere creditum criminari; postremo ne quid iam a me, ne quid ex meis commentariis quaereretur, ne aut oblivio mea aut memoria nimia videretur, ne denique aut neglegentia turpis aut diligentia crudelis putare-

44 tur. Sed tamen abs te, Torquate, quaero: cum indicatus tuus esset inimicus et esset eius rei frequens senatus et recens memoria testis, et[2] tibi, meo familiari et contubernali, prius etiam edituri indicium fuerint scribae mei, si voluisses, quam in codicem rettulissent, cur[3] cum videres aliter fieri,[4] tacuisti,[5] passus es, non mecum aut ut[6] cum familiarissimo[7] questus es aut, quoniam tam facile inveheris in ami-

---

[1] tota Italia *Madvig.* toti (-ae *e*) Italiae MSS.
[2] et *added by Halm.*   [3] cur *added by Nohl.*
[4] referri *Orelli.*
[5] cur tacuisti Σ *in margin,* πb[1]c[2]k, *editio Veneta.*
[6] ut *added by Clark.*
[7] familiarissimo *Clark.* familiari meo MSS. familiari tuo *Richter.*

but that they would be retained, as was the traditional practice, in the safe-keeping of individuals, I did not conceal it or retain it at home, but immediately ordered it to be copied by all the clerks, distributed everywhere and given full publicity and made known to the Roman people. I broadcast it throughout Italy and despatched it to all the provinces. I did not want anyone to be ignorant of the information which had been responsible for the salvation of us all. I say, therefore, that there is no 43 place in the whole world where the name of the Roman people is known that has not received a copy of this information. In that crisis, so sudden, so sharp, so stormy, I showed great foresight guided, just as I have said, not by my own resources but by divine inspiration. My purpose was, firstly, to stop anyone being able to remember only what suited him about the danger to the State or to any individual; secondly, to prevent anyone ever being allowed to discredit that information or complain that it was too readily accepted ; and finally, to stop an investigation depending any longer upon myself or upon my private notes, any semblance on my part of remembering or forgetting too much and any thought that my laxity was a scandal or my efficiency inhuman. This apart, 44 however, I ask you, Torquatus : your enemy's name was given, a crowded Senate and the memory of the event still fresh in their minds bore witness to it, and my clerks would even have shown the information to you, my friend and close companion, if you had wished, before recording it in the minutes ; why, then, when you saw the record being falsified, did you remain silent ? Why did you allow it ? Why did you not complain to me as a close friend or, since you

cos, iracundius et vehementius expostulasti ? Tu, cum
tua vox numquam sit audita, cum indicio lecto, de-
scripto, divolgato quieveris, tacueris, repente tantam
rem ementiare et in eum locum te deducas ut, ante
quam me commutati indici coargueris, te summae
neglegentiae tuo iudicio convictum esse fateare ?

45   Mihi cuiusquam salus tanti fuisset ut meam neg-
legerem ? per me ego veritatem patefactam conta-
minarem aliquo mendacio ? quemquam denique ego
iuvarem, a quo et tam crudelis insidias rei publicae
factas et me potissimum consule constitutas putarem?
Quod si iam essem oblitus severitatis et constantiae
meae, tamne amens eram ut, cum litterae posteritatis
causa repertae sint, quae subsidio oblivioni esse
possent, ego recentem putarem memoriam cuncti
46 senatus commentario meo posse superari ? Fero ego
te, Torquate, iam dudum fero, et non numquam
animum incitatum ad ulciscendam orationem tuam
revoco ipse et reflecto, permitto aliquid iracundiae
tuae, do adulescentiae, cedo amicitiae, tribuo parenti.
Sed nisi tibi aliquem modum tute constitueris, coges
oblitum me nostrae amicitiae habere rationem meae
dignitatis. Nemo umquam me tenuissima suspicione
perstrinxit quem non perverterim ac perfregerim.
Sed mihi hoc credas velim : non eis libentissime soleo
respondere quos mihi videor facillime posse superare.

attack your friends so readily, remonstrate with me more angrily or vigorously ? Seeing that your voice was never heard, that you did nothing and remained silent when the information had been read, copied and published, how can you suddenly invent a charge as serious as this and get yourself into a position in which before you convict me of tampering with the information you are on your own admission found guilty of the grossest negligence ?

Would anyone's safety have been so important to 45 me that I should neglect my own ? Would I debase with some falsehood the truth which my efforts had revealed ? In short, would I help anyone whom I thought to be the instigator of such a savage plot against the State, a plot at that planned during my consulship ? If, however, I had so quickly forgotten my severity and my resolve, was I so foolish as to think that the recollection of recent events by the whole Senate could be proved wrong by my private journal, when written records have been invented for the benefit of posterity as an aid against forgetfulness ? I suffer you, Torquatus, and have long done so, 46 and on a number of occasions I have restrained and curbed my urge to repay your speech in its own coin; I make some allowance for your temper, I make some concession to your youth, I make some sacrifice to our friendship, I pay some regard to your father; but if you do not lay some restraint upon yourself, you will force me to forget our friendship and take account of my own position. No one has ever touched me with the slightest hint of suspicion without my refuting him and exploding his story. Yet please take my word for this : I get the least pleasure from replying to those who seem to me the easiest to refute. You 47

47 Tu quoniam minime ignoras consuetudinem dicendi
meam, noli hac nova lenitate abuti mea, noli aculeos
orationis meae, qui reconditi sunt, excussos arbitrari,
noli id omnino a me putare esse amissum si quid est
tibi remissum atque concessum. Cum illae valent
apud me excusationes iniuriae tuae, iratus animus
tuus, aetas, amicitia nostra, tum nondum statuo te
virium satis habere ut ego tecum luctari et congredi
debeam. Quod si esses usu atque aetate robustior, essem idem qui soleo cum sum lacessitus ; nunc tecum
sic agam tulisse ut potius iniuriam quam rettulisse

48 gratiam videar. Neque vero quid mihi irascare
intellegere possum. Si, quod eum defendo quem tu
accusas, cur tibi ego non suscenseo, quod accusas eum
quem ego defendo ? " Inimicum ego," inquis, " ac-
cuso meum." Et amicum ego defendo meum. " Non
debes tu quemquam in coniurationis quaestione
defendere." Immo nemo magis cum de quo nihil
umquam est suspicatus quam is qui de aliis multa
cognovit.[1] " Cur dixisti testimonium in alios ? " Quia
coactus sum. " Cur damnati sunt ? " Quia creditum est. " Regnum est dicere in quem velis et defendere quem velis." Immo servitus est non dicere
in quem velis et non defendere quem velis. Ac si
considerare coeperis utrum magis mihi hoc necesse
fuerit facere an istud tibi, intelleges honestius te
inimicitiarum modum statuere potuisse quam me

49 humanitatis. At[2] vero, cum honos agebatur familiae

---

[1] cognovit *ac*[1], *Lambinus.* cogitavit *the other* MSS.
[2] At *cod. Salisb.* 34, *Lambinus.* Aut *T.* An *the other* MSS.

---

[a] For *amicitia,* see p. 307, n. *d.* For Cicero's personal
dislike of Sulla, see p. 307.
[b] The word *servitus,* like *regnum,* is part of the stock-in-
trade of popular political invective.

are very well aware of my normal manner of speaking, so do not strain my unparalleled forbearance in this case; do not think that the stings of my rhetoric have been drawn, they have only been sheathed; do not think that the loss has been all mine in any allowance or concession that I have made to you. The excuses made for the injury you have inflicted carry conviction with me—your quick temper, your youth, our friendship—and I have decided that you are not yet powerful enough for me to need to come to grips and do battle with you. If you were older and more experienced, I should behave as I usually do under provocation; but in this case I shall show by my behaviour towards you that I have tolerated the injury and not repaid it. Moreover, I cannot under- **48** stand why you are angry with me. If it is because I am defending a man whom you are accusing, why am I not angry with you for accusing the man whom I am defending? " I am accusing my enemy," you say. And I am defending my friend.[a] " You should be the last man to defend anyone accused of conspiracy." On the contrary, nobody should be more ready to defend one whom he has never suspected of anything than a man who has known much about others. " Why did you give evidence against others?" Because I had no choice. " Why were they convicted?" Because my evidence was accepted. " It is tyranny to pick and choose whom you wish to defend or attack." On the contrary, it is servitude [b] not to do so. If you start to consider which of the two of us was under the greater con- straint to act as he did, you will see that you could have set bounds to your enmity more creditably than I to my compassion. When your family's highest **49**

vestrae amplissimus, hoc est consulatus parentis tui,
sapientissimus vir familiarissimis suis non suscensuit,
pater tuus, cum Sullam et defenderent et laudarent ?
Intellegebat hanc nobis a maioribus esse traditam
disciplinam ut nullius amicitia ad pericula propulsanda
impediremur. At erat[1] huic iudicio longe dissimilis
illa contentio. Tum adflicto P. Sulla consulatus vobis
pariebatur, sicuti partus est ; honoris erat certamen ;
ereptum repetere vos clamitabatis, ut victi in campo
in foro vinceretis ; tum qui contra vos pro huius salute
pugnabant, amicissimi vestri, quibus non irascebamini,
consulatum vobis eripiebant, honori vestro repugna-
bant, et tamen id inviolata vestra amicitia, integro
officio, vetere exemplo atque instituto optimi cuius-
50 que faciebant. Ego vero quibus ornamentis adversor
tuis aut cui dignitati vestrae repugno ? Quid est
quod iam ab hoc expetas ? Honos ad patrem, insignia
honoris ad te delata sunt. Tu ornatus exuviis huius
venis ad eum lacerandum quem interemisti, ego
iacentem et spoliatum defendo et protego. Atque
hic tu et reprehendis me quia defendam et irasceris ;
ego autem non modo tibi non irascor sed ne reprehendo quidem factum tuum. Te enim existimo tibi
statuisse quid faciendum putares et satis idoneum
offici tui iudicem esse potuisse.[2]

---

[1] At erat *Halm.* Aderat *Ta.* Et erat *the other* MSS. Et
omitted by π.
[2] esse *added by Halm.* potuisse *T.* posuisse *the other* MSS.

---

[a] See p. 562.
[b] The young Torquatus acquired Sulla's rank and insignia
as a result of his successful prosecution. L. R. Taylor,
Party Politics in the Age of Caesar 114.

honour—your father's consulship—was at stake, your
father in his great wisdom was not angry with his
closest friends when they defended Sulla and sang
his praises. He knew that it was a custom inherited
from our ancestors that friendship for no man should
stop us from acting for the defence. But that earlier
dispute was very different from the present case.
On that occasion, if Publius Sulla were condemned,
your family could secure the consulship and this was
what happened. It was a struggle for office. You
went about shouting that you were suing for what
had been stolen from you, for victory in the Forum
after defeat in the Campus Martius.[a] On that
occasion, your closest friends were working against
you in his defence but they did not incur your anger;
they were taking the consulship from you and opposing your rise to office, but they still did this without
forfeiting your friendship, without breaking their
obligation to you, and were following the ancient
precedent and tradition of all the best men. In this 50
case, however, what distinctions of yours am I im-
perilling and what office of yours am I attacking?
What more are you now trying to get from Sulla?
His office went to your father and the insignia of his
office to you. Adorned with his spoils you come to
mutilate the man whom you have destroyed, and I,
as he lies there stripped, defend and protect him.[b]
Such are the circumstances in which you blame me
and are angry with me for defending him. Yet, far
from being angry with you, I do not even blame you
for what you have done. I think that you decided
for yourself what you thought should be done and
were able to be a perfectly competent judge of where
your duty lay.

51 At accusat C. Corneli filius et id aeque valere debet
ac si pater indicaret. O patrem Cornelium sapientem
qui, quod praemi solet esse in indicio, reliquerit, quod
turpitudinis in confessione, id per accusationem fili
susceperit! Sed quid est tandem quod indicat per
istum puerum Cornelius? Si vetera, mihi ignota, cum
Hortensio communicata, respondit Hortensius; sin, ut
ais, illum conatum Autroni et Catilinae, cum in campo
consularibus comitiis, quae a me habita sunt, caedem
facere voluerunt, Autronium tum in campo vidimus—
sed quid dixi vidisse nos? ego vidi; vos enim tum,
iudices, nihil laborabatis neque suspicabamini, ego
tectus praesidio firmo amicorum Catilinae tum et
52 Autroni copias et conatum repressi. Num quis est
igitur qui tum dicat in campum aspirasse Sullam?
Atqui, si tum se cum Catilina societate sceleris con-
iunxerat, cur ab eo discedebat, cur cum Autronio non
erat, cur in pari causa non paria signa criminis
reperiuntur? Sed quoniam Cornelius ipse etiam nunc
de indicando dubitat, et, ut dicitis, informat ad hoc
adumbratum indicium filium, quid tandem de illa
nocte dicit, cum inter falcarios ad M. Laecam nocte
ea quae consecuta est posterum diem Nonarum
Novembrium me consule Catilinae denuntiatione

---

[a] See p. xx.

The son of Gaius Cornelius is a prosecutor and that 51 ought to carry as much weight as if the father were laying the information. Wisdom indeed for Cornelius' father to forgo the reward usually given for an information but to incur the disgrace of a confession elicited through his son's prosecution! What is the information, I should like to know, that Cornelius is laying through that child of his? If they are old charges about which I am ignorant but Hortensius well informed, then Hortensius has answered them; but if, as you say, it is that attempt of Autronius and Catiline when they were planning a massacre at the consular elections over which I was presiding in the Campus Martius, it was Autronius whom we saw in the Campus Martius on that occasion.[a] Why did I say " we " saw? It was I who saw him. You at that time, gentlemen, felt no anxiety and harboured no suspicion, and it was I who on that occasion, under the protection of a stout guard of my friends, suppressed the forces of Catiline and Autronius and the attempt they were making. Surely, then, there is 52 not a single individual who says that Sulla dreamed of entering the Campus Martius on that occasion? If, however, he had at that time been an associate of Catiline in a criminal conspiracy, why did he desert him, why was he not with Autronius, why, if their circumstances were identical, does there not come to light the same evidence for a criminal charge? Cornelius is still reluctant to make a charge in person and, as you say, is priming his son with this flimsy accusation; what, then, does he say of the night of his visit at Catiline's invitation to Marcus Laeca's house in the street of the scythemakers on the 6th of November in my consulship—the night that was the

convenit ? quae nox omnium temporum coniurationis
acerrima fuit atque acerbissima. Tum Catilinae dies
exeundi, tum ceteris manendi condicio, tum discriptio[1] totam per urbem caedis atque incendiorum
constituta est; tum tuus pater, Corneli, id quod tandem aliquando confitetur, illam sibi officiosam provinciam depoposcit ut, cum prima luce consulem
salutatum veniret, intromissus et meo more et iure
amicitiae me in meo lectulo trucidaret.

53   Hoc tempore, cum arderet acerrime coniuratio,
cum Catilina egrederetur ad exercitum, Lentulus
in urbe relinqueretur, Cassius incendiis, Cethegus
caedi praeponeretur, Autronio ut occuparet Etruriam praescriberetur, cum omnia ornarentur,[2] instru-
erentur, pararentur, ubi fuit Sulla, Corneli ? num
Romae ? Immo longe afuit. Num in eis regionibus
quo se Catilina inferebat ? Multo etiam longius.
Num in agro Camerti, Piceno, Gallico, quas in oras
maxime quasi morbus quidam illius furoris perva-
serat ? Nihil vero minus. Fuit enim, ut iam ante
dixi, Neapoli, fuit in ea parte Italiae quae maxime
54 ista suspicione caruit. Quid ergo indicat aut quid
adfert aut ipse Cornelius aut vos qui haec ab illo
mandata defertis ? Gladiatores emptos esse Fausti
simulatione ad caedem ac tumultum ? " Ita prorsus ;
interpositi sunt gladiatores." Quos testamento patris deberi videmus. " Adrepta est familia. Quae si

---

[1] discriptio *Bücheler.* descriptio *mss.*
[2] ornarentur *Landgraf.* ordinarentur *mss.*

---

[a] *Cf. in Catilinam* 1. 8-10, pp. 40-42.
[b] A town in Umbria.

most critical and alarming occasion in all the crises of
that conspiracy ?[a] Then were decided the day for
Catiline's departure, the provision under which the
rest were to remain, the division of the whole city
into sectors for murder and arson. Then your father,
Cornelius, as he at long last admits, complaisantly
demanded for himself the responsibility for murdering
me in my bed when he came at dawn to pay his
respects to the consul and had in accordance with my
custom and the rights of friendship been admitted.

At this time, when the fire of the conspiracy was at **53**
its height, when Catiline was leaving for his army,
when Lentulus was being left in the city, when
Cassius was being put in charge of the arson and
Cethegus of the massacre, when Autronius was being
ordered to seize Etruria, when all the equipment was
being provided, and all the arrangements and preparations being made, where was Sulla, Cornelius ?
Not at Rome, was he ? No, far away. Not in the
area to which Catiline was taking himself off ? No :
much further away than that. Not in Camerinum,[b]
Picenum or Umbria, districts into which the infection
of that mad folly had swept in its full violence ?
Nothing is further from the truth. He was, as I have
already said, at Naples; he was in the part of Italy
which was least suspected of being involved in the
conspiracy. What information, then, or what charge **54**
is being laid either by Cornelius in person or by you
who act upon his instructions ? That gladiators
were bought on a pretext furnished by Faustus for
murder and riot ? " Yes, that's right ; gladiators
were introduced." We see that they were required
by his father's will. " The company was engaged in
a hurry. If this company had been missed, another

esset praetermissa, posset alia familia Fausti munus praebere." Utinam quidem haec ipsa non modo
iniquorum invidiae sed aequorum exspectationi satis
facere posset ! " Properatum vehementer est, cum
longe tempus muneris abesset." Quasi vero tempus
dandi muneris non valde appropinquaret. " Nec
opinante Fausto, cum is neque sciret neque vellet,
55 familia est comparata." At litterae sunt Fausti, per
quas ille precibus a P. Sulla petit ut emat gladiatores
et ut hos ipsos emat, neque solum ad Sullam missae
sed ad L. Caesarem, Q. Pompeium, C. Memmium,
quorum de sententia tota res gesta est. " At praefuit
familiae Cornelius, libertus eius."[1] Iam si in paranda
familia nulla suspicio est, quis praefuerit nihil ad rem
pertinet; sed tamen munere servili[2] obtulit se ad fer-
ramenta prospicienda, praefuit vero numquam, eaque
res omni tempore per Bellum, Fausti libertum, administrata est.

56   At enim Sittius est ab hoc in ulteriorem Hispaniam
missus ut eam provinciam perturbaret. Primum Sittius, iudices, L. Iulio C. Figulo consulibus profectus
est aliquanto ante furorem Catilinae et suspicionem
huius coniurationis; deinde est profectus non tum
primum sed cum in isdem locis aliquanto ante eadem
de causa aliquot annos fuisset, ac profectus est non
modo ob causam sed etiam ob necessariam causam,

---

[1] *libertus eius added by Clark.*
[2] Servili *Lag. 9, Madvig;* *better* Servi, *i.e.* Serv. Sullae.
Cf. 6, Clark.

---

[a] The suggestion is that the company was not up to a
successful performance as gladiators, let alone to fighting in
a revolution as the prosecution alleged was its purpose.

[b] Lucius Julius Caesar, consul in 64 ; Quintus Pompeius,
a nephew of Faustus Sulla and grandson of the Dictator ;

would be able to put on Faustus' games." I doubt whether this company could satisfy the expectation of his friends, let alone the ill-will of his enemies.[a] "Great haste was shown although the date of the games was a long way off." As if the date for giving the games was not in fact getting very close. "The company was acquired without telling Faustus, when he neither knew of it nor wanted it." There is a letter from Faustus in which he begs Publius Sulla to buy gladiators and specifies this very company ; and letters were sent not only to Sulla, but also to Lucius Caesar, to Quintus Pompeius and to Gaius Memmius,[b] and the whole transaction was conducted on the lines they suggested. "His freedman Cornelius was in charge of the company." Now, if no ground for suspicion lies in the acquisition of the company, it does not matter who was in charge of it. Apart from that, Cornelius offered his services to procure weapons—a slave's job—but he was never in charge and the whole time the arrangements were in the hands of Bellus, a freedman of Faustus.

"Sittius [c] was sent by him to Further Spain to stir up trouble in that province." Firstly, gentlemen, Sittius left when Lucius Julius and Gaius Figulus [d] were consuls some time before Catiline's mad folly and any suspicion of the recent conspiracy. Secondly, this was not the first time that he had gone there but some time previously he had been in that region on similar business for a number of years. He had good reason for going there, indeed a vital reason, having

Gaius Memmius, husband of Faustus Sulla's twin sister, Fausta.

[c] Publius Sittius, a Roman knight from Nuceria in Campania, believed to have Catilinarian sympathies.   [d] In 64.

magna ratione cum Mauretaniae rege contracta. Tum autem, illo profecto, Sulla procurante eius rem et gerente plurimis et pulcherrimis P. Sitti praediis venditis aes alienum eiusdem dissolutum est, ut, quae causa ceteros ad facinus impulit, cupiditas retinendae possessionis, ea Sittio non fuerit praediis deminutis.

57 Iam vero illud quam incredibile, quam absurdum, qui Romae caedem facere, qui hanc urbem inflammare vellet, eum familiarissimum suum dimittere ab se et amandare in ultimas terras! Utrum quo facilius Romae ea quae conabatur efficeret, si in Hispania turbatum esset? At haec ipsa per se sine ulla coniunctione agebantur. An in tantis rebus, tam novis consiliis, tam periculosis, tam turbulentis hominem amantissimum sui, familiarissimum, coniunctissimum officiis, consuetudine, usu dimittendum esse arbitrabatur? Veri simile non est ut, quem in secundis rebus, quem in otio secum semper habuisset, hunc in adversis et in eo tumultu quem ipse comparabat ab se dimitteret.

58 Ipse autem Sittius—non enim mihi deserenda est causa amici veteris atque hospitis—is homo est aut ea familia ac disciplina ut hoc credi possit, eum bellum populo Romano facere voluisse? ut, cuius pater, cum ceteri deficerent finitimi ac vicini, singulari exstiterit in rem publicam nostram officio et fide, is sibi nefarium bellum contra patriam suscipiendum putaret? cuius aes alienum videmus, iudices, non libidine, sed

---

important financial dealings with the king of Mauretania. Again, after Sittius' departure, while Sulla
was his agent and was managing his affairs, he sold
a large number of Publius Sittius' finest properties
and paid off his debts; thus the reason why the others
were driven to crime—the desire to remain in possession—did not exist for Sittius since part of his
property had already gone.[a] What is more, how 57
incredible, how absurd it was, that a man who
intended to unleash a massacre at Rome and burn
our city should send his closest friend off on business
to the ends of the earth! Was it to allow him to
achieve his purpose at Rome more easily, if there
were disturbances in Spain? These disturbances,
however, were taking place of their own accord without any such contact. Or did he think that in a crisis
as serious as this, in so novel, so dangerous, so seditious an enterprise, he should send off the man who
was most devoted to him, his dearest friend, and the
one most closely bound to him by ties of obligation,
by their close relationship and by long association?
It is not reasonable to suppose that in the midst of
adversity and a revolution of which he was himself the
instigator he would part with the man whom he had
always had with him in times of prosperity and peace.

Sittius himself—for I must not abandon the cause 58
of an old friend and host—is he the sort of man or are
his family and upbringing such as to make it credible
that he wished to make war upon the Roman people?
That a man whose father, when the others, his
borderers and neighbours, were in revolt,[b] displayed
a unique sense of his ties and loyalty to Rome,
planned to raise the standard of rebellion against
his country? We see, gentlemen, that his debts were

negoti gerendi studio esse contractum, qui ita Romae
debuit ut in provinciis et in regnis ei maximae
pecuniae deberentur ; quas cum peteret, non com-
misit ut sui procuratores quicquam oneris absente se
sustinerent ; venire omnis suas possessiones et patrimonio se ornatissimo spoliari maluit quam ullam mo-
59 ram cuiquam fieri creditorum suorum. A quo quidem
genere, iudices, ego numquam timui, cum in illa rei
publicae tempestate versarer. Illud erat hominum
genus horribile et pertimescendum qui tanto amore
suas possessiones amplexi tenebant ut ab eis membra
citius divelli ac distrahi posse diceres. Sittius numquam sibi cognationem cum praediis esse existimavit
suis. Itaque se non modo ex suspicione tanti sceleris
verum etiam ex omni hominum sermone non armis,
sed patrimonio suo vindicavit.

60   Iam vero quod obiecit Pompeianos esse a Sulla
impulsos ut ad istam coniurationem atque ad hoc
nefarium facinus accederent, id cuius modi sit intellegere non possum. An tibi Pompeiani coniurasse
videntur ? Quis hoc dixit umquam, aut quae fuit
istius rei vel minima suspicio ? " Diiunxit," inquit,
" eos a colonis ut hoc discidio ac dissensione facta
oppidum in sua potestate posset per Pompeianos
habere." Primum omnis Pompeianorum colonorum-
que dissensio delata ad patronos est, cum iam in-
veterasset ac multos annos esset agitata ; deinde ita a
patronis res cognita est ut nulla in re a ceterorum

---

^a For Sullan colonies, see also *pro Murena* 49, p. 250 and *in
Catilinam* 3. 14, p. 114. P. A. Brunt, *Italian Manpower*
225 B.C.–A.D. 14 300-312.

^b Men of influence to represent the interests of the com-
munity at Rome. The office was usually hereditary, and a
colony's first patrons were normally those who had super-
intended its foundation. Sulla was one of these ; see 62 below.

contracted not by riotous living but in the pursuit of business. He was in debt at Rome but very large sums were owing to him in the provinces and kingdoms. When he was collecting these debts, he would not allow his agents to incur any charge during his absence but preferred to have all his possessions sold and to be deprived of his very considerable inheritance rather than to subject any of his creditors to delay. I never feared men like him, gentlemen, 59 when I was involved in that storm which broke upon the Republic. The type of men who filled me with horror and deep fear were those who clung to their possessions so passionately that you might say that it was easier to rob and strip them of their limbs. Sittius never thought that his estates were related to him by blood. He therefore protected himself from being suspected of so heinous a crime and against all gossip at the cost of his patrimony rather than with arms.

Furthermore, I cannot understand what is the 60 nature of his charge that the inhabitants of Pompeii were instigated by Sulla to join that conspiracy and set their hand to this nefarious crime. Do you think that they did join the conspiracy? Who ever said this or was there even a hint of a suspicion of it? " Sulla," he says " set them at odds with the new settlers [a] in order to use the division and dissension he had caused to get control of the town with the aid of the inhabitants of Pompeii." In the first place, the whole quarrel between the inhabitants and the new settlers was reported to the patrons [b] when it had grown chronic and had been pursued for many years. Secondly, in an inquiry conducted by the patrons, Sulla's views were in complete agreement with those

373

sententiis Sulla dissenserit; postremo coloni ipsi
sic intellegunt, non Pompeianos a Sulla magis quam
61 sese esse defensos. Atque hoc, iudices, ex hac frequentia colonorum, honestissimorum hominum, intellegere potestis, qui adsunt, laborant, hunc patronum, defensorem, custodem illius coloniae si in omni
fortuna atque omni honore incolumem habere non
potuerunt,[a] in hoc tamen casu in quo adflictus iacet per
vos iuvari conservarique cupiunt. Adsunt pari studio
Pompeiani, qui ab istis etiam in crimen vocantur; qui
ita de ambulatione ac de suffragiis suis cum colonis
dissenserunt ut idem de communi salute sentirent.
62 Ac ne haec quidem P. Sullae mihi videtur silentio
praetereunda esse virtus, quod, cum ab hoc illa colonia deducta sit,[b] et cum commoda colonorum a fortunis Pompeianorum rei publicae fortuna diiunxerit,
ita carus utrisque est atque iucundus ut non alteros
demovisse sed utrosque constituisse videatur.

At enim et gladiatores et omnis ista vis rogationis
Caeciliae causa comparabatur. Atque hoc loco in L.
Caecilium, pudentissimum atque ornatissimum virum,
vehementer invectus est. Cuius ego de virtute et
constantia, iudices, tantum dico, talem hunc in ista
rogatione quam promulgarat non de tollenda, sed
de levanda calamitate fratris sui[c] fuisse ut consulere

---

[a] A reference to the lost consulship.
[b] A masterly euphemism for the violence attending the
foundation of the Sullan colonies.
[c] Lucius Caecilius Rufus, a half-brother of Sulla and
tribune in 63, proposed a bill to restore their civil rights to
Autronius and Sulla.
374

of the others. Finally, the new settlers themselves realize that Sulla was defending their interests no less than those of the inhabitants of Pompeii. This, 61 gentlemen, you can infer from the large crowd of the settlers in court, men of the highest standing who are supporting and showing their solicitude for their patron here in the dock, the defender and guardian of that colony. Even if they have not been able to preserve him in the possession of all his fortune and of every office,[a] it is their urgent wish that at least in the misfortune which now prostrates him he should through you be helped and kept from harm. The inhabitants of Pompeii who have been included in the charge by the prosecution have come to court to support him with no less enthusiasm. Although they quarrelled with the new settlers about promenades and elections, they were of one mind about their joint safety. And I do not think that even this is an 62 achievement of Publius Sulla that I should pass over in silence: that although he founded the colony and although political circumstances caused the privileged position of the new settlers to clash with the interests of the inhabitants of Pompeii,[b] he is held in such affection and is so popular with both parties that he is felt not to have dispossessed the one but to have established the prosperity of both.

"But both the gladiators and all that display of force were mustered to ensure the passage of Caecilius' bill."[c] At this point he launched a violent attack upon Lucius Caecilius, a man of total integrity and high distinction. All I say, gentlemen, about his character and his loyalty is that in the bill which he had proposed to alleviate, not to end, his brother's ruin he only wanted to help his brother, not to come

voluerit fratri, cum re publica pugnare noluerit;
promulgarit impulsus amore fraterno, destiterit fratris
63 auctoritate deductus. Atque in ea re per L. Caecilium Sulla accusatur in qua re est uterque laudan-
dus. Primum Caecilius—quid ?[1] " id promulgavit in
quo res iudicatas videbatur voluisse rescindere, ut re-
stitueretur Sulla." Recte reprehendis; status enim
rei publicae maxime iudicatis rebus continetur;
neque ego tantum fraterno amori dandum arbitror ut
quisquam, dum saluti suorum consulat, communem
relinquat. At[2] nihil de iudicio ferebat, sed poenam
ambitus eam referebat quae fuerat nuper superioribus legibus constituta. Itaque hac rogatione non iudicum sententia, sed legis vitium corrigebatur. Nemo
iudicium reprehendit, cum de poena queritur, sed
legem. Damnatio est enim iudicum, quae manebat,
64 poena legis, quae levabatur. Noli igitur animos
eorum ordinum qui praesunt iudiciis summa cum
gravitate et dignitate alienare a causa. Nemo labefactare iudicium est conatus, nihil est eius modi pro-
mulgatum, semper Caecilius in calamitate fratris sui
iudicum potestatem perpetuandam, legis acerbita-
tem mitigandam putavit. Sed quid ego de hoc plura
disputem ? Dicerem fortasse, et facile et libenter
dicerem, si paulo etiam longius quam finis cotidiani offici postulat L. Caecilium pietas et fraternus

---

[1] quid *Clark.* qui *mss.* qui si *Halm.*
[2] At *added by Orelli.*

---

into conflict with the State. Affection for his brother
inspired the proposal but he abandoned his plan in
response to his brother's request. In a situation in 63
which both men deserve our praise Lucius Caecilius
is used as a means of attacking Sulla. Firstly,
Caecilius : " he introduced a bill which gave the
impression that he wanted to reverse the decision of
the court in order to restore Sulla to his former
position." If so, then you are right to condemn him.
The stability of the constitution depends upon decisions of the courts more than anything else, and I do
not think that affection for a brother should count
for so much that a man may sacrifice the public safety
in the interests of his family. His proposal, however,
did not affect the verdict ; it only raised the question
of the penalty for bribery which had recently been
introduced in earlier legislation. This bill, therefore,
did not seek to reverse the court's decision, only to
rectify a defect in the law. No one complaining of a
penalty questions the court's decision, only the law.
The conviction—which was to stand—is the verdict
of the court ; the penalty—which was to be mitigated
—is fixed by the law. Do not then try to alienate 64
from our case the feelings of those orders [a] which
conduct the courts with such dignity and authority.
No one has tried to reverse a decision, no proposal
like that has been made ; Caecilius has always thought
that in the disaster of his brother's conviction the
authority of the court should be upheld but the
rigour of the law softened. But why should I prolong
this discussion ? I should perhaps say more, and say
it readily and willingly, if family feeling and affection
for his brother had driven Lucius Caecilius even a
little further than the scope of our ordinary obligations

amor propulisset, implorarem sensus vestros, unius
cuiusque indulgentiam in suos testarer, peterem veniam errato L. Caecili ex intimis vestris cogitatio-
65 nibus atque ex humanitate communi.   Lex dies fuit
proposita paucos, ferri coepta numquam, deposita est
in senatu.   Kalendis Ianuariis cum in Capitolium nos
senatum convocassemus, nihil est actum prius, et id
mandatu Sullae Q. Metellus praetor se loqui dixit
Sullam illam rogationem de se nolle ferri.   Ex illo
tempore L. Caecilius egit de re publica multa ;
agrariae legi, quae tota a me reprehensa et abiecta
est, se intercessorem fore professus est, improbis
largitionibus restitit, senatus auctoritatem numquam
impedivit, ita se gessit in tribunatu ut onere deposito
domestici offici nihil postea nisi de rei publicae com-
66 modis cogitarit.   Atque in ipsa rogatione ne per vim
quid ageretur, quis tum nostrum Sullam aut Caecilium verebatur ? nonne omnis ille terror, omnis seditionis timor atque opinio ex Autroni improbitate
pendebat ? Eius voces, eius minae ferebantur, eius
aspectus, concursatio, stipatio, greges hominum
perditorum metum nobis seditionesque adferebant.
Itaque P. Sulla hoc importunissimo cum honoris tum
etiam calamitatis socio atque comite et secundas
fortunas amittere coactus est et in adversis sine ullo
remedio atque adlevamento permanere.
67   Hic tu epistulam meam saepe recitas quam ego ad

---

^a See pp. xxiv-xxvii.

requires. I should appeal to your fellow-feeling, I should call as evidence the affection of each one of you for his family, I should ask pardon of your innermost thoughts and your common humanity for Lucius Caecilius' mistake. The law remained a proposal for 65 a few days, no attempt was ever made to carry it, and it was abandoned in the Senate. When I had convened the Senate on the Capitol on the 1st of January, it was the first business taken. The praetor, Quintus Metellus, said that he was speaking on instructions from Sulla who did not wish the proposal about himself to be put to the vote. Subsequently Lucius Caecilius has spoken frequently on matters of state. He declared that he would veto the agrarian bill which was condemned and rejected by me in its entirety.[a] He opposed its reckless proposals for the free distribution of land, but he never blocked the expressed opinion of the Senate, and his conduct during his tribunate when he had discharged the burden of his family obligations showed that his sole thought after doing this was for the welfare of the State. Who of us, moreover, was afraid at that time 66 of any use of violence over the bill itself, so far as Sulla or Caecilius was concerned ? Did not all terror at that possibility, all fear and expectation of sedition spring from the desperate recklessness of Autronius ? His were the utterances, his the threats which were on men's lips, his was the expression, his the rallies, the retinues and the gangs of desperados which caused us panic and disorder. Publius Sulla, therefore, with his disastrous colleague, both fellow-candidate and co-defendant, was compelled to forfeit his prosperity and to linger in adversity without remedy or relief.

At this point you repeatedly quote from the letter 67

Cn. Pompeium de meis rebus gestis et de summa re
publica misi, et ex ea crimen aliquod in P. Sullam
quaeris et, si furorem incredibilem biennio ante conceptum erupisse in meo consulatu scripsi, me hoc
demonstrasse dicis, Sullam in illa fuisse superiore
coniuratione. Scilicet ego is sum qui existimem Cn.
Pisonem et Catilinam et Vargunteium et Autronium
nihil scelerate, nihil audacter ipsos per sese sine P.

68 Sulla facere potuisse. De quo etiam si quis dubitasset
antea an[1] id quod tu arguis cogitasset, ut interfecto
patre tuo consul[2] descenderet Kalendis Ianuariis cum
lictoribus, sustulisti hanc suspicionem, cum dixisti
hunc, ut Catilinam consulem efficeret, contra patrem
tuum operas et manum comparasse. Quod si tibi ego
confitear, tu mihi concedas necesse est hunc, cum
Catilinae suffragaretur, nihil de suo consulatu, quem
iudicio amiserat, per vim recuperando cogitavisse. Neque enim istorum facinorum tantorum, tam atro-
cium crimen, iudices, P. Sullae persona suscipit.

69   Iam enim faciam criminibus omnibus fere dis-
solutis, contra atque in ceteris causis fieri solet, ut
nunc denique de vita hominis ac de moribus dicam.
Etenim de principio studuit animus occurrere mag-
nitudini criminis, satis facere exspectationi hominum,
de me aliquid ipso qui accusatus eram dicere; nunc
iam revocandi estis eo quo vos ipsa causa etiam
tacente me cogit animos mentisque convertere.

[1] an *E. Eberhard*. num *mss*.
[2] consul *editio Romana, O. Müller*. consule *mss*.

---

[a] For these sections, see pp. 310-311.
[b] An admission slipped in by Cicero so that it is hardly
noticed. It would be interesting to know what charges
remained unanswered.

that I sent to Gnaeus Pompeius *a* in which I set out my achievements in office and the supreme interest of the State. In it you look for some charge against Publius Sulla, and you say that by writing that the incredible folly conceived two years previously had erupted in my consulship I showed that Sulla had been in the earlier conspiracy. I am, of course, the very man to think that Gnaeus Piso, Catiline, Vargunteius and Autronius were incapable of any criminal or reckless act by themselves without Publius Sulla. Even if anyone had previously been in 68 doubt about Sulla or had in mind what you attribute to him—a plot to murder your father and enter the Forum as consul with lictors on the 1st of January— you removed all suspicion of this when you said that he had collected a force of thugs against your father in order to make Catiline consul. If I were to admit the truth of this allegation, then you must agree with me that when, as you maintain, he was supporting Catiline's campaign he had no thought of recovering by force the consulship which he had lost by the decision of the court. Furthermore, gentlemen, Sulla's character does not admit the allegation of such serious and dastardly crimes.

Now that I have refuted almost *b* all the charges, 69 I shall follow a procedure different from that usually adopted in cases and take my client's life and character last. At the outset I was all eagerness to come to grips with an accusation as important as this, to satisfy men's expectations and, since I had been accused, to say something on my own behalf. Now I must call your attention back to the subject to which, even if I were silent, the case itself turns your thoughts and feelings.

Omnibus in rebus, iudices, quae graviores maiores-
que sunt, quid quisque voluerit, cogitarit, admiserit,
non ex crimine, sed ex moribus eius qui arguitur est
ponderandum. Neque enim potest quisquam nostrum
subito fingi neque cuiusquam repente vita mutari aut
70 natura converti. Circumspicite paulisper mentibus
vestris, ut alia mittamus, hosce ipsos homines qui
huic adfines sceleri fuerunt. Catilina contra rem
publicam coniuravit. Cuius aures umquam haec re-
spuerunt, conatum esse audacter hominem a pueritia
non solum intemperantia et scelere sed etiam consuetudine et studio in omni flagitio, stupro, caede
versatum ? Quis eum contra patriam pugnantem
perisse miratur quem semper omnes ad civile latrocinium natum putaverunt ? Quis Lentuli societates
cum indicibus, quis insaniam libidinum, quis perversam atque impiam religionem recordatur qui illum aut
nefarie cogitasse aut stulte sperasse miretur ? Quis
de C. Cethego atque eius in Hispaniam profectione ac
de volnere Q. Metelli Pii cogitat cui non ad illius[a]
71 poenam carcer aedificatus esse videatur ? Omitto
ceteros, ne sit infinitum ; tantum a vobis peto ut
taciti de omnibus quos coniurasse cognitum est cogi-
tetis ; intellegetis unum quemque eorum prius ab sua
vita quam vestra suspicione esse damnatum. Ipsum
illum Autronium, quoniam eius nomen finitimum
maxime est huius periculo et crimini, non sua vita ac
natura convicit ? Semper audax, petulans, libidi-
nosus ; quem in stuprorum defensionibus non solum

---

[a] Cicero suggests that Cethegus had gone to Spain to
assassinate Quintus Metellus Pius, who was commander
there against Sertorius from 79 to 71. This accusation is not
substantiated elsewhere. Rome's only prison, the Tullianum
on the Capitoline hill, was used for the execution of Cethegus
and the other conspirators.

In any matter more serious or important than usual, gentlemen, a man's intentions, plans and acts must be judged by his character, not by the charges against him. No one of us can be moulded in an instant nor can his way of life be suddenly changed or his nature altered. Ponder for a moment in your 70 minds only these men—let us ignore other considerations—who were personally implicated in this crime. Catiline conspired against the State. What man's ears have ever refused to believe this charge, that a desperate attempt had been made by one whose self-indulgence and criminality allied with his habits and inclination had involved him from childhood in every sort of scandal, debauchery and murder ? Who is surprised that he fell fighting against his country, a man who was always generally believed to have been born for banditry against his fellow-citizens ? Who that remembers Lentulus' association with informers, his insane passions, his perverted and godless superstition, is surprised at the villainy of his plots or the folly of his ambitions ? Who thinks of Gaius Cethegus and his departure for Spain, and of his assault upon Quintus Metellus Pius, without believing that our prison was built for his punishment ? [a] I omit the 71 others or I should never finish. I only ask you to recollect in silence all those known to have been in the conspiracy. You will find that every single one of them stood condemned by his own life before your suspicion pronounced its verdict. Has not Autronius in particular—for his name is most closely associated with the charge against Sulla and his dangerous situation—been convicted by his own character and way of life ? Always foolhardy, aggressive and intemperate ; we know that when he was defending

verbis uti improbissimis solitum esse scimus verum
etiam pugnis et calcibus, quem exturbare homines
ex possessionibus, caedem facere vicinorum, spoliare
fana sociorum, comitatu[1] et armis disturbare iudicia,
in bonis rebus omnis contemnere, in malis pugnare
contra bonos, non rei publicae cedere, non fortunae
ipsi succumbere. Huius si causa non manifestissimis
rebus teneretur, tamen eum mores ipsius ac vita
convinceret.

72 Agedum, conferte nunc cum illius vita vitam P.
Sullae vobis populoque Romano notissimam, iudices,
et eam ante oculos vestros proponite. Ecquod est
huius factum aut commissum non dicam audacius,
sed quod cuiquam paulo minus consideratum videretur ? Factum quaero ; verbum ecquod umquam ex ore
huius excidit in quo quisquam posset offendi ? At
vero in illa gravi L. Sullae turbulentaque victoria
quis P. Sulla mitior, quis misericordior inventus est ?
Quam[2] multorum hic vitam est a L. Sulla deprecatus !
quam multi sunt summi homines et ornatissimi et
nostri et equestris ordinis quorum pro salute se
hic Sullae obligavit ! Quos ego nominarem—neque
enim ipsi nolunt et huic animo gratissimo adsunt—
sed, quia maius est beneficium quam posse debet civis
civi dare, ideo a vobis peto ut quod potuit, tempori
73 tribuatis, quod fecit, ipsi. Quid reliquae[3] constantiam
vitae commemorem, dignitatem, liberalitatem, mode-

---

[1] comitatu *Clark*. vi conatum (-u $\Sigma b\psi k$) *mss*. vi esse
conatum *Kasten*.
[2] Quam *added from Aulus Gellius 7. 16. 6*.
[3] reliquae *Richter*. reliquam *mss*.

---

[a] Violence was endemic in the Italian countryside, even in
times of peace. P. A. Brunt, *Italian Manpower 225 b.c.–a.d.
14* Appendix 8, 551-557.

immorality it was his practice to use not only the foulest language but his fists and feet as well. We know too that it was his practice to evict men from their properties, to murder his neighbours,[a] to plunder the shrines of allies, to break up the courts with a band of retainers and force of arms, in prosperity to disregard everybody, in adversity to fight loyal citizens, not to bow to the public good and not to give in to fortune herself. Even if the case against him were not proved by the most obvious facts, his life and character would still convict him.

Let us now compare with his life the life of Publius 72 Sulla, a life that you, gentlemen, and the Roman people know so very well. Place it before your eyes. Is there any act of his, any deed, that was—I shall not say over-rash—but that might be thought rather injudicious ? I say act; but did ever word fall from his lips which could offend anyone ? Why, even amid the cruelty and confusion of Lucius Sulla's [b] victory, who was there kinder, who more compassionate than Publius Sulla ? Think of all the lives he begged Lucius Sulla to spare ! Think of all the eminent and distinguished senators and knights for whose safety he stood surety with Sulla ! I might give you their names, for they are not unwilling and in their deep gratitude are here in court to support him. The service, however, that he gave is greater than what one citizen ought to be called upon to render to another, and I therefore ask you to appreciate that, although the times provided him with his opportunity, his was the responsibility for the use he made of it. What need have I to recall the firmness of purpose in 73 the rest of his life, his distinction, his generosity, his

[b] The Dictator.

rationem in privatis rebus, splendorem in publicis ?
quae ita deformata sunt a fortuna ut tamen a natura
inchoata compareant. Quae domus, quae celebratio
cotidiana, quae familiarium dignitas, quae studia
amicorum, quae ex quoque ordine multitudo ! Haec
diu multumque et multo labore quaesita una eripuit
hora. Accepit P. Sulla, iudices, volnus vehemens et
mortiferum, verum tamen eius modi quod videretur
huius vita et natura accipere potuisse. Honestatis
enim et dignitatis habuisse nimis magnam iudicatus
est cupiditatem ; quam si nemo alius habuit in consulatu petendo, cupidior iudicatus est hic fuisse quam
ceteri ; sin etiam in aliis non nullis fuit iste consulatus
amor, fortuna in hoc fuit fortasse gravior quam in
74 ceteris. Postea vero quis P. Sullam nisi maerentem,
demissum adflictumque vidit, quis umquam est
suspicatus hunc magis odio quam pudore hominum
aspectum lucemque vitare ? Qui cum multa haberet
invitamenta urbis et fori propter summa studia
amicorum, quae tamen ei sola in malis restiterunt,
afuit ab oculis vestris et, cum lege retineretur, ipse
se exsilio paene multavit. In hoc vos pudore, iudices,
et in hac vita tanto sceleri locum fuisse credatis ?[1]
Aspicite ipsum, contuemini os, conferte crimen cum
vita, vitam ab initio usque ad hoc tempus explicatam
75 cum crimine recognoscite. Mitto rem publicam,
quae fuit semper Sullae carissima ; hosne amicos,

[1] credatis *Zielinski*. creditis мss.

---

[a] The *lex Calpurnia* of 67 under which Sulla had been
charged with electoral corruption did not provide for exile
as one of the penalties. *Cf.* p. 174.

simplicity in private life and magnificence in public ?
They have been disfigured by ill-fortune but the out-
line sketched by Nature is still visible. What a house
he had, what crowds of visitors every day, what
distinction from his close associates, what devotion
from his friends, what a throng from every class in
society ! All this, won by long and arduous toil, a
single hour snatched from him. Publius Sulla
received, gentlemen, a deep and deadly wound, but
after all the sort of wound to which men thought that
one of his life and character was exposed. He was
held to have been over-ambitious for office and distinction ; if no other consular candidate nursed a
similar ambition, Sulla was held to have been more
ambitious than the rest ; but if there were others
who shared his desire for the consulship, fortune was
perhaps harder in his case than upon the rest. Who **74**
afterwards saw Sulla other than in deep depression,
cast down and crushed ? Who ever suspected that
he was avoiding men's gaze and the light of day more
out of resentment than from shame ? The city and
the Forum still held many attractions for him owing
to the deep devotion of his friends which was all that
was left for him amid his misfortunes, but he kept
out of your sight and, although he might legally have
remained in Rome, he virtually condemned himself
to exile.[a] Would you believe, gentlemen, that so
monstrous a crime had a place with such a sense of
honour and such a life ? Look at the man, examine
his expression, contrast the accusation with his life ;
with the charge in your minds review his life unfolded
from its beginning to the present day. I say nothing **75**
of the national interests which Sulla always held so
very close to his heart. Did he wish these friends,

talis viros, tam cupidos sui, per quos res eius secundae
quondam erant ornatae, nunc sublevantur adversae,
crudelissime perire voluit, ut cum Lentulo et Catilina
et Cethego foedissimam vitam ac miserrimam
turpissima morte proposita degeret ? Non, inquam,
cadit in hos mores, non in hunc pudorem, non in hanc
vitam, non in hunc hominem ista suspicio. Nova
quaedam illa immanitas exorta est, incredibilis fuit
ac singularis furor, ex multis ab adulescentia con-
lectis perditorum hominum vitiis repente ista tanta
76 importunitas inauditi sceleris exarsit. Nolite, iudices,
arbitrari hominum illum impetum et conatum fuisse
—neque enim ulla gens tam barbara aut tam immanis umquam fuit in qua non modo tot, sed unus
tam crudelis hostis patriae sit inventus—, beluae
quaedam illae ex portentis immanes ac ferae forma
hominum indutae exstiterunt. Perspicite etiam atque etiam, iudices,—nihil enim est quod in hac causa
dici possit vehementius—penitus introspicite Catilinae, Autroni, Cethegi, Lentuli ceterorumque mentis ;
quas vos in his libidines, quae flagitia, quas turpi-
tudines, quantas audacias, quam incredibilis furores,
quas notas facinorum, quae indicia parricidiorum,
quantos acervos scelerum reperietis ! Ex magnis et
diuturnis et iam desperatis rei publicae morbis ista
repente vis erupit, ut ea confecta et eiecta con-
valescere aliquando et sanari civitas posset ; neque

men of such quality and such eager supporters, men through whom he had once won his prosperity and who are now cushioning his adversity, did he wish them to meet the cruellest of deaths in order to let him live out an utterly wretched and contemptible life in the company of Lentulus, Catiline and Cethegus with the prospect of an ignominious death ? No ; that sort of suspicion does not square with a character like his, a sense of honour, a way of life like his, or a man like him. It was a new sort of enormity that sprang into being, an incredible madness that was unparalleled. Out of the host of vices accumulated by abandoned men from the days of their youth there suddenly blazed up that outrage of a crime without precedent. Do not think, gentlemen, that this attack and this **76** enterprise were the work of human beings—there never was race so barbarous or savage as to produce a single enemy of his country with the cruelty of these brutes, let alone a host as numerous. They were a sort of wild beast, sprung into being from monstrosities —animals clothed in human form. Scrutinize them intently, gentlemen—for there is nothing in this case that I can emphasize more strongly—look deep into the minds of Catiline, Autronius, Cethegus, Lentulus and the rest. What passions you will find there, what crimes, what immorality, what wanton reckless-ness, what madness beyond belief, what stains left by their crimes, what proofs of their murder of relations, what accumulations of evil doing ! Out of those gross, chronic and now desperate distempers of the Re-public there suddenly erupted that act of violence, and only when it had been digested and eliminated could the body-politic finally begin to mend and re-cover its well-being. There is not a single man who

enim est quisquam qui arbitretur illis inclusis in re
publica pestibus diutius haec stare potuisse. Itaque
eos non ad perficiendum scelus, sed ad luendas rei
77 publicae poenas Furiae quaedam incitaverunt. In
hunc igitur gregem vos nunc P. Sullam, iudices, ex
his qui cum hoc vivunt atque vixerunt honestissimorum hominum gregibus reicietis, ex hoc amicorum[1]
numero, ex hac familiarium dignitate in impiorum
partem atque in parricidarum sedem et numerum
transferetis ? Ubi erit igitur illud firmissimum praesidium pudoris, quo in loco nobis vita ante acta pro-
derit, quod ad tempus existimationis partae fructus
reservabitur, si in extremo discrimine ac dimicatione fortunae deseruerit,[2] si non aderit, si nihil
adiuvabit ?

78 Quaestiones nobis servorum accusator et tormenta
minitatur. In quibus quamquam nihil periculi suspicamur, tamen illa tormenta gubernat dolor, moderatur natura cuiusque cum animi tum corporis,
regit quaesitor, flectit libido, corrumpit spes, infirmat
metus, ut in tot rerum angustiis nihil veritati loci
relinquatur. Vita P. Sullae torqueatur, ex ea quaeratur num quae occultetur libido, num quod lateat
facinus, num quae crudelitas, num quae audacia. Nihil erroris erit in causa nec obscuritatis, iudices, si
a vobis vitae perpetuae vox, ea quae verissima et
79 gravissima debet esse, audietur. Nullum in hac causa
testem timemus, nihil quemquam scire, nihil vidisse,

---

[1] amicorum *Klotz.* hominum *mss.*

[2] deseruerit *codex Victorianus.* deseret *k.* deserit (-uit
b[1]*c*[2]) *the other mss.*

---

[a] Torture as a means of extracting information in legal
processes was rarely used at Rome and little store was set by
what it elicited.

would think that Rome could have endured longer while that poison remained within the Republic. You might say, then, that Furies drove those men on, not to complete their crime, but to pay the penalty of their punishment to the State. Will you 77 then, gentlemen, now cast Publius Sulla out into that crew, excluding him from these groups of honourable men who have associated and still associate with him ? Will you transfer him from this company of his friends and from these distinguished comrades to the party of wicked men, to the abode and company of traitors to their country ? What then will have become of that stoutest of defences, a sense of propriety ? Where will our past life serve to help us ? For what occasion will the reward of acquiring a good character be preserved, if in the moment of crisis and the struggle for our fortune it desert us, fail us and render us no aid ?

The prosecutor threatens us with the examination 78 of our slaves under torture.[a] Although we do not foresee any danger in this procedure, still the course of examinations under torture is steered by pain, is controlled by individual qualities of mind and body, is directed by the president of the court, is diverted by caprice, tainted by hope, invalidated by fear, and the result is that in all these straits there is no room left for truth. Let the life of Publius Sulla be put upon the rack. Let it be examined, whether any lawlessness is concealed in it, any crime hidden, any cruelty, any recklessness. There will be no mistake in the case, no uncertainty, gentlemen, if you listen to what should be the most truthful and convincing witness, the story of his entire life. There is no witness in this case of whom we are afraid ; we do not 79

nihil audisse arbitramur. Sed tamen, si nihil vos P.
Sullae fortuna movet, iudices, vestra moveat. Vestra
enim, qui cum summa elegantia atque integritate
vixistis, hoc maxime interest, non ex libidine aut
simultate aut levitate testium causas honestorum
hominum ponderari, sed in magnis disquisitionibus
repentinisque periculis vitam unius cuiusque esse
testem. Quam vos, iudices, nolite armis suis spoliatam atque nudatam obicere invidiae, dedere suspi-
cioni ; munite communem arcem bonorum, obstruite
perfugia improborum ; valeat ad poenam et ad salutem vita plurimum, quam solam videtis per se[1] ex sua
natura facillime perspici, subito flecti fingique non
posse.

80   Quid vero ? haec auctoritas—saepe[2] enim est de ea
dicendum, quamquam a me timide modiceque dicetur—quid ? inquam, haec auctoritas nostra, qui a
ceteris coniurationis causis abstinuimus, P. Sullam
defendimus, nihil hunc tandem iuvabit ? Grave est
hoc dictu fortasse, iudices, grave, si appetimus aliquid ; si, cum ceteri de nobis silent, non etiam nosmet
ipsi tacemus, grave ; sed, si laedimur, si accusamur,
si in invidiam vocamur, profecto conceditis, iudices,
ut nobis libertatem retinere liceat, si minus liceat
81 dignitatem. Accusati sunt uno nomine omnes[3] consulares, ut iam videatur honoris amplissimi nomen
plus invidiae quam dignitatis adferre. " Adfuerunt,"
inquit, " Catilinae illumque laudarunt." Nulla

---

[1] per se *Mommsen.* ipse *T.* ipsam *the other MSS.*
[2] saepe *Spengel.* semper *MSS.*
[3] omnes *added by Clark in this position ; before* uno *by*
Lambinus.

---

[a] See p. 4, n. *a.*

think that anyone knows anything, has seen anything, has heard anything. But if you are still not one whit moved by Publius Sulla's fate, gentlemen, be moved by your own. It is most important for you who have lived with the greatest propriety and integrity that the cases of honourable men should not be decided by the caprice, animosity or unreliability of witnesses, but that in important inquiries and unexpected charges each man's life should be his witness. Do not, gentlemen, deprive it of its proper weapons, do not lay it bare and expose it to jealousy and surrender it to suspicion. Strengthen the fortress shared by all loyal citizens, cut off the retreat of traitors. Let his life be the most telling witness to condemn or acquit a man; it alone, as you see, by its nature lends itself very readily to scrutiny, but cannot suddenly be changed or feigned.

Well then ? Shall my authority—for I must refer 80 to it constantly, although I shall do so hesitantly and with moderation—shall my personal authority, I say, give no help at all to Publius Sulla whom I am defending after I have refused the briefs for the other cases arising out of the conspiracy ? This is perhaps, gentlemen, an objectionable thing to say ; objectionable, if I have some motive ; if, when others are silent about me, I too am not silent, then that is objectionable ; but if I am attacked, if I am accused, if I am made the object of odium, you, of course, gentlemen, permit me to retain my freedom of speech, if not my good name. All the consulars were charged under a single head- 81 ing, so that the title of the highest magistracy now seems to attract more odium than respect. " They supported Catiline in court," he says, " and were character-witnesses for him." [a] No conspiracy had

393

tum patebat, nulla erat cognita coniuratio ; defen-
debant amicum, aderant supplici, vitae eius turpitudinem in summis eius periculis non insequeban-
tur. Quin etiam parens tuus, Torquate, consul reo
de pecuniis repetundis Catilinae fuit advocatus,
improbo homini, at supplici, fortasse audaci, at aliquando amico. Cui cum adfuit post delatam ad
eum primam illam coniurationem, indicavit se audisse
aliquid, non credidisse. " At idem non adfuit alio in
iudicio, cum adessent ceteri." Si postea cognorat ipse
aliquid quod in consulatu ignorasset, ignoscendum est
eis qui postea nihil audierunt ; sin illa res prima valuit,
num inveterata quam recens debuit esse gravior ?
Sed si tuus parens etiam in ipsa suspicione periculi sui
tamen humanitate adductus advocationem hominis
improbissimi sella curuli atque ornamentis et suis et
consulatus honestavit, quid est quam ob rem consu-
82 lares qui Catilinae adfuerunt reprendantur ? " At
idem eis qui ante hunc causam de coniuratione
dixerunt non adfuerunt." Tanto scelere astrictis
hominibus statuerunt nihil a se adiumenti, nihil opis,
nihil auxili ferri oportere. Atque ut de eorum
constantia atque animo in rem publicam dicam quorum tacita gravitas et fides de uno quoque loquitur
neque cuiusquam ornamenta orationis desiderat,
potest quisquam dicere umquam meliores, fortiores,
constantiores consularis fuisse quam his temporibus

---

[a] See p. 415 f.

[b] Magistrates who went into court to support a defendant
appeared in the full trappings of office. The curule chair
was used by all magistrates with *imperium*.

been revealed then, none was known. They were
defending a friend, supporting a suppliant, and in his
dire peril they did not reproach his life of infamy.
Furthermore, in his consulship your father, Torquatus,
was counsel for Catiline when he was answering a
charge of extortion.[a] Rogue he may have been, but
he was a suppliant; reckless perhaps, but he had
once been a friend. Inasmuch as he appeared for him
after that first conspiracy had been reported to him,
he indicated that he had heard something, but did
not believe it. " But he did not support him in court
in another trial, although the others did." If he had
subsequently discovered something which he did not
know when he was consul, then we must excuse those
who heard nothing later. But if that first piece of
information had any substance, ought it to have
carried more weight when it was old than when it
was fresh ? If, moreover, your father, even when
suspecting danger to himself, was still induced by
his kindly nature to give respectability to the body
which supported that unscrupulous wretch by appearing with the curule chair and both his personal and
his consular insignia,[b] is there any reason why the
consulars who supported Catiline should be blamed ?
" But the same men did not support those who were 82
put on trial for the conspiracy before Sulla." They
decided that they should give no support, no help, no
assistance to men involved in so heinous a crime. To
speak of their resoluteness and affection for their
country when their sense of responsibility and loyalty
—though silent—speak out for each one of them and
need no elaboration in anyone's speech, can anyone
say that there were ever better, braver, more
resolute ex-consuls than in this perilous crisis which

et periculis quibus paene oppressa est res publica ?
Quis non de communi salute optime,[1] quis non
fortissime, quis non constantissime sensit ? Neque
ego praecipue de consularibus disputo ; nam haec et
hominum ornatissimorum, qui praetores fuerunt, et
universi senatus communis est laus, ut constet post
hominum memoriam numquam in illo ordine plus
virtutis, plus amoris in rem publicam, plus gravitatis
fuisse ; sed quia sunt descripti consulares, de his
tantum mihi dicendum putavi quod satis esset ad
testandam omnium memoriam, neminem esse ex illo
honoris gradu qui non omni studio, virtute, auctoritate
incubuerit ad rem publicam conservandam.

83   Sed quid ego ? qui Catilinam non laudavi, qui reo
Catilinae consul non adfui, qui testimonium de coniuratione dixi in alios, adeone vobis alienus a sanitate,
adeo oblitus constantiae meae, adeo immemor rerum
a me gestarum esse videor ut, cum consul bellum
gesserim cum coniuratis, nunc eorum ducem servare
cupiam et animum inducam, cuius nuper ferrum ret-
tuderim flammamque restinxerim, eiusdem nunc
causam vitamque defendere ? Si medius fidius,
iudices, non me ipsa res publica meis laboribus et
periculis conservata ad gravitatem animi et constantiam sua dignitate revocaret, tamen hoc natura
est insitum ut, quem timueris, quicum de vita
fortunisque contenderis, cuius ex insidiis evaseris,
hunc semper oderis. Sed cum agatur honos meus

---

[1] optime *Spengel*. apertissime (aptissime *c*[1]) MSS.

---

[a] See *pro Murena* 51, p. 252.

nearly wrecked the Republic ? Who failed to display the utmost loyalty, bravery and resoluteness in his concern for the public safety ? And I do not refer exclusively to ex-consuls, for such praise is shared by the distinguished men who have been praetors and by the whole Senate, that by common consent there has never been, within the memory of man, in that body more valour, more patriotism, or a stronger sense of responsibility. Since, however, ex-consuls have been stigmatized, I thought that I should say about them just so much as would suffice to bear out what everyone remembers, that there was no one at that level of office who did not apply to the preservation of the Republic his whole energy, valour and influence.

What of my own conduct ? I did not testify to 83 Catiline's good character, I did not support Catiline after he had been indicted when I was consul,*a* I gave evidence about the conspiracy against other defendants. Do you think that I am so bereft of my wits, so forgetful of my resolve, so unmindful of the measures I took that, although I waged war upon the conspirators when I was consul, I now want to save one of their leaders and to persuade myself to defend the cause and life of the man whose sword I have only recently blunted and whose torch I have just extinguished ? In heaven's name, gentlemen, if even the Republic, preserved by my efforts and at my peril, did not have the influence to recall me to a sense of responsibility and firmness of purpose, it is still human nature always to hate the man of whom you have been afraid, against whom you have staked your life and fortune, and from whose toils you have escaped. Since the highest office of my career and

397

amplissimus, gloria rerum gestarum singularis, cum,
quotiens quisque est in hoc scelere convictus, totiens
renovetur memoria per me inventae salutis, ego sim
tam demens, ego committam ut ea quae pro salute
omnium gessi, casu magis et felicitate a me quam vir-
84 tute et consilio gesta esse videantur ? " Quid ergo ?
hoc tibi sumis," dicet fortasse quispiam, "ut, quia tu
defendis, innocens iudicetur ? " Ego vero, iudices,
non modo mihi nihil adsumo in quo quispiam re-
pugnet sed etiam, si quid ab omnibus conceditur, id
reddo ac remitto. Non in ea re publica versor, non
eis temporibus caput meum obtuli pro patria periculis omnibus, non aut ita sunt exstincti quos vici aut
ita grati quos servavi, ut ego mihi plus appetere
coner quam quantum omnes inimici invidique pati-
85 antur. Grave esse videtur eum qui investigarit coniurationem, qui patefecerit, qui oppresserit, cui senatus
singularibus verbis gratias egerit, cui uni togato
supplicationem decreverit, dicere in iudicio : " non
defenderem, si coniurasset." Non dico id quod grave
est, dico illud quod in his causis coniurationis non
auctoritati adsumam, sed pudori meo : " ego ille
coniurationis investigator atque ultor certe non defenderem Sullam, si coniurasse arbitrarer." Ego, iudices, de tantis omnium periculis cum quaererem

---

the unique glory of my achievements are involved and since the memory of the salvation won by my efforts is renewed each time a man is convicted in connexion with this crime, would I be so insane, would I induce people to think that what I did to secure the safety of us all was the product of chance and luck and not of my courage and statesmanship? " A further 84 point," perhaps someone will say; " do you arrogate to yourself the claim that a man should be acquitted because you are defending him ? " No, gentlemen; not only do I make no claim for myself that anybody would resist, but even if something is conceded to me by common consent, I relinquish it and hand it back. I am not involved in such a political situation, I have not risked my life for my country in every danger in such a time of crisis, those whom I have defeated are not so completely exterminated nor those whom I have saved so grateful, that I would try to grasp for myself more than all those who hate and envy me would allow. It seems to cause resentment that the 85 man who discovered the conspiracy, who exposed it, who suppressed it, whom the Senate thanked in a decree without precedent, the only civilian to whom a thanksgiving has ever been decreed,[a] should say in a trial : " I would not be defending him if he had been a conspirator." I am not saying anything objectionable, but I am saying what in these cases concerned with the conspiracy I would claim to say not on the strength of my authority but as a man of honour : " I who investigated and punished the conspiracy would certainly not be defending Sulla if I thought that he had been a member of it." When, gentlemen, I was investigating everything concerned with the great dangers threatening us all, was receiv-

omnia, multa audirem, crederem non omnia, caverem
omnia, dico hoc quod initio dixi, nullius indicio, nullius nuntio, nullius suspicione, nullius litteris de P.
Sulla rem ullam ad me esse delatam.

86 Quam ob rem vos, di patrii ac penates, qui huic urbi
atque huic rei publicae praesidetis, qui hoc imperium, qui hanc libertatem, qui populum Romanum,
qui haec tecta atque templa me consule vestro numine auxilioque servastis, testor integro me animo
ac libero P. Sullae causam defendere, nullum a me
sciente facinus occultari, nullum scelus susceptum
contra salutem omnium defendi ac tegi. Nihil de
hoc consul comperi, nihil suspicatus sum, nihil audivi.

87 Itaque idem ego ille qui vehemens in alios, qui in-
exorabilis in ceteros esse visus sum, persolvi patriae
quod debui; reliqua iam a me meae perpetuae con-
suetudini naturaeque debentur; tam sum misericors,
iudices, quam vos, tam mitis quam qui lenissimus; in
quo vehemens fui vobiscum nihil feci nisi coactus; rei
publicae praecipitanti subveni, patriam demersam
extuli; misericordia civium adducti tum fuimus tam
vehementes quam necesse fuit. Salus esset amissa
omnium una nocte, nisi esset severitas illa suscepta.
Sed ut ad sceleratorum poenam amore rei publicae
sum adductus, sic ad salutem innocentium voluntate
deducor.

88 Nihil video esse in hoc P. Sulla, iudices, odio dignum, misericordia digna multa. Neque enim nunc

---

[a] The first group comprises the conspirators executed in
Rome and those killed fighting with Catiline; the second,
those brought to trial later.

[b] For this appeal to the jury, see p. 309.

ing much information, was not believing everything, but was providing against every eventuality, I repeat what I said at the beginning, that no man's information, message, suspicion, or letter revealed to me anything implicating Publius Sulla.

Therefore, you gods of our fathers and of our 86 homes, who watch over this city and this State, who during my consulship brought your power and your assistance to the preservation of our empire, of our liberty, of the people of Rome, of our homes and our temples, I call you to witness that I am defending the case of Publius Sulla with my judgement uncorrupted and unfettered, that I am not knowingly concealing any crime, that I am not defending and hiding any attempt made upon the safety of us all. When I was consul I discovered nothing about my client, I suspected nothing, I heard nothing. I, the man who 87 appeared harsh towards some and implacable towards the others,[a] have discharged my obligation to my country. There now remains my obligation to my normal practice and to my nature. I am as compassionate as yourselves, gentlemen, as lenient as the mildest of men. When I shared your severity, I only acted under compulsion; the State was collapsing in ruins, I came to its aid; my country had been engulfed, I rescued it; we were led by pity for our fellow-countrymen to act with severity, but only so far as was necessary. The safety of all would have vanished in a single night, if I had not adopted such severity. If my patriotism led me to punish the criminals, my natural inclination leads me to save the innocent.

I see nothing in my client, Publius Sulla, that 88 deserves hatred, but much that merits compassion.[b]

propulsandae calamitatis suae causa supplex ad vos,
iudices, confugit, sed ne qua generi ac nomini suo nota
nefariae turpitudinis inuratur. Nam ipse quidem, si
erit vestro iudicio liberatus, quae habet ornamenta,
quae solacia reliquae vitae quibus laetari ac perfrui
possit ? Domus erit, credo, exornata, aperientur
maiorum imagines, ipse ornatum ac vestitum pristi-
num recuperabit. Omnia, iudices, haec amissa sunt,
omnia generis, nominis, honoris insignia atque ornamenta unius iudici calamitate occiderunt. Sed ne
exstinctor patriae, ne proditor, ne hostis appelletur,
ne hanc labem tanti sceleris in familia relinquat, id
laborat, id metuit, ne denique hic miser coniurati et
conscelerati et proditoris filius nominetur; huic puero
qui est ei vita sua multo carior metuit, cui honoris
integros fructus non sit traditurus, ne aeternam
89 memoriam dedecoris relinquat. Hic vos orat, iudices,
parvus, ut se aliquando si non integra fortuna, at ut
adflicta patri suo gratulari sinatis. Huic misero no-
tiora sunt itinera iudiciorum et fori quam campi et
disciplinarum. Non iam de vita P. Sullae, iudices, sed
de sepultura contenditur; vita erepta est superiore
iudicio, nunc ne corpus eiciatur laboramus. Quid
enim est huic reliqui quod eum in hac vita teneat, aut
quid est quam ob rem haec cuiquam vita videatur ?
Nuper is homo fuit in civitate P. Sulla ut nemo ei se

---

[a] His conviction for electoral corruption.
[b] *i.e.* in exile.

402

He has not sought refuge as a suppliant before you,
gentlemen, in order to avert his own ruin, but to save
his family and name from the stigma of criminal
disgrace. Even if he is acquitted by your verdict,
what marks of distinction does he have, what con-
solations for the remainder of his life from which he
can get pleasure and enjoyment? Of course his
house will be decorated, the busts of his ancestors
will be brought out, and he will resume his former
decorations and dress! No, gentlemen; all these
have been lost, all the insignia and marks of distinction belonging to his clan, his family, his office have
been lost in the disaster of a single verdict.[a] To
avoid being called destroyer of his country, traitor,
public enemy, to avoid leaving the stain of so heinous
a crime upon his family, that is his aim. His fear is
that his unhappy son here in court may be called the
son of a conspirator, a criminal, a traitor; his fear for
this boy, who is much dearer to him than his own life
and to whom he will not pass down intact the rewards
of his office, is that he will leave to him the eternal
memory of his disgrace. This little boy, gentlemen, 89
begs you to allow him at long last to congratulate his
father so far as his battered fortune permits, even if
he cannot do so with it intact. The ways to the
Forum and the courts are better known to this
unhappy boy than those to the Campus Martius and
places of instruction. It is no longer a question of the
life of Publius Sulla, gentlemen, but of the disposal
of his body. His life was taken by the earlier verdict,
our anxiety now is that his body may be cast out.[b]
What has he left to detain him in this life? What is
there to make anyone think this life of his a real life?
Only a short time ago Publius Sulla's position in the

neque honore neque gratia neque fortunis anteferret,
nunc spoliatus omni dignitate quae erepta sunt non
repetit ; quod fortuna in malis reliqui fecit, ut cum
parente, cum liberis, cum fratre, cum his necessariis
lugere suam calamitatem liceat, id sibi ne eripiatis
90 vos, iudices, obtestatur. Te ipsum iam, Torquate, ex-
pletum huius miseriis esse par erat et, si nihil aliud
Sullae nisi consulatum abstulissetis, tamen eo vos
contentos esse oportebat; honoris enim contentio vos
ad causam, non inimicitiae deduxerunt. Sed cum
huic omnia cum honore detracta sint, cum in hac fortuna miserrima ac luctuosissima destitutus sit, quid
est quod expetas amplius ? Lucisne hanc usuram eripere vis plenam lacrimarum atque maeroris, in qua
cum maximo cruciatu ac dolore retinetur ? Libenter
reddiderit adempta ignominia foedissimi criminis. An
vero inimicum ut expellas ? cuius ex miseriis, si esses crudelissimus, videndo fructum caperes maiorem
91 quam audiendo. O miserum et infelicem illum diem
quo consul omnibus centuriis P. Sulla renuntiatus est,
o falsam spem, o volucrem fortunam, o caecam
cupiditatem, o praeposteram gratulationem ! Quam
cito illa omnia ex laetitia et voluptate ad luctum et
lacrimas reciderunt, ut, qui paulo ante consul designatus fuisset, repente nullum vestigium retineret
pristinae dignitatis ! Quid enim erat mali quod huic
404

State was such that no one surpassed him in office, influence or fortune; but now, stripped of his whole position, he does not ask back what has been taken from him. He only entreats you not to take from him what fortune has left him in his adversity, the right to bewail his calamity with his father, his children, his brother and his relatives here in court. You, 90 Torquatus, should long ago have been satisfied with Sulla's misfortunes and, if you and your father had taken nothing from Sulla but his consulship, you should have been content with that; for it was competition for office, not enmity, that induced you to bring that case. Since, however, along with his office everything else has been taken from him, since he has been brought low by this most grievous and disastrous ill-fortune, what more can you desire? Do you want to take from him the right to enjoy this light of day, full as it is of tears and sorrow, in which he lingers amid calamity and tribulation? He will willingly surrender it on the spot if the disgrace of this foul charge is removed. Or do you wish to drive an enemy into exile? If you were the cruellest of men, you would get a greater satisfaction from seeing his distress than from hearing about it. What a sorry 91 and calamitous day that was on which Publius Sulla was duly declared consul by all the centuries,[a] how deceptive were his hopes, how fleeting his success, how blind his ambition, how premature the congratulations he received! How quickly all this changed from joy and pleasure to grief and tears, and suddenly left without a single trace of his former position the man who only a short while before had been a consul-designate! Was there any mis-

<hr />

[a] See Appendix A, p. 563.

spoliato fama, honore, fortunis deesse videretur ? aut
cui novae calamitati locus ullus relictus ?[1] Urget
eadem fortuna quae coepit, repperit novum maerorem, non patitur hominem calamitosum uno malo
adflictum uno in luctu perire.

92 Sed iam impedior egomet, iudices, dolore animi ne
de huius miseria plura dicam. Vestrae sunt iam
partes, iudices, in vestra mansuetudine atque humanitate causam totam repono. Vos reiectione interposita nihil suspicantibus nobis repentini in nos iudices
consedistis, ab accusatoribus delecti ad spem acerbi-
tatis, a fortuna nobis ad praesidium innocentiae
constituti. Ut ego quid de me populus Romanus
existimaret, quia severus in improbos fueram, laboravi
et, quae prima innocentis mihi defensio est oblata,
suscepi, sic vos severitatem iudiciorum quae per hos
mensis in homines audacissimos facta sunt lenitate ac
93 misericordia mitigate. Hoc cum a vobis impetrare
causa ipsa debet, tum est vestri animi atque virtutis
declarare non esse eos vos ad quos potissimum interposita reiectione devenire convenerit. In quo ego vos,

---

[1] relictus esset *mss.* (est *b*[1], esse *ms. of Stephanus*). esset
deleted by Clark.

---

[a] In the words of the scholiast (p. 84 *ed.* Stangl) " sensus
quidem multae obscuritatis est." We do not know why the
jury was constituted so hurriedly. Th. Mommsen, *Römisches
Strafrecht* 215, n. 5, finds evidence in this passage for some
unknown system of selecting jurors by a combination of
nomination and lot, but the word *fortuna* need not necessarily imply this. J. L. Strachan-Davidson, *Problems of the
Roman Criminal Law* 2. 98-99, suggests that the jurors
were the normal *editicii iudices* (see p. 306) and that the word

fortune that did not touch this man, robbed of his
reputation, office and fortune ? For what new
calamity has any room been left ? The same ill-
fortune has dogged him from the beginning, has
brought him new sorrow and does not permit the ill-
starred man to be stricken by a single blow and to
perish in a single affliction.

My mental anguish, gentlemen, prevents me now 92
from saying more about Sulla's misfortune. The part
is now yours to play, gentlemen, and I entrust the
whole case to your compassion and humanity. You
were hastily empanelled and have sat upon this case
after objections had been introduced when we were
not expecting them. You were selected by the
prosecution in the hope of a harsh verdict, you have
been chosen for us by fortune to protect innocence.[a]
I felt anxious about what the Roman people thought
of me because I had acted with severity towards
malefactors and I undertook the first defence of an
innocent man that was offered to me ; do you too,
then, temper with your lenience and compassion the
severity of the verdicts which have been passed during recent months upon the most brazen of criminals.
Not only should the case win this request from you on 93
its own merits, but it is in keeping with your spirit
and character to show that you are not the men upon
whom it was most advantageous for the prosecution
to alight after introducing their objections. In this

fortuna is justified by the ignorance or incompetence (*cf.
pro Plancio* 41) of the prosecution in making their selection,
or by the chance which left only some members of the panel
free for this case. Cicero wants to complain of the method of
selection and at the same time congratulate himself upon the
fine body of men that he sees before him, and *fortuna* serves
to bridge the inconsistency between the two insinuations.

iudices, quantum meus in vos amor postulat, tantum hortor ut communi studio, quoniam in re publica coniuncti sumus, mansuetudine et misericordia nostra[1] falsam a nobis crudelitatis famam repellamus.

[1] nostra Σ*k*.   vestra *the other* MSS.

case, gentlemen, I urge you with all the affection that I feel for you that, in a common effort since we have the same political objectives, we may by our clemency and compassion preserve ourselves from a false reputation for cruelty.

THE SPEECH IN DEFENCE OF
LUCIUS VALERIUS FLACCUS

INTRODUCTION

Lucius Valerius Flaccus [a] was a member of the *gens Valeria*, which had behind it a long tradition of public service [b] and which according to Cicero had provided the Republic with its first consul.[c] His father, also Lucius Valerius Flaccus, who is mentioned on a number of occasions in this speech, was prosecuted in 99 at the very end of his year of office as curule aedile by Gaius Appuleius Decianus, a tribune of 98.[d] He was then praetor, possibly in 96, and governor of Asia 95–94.[e] On the death of Marius he was made *consul suffectus* for 86 and was appointed to

[a] F. Münzer in Pauly-Wissowa, *Realencyclopädie* VIII A 1 (1955), L. Valerius Flaccus (179), 30-36. [b] 1, p. 434.

[c] 25, p. 468. He would have followed the story more accurately if he had said " a consul in the first year of the Republic." The shadowy figure, Publius Valerius Publicola, was elected *consul suffectus* to Tarquinius Collatinus in 509.

[d] Tribunes entered office on the 10th of December. This Decianus was a father of the younger Flaccus' prosecutor. See 77, p. 524. The grounds of the indictment are not known, nor is the outcome of the case. F. Münzer in Pauly-Wissowa, *Realencyclopädie* VIII A 1 (1955), L. Valerius Flaccus (178), 26.

[e] 55-59, pp. 502-506. See E. Badian, " Notes on Provincial Governors from the Social War down to Sulla's Victory," *Proceedings of the African Classical Associations* (1958), reprinted in *Studies in Greek and Roman History*, especially 86-87 and 97 ; also D. Magie, *Roman Rule in Asia Minor* 2. 1242, n. 1.

succeed him in the command against Mithridates, king of Pontus. He had already served in Asia and had been a popular governor there, so was an obvious choice. He went straight to the province but by 85 was dead, murdered by Gaius Flavius Fimbria, who had been assigned to him as a subordinate officer.[a]

The son accompanied his father to the East and in 85 after his father's murder took refuge with his uncle, Gaius Valerius Flaccus, who was at that time in Transalpine Gaul.[b] There he served under his uncle and later saw further service as a military tribune under Publius Servilius Vatia.[c] In 76 he was, probably as a *quindecimvir sacris faciundis*, a member of a sacred embassy dispatched under the leadership of Publius Gabinius to collect Sibylline oracles from Erythrae.[d] In 71 or 70 he was quaestor and served under Marcus Pupius Piso in Spain, service which in all likelihood extended into the following year, in which he would have been proquaestor. In 68 he was a subordinate commander under Quintus Caecilius Metellus Creticus, in 67 in Achaea and Crete and in 66 under Pompey in his campaign against the pirates.[e]

[a] E. Badian, "Waiting for Sulla," *Journal of Roman Studies* 52 (1962), reprinted in *Studies in Greek and Roman History*, especially 223 f.

[b] 63, p. 510. E. Badian, *op. cit.* (p. 413, n. *e*) 89.

[c] 5, 6 and 100, pp. 438, 446 and 550.

[d] Cf. *in Catilinam* 3. 9, p. 108, n. *c*.

[e] 6, 63 and 100, pp. 446, 510 and 550. Dio 36. 54. 3-4. The service under Pompey is not mentioned by Cicero in this speech—Pompey and Flaccus had quarrelled (see 14, p. 456 ; also p. 430). The words in 6, however, *bellum Cretense ex magna parte gessit*, suggest that Flaccus did not stay with Metellus throughout the war. See T. R. S. Broughton, *The Magistrates of the Roman Republic* 2. 156, n. 3.

PRO FLACCO

Sallust's description of him as a *homo militaris* [a] was in the light of this record of service no idle phrase.

He was then praetor in 63 [b] and in this office played a key rôle in the suppression of the Catilinarian conspiracy.[c] In the following year, while Pompey was organizing his conquests, Flaccus was propraetor and governor of Asia. There he succeeded Publius Servilius Globulus, who had taken the province over from Publius Orbius, and he was in his turn succeeded by Cicero's brother Quintus.[d] In this province he was, as had been his father before him, patron of the town of Tralles.[e]

On his return from Asia in 60 he was, together with Metellus Creticus and Gnaeus Cornelius Lentulus Clodianus, appointed envoy by decree of the Senate to urge various Gallic tribes not to join the Helvetii. It was on his return from this mission that he was brought before the extortion court to answer for his behaviour in his province.

The offence of " extortion," [f] as the phrase *res repetundae* is conventionally translated, embraced any exaction of money or property from provincials, foreigners or subjects by Roman officials. During

---

[a] *Bellum Catilinae* 45. 2. For the careers of men like Flaccus, see R. E. Smith, *Service in the Post-Marian Roman Army* 59 f.

[b] 6 and 100, pp. 446 and 550. The phrase in 100, *urbana iuris dictio*, does not mean conclusively that he was *praetor urbanus*. The subject matter of 6 suggests that he was in fact *praetor peregrinus*.

[c] 1, 5, 95 and 102, pp. 434, 438, 544 and 550. For the story in detail see pp. 13-30.

[d] 31, 43 and 100, pp. 474, 488 and 550.   [e] 52, p. 498.

[f] The Latin phrase means " recovery " and refers to the purpose of the court dealing with the offence rather than to the offence itself.

the first half of the second century when the Roman empire was undergoing rapid expansion, there were a number of ways in which satisfaction could be claimed by those who had been mistreated. Pecuniary damages could be claimed through civil procedure in front of a board of *recuperatores* chosen by the praetor. But if the complaint appeared to be serious, a magistrate or, more commonly, a tribune could arrange a hearing before the people. Failing that, a *quaestio extraordinaria* or special commission could be convened for the occasion. None of these methods proved entirely satisfactory and offences against provincials and foreigners continued to be committed.

Finally, in 149 the people's scandalous failure to bring Servius Sulpicius Galba to justice ensured that the current state of affairs should not be allowed to continue. Galba had been propraetor in Further Spain in 150 and during his period of office had behaved outrageously. A proposal that he should be brought before a special *quaestio* was defeated by the people, and the case against him went by default. As a direct result of this failure to bring a guilty man to book a new procedure now emerged. Lucius Calpurnius Piso, a tribune of 149, secured the passage of a law establishing Rome's first permanent criminal court, the *quaestio de rebus repetundis.*[a] The precise

---

[a] For the complexities of the extortion court procedure and its penalties, see A. N. Sherwin-White, " *Poena legis repetundarum,*" *Papers of the British School at Rome* 17 (1949), 5-25, with bibliography (to which should be added A. H. J. Greenidge, *The Legal Procedure of Cicero's Time*) ; M. I. Henderson, " The process *de repetundis,*" *Journal of Roman Studies* 41 (1951), 71-88 ; and A. N. Sherwin-White, " The Extortion Procedure Again," *Journal of Roman Studies* 42 (1952), 43-55.

provisions of the law are not known, but it is clear that the jurors were drawn from the senatorial order. It is also probable that the *praetor peregrinus* was the presiding officer and that the penalty was simple restitution of the financial loss.

Unfortunately Piso's legislation does not appear to have been of much assistance to the provincials. There is no evidence, though this may be the fault of defective sources, that the machinery provided by his law was used during the succeeding decade, and when it was used against Quintus Pompeius in 139 or 138 and against Lucius Aurelius Cotta in 138 the primary aim of the prosecution was not justice for provincials but the pursuit of political enemies within the Senate. The use of the court for this purpose was to continue for the rest of the Republican period.

A further dimension, too, was added during Gaius Gracchus' tribunates to the rôle of the court in the struggle for power at Rome.[a] Among the body of Gracchan legislation is a measure carried by another tribune, Manius Acilius Glabrio. It appears that Gaius Gracchus' original intention was that membership of the juries in this court should be shared by Senate and knights. It was to be the duty of the senators to supervise the actions of the equestrian *publicani* and of the knights to ensure that senatorial solidarity did not lead to the acquittal of guilty senators. In the end, however, sole control of the court was put in the hands of the knights. Glabrio's measure also assessed pecuniary damages at twice the sum involved in the complaint. Thereafter there

[a] At some date between 149 and 123 there was a *lex Iunia repetundarum* of a tribune Marcus Iunius but our source tells us nothing about this law.

continued until 70 a contest between the two orders
for control of the court. In 106 the consul, Quintus
Servilius Caepio, sponsored a judiciary law which
established mixed juries of senators and knights, only
to have it superseded by a *lex repetundarum* of a
tribune, Gaius Servilius Glaucia, at some date between 104 and 100. This law restored the court to
the knights. In 91 Marcus Livius Drusus, a tribune
of that year, endeavoured without success to re-estab-
lish mixed juries of senators and knights, and in 89
the tribune Marcus Plautius Silvanus created by his
lex Plautia a new system for the selection of jurors.[a]
Every year fifteen were to be chosen by each tribe
and the order from which the jurors came would be
irrelevant. The effect of this measure, since the
senatorial order held such control over voting in the
tribes, was to ensure that once again senators would
predominate in the court.[b]

In 81 the extortion court was again reconstituted
as one of the seven permanent courts, each the subject of a separate *lex Cornelia*, by the dictator Sulla.
Once more the Senate was given complete control of
the court but otherwise we have little information
about what changes Sulla made, a silence that may
indicate that there were no substantial alterations.
There may have been some minor adjustment to the

---

[a] It is not possible in an introduction of this length to
discuss in greater detail the complicated history of the
extortion court from 123 to 70. Reference may be made to
J. P. V. D. Balsdon, " The History of the Extortion Court at
Rome, 123–70 B.C.," *Papers of the British School at Rome*
14 (1938), 98–114, reprinted in R. Seager, Ed., *The Crisis of
the Roman Republic* 132-149 ; and E. S. Gruen, *Roman
Politics and the Criminal Courts 149–78 B.C.* 84 f.

[b] E. S. Gruen, *op. cit.* 221.

penalty, but firm evidence is lacking. Sulla's main contribution to the history of the court was a definitive re-statement of the relevant legislation.[a]

The jury before which Flaccus was tried was composed of twenty-five members each of the Senate, the knights and the *tribuni aerarii*.[b] The last-named were previously officers of the tribes and now formed a new class in the State with a property rating slightly below that of the knights. The panel was nine hundred strong and composed of equal numbers from each class. This tripartite composition of the juries had been established in 70 by the *lex Aurelia iudiciaria* of a praetor, Lucius Aurelius Cotta, whose law replaced Sulla's provisions and succeeded in removing the composition of juries from the arena of political strife for more than twenty years. Under the terms of the *lex Cassia tabellaria* of Lucius Cassius Longinus Ravilla, a tribune of 137, the jurors gave their verdict by ballot. A further measure was passed in the year of this trial by a praetor, Quintus Fufius Calenus, which required separate reports of the votes of the three classes. The president of the court was probably Titus Vettius (Sabinus).[c]

There was also passed in this year Caesar's *lex Iulia*

[a] Cicero, II *in Verrem* 1. 108.

[b] 4, p. 438, where the *tribuni aerarii* are classed by Cicero with the *equites* proper.

[c] 85, p. 534. T. B. L. Webster in the introductory note to his edition of the speech says Gnaeus Lentulus Clodianus, assuming that Gaius Antonius Hybrida too was tried for extortion. Antonius, however, is more likely to have been tried for *maiestas* with extortion and other charges as supporting accusations and Lentulus, who, we know, presided over the trial of Antonius, will therefore not have been in charge of the *quaestio de repetundis*. R. G. Austin, *pro Caelio* Appendix VII, 158-159.

repetundarum. This was a comprehensive measure which restricted donations to generals in the provinces, limited governors' powers to intervene in *liberae civitates*—free cities—and forbade them to wage war on their own responsibility.[a]

The province of Asia [b] had its origins in the will of Attalus III, the king of Pergamum, who made the Roman people heir to his kingdom. When he died in 133 Tiberius Gracchus saw to it that the bequest was accepted and planned to use some of the royal funds for his agrarian schemes. Before the end of the year a commission of five senators under Publius Cornelius Scipio Nasica was dispatched to organize the province, but their plans were disrupted by a revolt led by a certain Aristonicus, the illegitimate son of Attalus' predecessor. The country was eventually pacified and in 126 the settlement of the province was arranged by Manius Aquilius (consul in 129) with the aid of the ten members of a senatorial commission ; it was not, however, finally ratified until 125 or 124.

The city of Pergamum itself and the cities formerly subject to it received their freedom and immunity from taxation, and in all their arrangements the commission showed more interest in the new province as a political and strategic base than as a source of revenue. Their aim seems to have been the avoidance of further administrative commitments and they evinced little concern for financial gain.[c]

---

[a] See also p. 456, n. *a.* Flaccus was not tried under the provisions of this law.

[b] See in particular T. R. S. Broughton in T. Frank, *An Economic Survey of Ancient Rome* iv, part 4, and D. Magie, *Roman Rule in Asia Minor.*

[c] This attitude is in line with normal Roman imperial policy. Rome sought no major financial benefits from her

PRO FLACCO

But there were others at Rome who were more concerned with the prospect of additional revenues for implementing agrarian reform in Italy, and Gaius Gracchus, tribune in 123 and 122, effectively challenged the commission's policy.[a] More important for the future of Asia was the measure which gave the *publicani*, who had previously collected only minor taxes in the province, the right to collect the main tax for the whole of Asia. The contracts were to be sold at Rome by the censors for five years at a time and the Asiatic communities were thus deprived of the opportunity of bidding for the contracts themselves.[b]

Asia was extremely wealthy. Even after decades of oppression by dishonest governors and rapacious tax-gatherers and after three years' occupation by the army of Mithridates Cicero could still in 66 say that " in the richness of its soil, in the variety of its products, in the extent of its pastures and in the number of its exports " it was unsurpassed.[c] It was this wealth that fired the avaricious rapacity of Roman governors, officials and businessmen, and it was to prove in Cicero's words a *corruptrix provincia* [d]

Empire.   E. Badian, *Roman Imperialism in the Late Republic* 18.

[a] It was the acquisition of Asia with its colossal wealth that led Tiberius Gracchus to establish the principle that the provinces should be systematically exploited for the benefit of the Roman people. E. Badian, *op. cit.* 48 f.

[b] Mainly because the capital required was beyond their resources, but there were requirements, *e.g.* property in Italy to be put up as surety for the proper fulfilment of the contract, which they were not likely to be able to meet.

[c] *de imperio Gnaei Pompei* 14.

[d] *ad Quintum fratrem* 1. 1. 19.

to all too many of the Romans and Italians who came into touch with it.

For a time the Gracchan law-courts [a] worked well and dealt effectively with extortion,[b] but standards started to decline in the mid-90s and the system finally broke down because the *publicani* for whom the provinces proved so profitable came to dominate the very class which was in charge of the courts.[c] This meant that the men who held the largest financial stake in the province could hope for the protection of their fellow knights at Rome if accused of extortion. It meant, too, that an honest governor and his staff were at the mercy of the very men whose excesses it was their duty to curb and were liable on their return to Rome to face a trumped-up charge before a hostile jury.[d] Such scandalous partisanship did its best to see that oppression went unpunished and that a govenor's attempts to check it secured for him the punishment that should have gone to the men he had sought to restrain. This unchecked rapacity was to earn for Rome a bitter hatred and was alleged to have caused on a single day in 88 the death of eighty thousand members of the Roman and Italian community whom

[a] See p. 417.
[b] Cicero, I *in Verrem* 38. The notorious condemnation of Publius Rutilius Rufus was thirty years after the equestrian juries had first been established.
[c] *Cf.* Cicero, *pro Plancio* 23.
[d] In 92 Rufus (see above) was condemned and exiled. His crime was that he had attempted to defend the Asians against the depredations of the tax-gatherers while legate to Quintus Mucius. See Livy, *Periocha* 70. Senatorial rivals for power were another source of danger ; the court was in constant use as a means of eliminating political competitors. See p. 177.

the provincials slaughtered at a given signal from Mithridates.[a]

Once the situation had been restored the tax-gatherers returned to Asia and the Gracchan system of collecting taxes continued until it was ended by Julius Caesar in 48 or 47.[b] Even without the protection of equestrian juries in the years following Sulla's reorganization which returned control of the courts to the Senate in 81, the publicans' greed continued unabated.

During this period there were two groups of Romans and Italians concerned with Asia. One was resident in the province and consisted mainly of traders and the smaller bankers; the other consisted of men of wealth and high social standing, bankers on a large scale, who lived outside the province and transacted their business in it by means of local agents. Those who were resident in the province formed local associations and the existence of these associations is attested for a number of towns throughout the province.[c] Our limited evidence shows that these men followed a variety of trades and occupations; in this speech alone we have land-

[a] 60, p. 508. The number is exaggerated and no accurate figure can be given; " a few thousand " is the best that we can do. P. A. Brunt, *Italian Manpower 225 B.C.–A.D. 14* 224-227.

[b] The tax-gatherers would be in operation again by the end of the decade. This speech makes clear the extent to which the Romans recovered and consolidated their power after Lucullus' settlement, probably to be dated around 70. Much of it is taken up with the interests of Roman citizens.

[c] 71, p. 518: Pergamum, Smyrna and Tralles, which appear to have supported the most important Italian communities.

owners both resident and non-resident, bankers and money-lenders, and local agents.[a]

Such was the province governed by Flaccus and such were the fellow-citizens with whom he would have to deal.[b] The difficulties and dangers confronting a governor of Asia are described by Cicero in a famous letter to his brother.[c] Not only were the opportunities for personal profit virtually endless for a determined governor, but it was in his complaisance that there lay the danger of abuses by others. During office he was continuously subjected to influential pressures, and these pressures were liable to derive not so much from the tax-collection itself as from the other activities to which it used to lead.

The fact that the publicans collected tithes in kind and had to handle various commodities led to their involvement in trade as merchants dealing in these commodities. Furthermore, their contacts with the

[a] Resident landowners : 51 and 72, pp. 498 and 520 ; non-resident landowners : 46, p. 492 ; bankers and money-lenders : 34-35, 54 and 75, pp. 478-480, 502 and 524 ; agents : 46-48, pp. 492-496. This speech attests the power and the connexions of these provincial Romans. See in general J. Hatzfeld, " Les Italiens résidant à Délos," *Bulletin de Correspondance hellénique* 36 (1912), 5-218 and *Les Trafiquants italiens dans l'Orient hellénique* ; also T. P. Wiseman, *New Men in the Roman Senate 139 B.C.-A.D 14.*

[b] For an account of the life of a provincial governor emphasizing his heavy load of administrative and judicial work and the constant travel in which he was engaged, see A. J. Marshall, " Governors on the Move," *Phoenix* 20 (1966), 231-246. This account provides a valuable corrective to our sources with their emphasis upon military expansion and the fate of the more corrupt provincial magistrates.

[c] *ad Quintum fratrem* 1. 1. 32 f. Cicero's own order of priorities should be noted : in order to preserve the *concordia ordinum* the interests of the provincials must suffer.

individuals and communities liable to pay tax and their realization that personal profit was possible from mutually convenient financial arrangements led to their becoming money-lenders and bankers. Their expertise and the possession of trained personnel also enabled Roman and Italian businessmen to compete with the inhabitants for the right to collect local taxes.[a] The possibilities for extortion inherent in this system are not far to seek.

Our sources have to be treated with caution if they are to provide us with a reliable picture of the ethical standards current in Rome's provinces. They are biased against the equestrian juries, and the governors about whom we hear most are the most deplorable. Not every jury condemned an innocent governor or acquitted a guilty publican, and not every governor was a Verres. But it is fair to say that there were rich profits to be had by the unscrupulous in the province of Asia and all too many Romans from the governor downwards succumbed to the temptation of illicit gain.[b]

The prosecution had alleged that Flaccus levied an assessment on the cities of Asia for the construction of a fleet and then kept a large part of the sum contributed for himself.[c] Cicero sought to refute this charge by arguing that a decree of the Senate had permitted Flaccus to impose the levy, that a fleet was required because inhabitants of the province had been captured by pirates and that some ships had

[a] 91, p. 540.

[b] The problem of corruption in the provinces was never solved under the Republic. A steady flow of legislation attempted to control the system, but the evil was inherent in the system itself.

[c] 27-33, pp. 470-478.

in fact put to sea. He tried to avoid the charge that
Flaccus had not spent all the money on the fleet by
arguing that it was irrelevant that it had not been
entered in his accounts. This defence is quite unconvincing and we know that the imposition of a levy
with which to man a fleet was a recognized source of
income for governors.[a] Other allegations were that
he had extorted sums of money from the communities
of Acmona, Dorylaeum and Temnus [b] ; that at
Tralles he had appropriated money collected years
before by the cities of Asia to found a festival in
honour of his father [c] ; that he had misappropriated
gold collected by the Jewish community to send to
Jerusalem and the export of which he had forbid-
den [d] ; that Roman citizens had been victims of the
illegal exercise of his powers as governor : Decianus
who claimed that he had been denied justice, Sextilius Andro who claimed that Flaccus had taken an
inheritance that was rightly his and Falcidius who
alleged that fifty talents had been extorted from him
as the price of Flaccus' ratification of his right to
collect the revenues of Tralles.[e]

As in the defence of Murena and of Sulla, Cicero
was joined in his defence of Flaccus by Quintus
Hortensius Hortalus, that constant champion of
senators in trouble.[f] Once again Cicero spoke last
and made one of the emotional appeals to the jury
for which he was renowned and at which he was so
successful.[g] We learn from this speech that Horten-

[a] M. Rostovtzeff, *The Social and Economic History of the
Hellenistic World* 2. 963.

[b] 34-38, 39-41 and 42-51, pp. 478-484, 484-488 and 488-
498.   [c] 52-61, pp. 498-510.   [d] 66-69, pp. 514-518.

[e] 70-83, 84-89 and 90-93, pp. 518-532, 532-540 and 540-
544.   [f] See p. 179.   [g] 99 f., p. 548 f. See also p. 309.

sius had refuted the accusations brought by Mithridates of Pergamum[a] and had explained the reasons for the animosity shown towards Flaccus by the inhabitants of Tralles.[b] Hortensius may also have dealt with the charges made by other cities which Cicero mentions but does not refute,[c] and in a letter written in October the same year Cicero tells Atticus of Hortensius' eloquence on the subject of Flaccus' praetorship and of his own intense satisfaction at his account of the lead taken by Cicero in the suppression of the Catilinarian conspiracy.[d]

The speech that has come down to us is a shortened version of that delivered by Cicero at the trial[e] and, although it may not be counted one of his masterpieces, it is a work of considerable forensic skill. A decade earlier Cicero had defended Marcus Fonteius against a charge of extortion in Gaul and a comparison of the two speeches reveals a very similar approach to the task of securing the acquittal of a guilty governor. An account is given of the defendant's outstanding services to Rome: in this speech Flaccus is a Roman noble *par excellence*, the last of a long line to spend their lives in the service of the city and a provincial governor in the tradition of Rome's great proconsuls.[f] The charges are then flatly

[a] 41, p. 488.   [b] 54, p. 502.
[c] Tmolus and Cyme ; Milan fragment and 17, pp. 440 and 460.   [d] *ad Atticum* 2. 25. 1.
[e] Symmachus in Macrobius, *Saturnalia* 2. 1. 13. " Atque ego, ni longum esset, referrem in quibus causis, cum nocentissimos reos tueretur, victoriam iocis adeptus sit ; ut ecce pro L. Flacco, quem repetundarum reum ioci opportunitate de manifestissimis criminibus exemit. Is iocus in oratione non exstat, mihi ex libro Furii Bibaculi notus est, et inter alia eius dicta celebratur." *Cf.* p. 183.
[f] 1 and 28, pp. 434 and 470.

denied,[a] the prosecution's witnesses are discredited and an appeal is made to interests of state.

Yet Cicero's task in 59 was not as straightforward as he could have wished it. In the previous year he had written the letter to his brother Quintus and this letter complicated matters for him. It was clearly a letter for public consumption in which he instructed his brother at length in a governor's problems and duties in the province of Asia and it contained pious injunctions to Quintus on the subject of the special responsibilities he owed to Greeks.[b] This line made it difficult for Cicero to undermine their credit as bluntly as he would have liked, in a speech delivered not so many months later. Just as the Gauls who gave evidence against Fonteius were held to display the traditional unreliability of Gauls, so in this speech Cicero impugns the credibility of Greek witnesses both as a class and as individuals. He extricates himself, however, from his awkward position with no little skill. Firstly, he makes a clear-cut distinction between the literary and intellectual achievements of Greeks, which he readily acknowledges, and their reliability as witnesses.[c] Later in the speech he shifts his ground and draws a different distinction —between Asiatic Greeks and "true" Greeks.[d] Fortunately Flaccus had seen service in Greece [e] and Cicero is therefore able to produce native Greek witnesses to testify on Flaccus' behalf. He also produces Greek witnesses from other areas in which

[a] Cicero, de oratore 2. 105, says that in trials for extortion the charges must be flatly denied.

[b] ad Quintum fratrem 1. 1. 28.   [c] 9-12, pp. 450-454.

[d] 62-64 and 100, pp. 510-512 and 550.

[e] See p. 414 above. The prosecution no doubt ensured that witnesses favourable to Flaccus were hard to come by in Asia.

Flaccus had seen service with whom to combat the unreliable Asiatic Greeks of the prosecution.

The varied themes of the speech are reflected in its oratorical style. Flaccus the saviour of his country is described in the grand style,[a] but the prosecution witnesses are devalued by colloquial language and sarcasm.[b] For his own witnesses there is a brief return to the grand style,[c] but Cicero soon reverts to a lower key in passages where he ridicules the Mysians and Carians, uses proverbial sayings to poke fun at them and makes cheap appeals to the prejudices of his audience.[d] As in the case of the *pro Murena* this speech became a famous example of how to help your guilty client by a timely joke.[e] The speech ends with a return to the grand style for the appeal to interests of state and the emotional peroration to the jury.[f]

The case was heard in August [g] and Laelius [h] opened the first hearing with an account of the charges brought by the Asiatics and by Decianus and then dealt with the wrongs done to himself and to other Roman citizens. Hortensius replied and the hearing was concluded with the interrogation of witnesses. Laelius also opened the second hearing,

[a] 1, p. 434.

[b] 39 and 46, pp. 484 and 494 for colloquialisms ; 34 and 39, pp. 474 and 484 for sarcasm.

[c] 62-64, pp. 510-512. [d] 65, p. 512.

[e] Macrobius, *loc. cit.* See also p. 183, n. *a.*

[f] On the variety of styles matching the topics, see L. Laurand, *Le Style des discours de Cicéron* 316-318.

[g] For the date, see L. R. Taylor, " The Date and Meaning of the Vettius Affair," *Historia* 1 (1950), 48 following *ad Atticum* 2. 25. 1.

[h] For this account of the proceedings, see T. B. L. Webster's edition of the speech (p. vi and Appendix A).

was followed by Lucius Cornelius Balbus,[a] and Cicero
then completed the proceedings.

Laelius was the prime mover in the prosecution and
had as his colleague, in addition to Decianus and Balbus, a certain Lucceius. Cicero represents, as also
apparently had Hortensius, that the prosecution's
chief concern was to attack Flaccus, as they had
attacked Gaius Antonius, because he had actively
helped Cicero in the suppression of the Catilinarian
conspiracy ; and that by means of their attack on
Flaccus they hoped to smash Cicero himself. A
stronger motive seems to have been the desire of the
Triumvirs to eliminate Flaccus as a member of the
nobility opposing their interests,[b] and in Pompey's
case another motive was his genuine concern for
good provincial government. In Asia the view was
widely held that Pompey's hostility lay behind
Laelius' prosecution and the freedom with which he
had been able to prepare his case.[c] Cicero does not

---

[a] For the identification of this Balbus, see Valerius
Maximus 7. 8. 7 : " L. Valerius, cui cognomen Heptachordo
fuit, togatum hostem Cornelium Balbum expertus, utpote
opera eius et consilii compluribus privatis litibus vexatus ad
ultimumque subiecto accusatore capitali crimine accusatus,
praeteritis advocatis et patronis suis solum heredem reliquit "
and the scholiast (p. 93, ed. Stangl): " ⟨subscri⟩bentibus L.
Balbo et Appuleio Deciano " ; also F. Münzer in Pauly-
Wissowa, *Realencyclopädie* IV. 1 (1900), L. Cornelius Balbus
(69), 1260-1268 and R. Gardner's introduction to the speech
pro Balbo (Loeb Classical Library), 617. After his record of
numerous private cases against Flaccus he was now a devoted
adherent of Caesar and Pompey. It has been suggested that
Flaccus' nick-name may have been the subject of Cicero's joke.

[b] Even if they did not secure his condemnation, they
prevented him from becoming consul in 58.

[c] 14, p. 456. *Cf.* his disapproval of Antonius Hybrida's
administration in Macedonia ; see *ad Atticum* 1. 12. 1.

dare to deny this, and his brother Quintus was apparently unable to halt the proceedings against his predecessor in the province. Neither Pompey, whose subordinate Flaccus had been, nor Pupius Piso, whose quaestor he had been and who had been consul in 61, came forward to speak on his behalf. The only men under whom he had served who did speak up for him were Publius Servilius Vatia Isauricus and Quintus Caecilius Metellus Creticus, both opponents of the Triumvirs.[a]

In the face of these disadvantages Cicero makes the best use of the material available on his client's behalf; the maintenance of a fleet against the pirates rings true of a *homo militaris*, the ban on the export of gold may well have had sound economic reasons behind it,[b] Flaccus' legal decisions may have been perfectly good, even though they laid him open to personal revenge.

Yet, when everything has been said on Flaccus' behalf, even without Macrobius' explicit testimony, the picture is of a guilty man. The specific indictments of the prosecution go unanswered and in the place of any effective reply there are generalizations, evasions, sarcasm and appeals to prejudice. Combined with these tactics the partisan appeal for sympathy with those who helped Cicero in 63 does nothing to strengthen our belief in Flaccus' innocence.

Flaccus appears to have been acquitted and there is good reason to feel that he owed the favourable verdict more to his counsel's powers of persuasion

[a] 100, p. 550. See E. S. Gruen, *The Last Generation of the Roman Republic* 289-291.

[b] M. W. Frederiksen, "Caesar, Cicero and the Problem of Debt," *Journal of Roman Studies* 56 (1966), 133, n. 40.

than to any inherent strength of his case. The result of the trial is not recorded in any surviving source; Flaccus never held another magistracy and the consulship that he had been promised eluded him. In 57–56, however, he was a *legatus* of Lucius Piso in Macedonia ; apart from this reference to him in the speech *pro Plancio* [a] delivered in 54 he is not heard of again.

[a] 27.

PRO FLACCO

PRO L. FLACCO ORATIO

1　　Cum in maximis periculis huius urbis atque imperi, gravissimo atque acerbissimo rei publicae casu, socio atque adiutore consiliorum periculorumque meorum L. Flacco, caedem a vobis, coniugibus, liberis vestris, vastitatem a templis, delubris, urbe, Italia depellebam, sperabam, iudices, honoris potius L. Flacci me adiutorem futurum quam miseriarum deprecatorem. Quod enim esset praemium dignitatis quod populus Romanus, cum huius maioribus semper detulisset, huic denegaret, cum L. Flaccus veterem Valeriae gentis in liberanda patria laudem prope quingen-
2　tesimo anno rei publicae rettulisset ? Sed si forte aliquando aut benefici huius obtrectator aut virtutis hostis aut laudis invidus exstitisset, existimabam L. Flacco multitudinis potius imperitae, nullo tamen cum periculo, quam sapientissimorum et lectissimorum virorum iudicium esse subeundum. Etenim quibus auctoribus et defensoribus omnium tum salus

---

a The consulship. Flaccus had been praetor in 63 ; his colleague in the praetorship, Quintus Caecilius Metellus Celer, became consul in 60.

b Publius Valerius Publicola had expelled the Tarquins in 509 and had been made consul ; Lucius Valerius Publicola had been consul in 449 ; Lucius Valerius Flaccus had been consul in 195 and censor in 184 ; Lucius Valerius Flaccus had

SPEECH IN DEFENCE OF
LUCIUS VALERIUS FLACCUS

AMID the direst perils of Rome and of our Empire, in 1
that most grievous hour of crisis for the Republic,
Lucius Flaccus was my companion and helper in my
deliberations and my dangers. With his aid I rescued
you, your wives and your children from death ; our
temples and shrines, our city and Italy from devastation. I hoped, gentlemen, that I would be helping
Flaccus win the high honour of office,[a] not that I
would be protecting him from personal tragedy.
What reward of high office was there that the Roman
people would deny to him when it had always granted
such rewards to his ancestors ? This it had done from
that time when, almost five hundred years after the
foundation of the Republic, he had revived the
ancient glory won by the Valerii in their liberation of
our fatherland.[b] But if there had ever chanced to be 2
one to belittle the services of Lucius Flaccus, to
attack his personal courage or to begrudge him his
reputation, I reckoned that Flaccus would have to
submit to the verdict of the uneducated mob—
though this would not endanger him in any way—
rather than to the pick of our most intelligent men.
Of those who at that time were its authors and

been consul in 100, censor in 97, *interrex* and *magister
equitum* in 86 and *princeps senatus* in 85.

esset non civium solum verum etiam gentium defensa
ac retenta, neminem umquam putavi per eos ipsos
periculum huius fortunis atque insidias creaturum.
Quod si esset aliquando futurum ut aliquis de L.
Flacci pernicie cogitaret, numquam tamen existimavi,
iudices, D. Laelium, optimi viri filium, optima ipsum
spe praeditum summae dignitatis, eam suscepturum
accusationem quae sceleratorum civium potius odio
et furori quam ipsius virtuti atque institutae adulescentiae conveniret. Etenim cum a clarissimis viris
iustissimas inimicitias saepe cum bene meritis civibus
depositas esse vidissem, non sum arbitratus quemquam amicum rei publicae, postea quam L. Flacci
amor in patriam perspectus esset, novas huic inimici-
3 tias nulla accepta iniuria denuntiaturum. Sed quoniam, iudices, multa nos et in nostris rebus et in re
publica fefellerunt, ferimus ea quae sunt ferenda ;
tantum a vobis petimus ut omnia rei publicae subsidia, totum statum civitatis, omnem memoriam
temporum praeteritorum, salutem praesentium, spem
reliquorum in vestra potestate, in vestris sententiis,
in hoc uno iudicio positam esse et defixam putetis.
Si umquam res publica consilium, gravitatem, sapientiam, providentiam iudicum imploravit, hoc, hoc
inquam, tempore implorat. Non estis de Lydorum aut
Mysorum aut Phrygum, qui huc compulsi concitati-
que venerunt, sed de vestra re publica iudicaturi, de
civitatis statu, de communi salute, de spe bonorum

---

[a] Decimus Laelius was the son of the Laelius who had
been a subordinate commander under Pompey in Spain
and had been killed in the war with Sertorius. He served
with Pompey in the East, was tribune in 54 and a *praefectus
classis* with Pompey in 49-48.

[b] *i.e.* he did not need to obtain it by undertaking prosecutions.

guardians and had protected and preserved the safety not only of our own citizens but of the whole world, I never thought that among these very men one would hatch a scheme to endanger Flaccus' fortunes. But if there ever should appear a man to plan his destruction, I never thought, gentlemen, that Decimus Laelius,[a] the son of a fine gentleman, who had an excellent claim in his own right to reach the highest rank,[b] would undertake a prosecution more appropriate to the crazed hatred of criminals [c] than to his own good qualities and the standards he learnt as a young man. Having often seen men of distinction abandon feuds that were fully justified with fellow-citizens who had served the State well, I did not think that after Lucius Flaccus' devotion to his fatherland had been proved any true patriot would without provocation threaten him with a gratuitous quarrel. I have, 3 however, gentlemen, suffered many disappointments both in private affairs and in public [d] and so I submit to the inevitable. I only ask you to appreciate that every buttress of the State,[e] its whole constitution, all our recollection of times past, the safety of the present, our hope for the future, have been firmly placed in your hands and in your verdict in this one trial. If ever the Republic appealed for good sense, responsibility, intelligence and foresight in a jury, she appeals on this, I repeat, this occasion. It is not upon the land of the Lydians, Mysians and Phrygians who have been urged with bribes to come to Rome that you are going to give your verdict, but upon your own State, upon the fabric of the body-politic, the

---

[c] *i.e.* Catilinarians.   [d] See p. xxx.
[e] *Cf. ad Atticum* 1. 18. 3. Presumably the authority of the Senate and the *concordia ordinum.* See p. xxix.

omnium, si qua reliqua est etiam nunc quae fortium
civium mentis cogitationesque sustentet; omnia alia
perfugia bonorum, praesidia innocentium, subsidia
4 rei publicae, consilia, auxilia, iura ceciderunt. Quem
enim appellem, quem obtester, quem implorem?
Senatumne? At is ipse auxilium petit a vobis et
confirmationem auctoritatis suae vestrae potestati
permissam esse sentit. An equites Romanos? Indicabitis[1] principes eius ordinis quinquaginta quid cum
omnibus senseritis. An populum Romanum? At is
quidem omnem suam de nobis potestatem tradidit
vobis. Quam ob rem nisi hoc loco, nisi apud vos, nisi
per vos, iudices, non auctoritatem, quae amissa est,
sed salutem nostram, quae spe exigua extremaque
pendet, tenuerimus, nihil est praeterea quo confugere
possimus; nisi forte quae res hoc iudicio temptetur,
quid agatur, cui causae fundamenta iaciantur, iudices,
5 non videtis. Condemnatus est is qui Catilinam signa
patriae inferentem interemit; quid est causae cur
non is qui Catilinam ex urbe expulit pertimescat?
Rapitur ad poenam qui indicia communis exiti cepit;
cur sibi confidat is qui ea proferenda et patefacienda
curavit? Socii consiliorum, ministri comitesque

---

[1] Indicabitis *Clark*. Iudicabitis *mss*.

---

[a] The *subsidia* are, as above, senatorial authority and the
concordia ordinum which were Cicero's *consilia* or policy
against Catiline. When put into action by means of the
constitutional powers available as *auxilia*, they are *praesidia*; when in a judicial context as *iura*, they are *perfugia*.

[b] See p. 419.

[c] Cicero interprets the case as an attack upon those
involved in the suppression of the Catilinarian conspiracy.
For the background to the case, see p. 430.

safety of us all, the hope of loyal men—if any still remains to sustain the minds and spirits of courageous citizens. Every other refuge for loyal men, the protection of the innocent, the pillars of the State—policy, succour, justice—they have all perished.[a] Whom else am I to invoke, whom else entreat, whom **4** else implore? The Senate? The Senate is itself seeking your help and realizes that the enforcement of its authority has been entrusted to your decision. The Roman knights? Fifty of you, leading men of the order, will show what you and everyone else have felt.[b] The Roman people? They have entrusted to you all their power to help me. If, then, it is in this place alone and among you alone, gentlemen, through you alone that I have retained, I do not say my authority—for that is lost—but my chance of survival, which is hanging by the slender thread of a last hope, then there is no other place in which I can take refuge. Yet perhaps you do not see, gentlemen, what the purpose of this trial is, what is at stake, what is the case the foundations of which are now being laid.[c] The man has been condemned who did **5** away with Catiline as he led his standards against his fatherland.[d] Should not then the man who drove Catiline from Rome have good cause to be afraid? [e] The man is being rushed to punishment who obtained the information about the plan to destroy us all.[f] What reassurance can there be for the man who ensured the disclosure and publication of that information? Those who shared his decisions, his agents

---

[d] Gaius Antonius Hybrida, Cicero's consular colleague of 63. See pp. 28 and 430, n. c.

[e] Cicero himself.

[f] See *in Catilinam* 3. 5-6, pp. 104-106.

vexantur; quid auctores, quid duces, quid principes
sibi exspectent? Atque utinam inimici nostri ac
bonorum omnium mecum potius aestiment, utrum[1]
tum omnes boni duces nostri an[2] comites fuerint ad
communem conservandam salutem * * *

Fragmenta Scholiastae Bobiensis

Strangulatos maluit dicere.
Quod sibi meus necessarius Caetra voluit.
Quid vero Decianus?
Utinam esset proprie mea! Senatus igitur magna
ex parte * * *
Di, inquam, immortales Lentulum * * *

Fragmentum Mediolanense

* * * externum cum domestica vita naturaque constaret. Itaque non patiar, D. Laeli, te tibi hoc sumere
atque hanc ceteris in posterum, nobis in praesens
tempus legem condicionemque * * *
Cum adulescentiam notaris, cum reliquum tempus
aetatis turpitudinis maculis consperseris, cum privatarum rerum ruinas, cum domesticas labes, cum
urbanam infamiam, cum Hispaniae, Galliae, Ciliciae,
Cretae, quibus in provinciis non obscure versatus est,
vitia et flagitia protuleris, tum denique quid Tmoli-

---

[1] aestiment, utrum *Madvig.* tum est utrum Σχ. con-
tendant tum est utrum tamen *b*[1]. utrum tum est tum *B.*
contenderent utrum ѕ.
[2] aut Σ *in the margin.*

---

[a] Nothing is known of him. The name is not found elsewhere in Latin literature, but occurs twice in inscriptions.
[b] See 70-74, pp. 518-524. It would seem from the scholiast's
note (p. 95 ed. Stangl) that Cicero referred to Decianus' father

and his associates are being harried. What are those who shouldered the responsibility, the leaders, the principals to expect? I would rather have those who are my enemies and the enemies of all good men judge whether all good men were my leaders or my comrades in preserving the safety of us all.

Fragments preserved by the Scholiast of Bobbio

He preferred to say that they had been strangled.
What my relative Caetra [a] wanted for himself.
What then of Decianus? [b]
I wish that it were really mine! The Senate, then, to a large extent . . .
Immortal gods! I say . . . Lentulus . . . [c]

The Milan Fragment

. . . abroad . . ., corresponded with his life and character at home. I shall, therefore, not allow you, Decimus Laelius, to arrogate this right to yourself and impose this rule and condition upon us now and upon others in the future . . .

When you have branded his youth, when you have bespattered the rest of his life with the stains of disgrace, when you have published abroad the ruin of his private affairs, his personal shame, his infamous behaviour in Rome, the vices contracted and the crimes committed in Spain, Gaul, Cilicia and Crete, provinces in which he played no small rôle, then we shall finally hear what the people of Tmolus and

at this point. Of equestrian status himself, Decianus belonged to a senatorial family. For the family, see E. Badian, " P. Decius P. f. Subulo," *Journal of Roman Studies* 46 (1956), 95-96. [c] The conspirator. See p. 12.

tae et Lorymeni[1] de L. Flacco existiment audiemus. Quem vero tot tam gravesque provinciae salvum esse cupiant, quem plurimi cives tota ex Italia devincti necessitudine ac vetustate defendant, quem haec communis nostrum omnium patria propter recentem summi benefici memoriam complexa teneat, hunc etiam si tota Asia deposcit ad supplicium, defendam, resistam. Quid? si neque tota neque optima neque incorrupta neque sua sponte nec iure nec more nec vere nec religiose nec integre, si impulsa,[2] si sollicitata, si concitata, si coacta, si impie, si temere, si cupide, si inconstanter nomen suum misit in hoc iudicium per egentissimos testis, ipsa autem nihil queri vere de iniuriis potest, tamenne, iudices, haec ad breve tempus audita longinqui temporis cognitarum rerum fidem derogabunt? Tenebo igitur hunc ordinem defensor quem fugit inimicus, et accusatorem urgebo atque insequar et ultro crimen ab adversario flagitabo. Quid est, Laeli? num quid ea d . . d . . ea . . f . . . no qui quidem non in umbra neque in illius aetatis disciplinis artibusque versatus est? Etenim puer cum patre consule ad bellum est profectus. Nimirum etiam hoc ipso nomine aliquid . . ia sus * * *

---

[1] Lorymeni *Heinrich*. Loreni *M*. Dorylenses *Mommsen*.
[2] impulsa *Peyron*. iniuria *M*.

PRO FLACCO, fragment

Loryma [a] think of Lucius Flaccus. A man, however, whom so many important provinces want to be acquitted, to whose defence there has rallied a large number of citizens from the whole of Italy, bound to him by ties of long standing, whom this fatherland that we all share regards with affection because she remembers the outstanding service that he has recently rendered her, even though all Asia demand his punishment, I shall withstand her and defend him. If, moreover, it has not been the whole of Asia that has lent her title to this trial, nor the best nor the uncorrupted part; if she has not acted of her own free will, nor backed by right, custom, truth, conscience or integrity; but illegally, under incitement, provocation or compulsion, criminally, heedlessly, inspired by greed or caprice, by means of destitute witnesses, and if she cannot herself substantiate any complaint of her injuries, will this evidence that takes you a few minutes to hear shake your belief in what you have learnt over a period of many years? I shall, therefore, as counsel for the defence take the course which my opponent has avoided; I shall go over to the offensive against the prosecution and, seizing the initiative, demand to know the charge from my opponent. What then, Laelius? Surely ... who spent an active life, not at ease in the shade nor in the training or activities appropriate to his age? As a lad he went to the wars with his father, the consul.[b] Under this very head ... something ...

[a] Tmolus was a hill-town in Lydia; Loryma a town on the coast of Caria.

[b] In 86 when his father took over the command against Mithridates.
See p. 413.

CICERO

Versutissimum hominem et in fallendo exercitatissimum.

Quid est in testimonio vestro praeter libidinem, praeter audaciam, praeter amentiam, cum fortissimi et ornatissimi viri et ipsa victoria sit testis?

Nec mediocrem in re militari virtutem,[2] iudices.

Defendo[3] fortem egregiumque virum, magni animi, summi laboris, optimi consilii.

Multis ab adolescentia in bellis variisque versatum atque in primis bonum ductorem[4] et hominem, ut vere dicam, corpore, animo, studio, consuetudine natum atque aptum ad tempora belli militaremque rationem.

Huic hominum generi maiores nostri sic parcendum, iudices,[5] arbitrabantur, ut eos non modo in invidia, verum etiam in culpa defenderent. Itaque non solum recte factis eorum praemia sed etiam delictis veniam dare solebant.

Exsurgite, quaeso, viri optimi atque fortissimi legati amplissimae atque honestissimae civitatis, resistite per deos immortales eorum periuriis iniuriisque, quorum saepenumero telis resistitis.

Homo omnibus ornamentis virtutis et existimationis praeditus, qui mihi videtur quasi quoddam exemplar pristinae gravitatis et monimentum antiquitatis in re publica divinitus reservari.

---

[1] *These fragments are not printed by Clark and are placed here by Webster.*   [2] virtutem *Halm.* viri *MSS.*
[3] defendo *Webster.* defendendo *MSS*
[4] ductorem *Halm.* doctorem *MSS.*
[5] iudices *Halm.* iudicium *MSS.* iudicio *Klein.*

PRO FLACCO, fragments

A very crafty fellow and well-practised in deceit.[a]

What is there in your evidence except caprice, effrontery and sheer folly, seeing that the victory of a very gallant and distinguished man itself provides additional evidence ?

And no mean valour in arms, gentlemen.

I am defending a gallant and illustrious man, great-hearted, tireless and of outstanding common sense.

Engaged in many wars of various kinds from the time of his youth, a particularly fine leader and a man, to tell the truth, fitted in mind and body by his interests and experience for times of war and a life under arms.

Our ancestors thought, gentlemen, that this class of men should be treated with such concern that they defended them not only when they were victims of malice but even when they were in the wrong. Thus, they used not only to reward meritorious acts but also to pardon their misdeeds.[b]

Rise, please, noble men and gallant representatives of a magnificent and most honourable city, resist in heaven's name the lies and insults of those whose weapons you have many times withstood.

A man endowed with all the rewards of personal merit and high repute, a man, in my view, preserved in the State by divine providence as an example of old-time dignity and a memorial to a bygone age.

[a] This and the following fragment appear to refer to some of Laelius' Asiatic witnesses.

[b] *Cf.* p. 548, n. *a.*

CICERO

Quam benivolum hunc populo Romano, quam fidelem putatis ?[1]

Ingenita levitas et erudita vanitas.[2]

Fragmenta Scholiastae Bobiensis

Sed si neque Asiae luxuries infirmissimum tempus aetatis * * *

Ex hoc aetatis gradu se ad exercitum C. Flacci patrui contulit.

Tribunus militaris cum P. Servilio, gravissimo et sanctissimo cive, profectus.

Quorum amplissimis iudiciis ornatus quaestor factus est.

M. Pisone, qui cognomen frugalitatis, nisi accepisset, ipse peperisset.

Idem novum bellum suscepit atque confecit.

Non Asiae testibus, sed accusatoris[3] contubernalibus traditus.

6   Hunc igitur virum, Laeli, quibus tandem rebus oppugnas ? Fuit P. Servilio imperatore in Cilicia tribunus militum ; ea res siletur. Fuit M. Pisoni quaestor in Hispani ; vox de quaestura missa nulla est. Bellum Cretense ex magna parte gessit atque una cum summo imperatore sustinuit ; muta est huius temporis accusatio. Praeturae iuris dictio, res varia

---

[1] *From Arusianus Messus K. vii 458. This and the following fragment are printed by Clark at the end of his text and placed here by Schöll.*

[2] *From St. Jerome's commentary on Galatians i. 3.*

[3] accusatoris *Pluygers.* accusatoribus *ms.*

---

[a] *Cf. pro Murena 11-12, pp. 198-200.*
[b] See p. 414.   [c] See p. 414.   [d] In 71.

PRO FLACCO, fragments and 6

How kind do you think he was to the Roman people, how faithful ?

Unreliability is inborn, deceit is taught.

FRAGMENTS PRESERVED BY THE SCHOLIAST OF BOBBIO

But if neither the luxury of Asia ... the most susceptible years of his life.[a]

At this point in his life he transferred to the army of his uncle, Gaius Flaccus.[b]

He set out as military tribune with Publius Servilius,[c] a most venerable and highly respected citizen.

Honoured by their handsome opinions of him, he was elected quaestor.[d]

From Marcus Piso,[e] who would have earned the family name of Frugi for himself, had he not inherited it.

He also undertook and concluded a new war.[f]

Delivered, not to the witnesses from Asia, but to the prosecutor's lodgers.

Tell me then Laelius : on what grounds are you 6 attacking this man ? He was military tribune under Publius Servilius when commander in Cilicia. Nothing about this appointment. He was quaestor to Marcus Piso in Spain. Not a word about his quaestorship. He played a large part in the war in Crete and shared the responsibilities of the commander-in-chief. The accusations against this period of his life remain unspoken. His administration of

[e] Marcus Pupius Piso Calpurnianus, proconsul in Spain 71–69 and consul in 61.

[f] According to the scholiast (p. 96 ed. Stangl) Quintus Caecilius Metellus Creticus, who reduced the pirates in Crete (68–67) and under whom Flaccus served.

et multiplex ad suspiciones et simultates, non attingitur. At vero in summo et periculosissimo rei publicae tempore etiam ab inimicis eadem praetura laudatur. At a testibus laeditur. Ante quam dico a quibus, qua spe, qua vi, qua re concitatis, qua levitate, qua egestate, qua perfidia, qua audacia praeditis, dicam de genere universo et de condicione omnium nostrum. Per deos immortalis ! iudices, vos, quo modo is qui anno ante Romae ius dixerat anno post in Asia ius dixerit, a testibus quaeretis ignotis, ipsi coniectura nihil iudicabitis ? Cum[1] in tam varia iuris dictione tam multa decreta, tot hominum gratiosorum laesae sint[2] voluntates, quae est umquam iacta non suspicio —quae tamen solet esse falsa—sed iracundiae vox

7 aut doloris ? Et is est reus avaritiae qui in uberrima re turpe compendium, in maledicentissima civitate, in suspiciosissimo negotio maledictum omne, non modo crimen effugit ? Praetereo illa quae praetereunda non sunt, nullum huius in privatis rebus factum avarum, nullam in re pecuniaria contentionem, nullam in re familiari sordem posse proferri. Quibus igitur testibus ego hosce possum refutare nisi vo-

8 bis ? Tmolites ille vicanus, homo non modo nobis sed ne inter suos quidem notus, vos docebit qualis sit L. Flaccus ? quem vos modestissimum adulescentem, provinciae maximae sanctissimum virum, vestri ex-

---

[1] Cum *added by Clark.*
[2] sint *added by Clark.*

justice as praetor, a varied task and a prey in many
ways to suspicion and animosity, is not mentioned.
On the contrary, in a critical time of peril for the
Republic even his enemies extol that praetorship.
You say that it is attacked by witnesses. Before I
say who they are, what the hope, the pressure, the
motive that has stirred them up, what the frivolity,
the poverty, the treachery and the audacity with
which they are endowed, I shall speak about their
nature in general and about the position of us all.
In heaven's name, gentlemen, will you ask witnesses
about whom you know nothing how he administered
justice in Asia the year after he had done so in Rome
rather than judge for yourselves from what you can
infer ? His multifarious jurisdiction blocked numerous decrees and damaged the interests of many men
of influence but what single suspicion—unjustified
though it usually is—or what angry or indignant
criticism has ever been voiced against it ? Is the 7
man now a defendant to a charge of avarice who in
the midst of fat prizes shunned ill-gotten gain, who
in a land alive with slander and in transactions
fraught with suspicion remained unscathed not only
by criminal charge but also by the voice of slander ?
I pass over other facts that should not really be
omitted ; that no act prompted by greed in his private
affairs, no dispute about his financial dealings, no
scandal in his domestic life can be produced. What
witnesses, then, can I use to refute these men other
than yourselves ? Shall that villager from Tmolus, a 8
man unknown to his neighbours let alone to us, give
lessons to you on the character of Lucius Flaccus ?
You have acknowledged him to be a most unassuming
youth, your largest provinces to be the justest of men,

449

ercitus fortissimum militem, diligentissimum ducem, temperatissimum legatum quaestoremque cognoverunt, quem vos praesentes constantissimum senatorem, iustissimum praetorem atque amantissimum 9 rei publicae civem iudicastis. De quibus vos aliis testes esse debetis, de eis ipsi alios testis audietis? At quos testis? Primum dicam, id quod est commune, Graecos; non quo nationi huic ego unus maxime fidem derogem. Nam si quis umquam de nostris hominibus a genere isto studio ac voluntate non abhorrens fuit, me et esse arbitror et magis etiam tum cum plus erat oti fuisse. Sed sunt in illo numero multi boni, docti, pudentes, qui ad hoc iudicium deducti non sunt, multi impudentes, inliterati, leves, quos variis de causis video concitatos. Verum tamen hoc dico de toto genere Graecorum: tribuo illis litteras, do multarum artium disciplinam, non adimo sermonis leporem, ingeniorum acumen, dicendi copiam, denique etiam, si qua sibi alia sumunt, non repugno; testimoniorum religionem et fidem numquam ista natio coluit, totiusque huiusce rei quae sit 10 vis, quae auctoritas, quod pondus, ignorant. Unde illud est: " da mihi testimonium mutuum "? num Gallorum, num Hispanorum putatur? Totum istud Graecorum est, ut etiam qui Graece nesciunt hoc quibus verbis a Graecis dici soleat sciant. Itaque videte quo voltu, qua confidentia dicant; tum intelle-

your armies to be a soldier of outstanding bravery, a most painstaking leader and even-tempered subordinate commander and quaestor, from your own experience you judged him to be the most resolute of senators, the justest of praetors and the most patriotic of citizens. Will you listen to other witnesses about 9 men for whom you should yourselves be witnesses to others ? What witnesses ? you say. I shall first say— for this is the common factor—that they are Greeks. Not that I more than anyone else would disparage the trustworthiness of this nation. If ever there was one of us Romans not averse to that race in interest and by inclination, I think that I am he, and the more so when I had more leisure. There are among them many reliable, well-educated and honourable men who have not been summoned as witnesses to this trial, but there are also many with no sense of shame, uneducated and shifty who, I see, have for various reasons been stirred up. Still, I do say this for the Greek people as a whole : I grant them literature, the knowledge of many sciences, I do not deny the attractiveness of their language, their keenness of intellect or richness of expression ; and in short, I do not reject any other claims they make ; but that nation has never cultivated a scrupulous regard for honesty when giving evidence, and it is quite ignorant of the meaning, the importance or the value of anything to do with it. Where does the 10 saying come from " May I have a loan of your evidence ? " ? It's not from Gaul or Spain, is it ? It is so completely Greek that even those who do not know the language know the Greek for this saying. Watch their expression and effrontery when they speak ; then you will realize how few scruples they

getis qua religione dicant. Numquam nobis ad rogatum respondent, semper accusatori plus quam ad
rogatum, numquam laborant quem ad modum
probent quod dicunt, sed quem ad modum se expli-
cent dicendo. Iratus Flacco dixit M. Lurco quod, ut
ipse aiebat, libertus erat eius turpi iudicio condemnatus. Nihil dixit quod laederet eum, cum cuperet ;
impediebat enim religio; tamen id quod dixit quanto
11 cum pudore, quo tremore et pallore dixit ! Quam
promptus homo P. Septimius, quam iratus de iudicio
et de vilico ! Tamen haesitabat, tamen eius iracundiae religio non numquam repugnabat. Inimicus
M. Caelius quod, cum in re manifesta putasset nefas
esse publicanum iudicare contra publicanum, sublatus
erat e numero recuperatorum, tamen tenuit se neque attulit in iudicium quicquam ad laedendum nisi
voluntatem.

Hi si Graeci fuissent, ac nisi nostri mores ac disciplina plus valeret quam dolor ac simultas, omnes se
spoliatos, vexatos, fortunis eversos esse dixissent.
Graecus testis cum ea voluntate processit ut laedat,
non iuris iurandi, sed laedendi verba meditatur ;
vinci, refelli, coargui putat esse turpissimum; ad id se
parat, nihil curat aliud. Itaque non optimus quisque

---

[a] 88, p. 538.   [b] 100, p. 550.
[c] A board of from three to five members to whom provincial governors frequently referred cases between the tax-
collectors and provincials. A. H. J. Greenidge, *The Legal
Procedure of Cicero's Time* 124. *Cf.* 48, p. 494 for a case of
assessors arbitrating between provincials.

have. They never answer the question we put to
them but always give the prosecutor a fuller answer
than the question requires. They never worry how
to prove what they are saying but only how to get
themselves out of difficulties. Marcus Lurco gave
evidence when he was angry with Flaccus because, as
he said himself, his freedman had been convicted in a
case involving the loss of his rights. He said nothing
to harm Flaccus, although he longed to do so, because
his conscience prevented him ; and even what he did
say, he said with extreme reluctance, trembling all
over and ashen white. What a quick-tempered man 11
Publius Septimius [a] was and how angry he was at his
bailiff's sentence ! Yet he kept hesitating and his
conscience repeatedly did battle with his anger.
Marcus Caelius [b] was an enemy because he had been
removed from the roll of assessors,[c] for Flaccus had
thought it wrong for one tax-collector to sit in judgement upon another even when the case was clear-cut.
Even so, he contained himself and did not bring to
the trial anything to harm Flaccus except his desire
to do so.

If these men had been Greeks and if Roman character and training did not count for more than
animosity and enmity, they would all have said that
they had been plundered, harassed and evicted from
their property. When a Greek witness has come
forward and is in the box with the sole intention of
injuring someone, he does not think of the words of
his oath but of words that can injure. To get the
worst of it, to be proved wrong, to be refuted, he
thinks quite disgraceful ; he prepares himself against
this and this is the only thing he worries about. For
this reason there are chosen not all the best men and

nec gravissimus, sed impudentissimus loquacissimus-
12 que deligitur. Vos autem in privatis minimarum
rerum iudiciis testem diligenter expenditis ; etiam
si formam hominis, si nomen, si tribum nostis, mores
tamen exquirendos putatis. Qui autem dicit testimonium ex nostris hominibus, ut se ipse sustentat, ut
omnia verba moderatur, ut timet ne quid cupide, ne
quid iracunde, ne quid plus minusve quam sit necesse
dicat ! Num illos item putatis, quibus ius iurandum
iocus est, testimonium ludus, existimatio vestra tene-
brae, laus, merces, gratia, gratulatio proposita est
omnis in impudenti mendacio ? Sed non dilatabo
orationem meam ; etenim potest esse infinita, si mihi
libeat totius gentis in testimoniis dicendis explicare
levitatem. Sed propius accedam ; de his vestris[1] testibus dicam.
13 Vehementem accusatorem nacti sumus, iudices, et
inimicum in omni genere odiosum ac molestum ;
quem spero his nervis fore magno usui et amicis et rei
publicae ; sed certe inflammatus incredibili cupiditate hanc causam accusationemque suscepit. Qui
comitatus in inquirendo ! Comitatum dico ; immo
vero quantus exercitus ! quae iactura, qui sumptus,
quanta largitio ! Quae quamquam utilia sunt causae,
timide tamen dico, quod vereor ne Laelius ex his rebus
quas sibi suscepit gloriae causa putet aliquid oratione
mea sermonis in sese aut invidiae esse quaesitum.

[1] vestris *B.* nostris *the other* MSS.

---

[a] On behalf of the Triumvirs. See p. 430.

those who carry the most weight, but the most shameless and the fastest talkers. You, however, weigh up a witness carefully in private suits where the issues involved are trivial, and even if you are familiar with his appearance, his name, his tribe, you still think that you should look into his character. When one of us Romans gives evidence, what self-restraint he shows, what control over his language, what fear that he may display self-interest or ill-temper, or that he may say too little or too much! Surely you do not view in the same light those men to whom their oath before you is a joke, their evidence to you a game, your opinion of them a worthless nothing; who see in a shameless lie all their chances of honour, profit, influence and favour? I shall not, however, prolong my speech; it could be endless if I wanted to display the untrustworthiness of the whole nation in giving evidence. I shall, instead, move nearer home and speak about your witnesses in this case.

We have got an energetic prosecutor, gentlemen, and an enemy in every way offensive and dangerous. I hope that with all this energy he will be of great service to his friends and to the Republic, but he certainly undertook this case and prosecution inflamed by an unbelievable passion![a] What a staff he had for collecting the evidence! Staff do I say? No, what an army! What extravagance, what expense, what munificence! Although this is helpful to my case, I speak with hesitation because I am afraid that Laelius may think that in my speech some gossip or odium has been worked up against him owing to these activities which he has undertaken in his thirst for glory.

Itaque hanc partem totam relinquam ; tantum a vobis petam, iudices, ut, si quid ipsi audistis communi fama atque sermone de vi, de manu, de armis, de copiis, memineritis ; quarum rerum invidia lege hac recenti ac nova certus est inquisitioni comitum
14 numerus constitutus. Sed ut hanc vim omittam, quanta illa sunt quae, quoniam accusatorio iure et more sunt facta, reprehendere non possumus, queri tamen cogimur ! primum quod sermo[1] est tota Asia dissipatus Cn. Pompeium, quod L. Flacco esset[2] vehementer inimicus, contendisse a Laelio, paterno amico ac pernecessario, ut hunc hoc iudicio arcesseret, omnemque ei suam auctoritatem, gratiam, copias, opes ad hoc negotium conficiendum detulisse. Id hoc veri similius Graecis hominibus videbatur quod paulo ante in eadem provincia familiarem Laelium Flacco viderant. Pompei autem auctoritas cum apud omnis tanta est quanta esse debet, tum excellit in ista provincia quam nuper et praedonum et regum bello liberavit. Adiunxit illa ut eos qui domo exire nolebant testimoni denuntiatione terreret, qui domi stare non poterant, largo et liberali viatico commoveret.
15 Sic adulescens ingeni plenus locupletis metu, tenuis praemio, stultos errore permovit ; sic sunt expressa

---

[1] distributis partibus *before* sermo MSS., *but omitted by Scholiast. Cf. 15 below.*   [2] esset *Scholiast.* est MSS.

---

[a] The scholiast (p. 97 ed. Stangl) suggests that this law was either the *lex Vatinia de alternis consiliis reiciendis* or the *lex iudiciaria* of the praetor Quintus Fufius Calenus (see p. 419), but the reference is almost certainly to the *lex Iulia repetundarum* (see p. 419). The restriction mentioned is appropriate only to a *lex repetundarum* which, according to Valerius Maximus 8. 1. 10, also fixed the number of witnesses to be summoned. We know that this trial was held under the *lex Cornelia* (Cicero, *pro Rabirio Postumo* 9) and we must

I shall, therefore, omit all this part. I shall only ask of you, gentlemen, that, if you have heard with your own ears from any widespread rumour or gossip of force, violence, arms or troops, you will remember it. Owing to the scandal caused by those activities the number of assistants for collecting evidence was recently fixed by this new law.[a] Apart from this use 14 of violence, however, look at all the devices which we cannot condemn since they are in accordance with the rights and practices of prosecutors, but which we are nevertheless forced to deplore! Firstly, that the rumour was spread throughout the whole of Asia that Gnaeus Pompeius, being a bitter enemy of Lucius Flaccus, had pressed Laelius, a friend and close acquaintance of his father,[b] to summon Flaccus before this court and had used all his authority, influence, resources and power to achieve this end.[c] This seemed to Greeks the more likely because not long previously they had seen Laelius on friendly terms with Flaccus in that very province. Also, while Pompeius' authority is as universally recognized as it ought to be, it is particularly influential in that province which he has recently freed from war with the pirates and the kings.[d] He also used the device of frightening those who did not wish to leave home by issuing a witness-summons and those who were bankrupt he got moving with a liberal and generous travel allowance. So this talented young man prevailed 15 upon the wealthy by fear, the poor by the offer of a reward, the stupid by deception. That is how there

therefore conclude that the law had been promulgated by the time of this speech. M. Gelzer, *Caesar, Politician and Statesman* 93, n. 1. [b] See p. 429, n. *h*. [c] See p. 430. [d] Tigranes of Armenia and Mithridates of Pontus.

ista praeclara quae recitantur psephismata non sententiis neque auctoritatibus declarata, non iure iurando constricta, sed porrigenda manu profundendoque clamore multitudinis concitatae.

O morem praeclarum disciplinamque quam a maioribus accepimus, si quidem teneremus ! sed nescio quo pacto iam de manibus elabitur. Nullam enim illi nostri sapientissimi et sanctissimi viri vim contionis esse voluerunt ; quae scisceret plebes aut quae populus iuberet, submota contione, distributis partibus, tributim et centuriatim discriptis ordinibus, classibus, aetatibus, auditis auctoribus, re multos dies promulgata et cognita iuberi vetarique voluerunt.

16 Graecorum autem totae res publicae sedentis contionis temeritate administrantur. Itaque ut hanc Graeciam quae iam diu suis consiliis perculsa et adflicta est omittam, illa vetus quae quondam opibus, imperio, gloria floruit hoc uno malo concidit, libertate immoderata ac licentia contionum. Cum in theatro imperiti homines rerum omnium rudes ignarique consederant, tum bella inutilia suscipiebant, tum seditiosos homines rei publicae praeficiebant, tum

17 optime meritos civis e civitate eiciebant. Quod si haec Athenis tum cum illae non solum in Graecia sed prope cunctis gentibus enitebant accidere sunt solita,

---

<a> See Appendix A, pp. 559-561.

<b> The minimum length of time that had to elapse between the promulgation of a bill and its submission to the *comitia* was known as a *trinum nundinum*. The magistrate could of course set his *comitia* for a later date if he wanted to. There is no clear case of the use of the phrase that can settle the question of its length. Th. Mommsen, *Römisches Staatsrecht* 3. 373 and n. 1 and 375-377, argues that it was a period of twenty-four days ; A. K. Michels, *The Calendar of the Roman Republic* 202-206, that it was one of twenty-five days.

were extracted those fine resolutions which are read out to us. They are not based upon considered votes or affidavits nor safeguarded by an oath, but produced by a show of hands and the undisciplined shouting of an inflamed mob.

Oh, if only we could maintain the fine tradition and discipline that we have inherited from our ancestors ! But somehow it is now slipping out of our hands. Those wisest and most upright of our men did not want power to lie in the public meetings.[a] As for what the commons might approve or the people might order, when the meeting had been dismissed and the people distributed in their divisions by centuries and tribes into ranks, classes and age groups, when the proposers of the measure had been heard, when its text had been published well in advance and understood, then they wished the people to give their orders or their prohibitions.[b] In Greece, on the other 16 hand, all public business is conducted by the irresponsibility of a public meeting sitting down. And so—to pass over the modern Greece which has long since been struck down and laid low in its councils— that Greece of ancient times, once so flourishing in its wealth, dominion and glory, fell through this single evil, the excessive liberty and licence of its meetings. When untried men, totally inexperienced and ignorant, had taken their seats in the theatre, then they would decide on harmful wars, put troublemakers in charge of public affairs and expel from the city the citizens who had served it best. If behaviour 17 like this used to occur regularly in Athens when she outshone not just the rest of Greece but virtually the

Cf. A. W. Lintott, " *Trinundinum*," *Classical Quarterly* 15 (1965), 281-285.

quam moderationem putatis in Phrygia aut in Mysia
contionum fuisse ? Nostras contiones illarum nationum homines plerumque perturbant ; quid, cum soli
sint ipsi, tandem fieri putatis ? Caesus est virgis
Cymaeus ille Athenagoras qui in fame frumentum
exportare erat ausus. Data Laelio contio est.
Processit ille et Graecus apud Graecos non de culpa
sua dixit, sed de poena questus est. Porrexerunt
manus ; psephisma natum est. Hoc testimonium
est ? Nuper epulati, paulo ante omni largitione
saturati Pergameni, quod Mithridates qui multitudinem illam non auctoritate sua, sed sagina tenebat
se velle dixit, id sutores et zonarii conclamarunt.
Hoc testimonium est civitatis ? Ego testis a Sicilia
publice deduxi[1] ; verum erant ea testimonia non
18 concitatae contionis, sed iurati senatus. Qua re iam
non est mihi contentio cum teste, vobis, iudices,
videndum[2] est, sintne haec testimonia putanda.

Adulescens bonus, honesto loco natus, disertus cum
maximo ornatissimoque comitatu venit in oppidum
Graecorum, postulat contionem, locupletis homines et
gravis ne sibi adversentur testimoni denuntiatione
deterret, egentis et levis spe largitionis[3] et viatico
publico, privata etiam benignitate prolectat. Opifices

---

[1] deduxi *Halm.* dux *mss.*

[2] iudices, videndum *Klotz.* dividendum Σ. videndum
the other mss.   [3] legationis $b\chi^2k$.

---

[a] The foreigners at *contiones* would be mainly freedmen.
L. R. Taylor, *Party Politics in the Age of Caesar* 54.

[b] Asia was not a province that had a surplus of grain for
export. Many cities could not produce enough for their own
needs.

whole world, what restraint do you think has existed
in the public meetings of Phrygians and Mysians ?
If our own public meetings are often thrown into disorder by men of these nations,[a] what on earth do you
think happens when they are by themselves ? That
Athenagoras of Cyme was flogged for daring to
export corn during a famine.[b] A meeting was held
for Laelius. Athenagoras came forward and, being a
Greek among Greeks, did not say a word about his
crime but complained of his punishment. Up went
their hands ; a resolution was born. Is this evidence ?
The Pergamenes, recently feasted and a little earlier
glutted with every sort of bounty, those cobblers and
belt-makers, shouted their approval of what Mithridates [c] said he wanted, for he controlled that mob
not by his authority but by filling them with food.
Is this a city's evidence ? I summoned witnesses from
Sicily at public expense [d] ; their evidence, however,
was not that of an inflamed meeting but of a senate
on oath. In this case, then, it is not a question of 18
conflict between myself and a witness, but it is for
you, gentlemen, to see whether this ought to be
regarded as evidence at all.

A young man of standing, of honourable birth and
eloquent, comes with a large and splendidly accoutred
retinue into a town of Greeks, he requests a public
meeting, frightens the wealthy and the influential
men out of opposing him by the threat of a witness-
summons, entices the poor and the unimportant with
the hope of free gifts and with a travelling allowance
from public funds, even by a grant from his own
resources. What difficulty is there in stirring up

[c] He claimed to be a natural son of the king of Pontus and
served under him.   [d] Cf. II in Verrem 4. 137 f.

et tabernarios atque illam omnem faecem civitatum
quid est negoti concitare, in eum praesertim qui
nuper summo cum imperio fuerit, summo autem in
amore esse propter ipsum imperi nomen non potuerit?

19 Mirandum vero est homines eos quibus odio sunt
nostrae secures, nomen acerbitati, scriptura, decumae,
portorium morti, libenter adripere facultatem laedendi quaecumque detur! Mementote igitur, cum audietis psephismata, non audire vos testimonia, audire
temeritatem volgi, audire vocem levissimi cuiusque,
audire strepitum imperitorum, audire contionem[1]
concitatam levissimae nationis. Itaque perscrutamini
penitus naturam rationemque criminum; iam nihil
praeter spem,[2] nihil praeter terrorem ac minas reperietis.

20   * * * In aerario nihil habent civitates, nihil in vectigalibus. Duae rationes conficiendae pecuniae, aut
versura aut tributo; nec tabulae creditoris proferuntur nec tributi confectio ulla recitatur. Quam
vero facile falsas rationes inferre et in tabulas quod-
cumque commodum est referre soleant, ex Cn.
Pompei litteris ad Hypsaeum et Hypsaei ad Pompeium missis, quaeso, cognoscite.

LITTERAE POMPEI ET HYPSAEI

Satisne vobis coarguere his auctoribus dissolutam
Graecorum consuetudinem licentiamque impudentem

---

[1] contionem *editio Romana.* contentionem χ. contentionem et contionem *the other* MSS.   [2] speciem χ.

ᵃ The Latin word *faex*, like *sentina*—" bilge," was a
regular term for the urban proletariat and does not necessarily imply that they were down-and-out unemployables.
462

craftsmen, shopkeepers and all the dregs *a* of a city, particularly against a man who has recently held the supreme power and has not been able to attract deep affection to himself because of the very word " power " ? It is indeed surprising that men to whom 19 our axes *b* are a hated symbol, our name is gall, our pasture-tax, tithes and customs dues are death, gladly seize any opportunity for harming us that is offered ! Remember, then, that when you hear Greek resolutions, you are not hearing evidence ; you are hearing the wild decisions of a mob, the voice of every nonentity, the din of ignoramuses, an inflamed meeting of the most unstable of nations. Scrutinize thoroughly the nature and motivation of the charges ; you will find nothing there but the hope of one group and terrorization and threats against the other.

Suppose that a city has nothing in the treasury, 20 nothing in taxes ; then there are two ways of raising money—by raising a loan or by a poll-tax ; but no accounts of a creditor are produced and no imposition of a tax is offered in evidence. I invite you, however, to learn from the letter of Gnaeus Pompeius to Hypsaeus *c* and his reply to Pompeius how readily they submit false accounts and enter in the books whatever suits them.

The Letters of Pompeius and Hypsaeus are read

Do you feel that with these letters I am providing convincing evidence of the lax practices of Greeks

---

b The symbols of the magistrate's power of life and death which were carried by his lictors.
c Publius Plautius Hypsaeus, quaestor under Pompey in the East in 66 and proquaestor 64–62.

videmur ? Nisi forte qui Cn. Pompeium, qui prae-
sentem, qui nullo impellente fallebant, eos urgente
Laelio in absentem et in L. Flaccum aut timidos fuisse
21 aut religiosos putamus. Sed fuerint incorruptae
litterae domi ; nunc vero quam habere auctoritatem
aut quam fidem possunt ? Triduo lex ad praetorem
deferri, iudicum signis obsignari iubet ; tricesimo die
vix deferuntur. Ne corrumpi tabulae facile possint,
idcirco lex obsignatas in publico poni voluit ; at
obsignantur corruptae. Quid refert igitur tanto post
ad iudices deferantur, an omnino non deferantur ?

Quid ? si testium studium cum accusatore sociatum
est, tamenne isti testes habebuntur ? Ubi est igitur
illa exspectatio quae versari in iudiciis solet ? Nam
antea, cum dixerat accusator acriter et vehementer,
cumque defensor suppliciter demisseque responderat,
tertius ille erat exspectatus locus testium, qui aut sine
ullo studio dicebant aut cum dissimulatione aliqua
22 cupiditatis. Hoc vero quid est ? Una sedent, ex
accusatorum subselliis surgunt, non dissimulant, non
verentur. De subselliis queror ? una ex domo pro-
deunt ; si verbo titubaverint, quo revertantur non
habebunt. An quisquam esse testis potest quem
accusator sine cura interroget nec metuat ne sibi

and their shameless permissiveness ? Surely so, unless of course we think that men who needed no pressure upon them to deceive Pompeius to his face have, notwithstanding Laelius' insistence, become timid or developed scruples about deceiving Lucius Flaccus behind his back. Even suppose that the 21 documents were not falsified at home ; what value or credibility can they have now ? The law requires them to be delivered to the praetor within three days and to be sealed with the marks of the jurors. They were only delivered twenty-nine days later. The law requires the accounts to be held in official custody after they have been sealed so that they cannot easily be falsified ; but these have been falsified before they are sealed. What does it matter then whether they are delivered to the jury as late as this or whether they are not delivered at all ?

Again, if the witnesses have associated with the prosecutor, will they still be considered witnesses ? What has happened to that customary order of events that is usual at trials ? In the old days, when the prosecutor had spoken vigorously and forcefully and the defendant had replied with deprecation and humility, it was then the eagerly awaited turn of the witnesses who would speak with complete impartiality or with some concealment of their partisanship. But what are we to make of this ? They sit with the 22 prosecutors, they rise from their benches, they make no effort to hide their feelings, they show no embarrassment. Do I complain about benches ? They leave home with the prosecutors ; if they make one slip in their evidence, they will have no home to go back to. Can anyone be a witness when the prosecutor is not anxious about his examination and not

aliquid quod ipse nolit respondeat ? Ubi est igitur
illa laus oratoris quae vel in accusatore antea vel in
patrono spectari solebat : " bene testem interrogavit ;
callide accessit, reprehendit ; quo voluit adduxit ;
23 convicit et elinguem reddidit " ? Quid tu istum ro-
ges, Laeli, qui, prius quam hoc " Te rogo " dixeris,
plura etiam effundet quam tu ei domi ante praescri-
pseris ? Quid ego autem defensor rogem ? Nam aut
oratio testium refelli solet aut vita laedi. Qua dispu-
tatione orationem refellam eius qui dicit : " dedimus,"
nihil amplius ? In hominem dicendum est igitur, cum
oratio argumentationem non habet. Quid dicam in
ignotum ? Querendum est ergo et deplorandum, id
quod iam dudum facio, de omni accusationis iniquitate, primum de communi genere testium ; dicit
enim natio minime in testimoniis dicendis religiosa.
Propius accedo ; nego esse ista testimonia quae tu
psephismata appellas, sed fremitum egentium et
motum quendam temerarium Graeculae contionis.
Intrabo etiam magis. Qui gessit non adest, qui nu-
merasse dicitur non est deductus ; privatae litterae
nullae proferuntur, publicae retentae sunt in accusatorum potestate ; summa est in testibus ; hi vivunt
cum inimicis, adsunt cum adversariis, habitant cum

afraid that the witness may give a reply that is not the one he wanted ? What has happened to that fine testimonial to forensic skill that we used to look for in the prosecutor or counsel for the defence : " that was a good cross-examination ; he made a cunning approach, brought him up short ; he got him just where he wanted him ; he broke his story and left him speechless " ? What are you to ask that **23** witness, Laelius, who before the words " I ask you . . . " are out of your mouth, is going to pour out a story even longer than the one in which you have previously schooled him at home ? What am I to ask as counsel for the defence ? The usual course is either to disprove the evidence of witnesses or to impugn their reliability. How am I to disprove in my cross-examination the evidence of a man who says " we paid," and nothing else ? Since, then, the evidence does not permit analysis, I must make an attack on character. What am I to say against somebody who has never been heard of ? I must—as I have long been doing—bitterly deprecate the total injustice of the accusation, but first the character common to the witnesses ; for a people is giving evidence that is quite without scruples in what it says. I go further ; I say that what you call Greek resolutions are not evidence at all, but the clamour of the impoverished and some reckless impulse of a meeting of Greeklings. I shall go further still. The principal is not here, the man who is said to have counted the money has not been called ; no private letters have been produced and the public documents have been kept in the hands of the prosecution ; the decision lies with the witnesses ; they spend their time with Flaccus' enemies, they come into court with his opponents,

24 accusatoribus. Utrum hic tandem disceptationem et
cognitionem veritatis, an innocentiae labem aliquam
aut ruinam fore putatis? Multa enim sunt eius modi,
iudices, ut, etiam si in homine ipso de quo agitur
neglegenda sint, tamen in condicione atque in exemplo pertimescenda videantur.

Si quem infimo loco natum, nullo splendore vitae,
nulla commendatione famae defenderem, tamen civem a civibus communis humanitatis iure ac misericordia deprecarer, ne ignotis testibus, ne incitatis, ne
accusatoris consessoribus, convivis, contubernalibus,
ne hominibus levitate Graecis, crudelitate barbaris
civem ac supplicem vestrum dederetis, ne periculosam
imitationem exempli reliquis in posterum proderetis.

25 Sed cum L. Flacci res agatur, qua[1] ex familia qui
primus consul factus est primus in hac civitate consul
fuit, cuius virtute regibus exterminatis libertas in re
publica constituta est, quae usque ad hoc tempus
honoribus, imperiis, rerum gestarum gloria continuata
permansit, cumque ab hac perenni contestataque
virtute maiorum non modo non degeneraverit L.
Flaccus sed, quam[2] maxime florere in generis sui
gloria viderat, laudem patriae in libertatem vindi-
candae praetor adamarit, in hoc ego reo ne quod
perniciosum exemplum prodatur pertimescam, in quo
etiam si quid errasset, omnes boni conivendum esse
26 arbitrarentur? Quod quidem ego non modo non

---

[1] qua *Clark.* cuius *mss.* ex ea familia cuius *Madvig.*
[2] quam *B, Müller.* id quod Σχ. quod *c.* in qua *b¹k.*

---

[a] See p. 413, n. *c.*

they lodge with his accusers. Do you think that we 24
are going to have a debate and an inquiry into the
truth here or the demolition and destruction of innocence ? There are many things, gentlemen, that
are going to inspire fear of a general acceptance and
use as precedent, even if they should be ignored in
the case of the particular individual on trial.

If I were defending a man of low birth who has
lived in obscurity without any reputation to commend
him, but still a citizen, I would beg you citizens in the
name of his right to pity as a fellow human-being
not to surrender a fellow-citizen and your suppliant to
witnesses about whom you know nothing and who
have been stirred up against him, the assistants,
companions and lodgers of the prosecutor ; not to
surrender him to men who are Greeks in their unreliability and barbarians in their savagery ; not to
establish a dangerous precedent for others in the
future. It is, however, the position of Flaccus that 25
is at stake ; a man from a family whose first consul
was the first consul of the Republic,[a] whose valour
banished the kings and established liberty in the
State, and which to this day has maintained a succession of high offices, commands and glorious
achievement ; and not only has he not declined from
this continuous and well-attested excellence of his
ancestors, but he has also as praetor aspired to the
glory of confirming his fatherland in its liberty, the
act which he had seen to be the greatest of his
family's laurels. Am I then to fear that some
dangerous precedent may be established in the case
of this defendant, a man of whom all right-minded
citizens would think that any wrong he might have
done should be condoned ? Far from requesting that, 26

postulo, sed contra, iudices, vos oro et obtestor ut totam causam quam maxime intentis oculis, ut aiunt, acerrime contemplemini. Nihil religione testatum, nihil veritate fundatum, nihil dolore expressum, contraque omnia corrupta libidine, iracundia, studio, pretio, periurio reperientur.

27 Etenim iam universa istorum cognita cupiditate accedam ad singulas querelas criminationesque Graecorum. Classis nomine pecuniam civitatibus imperatam queruntur. Quod nos factum, iudices, confitemur. Sed si hoc crimen est, aut in eo est quod non licuerit imperare, aut in eo quod non opus fuerit navibus, aut in eo quod nulla hoc praetore classis navigarit. Licuisse ut intellegas, cognosce quid me consule senatus decreverit, cum quidem nihil a superioribus continuorum annorum decretis discesserit.

SENATUS CONSULTUM

Proximum est ergo ut opus fuerit classe necne quaeramus. Utrum igitur hoc Graeci statuent aut ullae exterae nationes, an nostri praetores, nostri duces, nostri imperatores ? Equidem existimo in eius modi regione atque provincia quae mari cincta, portibus distincta, insulis circumdata esset, non solum praesidi sed etiam ornandi imperi causa navigandum
28 fuisse. Haec enim ratio ac magnitudo animorum in maioribus nostris fuit ut, cum in privatis rebus suisque sumptibus minimo contenti tenuissimo cultu viverent,

---

ᵃ The Greek claim for ship-money was not admissible unless Flaccus had abused his *imperium*, and that was not for Greeks to say. M. I. Henderson, " The process *de repetundis*," *Journal of Roman Studies* 41 (1951), 79.

gentlemen, I beg and implore you to examine the whole case as acutely as possible and, as they say, with the most penetrating gaze. No evidence will be found that is based on scruples, none grounded on truth, none wrung out by suffering ; on the contrary, it will all have been falsified by passion, animosity, partiality, bribery and perjury.

Now that the general avarice of these men is 27 recognized, I shall move on to the particular complaints and accusations of Greeks. They complain that money was demanded from the cities on the strength of raising a fleet. We admit it, gentlemen. But if this measure is a crime, it is so either because it contained an illegal order, or a fleet was not required, or none put to sea during his praetorship. To show you that it was lawful, listen to the decree of the Senate passed in my consulship, although in fact it was no different from the previous decrees of successive years.

The Decree of the Senate is read

The next point, then, is to inquire whether a fleet was needed or not. Are Greeks or any foreign nation going to decide this or are our governors, our commanders, our generals going to make the decision ? [a] I personally think that in a district or province of this kind which was encircled by sea, dotted with harbours and encircled by islands, we had to have a fleet not only for protection but also to add distinction to our rule. The policy and high 28 principles of our ancestors provided that, although in their private lives and personal expenditure they were content with very little and lived in an extremely

471

in imperio atque in publica dignitate omnia ad
gloriam splendoremque revocarent. Quaeritur enim
in re domestica continentiae laus, in publica dignitatis. Quod si etiam praesidi causa classem habuit,
quis erit tam iniquus qui reprehendat? " Nulli erant
praedones." Quid? nullos fore quis praestare po-
29 terat? " Minuis," inquit, " gloriam Pompei." Immo
tu auges molestiam. Ille enim classis praedonum,
urbis, portus, receptacula sustulit, pacem maritimam summa virtute atque incredibili celeritate confecit; illud vero neque suscepit neque suscipere
debuit ut, si qua uspiam navicula praedonum appa-
ruisset, accusandus videretur. Itaque ipse in Asia,
cum omnia iam bella terra marique confecisset, classem tamen isdem istis civitatibus imperavit. Quod si
tum statuit opus esse cum ipsius praesentis nomine
tuta omnia et pacata esse poterant, quid, cum ille
decessisset, Flacco existimatis statuendum et facien-
30 dum fuisse? Quid? nos hic nonne ipso Pompeio
auctore Silano et Murena consulibus decrevimus ut
classis in Italia navigaret? nonne eo ipso tempore
cum L. Flaccus in Asia remiges imperabat, nos hic in
mare superum et inferum sestertium ter et quadra-
giens erogabamus? Quid? postero anno nonne M.
Curtio et P. Sextilio quaestoribus pecunia in classem
est erogata? Quid? hoc omni tempore equites in
ora maritima non fuerunt? Illa enim est gloria
divina Pompei, primum praedones eos qui tum cum
illi bellum maritimum gerendum datum est toto mari

---

frugal manner, yet splendour and magnificence were their standards in government and in the grandeur of public life.[a] In home life praise for self-restraint was the aim, in public life praise for impressiveness. If, however, he raised the fleet for protection as well, who will be so unfair as to blame him ? " There were no pirates." Who could guarantee that there would not be any ? " You are detracting, " he says, " from the glory of Pompeius." No, but you are increasing 29 his responsibility. He destroyed the fleets of the pirates, their cities, their harbours, their lairs, and brought peace to the sea with the utmost valour and unbelievable speed ; but he did not undertake, nor need he have undertaken, to accept the blame if a pirate-skiff appeared anywhere. Although he had by now brought to an end all the wars on land and sea, Pompeius himself in Asia still levied a fleet from those same cities. If, moreover, he decided that a fleet was needed at a time when his presence in person could keep everything safe and peaceful, what decision do you think Flaccus should have made and acted upon after Pompeius had left ? Did not 30 we here in Rome during the consulship of Silanus and Murena [b] resolve on the proposal of Pompeius himself that a fleet should be put to sea off Italy ? At the very time when Lucius Flaccus was conscripting rowers in Asia, were not we here in Rome spending 4,300,000 sesterces on the Adriatic and Tyrrhenian Seas ? Was not money spent on a fleet in the following year when Marcus Curtius and Publius Sextilius were quaestors ? Were not knights stationed along the coast throughout this period ? This is the superhuman achievement of Pompeius : firstly, that he brought under control all those pirates who at the

dispersi vagabantur redactos esse omnis in potestatem, deinde Syriam esse nostram, Ciliciam teneri,
Cyprum per Ptolemaeum regem nihil audere, praeterea Cretam Metelli virtute esse nostram, nihil esse
unde proficiscantur, nihil quo revertantur, omnis sinus,
promunturia, litora, insulas, urbis maritimas claustris
31 imperi nostri contineri. Quod si Flacco praetore
nemo in mari praedo fuisset, tamen huius diligentia
reprehendenda non esset. Idcirco enim quod hic
classem habuisset, existimarem non fuisse. Quid ?
si L. Eppi, L. Agri, C. Cesti, equitum Romanorum,
huius etiam clarissimi viri, Cn. Domiti, qui in Asia tum
legatus fuit, testimonio doceo eo ipso tempore quo tu
negas classem habendam fuisse, compluris a praedonibus esse captos, tamen Flacci consilium in remigibus
imperandis reprehendetur ? Quid si etiam occisus
est a piratis Adramyttenus homo nobilis, cuius est
fere nobis omnibus nomen auditum, Atyanas pugil
Olympionices ? hoc est apud Graecos, quoniam de
eorum gravitate dicimus, prope maius et gloriosius
quam Romae triumphasse. " At neminem cepisti."
Quam multi orae maritimae clarissimi viri prae-

---

[a] Cyprus, a pirate stronghold, was subject to Ptolemy, the
younger brother of Ptolemy Auletes, king of Egypt ; the
latter is known to have been on friendly terms with Pompey.

[b] Metellus was sent to deal with the Cretan pirates in 68.
Pompey, when he had been given control of the whole Mediterranean in 67 to deal with the pirates, tried to replace
Metellus with his own legate. Metellus refused to be ousted
and completed the conquest of Crete. He was present in
court to support Flaccus (see p. 550), hence the tactful phras-
ing : " it is the superhuman achievement of Pompey . . . that
Crete is ours by the valour of Metellus."

[c] Lucius Eppius: see J. Hatzfeld, *Les Trafiquants italiens
dans l'Orient hellénique* 128 ; Lucius Agrius : possibly
Lucius Agrius Publeianus, a *negotiator* at Ephesus, see

time when conduct of the war at sea was entrusted to him were roving all over it ; and secondly, that Syria is ours, Cilicia is held by us, thanks to King Ptolemy [a] Cyprus dares not move ; Crete, moreover, is ours by the valour of Metellus.[b] There is no base from which the pirates may sally forth, no lair to which they may return ; every inlet, promontory, beach, island, coastal city is held secure by the barriers of our Empire. If there had not been a single pirate at sea 31 during Flaccus' praetorship, his caution would still not deserve censure. I should think that there were no pirates for the very reason that he had raised a fleet. If I show by the evidence of Lucius Eppius, of Lucius Agrius, of Gaius Cestius, Roman knights,[c] and by the evidence of the distinguished Gnaeus Domitius,[d] who is here in court and was at the time a subordinate commander in Asia, that at the very time when according to you a fleet was unnecessary, many people had been captured by pirates, would Flaccus' action in conscripting rowers still be censured ? Even if there was killed by the pirates a member of the aristocracy of Adramyttium [e] whose name is known to almost all of us, Atyanas the boxer and victor at the Olympic games ? [f] To Greeks, since we are talking in terms of their sense of values, this is almost more important and glorious than a triumph is to Romans. "But you took no prisoners." How many distinguished men have been in charge of the

Hatzfeld, *op. cit.* 102 ; Gaius Cestius : for this family of *negotiatores* in the East and their connexion with the senatorial Cestii, see T. P. Wiseman, *New Men in the Roman Senate 139 b.c.–a.d. 14* 202 and 223-224.

[d] Gnaeus Domitius Calvinus, a legate of Flaccus in Asia, tribune in 59, praetor in 56 and consul in 53.

[e] A town in Mysia.   [f] In 72.

CICERO

fuerunt qui, cum praedonem nullum cepissent, mare
tamen tutum praestiterunt! Casus est enim in
capiendo, locus, ventus,[1] occasio; defendendi facilis
est cautio, non solum latibulis occultorum locorum sed
etiam tempestatum moderatione et conversione.

32 Reliquum est ut quaeratur utrum ista classis cursu et
remis, an sumptu tantum et litteris navigarit. Num
id igitur negari potest, cuius rei cuncta testis est
Asia, bipertito classem distributam fuisse, ut una pars
supra Ephesum, altera infra Ephesum navigaret?
Hac classe M. Crassus, vir amplissimus, ab Aeno[a] in
Asiam, his navibus Flaccus ex Asia in Macedoniam
navigavit. In quo igitur praetoris est diligentia
requirenda? in numero navium et in discriptione
aequabili[2] sumptus? Dimidium eius quo Pompeius
erat usus imperavit; num potuit parcius? Discripsit
autem pecuniam ad Pompei rationem, quae fuit
accommodata L. Sullae discriptioni. Qui cum in[3]
omnis Asiae civitates pro portione pecuniam[4] dis-
cripsisset, illam rationem in imperando sumptu et
Pompeius et Flaccus secutus est. Neque est adhuc

33 tamen ea summa completa. "Non refert." Vero;
quid lucretur? Cum enim onus imperatae pecuniae
suscipit, id quod tu crimen esse vis confitetur. Qui
igitur probari potest in ea pecunia non referenda

---

[1] ventus *Clark.* eventus *MSS.*
[2] aequabili Σ*b*[1]. aequali *the other MSS.*
[3] in *added by Lambinus.*
[4] pecuniam *Lambinus.* in provincias *MSS.*

---

[a] Aenus in Thrace.
[b] Possibly in an unsuccessful attempt to do a deal with
Pompey. P. A. Brunt, "'Amicitia' in the Late Roman
Republic," *Proceedings of the Cambridge Philological
Society* 11 (1965), 17, reprinted in *The Crisis of the Roman*

coast and rendered the sea safe without capturing a single pirate ? Chance, the locality, the wind and opportunity, all play their part in the taking of prisoners ; it is easy to take precautions to protect oneself, not only by means of dens in hidden retreats, but also by the dropping and shifting of gales. It remains to inquire whether that fleet put to 32 sea for a voyage under oars or was merely an entry of expenditure. Surely, then, it cannot be denied—the whole of Asia is witness to it—that the fleet was divided into two squadrons and one cruised above Ephesus and the other below. In this fleet the great Marcus Crassus sailed from Aenus to Asia *a* ; in these ships Flaccus sailed from Asia to Macedonia. *b* What shortcomings, then, were there in the praetor's actions ? In the number of the ships and the equable division of the expense ? He requisitioned half the number that Pompeius had used ; how could he possibly be more economical ? He divided the cost according to the allocation made by Pompeius which followed Lucius Sulla's assessment. Sulla had allotted the amount proportionally among all the cities of Asia and both Pompeius and Flaccus followed his method of levying the cost. And the full sum had still not been reached. "He makes no entry in the 33 books." True ; but what would he gain by that omission ? The moment he admits responsibility for levying the money, he confesses to what you are making grounds for an accusation. How, therefore, can you prove that by failing to account for this

Republic Ed. R. Seager ; but he may well only have been on a business trip. If Crassus left Italy in fear of Pompey (as Plutarch, *Pompey* 43. 2 alleges), why did he go to an area under Pompey's control ?

crimen sibi ipsum facere in qua crimen esset nullum,
si referret ? At enim negas fratrem meum, qui L.
Flacco successerit, pecuniam ullam in remiges im-
perasse. Equidem omni[1] fratris mei laude delector,
sed aliis magis gravioribus atque maioribus. Aliud
quiddam statuit, aliud vidit ; existimavit, quocumque
tempore auditum quid esset de praedonibus, quam
vellet subito classem se comparaturum. Denique hoc
primus frater meus in Asia fecit ut hoc sumptu
remigum civitates levaret ; crimen autem tum videri
solet cum aliquis sumptus instituit eos qui antea non
erant instituti, non cum successor aliquid immutat de
institutis priorum. Flaccus quid alii postea facturi
essent scire non poterat, quid fecissent videbat.

34 Sed, quoniam de communi totius Asiae crimine est
dictum, adgrediar iam ad singulas civitates ; ex quibus
sit sane nobis prima civitas Acmonensis. Citat praeco
voce maxima legatos Acmonensis. Procedit unus
Asclepiades. Prodeant ceteri.[2] Etiamne praeconem
mentiri coegisti ? Est enim, credo, is vir iste ut civitatis nomen sua auctoritate sustineat, damnatus
turpissimis iudiciis domi, notatus litteris publicis ;
cuius de probris, adulteriis ac stupris exstant Acmonensium litterae, quas ego non solum propter longi-
tudinem sed etiam propter turpissimam obscenitatem
verborum praetereundas puto. Dixit publice data

---

[1] omni *Müller*. Q. mss.   [2] ceteri *added by Faernus*.

---

[a] This argument is particularly unconvincing.
[b] Quintus Cicero was governor of Asia from 61 to 59.
[c] The prosecution had clearly made a point to which
Cicero had no ready answer. The obvious rebuttal of this

money he committed an offence when there would be no offence if he did account for it? [a] You say that my brother [b] who succeeded Lucius Flaccus did not levy any money for rowers. I am, of course, delighted at any tribute to my brother, but I would be more delighted at other more serious and more important tributes. He decided upon a different policy, he took a different view; he thought that whenever there was any report of pirates he would instantly man the fleet he required. In brief, my brother was the first governor of Asia to relieve the cities of this expense of rowers; but a man usually comes under attack when he levies new taxes, not when he makes some change from the taxes levied by predecessors. Flaccus could not know what others were going to do afterwards; what they had already done, he did see. [c]

Now that I have dealt with the charge made by the whole of Asia in common, I shall move on to the individual cities. Of these let me take first the city of Acmona. The usher calls the representatives from Acmona at the top of his voice. Out steps the solitary Asclepiades. Let the rest of the representatives come forward! Have you forced even the usher to lie? That, I suppose, is the man picked to uphold the reputation of his city with his personal authority, a man condemned there in cases involving loss of civil rights and branded in the official gazette. There is available a letter from Acmona about his offences of adultery and debauchery which I think should be omitted not only because of its length, but also because of the foul obscenity of its language. He

line of argument, if it could be made with conviction, was that Quintus did not need a fleet because the situation was so much improved.

drachmarum $\overline{\text{ccvi}}$. Dixit tantum, nihil ostendit, nihil
protulit; sed adiunxit, id quod certe, quoniam erat
domesticum, docere debuit, se privatim drachmarum
$\overline{\text{ccvi}}$ dedisse. Quantum sibi ablatum homo impudentissimus dicit, tantum numquam est ausus ut
35 haberet optare. Ab[1] A. Sextilio dicit se dedisse et a
suis fratribus. Potuit dare Sextilius; nam fratres
quidem consortes sunt mendicitatis. Audiamus igitur Sextilium; fratres denique ipsi prodeant; quam
volent impudenter mentiantur et, quod numquam
habuerint, dedisse se dicant; tamen aliquid fortasse
coram producti dicent in quo reprehendantur. " Non
deduxi," inquit, " Sextilium." Cedo tabulas. " Non
deportavi." Fratres saltem exhibe. " Non denun-
tiavi." Quod ergo unus Asclepiades fortuna egens,
vita turpis, existimatione damnatus, impudentia atque audacia fretus sine tabulis, sine auctore iecerit,[2]
id nos quasi crimen aut testimonium pertimesca-
36 mus?[3] Idem laudationem quam nos ab Acmonensi-
bus Flacco datam proferebamus falsam esse dicebat.
Cuius quidem laudationis iactura exoptanda nobis
fuit. Nam ut signum publicum inspexit praeclarus

[1] Ab *Angelius.* Aut Σ. At *the other* mss.
[2] iecerit *Victorius.* legerit mss.
[3] pertimescamus *editio Veneta.* pertimescimus mss. pertimescemus *s.*

---

[a] Asclepiades' story is that he paid the sum given to
Flaccus by Acmona out of his own pocket. He was not able
to raise the money himself, so had to borrow it from his
brothers and from Sextilius.
[b] Sextilius was a wealthy money-lender and probably a
member of a family known to have operated in Delos,
Chalcis, Naxos and Ephesus. For Delos, see J. Hatzfeld,
" Les Italiens résidant à Délos," *Bulletin de Correspondance
hellénique* 36 (1912), 78; also *Les Trafiquants italiens dans
l'Orient hellénique* 123.

said that the city had given 206,000 drachmae.[a] We
only have his word for it ; he gave no proof, produced
no evidence ; but he added—information that it was
certainly right for him to give since it concerned him
personally—that he had given the 206,000 drachmae
himself. The fellow has the barefaced effrontery to
say that a sum larger than he ever dared hope to
possess was taken from him. He says that he paid it 35
through Aulus Sextilius [b] and his own brothers.
Sextilius was able to pay it and I only mention this
because his brothers were his partners in beggary.
Let us, then, hear Sextilius and then let his brothers
appear in person; let them lie to their hearts' content
and let them say that they have given what they
have never possessed. Still, when they appear in
person perhaps they will trap themselves in something they say. " I haven't brought Sextilius," he
says. Produce the accounts. " I haven't brought
them either." Well, at least put your brothers on
show. " I didn't notify them." Are we, then, going
to be afraid of what has been tossed at us by the
solitary Asclepiades, a man without means, scandalous in his way of life, condemned by public opinion
and a fellow who relies without documents or anyone
to substantiate his story upon his nerve and effrontery,
as if they were a valid accusation or sworn evidence ?
He said too that the character testimonial given to 36
Flaccus by Acmona and introduced by us in evidence
was a forgery.[c] The loss of that testimonial at least
was my devout wish. For when this fine representa-

---

[c] For these testimonials, see A. H. J. Greenidge, *The Legal
Procedure of Cicero's Time* 489. By voluntarily abandoning
the *testimonium* on Flaccus' behalf, Cicero diminishes the
credibility of all the *testimonia* against Flaccus.

iste auctor suae civitatis, solere suos civis ceterosque
Graecos ex tempore quod opus sit obsignare dixit.
Tu vero tibi habeto istam laudationem; nec enim
Acmonensium testimonio Flacci vita et dignitas niti-
tur. Das enim mihi quod haec causa maxime postulat, nullam gravitatem, nullam constantiam, nullum
firmum in Graecis hominibus consilium, nullam denique esse testimoni fidem. Nisi vero hactenus ista
formula testimoni atque orationis tuae describi ac
distingui potest ut Flacco absenti aliquid civitates
tribuisse dicantur, Laelio praesenti per se agenti vi
legis, iure accusationis, opibus praeterea suis terrenti
ac minanti nihil temporis causa scripsisse aut obsig-
nasse videantur.

37   Equidem in minimis rebus saepe res magnas vidi,
iudices, deprehendi ac teneri, ut in hoc Asclepiade.
Haec quae est a nobis prolata laudatio obsignata erat
creta illa Asiatica quae fere est omnibus nota nobis,
qua utuntur omnes non modo in publicis sed etiam in
privatis litteris quas cotidie videmus mitti a publi-
canis, saepe uni cuique nostrum. Neque enim testis
ipse signo inspecto falsum nos proferre dixit, sed
levitatem totius Asiae protulit, de qua nos et libenter
et facile concedimus. Nostra igitur laudatio, quam
ille temporis causa nobis datam dicit, datam quidem
confitetur, consignata creta est; in illo autem testimonio quod accusatori dicitur datum ceram esse

---

ᵃ The argument is that Flaccus was elsewhere and so
unable to exert pressure upon Acmona to give him a forged
laudatio which, according to the prosecution, the city only
provided because it was forced to do so. Laelius, however,
was at Acmona and exerting pressure upon it, but still claims
that the evidence he obtained was true and not a false story
given to satisfy him.

tive of his city saw the state-seal he said that his fellow-citizens and the other Greeks put their seal on anything as expediency requires. Keep your testimonial, then ; the life and good name of Flaccus do not depend on evidence from Acmona. You are granting me what this case needs most : the proof that there is no weight, no reliability, no fixed purpose in Greeks and, in short, that their evidence is not to be trusted. Unless, of course, that principle laid down in your evidence and your address to the court can be defined and applied widely enough to say that the cities have made some concession to Flaccus' absence. For Laelius, however, who was present and acting in person with the force of the law and the rights of a prosecutor behind him, and who in addition was using his own resources to terrify and threaten them, they seem not to have written or sealed anything for reasons of expediency.[a]

I have myself, gentlemen, often seen trivial details **37** lead to the discovery and establishment of important facts, as in the case of this Asclepiades. This testimonial which we produced in evidence was sealed with that Asiatic clay with which we are almost all familiar. Everybody uses it on both public and private letters such as we see every day being sent by the tax-collectors, often to each one of us. The actual words of the witness after he had inspected it did not say that we were producing a false seal but cited the unreliability of the whole of Asia which we willingly and readily admit. Our testimonial which he says was given to us for reasons of expediency— he admits that it was given—was sealed with clay. On the evidence, however, that is said to have been given to the prosecutor we have seen that the seal is

38 vidimus. Hic ego, iudices, si vos Acmonensium decretis, si ceterorum Phrygum litteris permoveri putarem, vociferarer et quam maxime possem contenderem, testarer publicanos, excitarem negotiatores, vestram etiam scientiam implorarem; cera deprehensa confiderem totius testimoni fictam audaciam manifesto comprehensam atque oppressam teneri. Nunc vero non insultabo vehementius nec volitabo in hoc insolentius neque in istum nugatorem tamquam in aliquem testem invehar neque in toto Acmonensium testimonio, sive hic confictum est, ut apparet, sive missum domo est, ut dicitur, commorabor.[1] Etenim quibus ego laudationem istam remittam, quoniam sunt, ut Asclepiades dicit, leves, horum testimonium non pertimescam.

39 Venio nunc ad Dorylensium testimonium; qui producti tabulas se publicas ad Speluncas perdidisse dixerunt. O pastores nescio quos cupidos litterarum, si quidem nihil istis praeter litteras abstulerunt! Sed aliud esse causae suspicamur, ne forte isti parum versuti esse videantur. Poena est, ut opinor, Dorylai gravior quam apud alios falsarum et corruptarum litterarum. Si veras protulissent, criminis nihil erat, si falsas, erat poena. Bellissimum putarunt dicere

40 amissas. Quiescant igitur et me hoc in lucro ponere

---

[1] commorabor *b*[1]. commovebor *the other mss.*

---

of wax. If I thought, gentlemen, that you were being 38
influenced by the resolutions of Acmona and by the
letters of the rest of the Phrygians I would at this
point cry aloud and speak with all the passion I could
muster. I would summon the tax-collectors as witnesses, I would stir up the businessmen, I would
appeal too to your own experience. From the discovery that wax had been used I would be confident
that the audacious forgery of all the evidence had
been clearly detected and suppressed for good. As
it is, however, I shall not revile him too harshly, I
shall not fly into too great a passion at this fraud,
I shall not round on this prattler as if he were a witness of some account, nor shall I spend time on the evidence from Acmona, whether it has been forged here,
as appears to be the case, or whether it has been
sent from home as is their story. I shall not fear
the evidence of these men to whom I shall return
that testimonial, for they are, as Asclepiades says,
untrustworthy.

  I come now to the evidence of the people of 39
Dorylaeum.[a] When they were brought before us
they said that they had lost their public records near
Speluncae.[b] What gluttons for literature some
shepherds or other were if they stole only the documents from them ! But I suspect that there was a
different reason, not to make them appear rather too
naïve. The penalty for falsifying records by tampering with them is heavier, I think, at Dorylaeum than
elsewhere. If they had produced the genuine
records, there was nothing with which to accuse
Flaccus; if they forged, there was the penalty awaiting
them. They thought it a very smart idea to say that
they had been lost. So let them keep quiet and allow 40

atque aliud agere patiantur. Non sinunt. Supplet
enim iste nescio qui et privatim dicit se dedisse. Hoc
vero ferri nullo modo potest. Qui de tabulis publicis
recitat eis[1] quae in accusatoris potestate fuerunt non
debet habere auctoritatem ; sed tamen iudicium
fieri videtur, cum tabulae illae ipsae, cuicuimodi sunt,
proferuntur. Cum vero is quem nemo vestrum vidit
umquam, nemo qui mortalis esset audivit, tantum
dicit : " dedi," dubitabitis, iudices, quin ab hoc
ignotissimo Phryge nobilissimum civem vindicetis ?
Atque huic eidem nuper tres equites Romani honesti
et graves, cum in causa liberali eum qui adserebatur
cognatum suum esse diceret, non crediderunt. Qui
hoc evenit ut, qui locuples testis doloris et sanguinis
sui non fuerit, idem sit gravis auctor iniuriae publi-
41 cae ? Atque hic Dorylensis nuper cum efferretur
magna frequentia conventuque[2] vestro, mortis illius
invidiam in L. Flaccum Laelius conferebat. Facis iniuste, Laeli, si putas nostro periculo vivere tuos contubernalis, praesertim cum tua neglegentia factum
arbitremur. Homini enim Phrygi qui arborem[3] numquam vidisset fiscinam ficorum obiecisti. Cuius mors
te aliqua re levavit ; edacem enim hospitem ami-
sisti ; Flacco vero quid profuit ? qui valuit tam diu
dum huc prodiret, mortuus est aculeo iam emisso[4] ac

[1] recitat iis *k*. recitatis *V*. recitat his *Σb*. recitatur his
the other mss.
[2] conventuque *Kayser*. consensuque mss. consessuque
Paris. 7778 (m. 2), Naugerius (2). concursuque *Pluygers*.
[3] arborem *V, Scholiast*. arborem fici *the other* mss.
[4] emisso *V, Scholiast*. demisso *the other* mss.

[a] An action to establish a slave's freedom, the *vindicatio in
libertatem*, was heard by the *recuperatores*—assessors—when

me to count this a windfall and pass on to something else. They do not allow me. Some nonentity fills the breach and says that he gave the money personally. This is quite intolerable. A man who reads from those state accounts which have been in the hands of the prosecution ought not to carry conviction ; but there is still the semblance of a judicial process when those records, whatever they are like, are actually produced. When, however, a man whom none of you has ever seen, of whom no mortal man has ever heard, only says : " I gave the money," will you hesitate, gentlemen, to deliver a Roman aristocrat from this Phrygian about whom you know absolutely nothing ? Recently three Roman knights, men of honour and authority, did not believe him when in a case to decide a man's freedom he said that the claimant was his kinsman.[a] How does it happen that a man who was not a responsible witness of his grief for his kinsman and of his kinship is a credible informant of a wrong done to the State ? And when 41 not long ago this man from Dorylaeum was being borne to his burial in the company of a large crowd and gathering of your people, Laelius turned the odium of his death upon Lucius Flaccus. You are acting unjustly, Laelius, if you think that your companions' death endangers us, not least because we think that the cause of death was your carelessness. You threw a basket of figs at the Phrygian fellow who had never seen a fig-tree. His death was some relief to you, for you lost a voracious guest ; but what help was it to Flaccus ? The man who was in good health while he was in the witness-box died after he

at least one of the parties was a provincial. A. Watson, *The Law of Persons in the Later Roman Republic* 218.

dicto testimonio. At istud columen accusationis[1]
tuae, Mithridates, postea quam biduum retentus
testis a nobis effudit quae voluit omnia, reprensus, convictus fractusque discessit; ambulat cum lorica; metuit homo doctus et sapiens, ne L. Flaccus nunc se
scelere adliget, cum iam testem illum effugere non
possit, et, qui ante dictum testimonium sibi tempe-
rarit, cum tamen aliquid adsequi posset, is nunc id
agat ut ad falsum avaritiae testimonium verum
malefici crimen adiungat. Sed quoniam de hoc teste
totoque Mithridatico crimine disseruit subtiliter et
copiose Q. Hortensius, nos, ut instituimus, ad reliqua
pergamus.

42 Caput est omnium Graecorum concitandorum, qui
cum accusatoribus sedet, Heraclides ille Temnites,
homo ineptus et loquax, sed, ut sibi videtur, ita doctus ut etiam magistrum illorum se esse dicat. At,[2]
qui ita sit ambitiosus ut omnis vos nosque cotidie
persalutet, Temni usque ad illam aetatem in senatum
venire non potuit et, qui se artem dicendi traditurum
etiam ceteris profiteatur, ipse omnibus turpissimis
43 iudiciis victus[3] est. Pari felicitate legatus una venit
Nicomedes, qui nec in senatum ulla condicione pervenire potuit et furti et pro socio damnatus est. Nam
princeps legationis, Lysania, adeptus est ordinem
senatorium, sed cum rem publicam nimium amplecte-
retur, peculatus damnatus et bona et senatorium

---

[1] accusationis *V.* actionis *the other* MSS.
[2] At *Baiter.* Et MSS.
[3] victus *V.* convictus *the other* MSS.

---

[a] See p. 461, n. c.
[b] On the coast near Mount Sipylus.

had used his sting and completed his evidence. But that pillar of your prosecution, Mithridates,[a] was detained as a witness by us for two days, poured out everything he had to say and then went off, his evidence refuted, a beaten and a broken man. He walks about in a cuirass. The man, for all his intelligence and learning, is afraid that Lucius Flaccus is going to involve himself in a crime after Mithridates has gone into the box, and that a man who could control himself before Mithridates gave his evidence, when he could still have achieved something, is now going to add a true charge of a crime to the false evidence of extortion. Quintus Hortensius, however, has spoken in detail and at length about this witness and the whole of the charge involving Mithridates, so let me go on, as I planned, to what remains.

The man chiefly responsible for instigating all the 42 Greeks, sitting over there with the prosecution, is Heraclides of Temnus,[b] a silly chatterbox, but in his own opinion so knowledgeable that he even claims to be their teacher. A man, however, who is so eager to win goodwill that daily he greets every member of both sides in turn could not gain admission to the senate at Temnus even at his advanced age, and one too who claims that he will teach the art of speaking to others, has himself been convicted in all sorts of cases involving loss of civil rights. With him there 43 came Nicomedes, an equally propitious representative, who could not get into the senate on any terms and has been convicted of theft and of defrauding a partner. I have not yet mentioned Lysania, the head of the delegation, because he did reach the rank of senator but, when state property stuck to his fingers, he was condemned for embezzlement and lost both

nomen amisit. Hi tres etiam aerari nostri tabulas falsas esse voluerunt ; nam servos novem se professi sunt habere, cum omnino sine comite venissent. Decreto scribendo primum video adfuisse Lysaniam, cuius fratris bona, quod populo non solvebat, praetore Flacco publice venierunt. Praeterea Philippus est, Lysaniae gener, et Hermobius, cuius frater Pollis item pecuniae publicae est condemnatus. Dicunt se Flacco et eis qui simul essent drachmarum ccɪɔɔ ɪɔɔ

44 dedisse. Cum civitate mihi res est acerrima et con-ficientissima litterarum, in qua nummus commoveri nullus potest sine quinque praetoribus, tribus quae-storibus, quattuor mensariis, qui apud illos a populo creantur. Ex hoc tanto numero deductus est nemo, et cum illam pecuniam nominatim Flacco datam referant, maiorem aliam cum huic eidem darent in aedem sacram reficiendam se perscripsisse dicunt, quod minime convenit. Nam aut omnia occulte referenda fuerunt, aut aperte omnia. Cum perscri-bunt Flacco nominatim, nihil timent, nihil verentur ; cum operi publico referunt, idem homines subito eundem quem contempserant pertimescunt. Si praetor dedit, ut est scriptum, a quaestore numeravit, quaestor a mensa publica, mensa aut ex vectigali aut ex tributo. Numquam erit istuc simile criminis, nisi hanc mihi totam rationem omni et personarum genere et litterarum explicaris.

ᵃ Padding expense accounts is nothing new.

his property and his title of senator. These three men wanted the records of our treasury too to be falsified because they made a return that they had nine slaves when they had come without a single attendant.[a] I see that the first to witness the record of the decree was Lysania, whose brother's property was sold at public auction when Flaccus was praetor because he was in debt to the government. There is also Philippus, the son-in-law of Lysania, and Hermobius, whose brother Pollis has also been convicted for embezzlement. They say that they gave Flaccus and those with him 15,000 drachmae. I am dealing 44 with a very sharp city, one very careful in keeping its accounts, and one in which not a penny can be moved without the approval of five praetors, three quaestors and four bankers who are there elected by the people. Of all this number not one has been produced in court; and although they enter this sum as credited to Flaccus' personal account, they say that when they gave him another larger sum, they entered it to temple repairs. This is quite inconsistent; either all the payments ought to have been made secretly or all openly. When they enter a sum to Flaccus by name, they have no alarm or fear, but when they enter it to public works, the selfsame men suddenly become terrified of the man whom they had hitherto regarded with indifference. If the praetor authorized the sum as the record shows, he passed it for payment to the quaestor, the quaestor paid it from the local bank, and the bank got it from local taxation or a poll-tax. There will never be a semblance of a charge here unless you explain to me the principle behind the transactions with full details of the parties and accounts involved.

45 Vel quod est in eodem decreto scriptum, homines
clarissimos civitatis amplissimis usos honoribus hoc
praetore circumventos, cur hi neque in iudicio adsunt
neque in decreto nominantur? Non enim credo signi-
ficari isto loco illum qui se erigit Heraclidam. Utrum
enim est in clarissimis civibus is quem iudicatum hic
duxit Hermippus, qui hanc ipsam legationem quam
habet non accepit a suis civibus, sed usque Tmolo
petivit, cui nullus honos in sua civitate habitus est
umquam, res autem ea quae tenuissimis committe-
batur huic una in vita commissa sola est? Custos T.
Aufidio praetore in frumento publico est positus; pro
quo cum a P. Varinio praetore pecuniam accepisset,
celavit suos civis ultroque eis sumptum intulit. Quod
postea quam Temni litteris a P. Varinio missis cognitum atque patefactum est, cumque eadem de re Cn.
Lentulus, qui censor fuit, Temnitarum patronus,
litteras misisset, Heraclidam istum Temni postea
46 nemo vidit. Atque ut eius impudentiam perspicere
possitis, causam ipsam quae levissimi hominis animum in Flaccum incitavit, quaeso, cognoscite.

Fundum Cymaeum Romae mercatus est de pupillo
Meculonio. Cum verbis se locupletem faceret,
haberet nihil praeter illam impudentiam quam videtis, pecuniam sumpsit mutuam a Sex. Stloga, iudice
hoc nostro, primario viro, qui et rem agnoscit neque
hominem ignorat; qui tamen credidit P. Fulvi Nerati,

---

a Propraetor in 66.   *b* Propraetor in 65.

If, again, as was stated in this same resolution, the 45
most distinguished men in the city who had filled its
highest offices had been unjustly condemned by this
praetor, why are they neither here in court nor
named in the resolution? For I do not suppose that
there is a reference there to Heraclides who is rising
from his seat. Is he one of the most distinguished
citizens, the man whom Hermippus here in court had
condemned and imprisoned, who did not get his
position on this delegation from his fellow-citizens
but begged it all the way from Tmolus, who never
held any office in his own city, and who was never in
his whole life entrusted with any business except such
as was entrusted to the most insignificant individuals?
He was put in charge of the public corn-supply when
Titus Aufidius was praetor,*a* but after he had received
the money for the corn from the praetor Publius
Varinius *b* he concealed the payment from his fellow-
citizens and charged them too with the cost of the
corn. After this had been discovered and exposed at
Temnus by a letter from Varinius and after Gnaeus
Lentulus who was censor and patron of Temnus had
also sent a letter upon the same subject, no one ever
saw our Heraclides at Temnus again. And to enable 46
you to appreciate his shamelessness, listen, please, to
the reason why the anger of this nonentity was
aroused against Flaccus.

At Rome he bought an estate at Cyme from an
orphan Meculonius. Although he possessed nothing
but the effrontery that you are now seeing, he span
a story that he was a rich man, on the strength of
which he borrowed money from Sextus Stloga, a juror
in this case and an eminent man who realizes what
is going on and is not ignorant of the fellow. Still,

lectissimi hominis, fide. Ei cum solveret, sumpsit a
C. M. Fufiis, equitibus Romanis, primariis viris. Hic
hercule " cornici oculum," ut dicitur. Nam hunc
Hermippum, hominem eruditum, civem suum, cui
debebat esse notissimus, percussit. Eius enim fide
sumpsit a Fufiis. Securus Hermippus Temnum pro-
ficiscitur, cum iste se pecuniam quam huius fide
sumpserat a discipulis suis diceret Fufiis persolutu-
47 rum. Habebat enim rhetor iste adulescentes[1] quosdam locupletis, quos dimidio redderet stultiores quam
acceperat ; neminem tamen adeo infatuare potuit ut
ei nummum ullum crederet. Itaque cum Roma clam
esset profectus multosque minutis mutuationibus
fraudavisset, in Asiam venit Hermippoque percon-
tanti de nomine Fufiano respondit se omnem pecuniam Fufiis persolvisse. Interim, neque ita longo
intervallo, libertus a Fufiis cum litteris ad Hermippum
venit ; pecunia petitur ab Hermippo. Hermippus ab
Heraclida petit ; ipse tamen Fufiis satis facit absen-
tibus et fidem suam liberat ; hunc aestuantem et
tergiversantem iudicio ille persequitur. A recupera-
48 toribus causa cognoscitur. Nolite existimare, iudices, non unam et eandem omnibus in locis esse frau-
datorum et infitiatorum impudentiam. Fecit eadem
omnia quae nostri debitores solent ; negavit sese
omnino versuram ullam fecisse Romae ; Fufiorum se
adfirmavit numquam omnino nomen audisse ; Her-

----

[1] discipulos *Scholiast.*

----

[a] *Cf. pro Murena* 25, p. 214.

Stloga made the loan on the surety of another extremely distinguished man, Publius Fulvius Neratus. When Heraclides paid Stloga, he got the funds from two other eminent men, Gaius and Marcus Fufius, who were Roman knights. This is indeed a case of " picking out a crow's eye " as the saying goes.[a] He cheated Hermippus here who was a scholar, a fellow-citizen and a man who should have known all about him. It was on his guarantee that Heraclides got the money from the Fufii. Hermippus sets off for Temnus with an easy mind, since the rogue Heraclides said that he would repay the Fufii the money that he had borrowed on the guarantee of Hermippus with funds obtained from his students. For this teacher of rhetoric had some rich young men 47 to make half as stupid again as they were when he took them on, but he could never make them stupid enough to lend him a single penny. And so when he had secretly left Rome after cheating many people out of small loans, he arrived in Asia and in reply to Hermippus' inquiry about his debt to the Fufii said that he had repaid them the whole amount. Meanwhile, and not so long afterwards, a freedman came to Hermippus from the Fufii with a letter asking him to repay the money. Hermippus asks Heraclides for it, but pays the Fufii in Rome and so discharges his guarantee. Heraclides gets into a panic and does not know which way to turn, and Hermippus sues him. The case is heard by assessors. Do not think, 48 gentlemen, that the impudence of cheats and defaulters is not one and the same the whole world over. He did everything that our debtors usually do. He flatly denied that he had raised any second loan at Rome ; that he had ever heard of the name Fufius ;

mippum vero ipsum, pudentissimum atque optimum virum, veterem amicum atque hospitem meum, splendidissimum atque ornatissimum civitatis suae, probris omnibus maledictisque vexavit.[1] Sed cum se homo volubilis quadam praecipiti celeritate dicendi in illa oratione[2] iactaret, repente testimoniis Fufiorum nominibusque recitatis homo audacissimus pertimuit, loquacissimus obmutuit. Itaque recuperatores contra istum rem minime dubiam prima actione iudicaverunt. Cum iudicatum non faceret, addictus Hermippo et ab hoc ductus est.

49 Habetis et honestatem hominis et auctoritatem testimoni et causam omnem simultatis. Atque is ab Hermippo missus, cum ei pauca mancipia vendidisset, Romam se contulit, deinde in Asiam rediit, cum iam frater meus Flacco successisset. Ad quem adiit causamque ita detulit, recuperatores vi Flacci coactos et metu falsum invitos iudicavisse. Frater meus pro sua aequitate prudentiaque decrevit ut, si iudicatum negaret, in duplum iret; si metu coactos diceret, haberet eosdem recuperatores. Recusavit et, quasi nihil esset actum, nihil iudicatum, ab Hermippo ibidem mancipia quae ipse ei vendiderat petere coepit. M. Gratidius legatus, ad quem est aditum, actionem se daturum negavit; re iudicata stari ostendit placere. Iterum iste, cui nullus esset usquam consistendi locus, Romam se rettulit; persequitur

---

[1] vexavit *k*. vexat *the other* MSS.
[2] oratione *k*. ratione *the other* MSS.

---

[a] A subordinate officer of the governor in Asia 61–59.

but Hermippus himself, a most honourable and upright man and an old friend and host of mine, the most illustrious and distinguished man of his city, he abused with all sorts of insults and curses. But despite the fluent fellow's confident boasting in his speech with a veritable torrent of words, when the depositions of the Fufii and their entries were suddenly read out, his bold front turned to terror, his eloquence to silence. And so the assessors found a clear-cut case against him on the first day's hearing. When he did not pay the amount awarded, he was handed over to Hermippus who haled him off.

You now have the integrity of the man, the value of 49 his evidence and the whole reason for his hostility. He was released by Hermippus when he had sold Hermippus a few slaves, took himself off to Rome and then returned to Asia when my brother had already succeeded Flaccus. He went to my brother and gave him this account of the case: the assessors had been under pressure from Flaccus and in their fear had unwillingly given a false verdict. My brother, displaying his usual justice and good sense, determined that if Heraclides disputed the verdict he should have a new trial but with double the penalty; and if he said that they had been constrained by fear, he should have the same assessors. He refused and, as though he had not appealed and had not been condemned in the first place, he began to sue Hermippus in the same court for the slaves which he had sold him. Marcus Gratidius,[a] the governor's deputy before whom he appeared, refused him a hearing and indicated that his decision was that the verdict should stand. For a second time Heraclides, who had 50 nowhere to stay, took himself off to Rome; Hermip-

Hermippus, qui numquam istius impudentiae cessit.
Petit Heraclides a C. Plotio senatore, viro primario,
qui legatus in Asia fuerat, mancipia quaedam quae se,
cum iudicatus esset, per vim vendidisse dicebat. Q.
Naso, vir ornatissimus, qui praetor fuerat, iudex
sumitur. Qui cum sententiam secundum Plotium se
dicturum ostenderet, ab eo iudice abiit et, quod iudicium lege non erat, causam totam reliquit. Satisne vobis, iudices, videor ad singulos testis accedere
neque, ut primo constitueram, tantum modo cum universo genere confligere ?

51 Venio ad Lysaniam eiusdem civitatis, peculiarem
tuum, Deciane, testem ; quem tu cum ephebum
Temni cognosses, quia tum[1] te nudus delectarat, semper nudum esse voluisti. Abduxisti Temno Apol-
lonidem ; pecuniam adulescentulo grandi faenore,
fiducia tamen accepta, occupavisti. Hanc fiduciam
commissam tibi dicis ; tenes hodie ac possides. Eum
tu testem spe recuperandi fundi paterni venire ad testimonium dicendum coegisti ; qui quoniam testimonium nondum[2] dixit, quidnam sit dicturus exspecto.
Novi genus hominum, novi consuetudinem, novi libidinem. Itaque, etsi teneo quid sit dicere paratus,
nihil tamen contra disputabo prius quam dixerit.
Totum enim convertet atque alia finget. Quam ob
rem et ille servet quod paravit, et ego me ad id quod
adtulerit integrum conservabo.

52 Venio nunc ad eam civitatem in quam ego multa

---

[1] quia tum *Faernus.* qua tum *V.* qui tunc *Scholiast.*
[2] nondum *added by Faernus.*

---

[a] A subordinate officer of the governor in Asia in 62.
[b] Quintus Voconius Naso, praetor in 60.
[c] A town in Lydia between the rivers Hermus and Caicus.
[d] Tralles in Caria.

pus, who never gave in to his effrontery, follows him. Heraclides asks that eminent senator, Gaius Plotius,[a] who had been a deputy of the governor in Asia, for certain slaves which he said he had been illegally forced to sell when he had been condemned for debt. The distinguished ex-praetor, Quintus Naso,[b] is accepted as arbitrator. When, however, he indicated that he was going to give his decision in favour of Plotius, Heraclides rejected him as arbitrator and, because the action was not based on statute law, abandoned the whole case. Do you think, gentlemen, that I am tackling the individual witnesses adequately instead of doing battle only with the class as a whole, as was my original plan ?

I come to Lysania from the same city, your own 51 special witness, Decianus. You knew him as a youth at Temnus and because he delighted you then when stripped, you wanted to keep him stripped. You took him from Temnus to Apollonis.[c] You lent the lad money at a high rate of interest, but only after taking a security. You say that this security is forfeited to you; you hold it today and it belongs to you. You have forced him to come here to give evidence as a witness in the hope of recovering his family estate. He has not yet given his evidence, so I am waiting to see what he is going to say. I know the sort of man he is ; I know their ways and their disregard for the law. So even though I know what he is all ready to say, I shall not contradict him until he has spoken. Otherwise he will alter it all and make up something else. Let him, therefore, keep what he has got ready and I shall keep myself fresh for what he produces.

I come now to a city [d] whose interests I have often 52

CICERO

et magna studia et officia contuli, et quam meus frater
in primis colit atque diligit. Quae si civitas per viros
bonos gravisque homines querelas ad vos detulisset,
paulo commoverer magis. Nunc vero quid putem ?
Trallianos Maeandrio causam publicam commisisse,
homini egenti, sordido, sine honore, sine existu-
matione, sine censu ? Ubi erant illi Pythodori, Aetidemi, Lepisones,[1] ceteri homines apud nos noti, inter
suos nobiles, ubi illa magnifica et gloriosa ostenta-
tio civitatis ? Nonne esset puditum, si hanc causam
agerent severe, non modo legatum sed Trallianum
omnino dici Maeandrium ? Huic illi legato, huic
publico testi patronum suum iam inde a patre atque maioribus, L. Flaccum, mactandum civitatis
testimonio tradidissent ? Non est ita, iudices, non est
53 profecto. Vidi ego in quodam iudicio nuper Philo-
dorum testem Trallianum, vidi Parrhasium, vidi Ar-
chidemum, cum quidem idem hic mihi Maeandrius
quasi ministrator aderat subiciens quid in suos civis
civitatemque, si vellem, dicerem. Nihil enim illo
homine levius, nihil egentius, nihil inquinatius. Qua
re, si hunc habent auctorem Tralliani doloris sui, si
hunc custodem litterarum, si hunc testem iniuriae, si
hunc actorem[2] querelarum, remittant spiritus, com-
primant animos suos, sedent adrogantiam, fateantur
in Maeandri persona esse expressam speciem civitatis.

[1] Pythodori, Aetidemi, Lepisones *k, Faernus. The readings of the other* MSS. *are gibberish.* Archidemi *for* Aetidemi
Klotz. Epigoni *for* Lepisones *Baiter.*
[2] actorem *Camerarius.* auctorem MSS. *and Scholiast.*

[a] Pythodorus was a friend of Pompey and extremely
wealthy.
[b] According to the scholiast (p. 105 ed. Stangl) this is a
500

served with the greatest energy and of which my
brother is a particularly devoted admirer. If this
city had employed men of honour and influence to
report its grievances to you, I would show a little
more concern. But as it is—what am I to think?
That the inhabitants of Tralles have entrusted their
city's case to a squalid down-and-out like Maeandrius,
a fellow without position, reputation or property?
Where were the men like Pythodorus,[a] Aetidemus,
Lepiso and all the other men who are known to us and
highly regarded among their own people? What had
become of the city's usual magnificent and glorious
array? Was it not deplorable, if they were conducting this case seriously, that Maeandrius was their
representative or even a citizen of Tralles at all?
Would they have handed over to this representative,
to this witness for their city, Lucius Flaccus, their
patron as were his father and forebears before him,
to be the victim of their city's evidence? It cannot
be so, gentlemen, it cannot be so. I recently saw 53
Philodorus giving evidence for Tralles in some trial, I
saw Parrhasius, I saw Archidemus, and there too was
this same Maeandrius like a sort of " second "[b]
handing me ideas that I might care to use against
his fellow-citizens and his own city. There is nothing
more untrustworthy, more vile, more loathsome than
that man. If, then, the people of Tralles have this
man to vouch for their afflictions, to guard their
records, to bear witness to their wrongs, to voice their
complaints, let them calm their airs, curb their pride
and check their arrogance, let them admit that in the
character of Maeandrius is reproduced the nature of

metaphor from the gladiatorial games and the *ministrator*
handed the gladiators their weapons.

Sin istum semper illi ipsi domi proterendum et con-
culcandum putaverunt, desinant putare auctoritatem
esse in eo testimonio cuius auctor inventus est nemo.

Sed exponam quid in re sit ut quam ob rem ista
civitas neque severe Flaccum oppugnarit neque be-
54 nigne defenderit scire possitis. Erat ei Castriciano
nomine irata, de quo toto respondit Hortensius; invita
solverat Castricio pecuniam iam diu debitam. Hinc
totum odium, hinc omnis offensio. Quo cum venisset
Laelius ad iratos et illud Castricianum volnus dicendo
refricuisset, siluerunt principes neque in illa contione
adfuerunt neque istius decreti ac testimoni auctores
esse voluerunt. Usque adeo orba fuit ab optimatibus
illa contio ut princeps principum esset Maeandrius;
cuius lingua quasi flabello seditionis illa tum est
55 egentium contio ventilata. Itaque civitatis pudentis,
ut ego semper existimavi, et gravis, ut ipsi existimari
volunt, iustum dolorem querelasque cognoscite.
Quae pecunia fuerit apud se Flacci patris nomine a
civitatibus, hanc a se esse ablatam queruntur. Alio
loco quaeram quid licuerit Flacco; nunc tantum a
Trallianis requiro, quam pecuniam ab se ablatam
querantur, suamne dicant, sibi a civitatibus conlatam
in usum suum. Cupio audire. " Non," inquit, " di-

ᵃ Castricius was a member of a family with wide business
interests, *e.g.* in Rome, Sicily and Delos. J. Hatzfeld, " Les
Italiens résidant à Délos," *Bulletin de Correspondance
hellénique* 36 (1912), 24 and *Les Trafiquants italiens dans
l'Orient hellénique* 109.

his city. If, however, they have themselves always thought that he should be trampled upon and trodden underfoot at home, let them stop thinking that there is any value in evidence which no one has been found to authenticate.

I shall, however, explain what is at the root of that matter so that you can understand why that city has neither bitterly attacked Flaccus nor hotly defended him. It was angry with him over the debt to 54 Castricius,[a] but Hortensius has dealt with the whole of this affair. It had unwillingly paid Castricius the money that it had owed him for a long time. This was the source of all the hatred and all the bad feeling. When Laelius had come to Tralles with its angry citizens and had by his talk reopened the wound caused by the Castricius affair, the leading figures kept silent and refused to support the public meeting or to be a party to that resolution and evidence. In fact, the leading men boycotted that meeting so effectively that the most distinguished leading figure present was Maeandrius and that meeting of paupers was then fanned by his tongue as if by the bellows of sedition. Listen, then, to the 55 legitimate grievance and complaints of a decent, as I have always thought, and responsible city, as its inhabitants would have it considered. They complain that the money they had on deposit from other cities on the count of Flaccus' father had been taken from them. I shall raise the question of what authority Flaccus had later, but now I only ask the people of Tralles whether they say that the money which they complain was taken from them was their own and collected by them from other cities for their own use. I wish to hear. " We say," he says,

cimus." Quid igitur ? " Delatam ad nos, creditam
nobis L. Flacci patris nomine ad eius dies festos at-
56 que ludos." Quid tum ? " Hanc te," inquit, " capere non licuit." Iam id videro, sed primum illud
tenebo. Queritur gravis, locuples, ornata civitas,
quod non retinet alienum; spoliatam se dicit, quod id
non habet quod eius non fuit. Quid hoc impudentius
dici aut fingi potest ? Delectum est oppidum, quo in
oppido uno[1] pecunia a tota Asia ad honores L. Flacci
poneretur. Haec pecunia tota ab honoribus translata
est in quaestum et faenerationem ; recuperata est
57 multis post annis. Quae civitati facta est iniuria ? At
moleste fert civitas. Credo; avolsum[2] est enim praeter spem quod erat spe devoratum lucrum. At
queritur. Impudenter facit ; non enim omnia quae
dolemus, eadem queri iure possumus. At accusat
verbis gravissimis. Non civitas, sed imperiti homines
a Maeandrio concitati. Quo loco etiam atque etiam
facite ut recordemini quae sit temeritas multitudinis, quae levitas propria Graecorum, quid in contione
seditiosa valeat oratio. Hic, in hac gravissima et
moderatissima civitate, cum est forum plenum iudiciorum, plenum magistratuum, plenum optimorum
virorum et civium, cum speculatur atque obsidet rostra
vindex temeritatis et moderatrix offici curia, tamen

---

[1] uno *B, Angelius.* una Σ*b*[1]χ*ς.* universa *Clark.*
[2] avolsum Σ*b*[1]. amissum *the other* MSS.

" that it was not." And then ? " It was paid over
and entrusted to us on the count of Lucius Flaccus'
father for a festival and games in his honour."
Where does that bring you ? " You had no right to 56
take it." I shall consider that presently, but I shall
make this point first. A responsible, wealthy and
distinguished city is complaining because it does not
hold on to something that does not belong to it ; it
says that it has been robbed because it does not have
what it does not own. Can you imagine a more outrageous statement than this ? A town was selected
which was to be the sole repository of the money
collected from the whole of Asia for the celebrations
in honour of Lucius Flaccus. The whole of this money
was converted from these celebrations to lending at
interest for their own profit and it was only recovered
many years later. What injury has the city suffered ? 57
But the city is annoyed. I accept that, for the profit
was unexpectedly lost after it had already been swal-
lowed up in anticipation. But the city complains.
It does so quite unjustifiably, because we cannot
reasonably complain about everything that we do
not like. But it accuses Flaccus in the strongest
terms. Not the city, but the ignorant rabble stirred
up by Maeandrius. And I here repeatedly urge you
to remember the irresponsibility of the crowd, the
instability characteristic of Greeks and the force that
a seditious speech has in a public meeting. Here in
Rome, the most responsible and the most controlled
of cities, where the Forum is filled with courts,
magistrates, men of standing, loyal citizens, and
where the Senate-house that punishes our folly and
directs our sense of duty watches and overlooks the
Rostra, think of the storms that you see aroused even

quantos fluctus excitari contionum videtis ! Quid vos
fieri censetis Trallibus ? an id quod Pergami ? Nisi
forte hae civitates existimari volunt facilius una se
epistula Mithridatis moveri impellique potuisse ut
amicitiam populi Romani, fidem suam, iura omnia
offici humanitatisque violarent, quam ut filium testimonio laederent cuius patrem armis pellendum a suis
58 moenibus censuissent. Qua re nolite mihi ista nomina
civitatum nobilium opponere ; quos enim hostis haec
familia contempsit, numquam eosdem testis perti-
mescet. Vobis autem est confitendum, si consiliis
principum vestrae civitates reguntur, non multitudinis temeritate, sed optimatium consilio bellum ab
istis civitatibus cum populo Romano esse susceptum ; sin ille tum motus est temeritate imperitorum
excitatus, patimini me delicta volgi a publica causa
59 separare. At enim istam pecuniam huic capere non
licuit. Utrum voltis patri Flacco licuisse necne ?
Si licuit uti,[1] certe licuit, ad eius honores conlata,[2]
ex quibus nihil ipse capiebat, patris pecuniam recte
abstulit filius ; si non licuit, tamen illo mortuo non
modo filius sed quivis heres rectissime potuit auferre.
Ac tum quidem Tralliani cum ipsi gravi faenore istam
pecuniam multos annos occupavissent, a Flacco tamen
omnia quae voluerunt impetraverunt, neque tam
fuerunt impudentes ut id quod Laelius dixit dicere
auderent, hanc ab se pecuniam abstulisse Mithridatem. Quis enim erat qui non sciret in ornandis
studiosiorem Mithridatem quam in spoliandis Tralli-

[1] uti *added by Clark.*   [2] collatam *b[1]k, editio Veneta.*

---

[a] 17, p. 460.   [b] See p. 422.
[c] Because the games were never held.

here in our public meetings ! What do you think happens at Tralles ? Is it not what happened at Pergamum ?[a] These cities may perhaps wish it to be thought that they could be instigated more easily by a single letter of Mithridates[b] to violate the friendship of the Roman people, their own loyalty, all the laws of obligation and humanity, than to injure by their evidence a son whose father they had voted to drive from their walls by force of arms. Do not, then, 58 thrust at me those names of noble cities ; this family will never fear as witnesses the men whom it despised as enemies. And you must admit, if your cities are ruled by the councils of their leading men, that those cities declared war upon the Roman people not as a result of the impetuosity of the mob, but upon the decision of their best men. If, on the other hand, that rising was provoked by the rashness of ignorance, then allow me to distinguish between the crimes of the mob and the position of the city. But Flaccus 59 had no right to take that money. Do you maintain that Flaccus' father had a right or not ? If he had a right, as was certainly the case, to use money collected for the celebrations in his honour from which he got no personal benefit,[c] then the son was justified in taking his father's money. If, however, he did not have the right, after the father's death not only the son but any heir could take it quite legitimately. And even when the people of Tralles had put that money out on loan for many years at an exorbitant rate of interest, they still obtained everything they wanted from Flaccus and did not have the impertinence to assert, as did Laelius, that Mithridates had taken this money from them. Who did not know that Mithridates was more concerned to enrich the citizens

60 anis fuisse ? Quae quidem a me si, ut dicenda sunt,
dicerentur, gravius agerem, iudices, quam adhuc egi,
quantam Asiaticis testibus fidem habere vos conveniret ; revocarem animos vestros ad Mithridatici
belli memoriam, ad illam universorum civium Romanorum per tot urbis uno puncto temporis miseram crudelemque caedem, praetores nostros deditos,
legatos in vincla coniectos, nominis prope Romani
memoriam cum vestigio omni[1] imperi non modo
ex sedibus Graecorum verum etiam ex litteris esse
deletam. Mithridatem dominum,[2] illum patrem, illum conservatorem Asiae, illum Euhium, Nysium,
61 Bacchum, Liberum nominabant. Unum atque idem
erat tempus cum L. Flacco consuli portas tota Asia
claudebat, Cappadocem autem illum non modo re-
cipiebat suis urbibus verum etiam ultro vocabat.
Liceat haec nobis, si oblivisci non possumus, at tacere, liceat mihi potius de levitate Graecorum queri
quam de crudelitate ; auctoritatem isti habeant apud
eos quos esse omnino noluerunt ? Nam, quoscumque
potuerunt, togatos interemerunt, nomen civium Romanorum quantum in ipsis fuit sustulerunt. In hac
igitur urbe se iactant quam oderunt, apud eos quos
inviti vident, in ea re publica ad quam opprimendam
non animus eis, sed vires defuerunt ?[3] Aspiciant hunc
florem legatorum laudatorumque Flacci ex vera atque

---

[1] omni *added by Oetling* ; *after* cum *by Garatoni*.

[2] dominum. *The various* MSS. *readings are derived from the contraction which can be expanded into either* deum *or* dominum.

[3] defuerunt *Naugerius* (2). defecerunt et defuerunt Σ*bc*χ. defecerunt *k, Gruter.*

---

[a] Mithridates called himself Dionysus and is given here
the Dionysiac titles : Euhius from the cry of the Dionysiac
revellers ; Nysius from Nysa, where he is supposed to have

of Tralles than to despoil them? If, gentlemen, I 60
were saying what the facts require me to say, I should
be dealing more harshly than I have hitherto with
the degree of trust that you should place in Asiatic
witnesses; I should be taking your minds back to
recall the Mithridatic War, to the horror of that
barbarous massacre inflicted simultaneously upon all
Roman citizens in every city, to the surrender of our
praetors, the imprisonment of their officers and the
almost total obliteration of all memory of the name of
Rome and of every trace of our rule from the Greek
settlements and from their very records. They called
Mithridates Lord, Father, Saviour of Asia, Euhius,
Nysius, Bacchus, Liber.[a] That was the very time at 61
which all Asia was closing its gates to the consul
Lucius Flaccus, but was not only receiving the
Cappadocian[b] in its cities but even inviting him
spontaneously. Allow us, then, if we cannot forget
these events, at least to be silent about them; and
allow me to complain more about the unreliability of
Greeks than about their savagery. Are they to carry
weight with men whom they wanted to exterminate?
For they killed all the Roman civilians they could and
did away with the words " Roman citizen " so far as
was in their power. They are throwing their weight
about in this city which they hate, among men whose
sight they dislike, and in a state for whose destruction
they lacked not the will but the strength. Let them
look at these deputations to bear witness to Flaccus'

been born; Bacchus, another name for the god; and Liber,
an Italian deity of fertility and especially of wine, with whom
Dionysus was commonly identified.
   [b] Contemptuous because of the large number of Cappadocian slaves in Rome.

integra Graecia ; tum se ipsi expendant, tum cum his comparent, tum, si audebunt, dignitati horum anteponent suam.

62 Adsunt Athenienses, unde humanitas, doctrina, religio, fruges, iura, leges ortae atque in omnis terras distributae putantur ; de quorum urbis possessione propter pulchritudinem etiam inter deos certamen fuisse proditum est ; quae vetustate ea est ut ipsa ex sese suos civis genuisse ducatur,[1] et eorum eadem terra parens, altrix, patria dicatur, auctoritate autem tanta est ut iam fractum prope ac debilitatum 63 Graeciae nomen huius urbis laude nitatur. Adsunt Lacedaemonii, cuius civitatis spectata ac nobilitata virtus non solum natura corroborata verum etiam disciplina putatur ; qui soli toto orbe terrarum septingentos iam annos amplius unis moribus et numquam mutatis legibus vivunt. Adsunt ex Achaea cuncta multi legati, Boeotia, Thessalia, quibus locis nuper legatus Flaccus imperatore Metello praefuit. Neque vero te, Massilia, praetereo quae L. Flaccum militem[2] quaestoremque cognosti ; cuius ego civitatis disciplinam atque gravitatem non solum Graeciae, sed haud scio an cunctis gentibus anteponendam iure dicam ; quae tam procul a Graecorum omnium regionibus, disciplinis linguaque divisa cum in ultimis terris cincta Gallorum gentibus barbariae fluctibus adlu-

---

[1] ducatur *Clark.* dicatur *mss.*
[2] tribunum militum *Gulielmius, followed by Clark.*

---

[a] Flaccus had been there during his service with Metellus.
[b] Religion : Eleusinian Mysteries ; agriculture : story of Demeter and Triptolemus ; Athena's gift of the olive.
[c] Athena and Poseidon.
[d] Lycurgus was dated in antiquity to about 775.
[e] There are no grounds for reading *tribunum militum* " military tribune." E. Badian, " The Early Career of A. Gabinius (*cos.* 58 B.C.)," *Philologus* 103 (1959), 91.

character, the pick of the true, authentic Greece ; then let them weigh themselves, compare themselves with these men and then, if they dare, rate their own worth higher than theirs.

There are present men from Athens [a] where men **62** think civilization, learning, religion, agriculture,[b] justice and laws were born and spread thence into every land. Tradition relates that even the gods [c] competed for the possession of their city, so beautiful was it. It is so ancient that it is thought to have produced its own citizens, and the same soil is said to be their mother, their nurse and their home. Its prestige is so great that the present enfeebled and shattered renown of Greece is sustained by the reputation of this city. There are present men from **63** Sparta whose well-known and famous valour is thought to have derived its strength not only from their nature but also from their upbringing. They alone in the whole world have now lived for more than seven hundred years [d] with one set of customs and without ever altering their laws. There are also present a host of representatives from all Achaea, from Boeotia and from Thessaly where Flaccus was recently a subordinate commander under Metellus when he was commander-in-chief. And I do not omit you, Marseilles, who knew Lucius Flaccus as a soldier [e] and as quaestor.[f] I would be right in saying that in culture and reliability this city is the superior not only of Greece but probably of the whole world. Although it is far from any area inhabited by Greeks and cut off from their culture and language, and although it is surrounded at the edge of the world by Gallic tribes and washed by the waves of their

[f] See p. 414.

atur, sic optimatium consilio gubernatur ut omnes
eius instituta laudare facilius possint quam aemulari.
64 Hisce utitur laudatoribus Flaccus, his innocentiae
testibus, ut Graecorum cupiditati[1] Graecorum auxilio
resistamus.

Quamquam quis ignorat, qui modo umquam mediocriter res istas scire curavit, quin tria Graecorum
genera sint vere ? quorum uni sunt Athenienses,
quae gens Ionum habebatur, Aeolis alteri, Doris tertii
nominabantur. Atque haec cuncta Graecia, quae
fama, quae gloria, quae doctrina, quae plurimis arti-
bus, quae etiam imperio et bellica laude floruit,
parvum quendam locum, ut scitis, Europae tenet
semperque tenuit, Asia maritimam oram bello supera-
tam cinxit urbibus, non ut munitam[2] coloniis illam
65 gentem,[3] sed ut obsessam teneret. Quam ob rem
quaeso a vobis, Asiatici testes, ut, cum vere recordari
voletis quantum auctoritatis in iudicium adferatis,
vosmet ipsi describatis Asiam nec quid alienigenae de
vobis loqui soleant, sed quid vosmet ipsi de genere
vestro statuatis, memineritis. Namque, ut opinor,
Asia vestra constat ex Phrygia, Mysia, Caria, Lydia.
Utrum igitur nostrum est an vestrum hoc proverbium,
" Phrygem plagis fieri solere meliorem " ? Quid ?
de tota Caria nonne hoc vestra voce volgatum est,
" si quid cum periculo experiri velis, in Care[4] id potis-

[1] Graecorum cupiditati *added by Naugerius.* Graecis
Angelius.   [2] munitam *mss.* victam *Clark.*
[3] gentem *Bχc.* generaret Σ. augeret *b¹k.* gubernaret *i,*
Stangl. constringeret *Clark.*
[4] Care *s, Erasmus.* Caria Σ*bk.*

---

[a] The ring of Greek cities was between the sea and the
nearer parts of Asia, not between the nearer parts and the
further.
[b] Φρὺξ ἀνὴρ πληγεὶς ἀμείνων καὶ διακονέστερος " A Phrygian
512

barbarism, it is so well governed by the prudence of its aristocracy that it is easier for everyone to praise its institutions than to copy them. These are the 64 men whom Flaccus has as character-witnesses, and to testify to his innocence,—if I may combat the cupidity of Greeks with the aid of other Greeks.

And yet who that has ever taken the pains to acquire even a limited knowledge of this subject does not know that there are really three divisions of the Greek race ? The Athenians are one of these and were held to be Ionians ; the second were called Aeolians, and the third Dorians. This Greece in its entirety, distinguished as she was in repute, glory, learning, numerous arts, and also for her empire and renown in war, holds and always has held, as you know, only a small area of Europe. After conquering the coast of Asia in war and encircling it with cities she did not control her people by planting colonies but held them in siege.[a] I beg you, therefore, witnesses 65 for Asia, when you want to think over honestly what influence you bring to the court, to characterize Asia in your own minds and to remember not what foreigners usually say of you, but what you think of your own race yourselves. Your Asia, if I am not mistaken, consists of Phrygia, Mysia, Caria and Lydia. Is this proverb, then, ours or yours " Spare the rod and spoil the Phrygian " ? [b] And again, do you not have this saying about the whole of Caria, " If you want to make a risky experiment, try it first

is better and more obedient when beaten." ἐν Καρὶ τὸν κίνδυνον " Try danger on a Carian." Μυσῶν τὸν ἔσχατον " the farthest of Mysians." This last comes from Plato, *Theaetetus* 209 B and is deliberately misinterpreted by Cicero.

simum esse faciendum " ? Quid porro in Graeco
sermone tam tritum atque celebratum est quam, si
quis despicatui ducitur, ut " Mysorum ultimus " esse
dicatur ? Nam quid ego dicam de Lydia ? Quis
umquam Graecus comoediam scripsit in qua servus
primarum partium non Lydus esset ? Quam ob rem
quae vobis fit iniuria, si statuimus vestro nobis
66 iudicio standum esse de vobis ? Equidem mihi iam
satis superque dixisse videor de Asiatico genere
testium ; sed tamen vestrum est, iudices, omnia quae
dici possunt in hominum levitatem, inconstantiam,
cupiditatem, etiam si a me minus dicuntur, vestris
animis et cogitatione comprendere.

Sequitur auri illa invidia Iudaici. Hoc nimirum est
illud quod non longe a gradibus Aureliis haec causa
dicitur. Ob hoc crimen hic locus abs te, Laeli, atque
illa turba quaesita est ; scis quanta sit manus, quanta
concordia, quantum valeat in contionibus. Sic[1] sub-
missa voce agam tantum ut iudices audiant ; neque
enim desunt qui istos in me atque in optimum quemque incitent ; quos ego, quo id facilius faciant, non
67 adiuvabo. Cum aurum Iudaeorum nomine quotannis
ex Italia et ex omnibus nostris provinciis Hierosoly-
mam exportari soleret, Flaccus sanxit edicto ne ex
Asia exportari liceret. Quis est, iudices, qui hoc non
vere laudare possit ? Exportari aurum non oportere
cum saepe antea senatus tum me consule gravissime
iudicavit. Huic autem barbarae superstitioni resistere

---

[1] Sic *b¹k, Faernus.* Si Σ. *Omitted by the other* MSS.

---

[a] There is a pun on *aurum* and *Aurelium.* The Aurelian
steps and tribunal were near the temple of Castor. See E.
Nash, *Pictorial Dictionary of Ancient Rome 2.* 478-481.
[b] See p. 560.

on a Carian " ? Or again, is there a more hackneyed
and commonplace phrase in Greek than to say " the
farthest of the Mysians " of anyone you despise ?
And what am I to say about Lydia ? What Greek
ever wrote a comedy without giving the leading slave
part to a Lydian ? What injustice is there done to
you, then, if we decide to take you at your own
valuation ? I for my part feel that I have said 66
enough and more about witnesses from Asia as a
class, but it is your task, gentlemen, to form a mental
picture of everything that can be said about the
unreliability, instability and greed of these men even
if I have not dealt with them adequately.

Then there is that unpopularity over the Jewish
gold. This is presumably the reason why this case is
being heard not far from the Aurelian steps.[a] It
was for this particular charge, Laelius, that you
sought this site and that crowd. You know how vast
a throng it is, how close-knit, and what influence it
can have in public meetings.[b] I will speak in a
whisper like—this—, just loud enough for the jury to
hear; for there is no shortage of men to incite this
crowd against me and all the best men, but I shall not
help them by making it easier for them. It was the 67
practice each year to send gold to Jerusalem on the
Jews' account from Italy and all our provinces,[c] but
Flaccus issued an edict forbidding its export from
Asia. Who is there, gentlemen, who cannot genuinely
applaud this measure ? The Senate strictly forbade
the export of gold on a considerable number of
previous occasions, notably during my consulship.
To oppose this outlandish superstitition was an act of

[c] Every Jew paid a poll-tax of two drachmae to the
Temple in Jerusalem.

severitatis, multitudinem Iudaeorum flagrantem non
numquam in contionibus pro re publica contemnere
gravitatis summae fuit. At Cn. Pompeius captis
68 Hierosolymis victor ex illo fano nihil attigit. In primis
hoc, ut multa alia, sapienter ; in tam suspiciosa ac
maledica civitate locum sermoni obtrectatorum non
reliquit. Non enim credo religionem et Iudaeorum
et hostium impedimento praestantissimo imperatori,
sed pudorem fuisse. Ubi igitur crimen est, quoniam
quidem furtum nusquam reprehendis, edictum pro-
bas, iudicatum fateris, quaesitum et prolatum palam
non negas, actum esse per viros primarios res ipsa
declarat ? Apameae manifesto comprehensum ante
pedes praetoris in foro expensum est auri pondo c
paulo minus per Sex. Caesium, equitem Romanum,
castissimum hominem atque integerrimum, Lao-
diceae xx pondo paulo amplius per hunc L. Pedu-
caeum, iudicem nostrum, Adramytti c[1] per Cn.
69 Domitium legatum, Pergami non multum. Auri
ratio constat, aurum in aerario est ; furtum non
reprehenditur, invidia quaeritur ; a iudicibus oratio
avertitur, vox in coronam turbamque effunditur. Sua
cuique civitati religio, Laeli, est, nostra nobis.
Stantibus Hierosolymis pacatisque Iudaeis tamen

---

[1] c *transferred by Clark from after* hunc.

[a] Rome, not Jerusalem ; *cf.* 7, p. 448.
[b] *i.e.* he did not want to appear avaricious. This was in 64.
[c] Of the senate ; the basis of their approval of Flaccus'
edict.   [d] In Phrygia.
[e] To the west of Apamea.   [f] In Mysia.

firmness, and to defy in the public interest the crowd
of Jews that on occasion sets our public meetings
ablaze was the height of responsibility. But the
victorious Gnaeus Pompeius did not touch anything
in the Temple after his capture of Jerusalem. In this 68
he showed exceptional good sense—as he has on many
other occasions—in that he did not give his detractors
any opportunity for gossip in a city *a* so prone to
suspicion and slander. I do not believe that the
illustrious commander was restrained by the religious
susceptibilities of Jews and enemies, but out of
respect for public opinion.*b* Where, then, is there
any ground for accusing Flaccus? Nowhere do you
find any evidence of theft, you approve his edict, you
admit the previous decision,*c* you do not deny that
the investigation was held in public, and it is self-
evident that it was conducted by men of distinction.
At Apamea *d* a little less than a hundred pounds of
gold was seized as it was being exported and weighed
in the forum at the feet of the praetor through the
efforts of Sextus Caesius, a thoroughly upright and
honest Roman knight; at Laodicea *e* a little more
than twenty pounds was seized by Lucius Peducaeus who is here in court and a juror in this case;
at Adramyttium *f* a hundred pounds by Gnaeus
Domitius, one of Flaccus' subordinate officers; at
Pergamum not much. The account of the gold is 69
correct, it is in the treasury, there is no evidence of
theft, the sole intent is to create unpopularity. The
prosecution's address is not directed at the jury but is
playing to the gallery. Every city, Laelius, has its
own religious observances and we have ours. Even
when Jerusalem was still standing and the Jews at
peace with us, the demands of their religion were

istorum religio sacrorum a splendore huius imperi, gravitate nominis nostri, maiorum institutis abhorrebat; nunc vero hoc magis, quod illa gens quid de nostro imperio sentiret ostendit armis ; quam cara dis immortalibus esset docuit, quod est victa, quod elocata, quod serva facta.[1]

70 Quam ob rem quoniam, quod crimen esse voluisti, id totum vides in laudem esse conversum, veniamus iam ad civium Romanorum querelas ; ex quibus sit sane prima Deciani. Quid tibi tandem, Deciane, iniuriae factum est ? Negotiaris in libera civitate. Primum patere me esse curiosum. Quo usque negotiabere, cum praesertim sis isto loco natus ? Annos iam xxx in foro versaris, sed tamen in Pergameno. Longo intervallo, si quando tibi peregrinari commodum est, Romam venis, adfers faciem novam, nomen vetus, purpuram Tyriam, in qua tibi invideo, quod

71 unis vestimentis tam diu lautus es. Verum esto, negotiari libet; cur non Pergami, Smyrnae, Trallibus, ubi et multi cives Romani sunt et ius a nostro magistratu dicitur ? Otium te delectat, lites, turbae, praetor[2] odio est, Graecorum libertate gaudes. Cur

---

[1] serva facta *Sylvius.* servata *mss.* serva *Angelius.*
[2] praetor *Naugerius.* populus Romanus *mss.*

---

[a] Both their financial activities and their social and religious exclusiveness made the Jews unpopular, but there is no evidence in this passage that Flaccus was moved by animus against the Jews rather than by considerations of the economy of the province. It is clear that his action was not unusual and for the shortage of specie at this time, see p. 10. But interference with the dispatch of the sacred money could easily become an emotional issue and be exploited by Flaccus' enemies.

[b] It is difficult to reproduce the effect of this sentence in English. To a Roman audience *in foro* could only mean the Forum at Rome, and then Cicero adds the unexpected

incompatible with the majesty of our Empire, the dignity of our name and the institutions of our ancestors *a* ; and now that the Jewish nation has shown by armed rebellion what are its feelings for our rule, they are even more so; how dear it was to the immortal gods has been shown by the fact that it has been conquered, farmed out to the tax-collectors and enslaved.

Seeing, then, that what you tried to make into an **70** accusation has been completely transformed into a commendation, let us now come to the complaints of Roman citizens, and I should like to take Decianus' first. What injury, I ask you, did you suffer, Decianus? You are in business in a free city. Firstly, let me be inquisitive. How long, particularly in view of your birth, are you going to continue in business? For thirty years now you have practised at the Bar—I mean the Bar at Pergamum.*b* At infrequent intervals, when your interests take you abroad, you come to Rome, you bring a new appearance, an old name and Tyrian purple, which I envy you because you can be smart so long in one suit of clothes. But let it go; you like being in business. **71** Why not at Pergamum, Smyrna, Tralles, where there are many Roman citizens and justice is administered by our magistrate? You enjoy peace; you hate lawsuits, commotions, a praetor; you like the freedom of the Greeks. Why, then, are you the only man to

Pergameno. Decianus appears to have been in business at Apollonis and practised law at Pergamum. Being a *libera civitas* Apollonis would enjoy control of its finances, freedom from tribute and the use of its own laws. See A. H. J. Greenidge, *The Legal Procedures of Cicero's Time* 111. By conducting his business interests at Apollonis he would avoid the constraints of Roman jurisdiction.

ergo unus tu Apollonidensis amantissimos populi
Romani, fidelissimos socios, miseriores habes quam
aut Mithridates aut etiam pater tuus habuit umquam ? Cur his per te frui libertate sua, cur denique esse liberos non licet ? Homines sunt tota ex
Asia frugalissimi, sanctissimi, a Graecorum luxuria
et levitate remotissimi, patres familias suo contenti,
aratores, rusticani ; agros habent et natura perbonos
et diligentia culturaque meliores. In hisce agris tu
praedia habere voluisti. Omnino mallem, et magis
erat tuum, si iam te crassi agri delectabant, hic
alicubi in Crustumino aut in Capenati paravisses.
72 Verum esto ; Catonis est dictum "pedibus compensari pecuniam." Longe omnino a Tiberi ad
Caicum, quo in loco etiam Agamemnon cum exercitu
errasset, nisi ducem Telephum invenisset. Sed con-
cedo id quoque ; placuit oppidum, regio delectavit.
Emisses. Amyntas est genere, honore, existimatione,
pecunia princeps illius civitatis. Huius socrum,
mulierem imbecilli consili, satis locupletem, pellexit
Decianus ad sese et, cum illa quid ageretur nesciret,
in possessione praediorum eius familiam suam con-
locavit; uxorem abduxit ab Amynta praegnantem,
quae peperit apud Decianum filiam, hodieque apud
73 Decianum est et uxor Amyntae et filia. Num quid
harum rerum a me fingitur, Deciane ? Sciunt haec

---

^a Both are near Mount Soracte, to the north of Rome.
^b Cato meant that hard work makes up for lack of means,
but Cicero interprets it as meaning the more distant the land,
the cheaper it is.
^c Telephus guided Agamemnon and the Greek army to
Troy in return for Achilles healing his wound.
^d A good example of the additional pressures to which

make the people of Apollonis, so strongly attached to the Roman people and such faithful allies, more miserable than ever did Mithridates or even your own father ? Why do you not allow them to enjoy their freedom or even to be free at all ? They are the most thrifty and honest men in the whole of Asia, completely untouched by the extravagance and unreliability of Greeks, yeomen content with their lot, farmers and countrymen. Their land is naturally fertile and made more so by their careful toil and cultivation. This was the district in which you wanted an estate. Doubtless I would prefer it, and it was more like you, if you now wanted fertile land, that you should have acquired an estate somewhere in this area at Crustumium or at Capena.[a] I do not press 72 my point; there is a saying of Cato, " Distance lends cheapness." [b] It certainly is a long way from the Tiber to the Caicus, a place where even Agamemnon would have lost his way with his army, had he not found Telephus to direct him.[c] I let that pass too ; you liked the town and found the district delightful. You should have bought your estate. Amyntas is the leading man of that city in birth, position, reputation and wealth. Decianus got a hold over his mother-in-law, a woman of limited intelligence, though wealthy enough, and without her realizing what was happening he installed his slaves in possession of her estate.[d] He abducted Amyntas' wife who was pregnant and gave birth to a daughter in Decianus' house where both the wife and daughter of Amyntas still remain today. I am not making up any of this story, am I, Decianus? 73 All the aristocracy knows it, men of substance

magistrates were subject in the provinces in controlling the lawlessness of Roman private citizens.

omnes nobiles, sciunt boni viri, sciunt denique noti[1]
homines, sciunt mediocres negotiatores. Exsurge,
Amynta, repete a Deciano non pecuniam, non
praedia, socrum denique sibi habeat; restituat
uxorem, reddat misero patri filiam. Membra quidem,[2] quae debilitavit lapidibus, fustibus, ferro,
manus quas contudit, digitos quos confregit, nervos
quos concidit, restituere non potest; filiam, filiam
74 inquam, aerumnoso patri, Deciane, redde. Haec
Flacco non probasse te miraris? Cui, quaeso, tandem
probasti? Emptiones falsas, praediorum proscriptiones[3] cum aperta[4] circumscriptione fecisti. Tutor
his mulieribus Graecorum legibus ascribendus fuit;
Polemocratem scripsisti, mercenarium et administrum consiliorum tuorum. Adductus est in iudicium
Polemocrates de dolo malo et de fraude a Dione huius
ipsius tutelae nomine. Qui concursus ex oppidis
finitimis undique, qui dolor animorum, quae querela!
Condemnatus est Polemocrates sententiis omnibus;
inritae venditiones, inritae proscriptiones. Num re-
stituis? Defers ad Pergamenos ut illi reciperent in
suas litteras publicas praeclaras proscriptiones et emptiones tuas. Repudiant, reiciunt. At qui homines?
Pergameni, laudatores tui. Ita enim mihi gloriari
visus es laudatione Pergamenorum quasi honorem maiorum tuorum consecutus esses, et hoc te superiorem
esse putabas quam Laelium, quod te civitas Perga-

---

[1] noti *Clark*. nostri *MSS*.   [2] quidem *added by Clark*.
[3] praescriptiones $\Sigma^1 b$.
[4] cum aperta . . . his mulieribus *Clark*. cum mulieribus
(-erculis $B\chi$) aperta . . . his rebus (verbis $\chi\varsigma$) *MSS*.

---

[a] For the legal background to this episode, see A. J.
Marshall, " Romans under Chian Law," *Greek, Roman, and
Byzantine Studies* 10 (1969), 267 f.

know it, in short well-known men and traders in a small way alike know it. Bestir yourself, Amyntas, and demand back from Decianus not your money, not your estate, let him even have your mother-in-law; but let him restore your wife and return your daughter to her poor father. The limbs which he has maimed with stones, clubs and swords, the hands which he has crushed, the fingers which he has broken, the sinews which he has cut, these indeed he cannot restore; but, Decianus, return the daughter, the daughter I say, to her sorrowing father. Are you 74 surprised that Flaccus did not approve of this? Who, I ask you, did approve of your behaviour? [a] You made fraudulent purchases and registrations of the estate with bare-faced deceit. Under Greek law a guardian had to be appointed for these women. You appointed Polemocrates, your hireling and accomplice in your plans. Polemocrates was brought to trial by Dio for fraud and false pretences in respect of this guardianship. What a crowd there was from the neighbouring towns all around, what indignation, what complaints! Polemocrates was unanimously condemned and the sales and registrations declared invalid. You do not return the estates? Of course not. You take the transaction off to the people of Pergamum for them to enter in their public register your fine sales and registrations. They refuse and reject them. You ask: what men did this? The Pergamenes who used to sing your praises. For you gave me the impression of bragging about their praise as if you had attained the rank of your ancestors [b] and thought that you were superior to Laelius because

[b] He was of equestrian rank, his father a senator. See p. 278, n. b.

mena laudaret. Num honestior est civitas Pergamena
quam Smyrnaea? At ne ipsi quidem dicunt.

75 Vellem tantum habere me oti, ut possem recitare
psephisma Smyrnaeorum quod fecerunt in Castricium
mortuum, primum ut in oppidum introferretur, quod
aliis non conceditur, deinde ut ferrent ephebi, postremo ut imponeretur aurea corona mortuo. Haec
P. Scipioni, clarissimo viro, cum esset Pergami
mortuus, facta non sunt. At Castricium quibus verbis, di immortales! "decus patriae, ornamentum populi Romani, florem iuventutis "appellant. Qua re,
Deciane, si cupidus es gloriae, alia ornamenta cen-
76 seo quaeras; Pergameni te deriserunt. Quid? tu ludi
te non intellegebas, cum tibi haec verba recitabant:
"clarissimum virum, praestantissima sapientia, singulari ingenio"? Mihi crede, ludebant. Cum vero
coronam auream litteris imponebant, re vera non plus
aurum tibi quam monedulae committebant, ne tum
quidem hominum venustatem et facetias perspicere
potuisti? Ipsi[1] igitur illi Pergameni proscriptiones
quas tu adferebas repudiaverunt. P. Orbius, homo et
prudens et innocens, contra te omnia decrevit. Apud[2]
P. Globulum, meum necessarium, fuisti gratiosior.

77 Utinam neque ipsum neque me paeniteret! Flaccum
iniuria decrevisse in tua re dicis; adiungis causas
inimicitiarum, quod patri L. Flacco[3] aedili curuli pater
tuus tribunus plebis diem dixerit. At istud ne ipsi

[1] Ipsi *added by Clark.* Isti igitur Pergameni *Mommsen.*
[2] Apud *Lambinus.* in *P.* [3] Flacco *Orelli.* Flacci *P.*

---

[a] See p. 502, n. *a.*
[b] Publius Cornelius Scipio Nasica Serapio, consul in 138,
and the object of attack by Marcus Fulvius Flaccus for the
murder of Tiberius Gracchus. He went on an embassy to
Asia, where he died. [c] In 64.
[d] Publius Servilius Globulus, in 63. [e] See p. 413.

the city of Pergamum praised you. Surely the city of Pergamum is not more honourable than Smyrna? Not even its own citizens claim that.

I would like just to have the time to read out the 75 decree that the people of Smyrna passed in honour of Castricius [a] upon his death : firstly, that his body should be brought into the town—an honour not conferred upon others—secondly, that the young men should carry it, and finally, that a golden crown should be placed upon it. The famous Publius Scipio did not receive these honours when he died at Pergamum.[b] In heaven's name, the titles they give to Castricius ! They call him " the glory of his fatherland, the pride of the Roman people, the flower of the youth." So, if you are eager for glory, Decianus, I think that you had better look for other honours ; the Pergamenes were making fun of you. Did you not realize that you were being ridiculed 76 when they read out phrases like : " a man of distinction, of exceptional wisdom, of unique ability " ? Believe me, they were making fun of you. When they were putting a golden crown at the head of the text, they were really giving you no more gold than they would give a jackdaw. Could you not even then see through their fun and wit ? And so those Pergamenes rejected with their own hands the titles you brought to be registered. Publius Orbius,[c] a man of good sense and integrity, gave every decision against you. With my friend Publius Globulus [d] you were more successful—and how we both regret it ! You allege 77 that Flaccus' decision in your case was prejudiced and you add as your reasons for his hostility that your father when tribune of the commons brought to trial his father Lucius Flaccus who was curule aedile.[e]

quidem patri Flacco valde molestum esse debuit,
praesertim cum ille cui dies dicta est praetor postea
factus sit et consul, ille qui diem dixit non potuerit
privatus in civitate consistere. Sed si iustas inimicitias putabas, cur, cum tribunus militum Flaccus esset,
in illius legione miles fuisti, cum per leges militaris
effugere liceret iniquitatem tribuni ? Cur autem
praetor[1] te, inimicum paternum, in consilium vocavit ?
Quae quidem quam sancte solita sint observari scitis
omnes. Nunc accusamur ab eis qui in consilio nobis
78 fuerunt. " Decrevit Flaccus." Num aliud atque
oportuit ? " In liberos." Num aliter censuit senatus ? " In absentem." Decrevit, cum ibidem esses,
cum prodire nolles ; non est hoc in absentem, sed in
latentem reum.

SENATUS CONSULTUM ET DECRETUM FLACCI

Quid ? si non decrevisset, sed edixisset, quis posset
vere reprehendere ? Num etiam fratris mei litteras
plenissimas humanitatis et aequitatis reprehensurus
es ?[2] quas ea de muliere ad me[3] datas apud ⟨Pata-
ranos⟩[4] requisivit. Recita.

LITTERAE Q. CICERONIS

79 Quid ? haec Apollonidenses occasionem nacti[5] ad
Flaccum non[6] detulerunt, apud Orbium acta non sunt,

[1] praetor *A. Augustinus.* per *P.*
[2] es *added by Lambinus.*
[3] ea de muliere ad me *Clark.* easdem mulieri a me *P.*
[4] apud . . . *P.* Pataranos *Naugerius. Clark would prefer*
publicanos, *cf. 37.*
[5] occasionem nacti *Orelli.* occasione facta *P.*
[6] non *added by Lambinus.*

---

[a] In Cilicia in 78. [b] A town in Lycia.

That need not have caused much animosity even with the elder Flaccus himself, particularly since the defendant was later elected praetor and consul, while the plaintiff could not remain in the city even as a private citizen. If you thought the hostility justified, why did you serve in the legion of which Flaccus was a military tribune[a] although the military regulations allowed you to avoid service under a tribune prejudiced against you ? Why when he was praetor did he make you a member of his council although your fathers had been enemies ? You all know how scrupulously such bonds are observed, and now we are being accused by men who sat on our council. " Flaccus gave a ruling." There was nothing wrong in that, was there ? " Upon land belonging to a free city." The Senate did not forbid this action, did it ? " Against a man in his absence." He gave this ruling when you were there but refused to come into court ; that is not against a man in his absence but against a defendant who refuses to appear.

The Decision of the Senate and the Ruling of Flaccus are read

If he had given a ruling on his own authority and not supported by a decree of the Senate, who could reasonably blame him ? Surely you are not also going to criticize my brother's letter, brim-full of humanity and justice ? The letter which he wrote to me about this woman when he was ⟨at Patara⟩[b] was demanded by Laelius. Read it out.

The Letter of Quintus Cicero is read

Did not the people of Apollonis when the opportunity offered report these events to Flaccus ? Were

ad Globulum delata non sunt ? Ad senatum nostrum me consule nonne legati Apollonidenses omnia postulata de iniuriis unius Deciani detulerunt ? At haec praedia in censum dedicavisti. Mitto quod aliena, mitto quod possessa per vim, mitto quod convicta ab Apollonidensibus, mitto quod a Pergamenis repudiata, mitto etiam quod a nostris magistratibus in integrum restituta, mitto quod nullo iure 80 neque re neque possessione tua ; illud quaero sintne ista praedia censui censendo, habeant ius civile, sint necne sint mancipi, subsignari apud aerarium aut apud censorem possint. In qua tribu denique ista praedia censuisti ? Commisisti, si tempus aliquod gravius accidisset, ut ex isdem praediis et Apollonide et Romae imperatum esset tributum. Verum esto, gloriosus fuisti, voluisti magnum agri modum censeri, et eius agri qui dividi plebi Romanae non potest. Census es praeterea numeratae pecuniae c̄xxx. Eam opinor tibi numeratam non esse abs te. Sed haec omitto. Census es mancipia Amyntae neque huic ullam in eo fecisti iniuriam. Possidet enim ea mancipia Amyntas. Ac primo quidem pertimuit, cum te

---

a If we accept the authenticity of the words that fill the gap at the end of 80, and there seems to be no reason why we should not, the census will be that of 64–63.

Cicero asks four questions to establish whether this land was capable of being returned in the census : Does the *ius civile* apply to it ? Does Decianus have formal possession ? Can it be put up as a surety ? Can it be registered in the land of a tribe ?

Only Italian land could be formally held *iure Quiritium* ; publicans had to find security in land for the due performance

they not dealt with before Orbius and referred to Globulus ? Did not the representatives of Apollonis when I was consul refer to our Senate all the claims arising out of the injuries done by this one Decianus ? But you say you made returns of these estates in the census. I omit the fact that they belonged to others, that they had been taken by violence, that they were declared by the people of Apollonis not to belong to you, that the Pergamenes refused to register them, even that they were reinstated by our magistrates, that you held them without right either of ownership or of possession. I ask these questions : are those 80 estates capable of being returned in the census, do they admit of a legal right, are they in your formal possession or not, can they be entered as surety at the treasury or with the censor ?[a] Finally, in what tribe did you register those estates ? You rendered yourself liable, had some crisis occurred, to have those same estates assessed for tribute at both Apollonis and Rome. But let that pass ; you were full of your own importance, you wanted to be assessed for a large area of land, and land at that which cannot be divided among the Roman commons.[b] You also declared 130,000 sesterces in cash, but I think that your ready money was not your own. I let that go too. You declared Amyntas' slaves but you did not cause him any loss by doing so, for he still owns those slaves. Admittedly, he was afraid at first when he had heard that

of their contracts and that land had to be in Italy. Similarly, the tribes only held land in Italy ; how could Asiatic land be registered in the land of a tribe ?

[b] The point seems to be that Decianus wanted to ensure that his land in Asia was not liable to be bought for the Roman people under any agrarian proposals such as those of Rullus. *Cf.* p. xxiv.

audisset servos suos esse censum ; rettulit ad iuris
consultos. Constabat inter omnis, si aliena censendo
Decianus sua facere posset, eum maximam[1] habitu-
rum esse familiam. Responsum est, eius facta non
videri. Idem visum est postea Flacco, cum rem cog-
nosceret. Itaque decrevit.[2]

81 Habetis causam inimicitiarum, qua causa inflammatus Decianus ad Laelium detulerit hanc opimam
accusationem. Nam ita questus est Laelius, cum de
perfidia Deciani diceret : " qui mihi auctor fuit, qui
causam ad me detulit, quem ego sum secutus, is
a Flacco corruptus est, is me deseruit ac prodidit."
Sicine tu auctor tandem eum cui tu in consilio fuisses,
apud quem omnis gradus dignitatis tuae retinuisses,
pudentissimum hominem, nobilissima familia natum,
optime de re publica meritum in discrimen omnium
fortunarum vocavisti ? Scilicet[3] defendam Decianum,
qui tibi in suspicionem nullo suo delicto venit. Non
82 est, mihi crede, corruptus. Quid enim fuit quod ab
eo redimeretur ? ut duceret iudicium ? Cui sex horas
omnino lex dedit, quantum tandem ex his horis
detraheret, si tibi morem gerere voluisset ? Nimirum
illud est quod ipse suspicatur. Invidisti ingenio sub-
scriptoris tui ; quod ornabat facile locum quem pre-
henderat, et acute testis interrogabat ; aut fortasse
fecisset ut tu ex populi sermone excideres,[4] idcirco

---

[1] maximam *Lambinus.* maxima *P.*
[2] familiam ... decrevit *added by Lambinus from the
margin of an old* ᴍs. [3] Scilicet *P.* Si licet *Clark.*
[4] fecistis et tu et populi sermone exciperes *P* ; *corrected by
Manutius.*

---

[a] A successful prosecutor obtained a proportion of the
defendant's property.
[b] The most satisfactory explanation of this sentence is that
the proportions of time taken by the accusers' speeches were

you had declared his slaves and took legal advice. The unanimous opinion was that if Decianus was able to make other people's slaves his own by declaring them, he would have the largest household of any of us. Amyntas was given the opinion that the acts of Decianus were not legal. Subsequently Flaccus took the same view when he heard the case, and gave his ruling on this basis.

Now you have the cause of the enmity which fired 81 Decianus to place this profitable [a] accusation before Laelius. Laelius complained when speaking of the treachery of Decianus : " the man who was my informant, who laid the information before me, whose guidance I followed, was bribed by Flaccus and deserted and betrayed by me." Were you really responsible then for endangering the whole fortune of Flaccus on whose council you had sat and in whose company you had held all your public offices, a man of the highest integrity and of aristocratic birth, and one who had served the State devotedly ? Assuredly, I shall defend Decianus who has fallen under suspicion with you although he has done nothing wrong. He was not bribed, believe me. What could be got 82 from him in return ? That he should prolong the trial ? The law allowed him six hours in all ; how much of this do you think he would surrender, if he had wanted to please you ? [b] Of course, what he suspects himself is that you were jealous of the professional skill of your junior because he elaborated with ease the position which he had taken up and cross-examined the witnesses with penetration ; or perhaps he might have caused you to drop out of

allowed to vary provided that the total length permitted was not exceeded.

Decianum usque ad coronam applicavisti. Sed, ut
hoc haud veri simile est[1] Decianum a Flacco esse
83 corruptum, ita scitote esse cetera, velut quod ait
Lucceius, L. Flaccum sibi dare cupisse, ut a fide
se abduceret, sestertium viciens. Et eum tu accusas
avaritiae quem dicis sestertium viciens voluisse per-
dere ? Nam quid emebat, cum te emebat ? ut ad se
transires ? Quam partem causae tibi daremus ? An
ut enuntiares consilia Laeli ? qui testes ab eo pro-
dirent ? Quid ? nos non videbamus ? Habitare una ?
Quis hoc nescit ? Tabulas in Laeli potestate fuisse ?
Num dubium est ? An ne vehementer, ne copiose
accusares ? Nunc facis suspicionem ; ita enim dixisti
ut nescio quid a te impetratum esse videatur.

84 At enim Androni Sextilio gravis iniuria facta est
et non ferenda, quod, cum esset eius uxor Valeria
intestato mortua, sic egit eam rem Flaccus quasi ad
ipsum hereditas pertineret. In quo quid reprehendas
scire cupio. Quod falsum intenderit ? Qui doces ?
" Ingenua," inquit, " fuit." O peritum iuris hominem ! Quid ? ab ingenuis mulieribus hereditates
lege non veniunt ? " In manum," inquit, " con-

[1] haud veri simile est *Clark.* veri simile est haud veri
simile *P.*

---

[a] The name suggests a Roman citizen of Greek birth.
The *cognomen* is put here before the name of his *gens.*
According to the scholiast (p. 106 ed. Stangl) Valeria was a
freedwoman of Flaccus, but this is impossible because she is
ingenua. She will, in all likelihood, have been the daughter
of a freedman either of Flaccus' father or of his grandfather
and therefore in the *tutela legitima* of Flaccus. If she died
intestate, her estate would go first to her husband, provided
that she was in his *manus*, and then to Flaccus and other
members of his family. Flaccus must therefore show that
she was not in the *manus* of her husband.

[b] The point that his opponent is making begins to dawn

people's conversation, and so you steered Decianus right into the surrounding crowd. It is not likely that Decianus was bribed by Flaccus and, let me tell you, the other allegations are false—for example, 83 Lucceius' statement that Lucius Flaccus wanted to give him 2,000,000 sesterces as the price of suborning him. Do you accuse of rapacity a man who, according to you, wanted to waste 2,000,000 sesterces? What was he buying when he was buying you? Your defection to his side? What part of the case would we give you? Or was it your disclosure of Laelius' plans? Or of the witnesses he was putting on the stand? Did we not see for ourselves? That they were living with him? Is it not public knowledge? That the records were in Laelius' hands? That is not in doubt, is it? That you would press the charge less vigorously and less fully? Now you are raising a suspicion; for the way in which you have spoken suggests that he did get something from you.

You claim that a serious and intolerable injustice 84 has been done to Sextilius Andro [a] because, when his wife Valeria had died intestate, Flaccus dealt with the case as if her estate belonged to him. I want to know what you find wrong in that. Is it that his claim was false? How do you prove it? " She was free-born," he says. What an expert lawyer he is! Are not estates inherited legally from free-born women? " She had come under the charge of her husband." Ah! Now I begin to understand [b];

upon Cicero. He had not previously been aware of what his opponent was getting at, because he had taken it for granted that the marriage was *sine manu*. The fact that Cicero can plausibly argue that it had not entered his head that it might have been *cum manu* shows that this form of marriage was uncommon; and this to some extent confirms Cicero's point

venerat." Nunc audio; sed quaero, usu an coemptione? Usu non potuit; nihil enim potest de tutela legitima nisi omnium tutorum auctoritate deminui. Coemptione? Omnibus ergo auctoribus; in quibus 85 certe Flaccum fuisse non dices. Relinquitur illud quod vociferari non destitit, non debuisse, cum praetor esset, suum negotium agere aut mentionem facere hereditatis. Maximas audio tibi, L. Luculle, qui de L. Flacco sententiam laturus es, pro tua eximia liberalitate maximisque beneficiis in tuos venisse hereditates, cum Asiam provinciam consulari imperio obtineres. Si quis eas suas esse dixisset, concessisses? Tu, T. Vetti, si quae tibi in Africa venerit hereditas, usu amittes, an tuum nulla avaritia salva dignitate retinebis? At istius hereditatis iam Globulo praetore Flacci nomine petita possessio est. Non igitur impressio, non vis, non occasio, non tem-

that a woman did not come into the *manus* of her husband by *usus* except with the consent of all her guardians and this consent would have to be expressly given. A. Watson, *The Law of Persons in the Later Roman Republic* 20 f. *Coemptio*, too, to be valid would have to be with the consent of all her guardians. *Op. cit.* 24.

Cicero's argument is that since Valeria was not married *cum manu* she had no capacity to make a will. He denies that Flaccus usucapted, *i.e.* acquired ownership by virtue of uninterrupted possession for a certain length of time, the estate of Valeria, but he does not seek to deny that Flaccus treated the estate as if it belonged to him. He does not claim, however, that Flaccus did this as *agnatus proximus*—indeed there is no sign that he was a close relative of Valeria—and it is therefore likely that Flaccus' claim would be based on the idea that both he and the deceased belonged to the *gens Valeria*. A. Watson, *The Law of Succession in the Later Roman Republic* 181 f.

[a] Cicero now considers the possibility that Flaccus' accuser, who was entitled to the estate, did not press his claim at the time because Flaccus was praetor and it was not

but I ask whether the marriage was by cohabitation or by sale ? If it was a common-law marriage, that was not possible because no alteration in the status of a legal ward can be made without the consent of all the guardians. If it was a marriage by sale ? Then it was with the approval of all the guardians ; but surely you are not going to say that Flaccus was one of them. There only remains what he has kept on shouting from the roof-tops, that Flaccus should not when he was praetor have conducted business to which he was an interested party nor laid claim to the inheritance.[a] I hear that you, Lucius Lucullus, who are going to be a character-witness for Lucius Flaccus, came into very large legacies in return for your outstanding liberality and the great benefits conferred upon your friends when you were governor of Asia with the rank of proconsul. If anyone had said that they were his, would you have surrendered them ? You, Titus Vettius,[b] if a legacy comes to you in Africa, will you lose it from another man's use of it, or will you keep it as your own without any taint of rapacity or loss of your good name ? In fact the possession of that inheritance was claimed on Flaccus' behalf when Globulus was still praetor.[c] No pressure, then, no violence, no opportunity offered

85

proper for him to conduct business to which he was an interested party. He then asks T. Vettius whether, if an estate came to him in Africa, he would lose it to another *usu* or keep it without forfeiting his good name. This interpretation of the passage means that *usucapio hereditatis* was still in existence, but Cicero's failure to use it as an argument on his client's behalf suggests that it was regarded by this time as morally unjustified. A. Watson, *The Law of Property in the Later Roman Republic* 37 f.

[b] See p. 419.   [c] In 63.

pus, non imperium, non secures ad iniuriam faciendam
86 Flacci animum impulerunt. Atque eodem etiam
M. Lurco, vir optimus, meus familiaris, convertit
aculeum testimoni sui; negavit a privato pecuniam
in provincia praetorem petere oportere. Cur tandem,
M. Lurco, non oportet ? Extorquere, accipere contra
leges non oportet, petere non oportere numquam
ostendes, nisi docueris non licere. An legationes
sumere liberas exigendi causa, sicut et tu ipse nuper
et multi viri boni saepe fecerunt, rectum est, quod ego
non reprehendo, socios video queri ; praetorem, si
hereditatem in provincia non reliquerit, non solum
reprehendendum verum etiam condemnandum putas? "Doti," inquit, "Valeria pecuniam omnem suam
dixerat." Nihil istorum explicari potest, nisi os-
tenderis illam in tutela Flacci non fuisse. Si fuit,
quaecumque sine hoc auctore est dicta dos, nulla est.
87 Sed tamen Lurconem, quamquam pro sua dignitate
moderatus est in testimonio dicendo orationi[1] suae,
tamen iratum Flacco esse vidistis. Neque enim oc-
cultavit causam iracundiae suae neque reticendam
putavit ; questus est libertum suum Flacco praetore
esse damnatum. O condiciones miseras admini-
strandarum provinciarum, in quibus diligentia plena
simultatum est, neglegentia vituperationum, ubi
severitas periculosa est, liberalitas ingrata, sermo
insidiosus, adsentatio perniciosa, frons omnium fa-

---

[1] orationi *Bremius.* religioni *mss.* religiose orationi
Früchtel.

---

[a] The system of *liberae legationes* admitted the principle
that a magistrate with *imperium* might transact his own business in the provinces. Cicero had attacked it in 63, see
p. xxxviii.

by his term of office, no authority of his position prompted Flaccus to commit any act of injustice. And my friend, the excellent Marcus Lurco, has 86 aimed the sting of his evidence at the same target. He has said that a praetor ought not to seek money from a private citizen in his province. Tell me, Lurco; why not? He ought not extract it by force or accept it illegally; but you will never show that it is wrong for him to make a claim, unless you prove that it is made illegally. Is it right to accept missions at the public expense[a] for the purpose of recovering a private debt? Men of integrity, including yourself a short time ago, have often done so. I do not object to this practice although I see that the allies complain of it, but do you think that a praetor who does not renounce an inheritance in his province is not only morally culpable but also guilty of a criminal offence? " Valeria," he says, " had settled all her money upon him for a dowry."[b] None of those arguments can be developed unless you show that she was not a ward of Flaccus. If she was, any dowry settled without his consent is void. Nevertheless, you saw that, although Lurco with his 87 usual dignity kept his language within bounds when giving evidence, he was angry with Flaccus. He did not hide the cause of his anger nor did he think that he ought to keep it secret. He complained that his freedman had been condemned while Flaccus was praetor. What a wretched state the government of our provinces is in! Devotion to duty breeds animosity and negligence censure, firm action is dangerous and to be easy-going wins no thanks; their conversation is full of traps, their flattery dangerous

[b] She needed the consent of her guardians to do this.

miliaris, multorum animus iratus, iracundiae occul-
tae, blanditiae apertae, venientis praetores exspectant, praesentibus inserviunt, abeuntis deserunt!
Sed omittamus querelas, ne nostrum consilium in
88 praetermittendis provinciis laudare videamur. Litteras misit de vilico P. Septimi, hominis ornati, qui
vilicus caedem fecerat; Septimium ardentem iracundia videre potuistis. In Lurconis libertum iudicium ex edicto dedit; hostis est Lurco. Quid igitur?
hominum gratiosorum splendidorumque libertis fuit
Asia tradenda? an simultates nescio quas cum
libertis vestris Flaccus exercet? an vobis in vestris
vestrorumque causis severitas odio est, eandem
laudatis, cum de nobis iudicatis?

At iste Andro spoliatus bonis, ut dicitis, ad
89 dicendum testimonium non venit. Quid si veniat?
Decisionis arbiter C. Caecilius fuit, quo splendore
vir, qua fide, qua religione! obsignator C. Sextilius,
Lurconis sororis filius, homo et pudens et constans et
gravis. Si vis erat, si fraus, si metus, si circumscriptio,
quis pactionem fieri, quis adesse istos coegit? Quid?
si ista omnis pecunia huic adulescentulo L. Flacco
reddita est, si petita, si redacta per hunc Antiochum,
paternum huius adulescentis libertum seni illi Flacco
probatissimum, videmurne non solum avaritiae crimen effugere sed etiam liberalitatis laudem adsequi

---

[a] Cf. ad Quintum fratrem 1. 1. 15.
[b] See p. xxxvii, n. f.
[c] For Sextilii, one of whom married a sister of Marcus
Aufidius Lurco, tribune in 61, see J. Hatzfeld, " Les Italiens
résidant à Délos," *Bulletin de Correspondance hellénique* 36
(1912), 78 and *Les Trafiquants italiens dans l'Orient hellénique* 403.

and, although their faces all smile in friendship, the hearts of many seethe with anger; their fury is kept hidden, their flattery is unconcealed; they eagerly await the praetors' arrival, they are deferential to their faces and they abandon them the moment their backs are turned.[a] But let me omit these complaints or I may give the impression of applauding my own decision not to accept provinces.[b] Flaccus sent a **88** letter about the bailiff of that distinguished gentleman, Publius Septimius, when the bailiff had committed murder. You could see Septimius blazing with anger. He granted a trial of Lurco's freedman in the terms of his edict; Lurco is an enemy. What difference does that make? Was Asia to be surrendered to the freedmen of powerful and influential men? Or is Flaccus prosecuting some feud with your freedmen? Or do you dislike firm action when you or your friends are the defendants but applaud it when we are in the dock?

This Andro who, according to you, was despoiled of his property has not come to give evidence. What **89** if he were to come? The arbitrator who arranged the settlement was Gaius Caecilius. What a distinguished, scrupulous and conscientious man! Witness to the sealing was Gaius Sextilius, the son of Lurco's sister, a man of honour, reliable and responsible.[c] If there was violence, fraud, intimidation, cheating, who forced the agreement or compelled them to sanction it? Again, if all that money has been handed over to this youth Lucius Flaccus, if it was claimed and collected with the help of this Antiochus, the freedman of this young man's father, a man highly regarded by the elder Flaccus, are we not adding praise for exceptional liberality to the

singularem ? Communem enim hereditatem, quae
aequaliter ad utrumque lege venisset, concessit
adulescenti propinquo suo, nihil ipse attigit de
Valerianis bonis. Quod statuerat facere adductus
huius pudore et non amplissimis patrimoni copiis,
id non solum fecit sed etiam prolixe cumulateque
fecit. Ex quo intellegi debet eum contra leges
pecunias non cepisse qui tam fuerit in hereditate
concedenda liberalis.

90 At Falcidianum crimen est ingens ; talenta quinquaginta se Flacco dicit dedisse. Audiamus hominem. Non adest. Quo modo igitur dicit ? Epistulam mater eius profert et alteram soror; scriptum ad
se dicunt esse ab illo tantam pecuniam Flacco datam.
Ergo is cui,[1] si aram tenens iuraret, crederet nemo,
per epistulam quod volet iniuratus probabit ? At qui
vir ! quam non amicus suis civibus ! qui patrimonium
satis lautum, quod hic nobiscum conficere potuit,
91 Graecorum conviviis maluit dissipare. Quid attinuit
relinquere hanc urbem, libertate tam praeclara carere,
adire periculum navigandi ? quasi bona comesse
Romae non liceret. Nunc denique materculae suae
festivus filius, aniculae minime suspiciosae, purgat se
per epistulam, ut eam pecuniam quacum traicerat
non consumpsisse, sed Flacco dedisse videatur. At
fructus isti Trallianorum Globulo praetore venierant;
Falcidius emerat HS nongentis milibus. Si dat tan-

---

[1] cui *k, Graevius.* qui *the other* mss.

---

[a] A contract for the collection of local taxes, since governors
had power to review local contracts, but could not revise
contracts let by the censors at Rome.

dismissal of the charge of rapacity ? He renounced to his young relative a joint inheritance to which they had an equal claim in law and touched nothing himself from the estate of the Valerii. What he had decided to do, prompted by the good character of this young man and by the modest size of the inheritance, he not only did but he did it freely and generously. The renunciation of an inheritance with such liberality ought to show that a man did not take sums of money illegally.

Falcidius' charge, however, is serious. He says 90 that he gave Flaccus fifty talents. Let us hear the man. He isn't here. How does he tell us his story, then ? His mother produces a letter and his sister another, they say that he wrote to them that this huge sum of money had been given by him to Flaccus. Are you going to accept as proof of his story the unsworn testimony of a letter ? Even if he took the oath with his hand on an altar, no one would believe him. But what a man ! What a poor friend to his fellow-citizens ! He preferred to squander on dinners for Greeks the sizeable patrimony which he could have consumed here with us. What was the advan- 91 tage in leaving this city, in being parted from our glorious liberty or in facing the danger of a voyage ? As if he could not devour his substance at Rome ! Now this gay blade of a son at last clears himself in a written letter to his poor mother, a dear old lady who is quite unsuspecting, to make her think that he has not squandered the money which he had taken to Asia with him but has given it to Flaccus. But those tithes of Tralles had been up for sale when Globulus was praetor.[a] Falcidius had bought them for 900,000 sesterces. If he pays such a large sum to

tam pecuniam Flacco, nempe idcirco dat ut rata sit
emptio. Emit igitur aliquid quod certe multo pluris
esset ; dat de lucro, nihil detrahit de vivo. Minus
92 igitur lucri facit[1] ; cur Albanum venire iubet ? Cur
matri praeterea blanditur, cur epistulis et sororis et
matris imbecillitatem aucupatur, postremo cur non
audimus ipsum ? Retinetur, credo, in provincia.
Mater negat. " Venisset," inquit, " si esset de-
nuntiatum." Tu certe coegisses, si ullum firma-
mentum in illo teste posuisses ; sed hominem a
negotio abducere noluisti. Magnum erat ei certamen
propositum, magna cum Graecis contentio ; qui
tamen, ut opinor, iacent victi. Nam iste unus totam
Asiam magnitudine poculorum bibendoque superavit. Sed tamen quis tibi, Laeli, de epistulis istis
indicavit ? Mulieres negant se scire qui sit.[2] Ipse
igitur ille tibi se ad matrem et sororem scripsisse
93 narravit ? An etiam scripsit oratu tuo ? At vero M.
Aebutium, constantissimum et pudentissimum hominem, Falcidi adfinem, nihil interrogas, nihil eius
generum pari fide praeditum, C. Manilium ? qui profecto de tanta pecunia, si esset data, nihil audisse non
possent. His tu igitur epistulis, Deciane, recitatis,
his mulierculis productis, illo absente auctore laudato
tantum te crimen probaturum putasti, praesertim cum

---

[1] Minus . . . facit *deleted by Kayser, whom Clark follows.*
[2] qui sit *Clark.* quis is Σb^1. quis *the other* MSS. Quis is est
igitur ? Ipse ille *Orelli.* Ipse igitur ille Σb. is est igitur ?
Ille $\chi\varsigma$.

---

[a] What happened is not clear and it very much looks as if
Cicero is deliberately obscuring the situation by giving the
two sums in different currencies. It may have been that
Falcidius purchased the contract for 900,000 sesterces ($37\frac{1}{2}$
talents), but Flaccus annulled the contract and made Falcidius
buy it again at a higher price. Cicero alleges that the 50

Flaccus, it is only to secure the purchase. He is buying something, then, which would certainly be worth much more ; he pays out of income and does not draw upon his capital. His income, therefore, is smaller; but why does he order the sale of his Alban estate ? [a] Why, moreover, does he cajole his mother, 92 why does he prey in his letters upon the weakness of his sister and mother, and finally, why do we not hear him in person ? He is presumably detained in the province. His mother denies it. " He would have come," she says, " if a summons had been sent." You certainly would have compelled him to attend, if you had placed any reliance upon his evidence ; but you did not want to take the man away from his business. He had a hard fight and keen contest with the Greeks ahead of him, but I understand that they lie vanquished. Unaided, he defeated the whole of Asia in a drinking contest. But who told you about these letters, Laelius ? The women say that they do not know who it is. Did he tell you himself that he had written to his mother and sister ? Or did he even write at your request ? But are you not questioning 93 a man of Marcus Aebutius' reliability and sense of honour, a relative of Falcidius, and his equally trust-worthy son-in-law, Gaius Manilius ? These men surely could not fail to have heard about the payment of such a large sum of money. Did you then think, Decianus, that you would substantiate as serious a charge as this by reading out these letters, by producing these poor women, or by your eulogy of the absent writer ? It is highly unlikely ; for in failing to

talents was to ratify a purchase which was worth much more and that Falcidius could therefore pay the sum out of income without the need to sell his Alban estate.

ipse non deducendo Falcidium iudicium feceris plus
falsam epistulam habituram ponderis quam ipsius
praesentis fictam vocem et simulatum dolorem ?

94   Sed quid ego de epistulis Falcidi aut de Androne
Sextilio aut de Deciani censu tam diu disputo,[1] de
salute omnium nostrum, de fortunis civitatis, de
summa re publica taceo ? quam vos universam in hoc
iudicio vestris, vestris inquam, umeris, iudices, susti-
netis.   Videtis quo in motu temporum, quanta in
conversione rerum ac perturbatione versemur.   Cum
alia multa certi homines, tum hoc vel maxime moliuntur ut vestrae quoque mentes, vestra iudicia,
vestrae sententiae optimo cuique infestissimae atque inimicissimae reperiantur.   Gravia iudicia pro rei
publicae dignitate multa de coniuratorum scelere
fecistis.   Non putant satis conversam rem publicam,
nisi in eandem impiorum poenam optime meritos ci-
95 vis detruserint.   Oppressus est C. Antonius.   Esto ;
habuit quandam ille infamiam suam ; neque tamen
ille ipse, pro meo iure dico, vobis iudicibus damnatus
esset, cuius damnatione sepulcrum L. Catilinae flo-
ribus ornatum hominum audacissimorum ac domesticorum hostium conventu epulisque celebratum est.
Iusta Catilinae facta sunt ; nunc a Flacco Lentuli poenae per vos expetuntur.   Quam potestis P. Lentulo, qui vos in complexu liberorum coniugumque
vestrarum trucidatos incendio patriae sepelire cona-

----

[1] disputo *Faernus.* disputo. postulo χk. disputo (et
added by Σ^2) postulo *the other* MSS. disputo et expostulo *the*
MSS. *of Lambinus.*

----

[a] In the series of trials following Catiline's defeat and
death.   [b] See p. xxxvi.   [c] See pp. 12 and 21-23.

produce Falcidius you have given your judgement
that a forged letter will carry more weight than the
hypocritical words and feigned grief of Falcidius in
person.

Why do I spend so long discussing Falcidius' 94
letters, Sextilius Andro or Decianus' census-return,
when about the safety of all of us, the fortunes of the
citizen-body, the supreme welfare of the State I am
silent ? In this trial, gentlemen, you are carrying
it in its entirety upon your own, your very own
shoulders. You see in what times of revolution, in
what upheaval and turmoil we are living. Certain
men have a host of schemes afoot but their especial
aim is that your opinions too, your verdicts and your
votes should prove bitterly hostile to all the best
citizens. You have brought in many adverse verdicts
upon the crime of the conspirators and the Republic
deserved to have them.[a] They do not think that the
Republic has been effectively subverted until they
have dispossessed the citizens who have served her
best with the same punishment as that of those
traitors. Gaius Antonius has fallen victim.[b] No 95
matter ; he did have a certain ill-repute of his own ;
even so he would not have been convicted, had you
been his jurors—I say it and I have a right to say it.
On the day of his condemnation the tomb of Lucius
Catilina was decorated with flowers and was the
scene of a meeting and banquet of reckless desperados
and traitors to their country. Funeral rites were
performed for Catiline ; an attempt is now being made
to use you for visiting Lentulus' punishment upon
Flaccus. What sacrifice can you offer more welcome
to Publius Lentulus,[c] who tried to slay you in the
embraces of your wives and children and to bury you

CICERO

tus est, mactare victimam gratiorem quam si L. Flacci sanguine illius nefarium in vos[1] omnis odium satura-
96 veritis ? Litemus igitur Lentulo, parentemus Cethego, revocemus eiectos ; nimiae pietatis et summi amoris in patriam vicissim nos poenas, si ita placet, sufferamus. Nos iam ab indicibus nominamur, in nos crimina finguntur, nobis pericula comparantur. Quae si per alios agerent, si denique per populi nomen civium imperitorum multitudinem concitassent, aequiore animo ferre possemus ; illud vero ferri non potest, quod per senatores et per equites Romanos, qui haec omnia pro salute omnium communi consilio, una mente atque virtute gesserunt, harum rerum auctores, duces, principes spoliari omnibus fortunis atque civitate expelli posse arbitrantur. Etenim populi Romani perspiciunt eandem[2] mentem et voluntatem ; omnibus rebus quibus potest populus Romanus significat quid sentiat ; nulla varietas est inter homines
97 opinionis, nulla voluntatis, nulla sermonis. Qua re, si quis illuc me vocat, venio ; populum Romanum disceptatorem non modo non recuso sed etiam deposco. Vis absit, ferrum ac lapides removeantur, operae facessant, servitia sileant ; nemo erit tam iniustus qui me audierit, sit modo liber et civis, quin potius de praemiis meis quam de poena cogitandum putet.

O di immortales ! quid hoc miserius ? Nos qui P. Lentulo ferrum et flammam de manibus extorsimus, imperitae multitudinis iudicio confidimus, lectissimorum civium et amplissimorum sententias

---

[1] vos *editiones Veneta et Romana.* nos Σb^1. *Omitted by the other* MSS.

[2] eandem *Gulielmius.* eam (*omitted by* b^1) MSS. iam *Naugerius* (2).

---

[a] See pp. 430 and 438-440.

in the holocaust of your fatherland, than the sating of his evil hatred of us all with the blood of Lucius Flaccus ? Let us appease Lentulus, then, let us atone 96 for Cethegus, let us recall the exiled ; let us in our turn, if you wish, pay the penalty for an excess of devotion and a deep affection for our fatherland. We are now being named by informers, accusations are being forged against us, trials are being prepared for us.ᵃ If they were using others for these activities, even if they had roused the mob of ignorant citizens using the name of the people, we could bear it with greater equanimity ; but it is intolerable that they should believe that senators and Roman knights, whose single-minded valour united them in all these actions for our common safety, can despoil of all their fortunes and banish from the State the prime movers, leaders and principals in these events. They see that the spirit and will of the Roman people have not changed. The Roman people shows what it feels in every way it can ; men are unanimous in what they think, in what they want and in what they say. It is 97 for this reason that, if anyone calls me there, I come ; far from refusing to have the Roman people as arbitrator, I demand them. Let there be no violence —away with the swords and stones—let the hired gangs withdraw, let the slaves remain silent. No one who hears me, provided that he is a free man and a citizen, will be so unjust as not to think that I deserve reward rather than punishment.

Immortal gods ! What could be worse than this ? Are we, who tore the sword and the brand from the hands of Publius Lentulus and trusted the judgement of the ignorant crowd, afraid of the votes of the cream of our citizens and our most distinguished men ?

98 pertimescimus ! M'. Aquilium patres nostri multis
avaritiae criminibus testimoniisque convictum, quia
cum fugitivis fortiter bellum gesserat, iudicio li-
beraverunt. Consul ego nuper defendi C. Pisonem ;
qui, quia consul fortis constansque fuerat, incolumis
est rei publicae conservatus. Defendi item consul
L. Murenam, consulem designatum. Nemo illorum
iudicum clarissimis viris accusantibus audiendum sibi
de ambitu putavit, cum bellum iam gerente Catilina
omnes me auctore duos consules Kalendis Ianuariis
scirent esse oportere. Innocens et bonus vir et
omnibus rebus ornatus bis hoc anno me defendente
absolutus est, A. Thermus. Quanta rei publicae
causa laetitia populi Romani, quanta gratulatio consecuta est ! Semper graves et sapientes iudices in
rebus iudicandis quid utilitas civitatis, quid communis
salus, quid rei publicae tempora poscerent, cogita-
99 verunt. Cum tabella vobis dabitur, iudices, non de
Flacco dabitur solum, dabitur de ducibus auctori-
busque conservandae civitatis, dabitur de omnibus
bonis civibus, dabitur de vobismet ipsis, dabitur de
liberis vestris, de vita, de patria, de salute communi.
Non iudicatis in hac causa de exteris nationibus, non
de sociis ; de vobis atque de vestra re publica iudicatis.
100 Quod si provinciarum vos ratio magis movet quam
vestra, ego vero non modo non recuso sed etiam
postulo ut provinciarum auctoritate movemini.

---

[a] Consul in 101. He was tried for extortion and although
his guilt was acknowledged he was acquitted because of his
bravery in the Sicilian Slave War of 101. This was exploited
in dramatic fashion by his counsel, Marcus Antonius, who
displayed to the court the scars that the defendant had
received in battle. He later became notorious for his grue-
some death at the hands of Mithridates, who forced him to
swallow molten gold.   [b] See p. xxvii.   [c] See pp. 167-299.

Our ancestors discharged Manius Aquilius [a] who had 98
been proved guilty by a succession of witnesses on
numerous charges of extortion because he had
prosecuted with such energy the war against runaway
slaves. Recently, when I was consul, I defended
Gaius Piso [b] and because he had been a stout and
steadfast consul he was kept safe for the Republic.
In the same year I also defended Lucius Murena,
the consul-designate.[c] Even though his prosecutors
were men of distinction, not one member of that jury
thought that he should listen to a charge of electoral
corruption; for Catiline was already in the field and
I ensured that they all realized that two consuls were
required on the 1st of January. Aulus Thermus,[d] an
innocent and virtuous man, distinguished in every
way, was twice this year defended by me and acquitted. What pleasure the Roman people felt for
the Republic's sake, what rejoicing followed! In
reaching their decisions responsible and intelligent
jurors have always considered what the interests of
the citizens, the common safety and the circumstances
of the body-politic required. When the ballot is 99
given to you, gentlemen, it will not only be a ballot
to vote upon Flaccus, but also one to vote upon the
leaders and authors of the national safety, upon all
loyal citizens, upon your very selves, upon your
children, upon your lives, upon your fatherland and
upon the safety of us all. You are not giving your
verdict in this case upon the fate of foreign nations,
nor upon that of allies; you are giving it upon yourselves and your own country. If, however, the 100
provinces' judgement sways you more than your own,
far from objecting, I demand that you be swayed by

[d] We know nothing of the circumstances of these cases.

Etenim opponemus Asiae provinciae primum magnam partem eiusdem provinciae quae pro huius periculis legatos laudatoresque misit, deinde provinciam Galliam, provinciam Ciliciam, provinciam Hispaniam, provinciam Cretam; Graecis autem Lydis et Phrygibus et Mysis obsistent Massilienses, Rhodii, Lacedaemonii, Athenienses, cuncta Achaia, Thessalia, Boeotia; Septimio et Caelio testibus P. Servilius et Q. Metellus huius pudoris integritatisque testes repugnabunt; Asiaticae iuris dictioni urbana iuris dictio respondebit; annui temporis criminationem omnis aetas L. Flacci et perpetua vita defendet.

101 Et, si prodesse L. Flacco, iudices, debet, quod se tribunum militum, quod quaestorem, quod legatum imperatoribus clarissimis, exercitibus ornatissimis, provinciis gravissimis dignum suis maioribus praestitit, prosit quod hic vobis videntibus in periculis communibus omnium nostrum sua pericula cum meis coniunxit, prosint honestissimorum municipiorum coloniarumque laudationes, prosit etiam senatus

102 populique Romani praeclara et vera laudatio. O nox illa quae paene aeternas huic urbi tenebras attulisti, cum Galli ad bellum, Catilina ad urbem, coniurati ad ferrum et flammam vocabantur, cum ego te, Flacce, caelum noctemque contestans flens flentem obtestabar, cum tuae fidei optimae et spectatissimae salutem urbis et civium commendabam! Tu tum, Flacce, praetor communis exiti nuntios cepisti, tu inclusam in

---

^a 2nd/3rd of December.

their claim to consideration. We shall set against the province of Asia, firstly the large part of that province which has sent representatives and character-witnesses to help Flaccus at his trial; and then the provinces of Gaul, Cilicia, Spain and Crete. Against the Greeks of Lydia, Phrygia and Mysia, there will stand the Greeks of Massilia, Rhodes, Sparta, Athens, all Achaia, Thessaly and Boeotia. Publius Servilius and Quintus Metellus, witnesses to Flaccus' sense of honour and integrity, will rebut Septimius and Caelius. The administration of justice at Rome will reply to that in Asia. The whole career and entire life of Flaccus will refute a charge that only involves a single year. And, gentlemen, if it ought to be 101 counted in Lucius Flaccus' favour that he has shown himself worthy of his ancestors as military tribune, as quaestor, as lieutenant-general of élite armies in vital provinces under our most renowned com-manders-in-chief, let it also be counted in his favour that here before your own eyes amid the perils shared by us all, we two have suffered our dangers in concert. Let the eulogies of the boroughs and colonies that stand so high in our esteem, let the striking and sincere praise of the Senate and the Roman people be counted in his favour. What a night that was when 102 eternal darkness all but fell upon this city![a] The summons to war went forth to the Gauls, Catiline was marching on Rome, the conspirators were reaching for their swords and torches! There were tears in the eyes of us both as I implored you, Flaccus, in the name of heaven and of that night, and entrusted to your unquestioning and well-tried loyalty the safety of the city and its citizens. That was the night when as praetor, Flaccus, you seized the couriers bearing

litteris rei publicae pestem deprehendisti, tu periculorum indicia, tu salutis auxilia ad me et ad
senatum attulisti. Quae tibi tum gratiae sunt a me
actae, quae ab senatu, quae a bonis omnibus! Quis
tibi, quis C. Pomptino, fortissimo viro, quemquam
bonum putaret umquam non salutem verum honorem
ullum denegaturum? O Nonae illae Decembres quae
me consule fuistis! quem ego diem vere natalem
huius urbis aut certe salutarem appellare possum.
103 O nox illa quam iste est dies consecutus, fausta huic
urbi, miserum me, metuo ne funesta nobis! Qui tum
animus L. Flacci—nihil dicam enim de me—qui amor
in patriam, quae virtus, quae gravitas exstitit! Sed
quid ea commemoro quae tum cum agebantur uno
consensu omnium, una voce populi Romani, uno orbis
terrae testimonio in caelum laudibus efferebantur,
nunc vereor ne non modo non prosint verum etiam
aliquid obsint? Etenim multo acriorem improborum
interdum memoriam esse sentio quam bonorum.
Ego te, si quid gravius acciderit, ego te, inquam,
Flacce, prodidero. O mea dextera illa, mea fides,
mea promissa, cum te, si rem publicam conservaremus, omnium bonorum praesidio quoad viveres non
modo munitum sed etiam ornatum fore pollicebar.
Putavi, speravi, etiam si honos noster vobis vilior
104 fuisset, salutem certe caram futuram. Ac L. Flaccum
quidem, iudices, si, quod di immortales omen avertant, gravis iniuria adflixerit, numquam tamen

---

[a] Cf. *in Catilinam* 3. 2, p. 100 and n. *b*.

the destruction of us all, when you seized the letters containing the destruction of the Republic, when you brought the proofs of our perils and the means of our salvation to me and to the Senate. Remember the thanks that the Senate, that all loyal citizens, that I personally heaped upon you! Would it enter a man's head that any patriot would ever deny you or that brave man, Gaius Pomptinus, any honour, let alone acquittal? What a 5th of December that was in the year of my consulship! A day that I can truly call, if not the birthday of this city, at least the day of its salvation.[a] What a night it was that followed that 103 day! A night of good-fortune for Rome, but one of sorrow for me and of calamity, I fear, for us! What spirit Lucius Flaccus displayed at that time (for I shall omit all mention of myself), what love for his fatherland, what valour, what sense of responsibility! But why do I recall those deeds which the common consent of all men, the unanimous voice of the Roman people and the testimony of the whole world praised to the skies at the time? Now I fear that, far from counting in Flaccus' favour, they may do him harm. I realize that at times the memory of evil men is keener by far than that of good. It will be I who have betrayed you, Flaccus, if any greater harm befall you. Mine was the right hand, the assurance, the promises, when I undertook that if we preserved the Republic you could count for the remainder of your life upon the esteem as well as the protection of all loyal citizens. I thought, I hoped that, even if you did not think us worthy of honour, you would at least think us worthy of preservation. If, however, gentle- 104 men,—and may the immortal gods avert the omen— Lucius Flaccus does suffer any serious miscarriage of

prospexisse vestrae saluti, consuluisse vobis, liberis,
coniugibus, fortunis vestris paenitebit; semper ita
sentiet, talem se animum et generis dignitati et
pietati suae et patriae debuisse; vos ne paeniteat tali
civi non pepercisse, per deos immortalis, iudices,
providete. Quotus enim quisque est qui hanc in re
publica sectam sequatur, qui vobis, qui vestri simi-
libus placere cupiat, qui optimi atque amplissimi
cuiusque hominis atque ordinis auctoritatem magni
putet, cum[1] illam viam sibi videant expeditiorem ad
honores et ad omnia quae concupiverunt ?

Sed cetera sint eorum; sibi habeant potentiam, sibi
honores, sibi ceterorum commodorum summas facul-
tates; liceat eis qui haec salva esse voluerunt ipsis
105 esse salvis. Nolite, iudices, existimare eos quibus
integrum est, qui nondum ad honores accesserunt,
non exspectare huius exitum iudici. Si L. Flacco
tantus amor in bonos omnis, tantum in rem publicam
studium calamitati fuerit, quem posthac tam amentem
fore putatis qui non illam viam vitae quam ante
praecipitem et lubricam esse ducebat huic planae et
stabili praeponendam esse arbitretur ? Quod si
talium civium vos, iudices, taedet, ostendite; muta-
bunt sententiam qui potuerint; constituent quid agant
quibus integrum est; nos qui iam progressi sumus
hunc exitum nostrae temeritatis feremus. Sin hoc
animo quam plurimos esse voltis, declarabitis hoc
106 iudicio quid sentiatis. Huic, huic misero puero vestro

---

[1] cum *b¹k, Faernus. Omitted by the other MSS.* si sibi
Baiter.

---

[a] An attack upon the Caesarians.
[b] Flaccus' son, introduced to win the compassion of the
jury.
554

justice, even so he will never regret the foresight he displayed for your salvation and the measures he took for the well-being of yourselves, your children, your wives and your possessions. He will always feel that he owed this decision to the honour of his race, to his duty to his family and to his country; do you in the name of the immortal gods, gentlemen, see to it that you do not regret your failure to spare a citizen such as he. How many are there who follow this path in the Republic, who desire to please you and men like you, who regard highly the authority of every man and every order of standing and distinction, when they see that it offers them a shorter way to office and the fulfilment of their ambitions?

Let them have everything else.[a] Let them keep their ill-gotten power, their offices, the rich store of all their other benefits; but let those who wished Rome to be safe be safe themselves. Do not think, 105 gentlemen, that those who have not yet made up their minds, who have not yet attained office, are not awaiting the outcome of this trial. If Flaccus' affection for loyal citizens, his devotion to the Republic have been so great as to bring disaster upon him, who, do you think, will be so demented now as not to think that way of life which he previously considered steep and slippery preferable to the firm and level path that is ours? If, gentlemen, you are tired of citizens like him, show it. Those who can will change their minds; those who are not committed will decide what to do; we who have already set out on this path will accept these consequences of our foolhardiness. But if you want as many as possible to share our view, you will make your feelings clear in your decision. To this poor boy,[b] a suppliant to 106

ac liberorum vestrorum supplici, iudices, hoc iudicio
vivendi praecepta dabitis. Cui si patrem conservatis,
qualis ipse debeat esse civis praescribetis; si eripitis,
ostendetis bonae rationi et constanti et gravi nullum
a vobis fructum esse propositum. Qui vos, quoniam
est id aetatis ut sensum iam percipere possit ex
maerore patrio, auxilium nondum patri ferre possit,
orat ne suum luctum patris lacrimis, patris maerorem
suo fletu augeatis; qui etiam me intuetur, me voltu
appellat, meam quodam modo flens fidem implorat ac
repetit eam quam ego patri suo quondam pro salute
patriae spoponderim dignitatem. Misereminifamiliae,
iudices, miseremini fortissimi patris, miseremini fili;
nomen clarissimum et fortissimum vel generis vel
vetustatis vel hominis causa rei publicae reservate.

---

[a] The consulship.

you and to your children, gentlemen, you will by your decision give guidance in his way of life. If you acquit his father, you will show him by practical illustration what kind of citizen he ought to be; but if you take his father from him, you will show that you have offered no reward for a plan of life that has been virtuous, unwavering and responsible. He is now of an age to be affected by his father's grief, but not yet old enough to bring his father help, and so he begs you not to increase his grief by his father's tears nor his father's sorrow by his own weeping. He turns his eyes to me, his expression appeals to me for aid and somehow his tears call upon me to keep faith and look for that position of distinction *a* which I once promised to his father for saving our country. Have pity on his family, gentlemen, on a valiant father, have pity on the son. Whether it be for his family's sake or for his ancient lineage or for the man himself, preserve for the Republic an illustrious and gallant name.

APPENDIX A

THE *CONTIO* AND THE *COMITIA* [a]

In Cicero's time there was a clear distinction between these two bodies. The former was a public meeting which the citizens attended without being divided into their voting units of centuries or tribes, at which there might be present foreigners, slaves or women, and at which those present were not asked to vote; the latter was an assembly at which the citizen body of men only was divided into its voting groups and asked to vote upon any matter—electoral, legislative or judicial—that was put before it.

The *contio* was summoned by a dictator, consul, or, if both consuls were absent, by the urban praetor as an essential preliminary to the voting assemblies. If the assembly was meeting to elect magistrates, the only business of the *contio* was to give any necessary directions to the voters; but legislative and judicial assemblies were always preceded by meetings at which speeches explained the business in hand. A further purpose of the *contio* was for a magistrate to inform the people of matters of general interest, to warn them of dangers or to reprove them for depart-

[a] See L. R. Taylor, *Roman Voting Assemblies*, especially 15-33 for the *contio*, 84-106 for the *comitia centuriata*, 59-83 for the *comitia tributa*; and E. S. Staveley, *Greek and Roman Voting Assemblies* 121-235.

ing from the practices of their ancestors. Seven
orations of Cicero are the only extant examples of
speeches made in *contiones* [a] and of these the two
appearing in this volume—the second and third
against Catiline—are excellent examples of the
consul performing his duty of keeping the people
informed of events or warning them of danger to the
State.

The lower magistrates could only call meetings
concerning matters connected with their own office,
but the tribunes also had the right to summon
meetings and exercised it with great frequency as
they became responsible for much of the legislation at
Rome. There was little to distinguish a *contio* called
by a tribune from that summoned by a regular
magistrate except that a magistrate could speak only
from a platform that was augurally consecrated
ground, while no such restriction was laid upon a
tribune. Most *contiones* were held in the Comitium
and Forum, though a site in the Campus Martius
was also used for meetings preceding elections, and
the Circus Flaminius was frequently employed by
tribunes.

The part played by the audience at these meetings
was by no means passive and in a passage in the *pro
Flacco* [b] Cicero complains of the growing disorder
which made them more like the meetings or assemblies of the Greeks. [c] The disorders of Greek meetings were for some reason attributed by him to the
fact that the Greeks held their meetings seated in

---

[a] The Latin word *contio* means either the public meeting
or a speech made at it.   [b] 15-17, pp. 458-460.
[c] The Greeks had no distinction such as that beween the
contio and the *comitia*.

theatres and that men accustomed to the Greek practice had brought the resulting disorderly conduct with them to Rome.[a]

Although it is true that the urban proletariat by this time contained a considerable number of men to whom Roman traditions were alien, Cicero is exaggerating their influence when he attributes the growing violence of the times to the behaviour of Greeks in the *contiones*.

In the assemblies, both centuriate and tribal, the votes of groups, not of individuals, decided the matter in hand. This principle of voting in groups probably had its origin in the peculiar structure of early Roman society, but it persisted owing to the ease with which it could be made to serve the interests of a single group without violating the principle of full adult male suffrage.

The *comitia centuriata* was the assembly of the whole citizen body in its military organization of one hundred and ninety-three centuries and was believed to have been established by Servius Tullius, one of the kings of Rome. It was open to all citizens and was presided over with auspices by a consul or praetor or, if there were no consuls at the beginning of a year, by an *interrex* for the purpose of holding consular elections. In addition to its function of electing consuls, praetors and censors, it had once been the chief legislative body of the State and performed the judicial function of dealing with capital charges. After 218 it acted only rarely in its legislative capacity except to declare war and to confirm the power of the censors, and from the time of the Gracchi

[a] The Romans always stood at their meetings and assemblies.

onwards it acted as a court mainly to deal with charges of *perduellio*, the ancient form of treason. It met outside the *pomerium*, nearly always in the Campus Martius. It could not meet within the city boundary because the voters were regarded as soldiers, and no command could be given to troops inside the *pomerium*.

The composition of the one hundred and ninety-three centuries reflects that of the Roman army. There were eighteen centuries of *equites equo publico*, men who served as cavalry, of which six were formed from the ancient clan tribes of Romulus—Tities, Ramnes, and Luceres; known as the *sex suffragia*—and twelve more added to them by Servius Tullius. Secondly, there were one hundred and seventy centuries of *pedites*, the infantry who formed the bulk of the army. Their strength was divided into an equal number of centuries of *iuniores*, aged from seventeen to forty-six and liable for active service, and of *seniores*, aged from forty-six to sixty, fewer in numbers and liable only for home defence. They were also divided into five classes according to their property as assessed in the census. Thirdly, there were five unarmed centuries of which one comprised men who had no property or so little that it was not counted.

The further details of the assembly as organized by Servius Tullius need not detain us because at some date between 241 and 220 it was reorganized and, we are told, made more democratic. The centuries of the *pedites* became divisions of the thirty-five local tribes in which the census for allocation to classes was taken, and various other changes were made.

The reformed assembly voted in the following way.

APPENDIX A

There first voted a *centuria praerogativa*, a century chosen by lot, probably from the *iuniores* of the first class, and its vote was counted and announced before the remainder of the first class voted. The result of this century's vote had a telling effect upon elections because the Roman voters had the superstitious feeling that the man it chose was blessed by Heaven and that its vote was an omen for the outcome of the elections.[a] There then followed the vote and announcement of the result of the first class consisting of thirty-four *iuniores*, thirty-five *seniores*, twelve *equites*, and one of the unarmed centuries, then that of the *sex suffragia*, then successively that of the remaining four classes, consisting of one hundred centuries of *pedites* and four unarmed centuries. The divisions within these classes are not known, but the four unarmed centuries probably voted with the fifth class.

The vote of each century was announced before the next voted and the second class would often produce the decisive vote. As soon as a candidate secured a majority, he was declared elected. The Romans attached great importance both to priority of announcement[b] which could bring, in addition to the enhanced prestige, practical advantages, and to a favourable vote from all the centuries until a majority was obtained.[c] The complicated procedure of the

[a] *pro Murena* 38, p. 236. In 54 two of the consular candidates thought the influence of its vote worth 10,000,000 sesterces; see *ad Quintum fratrem* 2. 15. 4. The original intention of the practice was possibly to ensure a quick and decisive result to elections as numbers of candidates increased in the third century. [b] *pro Murena* 18, p. 206 and n. *c*.

[c] *pro Sulla* 91, p. 404. In his speech *de imperio Cn. Pompei* 2 Cicero proudly records that he was elected praetor by all the centuries three times in succession.

comitia lasted for many hours and, if the voting was not completed by sunset, it had to be continued on the next *dies comitialis* or day on which the calendar permitted *comitia* to be held.[a]

It has been said that the third-century reform of the centuriate assembly made it more democratic, but even after this reform had taken place it was still true of the assembly that the well-to-do mustered a voting strength disproportionate to their numbers. The voting units containing the wealthier citizens had a smaller complement than the rest, they were themselves more numerous and they voted before the others. Additional reforms were periodically mooted but nothing came of them.[b] The heavy weighting of votes in favour of the first class (eighty-two out of one hundred and ninety-three), the effect of the vote of the *centuria praerogativa* and the announcement of the vote of the first class before the second and subsequent classes had voted assured the timocratic nature of the assembly. It was theoretically possible to be elected by only a quarter of the total number of individual voters. A majority in ninety-seven out of a hundred and ninety-three centuries or eighteen of the thirty-five tribes could secure victory without a single vote in the remaining groups.

In the *comitia tributa*, also open to all citizens and presided over with auspices by a consul, praetor, or, in its judicial function, by a curule aedile, the people elected the curule aediles, quaestors and various

---

[a] See *pro Murena* 35, p. 232 for the possible effects of such interruptions. E. S. Staveley, *op. cit.* 189, estimates that the minimum time necessary for the election of a college of two was 6½ hours and the maximum 14½ hours. For a college of eight the figures are 8½ and 24½ hours respectively.

[b] *Cf. pro Murena* 47, p. 247 and n. *c*.

lower officers, passed any legislation that was not restricted to the *comitia centuriata* and sat in judgement upon any crime against the State punishable by no more than a fine.

The tribes which were the voting divisions in this assembly and from which it took its name were the four urban and thirty-one rural tribes to one of which every citizen belonged by virtue either of his place of residence or of the locality in which he owned property. Within the tribe, unlike the centuries with their group voting in units formed by division into census classes and age groups, each man had a vote of equal value.

The tribes appear to have voted simultaneously in elections and successively at legislative and judicial assemblies. After the votes had been counted, the results giving the candidates chosen by each tribe were announced, and as any man obtained a majority he was declared elected. As soon as the required number of places had been filled by those returned by a majority of the tribes, the assembly was dismissed without further announcement. As in the *comitia centuriata*, if the voting was not completed by sunset, it continued, usually on the next comitial day, and again great importance was attached by the Romans to priority of announcement and to being elected by all the tribes.

Finally, there was the *concilium plebis* which, although often called the *comitia tributa*, was strictly speaking not an assembly of the Roman people at all, because it was only attended by plebeians. It met without auspices under the presidency of a tribune or aedile of the plebs to elect tribunes and plebeian aediles, to pass legislation proposed by the tribunes

which were technically *plebiscita* but had the validity of *leges* since the *lex Hortensia* of 287, or to perform a judicial function similar to that of the *comitia tributa* but presided over by tribunes. There was, indeed, little difference between these two bodies apart from the fact that the former was composed of plebeians only while the latter was not so restricted, and from the office held by the presiding official.

APPENDIX B

THE *SENATUS CONSULTUM ULTIMUM* [a]

Any society, if it is to survive, must provide itself with adequate means of protection against both internal and external enemies. In the modern world the military forces of a State protect it from attack from without, while the police force is designed to deal with attempts to destroy it from within. In countries subject to the rule of law the size and nature of the police force and the way in which it conducts itself are regulated by law. Efforts to bring the enemies of society to justice are restricted by law to what society feels necessary for its preservation against those who would destroy it. Should, however, a situation arise in which a society's provisions prove inadequate to deal with an assault upon it, then there is no reason why society should acquiesce in its own destruction and not have recourse to exceptional measures to ensure its survival.

Whether these exceptional measures are legal or

[a] This title is commonly given to the *senatus consultum de republica defendenda* and derives from its use by Caesar, *de bello civili* 1. 5. 3. For the subject matter of this Appendix, see in particular H. Last in the *Cambridge Ancient History* ix. 82 f. and the *Journal of Roman Studies* 33 (1943), 94 f.; Ch. Wirszubski, *Libertas as a Political Idea During the Late Republic and Early Principate* 55 f.; A. W. Lintott, *Violence in Republican Rome* 149 f.; Th. N. Mitchell in *Historia* vol. 20 (see p. 580 below).

not depends upon the law of the State concerned. If the law provides for alternative measures when the normal procedure has proved unable to maintain law and order then these measures are legal. In Great Britain, for example, the Riot Act authorized repressive measures which were normally illegal.[a] In Rome the normal procedure against domestic enemies was the only one recognized by law. When this proves inadequate, there is a partial breakdown of the rule of law and it is meaningless, therefore, to ask whether a magistrate's actions are legal or not when this has occurred, because the criterion by which their legality may be judged no longer exists. The rightness of a magistrate's actions must now be judged by the speed with which they restore the reign of law and by the extent to which they infringe the rights of the citizen body. But more important than either of these criteria is the question: were the magistrates when they went beyond the bounds of legality justified in thinking that the danger to the community was so great that normal legal procedure was inadequate to deal with the situation?

If the constitution of a country provides for emergencies in which normal legal procedure is inadequate then the reading of the Riot Act or the

[a] Passed in 1714 and repealed in 1967, it provided that an unruly crowd, if it ignored a magistrate's warning that it must disperse within the hour, was to be regarded as felonious. It also granted the magistrates and those who assisted them in apprehending rioters a general indemnity in the event of any rioter being killed or injured. It is interesting to note that owing to uncertainty over the interpretation of its provisions the Act raised practical problems for men who sought to invoke it not dissimilar from those attending Roman magistrates relying upon the *senatus consultum ultimum*.

declaration of a State of Emergency or of Martial Law indicates that magistrates may now act in a way which would normally be illegal. But it is more difficult to say when magistrates at Rome were justified in non-legal action, because they were themselves responsible for making the decision when they could act in this way. The *senatus consultum ultimum* could only be passed after a consul had laid the matter before the Senate and had it discussed. The decree was an indication to the magistrates that the Senate felt that a situation could arise in which they might be required to ignore some of the limitations imposed by law upon their use of their *imperium* and to act in accordance with the maxim " salus rei publicae suprema lex esto." [a] It was still the magistrate's responsibility to decide when such a situation had arisen and what it justified him in doing, and those decisions were always liable to be challenged subsequently.[b] To this extent it is misleading to equate the passing of the decree with a declaration of Martial Law.

In the early Republic crises had been dealt with by the appointment of dictators, but with the growth of the Senate's powers in the third century this body viewed dictators with increasing disfavour and after 202 the dictatorship fell into a period of disuse.[c] During the second century the Senate met dangers by issuing special instructions to the regular magistrates and had done this on a number of occasions. The situation confronting it before the death of

[a] Cicero, *de legibus* 3. 8.
[b] Only in police states is he largely freed from this danger.
[c] Sulla's and subsequent dictatorships had a different purpose.

Gaius Gracchus was not so straightforward, and the Senate modified its practice to meet different circumstances. There was at the time no individual or body seeking to challenge society with force of arms, but nevertheless there was a threatening situation and the Senate tried to meet it by passing a decree urging the magistrates to defend the State. This was, of course, a normal duty of the magistrates, indeed the most important of their normal duties, and the decree therefore sought to give the executive additional backing by urging it to attend to the business for which it had been appointed.

The decree was addressed to those whom the Senate wished to take action, sometimes to both consuls, sometimes to one only and sometimes to a wider group of magistrates. Variations in its form were made to suit the situation with which it had to deal.[a] The right of the Senate to pass such a decree was never challenged, because the Senate might pass any resolution it wished provided that no veto was interposed. Although Caesar might argue that a situation did not justify the decree,[b] he never suggested that the Senate had gone beyond its powers.

The legal and political conflict that surrounded the use of this decree resulted from the vagueness of the exhortation to the magistrates, a vagueness which seriously undermined its value. The wording of the decree did not indicate to what extent there was implicit encouragement to take non-legal measures, nor to what lengths a magistrate could go in the contravention of the law.[c] The result was that

---

[a] The original form is to be found in Cicero, *Philippicae* 5. 34.   [b] *de bello civili* 1. 7. 5.
[c] This very vagueness would assist in preventing over-

opponents of action taken with the backing of the decree could indict individual magistrates for violating civil rights, while supporters pleaded interests of state and the authority of the Senate.

The right of a magistrate to decide when non-legal action was necessary and to use extraordinary measures of repression was felt to have been established by the acquittal of Lucius Opimius in 120. In the previous year Opimius had been consul and after the Senate had passed the *senatus consultum ultimum* he had executed citizens without trial in the course of crushing the supporters of Gaius Gracchus.[a] The effect of this verdict was to reassert the right of magistrates to take non-legal action with the backing of the decree after Gracchus' law of 123 had reaffirmed the right of appeal to the people in capital cases and the liability of magistrates who transgressed it to prosecution. It did not, however, establish any change in the legal position with regard to limitations upon the power of magistrates, and it was still every bit as much an infringement of the *leges de provocatione* to put a citizen to death without his first being able to exercise his right to be heard by the people.[b] Caesar's view of the way in which Cicero proposed to use the decree for the suppression of the Catilinarian conspiracy was highly critical.[c] He felt that

reaction by magistrates. If rebellion and the means of suppressing it sanctioned by law were to be too closely defined, the authorities might be tempted into an automatic harsh response when restraint and caution would have been more provident. [a] Livy, *Periocha* 61.

[b] Cicero, *de oratore* 2. 106 and 132; *de partitione oratoria* 104 f.

[c] For Caesar's attitude towards the *senatus consultum ultimum* and the purpose of the prosecution of Rabirius in 63, see p. xxviii.

summary punishment on the strength of the decree was incompatible with the Roman constitution.[a] He did not, however, maintain a consistent position because his own proposal for dealing with the conspirators, though less drastic, was just as much an infringement of citizens' rights as was Cicero's. He did not accept Cicero's assessment of the situation and the view that the conspirators were *hostes*, even though he was well aware of the dangers of adhering to strict constitutional procedure and himself held no brief for the Catilinarians. He felt that if the State resorted to unconstitutional measures in order to protect itself, a worse situation than that which it was seeking to remedy could result. If a consul could assume the power of life and death over citizens, there was nothing to stop proscriptions. The State could not afford to dispense with the established checks upon the power of magistrates or with safeguards for the civil rights of individual citizens.[b] It was not by chance that the word " regnum " was cast in Cicero's teeth by his opponents for what he had done in 63.[c]

Those who saw the decree as a means of ensuring the safety of the State in a time of civil disturbance felt that if it had been passed in appropriate circumstances two courses lay open to the magistrates. They could arm the people and lead them against citizens with the intention of killing them if they resisted efforts to bring them under control, and they could arrest them and execute them summarily or after an inquiry.

Cicero's own view was that Catiline and his fol-

---

[a] Sallust, *Bellum Catilinae* 51. 8, 17 and 41.
[b] *Ib.* 51. 25-36 ; *cf.* p. 26.
[c] *pro Sulla* 21 and 25, pp. 332 and 338.

lowers had by virtue of their actions made themselves
hostes and did not deserve to be treated as citizens.[a]
There were precedents for the Senate to name
citizens as *hostes*, and this they did to Catiline and
Manlius after Catiline had left Rome.[b] Enemies of
the Republic, however, were never named in the
decree, and the naming of *hostes* was an act which
was directed at enemies outside the city who might
constitute a military threat and quite separate from
passing the *senatus consultum ultimum*. Admittedly,
Cicero says that Catiline is a *hostis* in his first speech,[c]
but there is no mention of any official declaration,
and Catiline's presence in the Senate supports the
view that there was no such declaration at this time.

Defence of Cicero's actions subsequently could
only be made on the grounds that the crisis was so
acute that the legal procedure of accusation and trial
could not be followed without graver risks to society
than could reasonably be run by a magistrate whose
prime responsibility was society's preservation. The
crux of Cicero's action is the question : were the
Catilinarian prisoners put to death when their legal
right to a trial would endanger the State to an extent
that no magistrate could accept ? Sallust [d] says that
a plan was formed to rescue the prisoners by force
after it had been decided to keep them in custody.
Cato's reply [e] to Caesar's proposal that the prisoners
should be detained in various country towns suggests
that the possibility of their rescue was a serious
consideration during the debate and the gravity of

[a] *in Catilinam* 4. 10, p. 146.
[b] Sallust, *Bellum Catilinae* 36. 2-3.
[c] *in Catilinam* 1. 27-28, p. 60.
Bellum Catilinae 50. 1-2. [e] *Ib.* 52. 14 f.

the consequences had been stressed by Cato in an earlier passage.[a]

The fact of the matter was that during the last century of the Republic's existence the executive was on numerous occasions unable to maintain law and order without recourse to non-legal measures. The scale of the violence during this period required the concerted efforts of all magistrates to curb it, and had the *senatus consultum ultimum* set out the criteria by which the necessity for emergency measures could have been judged, the executive would have been encouraged to take stronger action to control it.

Even this would only have been a palliative. A more fundamental reason for failure to control violence was the direct conflict between the various elements in Roman society and the absence of any final arbiter between them. A strong executive was against the wishes of the ruling class and there were no officials standing above the political arena who could enforce the law impartially. The absence of such men was the main reason why republican Rome never had a police system adequate to enforce the rule of law.[b]

[a] *Bellum Catilinae*, 52. 4.
[b] P. A. Brunt, " The Roman Mob," *Past and Present* 35 (1966), 4-8, shows how certain constitutional factors favoured the growth of violence at Rome. For the effects of the absence of a garrison or police force, see Brunt, *op. cit.* 8-11 and C. Meier, *Res Publica Amissa* 157-159.

BIBLIOGRAPHY

Adcock, F. E. *Roman Political Ideas and Practice*, Ann Arbor, 1959.

Afzelius, A. " Zur Definition der römischen Nobilität in der Zeit Ciceros," *Classica et Mediaevalia* 1 (1938), 40-94.

" Zur Definition der römischen Nobilität vor der Zeit Ciceros," *Classica et Mediaevalia* 7 (1945), 150-200.

Allen, W., Jr. " Cicero's Governorship in 63 B.C.," *Transactions of the American Philological Association* 83 (1952), 233-241.

" The Acting Governor of Cisalpine Gaul in 63 B.C.," *Classical Philology* 48 (1953), 176-177.

" Cicero's Conceit," *Transactions of the American Philological Association* 85 (1954), 121-144.

Asconius Pedianus, Q. *Orationum Ciceronis quinque enarratio Ed.* A. C. Clark, Oxford, 1907.

Austin, R. G. *Ed.* Cicero : *pro Caelio* 3rd ed., Oxford, 1960.

Badian, E. " Notes on Provincial Governors from the Social War down to Sulla's Victory," *Proceedings of the African Classical Associations* (1958), 1-18. Reprinted in *Studies in Greek and Roman History*, Oxford, 1964.

" The Early Career of A. Gabinius (*cos.* 58 B.C.)," *Philologus* 103 (1959), 87-99.

" Caesar's *cursus* and the Intervals between Offices," *Journal of Roman Studies* 49 (1959), 81-89.

Roman Imperialism in the Late Republic 2nd ed., Oxford, 1968.

Publicans and Sinners, Oxford, 1972.

CICERO

Bailey, D. R. Shackleton. *Cicero's Letters to Atticus* 7 vols., Cambridge, 1964–1970.

Cicero, London, 1971.

Balsdon, J. P. V. D. " The History of the Extortion Court at Rome, 123–70 B.C.," *Papers of the British School at Rome* 14 (1938), 98-114. Reprinted in *The Crisis of the Roman Republic Ed.* R. Seager, Cambridge, 1969.

" *Auctoritas, Dignitas, Otium*," *Classical Quarterly* 10 (1960), 43-50.

" Roman History, 65–50 B.C. : Five Problems," *Journal of Roman Studies* 52 (1962), 134-141.

Boissier, G. *La Conjuration de Catilina* 7th ed., Paris, 1939.

Boulanger, A. " La Publication du *pro Murena*," *Revue des Études anciennes* 42 (1940), 382-387.

Broughton, T. R. S. *Roman Asia in An Economic Survey of Ancient Rome Ed.* Tenney Frank, Baltimore, 1938, 4. 499-916.

The Magistrates of the Roman Republic 2 vols., New York, 1951–1952 ; *Supplement*, New York, 1960.

Brunt, P. A. " Sulla and the Asian Publicans," *Latomus* 15 (1956), 17-25.

" Three Passages from Asconius," *Classical Review* 7 (1957), 193-195.

" The Equites in the Late Republic," *Second International Conference of Economic History*, Aix-en-Provence, 1962, vol. 1, *Trade and Politics in the Ancient World* 117-149. Reprinted in *The Crisis of the Roman Republic Ed.* R. Seager, Cambridge, 1969.

" The Army and the Land in the Roman Revolution," *Journal of Roman Studies* 52 (1962), 69-86.

" ' Amicitia ' in the Late Republic," *Proceedings of the Cambridge Philological Society* 11 (1965), 1-20. Reprinted in *The Crisis of the Roman Republic Ed.* R. Seager, Cambridge, 1969.

BIBLIOGRAPHY

"The Roman Mob," *Past and Present* 35 (1966), 3-27.

Italian Manpower 225 B.C.-A.D. 14, Oxford, 1971.

Cambridge Ancient History Ed. S. A. Cook, F. E. Adcock, and M. P. Charlesworth, vol. 9, Cambridge, 1932.

Cary, M. and Scullard, H. H. *A History of Rome*, London, 1975.

Corbett, P. E. *The Roman Law of Marriage*, Oxford, 1930.

Cousin, J. "Lex Lutatia de vi," *Revue historique de Droit français et étranger* 22 (1943), 88-94.

Crane, T. "Times of the Night in Cicero's First Catilinarian," *Classical Journal* 61 (1965-66), 264-267.

Criniti, N. *Bibliografia Catilinaria*, Milan, 1971.

Dorey, T. A. Ed. *Cicero*, London, 1964.

Drumann-Groebe. *Geschichte Roms* 6 vols., 2nd ed., Berlin and Leipzig, 1899-1929.

Earl, D. C. *The Political Thought of Sallust*, Cambridge, 1961.

The Moral and Political Tradition of Rome, London, 1967.

Frederiksen, M. W. "Caesar, Cicero and the Problem of Debt," *Journal of Roman Studies* 56 (1966), 128-141.

Frisch, H. "The First Catilinarian Conspiracy," *Classica et Mediaevalia* 9 (1947), 10-36.

Fuchs, H. "Eine Doppelfassung in Ciceros Catilinarischen Reden," *Hermes* 87 (1959), 463-469.

Gabba, E. "Cicerone e la falsificazione dei senatoconsulti," *Studi Classice e Orientali* 10 (1961), 89-96.

Gelzer, M. *Die Nobilität der römischen Republik*, Leipzig-Berlin, 1912. Reprinted in *Kleine Schriften* 1, Wiesbaden, 1962. English translation by R. Seager, *The Roman Nobility*, Oxford, 1969.

Caesar, der Politiker und Staatsman 6th ed., Wiesbaden, 1960. English translation by P. Needham, *Caesar, Politician and Statesman*, Oxford, 1968.

Cicero ; ein biographischer Versuch, Wiesbaden, 1969.

Greenidge, A. H. J. *Roman Public Life*, London, 1901.

The Legal Procedure of Cicero's Time, London, 1901.

and Clay, A. M. *Sources for Roman History 133-70 B.C.* 2nd ed. revised by E. W. Gray, Oxford, 1961.

CICERO

Griffin, M. "The Tribune C. Cornelius," *Journal of Roman Studies* 63 (1973), 196-213.

Gruen, E. S. *Roman Politics and the Criminal Courts 149-78 B.C.*, Harvard, 1968.

"Pompey, the Roman Aristocracy, and the Conference of Luca," *Historia* 18 (1969), 71-108.

"Notes on the 'First Catilinarian Conspiracy,'" *Classical Philology* 64 (1969), 20-24.

"Some Criminal Trials of the Late Republic : Political and Prosopographical Problems," *Athenaeum* 49 (1971), 54-69.

The Last Generation of the Roman Republic, Berkeley, 1974.

Gwatkin, W. E., Jr. "Cicero *in Catilinam* 1. 19," *Transactions of the American Philological Association* 65 (1934), 271-281.

Hall, U. "Voting Procedure in Roman Assemblies," *Historia* 13 (1964), 267-306.

Hardy, E. G. "A Catilinarian Date," *Journal of Roman Studies* 6 (1916), 56-58.

"The Catilinarian Conspiracy in its Context : a Re-Study of the Evidence," *Journal of Roman Studies* 7 (1917), 153-228. Reprinted as *The Catilinarian Conspiracy*, Oxford, 1924.

Some Problems in Roman History, Oxford, 1924.

Haskell, H. J. *This was Cicero : Modern Politics in a Roman Toga*, New York, 1942 ; London [1943].

Hatzfeld, J., "Les Italiens résidant à Délos," *Bulletin de Correspondance hellénique* 36 (1912), 5-21.

Les Trafiquants italiens dans l'Orient hellénique, Paris, 1919.

Hawthorn, J. R. "The Senate after Sulla," *Greece and Rome* 9 (1962), 53-60.

Heitland, W. *The Roman Republic* vol. 3, Cambridge, 1909.

Hellegouarc'h, J. *Le Vocabulaire latin des relations et des partis politiques sous la République*, Paris, 1963.

BIBLIOGRAPHY

Henderson, M. I. " *De commentariolo petitionis*," *Journal of Roman Studies* 40 (1950), 8-21.

" The Process *de repetundis*," *Journal of Roman Studies* 41 (1951), 71-88.

" The Establishment of the *Equester Ordo*," *Journal of Roman Studies* 53 (1963), 61-72. Reprinted in *The Crisis of the Roman Republic* Ed. R. Seager, Cambridge, 1969.

Hill, H. *The Roman Middle Class in the Republican Period*, Oxford, 1952.

Hoffmann, W. " Catilina und die römische Revolution," *Gymnasium* 66 (1959), 459-477.

Holmes, T. Rice. *The Roman Republic and the Founder of the Empire* vol. 1, Oxford, 1923.

Hough, J. N. " The *lex Lutatia* and the *lex Plautia de vi*," *American Journal of Philology* 51 (1930), 135-147.

How, W. W. and Clark, A. C. *Cicero : Select Letters* 2 vols., Oxford, 1925–1926.

Humbert, J. *Les Plaidoyers écrits et les plaidoiries réelles de Cicéron*, Paris, 1925.

Jones, A. H. M. " The Roman Civil Service (Clerical and Sub-clerical Grades)," *Journal of Roman Studies* 39 (1949), 38-55. Reprinted in *Studies in Roman Government and Law*, Oxford, 1960.

The Cities of the Eastern Roman Provinces 2nd ed., Oxford, 1971.

Kinsey, T. E. " Cicero, *pro Murena* 71," *Revue belge de Philologie et d'Histoire* 43 (1965), 57-59.

" A *Senatus Consultum* in the *pro Murena*," *Mnemosyne* 19 (1966), 272-273.

Laurand, L. *Études sur le style des discours de Cicéron* 3 vols., 4th ed., Paris, 1936–1938.

Linderski, J. " Cicero and Sallust on Vargunteius," *Historia* 12 (1963), 511-512.

Lintott, A. W. *Violence in Republican Rome*, Oxford, 1968.

Magie, D. *Roman Rule in Asia Minor* 2 vols., Princeton, 1950.

CICERO

Marshall, A. J. " Governors on the Move," *Phoenix* 20 (1966), 231-246.

" Romans under Chian Law," *Greek, Roman, and Byzantine Studies* 10 (1969), 255-271.

Meier, C. " Pompeius' Rückkehr aus dem Mithridatischen Kriege und die Catilinarische Verschwörung," *Athenaeum* 40 (1962), 103-125.

Res Publica Amissa, Wiesbaden, 1966.

Mello, M. " Sallustio e le elezioni consolari del 66 A.C.," *La Parola del Passato* 88 (1963), 36-54.

Michels, A. K. *The Calendar of the Roman Republic*, Princeton, 1967.

Mitchell, J. F. " The Torquati," *Historia* 15 (1966), 23-31.

Mitchell, Th. N. " Cicero and the *Senatus Consultum Ultimum*," *Historia* 20 (1971) 47-61

Mommsen, Th. *Römisches Staatsrecht* 3rd ed., Berlin, 1887–1888.

Römische Geschichte. English translation by W. P. Dickson, *The History of Rome* 5 vols. (vol. 4), London, 1894–1895.

Römisches Strafrecht, Leipzig, 1899.

Nash, E. *Pictorial Dictionary of Ancient Rome* 2 vols., London, 1961–1962.

Nicolet, C. " Le Sénat et les amendements aux lois à la fin de la République," *Revue historique de Droit français et étranger* 36 (1958), 260-275.

" *Confusio suffragiorum*," *Mélanges d'Archéologie et d'Histoire* 71 (1959), 145-210.

" *Consul togatus* ; Remarques sur le vocabulaire politique de Cicéron et de Tite-Live," *Revue des Études latines* 38 (1960), 236-263.

L'Ordre équestre à l'époque républicaine, Paris, 1966.

Nisbet, R. G. M. " The *commentariolum petitionis* : some Arguments against Authenticity," *Journal of Roman Studies* 51 (1961), 84-87.

Oxford Classical Dictionary Ed. N. G. L. Hammond and H. H. Scullard, 2nd ed., Oxford, 1970.

BIBLIOGRAPHY

Pauly, A., Wissowa, G. and Kroll, W. *Realencyclopädie für classischen Altertumswissenschaft*, Stuttgart, 1894– .

Gelzer, M. *L. Sergius Catilina* (23) II A 2 (1923), 1693–1711.

Münzer, F. *L. Licinius Murena* (123) XIII. 1 (1926), 446-449.

P. Cornelius Sulla (386) IV. 1 (1900), 1518–1521.

L. Valerius Flaccus (179) VIII A 1 (1955), 30-36.

Strasburger, H. *Nobiles* XVII. 1 (1936), 785-791.

Novus homo XVII. 1 (1936), 1223-1228.

Optimates XVIII. 1 (1939), 773-798.

Salmon, E. T. " Catiline, Crassus and Caesar," *American Journal of Philology* 56 (1935), 302-316.

Scullard, H. H. *From the Gracchi to Nero* 3rd ed., London, 1970.

Seager, R. " The First Catilinarian Conspiracy," *Historia* 13 (1964), 338-347.

Sherwin-White, A. N. *The Roman Citizenship*, Oxford, 1939.

" The Extortion Procedure Again," *Journal of Roman Studies* 42 (1952), 43-55.

" Poena legis repetundarum," *Papers of the British School at Rome* 17 (1959), 5-25.

Smith, R. E. *The Failure of the Roman Republic*, Cambridge, 1955.

Service in the Post-Marian Roman Army, Manchester, 1958.

Cicero the Statesman, Cambridge, 1966.

Stangl, T. Ed. *Ciceronis orationum scholiastae*, Vienna, 1912.

Stockton, D. L. *Cicero : A Political Biography*, Oxford, 1971.

Strachan-Davidson, J. L. *Cicero and the Fall of the Roman Republic*, New York and London, 1911.

Problems of the Roman Criminal Law, Oxford, 1912.

Sumner, G. V. " The Last Journey of L. Sergius Catilina," *Classical Philology* 58 (1963), 215-219.

CICERO

"The Consular Elections of 66 B.C.," *Phoenix* 19 (1965), 226-231.

"Cicero, Pompeius, and Rullus," *Transactions of the American Philological Association* 97 (1966), 569-582.

Syme, R. "The Allegiance of Labienus," *Journal of Roman Studies* 28 (1938), 113-125.

The Roman Revolution, Oxford, 1939.

Review of M. Gelzer, *Caesar, der Politiker und Staatsman* in *Journal of Roman Studies* 34 (1944), 92-103.

Sallust, Berkeley, 1964.

Taylor, L. R. "Caesar and the Roman Nobility," *Transactions of the American Philological Association* 73 (1942), 1-24.

Party Politics in the Age of Caesar, Berkeley, 1949.

The Voting Districts of the Roman Republic, Rome, 1960.

Roman Voting Assemblies, Ann Arbor, 1966.

Treggiari, S. *Roman Freedmen during the Late Republic*, Oxford, 1969.

Tyrrell, R. Y. and Purser, L. C. *The Correspondence of Cicero* 7 vols., var. eds., Dublin, 1901-1933.

Ward, A. M. "Politics in the Trials of Manilius and Cornelius," *Transactions of the American Philological Association* 101 (1970), 545-556.

"Cicero's fight against Crassus and Caesar in 65 and 63 B.C.," *Historia* 21 (1972), 244-258.

Waters, K. H. "Cicero, Sallust and Catiline," *Historia* 19 (1970), 195-215.

Watson, A. *The Law of Persons in the Later Roman Republic*, Oxford, 1967.

The Law of Property in the Later Roman Republic, Oxford, 1968.

The Law of Succession in the Later Roman Republic, Oxford, 1971.

Williams, P. *Le Sénat de la République romaine* 2 vols., Louvain, 1878-1883.

Wirszubski, Ch. *Libertas as a Political Idea at Rome*

BIBLIOGRAPHY

during the Late Republic and Early Principate, Cambridge, 1960.

" Cicero's *cum dignitate otium* : A Reconsideration," *Journal of Roman Studies* 44 (1954), 1-13. Reprinted in *The Crisis of the Roman Republic Ed.* R. Seager, Cambridge, 1969.

" *Audaces* : a Study in Political Phraseology," *Journal of Roman Studies* 51 (1961), 12-22.

Wiseman, T. P. " The Definition of *Eques Romanus*," *Historia* 19 (1970), 67-83.

New Men in the Roman Senate 139 B.C.-A.D. 14, Oxford, 1971.

Yavetz, Z. " The Living Conditions of the Urban Plebs in Republican Rome," *Latomus* 17 (1958), 500-517. Reprinted in *The Crisis of the Roman Republic Ed.* R. Seager, Cambridge, 1969.

" The Failure of Catiline's Conspiracy," *Historia* 12 (1963), 485-499.

INDEX OF PROPER NAMES

Achaea, 226, 414, 511

Achilles, 262, 520

Acilius Glabrio, M'., (Tr. Pl. 122 ?), 417

Acilius Glabrio, M'., (Cos. 67), 174

Acmona, 426, 479, 480, 481, 482, 483, 485

Adramyttium, 475, 517

Aebutius, M., 543

Aenus, 476, 477

Aeolians, 513

Aetidemus, 501

Aetolians, 225, 227

Africa, 160, 161, 227 ; the province, xix, 3, 50, 538

Amisus, 170

Amyntas, 521, 523, 529, 531

Ancona, 73

Andriscus, 226 (see also Philip the Pretender)

Andro : see Sextilius

Anio, River, 293

Annius Chilo, Q., 25, 115

Antiochus III, (king of Syria), 226, 227

Antiochus, (a freedman), 539

Antonius, M., (Cos. 99), 548

Antonius Creticus, M., (Pr. 74), 150

Antonius Hybrida, C., (Cos. 63), 114, 136, 238, 239 ; possible commissioner under Rullus' land bill, xxv ; consular candidate for 63, 4 ; suspected of Catilinarian sympathies, 5 ; won over by Cicero's exchange of provinces, xxxvi,

xxxvii, 5, 136 ; joint author with Cicero of law against electoral corruption, xxxviii, 174 ; leads army against Catiline in Etruria, xxxvi, 19, 28, 29 ; convicted of *maiestas*, xxxvi, 419, 430, 545

Antonius, M., (the Triumvir), 4, 178

Apamea, 516

Apennines, 28, 93

Apollonis, 499, 519, 521, 527, 529

Apulia, 15, 16, 115

Aquae Sextiae, Battle of, 127, 161

Aquilius, M'., (Cos. 129), 420

Aquilius, M'., (Cos. 101), 549

Archidemus, 501

Ariminum, 73

Aristonicus, 420

Aristotle, 266

Armenia, 170, 231, 457

Arpinum, 334, 338

Arretium, 251

Arrius, Q., (Pr. before 63), 15, 16

Asclepiades, 479, 480, 481, 483, 485

Asculum, 2, 339

Asia, 227, 229, 414, 477, 524 ; province, 169, 170, 415, 423, 425, 426, 428, 430, 443, 449, 457, 460, 479, 495, 496, 498, 499, 505, 509, 512, 521, 529, 539, 551 ; *corruptrix provincia*, 199, 201, 209, 421, 424, 427 ;

585

INDEX OF PROPER NAMES

origins, 420 ; Pompey's command, 473 ; Q. Cicero governor, 478 ; unreliability of, 428, 483, 509, 513, 514 ; Lucullus' command, 535
Athena, 510
Athenagoras, 461
Athenians, 266, 511, 513
Athenodorus, 268
Athens, 263, 511
Atlantic Ocean, 229
Attalus III, (king of Pergamum), 420
Attica, 232
Atticus, T. Pomponius, 176, 427
Atyanas, 475
Aufidius, T., (Pr. 67?), 493
Aurelia, lex, iudiciaria, (70), 172, 306, 419
Aurelia, via, 56, 75
Aurelian Steps, 514, 515
Autronius Paetus, P., (Cos. Desig. 65), consul designate, xix ; condemned for *ambitus* and loses consulship, 182, 203 ; part in " First Catilinarian Conspiracy," xx, xxi, 8, 365 ; possible commissioner under Rullus' land bill, xxv ; named by Allobroges, 349, 351 ; involved with Catilinarians, 24, 308, 312, 321, 323, 327, 331, 367, 379, 381, 383, 389 ; universally detested, 315 ; condemned for part in Catilinarian Conspiracy of 63, 305, 329 ; violence at trial, 311 ; proposal to restore rights, 374
Aventine, 35, 202, 203

Bacchus, 509
Balbus, T. Ampius, (Tr. Pl. 63), xxiv, xxvi
Balbus, L. Cornelius, (Cos. Suff. 40), 430
Bellus, (a freedman of Faustus Sulla), 369
Beneventum, Battle of, 205
Bestia, L. Calpurnius, (Tr. Pl. 62), 20, 144, 344
Bibulus, M. Calpurnius, (Cos. 59), xxxv
Bithynia, 229 ; and Pontus, (the province), xvii, 170
Black Sea, 226
Boeotia, 511

Bona Dea, xxx
Bosporus, Cimmerian, 231
Brundisium, xxxii, 484

Caecilius, C., 539
Caecilius, Q., 6, 7
Caecilius Rufus, L., (Tr. Pl. 63), xxiv, xxxvii, 303, 309, 310, 374, 375, 377, 379
Caelius, M., 453, 551
Caelius Caldus, C., (Cos. 94), 205
Caelius Rufus, M., (Pr. 48), 305
Caepio, Q. Servilius, (Cos. 106), 418
Caesar, C. Iulius, (Cos. 59), xvi, xxxiii, 302, 312, 423 ; and politics in the 60s, xviii, xxiii, xxv, xxvi, xxvii, xxxviii, 4, 5 ; and " First Catilinarian Conspiracy," xx, xxii ; and the prosecution of Rabirius, xxviii, xxix ; and Clodius, xxx ; member of " First Triumvirate," xxxiv, xxxv ; consulship in 59, xxxvi ; and the Catilinarian Conspiracy, 24, 26, 141, 142, 143, 145, 147 ; author of *lex Iulia repetundarum*, 419 ; and L. Cornelius Balbus, 430 ; view of the *senatus consultum ultimum,* 570, 571, 573
Caesar, L. Iulius, (Cos. 90), 150
Caesar, L. Iulius, (Cos. 64), 150, 151, 274, 368, 369
Caesius, Sext., 517
Caetra, 441
Caicus, R., 498, 521
Calpurnia, lex, de ambitu, (67), 42, 174, 247, 271, 303, 304, 386
Camerinum, 367
Campania, 369
Campus Martius, xxix, 69, 135, 243, 273, 293, 363, 403, 560, 562 ; scene of intended attack upon Cicero, 14, 45, 253, 287, 365
Capena, 521
Capitol, 90, 108, 121, 125, 159, 340, 379, 382
Cappadocians, 509
Capua, xxxvi, 16, 17, 28
Caria, 443
Carians, 429, 498, 513
Carthage, 160, 161, 227, 259, 280

INDEX OF PROPER NAMES

Cassia, lex, tabellaria, (137), 172, 307, 419

Cassius Longinus, C., (Cos. Desig. 41), 312

Cassius Longinus, L., 21, 23, 25, 109, 115, 119, 129, 153, 349, 351, 353, 367

Castor, (temple of), 514

Castricius, 502, 503, 525

Catilina, L. Sergius, (Pr. 68), xvi, xxxii, xxxvi, 309, 397, 439; defeat and death, xv, xxxvii, 29, 184, 304, 306, 400, 544; propraetor in Africa, xix; and "First Catilinarian Conspiracy," xx, xxi, 4, 8, 289, 312, 381; acquitted of charge *de vi,* xxiv; possible commissioner under Rullus' land bill, xxv; consular candidate in 63, xxxviii, 171, 249; and conspiracy of 63, xxxix, 14, 17-24, 28, 33, 35, 37, 39, 41, 43, 45, 47, 51, 53, 55, 59, 63, 65, 67, 69, 71, 72, 74, 75, 77, 81, 83, 85, 95, 97, 103, 113, 117, 119, 129, 139, 149, 153, 176, 177, 180, 181, 183, 193, 251, 253, 255, 285, 287, 291, 293, 295, 329, 331, 347, 365, 367, 369, 383, 389, 549, 551; family background, 2; and Sulla, 3; consular candidate in 64, 5, 207; career and character, 6, 9, 30; alleged crimes, 6, 7; policy, 10, 87; supporters, 11, 12, 13, 89, 91, 93; and slaves, 60, 109; and Allobroges, 105; tried and acquitted of extortion in 65, 311, 393, 395; decoration of his tomb, 545; a *hostis* of the State, 572, 573

Cato Censorius, M. Porcius, (Cos. 195), 176, 205, 227, 260, 261, 269, 336, 337, 520, 521

Cato Uticensis, M. Porcius, (Tr. Pl. 62), hostility towards Caesar, xxix, xxxiv, xxxv; denounces greed of taxgathers, xxxi, 265; leader in Senate of the extreme conservatives, xxxi; quaestor in 64, 5; threatened by Catiline, 14, 253; prosecutes Murena, 20, 175, 176, 183, 193, 201, 225, 231, 255, 257, 259, 261, 269,

271, 275, 281, 285, 289, 291; speaks in debate upon the fate of the Catilinarians, 25, 26, 573, 574; praises Cicero at the end of his consulship, 27; said to have succumbed to *ambitus* by 61, 173; a Stoic, 189, 263, 265, 267, 279; tribune in 62, 267

Catulus, Q. Lutatius, (Cos. 102), 233, 234

Catulus, Q. Lutatius, (Cos. 78), xvii, xxiii, xxix, xxxi, 3, 19, 24, 27, 128, 129, 305

Ceparius, M., 13, 27, 43, 115, 140, 346

Cephallenians, 226

Ceres, 238

Cestius, C., 475

Cethegus, C. Cornelius, xxv, 13, 19, 20, 21, 22, 23, 107, 109, 111, 115, 119, 129, 140, 149, 153, 305, 346, 367, 382, 383, 389, 547

Cicero, M. Tullius, (Cos. 63), 106, 124, 144, 147, 190, 217, 237, 258, 316, 336, 352, 380, 382, 407, 419, 438, 439, 440, 518, 520, 528, 533, 559; as statesman, xv, xvi; as advocate, xv, 310, 311, 431, 478, 481, 534, 535, 542; supports the *lex Manilia,* xvii; and Pompey, xviii, 130, 131; attacks the proposed annexation of Egypt, xxiii; attacks Rullus' land bill, xxiv, xxv, xxvi, xxvii; defends C. Piso, xxvii, xxxviii; defends Rabirius, xxviii, xxix; and the *concordia ordinum,* xxix, xxx, xxxi; and the "First Triumvirate," xxxv; defends Antonius Hybrida, xxxvi; enmity of Clodius, xxxvii; exchanges provinces with Antonius, xxxvii; carries law limiting *liberae legationes* to one year, xxxviii, 536; proposes thanksgiving of ten days in honour of Pompey, xxxviii; joint author of law against *ambitus,* xxxviii, 174; defines provisions of the *lex Calpurnia de ambitu,* xxxviii, 175; and the Catilinarian Conspiracy, xxxviii, xxxix, 15, 16, 17, 18,

INDEX OF PROPER NAMES

19, 22, 23, 24, 25, 28, 30, 171 ; renounces his province, xxxviii ; delivers *First Speech against Catiline*, xxxix, 16 ; delivers *Second Speech against Catiline*, xxxix, 11, 12, 19 ; delivers *Third Speech against Catiline*, xxxix, 24 ; delivers *Fourth Speech against Catiline*, xxxix, 26 ; attacked by Nepos, xxxix ; and Catiline in consular elections for 63, 4 ; elected consul for 63, 5 ; delivers speech *in toga candida*, 6 ; allegations of crimes committed by Catiline, 7, 8, 9 ; speech *pro Caelio*, 9 ; consular elections for 62, 14 ; defends Murena, 20, 170, 173, 179, 180, 181, 182, 183 ; and the Allobroges, 21 ; last day of his consulship, 27, 184 ; as orator, 30, 34, 310, 428, 429, 431, 542 ; defends himself against attack for executing the conspirators, 37, 60, 322 ; oldest surviving fragment of his writings, 44 ; holds office *suo anno*, 61 ; his version of Catiline's departure from Rome, 74 ; and Sullan colonists, 88 ; his civilian status, 96 ; and divine assistance, 98 ; his triumphal day, 100 ; and *leges de provocatione*, 146, 342 ; and Cato, 176 ; his policies, 177 ; and Sulpicius, 178, 182 ; and equestrians, 241 ; philosophical interests, 266 ; and L. Natta, 278 ; defends Sulla, 302, 303, 304, 307, 308, 309, 312, 322 ; gives evidence against Catilinarians, 305 ; native of Arpinum, 335 ; introduces shorthand to Rome, 354 ; defends Flaccus, 413, 414, 425, 426, 427, 428, 430, 431 ; brother Quintus governor of Asia, 415, 424 ; and Asia, 421 ; and *contiones*, 560 ; influence of foreigners at *contiones*, 560, 561 ; elected praetor by all the centuries, 563 ; and the *senatus consultum ultimum*, 571, 572, 573
Cicero, M. Tullius, (son of above), 136

Cicero, Q. Tullius, (Procos. Asia 61–58), 136, 415, 428, 431, 478, 479, 527
Cilicia, xvii, 3, 441, 447, 475, 526, 551
Cimber Gabinius, (P. Gabinius Capito), 106, 107
Cimbri, 56, 127, 161
Cincinnatus, L. Quinctius, (the Dictator), 34
Cinna, L. Cornelius, (Cos. 87–85), 108, 109, 127
Circus Flaminius, 560
Citium, 263
Claudius Caecus, Ap., (Cos. 307), 216
Claudius Pulcher, Ap., (Cos. 54), 355
Clodius Pulcher, P., (Tr. Pl. 58), xxx, xxxvii, 4, 312
Collatinus, Tarquinius, 413
Comitium, 560
Compitalia, 276
Concord, (temple of), 22, 25, 123, 155
Corinth, 225, 226
Corneliae, leges, (of the dictator Sulla), 418, 456
Cornelius, (a freedman), 369
Cornelius, C., (Tr. Pl. 67), xvii
Cornelius, C., 18, 42, 305, 321, 331, 365
Cornelius, C., (son of above), 307, 365
Coruncanius, Ti., (Cos. 280), 337
Cosconius, C., (Pr. 63), 354, 355
Cotta, L. Aurelius, (Cos. 144), 259, 261, 417
Cotta, L. Aurelius, (Pr. 70), xix, xx, xxii, 121, 172, 303, 306, 419
Cotta, M. Aurelius, (Cos. 74), 228
Crassus, M. Licinius, Dives, (Cos. 70), xvi ; consul in 70, xvi ; political activities in the 60s, xviii, xxiii, xxix, 4 ; and "First Catilinarian Conspiracy," xxi, xxii ; and Rullus' land bill, xxv, xxvi ; and Clodius, xxx ; and Asian tax-gatherers, xxxi, xxxv, xxxvi ; member of "First Triumvirate," xxxv, xxxvi ; and Catilinarian Conspiracy, xxxviii, 15, 24, 145 ; defends Murena, 179, 181, 197, 249 ; as orator, 180 ; sells house to Cicero,

309; goes to eastern Mediterranean, 477
Cretans, 280, 281
Crete, 16, 414, 441, 447, 474, 475, 551
Croton, 13
Crustumium, 521
Cumae, 108
Curio, C. Scribonius, (Cos. 76), xvi
Curio, L. Scribonius, (Tr. Pl. 149), 260
Curius, Q., 16, 18
Curius Dentatus, M'., (Cos. 290), 205, 225, 336, 337
Curtius, M., (Qu. 61), 473
Cyme, 427, 461, 493
Cynics, 281
Cynoscephalae, Battle of, 226
Cyprus, 263, 474, 475
Cyzicus, 229

Dardanus, (Peace of), 228
Decianus, C. Appuleius, (Tr. Pl. 98), 413, 440, 441
Decianus, C. Appuleius, 426, 429, 430, 441, 499, 519, 521, 523, 525, 528, 529, 531, 533, 543, 545
Delos, 502
Demeter, 510
Didius, T., (Cos. 98), 205
Dio, 523
Diogenes, (the Cynic), 281
Dionysus, 508, 509
Dolabella, P. Cornelius, (Cos. Suff. 44), 312
Domitia, lex, (104), xxix
Domitius Calvinus, Cn., (Cos. 53), 475, 517
Dorians, 513
Dorylaeum, 426, 485, 487
Drusus, M. Livius, (Tr. Pl. 91), 418
Dyrrachium, 312

Egnatia, 484
Egypt, xxiii, xxv, 474
Eleusinian Mysteries, 510
Ennius, Q., 224
Ephesus, 477
Epirus, 205
Eppius, L., 474, 475
Erythrae, 414
Etruria, in Catilinarian Conspiracy, 13, 14, 15, 18, 28, 37,

75, 104, 176, 330, 367; home of augury, 121
Euboea, 232
Euhius, (as title of Mithridates), 508, 509
Euripus, 232
Europe, 513

Fabia, (a Vestal Virgin), 3, 6, 7
Fabia, lex, 174
Falcidius, 426, 541, 542, 543, 545
Fausta, 369
Faustus Sulla, 367, 368, 369
Figulus, C. Marcius, (Cos. 64), 369
Fimbria, C. Flavius, (Cos. 104), 234
Fimbria, C. Flavius, (Leg., Lieut. 86–85), 414
Flaccus, M. Fulvius, (Cos. 125), 35, 150, 151, 524
Flaccus, M. Fulvius, 150
Flaccus, C. Valerius, (Cos. 93), 414, 447
Flaccus, L. Valerius, (Cos, 195), 434
Flaccus, L. Valerius, (Cos. 100), 37, 434
Flaccus, L. Valerius, (Cos. Suff. 86), 63, 413, 505, 509, 525, 527, 539
Flaccus, L. Valerius, (Pr. 63), xxxvii, 432, 443, 449, 453, 481, 482, 489, 517; assistance to Cicero the cause of his prosecution, xxxvii, 435, 437, 545, 547, 549, 553, 555; Triumvirs behind the prosecution, xxxvii, 430; arrested Catilinarians with the Allobroges, 22, 104, 105, 107, 115, 435; distinction of his family, 413, 427, 469; estranged from Pompey, 414, 431, 457; governor of Asia, 415, 424; trial for extortion, 419, 420, 426, 428, 430; charges brought against him, for embezzling money levied to raise a fleet, 425, 426, 470, 473, 475, 477, 479, by Sextilius Andro, 426, 532, 533, 534, 537, 539, by Falcidius, 426, 541, 542, 543, by Tralles, 427, 501, 503, 505, 507, by Laelius, 457, 487, 531, by Dorylaeum, 485, by Temnus, 491, by the Jews, 515, 518, by Decianus, 523;

589

defended by Cicero, 426 ; services to Rome, 427, 429, 437, 551 ; service in Europe, 428, 429, 511, 513 ; nick-name, 430 ; acquitted, 431 ; praetor in 63, 434, 475, 535 ; service with uncle, 447 ; supported by Metellus Creticus, 474 ; succeeded in Asia by Q. Cicero, 497 ; military tribune, 527 ; supported by Lucullus, 535

Flaminia, via, 22

Flamininus, T. Quinctius, (Cos. 198), 225, 226

Flavius, Cn., 215, 216

Flavius, L., (Tr. Pl. 60), xxvi, xxxiii

Flora, 238

Fonteius, M., (Propr. Transalp. Gaul 74–72), 427, 428

Forum, xx, xxi, 24, 25, 47, 64, 69, 122, 153, 211, 225, 243, 273, 275, 287, 293, 363, 505, 518, 560

Forum Aurelium, 57

Fufia, lex, iudiciaria, (59), 456

Fufius Calenus, Q., (Pr. 59), 419, 456

Fufius, C., 495, 497

Fufius, M., 495, 497

Fulvia, (wife of L. Julius Caesar, Cos. 90), 150

Fulvia, 16, 18

Fulvius Neratus, P., 495

Fulvius Nobilior, M., (Cos. 189), 225, 226

Furius, P., 13, 25, 115

Gabinius, A., (Tr. Pl. 67), xvii, xxiii, 312

Gabinius, P., (Pr. 89), 414

Gabinius Capito, P., 20, 21 22, 23, 27, 106, 107, 113, 115, 117, 140, 149, 153, 346

Galba, P. Sulpicius, (Pr. by 66), 206, 207

Galba, Ser. Sulpicius, (Cos. 144), 260, 261, 416

Gallus, C. Sulpicius, (Cos. 166), 269

Gaul, xxxiv, 13, 21, 241, 427, 441, 451, 551 ; Cisalpine, xxxvi, xxxvii, 18, 28, 72, 105, 171 ; Narbonese or Transalpine, xxxvi, 20, 28, 171, 297, 414

Gauls, (see also Allobroges), 428, 511, 551

Gellius Publicola, L., (Cens. 70), 27

Glaucia, C. Servilius, (Tr. Pl. 101 or 104?), 36, 37, 116, 117, 418

Globulus, P. Servilius, (Propr. Asia 63), 415, 524, 529, 535, 541

Gracchi, 63, 178, 561 ; C. Sempronius, (Tr. Pl. 123–122), xxxiv, 35, 110, 139, 146, 147, 151, 417, 421, 570, 571 ; Ti. Sempronius, (Tr. Pl. 133), 34, 35, 138, 139, 420, 421, 524

Gratidia, 2

Gratidianus, M. Marius, (Tr. Pl. ? 87), 2

Gratidius, M., (Leg., Lieut. 61–59), 497

Greece, Flaccus' service in, 428 ; ancient and modern contrasted, 458, 511 ; European and Asiatic contrasted, 513

Greeks, 428, 457, 461, 475, 489, 511, 519, 543 ; unreliability of Asiatic Greeks, 428, 429, 451, 453, 463, 467, 469, 483, 505, 509, 521 ; their complaints against Flaccus, 471 ; Europeans and Asiatics contrasted, 513, 551

Hannibal, 160, 227, 292

Helvetii, 415

Heraclides, (of Temnus), 489, 493, 495, 497, 499

Herennius, M., (Cos. 93), 233

Hermippus, 493, 495, 497

Hermobius, 491

Hermus, River, 498

Hortensia, lex, (287), 566

Hortensius Hortalus, Q., (Cos. 69) ; opposes *lex Gabinia*, xvii ; a leading Optimate, xxxi, 181 ; rival of Cicero at the Bar, 179, 180 ; defends Murena, 179, 181, 197, 249 ; defends Sulla, 307, 309, 310, 311, 317, 319, 325, 327, 335, 365 ; defends Flaccus, 426, 427, 429, 430, 489, 503

Hypsaeus, P. Plautius, (Qu. 66), 463

Ides, 47

Illyricum, xxxvi

Ionians, 513

Italy, xxiv, xxv, xxxiii, xxxiv,

INDEX OF PROPER NAMES

xxxv, 24, 37, 41, 45, 75, 93, 109, 117, 153, 160, 161, 205, 212, 218, 227, 229, 357, 367, 435, 443, 477, 515, 528, 529 ; addresses Cicero, 61

Iulia, lex, de agro Campano, (59), xxxvi

Iulia, lex, repetundarum, (59), 419, 456

Iunia, lex, repetundarum, (between 149 and 123), 417

Iunius, M., (Tr. Pl. by 123), 417

Janiculum, xxix
Jerusalem, 426, 515, 516, 517
Jews, 515, 517, 518, 519
Jugurtha, 205
Julia, (wife of P. Cornelius Lentulus Sura), 150, 151
Juno Sospita, 299
Jupiter, 123, 125, 133, 297 ; Optimus Maximus, 125 ; Stator, 43, 67 ; Stator, (temple of), 18, 32, 81

Labienus, T., (Tr. Pl. 63), xxiv, xxvi, xxvii, xxix, xxxvii
Laeca, M. Porcius, xxxix, 17, 19, 41, 81, 305, 321, 365
Laelius Sapiens, C., (Cos. 140), xxx, 268, 269
Laelius, D., (Tr. Pl. 54), 429, 430, 436, 437, 441, 443, 445, 447, 455, 457, 461, 465, 467, 482, 483, 487, 503, 507, 515, 517, 523, 527, 531, 533, 543
Laelius, D. (Leg., Lieut. ?76), 436
Lanuvium, 169, 298, 299
Laodicea, 517
Latium, 16
leges: see under names of authors
Lentulus, P. Cornelius, (Cos. Suff. 162), 110
Lentulus Clodianus, Cn. Cornelius, (Cens. 70), xvi, 493
Lentulus Clodianus, Cn. Cornelius, (Leg., Amb. 60), 415, 419
Lentulus Sura, P. Cornelius, (Pr. 63), 12, 19, 20, 21, 22, 23, 27, 28, 105, 106, 107, 109, 111, 113, 115, 117, 119, 125, 129, 137, 139, 140, 147, 149, 150, 151, 157, 329, 331, 342, 343, 346, 367, 383, 389

Lepidus, M. Aemilius, (Cos. 78), xviii, 127, 128, 306
Lepidus, M'. Aemilius, (Cos. 66), 17, 47, 53, 325
Lepiso, 501
Liber, 238, 509
Libera, 238
Lilybaeum, xxxviii
Longinus, C. Cassius, (Cos. 73), xvi
Longinus, L. Cassius, (Pr. 66), 13
Longinus Ravilla, L. Cassius, (Tr. Pl. 137), 172, 307, 419
Loryma, 443
Lucceius, L., (Pr. 67), 5
Lucceius, 430, 533
Lucullus, L. Licinius, (Cos. 74), xxxii, xxxiii, 176, 181, 228, 229, 231, 273, 423 ; close ties with Murena, 170, 171, 209, 211, 235 ; supports Flaccus, 535
Lurco, M. Aufidius, (Tr. Pl. 61), 453, 537, 538, 539
Lusitania, 260
Lutatia, lex, 305, 306
Lycia, 526
Lycurgus, 510
Lydia, 443, 498, 513, 515, 551
Lydians, 437, 515
Lysania, 489, 491, 499

Macedonia, xxxvi, xxxvii, 161, 205, 226, 432, 477
Macrobius, 431
Maeandrius, 501, 503, 505
Maelius, Spurius, 34
Magnesia, 227
Mallius Maximus, Cn., (Cos. 105), 233, 234
Manilius, C., (Tr. Pl. 66), xxiii ; author of law to give Pompey command in the East, xvi, xvii ; trials of, xxi ; author of bill to distribute the votes of freedmen, 246, 247, 248, 276
Manilius, C., 543
Manlius, C., xxxix, 13, 14, 16, 18, 19, 28, 29, 39, 43, 57, 65, 81, 85, 89, 183, 573
Manlius Capitolinus, M., (Cos. 392), 340
Marcellus, C. Claudius, (Pr. 80), 332, 333
Marcellus, C. Claudius, (Cos. 50), 332, 333

INDEX OF PROPER NAMES

Marcellus, M., 15

Marcellus, M., 53

Marcellus, M. Claudius, (Cos. 51), 54, 55

Marcius Rex, Q., (Cos. 68), xxxii, 16

Marius, C.,(Cos. 107), 37, 56, 116, 117, 126, 127, 205, 335, 337, 413

Marseilles, 19, 74, 83, 85, 511, 551

Mauretania, 371

Maximus Allobrogicus, Q. Fabius, (Cos. 121), 280, 281

Maximus Eburnus, Q. Fabius, (Cos. 116), 233, 235

Meculonius, 493

Mediterranean, xvii

Memmius, C., (Tr. Pl. 111), 139

Memmius, C., 369

Messala Niger, M. Valerius, (Cos. 61), 306, 333

Messala Rufus, M. Valerius, (Cos. 53), 355

Metellus Celer, Q. Caecilius, (Cos. 60), xxxi, xxxiii, xxxvi, xxxvii, 17, 28, 29, 52, 72, 73, 95, 304, 379, 434

Metellus Creticus, Q. Caecilius, (Cos. 69), xxxii, 16, 280, 414, 415, 431, 447, 474, 475, 551

Metellus Macedonicus, Q. Caecilius, (Cos. 143), 225, 226

Metellus Nepos, Q. Caecilius : see Nepos

Metellus Pius, Q. Caecilius, (Procos. Farther Spain 79–71), 382, 383

Metellus Pius Scipio, Q. Caecilius, 15

Minucius, 73

Mithridates, (of Pergamum), 427, 461, 489

Mithridates, (VI Eupator, king of Pontus), Pompey in command against him, xvii, 78 ; cost of war against him, 10 ; Sulla in command against him, 126 ; Sulla's agreement with him, 169 ; organization of his territory, 170 ; Lucullus in command against him, 176, 209 ; the fighting against him, 225, 227, 229, 231, 457, 508 ; Flaccus (governor of Asia 95–94) in command against him, 414, 443 ; his occupation of Asia, 421, 507, 521 ; his massacre

of Romans and Italians, 423 ; kills M'. Aquilius, 548

Mucius Scaevola, Q., (Cos. 95), 422

Mulvian Bridge, xxxix, 22, 105

Mummius, L., (Cos. 146), 225, 226

Murena, C. Licinius, (Leg., Lieut. 64–63), 171, 297

Murena, L. Licinius, (Pr. by 87), 170 ?, 229

Murena, L. Licinius, (Cos. 62), elected consul, xxxviii, 5, 14, 171, 187 ; tried for *ambitus*, xxxix, 20, 174, 175, 179 ; acquitted, xxxix, 184 ; supports death penalty for the Catilinarians, 25 ; in the field against the Catilinarians, 28 ; family background, 169 ; possibly a member of Lucullus' commission in Asia, 170 ; prosecuted by Cato, 176, 259 ; prosecuted by Sulpicius Rufus, 177 ; defended by Cicero, 180, 181, 189, 193, 257, 285, 295, 297, 308, 426, 549 ; probably guilty, 181 ; ties with both Cicero and Sulpicius, 182, 193, 195 ; date of trial, 183 ; comes to aid of Cato in 62, 184 ; consequences of conviction, 191 ; attack on private life, 199, 201 ; praetorian province, 207 ; outstanding experience as military commander, 209, 233 ; supported by Lucullus, 211, 235 ; helped electorally by his games, 237, 239, by his province, 240, 241 ; claim to consulship equal to that of Sulpicius, 243 ; Catiline his enemy, 251, 259 ; helped electorally by fear of Catiline, 255 ; consul in 62, 267, 473 ; grounds of accusation, 273, 277, 279

Mysia, 475, 513, 516, 551

Mysians, 429, 437, 461, 515

Naples, 303, 304, 331, 367

Naso, Q. Voconius, (Pr. 60), 499

Natta, L. Pinarius, (Pont. ca. 68–66), 278, 279

Nepos, Q. Caecilius Metellus, (Tr. Pl. 62), xviii, xxvii, xxxii, xxxix, 17, 27, 29, 53, 144, 184, 344

INDEX OF PROPER NAMES

Nicomedes, 489
Nicopolis, 230
Nigidius Figulus, P., (Pr. 56), 355
Nuceria, 369
Numa Pompilius, (king of Rome), 308, 335
Numantia, 160, 161, 259, 280
Nysa, 508, 509

Oceanus : see Atlantic
Octavius, Cn., (Cos. 87), 127
Olympic Games, 475
Opimius, L., (Cos. 121), 35, 151, 571
Orbius, P., (Propr. Asia 64), 415, 525, 529
Orestilla, Aurelia, 6
Orestinus, Q. Mucius, (Tr. Pl. 64), 4, 304
Ostia, 178, 207, 208
Otho, L. Roscius, (Tr. Pl. 67), 236, 237

Palatine, 32, 309
Panaetius, 269, 280
Parrhasius, 501
Patara, 527
Paulus, L. Aemilius, 17, 305
Paulus, L. Aemilius, (Cos. 168), 161, 225, 226, 283
Peducaeus, L., 517
Pergamenes, 461, 523, 525, 529
Pergamum, 420, 423, 427, 507, 517, 519, 523, 525
Perses, (king of Macedonia), 161, 225, 226
Petreius, M., 29
Pharsalus, 312
Philip, (V, king of Macedonia), 225, 226
Philip, (VI, king of Macedonia, the Pretender), 225, 226
Philippus, L. Marcius, (Cos. 91), 232, 233
Philippus, 491
Philodorus, 501
Philus, L. Furius, (Cos. 136), 269
Phoenix, 262
Phrygia, 484, 513, 516, 551
Phrygians, 437, 461, 485, 487, 512, 513
Picenum, 14, 17, 18, 72, 75, 95, 338, 339, 367
Piso, C. Calpurnius, (Cos. 67), xxvii, xxxviii, 24, 174, 246, 549
Piso, Cn. Calpurnius, (Qu. pro pr.

Spain 65–64), xx, xxi, xxii, 289, 381
Piso Caesoninus, L. Calpurnius, (Cos. 58), 432
Piso Frugi, C. Calpurnius, 136
Piso Frugi, L. Calpurnius, (Tr. Pl. 149), 416, 417
Piso Frugi Calpurnianus, M. Pupius, (Cos. 61), 180, 414, 431, 447
Pistoria, xxxvi, 29
Plato, 266, 267
Plautia, lex, de vi, 305, 306
Plautia, lex (89), 418
Plautius Silvanus, M., (Tr. Pl. 89), 418
Plotius, C., 499
Plutarch, 7
Polemocrates, 523
Pollio, Asinius, xxxvii
Pollis, 491
Pompeius Magnus, Cn., (Cos. 70), 161, 181, 309, 463, 465, 500, 517 ; consul in 70, xvi ; service in Spain, 436 ; command against pirates, xvii, 78, 473, 474, 477 ; command against Mithridates, xvii, 78, 231, 415, 436, 463, 473 ; political position in the 60s, xviii, xxiv, xxv, xxvi, xxvii, xxx, xxxii, 5, 29 ; relationships with Senate, xxxi, xxxiii ; hated by extreme conservatives, xxxii ; alliance with Caesar and Crassus, xxxiv, xxxv, xxxvi ; and Cicero, 8, 97, 130, 131, 311, 381 ; hostility to Flaccus, 414, 431, 457 ; concern for good provincial government, 430
Pompeius Strabo, Cn., (Cos. 89), 2
Pompeius, Q., (Cos. 141), 204, 205, 417
Pompeius, Q., 368, 369
Pompeius Rufus, Q., (Cos. 88), 126
Pompeius Rufus, Q., (Pr. 63), 17
Pomptinus, C., (Pr. 63), 22, 105, 107, 115, 553
Pontus, kingdom of, xvii, 78, 169, 225, 230, 414, 457, 461 ; and Bithynia, xvii, 170
Pontus, (the Black Sea), 229
Poseidon, 510
Postumus, C., 179, 255, 257, 258, 259, 273

INDEX OF PROPER NAMES

Praeneste, 16, 41
Ptolemy Auletes, (king of Egypt), 474, 475
Ptolemy, (younger brother of Auletes), 474
Publicius, 73
Pydna, Battle of, 161, 226
Pyrrhus, (king of Epirus), 205, 225, 226
Pythodorus, 500, 501

Quintilian, 98, 183

Rabirius Postumus, C., xxvii, xxviii, xxxviii
Reate, 105
Rhodes, 178, 268, 551
Rome, xvi, xvii, xviii, xix, xxiii, xxv, xxvii, xxxii, xxxviii, 6, 7, 13, 15, 17, 18, 19, 20, 21, 22, 27, 28, 30, 39, 43, 47, 56, 69, 75, 77, 79, 84, 85, 90, 92, 93, 96, 97, 102, 103, 104, 107, 109, 111, 117, 119, 121, 123, 127, 129, 131, 139, 141, 142, 143, 151, 153, 157, 163, 165, 169, 173, 183, 193, 208, 209, 215, 225, 235, 241, 257, 261, 273, 280, 283, 287, 292, 295, 299, 303, 304, 305, 310, 328, 334, 335, 341, 354, 367, 371, 372, 373, 390, 391, 400, 416, 420, 421, 422, 425, 427, 435, 441, 449, 493, 495, 497, 509, 516, 518, 519, 520, 541, 551, 553, 555, 560, 561, 568, 569, 573, 574
Romulus, 32, 67, 100, 120, 562
Rufus, P. Rutilius, (Cos. 105), 422
Rullus, P. Servilius, (Tr. Pl. 63), xxiv, xxv, xxxvii, 309

Sabines, 32, 217
Saenius, L., 16
Sallust, 6, 7, 11, 19, 30, 415, 573
Samnites, 205, 225
Sanga, Q. Fabius, 21
Saturnalia, 111, 119
Saturninus, L. Appuleius, (Tr. Pl. 100), xxviii, 36, 37, 63, 116, 139
Scaurus, M. Aemilius, (Cos. 115), 204, 205, 233, 235
Scipio Aemilianus Africanus Numantinus. P. Cornelius, (Cos. 147), xxx, 160, 161, 259, 268, 269, 280, 281, 283

Scipio Africanus, P. Cornelius, (Cos. 205), 160, 161, 227
Scipio Asiaticus, L. Cornelius, (Cos. 83), 227
Scipio Nasica Serapio, P. Cornelius, (Cos. 138), 34, 420, 524, 525
Sempronia, lex, de provinciis consularibus, (123), xxxiv
Sempronia, lex, ne de capite civium Romanorum iniussu iudicaretur, (123), 146, 147, 571
Senones, 73
Septimius, P., 453, 539, 551
Serranus, C. Atilius, 234
Sertorius, Q., (Pr. 83), xviii, 228, 229, 382, 436
Servilia, lex, repetundarum, (between 104 and 100), 418
Servilius Vatia Isauricus, P., (Cos. 79), xvi, xxix, 3, 414, 431, 447, 451
Servius : see Sulpicius, Rufus, Ser.
Sestius, P., (Qu. 63), 28, 55, 306
Sextilius, A., 480, 481
Sextilius, C., 538, 539
Sextilius, P., (Qu. 61), 473
Sextilius Andro, 426, 533, 539, 545
Sibylline books, 108, 109, 113, 414
Sicily, 461, 502
Silanus, D. Iunius, (Cos. 62), xxxviii, 5, 14, 291, 473 ; speaks in debate on fate of Catilinarians, 2, 140, 141, 143, 147
Sinope, 281
Sipylus, Mt., 488
Sittius, P., 310, 369, 371
Smyrna, 423, 519, 525
Soracte, Mt., 520
Spain, xxiii, 205, 228, 371, 382, 383, 414, 436, 441, 451 ; Farther, xxxiii, 260, 369, 416, 447
Speluncae, 485
Stagira, 266
Statilius, L., 20, 21, 22, 23, 107, 109, 111, 115, 140, 346
Stloga, Sex., 493
Stoics, 263, 268
Suetonius, xxiii, xxxiv
Sulla, L. Cornelius, (the Dictator), xviii, xxii, 2, 3, 13, 89, 109, 126, 127, 169, 229, 302, 385, 569 ; survival of his settle-

594

INDEX OF PROPER NAMES

ment, xvi, 477; return from the East, xviii; organization of courts, 5, 172, 418, 419; veterans' colonies, 11, 13, 40, 73, 88, 114, 115, 240, 241, 250, 251

Sulla, P. Cornelius, 305, 321

Sulla, P. Cornelius, (Cos. Desig. 65), 302, 303, 309, 310, 333, 369, 371, 379, 383, 387, 391, 395, 401, 403, 405, 407; elected consul for 65, xix, 302; prosecuted and condemned for *ambitus*, xix, 182, 303, 315, 362, 363, 386, 405; alleged involvement in "First Catilinarian Conspiracy," xx, xxi, 8, 309, 311, 313, 365, 381; stands apart from the Catilinarians in 63, 304, 367; accused as a conspirator, 305, 309, 312, 325; defended by Cicero, 307, 308, 310, 311, 317, 319, 323, 327, 329, 335, 393, 399, 426; named by the Allobroges, 349, 350, 351, 353; accused of inciting colonists at Pompeii, 372, 373, 375; bill introduced to restore his position, 377; life contrasted with that of Autronius, 385

Sulla, Ser. Cornelius, 305, 319

Sulla : see also Faustus

Sulpicius, C., (Pr. 63), 22, 109

Sulpicius Rufus, P., (Tr. Pl. 88), 126, 127

Sulpicius Rufus, Ser., (Cos. 51), 174, 179, 203, 211, 223, 246, 248, 249, 251, 255, 257, 277, 279; prosecutes Murena, 177, 178; elected quaestor, 170; consular candidate, 171, 182, 195, 243; aggrieved with Cicero, 182, 193; as lawyer, 197, 209, 215, 225; elected praetor, 233, 238

Sulpicius Rufus, Ser., 179, 255, 259

Syria, 226, 475

Tanusius, L., 6

Tarquinia, L., 24

Tarquinius Superbus, 108, 308, 335

Telephus, 520, 521

Temnus, 426, 489, 495, 499

Tenedus, 229

Terentia, (wife of Cicero), 136

Terracina, 13

Teutones, 127, 161

Thermopylae, 227

Thermus, A., 549

Thessaly, 511

Thrace, 476

Tiber, R., 104, 521

Tigranes, (king of Armenia), 230, 457

Tiro, (freedman of Cicero), 354

Titia, lex, (99?), 207

Tmolus, 427, 441, 443, 449, 493

Tongilius, 73

Torquatus, L. Manlius, (Cos. 65), xx; supports Catiline in 65, 4, 311; consul, 121, 303, 343

Torquatus, L. Manlius, (son of above), prosecutes Sulla in 66, xix; prosecutes Sulla, 8, 303, 307, 309, 310, 317, 319, 321, 323, 329, 334, 337, 343, 345, 347, 349, 351, 353, 357, 359, 362, 395, 405; close friend of Cicero, 307, 315; accuses Cicero of tyranny, 333; fails to secure right to prosecute Gabinius, 312

Torquatus, T. Manlius, (Cos. 340), 344

Tralles, 415, 423, 426, 427, 498, 501, 503, 507, 519, 541

Transpadanes, xxii, xxiii, xxvii

Triptolemus, 510

Troy, 520

Tubero, Q., 280, 281, 283

Tullia, (daughter of Cicero), 136

Tullia, lex, de ambitu, (63), 175

Tullianum, 27, 90, 96, 382

Tullus : see Volcacius

Tusculum, 336

Tyrrhenian Sea, 473

Umbrenus, P., 13, 21, 23, 25, 117

Umbria, 73, 75, 95, 104, 240, 241, 367

Valeria, 532, 533, 534, 537

Valerius Publicola, L., (Cos. 449), 434

Valerius Publicola, P., (Cos. Suff. 509), 413, 434

Vargunteius, L., 18, 42, 43, 305, 306, 319, 381

INDEX OF PROPER NAMES

Varinius, P., (Propr. Asia 65), 493
Vatinia, lex, de alternis consiliis reiciendis, (59), 456
Vatinius, P., (Tr. Pl. 59), xxxvi
Vercellae, 127, 161
Verres, C., (Propr. Sicily 73–71), 179, 425
Vesta, 159
Vestal Virgins, 3, 6, 109, 137, 149, 279

Vettius Sabinus, T., (Pr. 59), 419, 535
Volcacius Tullus, L., (Cos. 66), xix, xx, 3, 4, 47, 325
Volturcius, T., 13, 21, 22, 23, 24, 105, 107, 109, 113, 141
Volumnius, M., 6

Zama, Battle of, 160
Zeno, (of Citium), 263

Printed in Great Britain by R. & R. CLARK LIMITED, *Edinburgh*

THE LOEB CLASSICAL LIBRARY

VOLUMES ALREADY PUBLISHED

LATIN AUTHORS

AMMIANUS MARCELLINUS. J. C. Rolfe. 3 Vols.

APULEIUS: THE GOLDEN ASS (METAMORPHOSES). W. Adlington (1566). Revised by S. Gaselee.

ST. AUGUSTINE: CITY OF GOD. 7 Vols. Vol. I. G. E. McCracken. Vol. II. W. M. Green. Vol. III. D. Wiesen. Vol. IV. P. Levine. Vol. V. E. M. Sanford and W. M. Green. Vol. VI. W. C. Greene. Vol. VII. W. M. Green.

ST. AUGUSTINE, CONFESSIONS OF. W. Watts (1631). 2 Vols.

ST. AUGUSTINE: SELECT LETTERS. J. H. Baxter.

AUSONIUS. H. G. Evelyn White. 2 Vols.

BEDE. J. E. King. 2 Vols.

BOETHIUS: TRACTS AND DE CONSOLATIONE PHILOSOPHIAE. Rev. H. F. Stewart and E. K. Rand. Revised by S. J. Tester.

CAESAR: ALEXANDRIAN, AFRICAN AND SPANISH WARS. A. G. Way.

CAESAR: CIVIL WARS. A. G. Peskett.

CAESAR: GALLIC WAR. H. J. Edwards.

CATO AND VARRO: DE RE RUSTICA. H. B. Ash and W. D. Hooper.

CATULLUS. F. W. Cornish; TIBULLUS. J. B. Postgate; and PERVIGILIUM VENERIS. J. W. Mackail.

CELSUS: DE MEDICINA. W. G. Spencer. 3 Vols.

CICERO: BRUTUS AND ORATOR. G. L. Hendrickson and H. M. Hubbell.

CICERO: DE FINIBUS. H. Rackham.

CICERO: DE INVENTIONE, etc. H. M. Hubbell.

CICERO: DE NATURA DEORUM AND ACADEMICA. H. Rackham.

CICERO: DE OFFICIIS. Walter Miller.

CICERO: DE ORATORE, etc. 2 Vols. Vol. I: DE ORATORE, Books I and II. E. W. Sutton and H. Rackham. Vol. II: DE ORATORE, Book III; DE FATO; PARADOXA STOICORUM; DE PARTITIONE ORATORIA. H. Rackham.

CICERO: DE REPUBLICA, DE LEGIBUS. Clinton W. Keyes.

1

THE LOEB CLASSICAL LIBRARY

CICERO : DE SENECTUTE, DE AMICITIA, DE DIVINATIONE.
W. A. Falconer.

CICERO : IN CATILINAM, PRO MURENA, PRO SULLA, PRO
FLACCO. New version by C. Macdonald.

CICERO : LETTERS TO ATTICUS. E. O. Winstedt. 3 Vols.

CICERO : LETTERS TO HIS FRIENDS. W. Glynn Williams,
M. Cary, M. Henderson. 4 Vols.

CICERO : PHILIPPICS. W. C. A. Ker.

CICERO : PRO ARCHIA, POST REDITUM, DE DOMO, DE HA-
RUSPICUM RESPONSIS, PRO PLANCIO. N. H. Watts.

CICERO : PRO CAECINA, PRO LEGE MANILIA, PRO CLUENTIO,
PRO RABIRIO. H. Grose Hodge.

CICERO : PRO CAELIO, DE PROVINCIIS CONSULARIBUS, PRO
BALBO. R. Gardner.

CICERO : PRO MILONE, IN PISONEM, PRO SCAURO, PRO
FONTEIO, PRO RABIRIO POSTUMO, PRO MARCELLO, PRO
LIGARIO, PRO REGE DEIOTARO. N. H. Watts.

CICERO : PRO QUINCTIO, PRO ROSCIO AMERINO, PRO ROSCIO
COMOEDO, CONTRA RULLUM. J. H. Freese.

CICERO : PRO SESTIO, IN VATINIUM. R. Gardner.

[CICERO] : RHETORICA AD HERENNIUM. H. Caplan.

CICERO : TUSCULAN DISPUTATIONS. J. E. King.

CICERO : VERRINE ORATIONS. L. H. G. Greenwood. 2 Vols.

CLAUDIAN. M. Platnauer. 2 Vols.

COLUMELLA : DE RE RUSTICA, DE ARBORIBUS. H. B. Ash,
E. S. Forster, E. Heffner. 3 Vols.

CURTIUS, Q. : HISTORY OF ALEXANDER. J. C. Rolfe. 2 Vols.

FLORUS. E. S. Forster ; and CORNELIUS NEPOS. J. C. Rolfe.

FRONTINUS : STRATAGEMS AND AQUEDUCTS. C. E. Bennett
and M. B. McElwain.

FRONTO : CORRESPONDENCE. C. R. Haines. 2 Vols.

GELLIUS. J. C. Rolfe. 3 Vols.

HORACE : ODES AND EPODES. C. E. Bennett.

HORACE : SATIRES, EPISTLES, ARS POETICA. H. R. Fairclough.

JEROME : SELECT LETTERS. F. A. Wright.

JUVENAL AND PERSIUS. G. G. Ramsay.

LIVY. B. O. Foster, F. G. Moore, Evan T. Sage, A. C.
Schlesinger and R. M. Geer (General Index). 14 Vols.

LUCAN. J. D. Duff.

LUCRETIUS. W. H. D. Rouse. Revised by M. F. Smith.

MARTIAL. W. C. A. Ker. 2 Vols.

MINOR LATIN POETS : from PUBLILIUS SYRUS to RUTILIUS
NAMATIANUS, including GRATTIUS, CALPURNIUS SICULUS,
NEMESIANUS, AVIANUS, with "Aetna," "Phoenix" and
other poems. J. Wight Duff and Arnold M. Duff.

THE LOEB CLASSICAL LIBRARY

OVID : THE ART OF LOVE AND OTHER POEMS. J. H. Mozley.
OVID : FASTI. Sir James G. Frazer.
OVID : HEROIDES AND AMORES. Grant Showerman.
OVID : METAMORPHOSES. F. J. Miller. 2 Vols.
OVID : TRISTIA AND EX PONTO. A. L. Wheeler.
PETRONIUS. M. Heseltine ; SENECA : APOCOLOCYNTOSIS.
    W. H. D. Rouse.
PHAEDRUS AND BABRIUS (Greek). B. E. Perry.
PLAUTUS. Paul Nixon. 5 Vols.
PLINY : LETTERS, PANEGYRICUS. B. Radice. 2 Vols.
PLINY : NATURAL HISTORY. 10 Vols. Vols. I-V. H. Rack-
    ham. Vols. VI-VIII. W. H. S. Jones. Vol. IX. H. Rack-
    ham. Vol. X. D. E. Eichholz.
PROPERTIUS. H. E. Butler.
PRUDENTIUS. H. J. Thomson. 2 Vols.
QUINTILIAN. H. E. Butler. 4 Vols.
REMAINS OF OLD LATIN. E. H. Warmington. 4 Vols.
    Vol. I (Ennius and Caecilius). Vol. II (Livius, Naevius,
    Pacuvius, Accius). Vol. III (Lucilius, Laws of the XII
    Tables). Vol. IV (Archaic Inscriptions).
SALLUST. J. C. Rolfe.
SCRIPTORES HISTORIAE AUGUSTAE. D. Magie. 3 Vols.
SENECA : APOCOLOCYNTOSIS. Cf. PETRONIUS.
SENECA : EPISTULAE MORALES. R. M. Gummere. 3 Vols.
SENECA : MORAL ESSAYS. J. W. Basore. 3 Vols.
SENECA : NATURALES QUAESTIONES. T. H. Corcoran. 2 Vols.
SENECA : TRAGEDIES. F. J. Miller. 2 Vols.
SENECA THE ELDER : CONTROVERSIAE SUASORIAE. M.
    Winterbottom. 2 Vols.
SIDONIUS : POEMS AND LETTERS. W. B. Anderson. 2 Vols.
SILIUS ITALICUS. J. D. Duff. 2 Vols.
STATIUS. J. H. Mozley. 2 Vols.
SUETONIUS. J. C. Rolfe. 2 Vols.
TACITUS : AGRICOLA AND GERMANIA. M. Hutton ; DIALOGUS.
    Sir Wm. Peterson. Revised by R. M. Ogilvie, E. H.
    Warmington, M. Winterbottom.
TACITUS : HISTORIES AND ANNALS. C. H. Moore and J.
    Jackson. 4 Vols.
TERENCE. John Sargeaunt. 2 Vols.
TERTULLIAN : APOLOGIA AND DE SPECTACULIS. T. R. Glover ;
    MINUCIUS FELIX. G. H. Rendall.
VALERIUS FLACCUS. J. H. Mozley.
VARRO : DE LINGUA LATINA. R. G. Kent. 2 Vols.
VELLEIUS PATERCULUS AND RES GESTAE DIVI AUGUSTI.
    F. W. Shipley.

VIRGIL. H. R. Fairclough. 2 Vols.
VITRUVIUS : DE ARCHITECTURA. F. Granger. 2 Vols.

GREEK AUTHORS

ACHILLES TATIUS. S. Gaselee.
AELIAN : ON THE NATURE OF ANIMALS. A. F. Scholfield.
3 Vols.
AENEAS TACTICUS, ASCLEPIODOTUS AND ONASANDER. The
Illinois Greek Club
AESCHINES. C. D. Adams.
AESCHYLUS. H. Weir Smyth. 2 Vols.
ALICIPHRON, AELIAN AND PHILOSTRATUS : LETTERS. A. R.
Benner and F. H. Fobes.
APOLLODORUS. Sir James G. Frazer. 2 Vols.
APOLLONIUS RHODIUS. R. C. Seaton.
THE APOSTOLIC FATHERS. Kirsopp Lake. 2 Vols.
APPIAN'S ROMAN HISTORY. Horace White. 4 Vols.
ARATUS. *Cf.* CALLIMACHUS : HYMNS AND EPIGRAMS.
ARISTIDES. C. A. Behr. 4 Vols. Vol. I.
ARISTOPHANES. Benjamin Bickley Rogers. 3 Vols. Verse
trans.
ARISTOTLE : ART OF RHETORIC. J. H. Freese.
ARISTOTLE : ATHENIAN CONSTITUTION, EUDEMIAN ETHICS,
VIRTUES AND VICES. H. Rackham.
ARISTOTLE : THE CATEGORIES. ON INTERPRETATION. H. P.
Cooke ; PRIOR ANALYTICS. H. Tredennick.
ARISTOTLE : GENERATION OF ANIMALS. A. L. Peck.
ARISTOTLE : HISTORIA ANIMALIUM. A. L. Peck. 3 Vols.
Vols. I and II.
ARISTOTLE : METAPHYSICS. H. Tredennick. 2 Vols.
ARISTOTLE : METEOROLOGICA. H. D. P. Lee.
ARISTOTLE : MINOR WORKS. W. S. Hett. "On Colours,"
" On Things Heard," " Physiognomics," " On Plants,"
" On Marvellous Things Heard," " Mechanical Prob-
lems," " On Invisible Lines," " Situations and Names of
Winds," " On Melissus, Xenophanes, and Gorgias."
ARISTOTLE : NICOMACHEAN ETHICS. H. Rackham.
ARISTOTLE : OECONOMICA AND MAGNA MORALIA. G. C.
Armstrong. (With METAPHYSICS, Vol. II.)
ARISTOTLE : ON THE HEAVENS. W. K. C. Guthrie.
ARISTOTLE : ON THE SOUL, PARVA NATURALIA, ON BREATH.
W. S. Hett.

THE LOEB CLASSICAL LIBRARY

ARISTOTLE: PARTS OF ANIMALS. A. L. Peck; MOVEMENT
   AND PROGRESSION OF ANIMALS. E. S. Forster.
ARISTOTLE: PHYSICS. Rev. P. Wicksteed and F. M. Corn-
   ford. 2 Vols.
ARISTOTLE: POETICS; LONGINUS ON THE SUBLIME. W. Ham-
   ilton Fyfe; DEMETRIUS ON STYLE. W. Rhys Roberts.
ARISTOTLE: POLITICS. H. Rackham.
ARISTOTLE: POSTERIOR ANALYTICS. H. Tredennick; TOPICS.
   E. S. Forster.
ARISTOTLE: PROBLEMS. W. S. Hett. 2 Vols.
ARISTOTLE: RHETORICA AD ALEXANDRUM. H. Rackham.
   (With PROBLEMS, Vol. II.)
ARISTOTLE: SOPHISTICAL REFUTATIONS. COMING-TO-BE AND
   PASSING-AWAY. E. S. Forster; ON THE COSMOS. D. J.
   Furley.
ARRIAN: HISTORY OF ALEXANDER AND INDICA. 2 Vols.
   Vol. I. P. A. Brunt. Vol. II. Rev. E. Iliffe Robson.
ATHENAEUS: DEIPNOSOPHISTAE. C. B. Gulick. 7 Vols.
BABRIUS AND PHAEDRUS (Latin). B. E. Perry.
ST. BASIL: LETTERS. R. J. Deferrari. 4 Vols.
CALLIMACHUS: FRAGMENTS. C. A. Trypanis; MUSAEUS:
   HERO AND LEANDER. T. Gelzer and C. Whitman.
CALLIMACHUS: HYMNS AND EPIGRAMS, AND LYCOPHRON.
   A. W. Mair; ARATUS. G. R. Mair.
CLEMENT OF ALEXANDRIA. Rev. G. W. Butterworth.
COLLUTHUS. Cf. OPPIAN.
DAPHNIS AND CHLOE. Cf. LONGUS.
DEMOSTHENES I: OLYNTHIACS, PHILIPPICS AND MINOR
   ORATIONS: I-XVII AND XX. J. H. Vince.
DEMOSTHENES II: DE CORONA AND DE FALSA LEGATIONE.
   C. A. Vince and J. H. Vince.
DEMOSTHENES III: MEIDIAS, ANDROTION, ARISTOCRATES,
   TIMOCRATES, ARISTOGEITON. J. H. Vince.
DEMOSTHENES IV-VI: PRIVATE ORATIONS AND IN NEAERAM.
   A. T. Murray.
DEMOSTHENES VII: FUNERAL SPEECH, EROTIC ESSAY, EX-
   ORDIA AND LETTERS. N. W. and N. J. DeWitt.
DIO CASSIUS: ROMAN HISTORY. E. Cary. 9 Vols.
DIO CHRYSOSTOM. 5 Vols. Vols. I and II. J. W. Cohoon.
   Vol. III. J. W. Cohoon and H. Lamar Crosby. Vols. IV
   and V. H. Lamar Crosby.
DIODORUS SICULUS. 12 Vols. Vols. I-VI. C. H. Oldfather.
   Vol. VII. C. L. Sherman. Vol. VIII. C. B. Welles. Vols.
   IX and X. Russel M. Geer. Vols. XI and XII. F. R.
   Walton. General Index. Russel M. Geer.

DIOGENES LAERTIUS. R. D. Hicks. 2 Vols. New Introduction by H. S. Long.

DIONYSIUS OF HALICARNASSUS : CRITICAL ESSAYS. S. Usher. 2 Vols.

DIONYSIUS OF HALICARNASSUS : ROMAN ANTIQUITIES. Spelman's translation revised by E. Cary. 7 Vols.

EPICTETUS. W. A. Oldfather. 2 Vols.

EURIPIDES. A. S. Way. 4 Vols. Verse trans.

EUSEBIUS : ECCLESIASTICAL HISTORY. Kirsopp Lake and J. E. L. Oulton. 2 Vols.

GALEN : ON THE NATURAL FACULTIES. A. J. Brock.

THE GREEK ANTHOLOGY. W. R. Paton. 5 Vols.

THE GREEK BUCOLIC POETS (THEOCRITUS, BION, MOSCHUS). J. M. Edmonds.

GREEK ELEGY AND IAMBUS WITH THE ANACREONTEA. J. M. Edmonds. 2 Vols.

GREEK MATHEMATICAL WORKS. Ivor Thomas. 2 Vols.

HERODES. *Cf.* THEOPHRASTUS : CHARACTERS.

HERODIAN. C. R. Whittaker. 2 Vols.

HERODOTUS. A. D. Godley. 4 Vols.

HESIOD AND THE HOMERIC HYMNS. H. G. Evelyn White.

HIPPOCRATES AND THE FRAGMENTS OF HERACLEITUS. W. H. S. Jones and E. T. Withington. 4 Vols.

HOMER : ILIAD. A. T. Murray. 2 Vols.

HOMER : ODYSSEY. A. T. Murray. 2 Vols.

ISAEUS. E. S. Forster.

ISOCRATES. George Norlin and LaRue Van Hook. 3 Vols.

[ST. JOHN DAMASCENE] : BARLAAM AND IOASAPH. Rev. G. R. Woodward, Harold Mattingly and D. M. Lang.

JOSEPHUS. 9 Vols. Vols. I-IV. H. St. J. Thackeray. Vol. V. H. St. J. Thackeray and Ralph Marcus. Vols. VI and VII. Ralph Marcus. Vol. VIII. Ralph Marcus and Allen Wikgren. Vol. IX. L. H. Feldman.

JULIAN. Wilmer Cave Wright. 3 Vols.

LIBANIUS : SELECTED WORKS. A. F. Norman. 3 Vols. Vol. I.

LONGUS : DAPHNIS AND CHLOE. Thornley's translation revised by J. M. Edmonds ; and PARTHENIUS. S. Gaselee.

LUCIAN. 8 Vols. Vols. I-V. A. M. Harmon. Vol. VI. K. Kilburn. Vols. VII and VIII. M. D. Macleod.

LYCOPHRON. *Cf.* CALLIMACHUS : HYMNS AND EPIGRAMS.

LYRA GRAECA. J. M. Edmonds. 3 Vols.

LYSIAS. W. R. M. Lamb.

MANETHO. W. G. Waddell ; PTOLEMY : TETRABIBLOS. F. E. Robbins.

THE LOEB CLASSICAL LIBRARY

MARCUS AURELIUS. C. R. Haines.

MENANDER. F. G. Allinson.

MINOR ATTIC ORATORS. 2 Vols. K. J. Maidment and J. O. Burtt.

MUSAEUS: HERO AND LEANDER. *Cf.* CALLIMACHUS: FRAGMENTS.

NONNOS: DIONYSIACA. W. H. D. Rouse. 3 Vols.

OPPIAN, COLLUTHUS, TRYPHIODORUS. A. W. Mair.

PAPYRI. NON-LITERARY SELECTIONS. A. S. Hunt and C. C. Edgar. 2 Vols. LITERARY SELECTIONS (Poetry). D. L. Page.

PARTHENIUS. *Cf.* LONGUS.

PAUSANIAS: DESCRIPTION OF GREECE. W. H. S. Jones. 4 Vols. and Companion Vol. arranged by R. E. Wycherley.

PHILO. 10 Vols. Vols. I-V. F. H. Colson and Rev. G. H. Whitaker. Vols. VI-X. F. H. Colson. General Index. Rev. J. W. Earp.
Two Supplementary Vols. Translation only from an Armenian Text. Ralph Marcus.

PHILOSTRATUS: THE LIFE OF APOLLONIUS OF TYANA. F. C. Conybeare. 2 Vols.

PHILOSTRATUS: IMAGINES; CALLISTRATUS: DESCRIPTIONS. A. Fairbanks.

PHILOSTRATUS AND EUNAPIUS: LIVES OF THE SOPHISTS. Wilmer Cave Wright.

PINDAR. Sir J. E. Sandys.

PLATO: CHARMIDES, ALCIBIADES, HIPPARCHUS, THE LOVERS, THEAGES, MINOS AND EPINOMIS. W. R. M. Lamb.

PLATO: CRATYLUS, PARMENIDES, GREATER HIPPIAS, LESSER HIPPIAS. H. N. Fowler.

PLATO: EUTHYPHRO, APOLOGY, CRITO, PHAEDO, PHAEDRUS. H. N. Fowler.

PLATO: LACHES, PROTAGORAS, MENO, EUTHYDEMUS. W. R. M. Lamb.

PLATO: LAWS. Rev. R. G. Bury. 2 Vols.

PLATO: LYSIS, SYMPOSIUM, GORGIAS. W. R. M. Lamb.

PLATO: REPUBLIC. Paul Shorey. 2 Vols.

PLATO: STATESMAN, PHILEBUS. H. N. Fowler; ION. W. R. M. Lamb.

PLATO: THEAETETUS AND SOPHIST. H. N. Fowler.

PLATO: TIMAEUS, CRITIAS, CLITOPHO, MENEXENUS, EPISTULAE. Rev. R. G. Bury.

PLOTINUS. A. H. Armstrong. 6 Vols. Vols. I-III.

PLUTARCH: MORALIA. 17 Vols. Vols. I-V. F. C. Babbitt. Vol. VI. W. C. Helmbold. Vol. VII. P. H. De Lacy and

7

THE LOEB CLASSICAL LIBRARY

B. Einarson. Vol. VIII. P. A. Clement, H. B. Hoffleit. Vol. IX. E. L. Minar, Jr., F. H. Sandbach, W. C. Helmbold. Vol. X. H. N. Fowler. Vol. XI. L. Pearson, F. H. Sandbach. Vol. XII. H. Cherniss, W. C. Helmbold. Vol. XIII, Parts 1 and 2. H. Cherniss. Vol. XIV. P. H. De Lacy and B. Einarson. Vol. XV. F. H. Sandbach.

PLUTARCH: THE PARALLEL LIVES. B. Perrin. 11 Vols.

POLYBIUS. W. R. Paton. 6 Vols.

PROCOPIUS: HISTORY OF THE WARS. H. B. Dewing. 7 Vols.

PTOLEMY: TETRABIBLOS. *Cf.* MANETHO.

QUINTUS SMYRNAEUS. A. S. Way. Verse trans.

SEXTUS EMPIRICUS. Rev. R. G. Bury. 4 Vols.

SOPHOCLES. F. Storr. 2 Vols. Verse trans.

STRABO: GEOGRAPHY. Horace L. Jones. 8 Vols.

THEOPHRASTUS: CHARACTERS. J. M. Edmonds; HERODES, etc. A. D. Knox.

THEOPHRASTUS: DE CAUSIS PLANTARUM. G. K. K. Link and B. Einarson. 3 Vols. Vol. 1,

THEOPHRASTUS: ENQUIRY INTO PLANTS. Sir Arthur Hort. 2 Vols.

THUCYDIDES. C. F. Smith. 4 Vols.

TRYPHIODORUS. *Cf.* OPPIAN.

XENOPHON: ANABASIS. C. L. Brownson.

XENOPHON: CYROPAEDIA. Walter Miller. 2 Vols.

XENOPHON: HELLENICA. C. L. Brownson.

XENOPHON: MEMORABILIA AND OECONOMICUS. E. C. Marchant; SYMPOSIUM AND APOLOGY. O. J. Todd.

XENOPHON: SCRIPTA MINORA. E. C. Marchant and G. W Bowersock.

VOLUMES IN PREPARATION

GREEK AUTHORS

ARRIAN I. New version by P. Brunt.
LIBANIUS II. A. F. Norman.

LATIN AUTHORS

MANILIUS. G. P. Goold.

DESCRIPTIVE PROSPECTUS ON APPLICATION

CAMBRIDGE, MASS.	LONDON
HARVARD UNIV. PRESS	WILLIAM HEINEMANN LTD